"This book provides mental health professionals with a comprehensive, theory-based method for understanding the disorders in *DSM-5*. The utility of the Adlerian model is clear as each chapter incorporates theoretical concepts and techniques into a concise discussion of the disorder, case conceptualization, treatment considerations, and case studies. This updated edition should be required reading for professionals working with clients in a variety of settings."

Susan E. Belangee, Ph.D., LPC, private practice, Canton, Georgia

"In the third edition of their fine book *Psychopathology and Psychotherapy*, the editors Drs. Len Sperry, Jon Carlson, Jill Duba Sauerheber, and Jon Sperry do what they have done frequently in the past—they continue to fill a vacuum and shed light on areas of great interest and benefit. With clarity and precision these acclaimed authors, editors and academics, along with additional respected authors who contributed chapters, enlighten readers and provide solid and substantial information about treatment for various DSM-5 diagnoses from an Adlerian perspective. Those of us who work in the field can find our work enhanced greatly by reading and applying the knowledge presented in this book. I most highly recommend."

Debbie Joffe Ellis, private practice, New York City

"The editors of *Psychopathology and Psychotherapy: DSM-5 Diagnosis, Case Conceptualization, and Treatment* (3rd Edition)—Drs. Len Sperry, Jon Carlson, Jill Duba Sauerheber, and Jon Sperry—are to be congratulated for the development and timely release of a new resource for the conceptualization and treatment of a range of mental health disorders. Their book has captured the most recent evidence and thinking about mental health from an Adlerian perspective, and then deftly weaved in case examples, to highlight the value of this approach. This work will be of interest and value to psychotherapy trainees and practiced clinicians alike."

Keith S. Dobson, Ph.D., R. Psych., Professor of Clinical Psychology, University of Calgary, Canada; Past-President, International Association of Cognitive Psychotherapy

"*Psychopathology and Psychotherapy* begins each chapter with a captivating story, which moves to examine changes from *DSM-IV-TR* to *DSM-5*. This skillful examination of contrast evolves into conceptualization of dysfunction through an Adlerian perspective, giving clarity to how one might use current systems to inform practice, and embrace mental health. A must have reference for students and practicing clinicians."

J. Steve Hamm, Ed.D., LCPC, Indian Oaks Academy, Manteno, Illinois

"*Psychopathology and Psychotherapy* is a critical tool in assisting practitioners and practitioners-in-training to combine theory, practice, and diagnosis while incorporating a culturally sensitive framework. Rarely do we find books that allow us to directly apply a specific theoretical framework to our diagnostic work. This book will allow practitioners to broaden Adler's work to incorporate *DSM-5* and make specific suggestions on how diagnostic considerations can be linked to tailored treatment interventions for individual clients. A must read for current and developing Adlerians!"

Katherine Helm, Ph.D., Professor and Director of Graduate Programs in Psychology, Lewis University

Psychopathology and Psychotherapy

Psychopathology and Psychotherapy: DSM-5 Diagnosis, Case Conceptualization, and Treatment, Third Edition differs from other psychopathology and abnormal psychology books. While other books focus on describing diagnostic conditions, this book focuses on the critical link between psychopathology and psychotherapy. More specifically, it links diagnostic evaluation, case conceptualization, and treatment selection to psychotherapy practice. Research affirms that knowledge and awareness of these links is essential in planning and providing highly effective psychotherapy.

This third edition incorporates detailed case conceptualizations and treatment considerations for the DSM-5 diagnoses most commonly seen in everyday clinical practice. Extensive case studies illustrate the diagnostic, case conceptualization, and treatment process in a way that makes it come alive. Written by practicing clinicians with expertise in specific disorders, this book will be an invaluable resource to both novice and experienced clinicians.

Len Sperry, M.D., Ph.D. is Professor, Mental Health Counseling, Florida Atlantic University and Clinical Professor of Psychiatry and Behavioral Medicine at the Medical College of Wisconsin. He holds the post-doctoral Certificate in Psychotherapy from the Adler Institute—Chicago, and is a Life Fellow of the American Psychological Association and a Distinguished Life Fellow of the American Psychiatric Association. Of his 750 publications, 70 are books, of which nine are on psychopathology and its treatment.

Jon Carlson, Psy.D., Ed.D. is Distinguished Professor, Psychology and Counseling at Governors State University and a psychologist at the Wellness Clinic in Lake Geneva, Wisconsin. Jon has served as editor of several periodicals including the *Journal of Individual Psychology* and the *Family Journal*. He has authored 175 journal articles and 60 books and created over 300 professional trade videos and DVDs with leading professional therapists and educators.

Jill Duba Sauerheber, Ph.D., LPCC, EMDR Certified, Reality Therapy Certified, is Associate Professor in the Department of Counseling and Student Affairs at Western Kentucky University and has a private counseling practice. She has participated in the Harvard Graduate School of Education's Management Development Program, holds a certificate in Adlerian Psychology, and is the current President of the North American Society of Adlerian Psychology. Jill has also authored or coauthored over 35 journal articles, one edited book, and 15 book chapters.

Jon Sperry, Ph.D. is Visiting Assistant Professor, Mental Health Counseling, Florida Atlantic University and Counseling Specialist at Counseling and Psychological Services, Florida Atlantic University. Dr. Sperry holds a certificate in Adlerian Psychotherapy and is a Certified Addictions Professional. He serves as co-chair of the Theory, Research, and Training Section of the North American Society of Adlerian Psychology.

Psychopathology and Psychotherapy

DSM-5 Diagnosis, Case Conceptualization, and Treatment

Third Edition

Edited by
Len Sperry, Jon Carlson,
Jill Duba Sauerheber, and Jon Sperry

Routledge
Taylor & Francis Group

NEW YORK AND LONDON

First published 2015
by Routledge
711 Third Avenue, New York, NY 10017

and by Routledge
27 Church Road, Hove, East Sussex BN3 2FA

Routledge is an imprint of the Taylor & Francis Group, an informa business

© 2015 Taylor & Francis

First edition published 1993 by Routledge
Second edition published 1996 by Routledge

Library of Congress Cataloging in Publication Data
Psychopathology and psychotherapy : DSM-5 diagnosis, case conceptualization, and treatment / edited by Len Sperry [and three others]. -- Third edition.
pages cm
1. Psychology, Pathological. 2. Psychotherapy. 3. Psychiatry--Differential therapeutics. 4. Adler, Alfred, 1870-1937. 5. Diagnostic and statistical manual of mental disorders. I. Sperry, Len, editor of compilation.
RC454.S68 2015
616.89--dc23
2014006300

ISBN: 978-0-415-83872-6 (hbk)
ISBN: 978-0-415-83873-3 (pbk)
ISBN: 978-0-203-77228-7 (ebk)

Typeset in Minion Pro
by Saxon Graphics Ltd, Derby

Printed and bound in the United States of America by
Edwards Brothers Malloy on sustainably sourced paper

Contents

Contributors   xi
Foreword   xv
Preface   xvii
Acknowledgements   xix

1   Diagnosis, Case Conceptualization, Culture, and Treatment   1
    LEN SPERRY

2   Adlerian Case Conceptualization   15
    LEN SPERRY

3   Personality Disorders   27
    LEN SPERRY

    Avoidant Personality Disorder   30
    Borderline Personality Disorder   33
    Narcissistic Personality Disorder   37
    Obsessive-Compulsive Personality Disorder   39
    Schizotypal Personality Disorder   42
    Antisocial Personality Disorder   45
    Dependent Personality Disorder   48
    Histrionic Personality Disorder   51
    Schizoid Personality Disorder   54
    Paranoid Personality Disorder   56

4   Anxiety and Obsessive-Compulsive Disorders   63
    JILL DUBA SAUERHEBER AND JAMES ROBERT BITTER

    Separation Anxiety Disorder   68
    Selective Mutism   70
    Specific Phobias and Social Anxiety Disorder   73

Panic Attacks and Panic Disorder   75
Agoraphobia   77
Generalized Anxiety Disorder   80
Obsessive-Compulsive and Related Disorders   82
Body Dysmorphic Disorder, Trichotillomania, and Excoriation   85
Hoarding Disorder   89

5   Depression and Bipolar Disorders   95
PAUL R. RASMUSSEN AND DINKO ALEKSANDROF

Major Depressive Disorder   101
Disruptive Mood Dysregulation Disorder   105
Persistent Depressive Disorder (Dysthymia)   107
Bipolar Disorder   109
Bipolar II Disorder   115
Cyclothymia   117

6   Trauma- and Stressor-Related Disorders   123
BRET A. MOORE AND JOHN F. NEWBAUER

Reactive Attachment Disorder   127
Disinhibited Social Engagement Disorder   131
Post-Traumatic Stress Disorder   134
Acute Stress Disorder   142
Adjustment Disorders   145

7   Eating Disorders   151
MARY FRANCES SCHNEIDER

Anorexia Nervosa   153
Bulimia Nervosa   158
Avoidant/Restrictive Food-Intake Disorder   162
Binge-Eating Disorder   165
Pica and Rumination Disorder   171

8   Schizophrenia Spectrum and Other Psychotic Disorders   177
LEN SPERRY AND JON SPERRY

Schizophrenia and Schizophreniform Disorders   184
Delusional Disorders   194
Schizoaffective Disorder   197
Brief Psychotic Disorder   199
Substance/Medication-Induced Psychotic Disorders   201

9 Dissociative Disorders 205

JON SPERRY AND LEN SPERRY

Dissociative Identity Disorder 210
Dissociative Amnesia 213
Depersonalization/Derealization Disorder 215
Other Specified Dissociative Disorder 218
Unspecified Dissociative Disorder 220

10 Somatic Symptoms and Related Disorders 223

LAURIE SACKETT-MANIACCI AND MICHAEL P. MANIACCI

Somatic Symptom Disorder 226
Illness Anxiety Disorder 229
Conversion Disorder 232
Psychological Factors Affecting Other Medical Condition 235
Factitious Disorder 238

11 Sleep-Wake Disorders 243

JENNIFER N. WILLIAMSON AND DANIEL G. WILLIAMSON

Insomnia Disorder 246
Hypersomnolence Disorder 249
Narcolepsy/Hypocretin Deficiency 251
Sleep Apnea and Obstructive Sleep Apnea Hypopnea Syndrome 254
Central Sleep Apnea 255
Nightmare Disorder 259

12 Sexual Disorders 265

SHARYL M. TRAIL

Genito-Pelvic Pain/Penetration Disorder 270
Gender Dysphoria 273
Gender Dysphoria: Children 274
Paraphilic Disorders 278
Pedophilic Disorder 278

13 Neurodevelopmental and Conduct Disorders 285

LARRY MAUCIERI

Autistic Spectrum Disorder 292
Specific Learning Disorder 295

Attention Deficit Hyperactivity Disorder   298
Tourette's Syndrome   301
Conduct Disorder   303
Oppositional Defiant Disorder   305

14 Substance Use and Addictive Disorders   311
    MARK T. BLAGEN

    Alcohol Use Disorder   317
    Cannabis Use Disorder   320
    Opioid Use Disorder   323
    Stimulant Use Disorder   326
    Sedative, Hypnotic, or Anxiolytic Use Disorder   328
    Gambling Disorder   331

15 Neurocognitive Disorders   335
    MICHAEL P. MANIACCI AND LEN SPERRY

    Delirium   340
    Major or Mild Neurocognitive Disorder Due to Alzheimer's Disease   342
    Major or Mild Neurocognitive Disorder Due to Traumatic Brain Injury   344
    Major or Mild Neurocognitive Disorder Due to Parkinson's Disease   346
    Unspecified Neurocognitive Disorder   348
    Other Neurocognitive Disorders   350
    Other Disorders   351

    Index   357

List of Contributors

Editors

Len Sperry, M.D., Ph.D., ABPP is Professor, Mental Health Counseling, Florida Atlantic University and Clinical Professor of Psychiatry and Behavioral Medicine at the Medical College of Wisconsin. He holds the post-doctoral Certificate in Psychotherapy from the Adler Institute, Chicago, is a Life Fellow of the American Psychological Association and the American College of Preventive Medicine, and is a Distinguished Life Fellow of the American Psychiatric Association. Of his 750 publications 70 are books, of which nine are on psychopathology and its treatment.

Jon Carlson, Psy.D., Ed.D., ABPP is Distinguished Professor of Psychology and Counseling at Governors State University, Illinois, and a psychologist at the Wellness Clinic in Lake Geneva, Wisconsin. Jon has served as editor of several periodicals including the *Journal of Individual Psychology* and the *Family Journal*. He has authored 175 journal articles and 60 books and created over 300 professional trade videos and DVDs with leading professional therapists and educators

Jill Duba Sauerheber, Ph.D., LPCC, EMDR Certified, Reality Therapy Certified, is Associate Professor in the Department of Counseling and Student Affairs at Western Kentucky University and has a private counseling practice. She has participated in the Harvard Graduate School of Education's Management Development Program, holds a certificate in Adlerian Psychology, and is the current President of the North American Society of Adlerian Psychology. Jill has also authored or coauthored over 35 journal articles, one edited book, and 15 book chapters.

Jon Sperry, Ph.D. is Visiting Assistant Professor, Mental Health Counseling, Florida Atlantic University, and Counseling Specialist at Counseling and Psychological Services, Florida Atlantic University. Dr. Sperry holds a certificate in Adlerian Psychotherapy, and is a Certified Addictions Professional. He serves as co-chair of the Theory, Research, and Training Section of the North American Society of Adlerian Psychology.

Contributors

Dinko Aleksandrov, B.A. is a Doctoral student in Clinical Psychology at the Adler School of Professional Psychology in Chicago.

James Robert Bitter, Ed.D. is Professor of Counseling, Department of Counseling and Human Services, East Tennessee State University; Diplomate in Adlerian Psychology; author or co-author of four books and over 60 articles; former Editor of the *Journal of Individual Psychology*; founding faculty member of the Adlerian Training Institute.

Mark T. Blagen, Ph.D. is Assistant Professor, Governors State University, Illinois. He was a Certified Addictions Counselor, and has presented widely on addiction-related topics. Awards include a Faculty Excellence Award, Most Inspirational Professor Award, and an Award for Innovative Excellence in Teaching, Learning, and Technology.

Michael P. Maniacci, Psy.D. has a private practice of clinical psychology, and is a consultant. Dr. Maniacci is a graduate of the State University of New York at Stony Brook and the Alfred Adler Institute of Chicago. He has over 50 publications in the field, and has taught throughout the U.S. and Canada.

Larry Maucieri, Ph.D. is an Assistant Professor of Psychology and Counseling, Governors State University, Illinois, and affiliate clinical neuropsychologist at the Family Institute at Northwestern University. His research and clinical areas of specialty involve adult ADHD, traumatic brain injury, dementia, and psychometric assessment.

Bret A. Moore, Psy.D., ABPP is Adjunct Associate Professor of Psychiatry, University of Texas Health Sciences Center at San Antonio. Dr. Moore is licensed as a prescribing psychologist by the New Mexico Board of Psychologist Examiners. He is a Fellow of the American Psychological Association and author and editor of 12 books, many dealing with military psychology.

John F. Newbauer, Ed.D. is the Administrator for NASAP and ICASSI and a consulting psychologist. He is the former Director of Treatment and Diagnostic Services for the Allen County Superior Court in Fort Wayne, Indiana, co-founder and senior psychologist at Phoenix Associates, Inc., and former member of the Core Faculty of the Adler School of Professional Psychology in Chicago.

Paul R. Rasmussen, Ph.D. is staff psychologist at the Dorn VA Medical Center in Columbia South Carolina. He is a Diplomate in Adlerian Psychology, member of the Board and Faculty of the International Conference for Adlerian Summer Schools and Institutes (ICASSI), co-editor of the Clinical Strategies column for the *Journal of Individual Psychology*, and past North American Society of Adlerian Psychology (NASAP) COR member.

Laurie Sackett-Maniacci, Psy.D. has a private practice in Naperville, Illinois; drlauriemaniacci.com. She is a Consultant to the Rush-Copley Heart Institute Cardiac Rehab Center and provides education to various community organizations. She has worked in both psychiatric and medical settings.

Mary Frances Schneider, Ph.D. is Professor Emeritus, National-Louis University, in School and Clinical Psychology. She has a grant to study the spiritual and psychological needs of unaccompanied, detained children and adolescents. In addition to professional psychology publications she has written two young-adult novels, *Dear Cookie*, and *Molly McCumber I've Got Your Number*.

Sharyl M. Trail, Psy.D. is Lieutenant Commander, U.S. Public Health Service Commissioned Corps. Her areas of expertise include: trauma informed care; LGBT mental health; health disparities based on culture, race, and socioeconomic status; prevention models; healthcare administration and policy; and Adlerian topics including Social Interest and Social Equality.

Daniel G. Williamson, Ph.D., LPCC, NCC, HS-BCP and **Jennifer N. Williamson, Ph.D., LPCC, NCC, HS-BCP** are Associate Professors of Counseling and Human Services at Lindsey Wilson College in Columbia, Kentucky. They are Licensed Professional Counselors, nationally certified, and are recognized as Fulbright Specialists in Mental Health.

Foreword

More so today than perhaps at any time in the past, practitioners are inundated with multiple *professional demands* from distinct spheres of influence impacting their clinical practice. Some of their stressors stem from professional, regulatory, and statutory interests in protecting the public and insuring its safety. Mandatory continuing-education requirements for maintaining skills and licensure, HIPPA rules, informed-consent obligations, reporting mechanisms for abuse and neglect of vulnerable populations, and more and more stringent documentation requirements are a few of the more prominent *professional demands* that clinicians face. But, these are not the only such expectations that practitioners face.

Practitioners also face increased *clinical demands*. One of the most challenging of the contemporary clinical demands imposed upon practitioners is the emergence of the *DSM-5* and the need to integrate its directives into practice. As a much-awaited change and reorganization of diagnostic categories and the ever-expanding symptomatic criteria for various psychopathologies, the *DSM-5* has been received with much controversy and criticism (McHugh, 2013; Tavris, 2013; Satel, 2010; Greenberg, 2013; Frances, 2013; etc.), thus making it even more challenging for clinicians. While critiques of such creations as *DSM-5* will always be abundant, solutions will always be rarer. That observation serves as a reminder of the timeliness and clinical utility of this new edition of *Psychopathology and Psychotherapy*.

The regulatory, statutory, etc., *professional demands* will always evolve in keeping with the natural evolution of societal standards. Likewise, practitioners will always find it necessary to evolve in their thinking psychopathology as our conceptualization of it evolves. Such evolution will always be challenging, since practitioners are subject to the same principles of *cognitive ease* (Kahneman, 2011) as are all human beings. Nevertheless, practitioners do aspire to the status of master practitioner. It is in this domain that the authors have done a masterful job of helping to bring practitioners "up to speed" in dealing with the general complexities of clinical change in the air and those specific changes delineated in *DSM-5*.

Any reader of professional material who has published in the scientific literature understands the rigorous demands of such writing. Parsimonious command of language, conveying explicit meaning, conceptualization, etc. are all given requirements. But, also required in clinical writing for practitioners is coherence between theory, research, and practice. This is an area in which these authors excel. Their Adlerian theoretical frame of reference, combined with their knowledge and understanding of the "research" of

DSM-5 yields exceptionally sage and clinically logical guidance for practice. They have taken the professional consensus (such as it is with all its imperfections) of contemporary psychiatrists, represented in *DSM-5*, and integrated it with the guidance of the Adlerian frame of reference. In my opinion the Adlerian theoretical frame of reference transcends the changes made in (as well as the limitations of) *DSM-5*, in its ability to provide guidance for practitioners that facilitates their *dance with clients and patients through the therapeutic maze*. It is a truly valuable therapeutic tool, an instructional experience, and a thorough job well done.

In the interests of full disclosure, I have long been associated with the Adlerian movement and consider myself a neo-Adlerian. In that capacity, it has been my pleasure to know Len Sperry and Jon Carlson as colleagues and friends. They have my utmost respect and admiration for their innumerable contributions to psychology in general, the professional/scientific literature in particular, and to helping troubled souls make better and more tranquil lives.

Gerald J. Mozdzierz
Professor, Department of Psychiatry and Behavioral Neurosciences, Loyola University, Chicago, IL

References

Frances, A. (2013). *Saving Normal: Insiders revolt against out-of-control psychiatric diagnoses, DSM 5, big pharma and the medicalization of ordinary life*. New York: William Morrow.

Greenberg. G. (2013). *The Book of Woe: The DSM and the unmaking of psychiatry*. New York: Blue Rider Press/Penguin Group.

McHugh, P. (2013). 'McHugh derides DSM 5 for failure to progress'. Available at: http://psychiatristblog.blogspot.com/2013/07/wsj-paul-mchugh-derides-dsm5-for.html. *Shrink Rap*, July 13, accessed January 5, 2014.

Kahneman, D. (2011). *Thinking, Fast and Slow*. New York: Farrar, Straus and Giroux.

Satel, S. (2010). The physician's voice is only one of many. *American Journal of Transplantation*, 10(11), p. 2558.

Tavris, C. (2013). How Psychiatry went crazy. *The Wall Street Journal* (Saturday/Sunday, May 18–19), p. C1–C7.

Preface

The first edition of *Psychopathology and Psychotherapy* was published in 1993. It combined DSM-III-R criteria with the dynamic-behavioral-cognitive-systemic perspective of Adlerian Psychology. The second edition of *Psychopathology and Psychotherapy* appeared in 1996. It combined DSM-IV criteria with the Adlerian perspective. This third edition of *Psychopathology and Psychotherapy* appears in print some 18 years later and combines the Adlerian perspective with the recently released *DSM-5. Psychopathology and Psychotherapy: DSM-5 Diagnosis, Case Conceptualization, and Treatment, Third Edition* differs from most other books on abnormal psychology and psychopathology in its focus on the link between psychotherapy and psychopathology. More specifically it links diagnostic evaluation, case conceptualization, and treatment selection to psychotherapy practice. These links are essential in understanding the relationship between psychopathology and psychotherapy. Knowledge and awareness of these links is indispensable in providing effective clinical services.

Since *DSM-5* has been in development for nearly 20 years, it is not surprising that it includes a significant number of changes in both diagnoses and diagnostic criteria. One of our goals in *Psychopathology and Psychotherapy: DSM-5 Diagnosis, Case Conceptualization, and Treatment, Third Edition* was to include only the most common diagnostic conditions that present in outpatient practice. For this reason we have not covered a number of less common diagnostic conditions in *DSM-5*.

A second goal was to emphasize case conceptualization—previously known as case formulation—in this edition since case conceptualization is increasingly considered an indispensable component of effective clinical practice. A separate chapter (Chapter 2) describes and illustrates an integrative Adlerian case conceptualization model.

A third goal of this edition was to build on the strengths of the two previous editions, which were favorably received by students and clinicians. We have listened to the feedback of readers and incorporated it into the book's design. The reader will note that a common format or structure is used in Chapters 3 to 15. Each of these chapters includes the DSM-5 characterizations, along with an Adlerian case conceptualization and case examples for all disorders covered. At least one case example per chapter includes a full-scale case illustration that includes family constellation information and life-style convictions.

Finally, Dr. Carlson and I are pleased to welcome two coeditors, Jill Duba Sauerheber, Ph.D. and Jon Sperry, Ph.D., to this edition. Our hope was to produce a truly reader-friendly book that highlights and integrates the Adlerian perspective with *DSM-5*. We trust that this edition increases both your clinical knowledge and your clinical practice.

Len Sperry, M.D., Ph.D.
Jon Carlson, Psy,D., Ed.D.
Jill Duba Sauerheber, Ph.D.
Jon Sperry, Ph.D.

Acknowledgments

We want to thank the chapter authors for their contribution to this volume. Each has had to write in a style slightly different to what they are accustomed to. In order to assist the reader we created a common outline that we required each contributor to follow.

This is the third edition of this book and we want to thank the authors of the chapters in the two previous volumes for their initial contribution to the development of psychopathology and psychotherapy.

We want to thank Routledge Publishers, and especially George Zimmar, Ph.D., for their continued support of this project.

Finally, we thank Alfred Adler and Rudolf Dreikurs for providing a system of understanding all forms of human behavior, that is not only accurate but easily understood and explained. Two of us (LS & JC) were taught by Dr. Dreikurs, and one of us (LS) had the good fortune to be supervised by him and trained in his private practice.

1   Diagnosis, Case Conceptualization, Culture, and Treatment

Len Sperry

A 31-year-old married female presents for therapy with depression and a fear of seriously harming her younger son. What more would you want to know about her? What is your diagnostic impression and case conceptualization? What are your treatment recommendations? Alfred Adler dealt with such questions with a similar client when he consulted on Mrs. A., his most famous case. The Case of Mrs. A. is a great way to begin a discussion of the Adlerian Psychology perspective on psychopathology and psychotherapy.

Certainly, much more is known about the process of normal development and psychopathology than in 1931 when Adler's consultation took place. Similarly, the hope is greater that treatment interventions can more effectively reduce and even reverse psychopathological processes than in past decades. This chapter has three purposes: First, it describes Alfred Adler's basic view of normality and psychopathology, along with some observations that extend and clarify it. Second, it overviews some of the basic changes in the use of the new *Diagnostic and Statistical Manual, Fifth Edition (DSM-5)* (American Psychiatric Association, 2013). Next, it compares the atheoretical *DSM-5* with Adlerian Psychology theory and suggests how diagnostic considerations can be linked to treatment interventions. Because of the increasing importance of cultural factors in clinical practice today, their place in a case conceptualization is noted. Finally, there is an analysis of the Case of Mrs. A., with DSM-5 diagnoses and an Adlerian case conceptualization.

Alfred Adler's View

Alfred Adler was the founder of the psychological theory and system called Individual Psychology (Adler, 1956). Adler chose the term "Individual"—as its Latin derivation meant "indivisible"—referring to the essential unity of the person. Adler believed that the hallmark of the healthy, nonpathological person was the capacity to move through life meeting the various life tasks with courage and common sense. Adler called this hallmark "social interest." In no way did Adler imply that such an individual was perfect or fully self-actualized. Actually, healthy persons can use private logic, experience some discouragement and a sense of inferiority, for which they compensate in ways that are outside the reaches of social interest. The common perception is that imperfections and failures are part of the human condition. On the other hand, pathological persons believe that they must be perfect, and then justify their thinking and actions as the only way to achieve perfection. For Adler, all personality dysfunction was the outcome of erroneous conceptions of how to achieve personal superiority. For the most part, he believed that these faulty conceptions were formed early in one's life (Adler, 1956).

A neurotic disposition, Adler's term for the predisposing conditions that can result in psychopathology, stems from childhood experiences that are characterized either by overprotection or neglect, or by an admixture of both. From these experiences, the young child develops a set of psychological convictions—about self, the world and life goal, which becomes the life style—of his/her inability to develop mastery or cope with the tasks of life. These convictions are confounded and reinforced by the child's perception of a hostile, punishing, or depriving environment at home or school, or one that is subtly demanding or frustrating. Rather than providing encouragement to engage in other efforts involving mastery and achievement, these experiences leave the youngster feeling discouraged and fearful. Rather than experiencing trusting and loving relationships, the young child grows to become distrustful and manipulative. To compensate for these exaggerated feelings of insecurity and anxiety, the child becomes self-centered and uncooperative.

So what is a pathological or dysfunctional life style? The dysfunctional life style is an inflexible life style. In it, problem-solving is based upon a self-protective "private sense," rather than a more task-oriented and socially useful "common sense." Once this set of faulty psychological convictions has coalesced and self-protective patterns of coping are established, the individual has difficulty in seeing or responding to life in any other way. The end result is that an individual with such a style cannot productively cope with the tasks of life nor really enjoy the rewards of his/her labors, much less his/her relationships with others. In contrast, a set of psychological convictions and coping patterns that are shaped positively by the child's healthy experiences of mastery, creativity, and loving and pleasurable relationships will result in a flexible life style.

Adler presented a unitary theory of psychopathology, wherein the individual "arranges" symptoms uniquely to serve as excuses for not meeting the tasks of life or to safeguard self-esteem either by aggression or distancing from others (Carlson, Watts, & Maniacci, 2006).

Adler discriminated dysfunctional behavior along the dimensions of social interest and degree of activity. For instance, neurotics respond to the life tasks with "Yes—but." With the "yes," the individual acknowledges social responsibilities, and with the "but," symptoms are presented which excuse responsibility. Mosak (1984) described two types of "yes—but" responses: "Yes—but I'm sick," which is the classic response of the psychoneurotic; and, "Yes—but I defy it," the acting-out response of the character neurosis or personality disorder. On the other hand, psychotics respond to life tasks with "No," and cut themselves off from the common world. As to activity level, Adler noted a low degree is found in neurotic conditions such as depression and obsessive-compulsion, with a higher degree in anxiety neurosis, Schizophrenia, and alcoholics. The highest levels were in manics and sociopaths (Adler, 1964a).

Developments in the Adlerian View

Adler believed that three main components were common to all psychopathology: discouragement, faulty conceptions, and life-style beliefs (Carlson, Watts, & Maniacci,

2006). Furthermore, he posited that undeveloped social interest and personality dysfunction were basically the outcome of an erroneous way of living. This represents Adler's views of normality versus abnormality at the time of his death. It should be noted that at the outset of his career, Adler believed that psychopathology stemmed from various organ inferiorities. This was a rather biological and reductionistic position. Later, his view changed to a more intrapsychic view in which dysfunctional behavior was seen as a conflict between inferiority and superiority feelings. He described the "neurotic disposition" as the predisposing factor in the development of neurosis. The term "pampered life style" eventually replaced this term. Still later, Adler developed a more sociopsychological view in which psychopathology represented movement toward self-importance at the expense of the common good. In many respects, the last version of Adler's theory represented one of the first attempts at developing a holistic view of psychopathology (Adler, 1964b). Although it encompassed features from the biological (organ inferiority and organ dialect) and the social realms, it was primarily a theory of emotional development and dysfunction, which integrated all processes through the prism of the life style: "This is notably the case with the lungs, the heart, the stomach, the organs of excretion and the sexual organs. The disturbance of these functions expresses the direction that an individual is taking to attain his goal. I have called these disturbances the organ dialect, or organ jargon, since the organs are revealing in their own most expressive language the intention of the individual totality" (Adler, 1964b, p. 156).

Neufield (1954) differentiated the early psychosomatic approaches from the bio-psychosocial and integrative approaches like Individual Psychology. Most psychosomatic theories failed to fully appreciate the multi-faceted dynamics and interdependence of *all* of the biological, the psychological, and the social dimensions of human existence. Failure to appreciate all of these multi-faceted dimensions leads to the same narrow reductionism Neufield criticized in many early psychosomatic theories.

A tendency among those espousing an integrative theory has been to downplay some of these multi-faceted dynamics, particularly the biochemical and neuropharmacological ones. This is particularly true in the treatment of depressive disorders. A growing awareness is that depression is not a single entity but rather a spectrum disorder. As such, depression is currently viewed by many as a group of discrete illnesses that span a biopsychosocial continuum in which symptom patterns appear to be more influenced by biochemical factors at one end of the continuum and more by psychological factors at the other end (Sperry & Sperry, 2012). To illustrate the biopsychosocial perspective, a helpful procedure is to speculate about how a depressive disorder develops.

Based on recent research findings we can speculate that individuals who experience a Major Depressive Episode are in some ways genetically susceptible to depression, such that brain pathways and circuits dealing with emotions such as pleasure are fragile and poorly buffered from external influences. Add to this some early life traumas such as the loss or separation from a significant other—for instance a parent—that undermines self-confidence and esteem, and for which individuals respond with safeguarding patterns. Subjecting individuals to a severe psychological stressor at a later point in life is interpreted by them as a threat that in some way echoes their early experience of loss or separation. When existing social support systems and personal coping strategies or safeguarding methods are not sufficient to neutralize this stressor, the already compromised brain biochemistry is overtaxed, resulting in the familiar biological symptoms of depression such as sleep and appetite disturbance, psychomotor retardation, reduced energy, inability to experience pleasure, and somatic symptoms such as constipation and headache. This reduced physiological functioning serves to further reinforce the individuals' life-style beliefs about self, the world, and the future (Sperry, 2010; Sperry & Sperry, 2012).

Pancner (1985) suggested a similar hypothesis. On the other hand, Persistent Depressive Disorder (Dysthymia), previously called Dysthymia or Neurotic Depression, probably has more psychosocial loading than Major Depressive Disorder, which has more genetic and biological loading. Disorders like Persistent Depressive Disorder most often present with few biological symptoms and more dysfunctional life-style beliefs and coping skills. Thus, it is not surprising that such a disorder responds well to psychosocial therapies, while Major Depressive Disorder is more likely to respond to biochemical therapies such as antidepressant medications, often in conjunction with psychotherapy. Psychotherapy will be a necessary adjunctive treatment, assuming that a pampered life style or neurotic disposition interferes with functioning in life tasks. But, when little or no life-task dysfunction exists, as is sometimes the situation, then psychotherapy is less likely to be useful.

Case Conceptualization: Diagnostic, Clinical, Cultural, and Treatment Formulations

A case conceptualization is a way of summarizing diverse information in a brief, coherent manner for the purpose of better understanding and treating of the individual. Furthermore, a case conceptualization consists of four components: diagnostic formulations, clinical formulations, cultural formulation, and treatment formulations (Sperry, 2010; Sperry & Sperry, 2012).

A *diagnostic formulation* is a descriptive statement about the nature and severity of the individual's psychiatric presentation. The diagnostic formulation aids the clinician in reaching three sets of diagnostic conclusions: whether the patient's presentation is primarily psychotic, characterological, or neurotic; whether the patient's presentation is primarily organic or psychogenic in etiology; and, whether the patient's presentation is so acute and severe that it requires immediate intervention. In short, diagnostic formulations are descriptive, phenomenological, and cross-sectional in nature. They answer the "What happened?" question. For all practical purposes the diagnostic formulation lends itself to being specified with DSM-5 criteria and nosology.

A *clinical formulation*, on the other hand, is more explanatory and longitudinal in nature, and attempts to offer a rationale for the development and maintenance of symptoms and dysfunctional life patterns. Clinical formulations answer the "Why did it happen?" question. Just as various theories of human behavior exist, so do various types of clinical formulations exist: psychoanalytic, Adlerian, cognitive, behavioral, biological, family systems, biopsychosocial, or some combination. In this book, a combination of the Adlerian and biopsychosocial case conceptualizations is emphasized. In the following chapters it is designated as "Biopsychosocial–Adlerian Conceptualization."

A *cultural formulation* is a systematic review and explanation of cultural factors and dynamics that are operative in the presenting problems. It answers the "What role does culture play?" question. More specifically, it describes the client's cultural identity and level of acculturation. It provides a cultural explanation of the client's condition, as well as the impact of cultural factors on the client's personality and level of functioning. Furthermore, it addresses cultural elements that may impact the relationship between the individual and the therapist, and whether cultural or culturally sensitive interventions are indicated.

A *treatment formulation* follows from the diagnostic, clinical, and cultural formulations and serves as an explicit blueprint governing treatment interventions. Rather than answering the "What happened?" or "Why did it happen?" questions, the treatment formulation addresses the "What can be done about it, and how?" question.

The most useful and comprehensive case conceptualizations are integrative ones that encompass all four components: diagnostic, clinical, cultural, and treatment formulations (Sperry & Sperry, 2012; Sperry & Carlson, 2014). The format of the following chapters of this book will highlight integrative conceptualizations. The diagnostic formulation will emphasize DSM-5 criteria. The clinical formulation will emphasis Adlerian interpretations and dynamics, while the treatment formulation will suggest treatment goals and methods. Because DSM-5 is often incorporated into case conceptualizations today, the connection between DSM-5 and Adlerian dynamics will be evident throughout this book. Chapter 2 describes and illustrates how to develop Adlerian case conceptualizations.

Changes in *DSM-5*

The DSM diagnostic system has undergone some major changes since the second edition of this book was published in 1996. Most of these changes have involved adding or removing diagnoses and criteria. These will be described in subsequent chapters. However, there are also some major changes in the structure of the *DSM-5* (American Psychiatric Association, 2013), and these are briefly noted here.

Single-Axis Diagnoses

The most obvious change in *DSM-5* is the return to a single-axis diagnosis as it was in *DSM-I* and *DSM-II*. The multiaxial (5-axes) system was introduced in *DSM-III* and continued through *DSM-IV-TR*. Axis I was for coding clinical disorders and V codes, while Axis II was for coding personality disorders or mental retardation. Axis III was for coding general medical conditions that triggered or exacerbated the clinical disorder, and Axis IV was for specifying stressors that triggered or exacerbated the clinical disorder. Finally, Axis V was for coding the individual's current level of functioning and impairment on the Global Assessment of Functioning Scale (American Psychiatric Association, 2013).

The purpose of the former multiaxial system was to encourage clinicians to present a thorough description of clients and communicate it in a systematic way to other professionals, as well as to third-party payors such as HMOs and insurance companies. However, because there were drawbacks to this multiaxial approach, *DSM-5* returned to a one-axis system. One of the main drawbacks involved the personality disorders (Axis II). Although it was not the intent of earlier editions of *DSM*, the idea of making a diagnosis of a personality disorder became problematic for many clinicians. They were concerned that the diagnosis of a personality disorder would stigmatize the individual.

As a result, some clinicians did not specify an Axis II diagnosis, when it was present. This was complicated by the mistaken notion among therapists and third-party payors that personality disorders were untreatable. Consequently, some individuals who were diagnosed with personality disorders encountered problems securing treatment. Today, however, clients who meet the criteria for a personality-disorder diagnosis may now find it easier to navigate mental health treatment, as they will no longer be viewed as having a diagnosis that is more difficult to treat than other disorders.

Other drawbacks of the multiaxial system involved specifying medical conditions and V-code diagnoses. In *DSM-5*, medical conditions are no longer listed on a separate axis (Axis III). As a result, they are likely to have a more significant role in mental health diagnosis since they can be listed side-by-side with the mental disorder. Also, psychosocial and environmental stressors, previously listed on Axis IV of *DSM-IV*, are now listed alongside mental disorders and physical health issues. In fact, *DSM-5* has increased the number of "V codes" (designated as Z codes in ICD-10), which are considered nondisordered conditions that sometimes are the focus of treatment and often are reflective of a host of psychosocial and environmental issues (e.g., homelessness, divorce, etc.). Finally, the GAF score (Axis V) is gone. In place of this largely unreliable measure of functioning and impairment, *DSM-5* encourages the use of the World Health Organization Disability Assessment Schedule 2.0 (WHODAS 2.0).

In short, the former 5-axes system gave a hierarchical (multiaxial) view of a client's diagnostic presentation. Since Axis I came first, the assumption was that it should be the primary focus of treatment, and that diagnoses and information indicated in the other axes was of less importance in treatment planning. In contrast, the return of *DSM-5* to a single-axis diagnostic system has leveled the treatment playing field, so to speak.

Reporting and Specifying Diagnoses

One goal of the new *DSM-5* was to make the edition more clinician friendly. Accordingly, it acknowledges the value of case conceptualization and treatment planning, which no previous edition had. One way it accomplishes this is by changing the way of reporting diagnoses to a single-axis format. It includes specific rules for ordering and specifying diagnoses that reflect treatment considerations (American Psychiatric Association, 2013).

Because clients often have more than one diagnosis, it is important to consider their ordering. Clinicians now are expected to order or list diagnoses in a way that reflects the treatment process. This differs considerably from previous *DSM* editions where diagnoses were simply "ordered" by axes. Thus, the symptom disorder was always listed first, since that is where Axes I diagnoses were expected to be listed, while personality disorders were always listed second as Axis II diagnoses. In *DSM-5*, the first diagnosis is called the principal diagnosis. In an inpatient setting, this diagnosis is the one that led in the admission and is "ordered" first. In an outpatient setting, the principal diagnosis is the reason for the visit, or is the main focus of treatment. The secondary and tertiary diagnoses are listed in order of need for clinical attention. Take the example of a suicide attempt that results in a psychiatric hospitalization. If it is determined that the client's self-harming behavior was a frantic effort to avoid abandonment, the principal diagnosis is likely to be Borderline Personality Disorder, with secondary diagnoses of Relationship Distress with Intimate Partner (V61.10), followed by codes for her mood and substance disorders. However, when she is stabilized and referred for an outpatient substance-abuse treatment program, her principal diagnosis is likely to be the substance disorder, since it will be the main focus of treatment. There is an exception to this ordering rule: If a psychiatric diagnosis is due to a general medical condition, ICD coding rules require listing the medical condition before the psychiatric diagnosis related to the condition.

Subtypes are used to further clarify the diagnosis. In *DSM-5*, the designation "Specify whether" represents mutually exclusive groupings of symptoms, of which the clinician selects the most appropriate one. For example, Anorexia Nervosa has two different subtypes from which to choose: restricting type, or binge-eating/purging type. "Specifiers," on the other hand, are not mutually exclusive, so more than one can be used. Clinicians are expected to identify and list all the specifiers that apply. Anorexia Nervosa provides two specifiers: "in partial remission" or "in full remission." Some diagnoses will offer an opportunity to rate the severity of the symptoms. These are identified in the *DSM* as "Specify current severity." For the diagnosis of Anorexia Nervosa, there are four options of severity: mild, moderate, severe, or extreme (American Psychiatric Association, 2013).

DSM-5 also allows for more flexibility in rating severity through *dimensional diagnosis*. Some diagnoses offer greater options to clinicians when rating severity. For example, for the diagnosis of Schizophrenia the clinician may use the "Clinician-Rated Dimensions of Psychosis Symptom Severity" chart (American Psychiatric Association, 2013, pp. 743–744) to rate symptoms on a five-point Likert-like scale.

Psychosocial and Environmental Considerations

Assessment of a client's psychosocial and environmental stressors can provide a more complete view of the client's presenting problem. Besides identifying precipitant and stressors, a clinically useful assessment can provide diagnostic information helpful in treatment planning. This includes risk factors and protective factors such support system, education, work history, housing, economic circumstances, and access to healthcare (Sperry & Sperry, 2012). Whereas in previous *DSM* editions these factors were listed on Axis IV, they can now be indicated under "Other conditions that may be a focus of clinical attention" as V codes (which match ICD-9 CM) or Z codes (which match ICD-10 CM) (American Psychiatric Association, 2013).

Cultural Considerations

Because individuals from various cultures express themselves in different ways, symptoms can vary as a function of culture. To avoid misdiagnosis and facilitate treatment planning, *DSM-5* highlights "Cultural Related Diagnostic Issues" in the description of every diagnosis. It also offers the "Cultural Formulation Interview" (American Psychiatric Association, 2013). The interview format consists of 16 questions (11 for children) that are useful in eliciting a client's values, meaning of symptoms, explanatory model, and influences that have shaped the client's cultural worldview. From these a useful cultural formulation can be developed. Further, it offers definitions of various cultural syndromes.

Biological and Medical Considerations

Medical conditions can mimic mental disorders. For instance, a client may present with symptoms of sadness, fatigue, poor appetite, trouble concentrating, and trouble sleeping. Since this presentation meets the criteria for Major Depressive Disorder, should this diagnosis be given? Not necessarily, since this same symptom presentation can be caused by hypothyroidism (underactive thyroid). These symptoms are also common in chronic kidney disease. So, what is the diagnosis: Major Depressive Disorder, hypothyroidism, or chronic kidney disease? Today, all the mental health professions have adopted the biopsychosocial model. This model has influenced clinical practice such that mental health clinicians are expected to screen for the influence of biological and medical factors on a client's presenting problem. Besides a review of past records and an interview to screen for medical conditions, an adequate biopsychosocial assessment may include a referral for a medical evaluation, if there are concerns that a medical problem may be contributing to, or exacerbating, the client's presentation. In the past, a medical condition that contributed to the Axis I diagnosis would have been reported on Axis III. Today, it is reported with an ICD code along with the DSM-5 diagnosis (American Psychiatric Association, 2013).

Individual Psychology and DSM-5

Quite unlike other psychological systems, which are based on a pathology or disease-model, Adlerian theory is based on a growth-model. It emphasizes the element of discouragement in the dysfunctional individual rather than focusing primarily on psychopathological symptoms (Mosak, 1984). Similarly, because it is a psychology of use rather than of possession, Adlerian Psychology does not emphasize the diagnostic classification of symptoms. Instead, Adlerian clinicians emphasize the meaning, purpose, and use of dysfunctional thinking, behavior, and symptoms. Since the Adlerian approach emphasizes the psychological reasons or mechanisms that are considered to be important in explaining behavior and symptoms, it has a *psychodynamic focus*; and since it also emphasizes attitudes and beliefs about self and the world, it has a *cognitive focus*. Finally, because it emphasizes family constellation, social interactions, and psychological movement, it has a *systemic focus*. In short, for an Adlerian clinician, a clinical formulation integrates psychodynamic, cognitive, and systemic dynamics (Mosak & Maniacci, 1999). This emphasis on the clinical formulation does not mean that Adlerian clinicians underplay or fail to specify a diagnostic formulation and DSM diagnoses. Instead, Adlerian clinicians can assign a formal diagnosis, if requested by an insurance carrier or by clinic policy. Still, observations about the individual's movement, life-style convictions, and descriptions about the uniqueness of the individual are considered more useful than diagnostic categories.

Interestingly, Adler was apparently not averse to personality typing, a form of diagnosis. He characterized four personality types: the ruling, getting, avoiding, and the healthy, socially useful person. The first three types describe individuals who are discouraged and low in social interest, and each would be considered dysfunctional. Mosak (1959; 1971; 1979; 1984) has briefly described several other personality types and has provided in-depth analyses of the getting and controlling types. Adler considered the obsessive-compulsive neurosis to be the prototype of all neuroses, while the hysterical neurosis was the prototype for Freud. Indecisiveness and doubt, depreciation of others, god-like strivings, and focus on minutiae were the safeguarding methods that Adler routinely noted were used by his compulsive-neurotic patients in seeking their goal of personal superiority. He observed that various neurotic and psychotic individuals might use different safeguarding methods, but their movement was nevertheless the same: avoidance or rejection of the life tasks.

Unlike the Adlerian approach with its unitary theory of psychopathology, *DSM-5* describes 22 distinct diagnostic categories covering more than 300 mental disorders (American Psychiatric Association, 2013). Each disorder has a unique set of descriptive—rather than dynamic—diagnostic criteria. A DSM-5 diagnosis can be made when a match exists between the facts from a particular individual's history and clinical presentation and the diagnostic criteria for a particular mental disorder. In short, the DSM-5 system is based on a pathological model and a psychology of possession, while the Adlerian approach is based on a growth model and a psychology of use. Consequently, the Adlerian therapist might not be as concerned about making a DSM-5 type of descriptive diagnosis as he/she would be in understanding the individual's dynamics; that is, movement and life-style themes. But, just as differences exist between the two approaches, some important similarities also exist.

As the Adlerian approach strives toward an integrative-biopsychosocial understanding of the individual, *DSM-5* allows for a biopsychosocial view of the person. The obvious question is: How can DSM diagnostic categories be interrelated with the Adlerian view of personality? In what many consider to be a classic in the psychopathology literature, Mosak (1968) has helped a generation of clinicians to interrelate central themes or basic life-style convictions with DSM diagnostic categories. These central themes are determined from clinical observation, psychological testing, and particularly through early recollections. Mosak listed the eight most common themes: getter; controller; driver; to be good, perfect, right; martyrs; victims; "aginners"; feeling avoiders; and excitement seekers. He also interrelated combinations of these themes with 19 diagnostic categories. For example, the life style of a person who would be traditionally diagnosed with a depressive disorder would likely be a composite, in varying degrees of the getter, the controller, and the person needing to be right (Mosak, 1979). For the antisocial personality, the themes would likely be those of the getter, the "aginner," and excitement seeker.

From Diagnosis to Treatment

How does a clinician know whether a client is receiving the most appropriate clinical care? The current consensus favors treatment that is matched or tailored to the client's needs and expectations. Tailored treatment is a logical extension of cooperation between clinician and client in Adlerian Psychology. Tailored treatment is based on a comprehensive evaluation and integrative case formulation, as well as on a negotiated, mutual agreement about treatment expectations and methods.

Briefly, a comprehensive clinical evaluation usually includes the presenting complaints and their history, mental status, social and developmental history, health status, previous treatment, and the client's explanation of the condition and expectations for treatment. These last two items represent the client's formulation. In addition, the

Adlerian clinician would observe and elicit information on life tasks and on life-style themes and convictions. The integrative clinical formulation suggests the origins and meaning of the client's concerns. Because it is an integrative statement, it accounts for biological and familial predispositions; the client's coping skills; faulty life-style convictions; as well as interpersonal, occupational, and social-system factors. A DSM-5 diagnosis, problem list, statement of the client's motivation and capacity for treatment, impact of cultural factors, and prognosis round out the case conceptualization.

The negotiation process begins with the clinician acknowledging the client's own case conceptualization, and the similarities and differences from the clinician's case conceptualization. The ensuing discussion allows the clinician to educate the client about his/her illness and clarify misconceptions about it and the treatment process. Discussion of the client's expectations for the treatment process and outcomes facilitates negotiating a mutually agreeable direction for treatment and a therapeutic relationship based on cooperation. Then, the specifics of treatment selection can be discussed.

Case Example: The Case of Mrs. A. Revisited

As noted earlier, Alfred Adler's most famous case was that of Mrs. A. What follows is a summary and case conceptualization of the Case of Mrs. A., as it might be reported by a clinician today, along with diagnostic, clinical, cultural, and treatment formulations. The reader should note that Adler did not treat her nor even interview her. Instead, Mrs. A. was an ongoing patient of Dr. Hilda Weber. At a professional meeting of physicians in 1931, Adler was asked to comment on parts of Dr. Weber's written case study. In his consultation, Adler was able to deduce Mrs. A.'s life-style themes. Here is a contemporary rendering of this case using DSM-5 terminology. Her life-style themes are noted in the Biopsychosocial–Adlerian Case Conceptualization (clinical formulation) section.

Mrs. A. is a 31-year-old married housewife with two children, who presents with a dysphoric mood, a cleaning compulsion, a knife phobia, and a fear of seriously harming her younger son. She dates these progressively worsening symptoms of 18 months to a terrifying dream in which angels surrounded a coffin. But it appears the symptoms span the eight years of her marriage, probably beginning with her immense disappointment that her first child was a boy rather than a girl. In time she became jealous of her husband's popularity and friends, had difficulty relating to her neighbors, and as their marital discord increased, threatened to kill herself and her son if things did not change. Her vanity was severely wounded when a second son was born about three years later. Soon thereafter, a drunken neighbor threatened to kill her with a knife. She subsequently moved out of their home, taking her two children, and moved in with her parents. During her absence, her husband had a "nervous breakdown" and begged her to return to care for him. After she returned, her obsessive thoughts and compulsions incapacitated her to the point that she was referred for treatment. Following her suicidal threats, her husband took her for an evaluation, at which time she was diagnosed with a "nervous stomach," a psychosomatic condition. Psychotherapy was neither recommended nor requested. This was approximately four years ago.

She denies any family history of psychiatric illness, but reports alcoholism on her father's side of the family. Father was described as a construction worker who was impulsive, physically abusive, and a binge drinker. Her mother was described as hardworking but non-assertive. Marital conflict was precipitated by her father's drinking and loud threats to "cut everyone's throat." She was the third of eight children, four girls followed by four boys. Mrs. A. described herself as a child as being cheerful, fun loving, and well liked by everyone, except her oldest brother, whom she described as selfish and inconsiderate. She described her older sister as selfish, because she was silent and reserved, and was severely disciplined for small matters.

She reports being in excellent health as a child, doing well in school, and having many friends. She left high school before graduation—which was not uncommon among her female friends—and had a number of unskilled jobs before marrying. While she lived at home and worked, she did well. But when jobs necessitated, she lived away from home, and developed numerous somatic symptoms including a severe skin condition and an enlarged thyroid gland. After her physician insisted that she return to live at home, her symptoms subsided. Thereafter she was able to return to work, choosing male-oriented jobs. She explained she didn't want to work around things like fine glassware or china, since she dreaded breaking such items. One day, her father threatened to kill her with a shovel because her return home had become a financial drain on the family. She ran from the house and hid at a nearby church, vowing she would never return to live at home again. At the age of 21 she broke off an engagement of three years to a rather passive and clinging male. Soon thereafter, she met her husband while he was recuperating from wounds sustained in the military. He was all she had dreamed of in a mate: tall, handsome, and a non-drinker. Like the marriage, their courtship was conflicted. He left her, and she pursued him when she learned that she was pregnant with their child. A "shot gun" wedding followed. She reports that he refuses to help her with housework and assisting with care of their children. On the other hand, he did help in arranging treatment for her.

Diagnostic Formulation

Of primary concern is Mrs. A.'s obsession that she would hurt her child. Since such thoughts are not uncommon in mothers with Obsessive-Compulsive Disorder, it is likely that this obsessive thought primarily accounts for her current distress. The fact that the child's safety can be comprised by Mrs. A.'s impulsivity and affective instability (associated with her Borderline Personality Disorder) serves to exacerbate her distressing symptoms. Her depressed mood also appears to be contributing to her distress, particularly since she reported she had run out of her thyroid medication several days ago. The context in which her distress occurs is her relationship with her children, particularly her younger son.

Here are her DSM-5 diagnoses:

300.30 Obsessive-Compulsive Disorder with poor insight.
301.83 Borderline Personality Disorder.
293.83 [F06.31] Depressive Disorder due to hypothyroidism with mild severity.
V61.20 Parent–Child Problems Relational Problem.

Biopsychosocial–Adlerian Conceptualization Clinical Formulation

The influence of her hypothyroidism as well as her temperament (impulsivity and affective instability) are central in explaining Mrs. A.'s presenting concerns. They appear to exacerbate her current stressors, her psychological dynamics, and the lack of support she experiences from her family and her husband.

She views life as hostile, unfair, and overcontrolling. She sees herself as a victim who expects to be humiliated, but also believes that she is entitled to be treated differently. Therefore, she demands that others take care of her, and she utilizes obsessions, compulsions, and threats of harming herself and her child, to insure that her husband and family continue in their caretaking roles. Mrs. A. also utilizes interpersonal relationships as a means of gaining dominance and resisting submission, and so she would likely construe cooperation as conquest. Therefore, a clinician might anticipate that the development of cooperative therapeutic relationships would take some time and that the negotiation phase of therapy would be very important and could not be downplayed. Also, because Mrs. A. showed relatively little insight and psychological mindedness, and was rather ambivalent, the initial phase of treatment should not focus primarily on insight and interpretation. In short, a clinician would endeavor to gain Mrs. A.'s cooperation from the very onset by attending to her expectations of treatment and by encouraging her involvement, while being aware of her ambivalent, controlling, and entitled life style.

Cultural Formulation

Mrs. A. identifies herself as a working-class female of German descent who is reasonably well acculturated. She believes her problems are caused by the abuse she suffered at the hands of her father and that it "scarred" her for life. She also believes she is being punished by God, because she can't control her murderous thoughts and impulses. It appears that while some cultural factors have a limited role, personality factors are primarily operative.

Treatment Formulation

The initial focus of treatment would be to elicit Mrs. A.'s expectations for treatment, for the clinician's role, and for her role in treatment. A mutually agreed-upon treatment plan would then be negotiated. Presumably, the treatment plan would involve symptom reduction at first, followed by stabilization of marriage and family relations, and at the same time address the influence of her Borderline Personality features, particularly impulsivity and affective instability.

Because of her history of hypothyroidism and psychosomatic symptoms (nervous stomach), a medical evaluation would be arranged, and, if indicated, restarting her thyroid medication. A short course of treatment with a trial of an antidepressant, anti-obsessive-compulsive medication (i.e., Anafranil), and/or focused behavior therapy aimed at symptom reduction is indicated. In addition, whatever measures might be needed to insure that Mrs. A. did not harm her children or herself (such as consultation with a child protective services agency) would be advised. Then, because of the chronic severity of her condition, psychosocial stressors, as well as her Borderline Personality features, a course of individual supportive therapy, with adjunctive sessions involving her husband and/or children, as well as a consideration of group therapy, would be indicated. Half-hour sessions would probably be scheduled twice weekly until sufficient symptom reduction was achieved and a stable therapeutic relationship had developed.

In the second phase of treatment, sessions might be weekly and focus on longer-term-problem issues such as parent–child and marital relations, and her faulty life-style convictions about overcontrol and entitlement, as well as her need to somatize, her threats of acting out, masculine protest, and so on. Because of her personality features, particularly impulsivity and affective instability, it is likely Mrs. A. might prove to be a difficult patient. However, she would merit a fair to good prognosis, assuming she would continue in her commitment to treatment.

Concluding Note

This chapter began with a description of the Adlerian perspective on normality and psychopathology. Then, it presented some of the basic changes in the use of the *Diagnostic and Statistical Manual, Fifth Edition (DSM-5)* (American Psychiatric Association, 2013) in clinical practice. Next, it compared the atheoretical model of DSM-5 with the Adlerian Psychology model. It suggested how a clinician with an Adlerian perspective could incorporate DSM-5 in his/her case conceptualization to account for diagnostic and cultural factors as well as treatment considerations. Finally, a case conceptualization of the Case of Mrs. A. was presented to illustrate the relationships of DSM-5 and Adlerian theory. The intent of this chapter is to set the stage for the chapters to come.

References

Adler, A. (1956). In H.H. Ansbacher & R.R. Ansbacher (Eds.), *The Individual Psychology of Alfred Adler*. New York, NY: Harper & Row.

Adler, A. (1964a). *Superiority and Social Interest*. Evanston, IL: Northwestern University Press.

Adler, A. (1964b). In H.H. Ansbacher & R.R. Ansbacher (Eds.), *Problems of Neurosis. A Book of Case Histories*. New York, NY: Harper & Row.

Adler, A. (1969). *The Case of Mrs. A.: The Diagnosis of a Life Style* (2nd edn., with commentary by B. Shulman, M.D.). Chicago, IL: Alfred Adler Institute Publishers.

American Psychiatric Association (2013). *Diagnostic and Statistical Manual of Mental Disorders, Fifth Edition*. Arlington, VA: American Psychiatric Publishing.

Carlson, J., Watts, R., & Maniacci, M. (2006). *Adlerian Therapy: Theory and Practice*. Washington, DC: American Psychological Association.

Dreikurs, R. (1967). The psychological interview in medicine. In R. Dreikurs (Ed.), *Psychodynamics, Psychotherapy and Counseling* (pp. 75–102). Chicago, IL: Alfred Adler Institute.

Mosak, H. (1959). The getting type, a parsimonious social interpretation of the oral character. *Journal of Individual Psychology*, 15(2), pp. 193–198.

Mosak, H. (1968). The interrelatedness of the neuroses through central themes. *Journal of Individual Psychology*, 24(1), pp. 67–70.

Mosak, H. (1971). Lifestyle. In A. Nikelly (Ed.), *Techniques for Behavior Changes: Applications of Adlerian Theory* (pp.77–81). Springfield, IL: Charles C. Thomas.

Mosak, H. (1973). The controller: A social interpretation of the anal character. In H.H. Mosak (Ed.), *Alfred Adler: His Influence on Psychology Today*. Park Ridge, NJ: Noyes Press, pp. 43–52.

Mosak, H. (1979). Mosak's typology: An update. *Journal of Individual Psychology*, 35(2), pp. 92–95.

Mosak, H. (1984). Adlerian psychology. In R. Corsini and B. Ozaki (Eds.), *Encyclopedia of Psychology*. New York, NY: Wiley-Interscience.

Mosak, H. & Maniacci, M. (1999). *Adlerian Psychology: The Analytic-Behavioral-Cognitive Psychology of Alfred Adler*. Philadelphia, PA: Brunner/Mazel.

Neufield, I. (1954). Holistic medicine versus psychosomatic medicine. *American Journal of Individual Psychology*, 10(3 & 4), pp. 140–168.

Pancner, R. (1985). Impact of current depression research on Adlerian theory and practice. *Individual Psychology*, 41(3), pp. 289–301.

Shulman, B. (1969) Foreword to second edition. In F.G. Crookshank (Ed.), *The Case of Mrs. A*. Chicago, IL: Alfred Adler Institute, p. 9.

Slavik, S. & Carlson, J. (Eds.) (2006). *Readings in the Theory of Individual Psychology*. New York, NY: Routledge.

Sperry, L. (1996). Psychopathology and the diagnostic and treatment process. In L. Sperry & J. Carlson (Eds.), *Psychopathology and Psychotherapy: From DSM-IV Diagnosis to Treatment* (2nd edn.) (pp. 3–18). Washington, DC: Accelerated Development/Taylor & Francis.

Sperry, L. (2010). *Highly Effective Therapy: Developing Essential Clinical Competencies in Counseling and Psychotherapy*. New York, NY: Routledge.

Sperry, L. & Carlson, J. (2014). *How Master Therapists Work*. New York, NY: Routledge.

Sperry, L., Gudeman, J., Blackwell, B., & Faulkner, L. (1992). *Psychiatric Case Formulations*. Washington, DC: American Psychiatric Publishing.

Sperry, L. & Maniacci, M. (1992). An integration of DSM-III-R diagnoses and Adlerian case formulations. *Individual Psychology*, 48, pp. 175–181.

Sperry, L. & Sperry, J. (2012). *Case Conceptualization: Mastering This Competency With Ease and Confidence*. New York, NY: Routledge.

2 Adlerian Case Conceptualization

Len Sperry

In this age of accountability, effective clinical practice presumes that therapists can and will competently develop and utilize case conceptualizations. Previously called case formulations, a case conceptualization is the most important competency in psychotherapy. Basically, a case conceptualization is a method for understanding and explaining a client's presenting concerns, and a strategy for guiding the treatment process (Sperry, 2005; Sperry & Sperry, 2012). Chapter 1 introduced the four components of a case conceptualization and described it as a "bridge" to connect clinical assessment to treatment planning, interventions, and clinical outcomes. This chapter describes an integrative case conceptualization model, its premises, and its benefits. Then, it describes an Adlerian perspective on conceptualizing and planning psychotherapeutic treatment. A case example illustrates the discussion.

An Integrative Approach to Case Conceptualization

While the term case conceptualization is relatively new, the process of explaining case material is not, and the Adlerian explanatory model appears to have influenced other approaches. In fact, Adlerian Psychotherapy is compatible with a wide range of contemporary approaches (Ansbacher & Ansbacher, 1956). These approaches include the analytic, behavioral, cognitive-behavioral, constructivist, interpersonal, and systemic approaches (Mosak & Maniacci, 1999; Carlson, Watts, & Maniacci, 2006). For the most part, these approaches emphasize pattern and self–other schemas, such as self-view and world-view. Both of these are basic constructs in Adlerian theory and the basis of an integrative approach to Adlerian case conceptualization (Sperry, 1989). This is not to suggest that all approaches to case conceptualization are the same. Actually, there are elements that are unique in every approach, as well as elements that are common among the approaches. A truly integrative approach to case conceptualization captures the *common elements* of the various approaches while retaining the distinctive or *approach-specific* elements of each approach (Eells, 2007, 2010).

Basic Premises and Elements

In the opinion of many, case conceptualization is one of the most challenging clinical competencies to master. The perceived difficulty in developing an effective case conceptualization may be one reason why many therapists neither develop nor use case conceptualizations, or why they lack confidence in their ability to conceptualize cases. My experience is that both therapists and graduate students can easily and confidently master this competency in as little as two hours of training. The training approach involves learning an integrated model of case conceptualization based on common and distinctive elements; and that emphasizes the element of pattern, i.e., the maladaptive pattern.

Two basic premises underlie this integrative model. The first premise is that individuals unwittingly develop a self-perpetuating, maladaptive pattern of functioning and of relating to others. Inevitably, this pattern underlies the individual's presenting issues. Effective treatment always involves a change process in which the client and therapist collaborate to identify this pattern, break it, and replace it with a more adaptive pattern. At least two outcomes result from this change process: increased well-being, and resolution of the client's presenting issue.

The second premise is that pattern recognition and pattern change is at the heart of the case-conceptualization process. Pattern is the predictable, consistent, and self-perpetuating style and manner in which individuals think, feel, act, cope, and defend themselves (Sperry, Brill, Howard, & Grissom, 1996; Sperry, 2006). Pattern change involves three processes: (1) identify the maladaptive pattern; (2) relinquish the maladaptive pattern and replace it with a more adaptive pattern; and (3) maintain the adaptive pattern (Beitman & Yue, 1999).

The integrative case conceptualization described in this chapter is comprised of some 17 elements, which are identified in Tables 2.1 and 2.2. Table 2.1 lists and defines 12 elements that are common to most case conceptualization models. Table 2.2 lists and identifies five elements that are specific and unique to a given model or approach. For instance, family constellation and life-style convictions are unique Predisposing factors (or Predispositions) in the Adlerian model, while maladaptive beliefs and schemas are unique to the Cognitive Therapy model. Taken together, these 17 elements represent an integrative case conceptualization (Sperry & Sperry, 2012).

Table 2.1 Common Elements of an Integrative Case Conceptualization

Presentation	presenting problem and characteristic response to precipitants
Precipitant	trigger that activates the pattern, resulting in presenting problem
Pattern: maladaptive	inflexible, ineffective manner of perceiving, thinking, acting
Perpetuants	triggers that activate one's pattern, resulting in presentation
Cultural identity	sense of belonging to a particular ethnic group
Culture: acculturation and acculturative stress	level of adaptation to the dominant culture; stress rooted acculturation including psychosocial difficulties
Cultural explanation	beliefs regarding cause of distress, condition, or impairment
Culture versus personality	operative mix of cultural and personality dynamics
Treatment pattern	flexible, effective manner of perceiving, thinking, acting
Treatment obstacles	predictable challenges in the treatment process anticipated from the maladaptive pattern
Treatment—cultural	incorporation of cultural intervention, culturally sensitive therapy, or cultural therapy interventions when indicated
Treatment prognosis	prediction of the likely course, duration, and outcome of a mental health condition with or without treatment

Table 2.2 Approach-Specific Elements of an Integrative Case Conceptualization

Predisposition	factors that offer a theoretical explanation for adaptive and maladaptive functioning; includes risk factors, protective factors, and relevant strengths
Treatment goals	stated short- and long-term outcomes of treatment
Treatment focus	central therapeutic emphasis providing directionality to treatment that is keyed to the adaptive pattern
Treatment strategy	action plan and vehicle for achieving a more adaptive pattern
Treatment interventions	specific change techniques and tactics related to the treatment strategy for achieving treatment goals and pattern change

Strengths and Protective Factors

This integrative case conceptualization model accounts for strengths and protective factors as well as deficits and risk factors. The influence of client strengths and protective factors on Predisposition is particularly important in the Adlerian case conceptualization, as well as other positive therapeutic approaches that endeavor to account for and balance strengths and development with deficits and pathology. The relationship of Predisposition to Pattern, Perpetuants, Precipitant, and Presentation and the influence of deficits/risks and strengths/protective factors is depicted in Figure 2.1.

Benefits of an Integrative Approach

There are few, if any, case conceptualization approaches that are both comprehensive and relatively easy to learn and use (Eells, 2007). Some approaches are overly detailed in their attempt to be complete, while others leave out key factors for the sake of brevity. According to Eells (2007), the benefits of an integrative approach are that it includes key factors that are common to most approaches, while at the same time highlighting factors unique to a specific approach. For instance, it would be expected that an integrative approach would highlight Adlerian constructs such as family constellation, life-style convictions, and encouragement, but also include factors or elements common to other

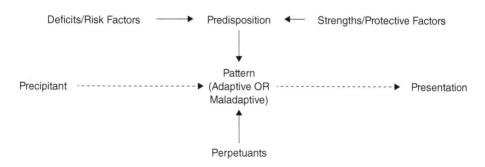

Figure 2.1 Relationship of Key Case Conceptualization Elements

approaches, such as presenting symptoms, precipitants, cultural factors, prognosis, etc. In contrast, an Adlerian case conceptualization that only included family constellation, life-style convictions (Predisposition), treatment goals, and interventions, such as encouragement and "acting as if," would be quite limited clinically, because it leaves out key elements that experts consider essential.

Adlerian Perspective, Assessment, and Approach to Case Conceptualization

Adlerian Perspective

Basic Adlerian constructs include life style, belonging, birth order, family constellation, private logic, social interest, life-style convictions, and basic mistakes. The Adlerian perspective assumes that the basic human motivation is to belong and develop social interest, i.e., willingness to contribute to the well-being of others. Development is influenced by family constellation, i.e., family dynamics, where individuals find a sense of belonging and self-worth, and birth order, i.e., psychological position in the family. Individuals create their own interpretation of life events derived from their unique subjective private logic, which becomes their life style, i.e., the cognitive map which guides their perceptions and actions. Their life style contains personalized convictions about self-view, world-view, and conclusions and life strategies that reflect their life narrative. Adler believed that high levels of social interest reflected mental health and well-being. Furthermore, problems in daily living are understood as the result of not experiencing a sense of belonging, or unhealthy ways of belonging.

Psychopathology is viewed as the way an individual "arranges" symptoms that serve as excuses for failing to meet "life tasks," i.e., one's responsibilities, and for safeguarding self-esteem. Psychopathology reflects discouragement and is manifested in clients' faulty life-style convictions, i.e., convictions that run counter to social interest, and are summarized as basic mistakes.

The Adlerian perspective is optimistic and focuses on assets, strengths, protective factors, and health, rather than on liabilities, deficits, and pathology. Psychotherapy is viewed as a learning process, based on encouragement, with the purpose of increasing a sense of belonging and social interest. The therapeutic relationship is characterized by mutual respect and equality. Client and practitioner are collaborative partners in the therapeutic endeavor, wherein the client is expected to assume an active role in the change process.

Adlerian Assessment

An Adlerian assessment emphasizes relevant Adlerian factors that add additional information to the diagnostic assessment, and facilitate the development of Adlerian-focused clinical and treatment formulations. Assessment focuses on both the current situations and predisposing factors, i.e., life-style analysis. This assessment includes gathering information about a client's family constellation and early developmental experiences, including early recollections. This information will assist the practitioner in deriving the individual's unique life-style convictions. Adler also posed three life tasks that all individuals strive to achieve: love, friendship, and work. Assessment focuses on the extent that a client has successfully or unsuccessfully approached these life tasks. Understanding clients' life styles permits practitioners to help clients better understand how their basic beliefs and perceptions influence their lifestyle and actions.

Three Adlerian constructs are critical to the assessment and case conceptualization process. Inferences are drawn from this data and are formulated into a case conceptualization statement. These constructs are:

Family Constellation

The family constellation includes information about a client's relationships with other family members, psychological birth order, family values, and the way the client found a sense of belonging in their family.

Helpful questions to elicit the family constellation are:

1. What was it like growing up in your household?
2. What was it like being the oldest (youngest, middle, or only) child in your family?
3. Describe your relationships with your parents. Which one were you most like? Of your siblings who was your mother's favorite? Father's favorite?
4. Describe the relationship between your parents. Who was the breadwinner? Who made the big decisions? How did they solve problems? Conflicts? Did they show affection openly? Who was the disciplinarian? Who did you go to when you got hurt or were frightened?
5. What were the family values? What were you expected to do (or be) when you grew up?
6. How would you describe your relationships with your siblings? Who got the best grades? Who was the most athletic? Had the most friends? Got into trouble the most? How are they doing now?

Early Recollections

Early recollections are a projective technique used to determine a client's self-view, view of others, world-view, and his or her overall strategy in dealing with others and with life's challenges. Early recollections also reflect the client's level of social interest, their movement toward life tasks, and their life-style convictions.

Here is a method for eliciting early recollections:

1. "Think back to your early life—before the age of nine—and tell me your first memory. It should be about a single experience that you specifically recall, rather than one that someone told you happened. Not a repeated experience but a single one."
2. If the client has difficulty identifying a memory, prompt him or her by asking about a memorable birthday, the first day of school, a specific vacation, etc.
3. For each memory: ask how old they were at the time; elicit the sequence of the memory; how it began and ended; who was involved; what each person was doing or saying; the most vivid moment in the sequence; what they felt at that moment; what they were thinking at that moment.

Life-style Convictions

Life-style convictions are conclusions about a client's inner world, derived from information about family constellation, birth order, early recollections, and overcompensation. In other approaches this is referred to as self–others schemas. They represent the individual basic pattern.

Here is a formula statement that summarizes the individual's self–others schemas and converts these convictions into a pattern:

1. I am … (self-view)
2. Life is …People are … (world-view)
3. Therefore…(life strategy or pattern for achieving a sense of belonging and meaning, which reflect self-view and world-view)

The client's "basic mistakes" are derived from these convictions, and reflected in the client's maladaptive pattern, which is essentially the life strategy.

Adlerian Approach to Case Conceptualization

An integrative Adlerian case conceptualization approach emphasizes both common and distinctive elements. Characteristic of this Adlerian approach to case conceptualization is the view of the clients' situational and longitudinal patterns. The conceptualization helps clients understand who they are, and how they become who they are. It also helps clients to increase awareness of their family dynamics and their life-style convictions, both of which are reflected in their maladaptive patterns. Treatment planning and implementation includes a plan to modify faulty life-style convictions and basic mistakes, and to increase social interest. Table 2.3 identifies and describes these five distinctive or signature elements.

Adlerian Case Conceptualization: Case Example

The process of constructing an Adlerian case conceptualization is illustrated here. Following background information, there is an assessment paragraph that identifies key

Table 2.3 Distinctive Elements of an Adlerian Case Conceptualization

Predisposition	family constellation: especially birth order and family environment life-style convictions: specifically early recollections, self- and world-view, and life strategy
Treatment goals	increase social interest and constructive action
Treatment focus	process situations triggered or exacerbated by mistaken beliefs and/or discouragement
Treatment strategy	modify life-style convictions
Treatment interventions	life-style assessment; early recollection analysis; encouragement; use of metaphor, stories, humor; acting "as if"; constructive action; paradox

information germane to this model. Then, a table summarizes the nine elements from the diagnostic, clinical, and cultural formulations, and the eight elements of the treatment formulation for that specific case. Finally, a narrative integrating this information is provided in a case conceptualization statement. The first paragraph reports the diagnostic and clinical formulation, the second paragraph reports the cultural formulation, and the third reports the treatment formulation.

Case of Geri

Geri is a 35-year-old African-American female who works as an administrative assistant. She is single, lives alone, and was referred by her company's human resources director for evaluation and treatment following three weeks of depression and social isolation. Her absence from work prompted the referral. Geri's symptoms began soon after her supervisor told her that she was being considered for a promotion. As a child, she reports isolating and avoiding others when she was criticized and teased by family members and peers. She is highly acculturated, and believes that her depression is a result of work stress and a "chemical imbalance" in her brain.

Adlerian Assessment

Besides diagnostic assessment information, the Adlerian assessment added the following: Geri had difficulty relating to her peers both in early life as well as currently. Geri is the oldest child and has a younger brother who is eight years younger than her. She is the psychological "only child." Geri reports that she was her father's favorite until her brother was born. As a child, she had difficulty relating to her peers while in school and was often criticized. She mentioned that her parents have been and continue to be unsupportive, demanding, and critical toward her. Three family values worth noting are "children are to be seen and not heard," "your worth depends on what you achieve in life," and "family secrets do not leave the family." Her earliest recollection involves feeling displaced and no longer wanted by her parents the day her mother brought her newborn brother home. Her father said it was the happiest day of his life, and Geri's reaction was to run out of the house and hide in her tree fort feeling angry, alone, sad, and rejected and thinking that nobody wanted her anymore. Another recollection was being told that what she painted in art class was awful, to which she felt sad and hurt. Table 2.4 summarizes the common and distinctive elements of an integrative Adlerian case conceptualization. Highlighted are the results of the Adlerian assessment (Predisposition) and treatment plan (treatment goals, treatment focus, treatment strategy, and treatment interventions).

Table 2.4 Case of Geri: Case Conceptualization Elements

Presentation	increased social isolation and depressive symptoms
Precipitant	her reaction to an impending job promotion and transfer out of a close-knit work group
Pattern: maladaptive	disconnects when feeling unsafe
Predisposition	*Family Constellation:* psychologically an only child; demanding and critical parents; teasing sibling; family valued achievement and secrecy; she modeled emotional distancing, and failed to develop social-relational skills *Life-style convictions:* I am inadequate and defective (self-view) Life is demanding, harsh, arbitrary, and unsafe (world-view) Therefore, avoid relationships and withdraw when feeling unsafe (life strategy) *Protective factors/strength* one trustworthy friend and Geri's dog; religious convictions; anticipation that she will qualify for a return-to-work accommodation re. her psychiatric disability
Perpetuants	maintained by her shyness, living alone, and generalized social isolation
Cultural identity	African-American conflicted about limited ethnic ties
Acculturation and acculturative stress	highly acculturated; no obvious acculturative stress
Cultural explanation	depression results from job stress and chemical brain imbalance
Culture versus personality	personality dynamics are significantly operative
Treatment pattern	connects while feeling safer
Treatment goals	decrease depression and discouragement; increase social interest; increase relational skills
Treatment focus	situations triggered/exacerbated by mistaken beliefs or discouragement
Treatment strategy	foster social interest and constructive action; support; interpretation; acting "as if"; medication
Treatment interventions	early recollection analysis; encouragement; acting "as if"
Treatment obstacles	"tests" practitioners; likely to resist group therapy; over dependence on therapists; difficulty with termination
Treatment—cultural	gender may be an issue, so assign supportive female practitioners
Treatment prognosis	good, if increased social connections, skills, and returns to work

Case Conceptualization Statement

Geri's increased social isolation and depressive symptoms *(Presentation)* seem to be her discouraged reaction to the news of an impending job transfer and promotion *(Precipitant)*, given her history of having critical and demanding people in her life. She avoids most relationships and has a history of isolating throughout her childhood *(Pattern)*. Geri's presenting problems are understandable when viewed from the perspective of her life style. Her style of relating with others mirrors the tentative and avoidant manner in which she related to family members. She sought a safe way to connect to family members without being criticized or having unreasonable demands put on her. She views herself as inadequate and defective as a person, and views life and others as demanding, harsh, arbitrary, and critical. Therefore, Geri found her place by avoiding most relationships, socially isolating, and overly investing in those she deems as trustworthy. This allowed her to avoid being criticized and helped her "feel safe." Her strategy of avoiding relationships and withdrawing anytime she feels unsafe works, but the price she pays to feel "safe" is high: she is lonely, has limited relational skills and experiences, and desires a close intimate relationship that seems unlikely. Some protective factors were identified that could positively impact treatment. She has a trusting relationship with a co-worker and has a dog whom she cares for. She holds strongly to religious convictions against suicide, and she will likely qualify for a return-to-work accommodation (ADA or Americans for Disabilities Act) because of her psychiatric disability *(Predisposition)*. Furthermore, her strategy of shyness, living alone, and social isolation serves to reinforce her maladaptive pattern *(Perpetuants)*.

She identifies herself as a middle-class African-American but is not involved with that community *(Cultural identity)*. She and her parents are highly acculturated and there is no obvious acculturative stress *(Acculturation)*. She believes that her depression is the result of stresses at work and a "chemical imbalance" in her brain *(Cultural explanation)*. There are no obvious cultural factors that are operative. Instead, it appears that Geri's personality dynamics are significantly operative in her current clinical presentation *(Culture versus personality)*.

The challenge for Geri is to function more effectively and feel safer in relating to others *(Treatment pattern)*. Decreasing discouragement and depressive symptoms, increasing social interest and social relating, and enhancing relational skills are the primary goals of treatment *(Treatment goals)*. The focus of treatment will be to analyze troublesome situations triggered or exacerbated by her by mistaken beliefs *(Treatment focus)*. The basic treatment strategy is to foster social interest and constructive action. Compatible treatment strategies include medication, support, and interpretation *(Treatment strategy)*. The practitioner will include support in the form of encouragement for Geri to engage and connect with her practitioner throughout the entire treatment process. Interpretation will be utilized regarding Geri's life-style convictions or basic mistakes, by analyzing and modifying her faulty convictions regarding her avoidance in order to feel safe. While Geri says she really wished she could be more comfortable talking with a neighbor, she will be encouraged to act "as if" she was comfortable. A referral will be made for a medication evaluation and, if indicated, medication monitoring will be arranged. Return to work can be facilitated by advocating for an ADA job accommodation by which Geri can return to work in a safer setting *(Treatment interventions)*. Some obstacles and challenges to treatment can be anticipated. Given her Avoidant Personality pattern, ambivalent resistance is likely. It can be anticipated that she would have difficulty discussing personal matters with practitioners, and that she would "test" and provoke practitioners into criticizing her for changing or canceling appointments at the last minute, being late, and that she might procrastinate, avoid feelings, and otherwise "test" the practitioner's trustability. Once trust in the practitioner is achieved, she is likely to cling to the practitioner and treatment and thus termination may be difficult unless her social support system outside therapy is increased. Furthermore, her pattern of avoidance is likely to make entry into and continuation with group work difficult. Therefore, individual sessions can serve as a transition into group, including having some contact with the group practitioner, who will presumably be accepting and non-judgmental. This should increase Geri's feeling of safety and make self-disclosure in a group setting less difficult. Transference enactment is another consideration. Given the extent of parental and peer criticism and teasing, it is anticipated that any perceived impatience and verbal or nonverbal indications of criticalness by the practitioner will activate this transference. Finally, because of her tendency to cling to others in whom she trusts, increasing her capacity to feel more confident in functioning with greater independence and increasing time between the last four to five sessions can reduce her ambivalence about termination *(Treatment obstacles).* Treatment progress does not seem dependent on cultural or even culturally sensitive interventions at this time. However, gender dynamics could impact the therapeutic relationship, given her strained relationship with her father and limited involvement with men since. Accordingly, female practitioners for both individual and group therapy appear to be indicated in the initial phase of treatment *(Treatment—cultural).* Assuming that Geri increases her self-confidence, relational skills and social contacts in and outside therapy, as well as returns to work, her prognosis is adjudged to be good; if not it is guarded *(Treatment prognosis).*

Concluding Note

Competency in case conceptualization is increasingly expected of psychotherapists today. An Adlerian approach to case conceptualization was described and illustrated here. This approach is based on a commonly used integrative model of case conceptualization. The characteristic features of this model are common elements and approach-specific elements, which were identified and described. The benefits of a comprehensive, integrative approach that combines both common and distinctive elements were also discussed. The basic premises of the Adlerian perspective, the Adlerian assessment approach, and the common and distinctive elements of an Adlerian case conceptualization were then discussed. This was followed by a detailed case example, which illustrated the integrative approach. Presumably, the use of this integrative model of Adlerian case conceptualization can increase a therapist's competence and confidence as well as treatment outcomes.

References

Ansbacher, H.L. & Ansbacher, R.R. (Eds.) (1956). *The Individual Psychology of Alfred Adler.* New York, NY: Harper & Row.

Beitman, B. & Yue, D. (1999). *Learning Psychotherapy*. New York, NY: Norton.

Carlson, J., Watts, R., & Maniacci, M. (2006). *Adlerian Therapy: Theory and Practice*. Washington, DC: American Psychological Association.

Eells, T. (2007). Comparing the methods. Where is the common ground? In T. Eells (Ed.), *Handbook of Psychotherapy Case Formulation* (2nd edn.) (pp. 412–432). New York, NY: Guilford.

Eells, T. (2010). The unfolding case formulation: The interplay of description and inference. *Pragmatic Case Studies in Psychotherapy*, 6(4), pp. 225–254.

Mosak, H. & Maniacci, M. (1999). *A Primer of Adlerian Psychology: The Analytic-Behavioral-Cognitive Psychology of Alfred Adler*. Philadelphia, PA: Brunner/Mazel.

Sperry, L. (1989). Integrative case formulations: What they are and how to write them. *Journal of Individual Psychology*, 45, pp. 500–507.

Sperry, L. (2005). Case conceptualization: A strategy for incorporating individual, couple, and family dynamics in the treatment process. *American Journal of Family Therapy*, 33, pp. 353–364.

Sperry, L. (2006). *Cognitive Behavior Therapy of DSM-IV-TR Personality Disorders* (2nd edn.). New York, NY: Routledge

Sperry, L. (2010). *Core Competencies in Counseling and Psychotherapy: Becoming a Highly Competent and Effective Therapist*. New York, NY: Routledge.

Sperry, L. (2011). Core competencies and competency-based Adlerian psychotherapy. *Journal of Individual Psychology*, 67, pp. 380–390.

Sperry, L. (2013). Family case conceptualization and medical conditions. *The Family Journal*, 21(1), pp. 74–77.

Sperry, L., Brill, P., Howard, K., & Grissom, G. (1996). *Treatment Outcomes in Psychotherapy and Psychiatric Interventions*. New York, NY: Brunner/Mazel.

Sperry, L. & Sperry, J. (2012). *Case Conceptualization: Mastering This Competency with Ease and Confidence*. New York, NY: Routledge.

3 Personality Disorders

Len Sperry

Jeffrey Dahmer was a sexual predator and serial killer notorious for cannibalizing (eating) many of his victims. He killed 17 males between 1978 and 1991, was sentenced to 15 consecutive life terms in 1992, and was subsequently killed by an inmate two years later. His early upbringing was unremarkable until aged six. Then, he underwent minor surgery, his brother was born, and he became increasingly withdrawn. After high school, he enrolled in college but dropped out after one quarter because of drinking and failure to attend class. Afterwards, he enlisted in the Army but was dishonorably discharged because of alcoholism. When his Army superior berated him and said he would never amount to anything, Dahmer is reported to have responded, "Just wait and see, someday everyone will know me." So what was his DSM diagnosis? Many speculated it was some kind of psychosis, while others—tongue in cheek—claimed it had to be Unspecified Eating Disorder (because of cannibalism)! Actually, it was Psychopathic Personality, which in DSM-5 terms is coded as Antisocial Personality Disorder.

I came to know Dahmer when I served as a psychiatric consultant during his trial (Sperry, 2011). From an Adlerian perspective, I was particularly impressed with the implication of Dahmer's statement that he would distinguish himself among other serial killers because of his cannibalism, and be known by "everyone." My Adlerian mentor, Rudolf Dreikurs, M.D., referred to this kind of inferiority-superiority striving as "being the first worst" instead of being the first best, in some socially useful endeavor. Today, he is considered one of the worst and most heinous serial killers.

You may be wondering why this book begins with personality disorders and not with anxiety or mood disorders, as nearly all psychopathology books do? Unlike other books that focus on describing and diagnosing mental conditions, this book *also* focuses on conceptualizing, planning, and implementing psychotherapeutic interventions. Personality disorders are described first in this book, because accumulating clinical and research evidence indicates that presenting problems and symptoms cannot be effectively assessed, conceptualized, or treated without an adequate understanding of the individual experiencing the problem or symptoms. For instance, depression can manifest quite differently in someone who fears and avoids relationships, as compared to someone who can more fully engage with others but is experiencing the loss of a job or a relationship. Another way of saying this is that there is no single clinical presentation of depression, but rather that the presentation of depression reflects an individual's unique personality dynamics. A diagnostic evaluation is effective to the extent that it identifies these personality dynamics, particularly when a personality disorder is present.

This chapter begins by describing the minor changes in *DSM-5*'s coverage of personality disorders. Then, it presents the Adlerian conceptualization of personality disorders. Finally, it describes and illustrates the diagnostic criteria and personality dynamics of the following personality disorders: Avoidant Personality Disorder; Borderline Personality Disorder; Narcissistic Personality Disorder; Obsessive-Compulsive Personality Disorder; Schizotypal Personality Disorder; Antisocial Personality Disorder; Dependent Personality Disorder; Histrionic Personality Disorder; Schizoid Personality Disorder; and Paranoid Personality Disorder.

Unlike other chapters in this book, that describe only the most common disorders in a diagnostic, this chapter provides an overview of all the specified DSM-5 personality disorders. This overview is necessarily brief. A fuller description of these disorders and their treatment is available in the *Handbook of the Diagnosis and Treatment of DSM-5 Personality Disorders* (Sperry, 2015).

Personality Disorders in *DSM-5*

Major changes were expected in how *DSM-5* (American Psychiatric Association, 2013) would characterize the personality disorders. Early indications was that at least four of the DSM-IV-TR personality disorders would be dropped, purportedly because of limited research support. In addition, the diagnosis of these disorders was to shift to a dimensional focus, rather than categorical focus as it had been in previous editions. However, when *DSM-5* appeared in May, 2013 the same criteria found in *DSM-IV-TR* were retained, and the anticipated changes appeared in Section III in a chapter entitled "Alternative DSM-5 Model for Personality Disorders." It appears that this, or some version of the "alternative model," may be incorporated in subsequent editions (*DSM-5.1* or *5.2*). For now, clinicians are expected to continue using the same criteria and the categorical method of making diagnoses as in *DSM-IV-TR*.

Retained in *DSM-5* was the earlier DSM definition of a personality disorder as an "enduring pattern of inner experience and behaviors that deviates markedly from the expectations of the individual's culture, is pervasive and inflexible … is stable over time, and leads to distress or impairment" (American Psychiatric Association, 2013, p. 645). While previous diagnostic criteria have been retained, there has been some updating of description of the various disorders. However, there is one substantive change. The diagnosis of Personality Disorder Not Otherwise Specified (NOS) has been replaced with Other Specified Personality Disorder (301.89) and Unspecified Personality Disorder (301.9).

Adlerian Conceptualization of Personality Disorders

Adler and Personality Structure

Alfred Adler did not discuss the personality disorders *per se*. However, based on his clinical experience, he did describe four different personalities based on the presence or absence of social interest. He called them the ruling type, the avoiding type, the getting type, and the socially useful type (1935). He also described levels of activity of personality, ranging from active to inactive. While not formally specifying it, Alder essentially advanced a two-dimensional theory of personality structure (social interest level and activity level), which was the basis for other Adlerians to develop personality typologies consistent with DSM categories.

Extension to DSM Personality Disorders

Combining Adler's insights about personality type in terms of social interest and activity level yields a four-fold personality typology. Accordingly, there is the ruling type (high active, low social interest); the avoiding type (low active, low social interest); the getting type (low active and high social interest); and socially useful type (high active, high social interest).

Mosak (1968, 1979) expanded this four-fold typology to eight types, which he correlated with DSM-II diagnostic codes. Sperry (1990) articulated these Adlerian psychodynamics for the personality disorders listed in *DSM-III-R*. Later, Sperry and Mosak (1993, 1996) collaborated to further describe Adlerian personality dynamics within a biopsychosocial framework. This book continues that framework, which is referred to as the Biopsychosocial–Adlerian Case Conceptualization.

Sperry (2002, 2011) extended the previous typologies but based them on the Adlerian dimensions of movement and activity level. Adler described movement and activity level as factors in determining personality (Ansbacher & Ansbacher, 1956). Karen Horney (1951) further extended Adler's initial observation. Horney noted that all behavior can be understood as movement in a social context. She also described three types of movement: toward, away from, and against. Adler also described a type of movement that he called "hesitating," i.e., movement back and forth, which today is commonly referred to as ambivalent. He also indicated that activity level was primarily active or passive (Ansbacher & Ansbacher, 1956; Clark & Butler, 2012).

The typology is based on four types of movement: toward, against, away, and ambivalent, along with two types of activity: active or passive. By combining these two dimensions, eight basic personality styles—and their derived personality disorders—can be articulated (Sperry, 2011). These are: the antisocial personality (against—active); the narcissistic personality (against—passive); the histrionic personality (toward—active); the dependent personality (toward—passive); the avoidant personality (away—active); the schizoid personality (away—passive); the passive-aggressive personality (ambivalent—active); and the obsessive-compulsive personality (ambivalent—passive). Millon (1969; Millon & Everly, 1985) considers the borderline, paranoid, and schizotypal personality disorders to be pathological extensions of the various eight basic styles. Accordingly, the Borderline Personality Disorder represents a decompensated extension of the histrionic, dependent, or the passive-aggressive personality, the Paranoid Personality Disorder is the decompensated extension of the antisocial, narcissistic or obsessive-compulsive personalities, and the Schizotypal Personality Disorder is the decompensated extension of the Schizoid Personality Disorder. It is important to note that movement and activity level reflect an individual's personality style. Finally, it is only when this style is habitually maladaptive and inflexible, i.e., marked by irresponsibility, lack of cooperation, and self-interest, that personality style is considered disordered. Parenthetically, Millon and Everly (1984) propose a similar typology based on the dimensions of instrumental behavior patterns and sources of reinforcement.

Clinical Presentation of the DSM Personality Disorders

We began this chapter by defining personality as enduring patterns of thinking, feeling, and behaving/interacting. In the ten personality disorders to be described, each disorder will be described in terms of its pattern of clinical presentation, case conceptualization, and treatment considerations.

The clinical presentation will be described by the observable pattern of the disorder in terms of its behavioral and interpersonal style, its thinking or cognitive styles, and its feeling or emotional style. This section reflects specific DSM-5 diagnostic criteria for each disorder.

The section on case conceptualization describes how the personality style and disorder develop and are maintained. A biopsychosocial framework will form the basis of this section. A biopsychosocial formulation is an integrative effort to combine biological, psychological, and social data to explain and predict behavior. Biological factors can include predispositions associated with temperament, heredity, and central nervous system functioning. Temperament can be thought of as the biologically determined subset of personality. Each individual enters the world with a distinctive pattern of response, dispositions, and sensitivities. Thomas and Chess (1977, 1984) have described infant and child temperament patterns, while Burks and Rubenstein (1979) have described the application of these temperament types in adults, particularly adults in psychotherapy.

Psychological factors that influence personality development can be described in cognitive, dynamic, or behavioral terms, and are the heart of a case conceptualization (Sperry & Sperry, 2012). The Adlerian perspective of personality development as a function of family constellation and life-style convictions is evident in this section. Specially, life-style convictions are derived from early recollections and refer to the individual's view of self, world, and life strategy. The Case of Ms. A. in the next section illustrates a full Adlerian case conceptualization.

Social factors will be described in terms of parenting style, parental injunction, as well as sibling, peer, and family relationship. In addition, those factors within the individual and the individual system and environment that reinforce and reconfirm this pattern and clinical presentation will be described.

AVOIDANT PERSONALITY DISORDER

Avoidant personalities are seemingly shy, lonely, hypersensitive individuals with low self-esteem. Although they are desperate for interpersonal involvement, they avoid personal contact with others because of their heightened fear of social disapproval and rejection sensitivity.

Clinical Presentation

The Avoidant Personality Disorder is characterized by the following behavioral and interpersonal styles, thinking or cognitive styles, and emotional or affective styles. The behavioral style of avoidant personalities is characterized by social withdrawal, shyness, distrustfulness, and aloofness. Their behavior and speech is both controlled and inactive, and they appear apprehensive and awkward. Interpersonally, they are rejection-sensitive. Even though they desire acceptance by others, they keep distance from others and require unconditional approval before being willing to "open up." They gradually "test" others to determine who can be trusted to like them.

DSM-5 Characterization

Individuals with this personality disorder are characterized by an unremitting pattern of being socially inhibited, feeling inadequate, and overly sensitive to the negative evaluations of others. This is because they view themselves as socially inept, unappealing, or inferior to others. They consistently avoid work activities that require close interpersonal contact, for fear of being criticized or rejected. They will not get involved with others unless they are certain of being accepted. Fearing they will be shamed or ridiculed, they are uncomfortable and act with restraint in intimate relationships. In anticipation of shame or ridicule, they are uncomfortable and are hesitant in intimate relationships. Similarly, they experience feelings of inadequacy and inhibition in new interpersonal situations. Not surprisingly, they refuse to take personal risks or engage in activities that may prove embarrassing (American Psychiatric Association, 2013).

Biopsychosocial–Adlerian Conceptualization

The following biopsychosocial formulation may be helpful in understanding how the Avoidant Personality pattern is likely to have developed. Biologically, these individuals commonly were hyperirritable and fearful as infants, and they most likely exhibited the "slow to warm" temperament (Thomas & Chess, 1977). Individuals with this personality pattern are also likely to have experienced various maturational irregularities as children. Their irregularities and their hyperirritable pattern are attributed to low arousal of their autonomic nervous system (Millon & Everly, 1985).

Psychologically, those with avoidant personalities typically view themselves as "See, I am inadequate and frightened of rejection." They are likely to view the world as some variant of the theme: "Life is unfair—people reject and criticize me—but, I still want someone to like me." As such, they are likely to conclude: "Therefore, be vigilant, demand reassurance, and if all else fails, fantasize and daydream about the way life could be." A common defense mechanism of the avoidant personality is fantasy. Thus, it is not surprising that avoidant personalities are major consumers of romance novels and soap operas.

Socially, predictable patterns of parenting and environmental factors can be noted for the avoidant personality disorder. The avoidant personality is likely to have experienced parental rejection and/or ridicule. Later, siblings and peers will likely continue this pattern of rejection and ridicule. The parental injunction is likely to have been: "We don't accept you, and probably no one else will either." They may have had parents with high standards and worried that they may not have met or would not meet these standards, and therefore would not be accepted.

This avoidant pattern is confirmed, reinforced and perpetuated by the following individual and systems factors: A sense of personal inadequacy and a fear of rejection leads to hypervigilance, which leads to restricted social experiences. These experiences, plus catastrophic thinking, lead to increased hypervigilance and hypersensitivity, leading to self-pity, anxiety and depression, which leads to further confirmation of avoidant beliefs and styles.

Treatment Considerations

In terms of treatment goals and strategies, there is little reported research on treating the avoidant personality. However, the goal of therapy is to increase the individual's self-esteem and confidence in relationship to others and to desensitize the individual to the criticism of others. Desensitization techniques appear to be much more useful and expedient in this regard. Assertiveness training and shyness training are reportedly very affective with the Avoidant Personality pattern (Turkat & Maisto, 1985). As with other personality disorders, medication can be useful for symptoms such as depression and anxiety associated with the avoidant pattern.

Case Example: Ms. A.

Ms. A. is a 35-year-old, African-American female who works as an administrative assistant. She is single, lives alone, and was referred by her company's human resources director for evaluation and treatment following three weeks of depression and social isolation. Her absence from work prompted the referral. Ms. A.'s symptoms began soon after her supervisor told her that she was being considered for a promotion. Ms. A. reports having difficulty relating to her peers, both in early life, as well as currently.

Family constellation

She is the older of two siblings, with a brother who is eight years younger than her. For all practical purposes, she was psychologically an only child. Ms. A. reports that she was her father's favorite until her brother was born. As a child, she had difficulty relating to her peers while in school and was often criticized. Typically, she responded by isolating and avoiding others. She mentioned that her parents were and continue to be unsupportive, demanding, and critical toward her. Three family values worth noting are "children are to be seen and not heard," "your worth depends on what you achieve in life," and "family secrets do not leave the family."

Early recollections

Her earliest recollection involves feeling displaced and no longer wanted by her parents the day her mother brought her newborn brother home. Her father said it was the happiest day of his life, and Ms. A.'s reaction was to run out of the house and hide in her tree fort feeling angry, alone, sad, and rejected, and thinking that nobody wanted her anymore. Another recollection involved being told that what she had drawn in art class was awful. Her response was to feel sad and hurt and conclude that something must be wrong with her if she couldn't draw.

Adlerian case conceptualization

Ms. A.'s increased social isolation and depressive symptoms seem to be her discouraged reaction to the news of an impending job transfer and promotion, given her history of having critical and demanding people in her life. She avoids most relationships and has a history of isolating throughout her childhood. Ms. A.'s presenting problems are understandable when viewed from the perspective of her life style. Her style of relating with others mirrors the tentative and avoidant manner in which she related to family members. She sought a safe way to connect to family members without being criticized or having unreasonable demands put on her. She views herself as inadequate and defective as a person, and views life and others as demanding, harsh, arbitrary, and critical. Therefore, Ms. A. found her place by avoiding most relationships, socially isolating, and overly investing in those she deems as trustworthy. This allowed her to avoid being criticized and helped her "feel safe." Her strategy of avoiding relationships and withdrawing whenever she feels unsafe works. However, the price she pays to feel "safe" is high: she is lonely, has limited relational skills and experiences, and desires a close intimate relationship that seems unlikely.

Treatment plan and implementation

Decreasing discouragement and depressive symptoms, increasing social interest and social relating, and enhancing relational skills are the primary goals of treatment. Interpretation will be utilized to process Ms. A.'s life-style convictions and basic mistakes. The focus will be on modifying her faulty convictions of avoidance to feel safe. Because of her discomfort in talking with a neighbor, she will be encouraged to act "as if" she were comfortable. A referral will be made for a medication evaluation and, if indicated, medication monitoring with be arranged.

BORDERLINE PERSONALITY DISORDER

Individuals with borderline personalities present with a complex clinical picture, including diverse combinations of anger, anxiety, intense and labile affect, and brief disturbances of consciousness such as depersonalization and dissociation. In addition, their presentation includes chronic loneliness, a sense of emptiness, boredom, volatile interpersonal relations, identity confusion, and impulsive behavior that can include self-injury or self-mutilation. Stress can even precipitate a transient psychosis. Some conceptualize this disorder as a level of personality organization rather than as a specific personality disorder (American Psychiatric Association, 2013).

Clinical Presentation

The borderline personality is characterized by the following behavior and interpersonal styles, cognitive style, and emotional style. Behaviorally, borderlines are characterized by physically self-damaging acts such as suicide gestures, self-mutilation, or the provocation of fights. Their social and occupational accomplishments are often less than their intelligence and ability warrant. Of all the personality disorders, they are more likely to have irregularities of circadian rhythms, especially of the sleep-wake cycle. Thus, chronic insomnia is a common complaint.

Interpersonally, borderlines are characterized by their paradoxical instability. That is, they fluctuate quickly between idealizing and clinging to another individual, to devaluing and opposing that individual. They are exquisitely rejection-sensitive, and experience abandonment depression following the slightest of stressors. Millon (2011) considered separation anxiety as a primary motivator of this personality disorder. Interpersonal relationships develop rather quickly and intensely, yet borderlines' social adaptiveness is rather superficial. They are extraordinarily intolerant of being alone, and they go to great lengths to seek out the company of others, whether in indiscriminate sexual affairs, late-night phone calls to relatives and recent acquaintances, or after-hours visits to hospital emergency rooms, with a host of vague medical and/or psychiatric complaints.

Their cognitive style is described as inflexible and impulsive (Millon, 2011). Inflexibility of their style is characterized by rigid abstractions that easily lead to grandiose, idealized perceptions of others, not as real people, but as personifications of "all good" or "all bad" individuals. They reason by analogy from past experiences and thus have difficulty reasoning logically and learning from past mistakes. Because they have an external locus of control, borderlines usually blame others when things go wrong. By accepting responsibility for their own incompetence, borderlines believe they would feel even more powerless to change circumstances. Accordingly, their emotions fluctuate between hope and despair, because they believe that external circumstances are well beyond their control (Shulman, 1982). Their cognitive style is also marked by impulsivity, and just as they vacillate between idealization and devaluation of others, their thoughts shift from one extreme to another: "I like people; no, I don't like them"; "Having goals is good; no, it's not"; "I need to get my life together; no, I can't, it's hopeless." This inflexibility and impulsivity complicates the process of identity formation. Their uncertainty about self-image, gender identity, goals, values, and career choice reflects this impulsive and flexible stance.

Gerald Adler (1985) suggested that borderlines have an underdeveloped evocative memory. As a result, they have difficulty recalling images and feeling states that could structure and soothe them in times of turmoil. Their inflexibility and impulsivity are further noted in their tendency toward "splitting." Splitting is the inability to synthesize contradictory qualities, such that the individual views others as all good or all bad, and utilizes "projective identification," that is, attributing his or her own negative or dangerous feelings to others. Their cognitive style is further characterized by an inability to tolerate frustration. Finally, micropsychotic episodes can be noted when these individuals are under a great deal of stress. These are ill-defined, strange thought processes, especially noted in response to unstructured rather than structured situations, and may take the form of derealization, depersonalization, intense rage reactions, unusual reactions to drugs, and intense brief paranoid episodes. Because of difficulty in focusing attention, and subsequent loss of relevant data, borderlines also have a diminished capacity to process information.

The emotional style of individuals with this disorder is characterized by marked mood shifts from a normal or euthymic mood to a dysphoric mood. In addition, inappropriate and intense anger and rage may easily be triggered. On the other extreme are feelings of emptiness, a deep "void," or boredom.

DSM-5 Characterization

Individuals with this personality disorder are characterized by an unremitting pattern of unstable relationships, emotional reactions, identity, and impulsivity. They engage in frantic efforts to avoid abandonment, whether it is real or imagined. Their interpersonal relationships are intense, unstable, and alternate between the extremes of idealization and devaluation. They have chronic identity issues and an unstable sense of self. Their impulsivity can result in self-damaging actions such as reckless driving or drug use, binge-eating, or high-risk sex. These individuals engage in recurrent suicidal threats, gestures, acting out, or self-mutilating behavior. They can exhibit markedly reactive moods, chronic feelings of emptiness, emotional outbursts, and difficulty controlling their anger. They may also experience brief stress-related, paranoid thinking, or severe episodes of dissociation (American Psychiatric Association, 2013).

Biopsychosocial–Adlerian Conceptualization

The following biopsychosocial formulation may be helpful in understanding how the borderline personality pattern is likely to have developed. Biologically, borderlines can be understood in terms of the three main subtypes: borderline-dependent, borderline-histrionic, and borderline-passive-aggressive. The temperamental style of the borderline-dependent type is that of the passive-infantile pattern (Millon, 2011). Millon hypothesized that low autonomic-nervous-system reactivity plus an overprotective parenting style facilitates restrictive interpersonal skills and a clinging relational style. On the other hand, the histrionic subtype was more likely to have a hyper-responsive infantile pattern. Thus, because of high autonomic-nervous-system reactivity and increased parental stimulation and expectations for performance, the borderline-histrionic pattern was likely to result. Finally, the temperamental style of the passive-aggressive borderline was likely to have been the "difficult child" type noted by Thomas and Chess (1977). This pattern, plus parental inconsistency, marks the affective irritability of the borderline-passive-aggressive personality.

Psychologically, borderlines tend to view themselves, others, the world, and life's purpose in terms of the following themes. They view themselves by some variant of the theme: "I don't know who I am or where I'm going." In short, their identity problems involve gender, career, loyalties, and values, while their self-esteem fluctuates with each thought or feeling about their self-identity. Borderlines tend to view their world with some variant of the theme: "People are great; no, they are not"; "Having goals is good; no, it's not"; or, "If life doesn't go my way, I can't tolerate it." As such, they are likely to conclude: "Therefore keep all options open. Don't commit to anything. Reverse roles and vacillate thinking and feelings when under attack." The most common defense mechanisms utilized by Borderline Personality Disordered individuals are regression, splitting, and projective identification.

Socially, predictable patterns of parenting and environmental factors can be noted for the Borderline Personality Disorder. Parenting style differs depending on the subtype. For example, in the dependent subtype, overprotectiveness characterizes parenting, whereas in the histrionic subtype, a demanding parenting style is more evident, while an inconsistent parenting style is more noted in the passive-aggressive subtype. But because the borderline personality is a syndromal elaboration and deterioration of the less severe Dependent, Histrionic, or Passive-Aggressive Personality Disorders (Millon, 2011), the family of origin in the borderline subtypes of these disorders is likely to be much more dysfunctional, increasing the likelihood that the child will have learned various self-defeating coping strategies. The parental injunction is likely to have been, "If you grow up and leave me, bad things will happen to me (parent)."

This borderline pattern is confirmed, reinforced, and perpetuated by the following individual and systems factors: Diffuse identity, impulsive vacillation, and self-defeating coping strategies lead to aggressive acting out, which leads to more chaos, which leads to the experience of depersonalization, increased dysphoria, and/or self-mutilation to achieve some relief. This leads to further reconfirmation of their beliefs about self and the world, as well as reinforcement of the behavioral and interpersonal patterns.

Treatment Considerations

The Borderline Personality Disorder is becoming one of the most common Axis II presentations seen in both the public sector and in private practice. It can be among the most difficult and frustrating conditions to treat. Clinical experience suggests that it is important to assess the individual for overall level of functioning and for subtype. The higher-functioning borderline-dependent personality has a higher probability for collaborating in psychotherapeutic treatment than the lower-functioning borderline-passive-aggressive personality. Higher-functioning borderlines possibly may be engaged in insight-oriented psychotherapy without undue regression and acting out. Masterson (1976) suggested that rather than using traditional interpretation methods with borderlines, the therapist should utilize confrontational statements in which borderlines are asked to look at their behavior and its consequences.

With lower-functioning patients, treatment goals may be much more limited. Here, the focus of treatment would be on increasing day-to-day stable functioning. Treatment strategies and methods are varied for the treatment of borderline subtypes. Strategies range from long-term psychotherapy, lasting two or more years, to rather short-term formats in which sessions are scheduled biweekly or even monthly, except when crises arise. Task-oriented group therapy has been shown to be a useful adjunct, as well as a primary treatment in and of itself (Linehan, 1987).

The rationale for group therapy with the borderline is that the intense interpersonal relationship that forms between the therapist and the patient, and serves as the trigger for so much acting out, is effectively reduced in a group format. Whether seen individually or in a group format, the therapist does well to clearly articulate treatment limits and objectives. For the lower-functioning borderlines and the histrionic and passive-aggressive subtypes, a particularly useful procedure is to employ a written treatment contract. Antidepressants are often used with borderline patients and are particularly aimed at target symptoms such as insomnia, depression, or anxiety disorders. Low-dose neuroleptics are often utilized as well.

Case Example: Mr. B.

Mr. B. is a 29-year-old unemployed male who was referred to the hospital emergency room by his therapist at a community mental health center after two days of sustained suicidal gestures. He appeared to function adequately until his senior year in high school, when he became preoccupied with transcendental meditation. He had considerable difficulty concentrating during his first semester of college and seemed to focus most of his energies on finding a spiritual guru. At times, massive anxiety and feelings of emptiness swept over him, which he found would suddenly vanish if he lightly cut his wrist enough to draw blood. He had been in treatment with his current therapist for 18 months and become increasingly hostile and demanding as a patient, whereas earlier he had been quite captivated with his therapist's empathy and intuitive sense. Lately, his life seemed to center on these twice-weekly therapy sessions. Mr. B.'s most recent suicidal gesture followed the therapist's disclosure that he was relocating to a new job in another state.

NARCISSISTIC PERSONALITY DISORDER

Although often symptom free and well functioning, the narcissistic personality is chronically unsatisfied due to a constant need for admiration and habitually unrealistic self-expectations. The narcissist is impulsive and anxious, has ideas of grandiosity and "specialness," becomes quickly dissatisfied with others, and maintains superficial, exploitative interpersonal relationships. Under stress and when needs are not met, the narcissist may become depressed, develop somatic symptoms, have brief psychotic episodes, or display extreme rage.

Clinical Presentation

The narcissistic personality is characterized by the following behavioral and interpersonal style, cognitive style, and affective style. Behaviorally, narcissistic individuals are seen as conceited, boastful, and snobbish. They appear self-assured and self-centered, and they tend to dominate conversation, seek admiration, and act in a pompous and exhibitionistic fashion. They are also impatient, arrogant, and thin skinned or hypersensitive. Interpersonally, they are exploitive and use others to indulge themselves and their desires. Their behavior is socially facile, pleasant, and endearing. However, they are unable to respond with true empathy to others. When stressed, they can be disdainful, exploitive, and generally irresponsible in their behavior.

Their thinking style is one of cognitive expansiveness and exaggeration. They tend to focus on images and themes rather than on facts and issues. In fact, they take liberties with the facts, distort them, and even engage in prevarication and self-deception to preserve their own illusions about themselves and the projects in which they are involved. Their cognitive style is also marked by inflexibility. In addition, they have an exaggerated sense of self-importance and establish unrealistic goals of power, wealth, and ability. They justify all of this with their sense of entitlement and exaggerated sense of their own self-importance.

Their feeling or affective style is characterized by an aura of self-confidence and nonchalance, which is present in most situations except when their narcissistic confidence is shaken. Then, they are likely to respond with rage at criticism. Their feelings toward others shift and vacillate between overidealization and devaluation. Finally, their inability to show empathy is reflected in their superficial relationships with minimal emotional ties or commitments.

DSM-5 Characterization

Individuals with this personality disorder are characterized by an unremitting pattern of self-centeredness and grandiosity. More specifically, they have an exaggerated sense of their own abilities and achievements. They may have a constant need for attention, affirmation, and praise. Typically, they believe they are unique or special and should only associate with others of the same status. They are likely to have persistent fantasies about attaining success and power. These individuals can exploit others for personal gain. A sense of entitlement and the expectation of special treatment is common. They may come across as snobbish or arrogant. They appear to be incapable of showing empathy for others. In addition, they can be envious or think that others are envious of them (American Psychiatric Association, 2013).

Biopsychosocial–Adlerian Conceptualization

The following biopsychosocial formulation may be helpful in understanding how the Narcissistic Personality Disorder is likely to have developed. Biologically narcissistic personalities tend to have hyper-responsive temperaments (Millon, 2011). As young children they were likely to be viewed by others as being special in terms of looks, talents, or "promise." Often, as young children, they had early and exceptional speech development. In addition, they were likely keenly aware of interpersonal cues. Psychologically, the narcissists' view of themselves, others, the world, and life's purpose can be articulated in terms of the following themes: "I'm special and unique, and I am entitled to extraordinary rights and privileges whether I have earned them or not." Their world-view is a variant of the theme: "Life is a banquet table to be sampled at will. People owe me admiration and privilege." Their goal is: "Therefore, I'll expect and demand this specialness." Common defense mechanisms utilized by the narcissistic personality involve rationalization and projective identification.

Socially, predictable parental patterns and environmental factors can be noted for the narcissistic personality. Parental indulgence and overevaluation characterize the narcissistic personality. The parental injunction was likely to be: "Grow up and be wonderful—for me." Often they were only children, and, in addition, may have sustained early losses in childhood. From an early age they learned exploitive and manipulative behavior from their parents. This narcissistic pattern is confirmed, reinforced, and perpetuated by certain individual and systems factors. The illusion of specialness, disdain for others' views, and a sense of entitlement lead to an underdeveloped sense of social interest and responsibility. This, in turn, leads to increased self-absorption and confirmation of narcissistic beliefs.

Treatment Considerations

In terms of treatment goals, a decision needs to be made as to whether the treatment is short term and crisis oriented, or long term and focused on personality restructuring. Crisis-oriented psychotherapy usually focuses on alleviation of the symptoms, such as anxiety, depression, or somatic symptoms associated with the narcissistic injury or wound. This injury occurs when others fail to respond to the narcissist's sense of entitlement and specialness. Empathic mirroring or reflection and soothing are the treatments of choice (Kohut, 1971). The goals of longer-term therapy involve the restructuring of personality. These goals include increasing empathy, decreasing rage and cognitive distortions, and increasing the individual's ability to mourn losses. Treatment methods and strategies include empathic mirroring (Kohut, 1971), anger management, cognitive restructuring, and empathy training, as well as interpretation. When marital issues are involved, couples therapy has been shown to be a useful treatment modality (Feldman, 1982). Medication management is directed at treatable symptoms such as depression, anxiety, etc. (Reid, 1989). Clinicians have noted that the majority of narcissistic personalities who present for treatment are interested only in having the narcissistic wound soothed; then they leave treatment.

Case Example: Mr. N.

Mr. N. is a 32-year-old male who presented for therapy after his wife of six years threatened to leave him and because his employer was pressuring him to resign his position as a sales executive for a condominium project. Apparently, Mrs. N. had told her husband that he loved himself "a hundred times more than you love me." Mr. N. dismissed this by saying he needed to buy $600 suits because his job demanded that he look his best at all times and that he was "tall, dark, handsome, and sexy, all any woman could want in a man." Mr. N. denied that he used scare tactics, exaggerated claims, or other pressure-selling techniques with customers. "Sure, I'm a bit aggressive, but you don't get into the 'Millionaire's Club' by being a wimp." He added that his employer would "go belly up without me," and that he was too important to be dismissed for such petty reasons.

OBSESSIVE-COMPULSIVE PERSONALITY DISORDER

Obsessive-Compulsive Personality Disordered individuals are described as inhibited, stubborn, perfectionistic, judgmental, overconscientious, rigid, and chronically anxious. Characteristically, they are people who avoid intimacy and experience little pleasure from life. They may be successful, but at the same time are indecisive and demanding. Often they are perceived as cold and reserved. Unlike the Axis I Obsessive-Compulsive Disorder, ritualistic compulsions and obsessions do not characterize this personality disorder.

Clinical Presentation

The Obsessive-Compulsive Personality Disorder can be recognized by the following behavior and interpersonal styles, cognitive style, and emotional style. Behaviorally, this disorder is characterized by perfectionism. Individuals with this disorder are likely to be workaholics. In addition to dependability, they tend to be stubborn and possessive. They, like passive-aggressive-disordered individuals, can be indecisive and procrastinating. Interpersonally, these individuals are exquisitely conscious of social rank and status and modify their behavior accordingly. That is, they tend to be deferential and obsequious to superiors, and haughty and autocratic to subordinates and peers. They can be doggedly insistent that others do things their way, without an appreciation or awareness of how others react to their insistence. At best, they are polite and loyal to the organizations and ideals they espouse.

Their thinking style can be characterized as constricted and rule based. They have difficulty establishing priorities and perspective. They are "detail" people and often lose sight of the larger project. In other words, they "can't see the forest for the trees." Their indecisiveness and doubts make decision-making difficult. Their mental inflexibility is matched by their non-suggestible and unimaginative style, suggesting they have a restricted fantasy life. Like passive-aggressive individuals, the obsessive-compulsives have conflicts between assertiveness and defiance, and pleasing and obedience.

Their emotional style is characterized as grim and cheerless. They have difficulty with the expression of intimate feelings such as warmth and tenderness. They tend to avoid the "softer" feelings, although they may express anger, frustration, and irritability quite freely. This grim, feeling-avoidant demeanor shows itself in stilted, stiff relationship behaviors.

DSM-5 Characterization

Individuals with this personality disorder are characterized by an unremitting pattern of perfectionism, orderliness, and control, instead of flexibility, openness, and efficiency. They are overly preoccupied with details, rules, and schedules. Their perfectionism interferes with completing tasks, due to their overly strict standards. They are overly devoted to work and productivity to the exclusion of leisure activities and friendships. When it comes to matters of values, morality, or ethics, these individuals are inflexible, scrupulous, and overconscientious. Often, they are unable to discard worn-out or worthless objects that have no sentimental value. They will not delegate tasks or work with others unless it can be on their terms. Not surprisingly, these individuals are also rigid and stubborn. Finally, they are misers with money, and it is hoarded in the event of future catastrophes (American Psychiatric Association, 2013).

Biopsychosocial–Adlerian Conceptualization

The following biopsychosocial formulation may be helpful in understanding how the Obsessive-Compulsive Personality Disorder is likely to have developed. Biologically, these individuals were likely to have exhibited an anhedonic temperament as an infant (Millon, 2011). Interestingly, firstborn children have a greater propensity for developing a compulsive style than other siblings (Toman, 1961).

Psychologically, these individuals view themselves, others, the world, and life's purpose in terms of the following themes. They tend to view themselves with some variant of the theme: "I'm responsible if something goes wrong, so I have to be reliable, competent, and righteous." Their world-view is some variant of the theme: "Life is unpredictable and expects too much." As such, they are likely to conclude, "Therefore, be in control, right, and proper at all times." Socially, predictable patterns of parenting and environmental conditioning are noted for this personality. The parenting style they experienced could be characterized as both consistent and overcontrolled. As children they were trained to be overly responsible for their actions and to feel guilty and worthless if they were not obedient, achievement oriented, or "good." The parental injunction to which they were most likely exposed was: "You must do and be better to be worthwhile."

This obsessive-compulsive pattern is confirmed, reinforced, and perpetuated by the following individual and systems factors: Exceedingly high expectations plus harshly rigid behavior and beliefs, along with a tendency to be self-critical, lead to rigid rule-based behavior and avoidance of social, professional, and moral unacceptability. This in turn further reconfirms the harshly rigid behaviors and beliefs of this personality.

Treatment Considerations

The Obsessive-Compulsive Personality Disorder (OCD) has a long tradition of treatment, dating back to Freud's case of the "Rat Man" and Adler's "Case of Mrs. A." Note that OCD is a symptom disorder, while the Obsessive-Compulsive Personality Disorder is a personality disorder. Since the "Rat Man" exhibited both symptom and personality disorders, many who have read Freud's account of this case and its treatment have incorrectly assumed that both disorders are the same and are treated the same. They are not the same condition, but in about one-third of cases, both disorders have been shown to be present (Jenike, Baer, & Minichiello, 1990). When both disorders are present together, treatment has been shown to be much more challenging than if only OCD is present.

The goals of treatment include increased cognitive constriction and increased feeling expression, so that a more reasonable balance can be obtained between thoughts and feelings. Treatment strategies for the Obsessive-Compulsive Personality Disorder usually involve long-term, insight-oriented therapy. Unlike the Obsessive-Compulsive Disorder, where antidepressants plus behavior therapy can result in amelioration of obsessions and compulsions in a relatively short period of time, the Obsessive-Compulsive Personality Disorder does not lend itself to short-term treatment outcomes. However, Salzman (1968) and Turkat and Maisto (1985) offered dynamic and cognitive behavior intervention that has proved effective. Medication is usually not needed with this disorder but may be effective for treatable symptoms such as depression and anxiety.

Case Example: Mr. O.

Mr. O. is a 37-year-old male business executive who wanted to begin a course of psychotherapy because his "whole world was closing in." He gave a history of longstanding feelings of dissatisfaction with his marriage, which had worsened in the past two years. He described his wife's increasing demands for time and affection from him, which he believed was a weakness she had. His professional life also had become conflicted when his partner of ten years wanted to expand their accounting firm to another city. Mr. O. believed this proposal was fraught with dangers, and had come to the point of selling out his share of the business to his partner. He knew he had to make some decisions about his marriage and his business but found himself unable to do so. He hoped therapy would help with these decisions. He presented as neatly dressed in a conservative three-piece gray suit. His posture was rigid and he spoke in a formal and controlled tone with constricted affect. His thinking was characterized by preoccupation with details and was somewhat circumstantial.

The reader is referred to the Case of Mrs. A., Adler's (1969) most famous case, for a detailed description and formulation of the Obsessive-Compulsive Disorder. It so happened that Mrs. A. manifested a moderately severe Borderline Personality Disorder.

SCHIZOTYPAL PERSONALITY DISORDER

In addition to having features similar to that of the Schizoid Personality Disorder, the schizotypal disorder is characterized by eccentric behavior and peculiar thought content. Schizotypals describe strange intrapsychic experiences, think in odd and unusual ways, and are difficult to engage. Yet, none of these features reach psychotic proportions. It has been suggested that the schizotypal personality is one of the schizophrenic spectrum disorders because schizophrenia occurs with increased frequency in family members of the schizotypal.

Clinical Presentation

The Schizotypal Personality Disorder is typically recognized by the following behavior and interpersonal styles, cognitive styles, and emotional styles. Behaviorally, schizotypals are noted for their eccentric, erratic, and bizarre mode of functioning. Their speech is markedly peculiar without being incoherent. Occupationally, they are inadequate, either quitting or being fired from jobs after short periods of time. Typically, they become drifters, moving from job to job and town to town. They tend to avoid enduring responsibilities, and in the process lose touch with a sense of social propriety.

Interpersonally, they are loners with few if any friends. Their solitary pursuits and social isolation may be the result of intense social anxiety, which may be expressed with apprehensiveness. If married, their style of superficial and peripheral relating often leads to separation and divorce in a short period of time.

The cognitive style of schizotypals is described as scattered and ruminative, and is characterized by cognitive slippage. Presentations of superstitiousness, telepathy, and bizarre fantasies are characteristic. They may describe vague ideas of reference and recurrent illusions of depersonalizing, derealizing experiences without the experience of delusions of reference, or auditory or visual hallucinations.

Their affective style is described as cold, aloof, and unemotional with constricted affect. They can be humorless individuals and difficult to engage in conversation, probably because of their general suspicious and mistrustful nature. In addition, they are hypersensitive to real or imagined slights.

DSM-5 Characterization

Individuals with this personality disorder are characterized by an unremitting pattern of social and interpersonal deficits, with significant discomfort and limited capacity for relationships, as well as by perceptual distortions and eccentric behavior. They experience ideas of reference as well as unusual beliefs and thinking that influence their behavior, and that are inconsistent with their subculture. They also experience unusual perception, such as bodily illusions, and odd speech thinking. These individuals are prone to suspiciousness and paranoid ideation. They exhibit inappropriate or constricted emotions, and behavior that is odd, peculiar, or eccentric. With few exceptions, they lack close friends or confidants except for first-degree relatives. When they are around others, they experience excessive social anxiety that is not diminished by familiarity and is associated with suspicion and fears (American Psychiatric Association, 2013).

Biopsychosocial–Adlerian Conceptualization

The following biopsychosocial formulation may be helpful in understanding how the Schizotypal Personality Disorder is likely to have developed.

This personality disorder is described by Millon (2011) as a syndromal extension or deterioration of the Schizoid or the Avoidant Personality Disorders. As such, a useful procedure is to describe the biological and temperamental features of both of these subtypes. The schizoid subtype of a schizotypal personality is characterized by a passive-infantile pattern, probably resulting from low autonomic-nervous-system reactivity and parental indifference that led to impoverished infantile stimulation. On the other hand, the avoidant subtype is characterized by the fearful infantile temperamental pattern (Millon, 1981). This probably resulted from the child's high autonomic-nervous-system reactivity, combined with parental criticalness and depreciation that was further reinforced by sibling and peer depreciation. Both subtypes of the schizotypal personality have been noted to have impaired eye-tracking motions, which is a characteristic shared with schizophrenic individuals.

Psychologically, the schizotypals view themselves, others, the world, and life's purpose in terms of the following themes. They tend to view themselves by some variant of the theme: "I'm on a different wavelength than others." They commonly experience being selfless; that is, they experience feeling empathy, estranged, and disconnected or dissociated from the rest of life. Their world-view is some variant of the theme: "Life is strange and unusual, and others have special magical intentions." As such, they are likely to conclude: "Therefore, observe caution while being curious about these special magical intentions of others." The most common defense mechanism utilized by them is undoing, the effort to neutralize "evil" deeds and thoughts by their eccentric, peculiar beliefs and actions.

Socially, predictable patterns of parenting and environmental factors can be noted for the Schizotypal Personality Disorder. The parenting patterns noted previously of the cold indifference of the schizoid subtype, or the deprecating and derogatory parenting style and family environment of the avoidant subtype are noted. In both cases, the level of functioning in the family of origin then would be noted in the Schizoid Personality Disorder or the Avoidant Personality Disorder. Fragmented parental communications are a feature common to both subtypes of the Schizotypal Personality Disorder. The parental injunction is likely to have been "You're a strange bird."

Treatment Considerations

Individuals with Schizotypal Personality Disorder find it very difficult to engage and remain in a psychotherapeutic relationship. Typically, they are on medication and may be referred for adjunctive psychotherapy. Accordingly, the focus of treatment is on "management" rather than on "treatment." Thus, instead of attempting personality restructuring, the realistic treatment goal for the schizotypal personality is to increase the individual's ability to function more consistently, even though on the periphery of society. Specifically, successful management will likely incorporate psychoeducational or social-skills training with supportive psychotherapeutic methods. Reid (1989) noted that if these patients can remain in long-term treatment, they may be able to increase their ability to function more consistently and with less disease. He reports that homogeneous groups can occasionally be a useful adjunct to individual treatment. In terms of medication, low-dose neuroleptics have been found to be useful for the schizotypal personality, even in the absence of psychotic features. Yet, it should be noted that medication compliance is particularly a problem with the Schizotypal Personality Disorder.

Case Example: Ms. B.

Ms. B. is a 46-year-old single female who was referred to a community mental health clinic by her mother because Ms. B. had no interests, friends, or outside activities and was considered by neighbors to be an "odd duck." Ms. B.'s father had recently retired, and because of a limited pension, the parents were having difficulty in making ends meet, since Ms. B. had been living with them for the past eight years after she had been laid off from an assembly-line job she had held for about ten years. The patient readily admitted she preferred to be alone but denied that this was a problem for her. She believed that her mother was concerned about her because of what might happen to the patient after her parents' deaths. Ms. B. was an only child who had graduated from high school with average grades but had never been involved in extracurricular activities while in school. She had never dated, and mentioned she had a female friend whom she had not talked with in four years. Since moving back with her parents, she stayed in her room, preoccupied with books about astrology and charting her astrological forecast. On examination, she was an alert, somewhat uncooperative female appearing older than her stated age, with moderately disheveled hair and clothing. Her speech was monotonal and deliberate. She achieved poor eye contact with the examiner. Her thinking was vague and tangential, and she expressed a belief that her fate lay in "the stars." She denied specific delusions or perceptual abnormalities. Ms. B.'s affect was constricted, except for one episode of anger when she thought the therapist was being critical.

ANTISOCIAL PERSONALITY DISORDER

Antisocial behavior tends to begin in childhood or early adolescence and is characterized by aggressiveness, fighting, hyperactivity, poor peer relationships, irresponsibility, lying, theft, truancy, poor school performance, runaway behavior, inappropriate sexual activity, as well as drug and alcohol abuse. As adults, assaultiveness, self-defeating impulsivity, hedonism, promiscuity, unreliability, and continued drug and alcohol abuse may be present. Criminality may be involved. These individuals fail at work, change jobs frequently, tend to receive dishonorable discharges from the military, are abusing parents and neglectful spouses, have difficulty maintaining intimate relationships, and may be convicted and spend time in prison. Antisocial Personality Disordered persons are frequently anxious and depressed and show both conversion symptoms and factitious symptoms. Antisocial behavior often peaks in the late adolescence and early twenties and lessens in the late thirties. This is primarily a diagnosis of males, the prevalence rate being approximately 4:1 males to females.

PSYCHOPATHY, SOCIOPATHY, AND ANTISOCIAL PERSONALITY DISORDER

Psychopaths, sociopaths, and antisocial personalities can engage in criminal behavior. For this reason, some clinicians use the terms psychopath and sociopath interchangeably. Because research indicates some notable differences in behavior and in etiology, others prefer to differentiate psychopathy and sociopathy (Hare, 1993; Walsh & Wu, 2008). For example, Hare (1993) identifies specific deficits in psychopaths that distinguish them from sociopaths. These include interpersonal deficits, i.e., grandiosity, arrogance, and deceitfulness, as well as affective deficits, i.e., lack of guilt and empathy. Specifically, psychopaths are characterized by a global empathic deficit. In contrast, sociopaths can emotionally attach to others, and may feel badly when they hurt those individuals to whom they are attached. Yet, sociopaths can lack empathy and attachment toward society, and are not likely to feel guilt in harming a stranger or breaking laws. So while both psychopaths and sociopaths are capable of committing heinous crimes, the psychopath would commit crimes against family members or "friends" (as well as strangers) and feel little to no remorse. In terms of etiology, research suggests that psychopathy is more of an innate and genetic phenomenon, whereas sociopathy is more the result of environmental factors such as poverty, exposure to violence, and overly permissive or neglectful parenting (Stout, 2005).

Currently, Antisocial Personality Disorder is both a legal designation and DSM diagnosis that can be applied to both psychopaths and sociopaths (Walsh & Wu, 2008).

Clinical Presentation

The Antisocial Personality Disorder is recognizable by the following behavior and interpersonal style, cognitive style, and emotional style. The behavioral style of antisocial personalities is characterized by poor job performance, repeated substance abuse, irresponsible parenting, persistent lying, delinquency, truancy, and violations of others' rights. Antisocial Personality Disordered individuals are also noted for their impulsive anger, hostility, and cunning. They are forceful individuals who regularly engage in risk-seeking and thrill-seeking behavior. Their interpersonal style is characterized as antagonistic and belligerent. They tend to be highly competitive and distrustful of others and thus poor losers. Their relationships may at times appear to be "slick" as well as calculating. The flavor of this DSM-5 diagnosis still retains some of the "criminal" diagnostic category. Yet, these criteria can also characterize the behavior of successful businessmen, politicians, and other professionals, who could be described as ambitious, hard driving, and successful.

The cognitive style of the antisocial personality is described as impulsive and cognitively inflexible as well as externally oriented. Because they are contemptuous of authority, rules, and social expectations, they easily rationalize their own behavior. Their feelings or emotional style are characterized by shallow, superficial relationships that involve no lasting emotional ties or commitments. They avoid "softer" emotions such as warmth and intimacy because they regard these as signs of weakness. Guilt is seldom if ever experienced. They are unable to tolerate boredom, depression, or frustration and subsequently are sensation-seekers. They are callous toward the pain and suffering of others and show little guilt or shame over their own deviant actions.

DSM-5 Characterization

Individuals with this personality disorder are characterized by an unremitting pattern of disregarding and violating the rights of others. They disrespect and disregard laws and social norms, and regularly engage in acts that are grounds for arrest. These individuals lie, are deceitful, and will take advantage of others for pleasure or for personal profit. They are impulsive and fail to plan ahead. They are also irritable and aggressive, which results in physical fights or assaults. It is not surprising that these individuals disregard the safety of others as well as of themselves. Their irresponsibility is demonstrated by their failure to engage in consistent work behavior and failure to meet financial obligations. Furthermore, their lack of remorse is shown by their indifference in having hurt, mistreated, or stolen from others (American Psychiatric Association, 2013).

Biopsychosocial–Adlerian Conceptualization

The following biopsychosocial formulation may be helpful in understanding how the antisocial personality is likely to have developed. Biologically, antisocial personalities manifested "difficult child" temperaments (Thomas & Chess, 1977). As such, their patterns were unpredictable, they tended to withdraw from situations, showed high intensity, and had a fairly low, discontented mood. This ill-tempered infantile pattern has been described by Millon (2011) as resulting in part from a low threshold for limbic stimulation and a decrease in inhibitory centers of the central nervous system. Their body types tend to be endomorphic (lean) and mesomorphic (muscular) (Millon, 2011).

Psychologically, these individuals have a unique view of themselves, others, and the world. They tend to view themselves with some variant of the theme: "I am cunning and entitled to get whatever I want." In other words, they see themselves as strong, competitive, energetic, and tough. Their view of life and the world is a variant of the theme: "Life is devious and hostile, and rules keep me from fulfilling my needs." Not surprisingly their life's goal has a variant of the theme: "Therefore, I'll bend or break these rules because my needs come first, and I'll defend against efforts to be controlled or degraded by others." Acting out and rationalization are common defense mechanisms used by the antisocial personality.

Socially, predictable parenting styles and environmental factors can be noted for the Antisocial Personality Disorder. Typically, the parenting style is characterized by hostility and deficient parental modeling. Or, the parents might have provided such good modeling that the child could not or refused to live up to high parental standards. The parental injunction is that, "The end justifies the means." Thus, vindictive behavior is modeled and reinforced. The family structure tends to be disorganized and disengaged. The antisocial pattern is confirmed, reinforced, and perpetuated by the following individual and systems factors: The need to be powerful and the fear of being abused and humiliated leads to a denial of "softer" emotions plus uncooperativeness. This, along with the tendency to provoke others, leads to further reinforcement of antisocial beliefs and behaviors.

Treatment Considerations

In terms of treatment goals, these individuals are usually not interested in presenting for treatment or are resistant to treatment if they are forced by the courts, employers, or other agencies. Individual therapy, in and of itself, has proved to be remarkably ineffective with these individuals. However, special residential treatment programs have shown some promise (Reid, 1989). If the antisocial personality is able to engage in psychotherapy, a clear sign of progress is noted with the appearance of depressive features.

Case Example: Mr. A.

Mr. A. is a 24-year-old Hispanic male who presented late in the evening to the emergency room at a community hospital, complaining of a headache. His description of the pain was vague and contradictory. At one point he said the pain had been present for three days, while at another point it was "many years." He indicated that the pain led to violent behavior and described how, during a headache episode, he had brutally assaulted a medic while he was in the Air Force. He gave a long history of arrests for assault, burglary, and drug dealing. Neurological and mental status examinations were within normal limits except for some mild agitation. He insisted that only Darvon—a narcotic—would relieve his headache pain. The patient resisted a plan for further diagnostic tests or a follow-up clinic appointment, saying unless he was treated immediately "something really bad could happen."

DEPENDENT PERSONALITY DISORDER

The Dependent Personality Disorder is characterized by a pervasive pattern of dependent and submissive behaviors. Those of this disorder are excessively passive, insecure, and isolated individuals who become abnormally dependent on one or more persons. While initially acceptable, this dependent behavior can become controlling, appear hostile, and even blend into a passive-aggressive pattern. This disorder is more common in females (2:1 females to males). In females the dependent style often takes the form of submissiveness, while in males the dependent style is more likely to be autocratic, such as when the husband and boss depends on his wife and secretary to perform essential tasks which he himself cannot accomplish. In either case, this disorder is likely to lead to anxiety and depression when the dependent relationship is threatened.

Clinical Presentation

The clinical presentation of the Dependent Personality Disorder can be described in terms of behavioral and interpersonal style, thinking style, and feeling style. Dependent personalities' behavioral and interpersonal styles are characterized by docility, passivity, and non-assertiveness. In interpersonal relations, they tend to be pleasing, self-sacrificing, clinging, and constantly requiring the assurance of others. Their compliance and reliance on others lead to a subtle demand that others assume responsibility for major areas of their lives.

The thinking or cognitive style of dependent personalities is characterized by suggestibility. They easily adopt a Pollyannaish attitude toward life. Furthermore, they tend to minimize difficulties, and because of their naiveté are easily persuadable and easily taken advantage of. In short, this style of thinking is uncritical and unperceptive.

Their feeling or affective style is characterized by insecurity and anxiousness. Because they lack self-confidence, they experience considerable discomfort at being alone. They tend to be preoccupied with the fear of abandonment and disapproval of others. Their mood tends to be one of anxiety or fearfulness, as well as having a somber or sad quality.

DSM-5 Characterization

Individuals with this personality disorder are characterized by an excessive and unremitting need to be cared for, and cling to others because of their fear of separation. They constantly seek the advice and reassurance of others when making decisions. More than anything, they want others to take responsibility for most major areas of their lives. Not surprisingly, they seldom express disagreement with others for fear they will lose their support and approval. Because they lack confidence in their own judgment and ability, they have difficulty starting projects and doing things on their own. These individuals will even engage in actions that are difficult and unpleasant in order to receive support and caring from others. Because of unrealistic fears of being unable to take care of themselves, they feel helpless or uncomfortable when faced with being alone. When a close relationship is about to end, they immediately seek out another caring and supportive relationship. Finally, they become preoccupied with fears of being left to take care of themselves (American Psychiatric Association, 2013).

Biopsychosocial–Adlerian Conceptualization

The following biopsychosocial formulation may be helpful in understanding how the Dependent Personality Disorder is likely to have developed. Biologically, these individuals are characterized by a low energy level. Their temperament is described as melancholic. As infants and young children they were characterized as fearful, sad, or withdrawn. In terms of body types they tend to have more endomorphic builds (Millon, 2011).

Psychologically, dependent personalities can be understood and appreciated in terms of their view of themselves, their world-view, and their life goal. The self-view of these individuals tends to be a variant of the theme: "I'm nice, but inadequate (or fragile)." Their view of self is self-effacing, inept, and self-doubting. Their view of the world is some variant of the theme: "Others are here to take care of me, because I can't do it for myself." Their life goal is characterized by some variant of the theme: "Therefore, cling and rely on others at all cost."

The social features of this personality disorder can be described in terms of parental, familial, and environmental factors. The dependent personality is most likely to be raised in a family in which parental overprotection is prominent. It is as if the parental injunction to the child is "I can't trust you to do anything right (or well)." The dependent personality is likely to have been pampered and overprotected as a child. Contact with siblings and peers may engender feelings of unattractiveness, awkwardness, or competitive inadequacy, especially during the preadolescent and adolescent years. These can have a devastating impact on the individual, and further confirm the individual's sense of self-deprecation and doubt. This personality is reinforced and becomes self-perpetuating by a number of factors: a sense of self-doubt, an avoidance of competitive activity; and particularly by the availability of self-reliant individuals who are willing to take care of and make decisions for the dependent person in exchange for the self-sacrificing and docile friendship of the dependent personality.

Treatment Considerations

The differential diagnoses for this personality disorder include the Histrionic Personality Disorder and the Avoidant Personality Disorder. Common diagnoses that are associated with the Dependent Personality Disorder include the Anxiety Disorders, particularly Simple and Social Phobias, and Panic Disorders with or without Agoraphobia. Other common DSM-5 disorders include Hypochondriasis, Conversion Disorders and

Somatization Disorders. The experience of loss of a supportive person or relationship can lead to a number of affective disorders including Persistent Depressive Disorder and Major Depressive Episodes. Finally, because dependent personalities can have lifelong training in assuming the "sick role," they are especially prone to the Factitious Disorders.

In general, the long-range goal of psychotherapy with a dependent personality is to increase the individual's sense of independence and ability to function interdependently. At other times, the therapist may need to settle for a more modest goal: that is, helping the individual become a "healthier" dependent personality. Treatment strategies typically include challenging the individual's convictions or dysfunctional beliefs about personal inadequacy, and learning ways in which to increase assertiveness. A variety of methods can be used to increase self-reliance. Among these are providing the dependent person directives and opportunities for making decisions, being alone, and taking responsibility for his or her own well-being.

Case Example: Ms. D.

Ms. D. is a 34-year-old single, white female with a two-year history of partially treated panic attacks. Her panic symptoms began approximately three years previously and consisted of symptoms of hyperventilation, palpitations, lightheadedness, and a feeling of dread while she was working around her apartment. Because she believed she was having a heart attack, she called for an ambulance and was taken to the emergency room of a local hospital. A heart attack was ruled out and she was referred to her primary care physician to be treated for anxiety symptoms. Over the course of the next several months, she was treated with Valium and the physician insisted she get psychotherapy. She did not, however, follow up with the recommendation for psychotherapy until 19 months after her first symptoms continued, and because of anticipatory anxiety of further panic attacks, she became increasingly homebound and agoraphobic. Over this period of time she became more moody, irritable, fatigued, and tearful, and she had difficulty with initial insomnia as well as early morning awakening.

Ms. D. is the younger of two siblings. Her brother was described as a successful attorney. Her parents were both alive, and since the panic attacks had begun, she moved back into her parents' home. She described both her parents as caring, concerned, and "my best friends." Ms. D. had graduated from college and went on to complete a master's degree in education. Subsequently, she worked for four years as an elementary school teacher before her first symptoms occurred. Since then she had taken an indefinite leave of absence from her job. She reported being sickly as a young child and being taken by mother from doctor to doctor for various minor ailments. Even though she was a good student at school and had some friends, she preferred to come home after school and help Mother around the house with the house cleaning and chores.

The following early recollections were reported: At age six she remembers her first day of going to school by herself. "I was proud. My mother said I could walk to school by myself. But when I turned the corner, I saw her out of the corner of my eye, following me." She recalls looking over her shoulder and seeing her mother behind a tree, and feeling flustered and angry, and at the same time relieved that her mother was there. She remembers thinking, "Why can't she let me do this by myself?"

She remembers at age four getting her first puppy. "It was a mixed collie and a shepherd. Little Fluffy couldn't make it down the driveway on its own. When I tried to take him for a walk his legs just collapsed and he began to pant. So Fluffy became dependent on everyone. I had to pick him up and I said, 'He's too tired to do it by himself.'" She recalls bending down and picking up her dog and thinking "He's too tired," and feeling love for her puppy, and love and appreciation from him.

At age five she recalls her mother asking her to go to the corner store to get some stamps. "She gave me instructions on how to cross the street, get change from the cashier, and put the money in the stamp machine. But when I went over to the stamp machine, I couldn't reach the coin slot because it was too high off the ground." Ms. D. recalls standing in front of the machine and trying to get it to work, but not being able to reach the coin slot, and feeling puzzled and nervous, wondering if someone would see her and try to help her.

Ms. D.'s presenting symptoms, her early childhood and family history, and her early recollections are all suggestive of the clinical presentation and dynamics of the Dependent Personality Disorder. Not only was Ms. D. overly dependent on her parents, she also became quite dependent on the Valium that she was prescribed for panic symptoms. The case of Ms. D. is prototypic of many individuals who present with panic, Agoraphobia, and depressive features. That is, the Dependent Personality Disorder is the most common personality disorder in individuals presenting with panic and agoraphobic symptoms.

HISTRIONIC PERSONALITY DISORDER

Histrionic personalities may initially seem charming, likable, energetic, and seductive, but as time passes they are likely to be seen as emotionally unstable, immature, and egocentric. This personality style and disorder predominates in females, and presents with a caricature of femininity in dress and manner.

Clinical Presentation

The clinical presentation of the Histrionic Personality Disorder can be characterized by the following behavioral and interpersonal style, thinking style, and feeling style. The behavioral style is characterized as charming, dramatic, and expressive, while also being demanding, self-indulgent, and inconsiderate. Persistent attention-seeking, mood lability, capriciousness, and superficiality further characterize their behavior. Interpersonally, these individuals tend to be exhibitionistic and flirtatious in their manner, with attention-seeking and manipulativeness being prominent.

The thinking or cognitive style of this personality can be characterized as impulsive and thematic, rather than being analytical, precise, and field-independent. In short, their tendency is to be non-analytic, vague, and field-dependent. They are easily suggestible and rely heavily on hunches and intuition. They avoid awareness of their own hidden dependency and other self-knowledge, and tend to be "other-directed" with respect to the need for approval from others. Therefore, they can easily dissociate their "real" or inner self from their "public" or outer self. Their emotional or affective style is characterized by exaggerated emotional displays and excitability, including irrational outbursts and temper tantrums. Although they are constantly seeking reassurance that they are loved, they respond with only superficial warmth and charm and are generally emotionally shallow. Finally, they are exceedingly rejection-sensitive.

DSM-5 Characterization

Individuals with this personality disorder are characterized by an unremitting pattern of attention-seeking and emotionality. They tend to be uncomfortable in situations where they cannot be the center of attention. Their emotional reactions tend to be shallow and rapidly shifting. Typically, they draw attention to themselves with the way they dress. Their manner of speech tends to be impressionistic with few details. These individuals are easily influenced by others or circumstances. They are likely to perceive relationships as more intimate than they really are. They often engage in provocative and inappropriate seductive sexual behavior. Furthermore, they are dramatic and overly exaggerate their emotional expressions (American Psychiatric Association, 2013).

Biopsychosocial–Adlerian Conceptualization

The following biopsychosocial formulation may be helpful in understanding how the Histrionic Personality Disorder develops. Biologically and temperamentally, the Histrionic Personality Disorder appears to be quite different from the Dependent Personality Disorder. Unlike the dependent personality, histrionic personality is characterized by a high energy level and emotional and autonomic reactivity. Millon and Everly (1985) noted that histrionic adults tended to display a high degree of emotional lability and responsiveness in their infancy and early childhood. Their temperament then can be characterized as hyper-responsive and externally oriented for gratification.

Psychologically, Histrionic Personality Disorder has the following characteristic view of self, world-view, and life goal. The self-view of the histrionic will be some variant of the theme: "I am sensitive and everyone should admire and approve of me." The world-view will be some variant of: "Life makes me nervous, so I am entitled to special care and consideration." Life goal is some variant of the theme: "Therefore, play to the audience, and have fun, fun, fun."

In addition to biological and psychological factors, social factors such as parenting style and injunction, and family and environmental factors, influence the development of the histrionic personality. The parental injunction for the histrionic personality involves reciprocity: "I'll give you attention, if you do X." A parenting style that involves minimal or inconsistent discipline helps insure and reinforce the histrionic pattern. The histrionic child is likely to grow up with at least one manipulative or histrionic parent who reinforces the child's histrionic and attention-seeking behavior. Finally, the following sequence of self and system perpetuants are likely to be seen in the Histrionic Personality Disorder: denial of one's real or inner self; a preoccupation with externals; the need for excitement and attention-seeking which leads to a superficial charm and interpersonal presence; and the need for external approval. This, in turn, further reinforces the dissociation and denial of the real or inner self from the public self, and the cycle continues.

Treatment Considerations

The differential diagnosis of the Histrionic Personality Disorder includes the Narcissistic Personality Disorder and the Dependent Personality Disorder. It also includes the Histrionic-Borderline Disorder, which is a decompensated version of the Histrionic Personality Disorder, and, according to Millon (2011), the Histrionic-Antisocial Personality Disorder. Associated diagnoses include: Persistent Depressive Disorder, Social Anxiety Disorder, and Obsessive-Compulsive Disorder. In addition, Major Depression and Bipolar Disorders are common in the decompensated Histrionic Personality Disorder.

The treatment of the Histrionic Personality Disorder may present a considerable challenge to the clinician. For the purposes of this discussion, we will limit ourselves to some general considerations about treatment goals, limits, and medications. General treatment goals include helping the individual integrate gentleness with strength, moderating emotional expression, and encouraging warmth, genuineness, and empathy. Because the histrionic personality can present as dramatic, impulsive, seductive, and manipulative with potential for suicidal gestures, the clinician needs to discuss the matter of limits early in the course of therapy regarding professional boundaries and personal responsibilities. Some histrionic personalities, particularly those who bear some resemblance to "Hysteroid Dysphoria," respond to certain antidepressant agents, particularly Parnate and Nardil (Liebowitz & Klein, 1979). Otherwise, unless a concurrent acute psychotic or Major Depressive Episode is present, psychotherapy is the principal mode of treatment.

Case Example: Ms. H.

Ms. H. is a 19-year-old female undergraduate student who requested psychological counseling at the University Health Services for "boyfriend problems." Actually, she had taken a nonlethal overdose of minor tranquilizers the day before coming to the Health Services. She said she took the overdose in an attempt to kill herself because "life wasn't worth living" after her boyfriend had left the afternoon before. She was an attractive, well-dressed woman adorned with makeup and nail polish, which contrasted sharply with the very casual fashion of most coeds on campus. During the initial interview she was warm and charming, maintained good eye contract, yet was mildly seductive. At two points in the interview she was emotionally labile, shifting from smiling elation to tearful sadness. Her boyfriend had accompanied her to the evaluation session and asked to talk to the therapist. He stated the reason he had left the patient was because she made demands on him which he could not meet, and that he "hadn't been able to satisfy her emotionally or sexually." Also, he noted that he could not afford to "take her out every night and party."

SCHIZOID PERSONALITY DISORDER

Individuals with Schizoid Personality Disorders tend to be reclusive individuals who have little desire or capacity for interpersonal relationships and derive little pleasure from them. Yet, they can perform well if left alone. For instance, they make excellent night watchmen and security guards. They have little emotional range, they daydream excessively, and appear to be humorless and aloof. Research evidence does not confirm the belief that the schizoid personality has an increased risk of developing a schizophrenic pattern (Grinspoon, 1982).

Clinical Presentation

The Schizoid Personality Disorder is characterized by the following behavior and interpersonal styles, thinking or cognitive styles, and emotional or affective styles. The behavioral pattern of schizoids can be described as lethargic, inattentive, and occasionally eccentric. They exhibit slow and monotone speech and are generally non-spontaneous in both their behavior and speech. Interpersonally, they appear to be content to remain socially aloof and alone. These individuals prefer to engage in solitary pursuits, they are reserved and reclusive, and rarely respond to others' feelings and actions. They tend to fade into the social backdrop and appear to others as "cold fish." They do not involve themselves in group or team activity. In short, they appear inept and awkward in social situations.

Their thinking style can be characterized as cognitively distracted. That is, their thinking and communication can easily become derailed through internal or external distraction. This is noted in clinical interviews, when these patients have difficulty organizing their thoughts, are vague, or wander into irrelevance such as the shoes certain people prefer (Millon, 2011). They appear to have little ability for introspection, nor ability to articulate important aspects of interpersonal relationships. Their goals are vague and appear to be indecisive.

Their emotional style is characterized as being humorless, cold, aloof, and unemotional. They appear to be indifferent to praise and criticism, and they lack spontaneity. Not surprisingly, their rapport and ability to empathize with others is poor. In short, they have a constricted range of affective response.

DSM-5 Characterization

Individuals with this personality disorder are characterized by an unremitting pattern of detachment from others and restricted emotional expression. They do not desire nor enjoy close relationships, including family relationships. Except for first-degree relatives, they are unlikely to have close friends or confidants. These individuals typically choose solitary activities, and have little, if any, interest in sexual relations. Not surprisingly, they seem indifferent to the feedback, including criticism, of others. They experience little, if any, pleasure in most activities. Instead, they exhibit emotional coldness, detachment, or flat affect (American Psychiatric Association, 2013).

Biopsychosocial–Adlerian Conceptualization

The following biopsychosocial formulation may be helpful in understanding how the schizoid personality develops. Biologically, the schizoid personality was likely to have had a passive and anhedonic infantile pattern and temperament. Millon (2011) suggested that this pattern results, in part, from increased dopaminergic postsynaptic limbic and frontal lobe receptor activity. Constitutionally, the schizoid is likely to be characterized by an ecomorphic body type (fragile and delicate) (Sheldon, Dupertius, & McDermott, 1954).

Psychologically, schizoids view themselves, others, the world, and life's purpose in terms of the following themes. They view themselves by some variant of the theme: "I'm a misfit from life, so I don't need anybody. I am indifferent to everything." For schizoid personalities, the world and others are viewed by some variant of the theme: "Life is a difficult place and relating to people can be harmful." As such, they are likely to conclude, "Therefore, trust nothing and keep a distance from others and you won't get hurt." Alexandra Adler (1956) further describes these life-style dynamics. The most common defense mechanism utilized by them is intellectualization.

Socially, predictable patterns of parenting and environmental factors can be noted for schizoids. Parenting style is usually characterized by indifference and impoverishment. It is as if the parental injunction was: "You're a misfit," or, "Who are you, what do you want?" Their family pattern is characterized by fragmented communications and rigid, unemotional responsiveness. Because of these conditions, schizoids are grossly under-socialized and develop few if any interpersonal relating and coping skills. This schizoid pattern is confirmed, reinforced, and perpetuated by the following individual and systems factors: Believing themselves to be misfits, they shun social activity. This plus social insensitivity leads to reinforcement of social isolation and further confirmation of the schizoid style.

Treatment Considerations

Included in the differential diagnosis of the Schizoid Personality Disorder are the following personality disorders: the Avoidant Personality Disorder, Schizotypal Personality Disorder, and the Dependent Personality Disorder. The most common symptom disorders associated with the Schizoid Personality Disorder are: Depersonalization Disorder, the Bipolar and Unipolar Disorders, Obsessive-Compulsive Disorder, Hypochondriasis, Schizophreniform, and Disorganized and Catatonic Schizophrenias.

Schizoid personalities rarely volunteer for treatment unless decompensation is present. However, they may accept treatment if someone, like a family member, demands it. Treatment goals are focused on symptom alleviation rather than on restructuring of personality. Treatment strategy involves a crisis and supportive approach, as well as providing a consistent and supportive therapeutic interaction. Medications, particularly the neuroleptics, do not appear to be useful with schizoid personality unless some psychotic decompensation has been noted (Reid, 1989).

Case Example: Mr. S.

Mr. S. is a 19-year-old freshman who met with the director of the introductory psychology course program to arrange an individual assignment in lieu of participation in the small-group research-project course requirement. Mr. S. told the course director that because of a daily two-hour commute each way, he "wouldn't be available for the research project," and that he "wasn't really interested in psychology and was only taking the course because it was required". Upon further inquiry, Mr. S. disclosed that he preferred to commute and live at home with his mother, even though he had the financial resources to live on campus. He admitted he had no close friends nor social contacts, and preferred being a "loner." He had graduated from high school with a "B" average, but did not date or participate in extracurricular activities, except the electronics club. He was a computer science major, and "hacking" was his only hobby. Mr. S.'s affect was somewhat flattened and he appeared to have no sense of humor and failed to respond to attempts by the course director to make contact through humor. There was no indication of a thought nor perceptual disorder. The course director arranged for an individual project for the student.

PARANOID PERSONALITY DISORDER

Paranoid personalities are aloof, emotionally cold individuals who display unjustified suspiciousness, hypersensitivity, jealousy, and a fear of intimacy. In addition they can be grandiose, rigid, contentious, and litigious. Because of their hypersensitivity to criticism and tendency to project blame on others, they tend to lead isolated lives and are often disliked by others. Millon (2011) conceived of the Paranoid Personality Disorder as a pathological syndromal continuation of the Narcissistic Personality Disorder, the Antisocial Personality Disorder, or the Obsessive-Compulsive Personality Disorder. As a result, the clinical presentation of the paranoid personality takes on characteristics of these three respective precursors.

Clinical Presentation

The Paranoid Personality Disorder is characterized by the following behavior interpersonal styles, cognitive style, and emotional style. Behaviorally, paranoid individuals are resistive of external influences. They tend to be chronically tense, because they are constantly mobilized against perceived threats from their environment. Their behavior also is marked by guardedness, defensiveness, argumentativeness, and litigiousness. Interpersonally, they tend to be distrustful, secretive, and isolative. They are intimacy-avoiders by nature, and repudiate nurturant overtures by others.

Their cognitive style is characterized by mistrusting preconceptions. They carefully scrutinize every situation encountered and scan the environment for "clues" or "evidence" to confirm their preconceptions, rather than objectively focus on data. Thus, while their perception may be accurate, their judgment often is not. The paranoid personalities' prejudices mold the perceived data to fit their preconceptions. Thus, they tend to disregard evidence that does not fit their preconceptions. When under stress, their thinking can take on a conspiratorial or even delusional flavor. Their hypervigilance and need to seek evidence to confirm their beliefs lead them to have a rather authoritarian and mistrustful outlook on life.

The affective style of the paranoid personalities is characterized as cold, aloof, unemotional, and humorless. In addition, they lack a deep sense of affection, warmth, and sentimentality. Because of their hypersensitivity to real or imagined slights, and their subsequent anger at what they believe to be deceptions and betrayals, they tend to have few, if any, friends. The two emotions they experience and express with some depth are anger and intense jealousies.

DSM-5 Characterization

Individuals with this personality disorder are characterized by an unremitting pattern of distrust and suspicion, and interpret others' motives as harmful. Without sufficient basis, they suspect that others are exploiting, harming, or deceiving them. They are obsessed with unfounded doubts about the loyalty of friends and associates. Because of their unfounded fears, they are reluctant to confide in others. They are likely to interpret otherwise benign remarks and situations as threatening and dangerous. Not surprisingly, they are unforgiving of slights, insults, and injuries. These individuals are quick to react angrily or to counterattack when they believe that their character or reputation is being attacked. They are likely to continually suspect, without justification, that their spouse or sexual partner is unfaithful (American Psychiatric Association, 2013).

Biopsychosocial–Adlerian Conceptualization

The following biopsychosocial formulations may be helpful in understanding how the Paranoid Personality Disorder is likely to have developed. Biologically, a low threshold for limbic system stimulation and deficiencies in inhibitory centers seem to influence the behavior of the paranoid personality. The underlying temperament can best be understood in terms of the subtypes of the paranoid disorder. Each of three subtypes is briefly described in terms of their underlying temperament, and correlative parental and environmental factors. In the narcissistic type, a hyper-responsive temperament and precociousness, parental overvaluation and indulgence, as well as the individual's sense of grandiosity and self-importance probably result in deficits in social interest and limited interpersonal skills. The antisocial type of the paranoid personality is likely to possess a hyper-responsive temperament. This, plus harsh parental treatment, probably contributes to the impulsive, hedonistic, and aggressive style of this type. In the compulsive type, the underlying temperament may have been anhedonic. This, as well as parental rigidity and overcontrol, largely accounts for the development of this type. Finally, a less common variant is the paranoid passive-aggressive type. As infants, these individuals usually demonstrated the "difficult child" temperament, and later temperament is characterized by affective irritability. This plus parental inconsistency probably accounts in large part for the development of this type (Millon, 2011).

Psychologically, paranoid individuals view themselves, others, the world, and life's purpose in terms of the following themes. They tend to view themselves by some variant of the theme: "I'm special and different. I'm alone and no one likes me because I'm better than others." Life and the world are viewed by some variant of the theme: "Life is unfair, unpredictable, and demanding. It can and will sneak up and harm you when you are least expecting it." As such, they are likely to conclude: "Therefore, be wary, counterattack, trust no one, and excuse yourself from failure by blaming others." The most common defensive mechanism associated with the paranoid disorder is projection.

Socially, predictable patterns of parenting and environmental factors can be noted for the Paranoid Personality Disorder. For all the subtypes the parental injunction appears to be "You're different. Don't make mistakes." Paranoid Personality Disordered individuals tend to have perfectionistic parents who expose these children to specialness training. This, plus the parental style that has been articulated for the subtypes of the disorder and parental criticism, leads to an attitude of social isolation and hypervigilant behavior. To make sense of the apparent contradiction between being special and being ridiculed, the children creatively conclude that the reason they are special and that no one likes them is because they are better than other people. This explanation serves the purpose of reducing their anxiety and allowing them to develop some sense of self and belonging.

This paranoid pattern is confirmed, reinforced, and perpetuated by the following individual and systems factors: A sense of specialness, rigidity, attributing malevolence to others, blaming others, and misinterpreting motives of others leads to social alienation and isolation, which further confirms the individual's persecutory stance.

Treatment Considerations

Included in the differential diagnosis of the Paranoid Personality Disorder are the following personality disorders: Antisocial Personality Disorder, Narcissistic Personality Disorder, Obsessive-Compulsive Personality Disorder, and Passive-Aggressive Personality Disorder. The most common symptom disorders associated with the Paranoid Personality Disorder are Generalized Anxiety Disorder, Panic Disorder, and Delusional Disorder. If a Bipolar Disorder is present, an irritable manic presentation is likely. Decompensation into Schizophrenic reaction is likely. The Paranoid and Catatonic subtypes of Schizophrenia are most commonly noted.

Until recently, the prognosis for treatment of the Paranoid Personality Disorder was considered guarded. Today more optimism prevails in achieving these goals of treatment: increasing the benignness of perception and interpretation of reality, and increasing trusting behavior. The social-skills training intervention described by Turkat and Maisto (1985) focuses on changing the internal processes of attention, processing, response emission, and feedback from a pathological to a non-pathological mode of perceiving and thinking. In essence, individuals are taught how to reduce their perceptual scanning and attending to inappropriate cues, to attending to more appropriate cues; and rather than using idiosyncratic logic and misinterpretation to process their cues, they learn to use more common logic and a more benign interpretation of cues. In so doing they are able to respond in a more socially graceful fashion and are more likely to interpret feedback, including criticism, as constructive. This social-skills intervention approach can be combined with insight-oriented therapy to achieve positive therapeutic outcomes. Medication, particularly lower-dose neuroleptics, have been shown useful for decreasing anxiety secondary to loss of control (Reid, 1989).

Case Example: Mr. P.

Mr. P. is a 59-year-old male referred for psychiatric evaluation by his attorney to rule out a treatable psychiatric disorder. Mr. P. had entered into five lawsuits in the past two and one-half years. His attorney believed that each suit was of questionable validity. Mr. P. was described as an unemotional, highly controlled male who was now suing a local men's clothing store "for conspiring to deprive me of my consumer rights." He contends that the store manager had consistently issued bad credit reports on him. The consulting psychiatrist elicited other examples of similar concerns. Mr. P. has long distrusted his neighbors across the street and regularly monitors their activity, since one of his garbage cans disappeared two years ago. Mr. P. took an early retirement from his accounting job one year ago because he could not get along with his supervisor, whom he believed was faulting him about his accounts and paperwork. Mr. P. contends he was faultless. On examination, Mr. P.'s mental status is unremarkable except for constriction of affect and a certain hesitation and guardedness in his response to questions.

Concluding Note

Clinicians and students are likely to be surprised at the changes in the personality disorders section of *DSM-5*. Taken together, these changes encourage clinicians to assess, diagnose, and treat the person presenting with a mental disorder, rather than merely diagnosing and treating a mental disorder. This is radical shift from previous *DSM* editions. Integrating the Adlerian perspective and case conceptualization with the focus of *DSM-5* on personality functioning and traits, can increase the likelihood that clinicians and their patients/clients will achieve better clinical outcomes.

References

Adler, A. (1935). The fundamental views of Individual Psychology. *International Journal of Individual Psychology*, 1(1), pp. 5–8.

Adler, A. (1956). In H.H. Ansbacher and R.R. Ansbacher (Eds.), *The Individual Psychology of Alfred Adler*. New York, NY: Harper & Row.

Adler, Alfred (1964). *Superiority and Social Interest: A Collection of Later Writings* (H.L. & R.R. Ansbacher (Eds.). Evanston, IL: Northwestern University Press.

Adler, Alexandra (1956). Problems in psychotherapy. *American Journal of Individual Psychology*, 12, pp. 12–24.

Adler, G. (1985). *Borderline Psychopathology and Its Treatment*. New York, NY: Jason Aronson.

American Psychiatric Association (2013). *Diagnostic and Statistical Manual of Mental Disorders, Fifth Edition*. Arlington, VA: American Psychiatric Publishing.

Burks, J. & Rubenstein, M. (1979). *Temperament Styles in Adult Interaction: Applications to Psychotherapy*. New York, NY: Brunner/Mazel.

Clark, A. & Butler, C. (2012). Degree of activity: Relationship to early recollections and safeguarding tendencies. *Journal of Individual Psychology*, 68, pp. 136–147.

Feldman, L. (1982). Dysfunctional marital conflict: An integrative interpersonal-intrapsychic model. *Journal of Marital and Family Therapy*, 8, pp. 417–428.

Grinspoon, L. (Ed.) (1982). The schizophrenic disorders. In *Psychiatric Update, Vol. I.* (pp. 822–855). Washington, DC: American Psychiatric Publishing.

Hare, R.D. (1993). *Without Conscience: The Disturbing World of Psychopaths Among Us*. New York, NY: Pocket Books.

Hopwood, C.J., Malone, C., Ansell, E.B., Sanislow, C.A., Grilo, C.M., McGlashan, T.H., Pinto, A., Markowitz, J.C., Shea, M.T., Skodol, A.E., Gunderson, J.G., Zanarini, M.C., & Morey, L.C. (2011). Personality assessment in DSM-V: Empirical support for rating severity, style, and traits. *Journal of Personality Disorders*, 25, pp. 305–320

Jenike, M., Baer, L., & Minichiello, W. (1990). *Obsessive Compulsive Disorders: Theory and Management* (2nd edn). Chicago, IL: Yearbook Medical.

Kohut, H. (1971). *The Analysis of the Self*. New York, NY: International Universities Press.

Horney, K. (1951). *Neurosis and Human Growth*. London: Routledge & Kegan Paul.

Liebowitz, M. & Klein, D. (1979). Hysteroid dysphoria. *Psychiatric Clinics of North American*, 2, pp. 555–575.

Linehan, M. (1987). Dialectical behavior therapy: A cognitive behavioral approach to parasuicide. *Journal of Personality Disorders*, 1, pp. 328–333.

Masterson, J. (1976). *Psychotherapy of the Borderline Adult: A Developmental Approach*. New York, NY: Brunner/Mazel.

Millon, T. (1969). *Modern Psychopathology: A Biosocial Approach to Maladaptive Learning and Functioning*. Philadelphia, PA: Saunders.

Millon, T. (2011). *Disorders of Personality: Introducing a DSM/ICD Spectrum From Normal To Abnormal*. New York, NY: John Wiley & Sons.

Millon, T. & Everly G. (1985). *Personality and Its Disorders: A Biosocial Learning Approach*. New York, NY: John Wiley & Sons.

Morey, L.C., Hopwood, C.J., Markowitz, J.C., Gunderson, J.G., Grilo, C.M., McGlashan, T.H., Shea, M.T., Yen, S., Sanislow, C.A., Ansell, E.B., & Skodol, A.E. (2012). Comparison of alternative models for personality disorders, II: 6-, 8- and 10-year follow-up. *Psychological Medicine*, 42, pp. 1705–1713.

Mosak, H. (1968). The interrelatedness of the neurosis through central themes. *Journal of Individual Psychology*, 24, pp. 67–70.

Mosak, H. (1979). Mosak's typology: An update. *Journal of Individual Psychology*, 35, pp. 92–95.

Oldham, J. (2005). Personality disorders: Recent history and future directions. In J. Oldham, A. Skodol, & D. Bender (Eds.), *The American Psychiatric Publishing Textbook of Personality Disorders* (pp. 3–16). Washington, DC: American Psychiatric Publishing.

PDM Task Force (2006). *Psychodynamic Diagnostic Manual*. Silver Spring, MD: Alliance of Psychoanalytic Organizations.

Reid, W. (1989). *The Treatment of Psychiatric Disorders: Revised for the DSM-III-R*. New York, NY: Brunner/Mazel.

Salzman, L. (1968). *The Obsessive Personality: Origins, Dynamics, and Therapy*. New York, NY: Science House.

Sheldon, W., Dupertius, C., & McDermott, E. (1954). *Atlas of Men: A Guide for Somatotyping the Adult Male at All Ages*. New York, NY: Harper & Row.

Shulman, B. (1982). An Adlerian interpretation of the borderline personality. *Modern Psychoanalysis*, 7(2), pp. 137–153.

Sperry, L. (1990). Personality disorders: Biopsychosocial descriptions and dynamics. *Individual Psychology*, 48(2), pp. 193–202.

Sperry, L. (2002). DSM-IV: Making it more clinician-friendly. *Journal of Individual Psychology*, 58, pp. 434–481.

Sperry, L. (2011). Duped, drugged, and eaten: Working with the Jeffrey Dahmers of the world. In J. Kottler & J. Carlson, (Eds.), *Duped: Lies and Deceit in Psychotherapy* (pp. 47–56). New York, NY: Routledge.

Sperry, L. (2011). Personality disorders: A quick and reliable method for screening and diagnosing Axis II disorders through observation and interview. In H. Rosenthal (Ed.), *Favorite Counseling and Therapy Techniques* (pp. 291–298). New York, NY: Routledge.

Sperry, L. (2015). *Handbook of the Diagnosis and Treatment of DSM-5 Personality Disorders* (3rd edn.). New York, NY: Routledge.

Sperry, L. & Mosak, H. (1993). Personality Disorders. In L. Sperry & J. Carlson (Eds.), *Psychopathology and Psychotherapy: From Diagnosis to Treatment* (pp. 299–367). Munice, IN: Accelerated Development.

Sperry, L. & Mosak, H. (1996). Personality Disorders. In L. Sperry & J. Carlson (Eds.), *Psychopathology and Psychotherapy: From DSM-IV Diagnosis to Treatment* (2nd edn.) (pp. 279–335). Washington, DC: Accelerated Development/Taylor & Francis.

Sperry, L. & Sperry, J. (2012). *Case Conceptualization*. New York, NY: Routledge.

Stout, M. (2005). *The Sociopath Next Door: The Ruthless Versus the Rest of Us*. New York, NY: Broadway Books.

Thomas, A. & Chess, S. (1977). *Temperament and Development*. New York, NY: Brunner/Mazel.

Thomas, A. & Chess, S. (1984). *Origins and Evolution of Behavior Disorders*. New York, NY: Brunner/Mazel.

Toman, W. (1961). *Family Constellation: Theory and Practice of a Psychological Game*. New York, NY: Springer.

Turkat, I. & Maisto, S. (1985). Personality disorders: Application of the experimental method to the formulation and modification of personality disorders. In D.H. Barlow (Ed.), *Clinical Handbook of Psychological Disorders* (pp. 187–202). New York, NY: Guilford.

Walsh, A. & Wu, H.H. (2008). Differentiating antisocial personality disorder, psychopathy, and sociopathy: Evolutionary, genetic, neurological, and sociological considerations. *Criminal Justice Studies*, 2, pp. 135–152.

4 Anxiety and Obsessive-Compulsive Disorders

Jill Duba Sauerheber and James Robert Bitter

The basic feeling state associated with anxiety disorders is fear. Fear is a survival emotion, highly connected to evolutionary development and hardwired into the brain for the protection and safety of the individual (Millon, 1990; Rasmussen, 2010). In situations that are actually dangerous or perceived as such, fear is stimulated through one or more of the five senses that send signals to and fire the neurons in the lateral amygdala. Over the many years of childhood, our learned responses to fear-activating experiences are stored in the lateral amygdala and flow easily and instantly to the central nucleus of the amygdala, where the cranial nervous system activates the defenses of freezing, fleeing, or fighting. The heart starts pumping, breathing gets shorter, adrenaline is flowing, and the body jumps into action or freezes.

From an evolutionary perspective, fear is an adaptive emotion that requires the person to act in defense of self—even if that act is freezing in one's tracks (Rasmussen, 2010). The individual perceives what is believed to be real danger, a threat to safety and survival, and personal defenses are activated. While these personal defenses tend to be learned responses, they also involve an almost instantaneous assessment too: What is the best thing to do to ensure my safety, perhaps the safety of those around me, and my/our future(s)?

Beck and Emery (1985) distinguish fear from anxiety by renaming the experience of fear as a *cognitive* assessment of a threatening situation. Anxiety is then the emotional reaction to this assessment. To be sure, this distinction has great value for those who work with anxiety from a cognitive-behavioral perspective, and Adlerian therapists who focus on private logic can certainly work within this definition. Rasmussen (2010) and Rasmussen and Dover (2007), however, also distinguish fear and anxiety without losing the emotional adaptation to threat that fear actually is. In their model, fear is a compelling emotion, an actual declaration that "there is danger," a threat to safety or survival, that needs to be addressed with escape, avoidance, and other protective responses. Anxiety is still fear, but its basic characteristic is putting one on alert and making one vigilant in *anticipation* of danger. The *DSM-5* (American Psychiatric Association, 2013) adopts this latter perspective and adds that anxiety exists when the fear is out of proportion to the event or situation to which it pertains and persists beyond a reasonable time.

In this sense, anxiety falls into the realm of the individual's *private logic*, a core set of beliefs and convictions that are outside of the common sense for the culture in which the person lives. Let's say one person hits another person with a baseball bat: Pain is what results from the actual hit; suffering is the story the person constructs about the event and the pain. Similarly, fear is the result of actually being in and/or perceiving danger or an immediate threat to personal safety; anxiety is the story that evolves from such fear experiences.

In this chapter, we will define anxiety and obsessive-compulsive and related disorders in general and link this understanding to an Adlerian perspective. We will offer specific descriptions of Separation Anxiety Disorder, Selective Mutism, Specific Phobia, Social Anxiety Disorder, Panic Disorder, Agoraphobia, and Generalized Anxiety Disorder—in the order they appear in *DSM-5*. Similar descriptions will be provided for Obsessive-Compulsive Disorder, Body Dysmorphic Disorder, Trichotillomania, and Excoriation (grouped because of similar dynamics), and Hoarding Disorder.

Definitions and Processes Related to Anxiety and Obsessive-Compulsive Disorders added to the *DSM-5* differentiates fear from anxiety in a manner similar to our discussion above. Fear is an emotional response to a threat or attack on one's personal sense of safety. Anxiety is anticipatory, excessive to the concern or situation, and persists beyond developmentally appropriate periods. Anxiety almost always leads to some kind of avoidance behaviors that are intended to reduce the fear and worry. People who suffer from anxiety tend to be pessimistic and overestimate the danger they seek to avoid. Panic is a specific type of fear response characterized by acute physiological fear responses, including accelerated heart rate, sweating, shaking, shortness of breath, and light-headedness, among other symptoms, as well as feelings of unreality or depersonalization and fears of losing control, going crazy, or dying. A panic attack is not a coded disorder. If, however, the individual has repeated panic attacks and begins to fear their recurrence or significantly adjust life activities to avoid the panic attacks, then the person may meet criteria for Panic Disorder, which is a coded diagnosis. Sperry (1996) notes that panic attacks occur "in the third decade of life and within six months of a stressful life event … Individuals with panic disorders tend to display poor problem-solving ability" (p. 166). Anxiety disorders are diagnosed in women more than men and are highly correlated with feelings of helplessness and a loss of confidence in and hope for the future. The more generalized and overwhelming the experience of panic and anxiety, the worse the prognosis for treatment.

Obsessions are recurring thoughts or urges, sometimes images, which persist over time, which are undesired and intrude on the person's life. They are distinguished from delusions, because the individual is able to reality-test the thoughts and recognize them as irrational. Obsessions produce anxiety in the individual and generally lead to efforts that are intended to reduce the worry or fear. *Compulsions* are repeated behaviors or mental processes that the person feels driven to do in response to obsessions. They are one way in which the individual tries to control the worry or anxiety. When successful, compulsive behavior processes involve recognition of the anxiety-producing obsession, engagement in corrective activities, and a temporary reduction in anxiety. For example, a person whose anxiety goes up at the thought of being invaded by germs might engage in compulsive washing on a regular schedule to control or reduce the anxiety. Those who suffer from obsessions and compulsions tend to come from the middle and upper class—and tend to be smarter than people with generalized anxiety disorders (Sperry, 1996).

The issue of control in anxiety and the obsessive-compulsive disorders cannot be ignored: It is central to almost every aspect of these disorders. These control issues are present in two forms: being *out of control* or *attempts to regain control*. Regardless of whether the fear response leads to fight, flight (fleeing or avoiding), or freeze, the disorders we are addressing here can be further delineated into their control functions.

In Figure 4.1, the anxiety and obsessive-compulsive disorders are divided into their control functions. Keeping in mind that dread, fear, and anxiety serve to put the individual on alert and to activate defensive, safeguarding positions, Separation Anxiety Disorder can be used as either a method of *fighting* the fear (an assertive stance that the attachment figure must stay with the person) or as a *fleeing* and *avoiding* function (e.g., running back to a safe person or place). Selective Mutism used to be called "Elective Mutism" *(DSM-III-R)*, and in either description, it is a fighting decision not to communicate with people who, or in places (often school) that, do not feel safe to the individual or child. The *flight* disorders are characterized by overwhelming feelings of being out of control, with no specific way to avoid the fearful situation. The *freeze* disorders (related to panic and phobias) stop people in their tracks, usually from an acute confrontation or anticipation of the feared stimulus.

Specific phobias, such as the obsessive-compulsive disorders, can also serve as a way to fight or control anxiety. Unlike the "out of control" disorders, the person with a specific phobia has identified what to fear, and as long as he or she can keep a distance

Feelings of:

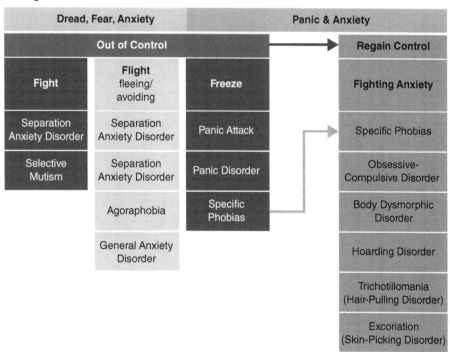

Figure 4.1 Control Processes and Their Uses in Anxiety and the Obsessive-Compulsive Disorders

or avoid the feared stimulus, the individual is OK. Still, to keep on top of the anxiety, to control it, people with phobias must occasionally confront the fear, or at least mentally re-examine and consider it. A similar function is at the heart of the rest of the obsessive-compulsive disorders. The fear, panic, or anxiety is located in a part of the body, a situation, or a process; one the person can continuously address and control through specific behaviors.

Adlerian Conceptualization

Adler (1927, 1959) identified three life tasks that all people must address: the social task, because we are all connected to the human community and must find ways to cooperate for survival and growth; the work or occupation task, because we must all decide what to do with our time on earth and find meaning in contribution; and the task of intimacy, because we are biologically driven to reproduce, and we must learn to get along with the other gender as well as members of our own sex. These tasks are universal, and challenge humanity regardless of the era in which a person lives or the culture or gender to which a person belongs. They exist because all of us are connected to the human condition, and are part of the human system: We are socially embedded, and these tasks demand a social answer. In general, those who address these tasks cooperatively and with courage, do better than those who retreat from these human demands. Those who act with courage and cooperation tend to develop what Adlerians call a "community feeling" (Ansbacher, 1992) and engage with others with an interest in their wellbeing (Sweeney, 2009). They live in such a way as to ensure mental health.

The opposite of such social interest is self-absorption. It is turning away from the demands of life and contributions to others in favor of a protective stance. Worry and anxiety are ways in which the individual turns inside. Adler (1964a; as cited in Ansbacher & Ansbacher, 1956) noted that anxiety is a safeguarding mechanism, protecting the individual from feelings of failure, inferiority, or diminished self-esteem, that results from a lack of courage when facing necessary tasks in life. In this sense, anxiety provides the individual with an *excuse* for *retreat* in the face of challenge: Life is perceived as dangerous, and the declaration "I am afraid" keeps the person from acting effectively. For Adlerians, anxiety is a mistaken solution to the problems of life, not the problem itself. Anxiety reflects discouragement in living; people literally frighten themselves out of living fully and courageously.

Mosak (1968) identified the central themes that tend to constitute the private logic of the anxious person. These themes include the convictions that the person:

- must be in control or all may be lost
- must stay on top of things as if one is driven to overly ambitious behavior
- must be good, perfect, or right in order to act; otherwise, failure and loss of self-esteem are imminent.

Mosak also notes that those with phobias also need something to be against. The person stands against that which stimulates the phobia, but also against all those from whom consensual validation would suggest the fear is excessive. Still, the phobic individual knows better than anyone else what the potential danger is, and she or he takes a stand against that danger: The individual would be willing to do anything, short of dying, to eliminate the fear-producing object, place, or person.

In addition to the desire to control or avoid being controlled, those with obsessive-compulsive and related disorders are also driven *feeling-avoiders*. Feelings are messy, and the energy in them can propel a person to act in spontaneous ways that are not pre-planned. The compulsive activities that control anxiety are known and predictable: They reduce fear, give one a sense of accomplishment, and focus the person on rational approaches to living. The obsessive-compulsive person may lack a social presence and feel comfortable only in intellectual endeavors or concrete activities.

Systemically, anxiety and the obsessive-compulsive disorders are always enacted in the presence of others. As such, it is never just the individual who suffers. Spouses, children, extended family, colleagues, coworkers, and friends are impacted by the individual's expression of anxiety. The personal and social goals or purposes of anxiety constitute a broad range of interactional motivation. The purpose of anxiety can be as simple as the seeking of sympathy or as complex as the desire to put others in service to the anxious person. Anxiety can act as a demand to get what one wants, or it can be used to control the movement and activities of others. It is not uncommon in a family with a parent who worries excessively for there to be one child who does whatever can be done to eliminate the worry and another child to provoke worry through misbehavior (Bitter, 2009, 2013).

Rasmussen (2010) starts with the premise that all people seek to be *happy*, indeed to feel happy. He calls this desired endpoint the *Z-factor*. All events and activities, therefore, are appraised by the individual in relation to the probability that one can reach happiness. I go to a movie with friends; I anticipate that we will have fun and enjoy the movie and post-movie conversation; the night turns out as expected, and *voilà*! Happiness validates me and the experience. What happens, however, if the prospect of going to a movie is assessed to be dangerous to my sense of wellbeing, my self-esteem? What if I anticipate that no one will want to go with me, or the movie won't be any good, or I will be stuck in a crowd with nothing to say and no one caring what I think? In such a case, I may generate the compelling emotion of anxiety to keep myself from going out and risking a social disaster. What does anxiety in this situation have to do with happiness, the *Z-factor*? Anxiety may not be good, but it is certainly better than total social failure or humiliation or exposure as worthless. *Better* is not always good; it does not always end in happiness, but better is sometimes good enough. Sometimes, it is the best one can expect.

Adlerians believe in the unity of the personality. People strive for goals that ensure survival and safety, organize personal movement toward an anticipated sense of success, a *felt* +, and support a style of living that is unique to the individual. In this sense, Adlerians believe in holism, the study of the person's way of being and movement in his or her social contexts and culture. They also approach the mind and body as a unity, with each aspect of human functioning in recursive relationship to the other parts. It is this holistic model that defines an Adlerian approach to biopsychosocial conceptualizations of cases (Sperry & Sperry, 2012).

Biologically, *DSM-5* tends to address genetic factors in the various anxiety and obsessive-compulsive and related disorders—and little else. The mind is often treated as a separate entity from the individual, and the most common psychiatric treatment is, therefore, psychopharmaceutical. The National Institutes of Health's (2010) *Treating Anxiety Disorders* notes that the medications most used in treatment include antidepressants, especially selective serotonin reuptake inhibitors (SSRIs); anti-anxiety medications (anxiolytic agents), like benzodiazepines that slow the activities of the central nervous system, in particular alprazolam (Xanax), clonazepam (Klonopin), diazepam (Valium), and lorazepam (Ativan); and beta blockers, including atenolol (Tenormin) and propranolol hydrochloride (Inderal).

There is a current focus within the Adlerian community on the negative and often dangerous effects of psychotropic drugs (see Breggin, 2008). Because of both a belief in mind–body holism and the fact that many Adlerian therapists are not psychiatrists, Adlerian treatment is likely to include a broader approach to biological contributions to and interventions in anxiety disorders. Although not an Adlerian, Mark Hyman (2008) has identified seven keys to wellness in his *UltraMind* solution. These keys are: embracing nutrition, balancing hormones, cooling off inflammation, fixing digestion, enhancing detoxification, boosting metabolism, and calming your mind. Together with a therapeutic focus on correcting private logic and ineffective central themes (the psychological) and addressing the goals and purposes of the individual (the social), Adlerian therapy starts with a *life-style assessment* (Eckstein & Kern, 2002; Powers & Griffith, 1987, 2012; Shulman & Mosak, 1988) and seeks to reorient the anxious person toward a more fully lived life with physical wellness, psychological toughness, and social connectedness (Carlson, Watts, & Maniacci, 2006; Sweeney, 2009).

Below, we describe each of the Anxiety Disorders before addressing the Obsessive-Compulsive and Related Disorders toward the end of the chapter. The Anxiety Disorders are listed in the order they appear in *DSM-5* (American Psychiatric Association, 2013), starting with Separation Anxiety Disorder and followed by Selective Mutism, Specific Phobias, Social Anxiety Disorder, Panic Disorder (and panic attacks), Agoraphobia, and Generalized Anxiety Disorder.

SEPARATION ANXIETY DISORDER

Clinical Presentation

Separation Anxiety Disorder is normal in very young children (12–18 months), but it may become problematic when the child reaches pre-school age. The fear of leaving home or being separated from major attachment figures often starts in childhood or adolescence after what is perceived as a major loss, and though it comes and goes, it can cause impairment in occupational, social, and other areas of life functioning and linger through adulthood. Individuals with Separation Anxiety Disorder experience extreme distress when anticipating separation from people or situations to which they have attached a sense of safety. They are not agoraphobic; they can leave home in company of a safe attachment figure, but they may put up quite a resistance to leaving home on their own. They can be demanding of the attachment figure, throw fits and tantrums, and/or may use vomiting, headaches, illness, or nightmares to keep attachment figures close.

Individuals with Separation Anxiety Disorder often resist staying with others, worry about strangers, and seek to avoid going to school—with girls doing the latter more than boys. When separation anxiety persists into adulthood, it is usually aimed at specific individuals (parents or a spouse) whom the individual believes must be kept close in order for the person to be safe.

DSM-5 Characterization

Separation Anxiety Disorder may be the result of some experience of loss (a pet or an individual), and though it may be normal for infants and toddlers, it becomes problematic when a child reaches pre-school age. Children and adolescents with separation anxiety worry about losing people close to them, impending dangers for self or others, and illness or injury. They often have nightmares and feel a need to sleep with or be close to significant adults in their lives. Young people can develop the disorder at any time during childhood or adolescence, and it is the most diagnosed anxiety disorder in young people under the age of 12. The disorder must be present for at least four weeks in children and six months in adults.

Biopsychosocial–Adlerian Conceptualization

The *DSM-5* (American Psychiatric Association, 2013) suggests that this disorder may be inherited. If it develops in childhood or adolescence, the prevalence will be stronger in young children (about 4% of the population) and tends to lessen as the person gets older. Parents who feel sorry for the child or give into demands tend to reinforce the anxiety as a way to maintain the child's perceived sense of safety. Girls will use the disorder to avoid school more than boys will; boys will tend to experience the anxiety when feeling a demand to leave home alone, when left alone, or when expected to act independently of others.

Separation anxiety is a relational fear, and as such, it places a demand on the attachment figure to be both present and engaged in keeping the child or person safe. This fear does not have to be altogether without merit. A death in the family, the loss of significant family members because of travel or moving, or the loss of a pet can set up in the young person a sense of vulnerability. When children are very little, they may not know what is safe and what isn't, so it is natural for them to form a tight bond with the person or people who provide for their survival. Some parents, too, approach life as if it is dangerous, and their attitudes and interactive patterns can reinforce similar fears in children. Indeed, pampering and overprotection are common parental responses to separation anxiety.

As children and adolescents get older, however, Adlerians tend to focus on the demand/control aspect of the disorder. What does the anxiety help the person, regardless of age, avoid? Who does the person put in his or her service? What interactive sequential patterns merely reinforce the fear that both the person and the attachment figure may share? With separation anxiety, the child goes out of control in order to control another; as the person gets older, the methods of going out of control may become more sophisticated, but the purpose is still to get someone else to be responsible for the individual's safety.

Treatment Considerations

Separation Anxiety Disorder is a relational disorder, and as such, successful therapy almost always involves family interventions. When young children start to exhibit anxiety about being away from home or family members, it is essential for parents to adopt a calm, optimistic orientation to life that models the belief that life will be OK. Too often, however, children with separation anxiety have parents who are concerned or worried about separating from the child. Helping parents with separation anxiety to identify the circumstances that elicit their anxiety is the first step. A child's ability to tolerate separations should gradually increase over time as he or she is exposed to the feared events. Start with 15 minutes during which a child is left with a friend or babysitter, and increase it slowly over weeks. Help the parents to be unimpressed with crying or screaming. At times when the child is calm, encourage him or her to feel competent and capable, as well as coaching the child to discuss their feelings with an adult who acknowledges them but also promotes recovery through calm reassurance.

> ### Case Example: Jamie
>
> Jamie is a four-year-old female, and has been, according to her mother, shy, timid, and quiet most of her young life. She does not like to go outside with other kids or go to play dates. When other children are invited into their home, Jamie stays "attached to her mother's dress," and refuses to speak to or play with the other child. These guests rarely come back. When her mother enrolled her in pre-school, Jamie cried and threw herself on the floor of her bedroom, refusing to let her mother dress her or to leave her room. When her mother tried to walk away from her, she cried and screamed until her mother came to hold her, at which point she settled right down. Her mother still took her to the pre-school, and Jamie cried the whole way in spite of her mother's reassurances. At the pre-school, she cried for over two hours, before the teacher called the mother to come to take her home. At night, Jamie has frequent nightmares which she "can't remember," but which upset her to the point of needing to sleep with her mother. When asked to a birthday party of a friend, she developed a severe stomachache, which cleared up shortly after the party was over. When Adlerians ask what the purpose of this anxiety is, the answer can be found in what people do with her. Because of her anxiety, Jamie gets her own way much, if not most, of the time. She often gets her mother in her service, and she defeats the requirements of others. The idea that life is scary is reinforced by the pampering and overprotection of the attachment figure.

SELECTIVE MUTISM

Clinical Presentation

Selective Mutism is a rare tactic, used primarily by young children, who seek to control people or situations they fear by adopting a stubborn, but powerful, stance. The child simply refuses to speak to a given person or in a specific situation that triggers significant distress in that child. While the disorder may develop in early childhood at home, it usually does not get diagnosed until the child is in a demanding situation, such as school. It is in these demanding situations that the refusal to speak can lead to impairment in work, social activities, or other areas of life. Selective Mutism is not diagnosed if there is a neurological problem with the child's speech or if the child is immigrating from a county that speaks a different language.

DSM-5 Characterization

Selective Mutism is one of the least-researched tactics for handling anxiety. Neither prevalence nor the etiology is known. Children who use this process may have subtle receptive language difficulties, but there are no conclusive studies of this linkage or the causal relationship that may exist. Children who develop Selective Mutism generally do so before the age of five. Some children may outgrow the use of the tactic (the disorder), but nothing is really known about the normal course of the disorder over time. The disorder must be enacted for at least one month, not all of which need be in a school setting.

Biopsychosocial–Adlerian Conceptualization

Selective Mutism shares some qualities with Social Anxiety Disorder, though one does not lead to the other. Such children, in addition to neither initiating speech nor responding to others with speech, may also exhibit excessive shyness, fear of social embarrassment, clinging, temper tantrums, or other mild forms of opposition. Parents of children who use Selective Mutism are often overprotective and more controlling than the parents of children who have other anxiety disorders or no anxiety at all. Due to its rarity, most children with this disorder are also diagnosed with another anxiety disorder, usually Social Anxiety Disorder.

Selective Mutism is usually a purposeful choice made by the child in an effort to, perhaps, control anxiety, but more often to control others who are placing demands on the child that are unwanted. Using Dreikurs' (1950) typology, the child is engaged in a passive power struggle with some adults in certain situations. The child seeks to demonstrate that he or she is the boss of his or her own life, and no one can make the child speak if he or she does not want to do so. Parents and teachers who are confronted with this behavior will typically engage in mistaken interactions (Bitter, 2009) that include coaxing, demanding, and arguing, as well as attempts to control the child. These mistaken interactions simply reinforce in the child that the power struggle is working— and that it should be maintained.

Treatment Considerations

Because Selective Mutism tends to develop in young children, the treatment of choice is family therapy. Parents need to address the disorder as the child's mistaken coping mechanism rather than an inability to speak. Helping parents bypass the power struggle and become calm, supportive, encouragers is an essential step. Neither speaking for the child nor demanding that the child talk will work. Instead, parents and teachers can help the child by asking questions once, and then allowing natural or logical consequences to occur. For example, if a child is fond of ice cream, asking the child if he or she would like some ice cream, in a situation where the child has not been talking, requires the child to speak or lose out on the opportunity. Or a teacher can tell a child that the parents have left a gift for him or her that the child can have if the child asks for it in a clear voice. Again, these interventions only work if the adult is calm, kind, and generally supportive.

In rare circumstances where the environment in which the child does not speak is simply not supportive, it may be useful to change the environment, seek a different classroom or a different school. Addressing the behavior early, however, is important, because as children advance to late childhood and adolescence, they can simply become used to not speaking, and stubborn quietness becomes a style of living; that is, the Selective Mutism develops into a social anxiety disorder or depression.

Case Example: Jeremy

Jeremy is in the second grade. He reportedly spoke, though in a limited way, with his first-grade teacher, but he has not spoken a word at school since the beginning of the school year. He speaks at home and in church or when out in the local community with his family, but he will not speak at school. His teacher has done everything from "call on him regularly" to asking him to sit with her in the front of the room. She has given him discipline slips to take home, and he has been to see the school counselor, with whom Jeremy also will not speak. He does some school work at school, and he does all of his homework, but he will not turn it in. The teacher searches his desk and backpack for it, and then she scolds him for not turning it in. He has told his grandfather that he does not like the teacher. Jeremy was in a children's play about Noah's Ark at his church, and he had one line to say, which he had practiced regularly and delivered well in rehearsals. When the Sunday afternoon performance arrived, Jeremy was ready and in costume. From the stage, he noticed another child from his classroom come into the audience. Jeremy sat down, refused to participate in the play, and did not speak again until he was home. Jeremy's Selective Mutism is a power-struggle tactic, probably aimed at his teacher, but possibly at the whole school too. He uses the tactic because it works. His opposition is frustrating to family and school personnel, but he does not seem greatly distressed by it at all. Still, when asked why he does this, he will report feeling scared. Adlerians know it is a power struggle, because the adults in his life report feeling angry, challenged, and often defeated. His stubbornness is more than a bid for attention. It is intended to win in a battle of "who controls who."

SPECIFIC PHOBIAS AND SOCIAL ANXIETY DISORDER

Clinical Presentation

Given the similar nature of both Specific Phobia and Social Anxiety Disorder, we will discuss them together and will close by clarifying the differences. Persons diagnosed with these disorders experience fear and anxiety that causes significant distress, causing impairment in social, occupational, and other areas of their life functioning. These disorders are common in younger persons (with an average age for Specific Phobia between 7 and 11; and around 13 for Social Anxiety Disorder).

Individuals with a Specific Phobia or Social Anxiety Disorder have an extreme fear of an object or situation (social situations in the case of Social Anxiety Disorder). Their fears and degree of anxiety do not match the danger or reality of the situation. Because their anxiety is so severe, they may make significant life changes in order to avoid the situation (relocation, turning down a high-paying job promotion because of the public speaking required, refusing to go to work or school). People with Social Anxiety Disorder are concerned about how they are being perceived and thought of by others. They are very worried about coming across in negative ways, such as being stupid, foolish, nasty, or threatening and menacing. Persons with Social Anxiety Disorder—and in some cases, those with Specific Phobias—may be perceived as "introverts" or self-absorbed due to the amount of attention they put on the fear of either avoiding or having to engage in a situation that is causing the fear.

DSM-5 Characterization

Individuals diagnosed with Specific Phobia and Social Anxiety Disorder experience anxiety or fear about an object or situation. Children with these disorders may express their fear in a multitude of flight or fight behaviors, including tantrums, crying, or clinging. In the case of Social Anxiety Disorder, children must experience it with peers and not just in relation to significant adults. In both cases, the fear is avoided at multiple costs, is persistent, lasting at least six months, and is out of proportion to the actual risk or danger. Specific Phobias are coded according to the feared stimulus (i.e., animal, natural environment, blood injection injury, situations, or other). Phobias are more likely in developed countries than under-developed ones, and women are twice as likely as men to report phobic experiences.

Biopsychosocial–Adlerian Conceptualization

Biologically, this disorder may be hereditory in origin. That is, persons with this disorder may have relatives who struggle with a similar condition. In addition, persons may tend to have behavioral inhibitions, and in the case of persons with Social Anxiety Disorder, may have a history of fearing negative evaluations. Finally, persons with this disorder may have a history of experiencing disturbing events and may have experienced childhood mistreatment and/or abuse.

Adler (1964b) noted that "individuals, perpetually comparing themselves with the unattainable ideal of perfection, are always possessed and spurred on by a sense of inferiority" (p. 35–36). People with these disorders believe that their imperfections (or lack of courage to cross over bridges, to come face to face with a spider, to engage with others) are so strong that they simply cannot overcome or face their fears. In addition, these individuals have a limited ability and/or desire for cooperation. People with phobias or Social Anxiety Disorder give up on certain aspects of life, and lose trust in life and in the relationships that can help sustain and support them in difficult situations. Asking what Adler (1927) and Dreikurs (1997) called "The Question," "How would life be different if you did not have this anxiety?" is the surest way to discover the purpose of the phobia or the fear of social situations. What the person says they would be doing is exactly what they want to avoid. Taking this a step further, how does this phobia allow the individual to hide from or evade one of his or her most embarrassing weaknesses? That is, if the individual spends this degree of fear on a designated stimulus, he or she does not have to gain the courage to address a major felt sense of inferiority in some particular area of his or her life. And finally, by focusing the anxiety on an object, event, or situation, the person ignores or avoids the larger, more general anxiety felt toward life itself.

By contrast, those with Social Anxiety Disorder have declared the life task that they are avoiding. Unlike Specific Phobias, Social Anxiety Disorder puts the individual in retreat from others. The fear of being judged or criticized or of making mistakes and embarrassing oneself puts the person in retreat from others. Again, if the individual can get someone else to help them navigate social situations, they can often go out and engage with others, but there is always the demand that someone else take care of them.

Treatment Considerations

Since the purpose of social anxiety is to avoid focusing on one's sense of inferiority, treatment should begin with a life history, including a life-style assessment. Findings will elicit less than positive events that the client experienced as self-depreciating. The goals of therapy would also include increasing insight about one's family-of-origin, experiences in one's early social system, as well as how the anxiety serves a purpose in avoiding the real pain. Additional therapy goals would include increasing social interest and self-esteem. Findings will suggest areas and events that prompted the client to begin avoiding.

Case Example: Jose R.

Jose is a 50-year-old male who came for therapy with his wife after he became sick the morning of his daughter's wedding, which almost prevented him from taking part in the event. His wife stated that she was getting "tired of not being able to do anything remotely social with Jose without him either putting up a big fuss or getting physically ill before the event." While Jose remarked that he has always attended the events, such as two family reunions last year, his daughter's wedding and a Christmas work party, he reported feeling "extremely ill before going" and "absolutely dreading the events." He would typically experience fear the day of the event, which would prevent him from "keeping his head on straight" or being able to concentrate on anything else. He would feel nauseated and would have to "lay down and sleep." In order to get through the events, he has been taking an Ibuprofen PM, which seems to set him at some ease. Jose mentioned that he "hates social situations," and is very concerned with "saying the wrong thing or doing something stupid." In addition, Jose remarked that just recently he feels "stalled in the bathroom"; he is unable to urinate when others are present in the public restroom. It would be easy to suggest that the goal of Jose's social anxiety disorder is to avoid events where he will have to engage with others. At the moment, however, Jose is going to these events. He is self-medicating, but he is pushing himself to go. What is the purpose, then, of his anxiety? The most likely possibility is that he uses it to keep his spouse engaged with him, to get her to take care of and be concerned for him when they are out. It may also develop into a more restrictive existence, one in which he finally says he simply isn't going to these events at all. It is almost as if he is building a case for withdrawal. All of this reflects a lack of courage in social situations, a fear that he is not good enough to participate fully in life.

PANIC ATTACKS AND PANIC DISORDER

Clinical Presentation

Specific Phobias signal a cautionary, hesitating approach to life. Panic attacks, on the other hand, freeze people in place, stop any movement, and often immobilize the individual. A panic attack, in and of itself, is not a coded disorder. It is merely a description of an intense fear that surges unpredictably and peaks within a few minutes. Panic attacks include four or more physiological and psychological experiences, including heart palpitations, trembling/shaking, shortness of breath or the experience of suffocating, numbness or tingling sensations, and fear of losing control, going crazy, or dying. Such attacks rarely occur in children before puberty; females have these attacks more often than men; and the risk of such attacks decreases with age.

When unexpected panic attacks become recurrent, and the individual begins to fear the possibility of such attacks or engages in significant useless changes in behavior in an effort to avoid the intense fear, then the panic attacks rise to the level of a panic disorder.

DSM-5 Characterization

Individuals diagnosed with Panic Disorder have recurrent panic attacks that include at least four physiological or psychological experiences. In addition to conditions already listed above, the person may also experience sweating, choking sensations, chest pain or discomfort (sometimes confused with a heart attack), nausea, dizziness, or chills or hot flashes. Some cultures also recognize symptoms of tinnitus, soreness in the neck, headaches, screaming, or crying, but *DSM-5* (American Psychiatric Association, 2013) does not recognize these as symptoms that count in terms of coding the disorder. In addition to recurring panic attacks, the disorder requires that either the person begins to have an ongoing fear (at least one month) of additional attacks or their consequences, or the person engages in maladaptive processes in an attempt to avoid future attacks.

Biopsychosocial–Adlerian Conceptualization

Biologically, a panic attack recreates the same fear response in the brain and body that would occur in the face of an actually dangerous stimulus. The difference is that the panic attack appears to emerge out of nowhere, for no reason. The body goes into the same protective mode that has developed as part of our evolutionary development. A sensitivity to certain medical conditions (e.g., asthma or heart problems) can stimulate a panic attack. Panic Disorder or even panic attacks within the last 12 months can be an indicator of suicide risk.

Just as a panic attack brings everything in a moment to a halt and freezes the person and life in place, those with a panic disorder begin to freeze in other aspects of life. Like all other anxieties, panic is enacted in social relationships, and is usually a call for help. The person does not feel strong enough to handle life, and so she or he flees to others, demanding that they take care of him or her (Adler, 1932). In this sense, panic is not a response, but rather an initiation. In what must feel like a return to childhood, the person temporarily freezes and then flees to someone stronger and more capable for care. Because such fear is deeply rooted in the individual weakness of the species and too often nurtured in a pampering or harsh childhood environment, the person begins to discover that fearful experiences allow one to retreat until a way to meet and triumph over one's situation can be found.

Treatment Considerations

A panic attack is not a disorder, but many panic attacks across an extended period of time coupled with increasing fear of future panic attacks is a disorder. The effect of the disorder is to orchestrate a retreat from the demands of life—in effect, to freeze the person in place while life goes on. If an attack is caught early, supportive family or friends can be enlisted to help calm the person when it occurs. Symptoms can be addressed in therapy by simulating the experience (e.g., intentional hyperventilation, running to increase heart rates, or spinning to cause dizziness) and then paying attention to what the person does to become calm again. For severe panic attacks, selective serotonin reuptake inhibitors used for a short period of time have been shown to be effective in relieving symptoms. The main focus of therapy, however, must be on the unfreezing of experience and developing strategies for fully living the life the client intends of him or herself.

Case Example: Tommy T.

Tommy is a 61-year-old male who recently decided to retire after 35 years of working as a pharmacist in what had originally been his father's store on the corner of Washington and 1st Avenue. Tommy was his father and mother's only son, and he had been helped all the way through college with special tutors and a support team in his extended family. He had started to feel pessimistic about his life when he was 12 years old and had to go to summer school for the first time to make up scores in math. He began to have anxiety over testing, but he managed with "special" help to get through. His father had him working at his pharmacy when he was not in school, so getting a Pharmacy post-graduate degree was actually easier for him than passing high school math. At 26, he became a pharmacist, working side-by-side with his father. At the age of 27, he met a young woman at that very store, had a whirl-wind romance with her, and at her suggestion, they were married a month after their first date. She got pregnant immediately, stayed at home to raise a family that would quickly have three kids. Tommy worked six days a week, and he was happiest at work. At home, he did what he was told, spent little time with the children, all of whom grew up and moved on with their lives.

On the day of Tommy's retirement, his wife announced that she was getting a divorce, and that she was taking everything. Tommy was to move out to their summer cottage, and she would take their home of 34 years. Tommy did what he was told. He began to feel the walls of the cottage close in on him. He couldn't breathe. He decided to stop smoking, and he went cold turkey for two days. On the second day, he went to a mall, and while there he had a panic attack. He fell to his knees and began choking on nothing. He was sweating, and his heart was pounding. He felt terrified, like he was going to die.

Over the next six weeks, Tommy had regular panic attacks. They came on almost anywhere. In the mall, at the cottage, while driving, while playing golf. He began to fear that he would not make it through the day. He called friends at all hours of the day and night, asking for help. His friends started to avoid his calls—and in some cases, they even blocked his calls.

To be sure, Tommy T.'s life has been turned upside down. He was totally pampered and cared for as a child, never having to struggle. His work and marriage were fixtures in his life that were dependable and stable. Now, he is lost. He does not know what to do, and he knows that he is unprepared to take care of himself. So he calls for help. He almost demands help. He is in a state of panic, after all.

AGORAPHOBIA

Clinical Presentation

Agoraphobia is an intense fear of going out into the public, of open or perceived enclosed space, and/or of various forms of transportation. It generally involves a retreat to one's home or to a part of one's home that is deemed safe. Although there can be some similarities to Social Anxiety Disorder, people with Social Anxiety Disorder can usually force themselves to go out into the world to complete necessary tasks, but the agoraphobic finds it hard to ever leave home.

People with Agoraphobia avoid going out of their safe zones because they believe that life is dangerous, and out in the open there may be no escape and no help. In some cases, especially with the elderly, the fear of going out can be associated with a fear of incapacitating or humiliating symptoms, such as falling or incontinence. Even in the case of the elderly, the fear must be seen as clearly excessive in relation to the avoided situation or experience.

DSM-5 Characterization

Individuals diagnosed with Agoraphobia must exhibit a marked fear of at least two situations from a range that includes public transportation, marketplaces, shops, theaters, standing in lines, or simply being away from home. The avoidance of these situations is the result of feeling there will be no escape from them or believing that there will be no one to help if they start to panic. These situations must always evoke fear in the person for Agoraphobia to be diagnosed, and if they cannot be avoided, they can only be endured with either extreme anxiety or the help of a companion. The Agoraphobia must be out of proportion to the situations of concern, and the fear must be present for at least six months. Agoraphobia is often comorbid with panic attacks or Panic Disorder.

Biopsychosocial–Adlerian Conceptualization

Biologically, Agoraphobia is considered to be the most likely phobia to be inherited. Panic attacks tend to precede Agoraphobia in 30% to 50% of the social and clinical samples. Initial onset of the disorder tends to happen in late adolescence or early adulthood; however, it can re-emerge after the age of 40. Full remission is rare. Any severe life events that threaten the individual's sense of safety can trigger Agoraphobia. Death in the family, separation, abuse of any kind, experiencing a trauma are a few of the stressors that can set off an agoraphobic response. As with other anxiety disorders, those with Agoraphobia tend to have a sensitivity to anxiety, with the experience of being "fearful" extending over many years in multiple situations.

Agoraphobia is a coping process for people who are in full flight and retreat from the demands of life. While there is no guarantee for anyone that life will work out in the end, Adlerians know that life is more fully lived when we act "as if" life will work out. Such optimism is expressed by a character in the movie *The Best Exotic Marigold Hotel* (Madden, 2012) when he says, "Life always works out in the end. If life is not working out, it most definitely is not the end." By contrast, the person with Agoraphobia believes that there is no chance life will work out. In a special adaptation of Murphy's Law, the Agoraphobic believes that anything that can go wrong already has and will continue incessantly to do so. In a sense, the person with Agoraphobia commits social suicide, withdrawing to home, retreating from life, and waiting impatiently for the body to catch up.

Other anxiety disorders are often used to avoid certain life tasks or demands that put the individual in a special state of vulnerability. With Agoraphobia, however, the person avoids facing and failing at all of the life tasks, leading to almost certain impairment in social, occupational, and intimate relationships. Still, the anxiety is not universal or beyond the individual's control, because it disappears when the person is at home or in a safe zone.

Treatment Considerations

With Agoraphobia, treatment involves the slow development of courage. Something in the person's past convinced him or her that life itself was unsafe. The treatment goal is not to reverse this often permanent conviction, but to learn to manage it and to move forward. Courage is not about having a life without fear: It is about moving forward in spite of the fear. Severe Agoraphobia can sometimes look like panic, and again, selective serotonin reuptake inhibitors can be effective because of their anti-panic properties when used in a focused manner for a short period of time. Entering into the world with the support of a confidant (family member or friend) can also be helpful, as are support groups, phone support, or online help accessed through a smartphone. Courage comes with practice, so it is often advisable to start with behavioral courage, taking actual steps to move into the world coupled with practices associated with systematic desensitization. It is essential that the person does not bolt from the behavioral experience in a state of panic, reinforcing the Agoraphobia, but stays in the fear-inducing situation until calm is achieved.

Behavioral courage is, however, merely the first level of practice. It lays the foundation for the courage to face what has happened in one's life and to reconsider the mistaken notions and orientations involved in one's style of living. A life-style assessment and early recollections are key to unlocking these aspects of the person's life (Powers & Griffith, 2012).

Case Example: Mary B.

Mary B. was raised in a strict Catholic home, where every danger was constantly stressed and reinforced. Mary was the youngest of five children and the only girl. Her father was largely absent from home, and he suffered from alcoholism and violent outbursts. Mary was her mother's little girl. Mary was sent to Catholic school starting in kindergarten, and she enrolled in an all-girl Catholic high school. Virginity was stressed at home and school, and boys were portrayed as simultaneously dangerous and protective. Mary did not date. When she went outside of the home, she was always accompanied by her mother or her oldest brother, whom she adored. Mary went to a private women's college, paid for by insurance from the death of her father. Shortly after her junior year, her brother died, a war casualty. Soon after his death, Mary met a boy at an extension course, who reminded her so much of her deceased brother. At the end of college, she married him, "because he insisted." Years later, she would often say to people that she should have followed through with her desire to become a Carmelite nun.

Early in her marriage, Mary began to have panic attacks, especially around the requirement to engage sexually with her husband. She went to a counselor by herself, but the panic attacks continued, and the husband saw no use in continuing counseling. Mary's fear of sexuality led her to claim a bedroom in their home for herself, and she and her husband seldom slept in the same room. He lost himself, more and more, in his work—and in alcohol. Mary left home less and less, and by her late 20s, she could not go outside without experiencing intense fear. It was her mother who came to stay with her and to care for her. In this case, Mary is retreating from everything: from intimacy, social relationships, and work. She also claims her place as the youngest child and only girl to put her mother in her service. Even her belief that she should have become a Carmelite nun reflects the desire to retreat from life and adulthood, to have only manageable tasks, like prayer, and to have the care of others.

GENERALIZED ANXIETY DISORDER

Clinical Presentation

Generalized Anxiety Disorder is diagnosed when individuals experience anxiety that causes significant distress, which maybe transient, as well as impairment in occupational, social, and other areas of life functioning. Individuals with Generalized Anxiety Disorder are characterized as "worrywarts," pessimists, and sometimes complainers. They may also appear irritable, grouchy, and touchy. They may be overly worried and concerned about the well-being of family members or friends, particularly in cases where life circumstances have been challenging. They also may experience undue anxiety about everyday tasks, life happenstances, and insignificant matters (e.g., folding laundry, reading e-mails). Such individuals appear restless, uneasy, and unsettled. In addition, their disposition and excessive worrying may induce negative reactions in others.

Individuals with Generalized Anxiety Disorder often experience absentmindedness and inattentiveness, making it difficult to complete and follow through with tasks. They will likely experience physical symptoms, such as becoming easily drained and tired and/or muscle tension. Despite their fatigue, they may find it difficult to acquire effective and replenishing sleep, struggling to fall or remain asleep.

DSM-5 Characterization

Individuals diagnosed with Generalized Anxiety Disorder can be characterized by extreme and unwarranted worry and anxiety that is difficult to regulate and reduce. They may be nervous about future events, and how others will perceive their performance. These individuals may become easily exhausted and fatigued, and yet may struggle with insomnia and unsatisfying sleep. They are likely to experience agitation, irritability, and difficulty in concentrating or focusing on tasks. In addition, muscle tension is common. These cognitive, emotional, and physical symptoms are not related or attributed to the effects of a substance or other medical condition, nor can the symptoms be characterized by another mental disorder.

Biopsychosocial–Adlerian Conceptualization

The *DSM-5* (American Psychiatric Association, 2013) suggests that this disorder may be genetic in origin, accounting for up to one-third of the etiology. However, susceptibility toward the disorder also may include temperamental factors such as harm avoidance, pessimistic affectivity, and behavioral reservations. Women are diagnosed with the disorder more than men, and those who live in developed countries and are of European descent are more likely than those from non-Caucasian cultures and under-developed countries to receive the diagnosis.

They are persistently fearful and negative about their future (i.e., mortality). In addition, they are equally disturbed by the realization that they only have limited control over others and events. However, from an Adlerian perspective, the individual is the "agent in the situation" and is not simply being exposed to an "array of forces" (Dreikurs, 1955, p. 56). Psychologically, individuals with Generalized Anxiety Disorder have a view of themselves, others, the world and life's purpose that can be expressed as: "Yes, but I'm sick." That is, the symptoms of anxiety are purposeful and useful. Anxiety is useful in that it provides a safeguard of self-esteem (Adler, 1964a; Carlson et al., 2006), against criticism and feedback from others, and from individual self-critiques. If they remain anxious and worrisome, it makes it difficult to take risks in any area of the life tasks (Sperry, 1987).

Individuals with Generalized Anxiety Disorder have carried patterns from childhood. It is not uncommon for such children to be overprotected. Dealing with defeat, critique, and responsibility is difficult for them even as young persons. They may use anxiety-type symptoms to get their way (or backing out of accepting and dealing with defeat), convincing their parents that they are incapable of carrying out particular tasks (e.g., going to school or assuming household chores). Parental pampering provides additional reinforcement that the child will be neither successful in their activities nor strong enough to take risks. A consequence of such a position is that the child, and then later the adult, is often enmeshed with other members of the family.

Treatment Considerations

As the counselor begins to establish a relationship with the client, he or she would want to be mindful of not becoming wrapped up in the client's misery and therefore falling trap to a position of "pampering" and/or collaborative excuse-making with the client. This not only sets the tone and expectation for the process, but if done so empathetically, begins to model that critique and feedback can be experienced in safe place, and is required for symptom reduction. The goals for therapy would involve increasing longer periods of time experiencing restfulness; increased mood (i.e., happiness, contentment); increased ability to cope with stressors and anxiety; increased tolerance for perceived "rejection" and the unknown; and increased attention and focus. Another treatment goal includes increasing awareness and insight regarding how their symptoms have been useful to them in creating safeguards against partaking in life's challenges. Treatment strategies include stress and relaxation management, countering tactics such as providing alternative explanations and substituting useful beliefs (Carlson et al., 2006), instruction on self-soothing, as well as interpretation. The counselor also helps the client make connections between his or her life style and earliest memories, family constellation, assets and strengths, and basic mistakes (Carlson et al., 2006). Such insight is meant to help the client reorient himself or herself to the life tasks.

Case Example: Bob J.

Bob is a 46-year-old male who presented for therapy after he began experiencing intense fatigue and other physical symptoms that were making "his life difficult." He felt too tired to maintain a job that required eight hours a day on his feet. Bob also was beginning to experience tension with his wife, particularly because he was more and more unwilling to do things with her. Bob "felt bad" but said that it's hard to "enjoy anything in life now." Bob explained that he has always worried "about the little things," even as a teenager, but his anxiety about "small things was invading" his life. He found himself getting worried about when he would get the cars washed, if his 16-year-old daughter would get in an accident now that she had acquired a driver's license, and when or if he would be able to retire in 20 years. Bob also noted that he tries to go to bed by eight pm and takes over-the-counter medication so that he can get a "decent rest." When asked "The Question" (Dreikurs, 1997), "What would be different in your life if you did not have this anxiety?", Bob answered that he thought he might get ahead in his work, feel more like doing things with others, and, "oh, get more sleep." An initial Adlerian assessment indicates that Bob is using his anxiety to safeguard himself against possible failure or lack of advancement at work; to avoid family and social interactions where he lacks the courage to participate; and to reinforce a lack of confidence in self and life. His private logic maintains that he has no control over life and, therefore, himself, and because life can get seriously out of control quickly, he needs to focus almost entirely on these pessimistic possibilities.

OBSESSIVE-COMPULSIVE AND RELATED DISORDERS

Obsessive-Compulsive and Related Disorders all involve recurrent and persistent thoughts, mental acts, or behaviors that people feel driven to enact. In general, these disorders are an attempt to fight general anxiety by focusing on repeated thoughts and acts that can then be addressed and controlled.

OBSESSIVE-COMPULSIVE DISORDER

Clinical Presentation

Obsessions are unwanted, repeated, persistent thoughts, images, or urges that the individual cannot ignore and that produce some level of anxiety or distress. More often than not, obsessive thoughts are linked to compulsive mental processes or behaviors that the person feels he or she must do. Much of the time, compulsions are related to body functions or body experiences. A person with obsessive thoughts about dirt or germs may feel driven to wash him or herself multiple times an hour. Because there is preciseness to both the thoughts and the actions, compulsions tend to occur on a relatively regular schedule. The individual may wash their hands and arms every 15 minutes or a person may re-set a room every time upon entering.

DSM-5 Characterization

Individuals diagnosed with Obsessive-Compulsive Disorder must experience either obsessions or compulsions or both. In addition, the individual must be making an attempt to ignore the obsessions and/or reduce the anxiety, often by enacting the compulsion. The compulsion, however, is not realistically designed to handle or prevent the distress or the compulsive behaviors are clearly excessive. The diagnosis requires the obsessions and compulsions to be time consuming, taking up more than an hour per day, and they must cause significant distress or impairment in social, occupational, or other forms of functioning. Approximately 30% of males who develop the disorder in childhood will also meet the criteria for Tic Disorder. About half of those diagnosed with OCD will entertain suicidal thoughts at some time during the course of the disorder.

Biopsychosocial–Adlerian Conceptualization

People with OCD were more than twice as likely to have an immediate adult family member with OCD than not, with genetics affecting perhaps some of the familial tie. Sexual or physical abuse or trauma in early childhood increases the risk of the development of OCD. Psychologically, obsessions and compulsions always reflect negativity and a need for order. The issue of control is paramount in the person's life. The practice of obsessive-compulsive processes is a distraction from relationships and tasks in which others engage on a daily basis. Males are more likely to have early (childhood/adolescence) onset of the disorder, more likely to have a comorbid Tic Disorder, and more likely to entertain inappropriate thoughts or seek symmetry in everything. Females tend to be more focused on body images or cleaning processes.

People with Obsessive-Compulsive Disorder use anxiety in one of two ways: It can be an excuse for avoiding or derailing their participation in necessary tasks in life—especially related to work or intimacy and family relationships; and it can be the assumption of a privileged or powerful position in social and family relationships that serve to assert the necessity of perfection and the individual's need to pursue it.

It is this development of an obsession or compulsion that diverts the insecure person from the more important life tasks of friendship, family, and work. By engaging in these more manageable processes, the individual retreats from more cooperative and life-sustaining efforts to keep busy with less meaningful tasks. Those with OCD invest these obsessions and compulsions with such significance and importance that they must be performed in a ritualistic and often perfect manner. Further, they are the only people who can perform the tasks adequately, thereby elevating themselves and their efforts above the everyday activities and needs of others.

Treatment Considerations

The first consideration in treatment is whether the obsessions and/or compulsions are disturbing to anyone, to the client, or to those with whom the client must interact. In rare cases, no one is particularly disturbed by the thoughts or behaviors, and there is nothing that really needs to be done. In such cases, usually a compulsion is effective at controlling the anxiety.

When compulsive acts do not control the anxiety, or the thoughts and behaviors actually disturb the client or those with whom the client is involved, then treatment is warranted and generally proceeds with desensitization to anxiety-provoking stimuli followed by addressing those tasks of life that the OCD allows the client to avoid. In severe cases of anxiety associated with obsessions or compulsions, selective serotonin reuptake inhibitors, sometimes at fairly high dosages, have been used.

Behavioral therapists call the first step in treatment "Exposure and Ritual Prevention" therapy: It involves exposure to low-level anxiety stimuli without engaging in the compulsive response. Let us say that a person feels infected by the presence of germs and has developed a hand-washing response. Therapy might start with a relative low level of exposure (a doorknob or a book handled by someone else) coupled with support for avoiding hand washing until the person feels calm again. In the case of Jack (below), it might involve support for entering his house and greeting his wife and children without checking to see what part of his home is out of place.

In the end, all obsessive-compulsive rituals are designed to be a retreat from the social, work, or intimacy tasks that Adler believed were central to all of life. Again, this process of discovery is greatly aided by a life-style assessment and the interpretation and understanding of early recollections (Powers & Griffith, 2012).

Case Example: Jack N.

Jack was a 45-year-old male who had attended Columbia University and majored in Journalism. He had worked at several newspapers before joining a city broadcast-news organization, where for several years he was both a weekend anchor and the male host of a morning news and entertainment program. Jack was a handsome man with a great television presence that made both guests and the audience feel at ease. It was during a morning interview with a psychiatrist who had recently written a book on Obsessive-Compulsive Disorder that Jack began to believe that he might have the disorder. He actually said so on the air, which led the station management to suggest that he take a camera team to his home to demonstrate what he believed may be his compulsive behaviors.

Jack was married, and he and his wife had two teenage daughters. They lived in a rather lavish two-story apartment in the city, that had large picture windows and beautiful wood floors. Twenty-two oriental rugs of varying sizes covered the floors, and all of these rugs had woven fringe on each end. The minute that Jack entered the apartment, he felt compelled to make sure that each strand of fringe was perfectly straight. He had a flipping process for the smaller rugs that lined up some of the fringe, but in all cases, he would use one of seven combs he had purchased or made to comb out the fringe on each side of each rug. While moving from rug to rug, he would also straighten out figurines on his mantel, move chairs and table back into place, or put papers and the mail in neat piles. The process took over two hours every time he came home. He knew it was unreasonable for him to expect such order, especially with two teenage daughters, but his anxiety would be overwhelming if he did not engage in his "rituals."

The camera crew caught a glimpse of his daughters' rooms, and, as might be guessed, both rooms were a mess—or as Jack described them, "a disaster." He would occasionally sneak into "the girls' rooms" when they were gone and clean every inch, putting everything in its correct place. The cleaning did not usually last all day, and his daughters never commented on it. No one bothered Jack anymore when he was straightening the house. His wife would occasionally greet him, but even that seemed to be ignored while he went about the process of straightening up.

Jack was considered one of the most engaging personalities on television in New York City, but at home, he hardly interacted with his spouse or his daughters, who long ago had given up on getting Dad to participate in the real life of the family. What becomes clear is that Jack is in retreat from family life. His obsession with orderliness and his compulsion to straighten everything when he comes home occupies and fills his time so that he does not have to be a responsible spouse or a parent. He elevates his compulsion over connection with family and the activities of others. If the family were to simply remove all the rugs, Jack would slip into an anxiety attack that would incapacitate him even more. It is the back-up plan if what Adler (1932/1970) called "the compulsion neurosis" does not work out.

BODY DYSMORPHIC DISORDER, TRICHOTILLOMANIA, AND EXCORIATION

Clinical Presentation

People diagnosed with Body Dysmorphic Disorder focus on a part of the body that seems to be problematic to them in spite of the fact that the perceived condition is not consensually validated by others. For example, a person with a perfectly healthy, full head of hair may believe that they are developing baldness that no one else can detect. Trichotillomania is a hair-pulling disorder in which repeated tugging at one's hair actually results in hair loss; repeated attempts to reduce or eliminate the hair-pulling have no effect. Excoriation is a skin-picking disorder in which repeated picking leads to lesions. Again, repeated attempts to reduce or eliminate the disorder fail. In each of these cases, the degree of preoccupation, though it may be transient, causes significant distress or impairment in occupational, social, and other areas of life.

While the latter two may appear to have a lot in common with addictive processes, the element that really holds these three disorders together is that they are primarily used by women. When males have Body Dysmorphic Disorder, their preoccupation tends to focus on either genital or muscle dysmorphia. Women's preoccupations include a wide range of appearance-based concerns, many of which are heightened in Western cultures and for which cosmetic procedures are both sought and readily available. Trichotillomania and Excoriation are almost exclusively female disorders, at a conservatively estimated rate of 90% and 75% respectively. These latter disorders also involve physical pain and suffering, not necessarily associated with Body Dysmorphic

Disorder. Given the sense of personal inadequacy and inferiority feelings associated with these disorders, it hard not to see the gender and cultural mandates that support these acts of self-depreciation and self-harm. Indeed, in Western cultures, these disorders are almost certainly a result and reflection of the sexism that exists in society.

All three of these disorders locate and focus attention on specific, concrete aspects of the person's body. In this sense, the anxiety is also located in a specific area and is addressed—and often controlled—by focusing remediation in one part of the individual's anatomy. Even though this effort at control is doomed to failure, it is still better than living with free-floating anxiety. Because the underlying processes associated with these disorders are similar, we shall focus the rest of this section on Body Dysmorphic Disorder.

Persons who are diagnosed with Body Dysmorphic Disorder are ashamed of how they look, often embarrassed about the amount of focus that they must put on their appearance. They also believe that others perceive them as they do themselves, and that others are mocking them for these perceived defects. Because of the shame they experience, as well as for the belief that others are noticing them for their perceived defects, they may appear to be introverted, quiet, and reserved. They likely do not have close, intimate friendships because of their shame, low self-esteem, and related social anxiety. They also may incorrectly and negatively interpret the facial expressions of others, especially in situations where the social cues are vague. On the other hand, these same people may connect with others in an effort to seek reassurance about their looks or perceived defects. Engaging in repetitive behavioral and mental acts that are time consuming and difficult to resist are normative, even though engaging in these behaviors does not provide relief and typically only increases feelings of anxiety and disgust in one's self-evaluation. Such behaviors might include excessive grooming and exercise; camouflaging (e.g., using excessive make-up and clothing to hide perceived defects); and skin picking. They may engage in compulsive shopping for beauty products, and may be preoccupied with what to wear. It is not uncommon for people with this disorder to seek cosmetic measures (or tan excessively) to hide perceived defects. Some of these behaviors may lead to real physical damage including ruptured blood vessels, melanomas, and other skin infections.

The focus of this disorder is always on a specific part of the body, usually the face, skin, or hair. The disdain, however, can be focused on any part of the body or on a perceived sense of asymmetry. People with this disorder tend to be perfectionistic and depressed. Those who seek cosmetic surgery typically end up feeling the same or worse.

DSM-5 Characterization

Individuals diagnosed with Body Dysmorphic Disorder can be characterized by fixation and concern about perceived imperfections and flaws in their physical appearance, even though these defects go unrecognized or seem minor to others. Some individuals are specifically concerned with having a deficient body build or muscle mass. They also have developed and engaged in repeated patterns in response to their concerns about their appearance. Such repeated behaviors might include mirror checking, extreme and unnecessary grooming, exercising, or picking at their skin. In addition, individuals also will engage in approval-seeking behaviors about their appearance from others. Mental acts of comparing personal appearance to that of others are common. These repeated behavioral and mental acts cause enough distress to impact social, occupational, and other areas of functioning.

Preoccupation with appearance cannot be related or attributed to concerns about weight or body fat in persons who have been diagnosed with an eating disorder. Persons with Body Dysmorphic Disorder may differ in their level of insight. In addition, people diagnosed with this disorder may have problems with executive functioning and visual processing.

Biopsychosocial–Adlerian Conceptualization

Biologically, this disorder may be genetic in origin, with a higher prevalence among those who have first-degree relatives diagnosed with Obsessive-Compulsive Disorder. In addition, the disorder is often associated with childhood abuse and neglect, is cross-cultural, and may be experienced across the lifespan.

While people with Body Dysmorphic Disorder may suffer from deficits in executive functioning and/or visual processing, the fundamental conclusion they have drawn is that they are flawed or disabled. Further, they have found and identified the flaw, so it can become the matter of focus that dominates their lives. Cognitively, the disorder is linked to the beliefs that appearances are important and perfection is required. Further, this imperfect personal appearance defines who they are, how others see them, and what they must do to handle life: "I'm defective and unique, and while I will keep trying, it is likely that I will never be able to find a worthy place among others." Their world-view may be: "The world and others are unsafe. I'd still like to fit in, but people find me disgusting. I find myself disgusting." This disorder is a tactic for controlling general anxiety; that is, the anxiety is named and defined, and rituals and processes are developed to keep the anxiety at a manageable level. Even the anticipated criticism of others is controlled: "I know that I am ugly and utterly despicable; by focusing on it, I manage the criticism and evaluate myself to avoid the criticism of others."

There are predictable social and environmental factors that can be noted for the Body Dysmorphic Disorder. Parental neglect and abuse are common. The child may have grown up in a setting where he or she had limited opportunities to prepare and deal with the various life tasks. They may have never "fit in" within the family, the school, or other social settings (Croake & Myers, 1985). The child may have developed repetitive patterns of evasion in relation to parental expectations. He or she may have become an expert at getting parents to give up. As a consequence, parents may have developed a discouraged relationship with the child: "I don't know what to do. I have tried to express my hope and belief in you, but nothing works. I am very tired, and I feel like I am giving up on you too." Low self-esteem and limited social interest and personal responsibility turn the child toward self-absorption, in this disorder focused on appearance.

Treatment Considerations

Regardless of whether the client in fact had observable physical deformities, Adlerians would seek to help the individual reorient his or her attitude toward the flawed area (whether it actually exists or not). The counselor would establish a relationship with the client by mirroring, reflecting, and soothing. The client's experience of extreme distress and possibly years of self-hate and disgust are considered and respectfully listened to. The goals of therapy would involve restructuring one's view of the need to be perfect. Other goals might include increasing self-contentment (or focus on areas of self that one is satisfied with); decreasing cognitive distortions; increasing awareness about what others like about the client; increasing ability to grieve one's childhood as well as the perceived loss of a "perfect" body; and increasing ability to self-soothe. Given the client's level of insight, one treatment method would include helping the client make connections between his or her life style and earliest memories, family constellation, assets and strengths, and basic mistakes (Carlson et al., 2006). Such insight is meant to help the client reorient himself or herself to the life tasks. In addition, coping strategies and self-soothing techniques would be taught, homework might be given, such as encouraging the client to partake in some volunteer activity (i.e., volunteering at a nursing home or animal shelter).

Case Example: Sadie K.

Sadie is a 24-year-old female who presented for therapy after her mother threatened to kick her out of the house if she did not get a job and do something with her life. Apparently, Sadie has applied for jobs online, but even after being hired, she has either been late on the first day and fired or has never shown up. Sadie's mother is also concerned because Sadie didn't have "a social life like other kids her age" and seemed "selfishly focused on herself." Sadie confesses that she "even has a hard time coming to therapy, because she feels so ugly and doesn't want others in the lobby to see her." On one occasion, Sadie mentions that it took her two hours to get ready for the counseling session, despite having nowhere else to go that day. She reports years of self-disgust about the size of her thighs, her stringy hair, and her acne. (The client is estimated to be a size 6, is dressed in an attractive outfit, has a nicely trimmed hairstyle and appears to have a "healthy tan."). Despite spending most of her childhood savings on manicures, facial scrubs, waxing, and the most expensive beauty products, Sadie never feels as "good looking" as even the most average girl on the street. She was ready to give up, but told herself that she really wanted to "get better." Sadie's anxiety about her appearance and the time she consumes correcting her perceived defects helps her to avoid the tasks presented by work, friends, and family; she protects herself from failure in these areas by being "too busy" to participate. Because these tasks also have a great deal to do with how she sees herself as a person and how her worth in life is measured, she winds up with low self-esteem and a lack of real connections. Her anxiety becomes an excuse, a reason for her inability to contribute to the life of others, and by so doing, becomes of no value to them.

HOARDING DISORDER

Clinical Presentation

The Hoarding Disorder is a compulsion to save everything or to keep an excess of certain items. Hoarding is an anxiety disorder because of the significant worry and distress associated with getting rid of or parting with possessions. The goal is often to save items that are deemed necessary to maintaining a safe environment for self and others. Hoarding can simply be the unwillingness to part with anything one has, or it can often be combined with excessive acquisition of unneeded items for which there is little or no available space. The result of hoarding is always significant amounts of clutter that limits the living space of the individual and other family members. Any empty or uncongested space is either an area still to be filled with additional items or areas that a third party (usually a family member) keeps "picked up." Individuals who hoard experience a significant degree of preoccupation that may be transient, but that causes distress and impairment in occupational, social, and other areas of life functioning. Individuals with a hoarding disorder may seem to be "normal" in public. That is, the Hoarding Disorder is not easily detected in everyday interpersonal interactions. However, when family and friends are aware of the hoarding, distress characterizes both the individual as well as the person's close relationships. This is particularly true for individuals who have limited insight into their disorder. Individuals with a Hoarding Disorder experience tentativeness in making decisions; they often are perfectionistic, have difficulty organizing their lives and following through with plans. They procrastinate and are easily distracted. They are convinced that the items they have collected or are buying have intrinsic value and can be used. They also may feel emotionally connected to these items, or they will claim that they do not want items to go to waste. These attachments and beliefs make it difficult for individuals to part with their belongings. They continue to save and buy, regardless of space in their homes. They may not be aware of the dangerous or even unsanitary living environment the clutter can create.

DSM-5 Characterization

Individuals diagnosed with Hoarding Disorder have a persistent and strong desire to keep and save items. They experience anguish when confronted with a need to discard items, regardless of their worth or necessity, or available space in their living area. 80% to 90% of those with Hoarding Disorder engage in an excessive acquisition. While some studies suggest that this disorder is more prevalent in males, clinical samples are predominantly women, who are more likely to engage in excessive acquisition than males. In both genders, the disorder is seen more frequently among the elderly, even though the hoarding may have started when the person was quite young. The clutter that causes significant distress for the individual and family members takes time to reach a significant level; when people are younger, family members/spouses often try to clean up the environment in an effort to help the individual.

Biopsychosocial–Adlerian Conceptualization

Biologically, this disorder may have some genetic predispositions, and there is also evidence of familial influences; 50% of those who hoard have a relative who also hoards. Psychologically, individuals who hoard worry that they will be without needed items or that desired items will be taken away from them. They believe that the minute something is discarded it will be essential to have it back, and, of course, then it will be too late. Family and friends may try to help an individual by clearing away clutter, but this only increases the distress in the person and often leads to the reclaiming or repurchasing of "needed" items.

Psychologically, persons who hoard are anxious and fearful about partaking in life tasks, friendships, occupation/vocation, and intimacy with others. That is, they typically believe that they are not adequate enough to make successful contributions in the life tasks. Further, their world-view is something along the lines of "The world is not safe." The origins of this world-view may vary. Persons may have been neglected and abused, or have grown up believing and/or sensing they never had enough. However, the ultimate goal of hoarding is to protect them from failing or from conflict in any of the life tasks. Persons who hoard fulfill this goal by spending more time collecting and spending time with their items than they do in social interaction. This disengagement from others makes intimacy and cooperation often impossible, which again, protects them from what they fear the most: failing. While the act of collecting and saving is essentially a way of keeping anxieties at bay, it also is often considered something that individuals believe they are good at.

Treatment Considerations

Since the purpose of hoarding is a protective device, the counselor is behooved to consider the complex history, including the pain and intense anxiety that is being safeguarded. Empathy and positive social regard for the client is essential (Carlson et al., 2006). The goals of therapy involve increasing insight about the client's family or origin, encouraging social-interest and increased self-esteem, and addressing how symptoms are purposeful. Treatment methods and strategies include stress and relaxation management, making connections between the life-style assessment and how they are using their symptoms, countering tactics such as providing alternative explanations and substituting useful beliefs (Carlson et al., 2006), instruction on self-soothing, as well as interpretation. When family members are involved or living with the client, inviting them to counseling may also be helpful.

Case Example: Mandy

Mandy is a 57-year-old female who presented for therapy after she began experiencing discord in her marriage. Apparently, her husband told her that he was "aggravated for taking the slack of making the money and taking care of the house." Mandy agreed that she was not taking on her part of the responsibilities, but she claimed that she was "always exhausted and can only manage getting up in the morning, watching television all day, and then going back to bed at night." After a few sessions, Mandy told the therapist that they also had "another problem." She explained that they were "hoarders." She further explained that cleaning up the house was extremely overwhelming for her. The bathroom and one of the two bedrooms were no longer accessible because of the clutter in the house. She further explained that there was a narrow path going from her bedroom to the couch in the living room. Mandy reported that she wanted to do something about this but was "too tired to think about what to get rid of," as so much of it was "sentimental" to her. In this case, Mandy is more than preoccupied. Indeed, she is fully occupied with things to the point of being able to avoid friendships, a relationship with her husband, and any sort of occupation that would help her feel like she was contributing something to life and the well-being of others. Her anxiety is an excuse for non-engagement, and her focus on hoarding helps her, literally, to build a physical wall between herself and others.

Treating Anxiety Disorders and Obsessive-Compulsive Disorders: Other Comments

Treatment Options for Adults in Flight

Separation Anxiety in adolescents and adults, Social Anxiety, Agoraphobia, and Generalized Anxiety Disorders are all forms of flight. The primary goal is to avoid problems or tasks in which the person feels a weakness or an insecurity and the anticipation that she or he might fail or not be good enough. The goal of avoidance is generally aimed at one of three life tasks: *Social relationships, occupation* or work, and *intimacy* with spouse or family members (Adler, 1927/1959). There are two assessment processes that Adlerians use to discover the purpose of these anxieties: "The Question" (Adler, 1927) and what Dreikurs (1997) called an "objective investigation" or life-style assessment (Powers & Griffith, 1987, 2012; Shulman & Mosak, 1988). "The Question" would be phrased: "What would you be doing, how would your life be different, if you did not have this anxiety?" The person's answer will often point directly at one of the three life tasks the person most wants to avoid. Similarly, an investigation of the individual's family of origin, developmental and coping process, and early recollections can all lead to clues about the purpose and goals of the symptom. It is not so much about avoiding feared situations as it is about avoiding a personal sense of failure. Understanding, however, is not the endpoint: it is the starting point. With understanding, change becomes an option. Options become possible. Encouragement starts with inviting clients to change their relationship with anxiety. Up to this point, anxiety has dominated their life and dictated what the person could and couldn't do. It was all-powerful.

Another safeguarding mechanism is when people frighten themselves out of doing things. They could simply decide not to do these things, but then they might have to face their complexes and admit them. With anxiety as a mechanism, they claim they are too afraid to try (Carlson, Watts, & Maniacci, 2006, p. 61).

Courage is not getting fear to go away: It is a decision not to let it dominate one's life. It is a decision to let fear and courage coexist. A counselor might even invite a client to thank the fear for offering protection over the years, but also to state one's determination to move on. What internal and external resources would the client need? What would steps toward a more courageous life look like? How would social interest be involved?

Panic attacks, Panic Disorder, and many Specific Phobias are designed to stop people in their tracks, to freeze them in place and not allow movement. Indeed, the panic often feels like one's very life is in danger. The first step is usually to help the client calm down, to reduce the overload of fear. Carlson, Watts, and Maniacci (2006) suggest two interventions to help reduce panic and high levels of anxiety: *Naming the Demon* and *Taking Over*. Naming the Demon proceeds from the idea that if you can name something, you start to control it. It is the answer to "What is happening to me?!?!" "I know you're scared, but what you're experiencing is called panic. It will stop shortly. Trust me" (p. 148). When someone actually knows what is happening and stays calm, the emergency quickly passes: Naming the Demon robs the Demon of its power.

When people freeze, they are often lost, unsure of what to do or where to go. In these moments, it helps to have someone, who is not lost, take over. "OK, here is what we are going to do. First, we will …" (p. 149). What the counselor proposes should be concrete and capable of being implemented immediately. "First, we are going to just breathe normally"; "First, we are going to sit up"; "First, I want you just to look at me, and see that I am smiling and that we are OK." Knowing when to stop taking over and hand the reins back to the individual is also important, but as long as social interest is guiding the intervention, the counselor will not send the person in a direction that will harm them in any way.

Tactics such as Specific Phobias, OCD, Body Dysmorphic Disorder, Hoarding, Trichotillomania, or Excoriation are designed to control anxiety by creating an alternative set of concerns or activities that will consume the individual's time. All of them reflect a level of self-absorption that is the antithesis to social interest. Implied in these tactics is a threat that people either take the individual's fears and control processes seriously, or the individual will lose everything in the anxiety that is sure to follow. Again, the processes the person uses to control the anxiety keep that person far too busy to address the social and occupational tasks of everyday life. While looking busy, consumed, or focused on a specific fear, the individual avoids the demands of family and work. Again, asking *"The Question"* or conducting a *life-style assessment* is the fastest way to ascertain the avoidance and the goal behind the anxiety.

Concluding Note

Anxiety Disorders and the Obsessive-Compulsive and Related Disorders are always about avoiding people, activities, or events in which the person fears that they would fail or be exposed as weak and ineffective, or lose face in front of others. In one sense, anxiety removes people from the field of play, but in another sense, it calls the person to battle. The anxious person has not given up; they have not thrown in the towel. They still want life to work out for them. It is in this hope, this desire, that the possibility of re-engagement emerges—however slowly. It is within a secure therapeutic relationship that alternative convictions, assessments, and engagements can be explored.

References

Adler, A. (1927). *The Practice and Theory of Individual Psychology.* New York, NY: Harcourt, Brace.

Adler, A. (1932). *What Life Should Mean to You.* London: George Allen & Unwin.

Adler, A. (1959). *Understanding Human Nature* (B. Wolfe, Trans.). New York, NY: Premier Books. (Original work published 1927.)

Adler, A. (1964a). *Problems of Neurosis.* New York, NY: Harper & Row.

Adler, A. (1964b). *Social Interest: Adler's Key To the Meaning Of Life.* Boston, MA: Oneworld Publications.

Adler, A. (1970). Compulsion neurosis. In H.L. Ansbacher & R.R. Ansbacher (Eds.), *Superiority and Social Interest: Alfred Adler: A Collection of Later Writings* (pp. 112–138). Evanston, IL: Northwestern University Press. (Original work published 1931.)

American Psychiatric Association (2000). *Diagnostic and Statistical Manual of Mental Disorders, Fourth Edition (Text Revision).* Washington, DC: American Psychiatric Publishing.

American Psychiatric Association (2013). *Diagnostic and Statistical Manual of Mental Disorders, Fifth Edition.* Arlington, VA: American Psychiatric Publishing.

Ansbacher, H.L. (1992). Alfred Adler's concepts of community feeling and social interest and the relevance of community feeling for old age. *Individual Psychology*, 48, pp. 402–412.

Ansbacher, H.L. & Ansbacher, R.R. (Eds.) (1956). *The Individual Psychology of Alfred Adler.* New York, NY: Basic Books.

Beck, A.T. & Emery, G. (1985). *Anxiety Disorders and Phobias.* New York, NY: Basic Books.

Bitter, J.R. (2009). The mistaken notions of adults with children. *Journal of Individual Psychology*, 65(4), pp. 135–155.

Bitter, J.R. (2013). *Theory and Practice of Family Therapy and Counseling* (2nd edn.). Belmont, CA: Brooks/Cole-Cengage.

Breggin, P.R. (2008). *Medication Madness: A Psychiatrist Exposes the Dangers of Mood-Altering Medications.* New York, NY: St. Martin's Press.

Carlson, J., Watts, R.E., & Maniacci, M. (2006). *Adlerian Therapy: Theory and Practice.* Washington, DC: American Psychological Association.

Croake, J.W. & Myers, K.M. (1985). Goal diagnosis in psychiatric consultation. *Individual Psychology*, 41(4), pp. 496–509.

Dreikurs, R. (1948). The socio-psychological dynamics of physical disability. In R. Dreikurs (Ed.), *Psychodynamics, Psychotherapy, and Counseling: Collected Papers of Rudolf Dreikurs* (pp. 171–192). Chicago, IL: Alfred Adler Institute.

Dreikurs, R. (1950). The immediate purpose of children's misbehavior, its recognition and correction. *Internationale Zeitschrift für Individual-Psychologie*, 19, pp. 70–87.

Dreikurs, R. (1953). *Fundamentals of Adlerian Psychology.* Chicago, IL: Alfred Adler Institute.

Dreikurs, R. (1955). Minor psychotherapy: A practice psychology for physicians. In R. Dreikurs (Ed.), *Psychodynamics, Psychotherapy, and Counseling: Collected Papers of Rudolf Dreikurs* (pp. 49–64). Chicago, IL: Alfred Adler Institute.

Dreikurs, R. (1997). Holistic medicine. *Individual Psychology*, 53, pp. 127–205.

Eckstein, D. & Kern, R. (2002). *Psychological Fingerprints: Lifestyle Assessment and Interventions* (5th edn.). Dubuque, IA: Kendall Hunt.

Hyman, M. (2008). *The UltraMind solution: Fix Your Broken Brain by Healing Your Body First.* New York, NY: Scribner.

Kottman, T. (2002). *Partners in Play: An Adlerian Approach to Play Therapy* (2nd edn.). Alexandria, VA: American Counseling Association.

Kottman, T. (2010). *Play Therapy: Basics and Beyond* (2nd edn.). Alexandria, VA: American Counseling Association.

Madden, J. (Director) (2012). *The Best Exotic Marigold Hotel*. United Kingdom: Participant Media.

Millon, T. (1990). *Toward a New Personology: An Evolutionary Model*. New York, NY: John Wiley & Sons.

Mosak, H.H. (1968). The interrelatedness of the neuroses through central themes. *Journal of Individual Psychology*, 24, pp. 67–70.

National Institutes of Health (2010). Treating anxiety disorders. NIH medline plus, 5 (3), p. 15. Retrieved from http://www.nlm.nih.gov/medlineplus/magazine/issues/fall10/articles/fall10 pg15.html.

Powers, R.L. & Griffith, J. (1987). *Understanding Lifestyle: The Psycho-Clarity Process*. Chicago, IL: Americas Institute of Adlerian Studies.

Powers, R.L. & Griffith, J. (2012). *The Key to Psychotherapy: Understanding the Self-Created Individual*. Port Townsend, WA: Adlerian Psychology Associates.

Rasmussen, P.R. (2010). *The Quest to Feel Good*. New York, NY: Routledge.

Rasmussen, P.R. & Dover, G. J. (2007). The purposefulness of anxiety and depression: Adlerian and evolutionary views. *Journal of Individual Psychology*, 62(4), pp. 366–396.

Shulman, B.H. & Mosak. H.H. (1988). *Manual for Lifestyle Assessment*. Muncie, IN: Accelerated Development.

Sperry, L. (1987). Common psychiatric presentations in clinical practice: *DSM-III* and dynamic formulations. *Individual Psychology*, 43(2), pp. 133–143.

Sperry, L. (1996). Anxiety disorders I. In L. Sperry & J. Carlson (Eds.), *Psychopathology and Psychotherapy: From DSM-IV Diagnosis to Treatment* (pp. 163–178). Washington, DC: Accelerated Development.

Sperry, L. & Sperry, J. (2012). *Case Conceptualization: Mastering This Competency With Ease and Confidence*. New York, NY: Routledge.

Sweeney, T.J. (2009). *Adlerian Counseling and Psychotherapy: A Practitioner's Approach* (5th edn.). New York, NY: Routledge.

5 Depression and Bipolar Disorders

Paul R. Rasmussen and Dinko Aleksandrof

The *Diagnostic and Statistical Manual of Mental Disorders*, published by the American Psychiatric Association, is considered to provide the official nomenclature for diagnosis and research. Since its introduction in 1952, it has undergone numerous changes and seen several different editions. Most recently, the American Psychiatric Association introduced its latest version—*DSM-5* (American Psychiatric Association, 2013), which intended to advance clinical practice and empirical research by further improving the diagnostic criteria for mental disorders.

During its evolution as a psychological theory, the school of Individual Psychology (IP) has sought ways to incorporate the nomenclature system of the *DSM* into its conceptual framework. Aside from the numerous works published in the literature, the *Journal of Individual Psychology* devoted a special issue in 2002 to the connection between the *DSM* and Individual Psychology. As Maniacci (2002) notes, the five axes of the DSM system largely resemble the biopsychosocial and holistic perspectives espoused by Individual Psychology.

The current chapter will provide an overview of the changes in *DSM-5* for the depressive and bipolar disorders. It will also introduce the reader to the way Adlerian theorists might conceptualize depression, mania, and related conditions. In doing so, the chapter will offer a way of integrating the DSM nomenclature system into the theory of Individual Psychology, particularly its understanding of psychopathology. The disorders covered in this chapter include Major Depressive Disorder, episodic and recurrent; Disruptive Mood Dysregulation Disorder; Persistent Depressive Disorder (Dysthymic Disorder); Bipolar I Disorder; Bipolar II Disorder; and Cyclothymic Disorder.

An Adlerian View

Several factors contribute to the expression of "problems in living" and to DSM-based clinical conditions, which may or may not be different. While some conditions are more medical, implying a physical pathology in need of medical intervention, more often psychological/emotional problems emerge as a consequence of one's inability to adequately overcome life challenges. This model emphasizes a *"psychology of use"* perspective rather than a *"psychology of possession"* view. In this perspective it is understood that symptoms emerge because they are useful to the individual; they may not be *optimally* useful, but they help to resolve or overcome an *immediate* challenge. A "psychology of possession" view holds that symptoms emerge as the outcome of a physical process that is essentially unrelated to one's orientation to life. While physiology could be the singular, etiological problem, it is believed that most conditions emerge not simply as the outcome of a physiological process, although physiology must be involved, but as a means of helping the individual to deal with the challenge. The fact that there is no perfect physical balance, and because physiology changes in response to psychological processes, yields support for the "use" perspective when working with an individual's orientation to life. The notion of "coping skills" is often referred to in psychology, and this is essentially what is being referred to here; however, it is more than simple coping that is of concern. Problems emerge when one is unable to "overcome" effectively the challenges faced, which occurs because the challenge is overwhelming or, more often, the preparation for overcoming is inadequate; thus it is not simply a matter of coping, it is an issue of overcoming or not overcoming.

Symptoms represent immediate solutions/adaptations to immediate demands. They include feelings (emotions), which compel actions (behaviors) implemented in response to a challenge; that we call these adaptations "pathological" stems from the fact that they are: 1) often painful and thus distressing; 2) they are optimally ineffective in overcoming the challenge; and 3) they often contribute to a worsening of one's quality of life. Taken together these outcomes satisfy the general standard for diagnosis in the *DSM*. Specifically, these optimally ineffective adaptations contribute to a disruption in one's ability to meet the demands (i.e., "common sense," guiding lines") of one's social, occupational, and familial responsibilities. Many forget that this is the critical factor in diagnosing a DSM disorder: it is not just the presence of symptoms, but the disruption of life associated with the symptoms.

Indeed, some individuals, given their circumstance in life, face more Axis IV challenges than others and/or are more easily overwhelmed by the demands of life, and have fewer options in overcoming those demands. This is the point at which society, as the organization, must respond to those needs and create solutions and opportunities. But, it is also the responsibility of each individual to contribute to the overall welfare of the community and to make optimal accommodations to the challenges faced—which requires social interest.

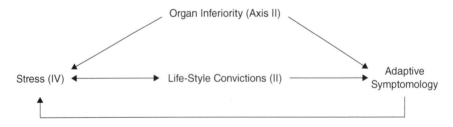

In this model: Stresses are the events/circumstances that need to be dealt with (i.e., the challenges to overcome).

Life-style convictions refers to beliefs one has about how life should/shouldn't go and include one's private logic. Organ inferiorities are physical factors that impact the adaptive, striving process.

Figure 5.1 The Psychology of Use Model

Noteworthy is the fact that symptoms in psychological disorders are typically emotions felt and actions implemented. Symptoms are not directly cognitive. Cognitions are more often the assumptions one has about life, which do not align well with external demands and events and thus create the circumstance for emotionally compelled actions. A close look at *DSM* will reveal that Axis I conditions/criteria are almost exclusively feelings and behaviors, while Axis II criteria are generally attitudes, beliefs, and other forms of cognition.

While there are many criticisms of the new *DSM-5*, one of the most unfortunate changes may be that it has taken the person out of the discussion of clinical disorder. In *DSM-5*, while personality disorders remain included, their role in helping us to explain clinical conditions appears to have been minimized. This is indeed unfortunate. But, it is the case that most clinicians did not use Axis II in their conceptualizations and focused primarily on Axis I; the 5-axial symptom was dropped, not because it wasn't useful, but because it wasn't used (Grohol, 2013). That it wasn't used might have been because most clinicians thought only in terms of disorder of personality and not, as Theodore Millon (1990, 1999) has tried to convey, as styles of personality that render an individual more or less prone to clinical conditions. Hopefully *DSM-5* does not throw the critical baby out with the bathwater. As Sir William Osler argued, to understand the condition, the doctor must understand the person. While this may not be the case in the new DSM approach, the truth of this statement remains as important now as it was in 1932 when Osler presented it (Arney & Bergen, 1984).

Important in the IP model is the role of *discouragement*. This seemingly simple term is important because it describes the circumstance of the human experience that often produces clinical outcomes. Given the goals of overcoming challenges and securing validation, it is reasonable to assume that one is at times encouraged, hopeful, and even enthused, and at other times discouraged ... discouraged about the ability to overcome burden and challenges, and discouraged about the ability to fulfill ambitions (i.e., to resolve the felt minus and produce the felt plus). The nature of one's discouragement will show up in a person's life at different times as periods of fear, anxiety, anger, self-contempt, guilt, or depression and in the form of other clinical and sub-clinical conditions. While many contemporary mental health professionals, particularly those more medically oriented, will have a problem with the following statement, an Adlerian-oriented therapist/theorist would accept this as common knowledge ... *clients come to see us not because they are disordered but because they are discouraged*. The nature of the discouragement can be seen in the nature of the symptoms (Rasmussen, 2010). For instance, before one can be said to be fully discouraged, he or she may feel and express complaint about having to overcome a burden, which reflects frustration. It may be that the individual is striving to identify the presence or nature of a challenge or threat, and this would require anxiety. The person may be actively fighting to overcome a burden that he or she does not think fair or reasonable, and this would require anger. If the individual has no idea what to do, but knows that something must be done, the feeling is panic in the immediate and anguish when profound and prolonged. It may be that the individual is hoping to sidestep the necessity of facing the burden, which would require another more pressing problem; it would require a crisis, which could be experienced as interpersonal crisis (e.g., family conflict), work crisis (e.g., problem with the boss), or health crisis (e.g., somatic symptoms, insomnia, etc.). In the face of stress, the individual is compelled to act, and different actions require different emotional states. To energize our actions, we feel the emotions we need given the demands of the situation and our perceived options. This isn't to suggest that those crises are not real; they may be very real and completely independent of life style. Yet, the advantage of a crisis, however extreme, is that it creates the necessity of ignoring other issues and allows one to make decisions that may be difficult to make in the absence of a crisis. For instance, it may be hard to tell a relationship partner that one is tired of the relationship and ready to move on; however, in the face of a crisis the relationship may be more easily terminated. Indeed, many relationship partners will subtly undermine a relationship and end that relationship when his or her partner, often in some state of distress, confronts him or her about the problems.

It is important to point out that our ability to explain the emergence of a depression, mania, or any other condition, as an adaptive mechanism implemented to help deal with life challenges is not to suggest that it is not a "real thing." To be sure, all psychological processes require physical processes, so the distinction between a psychological condition and a physiological condition is nearly irrelevant. What those suffering from a clinical condition may fail to appreciate is that their biology is simply responding to the circumstance in order to help them manage their life. Even in the face of a clear physical abnormality, the individual remains a holistic individual moving through time and circumstance with the goal of creating plus states and minimizing minus states.

To many people, psychological explanations often serve to suggest that the "disorder" is either a manipulated outcome or a sign of weakness. Those depressed, for instance, will often reject such an explanation because it suggests that they are responsible for the depression, when they would prefer to view themselves as the victims of either circumstance or bad biology. What they may fail to appreciate is how their biology is reacting to the circumstance in order to help them manage their life situation. Medical professionals may reject such an explanation because it could imply that their treatment is misguided and perhaps even unnecessary. However, a variety of treatments can be helpful given our understanding of these adaptive, useful mechanisms, including medications. Indeed, it may be necessary to introduce medicines in order to inhibit the emotions compelling destructive behaviors. But, we should hope that these treatments do not limit our understanding of the condition. As an example, we might simply explain depression as a genetically mediated, chemical imbalance, which must then be treated with other chemicals designed to help restore that balance. While this could be the case, we would argue that in the majority of mood disorder cases such explanations are inadequate and potentially dangerous. If, for example, the medical explanation implies that a person does not have control or influence over life experience, when in fact they may have both, the individual may cease to assert that influence. Further, if the condition is explained as one that can only be treated medically, when those medical treatments don't provide the life satisfaction and joy the individual seeks, the depth of the discouragement may increase and the hopefulness be dashed. It could also be that the "out-of-balance" chemicals might be very much "in balance" as it relates to meeting the current needs of the individual, which may be a retreat from a hopeless situation. That a condition is genetic is irrefutable; what in the human condition is not mediated by genetics? Is it not in our genetics to adapt to states of distress? Of course it's genetic, there is no way that it could not be; but to simply say "it's genetic" is not enough. To be sure, our ability to explain depression and other conditions as adaptive, purposeful reactions to environmental demand mediated by life-style orientation in no way negates the role of biology or the potential usefulness of medicine to help alleviate the discomfort of the condition and subsequently to limit counter-productive reactions implemented to resolve the felt minus state. Nor does it suggest that it is an equal playing field and that temperamental, genetic, and other physical factors are not involved (consider organ inferiorities) or are the same for everyone. It is not an equal playing field (consider the descriptions of temperament by Cloninger et al. (1993), and by Thomas and Chess (1977)) and for a variety of reasons some are more vulnerable to these conditions than are others. Indeed, differences in physical appearance, intelligence, energy level, creativity, persistence, and other qualities influence the development and expression of life-style attributes, thus the paths that may lead one to a depression or mania are infinite. Given the complexity, many prefer to view depression, for instance, as simply a physical "disorder" that caught them unaware, which represents a bad family legacy of which they are now the latest victims. While this could be accurate, there is more to the explanation. Having a relative who struggles with mental health issues does not create inevitability, nor explain why one struggles with similar afflictions. Humans all have similar genes, although in unique combinations, and can only react in human ways (e.g., we cannot flap our wings and fly from trouble). Understanding the genetic predispositions and necessary physical processes is helpful and useful; yet, from the IP perspective we must consider the individual's convictions, goals, and private logic, and movement through time and circumstance.

Mood Disorders and *DSM-5*

Several factors changed from *DSM-IV-TR* to *DSM-5*. One of the most-discussed topics in the mood disorders category has been the elimination of the bereavement exclusion. Per *DSM-IV-TR*, a person did not receive a Major Depressive Episode (MDE) diagnosis if his/her symptoms could be accounted for by bereavement (American Psychiatric Association, 2000). However, researchers claim that there has not been much empirical evidence for this bereavement exclusion (Zisook et al., 2012). More specifically, those involved in the revision argue that the clinical symptomatology of depression following death of a loved one is not much different compared to depression triggered by other adverse life events. Individuals who experience "normal grief" are believed to preserve their level of adaptive functioning, while others experience a significant compromise in that functioning. Shear (2009) and Lamb, Pies, and Zisook (2010) argue that even though grief presents with similar emotions to depressive disorders, it is characteristically different. For instance, grief includes the "pangs" of grief associated with thoughts or reminders of the deceased, which is different than the more persistent, pervasive sadness of MDE. Further, grief is often accompanied by positive emotions and humor, which is not characteristic of MDE. Grief also includes preoccupation with thoughts and memories of the deceased, rather than the self-critical or pessimistic ruminations seen in MDE. In addition, the bereavement exclusion is not part of the ICD symptoms for depression, nor was it part of *DSM-I* and *DSM-II*. Nonetheless, the DSM-5 Mood Disorders Workgroup has decided to eliminate the bereavement exclusion from the new edition of the manual. What is common, and relevant to our discussion, is the sadness associated with loss, which in the case of bereavement is a loved one and in non-bereavement depression is loss of hope, and subsequent retreat from life obligations.

Another change to the mood disorders is the addition of Disruptive Mood Dysregulation Disorder (DMDD), which did not exist in *DSM-IV-TR*. This is a severe and chronic expression of anger, rage, hostility, and irritability, expressed verbally and/or physically (American Psychiatric Association, 2013). This condition reflects the variety of ways that mood disorders can be expressed, underscoring the fact that there is not a pure form of the different clinical conditions represented in *DSM*. This fact is consistent with the IP conceptualization of psychopathology.

Much evidence exists in the empirical literature that anxiety is the most comorbid condition in mood disorders. In *DSM-IV-TR*, there is no anxiety specifier for mood disorders and, therefore, clinicians are forced to add a second diagnosis on Axis I in order to indicate that the patient is experiencing clinical levels of anxiety in addition to the depressive disorder. The problem, however, is that the anxiety disorders have their own specific criteria and, often times, patients who have anxiety comorbid with mood disorder do not fully meet the criteria for an anxiety disorder. Consequently, clinicians assign them a diagnosis of Anxiety NOS as a second diagnosis on Axis I. One solution that was proposed for *DSM-5* was to add an anxiety clinical scale to the mood disorders in order to prevent this overuse of Anxiety NOS.

Similarly, there have been many reports during the last decades about patients who present with clinically significant levels of depression and anxiety but who do not meet full criteria for either mood or anxiety disorders. Often times, those would be labeled as NOS or Adjustment Disorder. The DSM-5 Mood Disorders Workgroup, however, proposed that a Mixed Anxiety Depressive Disorder be included as an official and separate diagnosis. The proposed criteria for this condition would require at least two weeks of combined anxiety and depression symptoms. These proposed changes were accepted, and the *DSM-5* includes "anxious distress" as a specifier for the depressive disorders as well as the bipolar and related disorders.

As part of the general *DSM-5* changes, the Mood Disorders Workgroup has been asked to add a severity dimension to its disorders. So far, it has proposed two measures that will aid the clinician to determine disorder severity for MDD and Bipolar. The first measure is the Patient Health Questionnaire (PHQ-9; Kroenke, Spitzer, & Williams, 2001), which assesses depressive symptoms. The other measure they have recommended is the Clinical Global Impression Scale (CGI; Busner & Turgum, 2007), to be used for the severity of Bipolar Disorder.

Another condition that was under further examination by the DSM Task Force was Melancholia. In the empirical literature, researchers seemed to disagree as to whether or not Melancholia should be a distinct mood disorder in *DSM-5* or remain as a specifier. Proponents of the former view believe that, as a separate condition, Melancholia has better predictive validity for prognosis and treatment than the other mood disorders and represents a more homogenous category, which makes it better for research. In contrast, proponents of the latter view disagreed, claiming that there is not enough research supporting the argument that Melancholia has superior predictive validity to other mood disorders and specifiers. For instance, Hypercortisolemia is not specific to Melancholia and is present in other conditions as well. This piece of evidence speaks against the argument that Melancholia represents a more homogenous cluster of symptoms. Because this issue was not resolved, Melancholia remains a specifier in *DSM-5* rather than being a separate mental disorder.

MAJOR DEPRESSIVE DISORDER

Clinical Presentation

Depression itself is a normal emotional reaction to perceived loss and hopelessness. In *clinical depression*, which indicates *Major Depressive Disorder* (MDD), the experience of depression is more severe and more chronic, and significantly disrupts the individual's ability to meet normal demands of life. To many clinicians, clinical depression is considered a medical illness in need of medical intervention. To other mental health professionals this may be an exaggeration of the role of physiology and the role of the medical provider; yet, depression, like any clinical condition, includes important physical processes and can be positively impacted by the introduction of various medicines. The controversy emerges in whether the physical processes reflect genetically mediated physical differences occurring independent of experience, adapted physical changes (i.e., learning processes) that have emerged in relation to experience or reactive physical processes necessary to meet immediate challenge. Of course, the experience of any feeling state requires necessary physical mediators, and in the case of the depression, the individual experiences a functional decrease in critical neurochemicals mediated by changes in the hypothalamic-pituitary axis (Grisel, Rasmussen, & Sperry, 2006). Most notable over recent years is the role of norepinephrine and serotonin. More recently the importance of dopamine in depression has been considered.

DSM-5 Characterization

The symptoms of depression include feelings of sadness, emptiness and hopelessness, loss of interest or pleasure in typically enjoyed activities, weight loss or weight gain associated with change in appetite, insomnia at night and hypersomnia during the day. Other symptons include psychomotor agitation interspersed with periods of psychomotor retardation, fatigue or loss of energy, feelings of worthlessness and/or guilt, concentration problems and/or indecisiveness, and thoughts of death, including thoughts of suicide. Depression is mixed with a variety of other emotions, each serving to compel the individual into some useful, adaptive action. Importantly, the symptoms are distressing and impair the individual's ability to function in important areas of life, and it is because of this that the condition constitutes a "disorder."

Biopsychosocial–Adlerian Conceptualization

From an Adlerian perspective, depression represents retreat from what is perceived to be a hopeless circumstance (Rasmussen, 2010). Indeed, depression as an emotion compels withdrawal from a situation perceived as overwhelming. That hopelessness is a primary characteristic of depression supports this position. This retreat often follows periods of anxiety and perhaps anger—emotions that compel efforts to overcome circumstantial challenges. When efforts compelled by those emotions prove ineffective, the individual may give up hope and withdraw. While retreat may be a useful reaction to a hopeless situation, in the case of many depressions, the retreat is ultimately unnecessary as relative solutions may be available. Further, giving into a depression (allowing the retreat) provides some immediate relief from burdensome social and personal expectations and responsibilities, while at the same time not requiring an accommodation in one's life-style convictions or behavioral habits. In this context, depression, which is indeed painful and often debilitating, is serving as a safeguard against the obligation to alter convictions and act with greater social interest. As suggested by Slavik and Croake (2001), while people desire to give up their symptoms, they do not want to alter their goals or accept themselves as inferior.

When one's ambitions and expectations (i.e., fictional goals) are not being fulfilled, which emerges from own private interpretation of the circumstance, depression and varying degrees of retreat ensue. Important in this conceptualization is the understanding that one's objective reality may be quite positive. However, if that reality conflicts with one's more basic life-style desires, depression is possible and perhaps probable. From the IP perspective, those basic desires are often *unconscious*, which suggests that they are unarticulated goals. For instance, one may state that one desires to work hard, be responsible, get along with and be helpful to others, and that one is satisfied with one's current intimacies. At that *deeper*, unarticulated level of processing, that person may prefer to avoid work and other responsibilities, may find others generally insufferable, and may desire to give into and pursue carnal desires. This reflects both a continuation of the basic *infantile orientation* to life, which includes a desire to avoid burdens and derive pleasures (Rasmussen, 2012; Adler, 1959), and a failure to have accepted and met the basic tasks of life.

Of course, this requires biological processes and includes primarily the activities of the hypothalamic-pituitary axis (Grisel, Rasmussen, & Sperry, 2006). Stress in this circumstance is created by the inconsistency between the private and infantile desire to avoid life-task responsibilities and to pursue more self-bounded activities. Stress, in the case of depression, is managed via hopeless retreat; this allows the individual some relief from the burdensome responsibilities and, secondarily, provides some sympathy and perhaps accommodation by others. Given the physiological processes involved, the symptoms are indeed very real and often very painful. They are not very often spontaneous physical processes; these physical processes reflect the adaptive, purposeful reaction of the individual to a minus state.

Because life circumstance is ever changing and the desire to overcome distress is constant, we should expect to see symptoms that would appear contradictory. Some symptoms indicate social retreat and hopelessness, while others indicate subtle and blatant efforts to solicit rescue, to prompt compliance of others, or to compel the self into greater effort. It is important to note that these subtle expressions of sadness or disappointment prompt compassion and associated behaviors in others; that is, they elicit assistance. In the best of situations, the response of an individual to stress (i.e., actions energized by emotion) serves to help overcome the challenge in some optimally effective manner, "optimal" implying that the response 1) resolves and perhaps eliminates the problem, and 2) does not unnecessarily increase the probability of that problem re-emerging, or 3) create other problems with which the individual will then have to contend. More often, individuals enact responses that provide only momentary relief—thus proving to be immediately adaptive or useful. Or react in ways that almost guarantee a return of that problem and often the emergence of other problems. From an IP perspective, these suboptimal reactions are without social interest and subsequently exploit the welfare of others. For example, anger can prompt compliance in another, yet creates relationship problems. Indeed, humans tend to be focused on making things better, and don't act in their "optimal" interest (Rasmussen, 2010). The fact is that *better is always better, but a better state may fall quite short of a good state*. Indeed, things can be better and remain quite bad. In the case of depression, the withdrawal serves to remove one from an unwinnable battle, thus helping the person feel better. However, because the battle continues, a true plus is not often an option.

Treatment Considerations

Treatment of an episodic depression can often be rather straightforward. To be sure, medications can be used to help block the physiological process, mediating the painful feelings, and this can help the psychotherapeutic process by allowing the therapist and patient to focus on life style, less distracted by the painful emotions. There are several medications currently used to treat depression, including those that act on serotonin (SSRIs, e.g., fluoxetine, paroxetine, sertraline, citalopram, and escitalopram), serotonin and norepinephrine (SNRIs, e.g., duloxetine and venlafaxine), those that act on serotonin and dopamine (NDRIs, e.g., bupropion), older medicines such as mirtazapine, tranylcypromine, and phenelzine. For many patients the emotional relief derived from the medications is sufficient and minimizes the perceived need for therapy. For others, the relief is often short lived: frequent medication changes are necessary, and the necessity of coping with iatrogenic effects becomes nearly inescapable. While all individuals can grow and develop to make painful emotional symptoms less necessary, some may prefer to remain with a medical solution and it is each person's choice concerning commitment to treatment.

For those who experience episodic depression, psychotherapy can help to bolster the individual's resistance to stress created by challenges. In most cases of episodic depression, the individual is functioning either with an expansive enough life style that most challenges are managed well, or has existed within an environment in which life-style vulnerabilities are not expressed, yet currently is facing a period of hopelessness. In either condition, the individual likely possesses skills that can be extended to the challenge or can alter private logic assumptions sufficiently to create a reduction in depressive symptoms and vulnerability. Treatment will invariably include an adjustment to one's convictions concerning how life should go and a recommitment to acting with social interest and in line with the common tasks of life.

Unlike treatment of episodic depression, which can often extend a person's life-style assets to address current challenges, treatment of a recurrent depression may require more extensive assessment of life-style convictions and developed mistaken beliefs. Just as medicines can be used to treat the emotional aspects of other clinical conditions, medications can be used to treat recurrent depression (see the list of medications for depression presented above). However, the assumption that medicines are necessary and likely to remain necessary may be extreme.

~~Life-style convictions and thus one's style of movement through time and~~ circumstance can change, and thus can one's vulnerability to debilitating depression. However, in the case of recurrent depressions, the therapist will have to work with the patient to uncover and alter the convictions and mistaken beliefs that are leaving the individual recurrently hopeless. For some depressed individuals a comprehensive life-style analysis can help to uncover for the patient extreme beliefs and convictions creating the perception of hopelessness. With this understanding of the unarticulated rules and expectations of life, the individual is prepared to alter his or her orientation to life in a way in which depression is less necessary and less likely.

Case Example: Michelle

Michelle is 43 years old and has struggled for many years with depression. People who know Michelle view her as indeed fortunate. She is viewed as attractive and is in what appears to be an ideal marriage. She has two children, who appear by all accounts to be obedient and capable. Financially she is well off; both she and her spouse are successful professionals. Those who know of her struggles with depression cannot understand why, and it is assumed that her depression reflects an unfortunate genetic condition creating a biochemical imbalance, and to some extent this may be true. She has a long history of trying different medicines, all of which work for a period of time but eventually lose their effectiveness.

An IP conceptualization of Michelle considered those unarticulated life-style beliefs, accessed via consideration of Michelle's childhood experiences and early recollections. To begin, Michelle is an only child raised in a very "traditional" home. Her father worked as a businessman and her mother remained at home to raise their child. There were attempts to have more children, but without success. As a result, Michelle received a great deal of investment by her mother, which may have been less had other children been brought into the home. Her mother was described as loving and caring but also as prone to periods of anger and depression (which is attributed to her life not having gone as she had hoped). Her father was likewise viewed as loving and caring and tended to indulge Michelle with gifts and special opportunities. In many ways Michelle was pampered by her parents, but also felt occasionally abandoned by her mother when her mother went through her own depressed episodes. Michelle describes her own depression as having been a genetic "gift" from her mother. Her father passed away some years ago, but her mother is still alive and lives nearby. They remain close and talk every day and see each other several times a week.

Michelle is an attorney and reports that she enjoys the work, but admits that she dreams of being able to retire and live on a tropical island, existing in a constant state of relaxation; for some time, her depression has prevented her from doing full-time work. Michelle's early recollections relate to her being the center of attention and receiving gifts and admiration from her parents and grandparents. In one memory, it is her birthday and she is sitting in her favorite chair and her family is singing "Happy Birthday" to her, each holding a gift to present her after the song. Vivid in the memory is "everyone looking at me with happy smiles." The feeling she associates with the recollection is "absolute joy!" This suggests an individual who desires the investment and indulgence of others, but not for doing anything other than being present for that indulgence.

Michelle's current life circumstance conflicts with her more basic desires. While she wants to be a good mother, a good spouse, a good friend, and a good professional (and during college wanted to be a good student), these are *common sense* goals, which suggest goals that she knows that she *should* value (because they are commonly considered to be good values). However, as a child who appears to have been indulged and made to feel quite special by those around her, regardless of her efforts, the burdens to remain "special" have proven quite taxing and she struggles with recurrent feelings of discouragement manifested as depression.

The fact is that Michelle does not feel that she is valuable and significant unless others are treating her as someone special. While feeling special was easy to derive in childhood, in her adult life it has been far harder to achieve. While she is able to do many wonderful things, rather than receiving unconditional smiles from those in her life, what she perceives are expressions of demand and expectation. Her depression provides her an attitude of hopeless indifference to the demand and expectations of others. It has been the case that the only time she feels the specialness she desires is when she achieves something significant, or one of her children achieves. Most of her life is spent trying to please others. Michelle recognizes, as well, that during her "dark periods" she also feels some specialness as others try to help her through her struggles; she also recognizes the sense of relief she feels when the depression "takes over" and she abandons any investment in the thing she knows she should be doing; but the relief, she admits, is tainted by guilt and self-reproach.

While medicines have been helpful to Michelle, because her basic life-style orientation conflicts with the demands of reality, periods of depressed retreat are nearly inevitable without a change in orientation. While Michelle could seek an environment that might better accommodate her fictional goals, this is unlikely as an adult and she is not inclined to abandon her connection with those close to her. For Michelle, the task is to alter her orientation to life in such a way that joys and satisfactions are created not by the admiration and accommodations that she receives but from the contributions that she makes. To be sure, Michelle will need to be attentive to the demands and expectations that she accepts. She has, for many years, taken on tasks in order to elicit validation and then feels burdened by the excessive responsibility. What Michelle desires is to feel valued and important; The extent to which this is dependent on her ability to manage the reactions of others, proves problematic.

DISRUPTIVE MOOD DYSREGULATION DISORDER

Clinical Presentation

In Disruptive Mood Dysregulation Disorder (DMDD), we see a young person (aged seven to 18 years) who is essentially fighting off depression, or at least fighting to overcome perceived burdens. While anxiety reflects the individual's awareness of a burden to overcome, expressed frustration, irritability, and anger reflect the individual's efforts to impact what are perceived as obstacles to one's desired state (Rasmussen, 2010; Rasmussen & Dover, 2006), which is invariably a state of relief, indulgence, or validation. We may refer to these outbursts as tantrums, but we appear to have reserved that term for very young children who do not know better. Importantly, there is nothing in the normal developmental sequence that would require one to abandon a strategy that may have proven effective—effective in this context relating to immediate rather than optimal outcomes. Outbursts of anger serve several purposes, including 1) compelling others to comply with one's desire (e.g., the exasperated parent who says, "OK, fine! If you'll just calm down!!"), 2) creating a sense of victimization that may justify later behaviors (e.g., the child who storms off muttering, "I hate my parents! They are so unfair!! I'll show them!!"), and, relatedly, 3) compelling revenge (e.g., knocked-over lamps, kicked-in walls, etc.; Dreikurs & Soltz, 1964). When anger fails to produce the desired outcomes, the individual may then retreat into a depressed state, which includes withdrawal. In the case of DMDD, the child has not yet abandoned anger as a reactive strategy. That children diagnosed with DMDD are at greater risk of developing either Anxiety or Unipolar Depression underscores the relationship between anxiety, anger, and depression (American Psychiatric Association, 2013).

DSM-5 Characterization

The primary characteristic of Disruptive Mood Dysregulation Disorder is chronic irritability, which contributes to recurrent frustrations and temper outbursts. The young person diagnosed with DMDD experiences multiple episodes of expressed temper per week. The symptoms have been present for at least a year and the irritability and temper has been expressed across at least two settings, such as at home or at school or work, and contributes to significant functional disruption in those environments.

DMDD was included in *DSM-5* primarily as a means of accounting for the behavior of a pediatric population who under *DSM-IV* would have been diagnosed with Bipolar Disorder, a diagnosis now reserved for adults. It is included in the section on depressive disorders because it is believed that children with these symptoms are more likely to develop Unipolar Depression or Anxiety Disorder rather than Bipolar Disorder (American Psychiatric Association, 2013).

Biopsychosocial–Adlerian Conceptualization

From the IP perspective, this condition reflects purposeful behaviors, compelled by different emotions. Each child is striving to overcome burdens and to derive feelings of validation, pleasure, and significance. At times the burdens are common burdens that are inevitable in life. At other times, the burdens are common and arguably reasonable, yet the willingness to face them and to overcome them in a responsible way is non-existent; not because one can't, but because one has not been prepared during early childhood to meet those obligations. The simple fact is that mental health, which includes emotional regulation, requires the willingness to face burdens and to seek joys and validation in socially responsible ways. This is not necessarily the natural inclination for young children, and many children express great efforts to avoid feelings of burden, disappointments or of failures. For children diagnosed with DMDD, the remnants of childhood behaviors have persisted and are contributing to current difficulties.

Treatment Considerations

Individual Psychology is particularly well suited to treating DMDD. While this can be challenging to those who deal with the disruptive child, the introduction of encouragement and patience along with logical consequences is critical. When the disruption no longer serves a useful purpose and the child is taught alternative means for deriving a place in the family and eliciting feelings of validation, disruption will prove unnecessary. It is likely, and new research will hopefully show this, that it will not be enough to treat simply the individual child, but to address family dynamic patterns that promote the disruptive behaviors.

Case Example: Billy

Billy is 14 years old and was recently diagnosed with DMDD. Billy has an older sibling who is the model of good behavior; subsequently his parents are inclined to believe that Billy's behaviors reflect a physical disorder mediated by genetics. The fact that their first child is well behaved is evidence to them that their parenting approach is appropriate and effective. What they do not appreciate is the need for Billy to establish himself as different than his older sibling. Often when there are two children in the family, the second will be the polar opposite of the first sibling. If one is the perfect "good" child, the second may very well be the perfect "bad" child. While Billy has been emotional his entire life, he has been able to use his extreme reactions to manage his position in the family. Further, Billy often feels tremendous discouragement over his inability to do all the things that his "perfect" older sibling is able to do. This discouragement is expressed as anxiety, irritability, and tantrums, which often serve to perpetuate the feeling of victimization and allow some relief from the responsibility he perceives; responsibilities that are easily fulfilled by his sibling but that are perceived as overwhelming to him.

PERSISTENT DEPRESSIVE DISORDER (DYSTHYMIA)

Clinical Presentation

Persistent Depressive Disorder (Dysthymia) represents a more chronic (two years or more), less intense state of depression. Indeed, in this condition, the depressive retreat is the life style and not simply a retreat mediated by the life style. Those persistently depressed have embraced the position of "flying under the radar." Success in life requires effort, sacrifice, cooperation, and courage. In the absence of these qualities one is quickly overwhelmed by life demands, and that crisis is manifested in different symptoms. For some, the safe position in life is minimal commitments, expectations, and conflicts. Indeed, while one may dream of great accomplishments, the efforts to fulfill expectations or the skill required may be insufficient, and rather than risk the chance of painful outcomes (e.g., shame, embarrassment, guilt, anxiety, etc.), it is better to simply get through life without bringing unnecessary attention upon the self or allowing for burdensome expectations. If the objective is safety from social ridicule, embarrassment, or expectation, then a chronic detachment or retreat may be necessary and valuable.

DSM-5 Characterization

The major feature of Dysthymia is chronic depression in which the person feels depressed "more days than not," and this has persisted for "at least two years" (American Psychiatric Association, 2013, p. 168). During that period, the individual struggles with maintaining a healthy diet, and suffers poor sleep, lack of energy, poor self-esteem, poor concentration, and chronic feelings of hopelessness.

Biopsychosocial–Adlerian Conceptualization

For the individual with PDD, life style reflects a general surrender to the disappointments of life or a basic disengagement from the demands, expectations and disappointments of life. This surrender emerges as the result of expectations that are too unrealistic ("In order to have worth, I must be always social and popular, and I am not," or "I must not do anything to bring unwanted attention to myself"), or the outcome of being faced with challenges that one feels overwhelmed by ("I could never function at the level of expectations that others seem to meet so easily," "life is just too much").

Mosak and Maniacci (2006) discussed the dilemma of the dysthymic condition as the conflict associated with "chasing two rabbits at the same time." Rather than catching either rabbit, the individual stands in one spot trying to decide what to do. In the case of the PDD patient, one rabbit may be the desire to do the right thing, to meet obligations and be responsible, while the other rabbit is the desire to pursue self-bounded interests, which might exclude morality and obligation to others. Rather than choosing one course over another, the individual stands in the middle doing neither, while feeling some degree of sadness over the loss of both. Thus the individual feels conflicted and by remaining in the state of relative conflict does not have to sacrifice an ideal or put oneself in a position that one might prefer to avoid.

Treatment Considerations

Treatment of PDD will require the patient to make the decision to pursue one ambition over another. This will often require periods of sadness and disappointment as one option is abandoned, and perhaps the development of skills that had not previously been acquired. For Mrs. L. in the following case example, the challenge will be to accept herself as less than her own ideal as a mother, while also developing the skills to be the best mother that she, herself, can be. Thus, Mrs. L. will have to sacrifice her ideal, while at the same time develop parenting skills that she has thus far not mastered. Given the chronic nature of the persistent depressions, patients may benefit from engagement in a more thorough life-style assessment and analysis. For instance, by coming to a better understanding of how her life style emerged, given developmental experiences, Mrs. L. may be in a better position to abandon the idealized version of motherhood which she herself invented

---

Case Example: Mrs. L.

Mrs. L. is a middle-aged woman struggling with persistent depression whilst raising an adopted daughter, who is proving to be quite a handful. Her husband, who had years ago encouraged the adoption, is a nice enough fellow, but not highly involved in the parenting process. Mrs. L., who admitted to being a rather ambivalent mother, knows she needs to be more involved in her daughter's life. She has for years believed that to be a good mother she needs to be involved in parent–teacher associations, girl scouts, youth sports, etc. (i.e., "a good mother is actively involved in her child's life"). However, she has always found involvement in large groups and organizations unpleasant and anxiety provoking and she has tended to avoid them. We see the woman focused on two rabbits, to use Mosak and Maniacci's metaphor. On one hand, she feels a need to be a particular type of mother; on the other hand, a desire to be free of social burden and obligation. What she has done instead is neither, but continually castigates herself for 1) failing as a mother and 2) not being true to her basic tendencies and obligating herself to a task she would prefer to avoid. The net result then is a sad detachment from the obligations of life and personal dreams and ambitions.

The challenge for Mrs. L. is to alter her fictional goals or alter her commitment to the common sense goals. While not everyone can meet the expectations of the *perfect mother*, who is engaged in all aspects of a child's life, and this may not even be the best way to be in a child's life, it may be necessary for Mrs. L. to increase her involvement in her daughter's life. This may require learning new skills or learning to deal with anxiety that has interfered with her ability to be more involved. However, she should also accept that her style of parenting is not the common approach. What is important is that she encourages her daughter to face the challenges that life presents.

BIPOLAR DISORDER

Nusslock and Frank (2011) report that 40% to 50% of people with Major Depressive Disorder (MDD) display hypomanic symptoms (i.e. subthreshold bipolarity) throughout their life. Because these symptoms are not necessarily concurrent with an MDD, the DSM-IV-TR criteria for a mixed episode are not met. Furthermore, these individuals are reported to have more general impairment and are more likely to convert to a Bipolar I diagnosis over time. Additionally, they experience a more severe course of the illness, tend to have higher rates of comorbid conditions, and have more depressive episodes. Consequently, the DSM-IV-TR diagnostic criteria needed to change in order to better account for their condition.

One of the significant changes to *DSM-5* is the statement made by the addition of Disruptive Mood Dysregulation Disorder. This condition was added to account for the pattern of behaviors expressed by many young children who were often diagnosed with Bipolar Disorder in DSM-IV-TR criteria. However, because of the association with anxiety, irritability, anger, and depression, this disorder is classified as a depressive disorder.

BIPOLAR I DISORDER

Clinical Presentation

The classic bipolar patient is an individual who goes through periods of mania, typically followed by periods of hopeless depression. During the manic phase, the individual displays considerable enthusiasm that may be described as euphoric and perhaps joyful. During this manic period, the individual typically experiences hopefulness, confidence, and expansive self-esteem, often to the point of grandiosity. The individual often acts impulsively and fails to consider the consequences of chosen actions. Thinking is expansive and characterized by creativity and distractibility. The enthusiasm contributes to sleeplessness, pressured speech, and increased social participation and to extreme choices that would not be made during non-manic periods. Unfortunately for the manic individual, consequences are not carefully considered during periods of enthusiasm, and choices made during the manic period contribute to intensified periods of hopelessness and despair.

DSM-5 Characterization

The typical manic episode as described in the *DSM* includes a "period of abnormally and persistently elevated, expansive, or irritable mood and abnormally and persistently increased goal-directed activity or energy, lasting at least 1 week and present most of the day" (p. 124). The mania itself includes elevated self-esteem and grandiosity, decreased need for sleep, increased talkativeness, flight of ideas or sense of racing thoughts, distractibility, goal-directed behavior, and engagement in activities that have the potential for painful consequences. These symptoms reflect the emotional and behavioral strategies of individuals striving to overcome challenges and create feelings of worth and excitement. That these reactions often create immediate solutions to periods of discouragement reinforces their expression; that they lead to other problems makes them "dis"ordered.

Biopsychosocial–Adlerian Conceptualization

Bipolar depression, as the name implies, suggests two poles of the discouragement dimension. At one end the individual is highly discouraged over his or her inability to overcome the myriad challenges that life presents, and subsequently retreats into a state of hopelessness. This might include the inevitable challenges and burdens of life, but in the case of the bipolar-diagnosed individual, burdens that are very often the consequence of one's life-style and choices made while at the opposite end of that continuum. At that other end, the individual experiences enthusiasm. This "enthusiasm" includes high energy and obsessional focus on specific goals pursued without sufficient consideration of the challenges or potential consequences. Based on their research, Peven and Shulman (1983) identified that high achievement expectations from the self, and familial expectations, are common in Bipolar Disorder. Just as the word "discouragement" may appear to be a minimization of the notion of "depression," so too might the term "enthusiasm" fail to capture what many view as "mania." However, it is valuable to point out that if an individual with unbridled enthusiasm, high energy, and focused attention produces positive outcomes, this period of high activity is not often described, nor diagnosed, as mania. Just as the term "depression" is reserved for more severe forms of discouragement, "mania" appears reserved for those episodes of enthusiasm and focus that lead to negative consequence, which includes interpersonal conflicts and eventual states of despair and hopelessness. The difference may be in the quality of the conditions, or the quantity or intensity of the symptoms, the physiological sensitivities of the individual, or the difference might lie specifically in the descriptive frame of reference used by the individual offering explanation. But, to be sure, people do differ in temperament, cognitive complexity, and biological sensitivities, and those differences will impact the life-style orientation of the individual.

Peven and Shulman (1983) reported detailed clinical data on 17 cases of Bipolar Disorder. This invaluable study remains a significant contribution to the IP literature. They concluded that individuals with Bipolar: had low self esteem; blamed themselves for their failures (internal locus of control); were often firstborn or only children; viewed the world in extremes (all-or-nothing cognitive style); experienced the world through their emotions and were excitement seekers; and were high-achievement seekers—but resented family values that prioritize high achievement. In her historical review of the literature, Peven (1996) added that: "(a) bipolars have strong affiliative tendencies, (b) bipolars have a high achievement motive, (c) bipolars seem to have little faith in themselves and their ability to solve life's problems in a straightforward fashion, and (d) bipolars' attitudes and energies shift from one extreme to another" (p. 93).

The nature of development and the resulting life-style convictions, private logic, and learned tendencies are going to impact basic temperament in a way to render one more or less vulnerable to the conditions described as depression or mania. So, the question is, what might the life-style factors be that leave one more vulnerable to what becomes described as mania or bipolar depression? This is not a simple or straightforward explanation, as several factors combine, leading to the expression of the condition. What is common is an imperfect individual in a state of movement through time and circumstance, striving to find opportunities for validation and joy, and obligated to face the inevitable challenges of life. Often this is simple; however, given the unique differences between individuals and the complexity with which one can contrive challenges and solutions, this can become more complicated.

In some cases the individual's perception and interpretation of circumstance becomes so convoluted and bizarre that he or she violates common notions of rationality. In such cases, the movement and compensations may appear delusional or psychotic, perhaps characterizing Schizoaffective Disorder or Schizophrenia. It is important to note that unbiased rationality is not a natural human quality and all individuals are prone to some degree of irrationality, including delusional thinking. Where the line exists demarcating common forms of irrationality and deluded belief or psychotic thought from neurological pathology is difficult, if not impossible, to ascertain. In some cases, the structure of the neurological system may be so deranged that rational thinking is not possible. In many other cases, the neurological system functions as it should; yet the life style of the individual is such that bizarre thoughts and erratic behaviors occur. Many might argue that in the case of the Bipolar I patient the line has been crossed and we are dealing with a neurological condition. While this may be true, the IP position asserts that even then, the goal-driven movement and striving of the individual remains, albeit constrained by the unique physiology. In the old DSM model, this includes the Axis III component, which is part of the overall life style.

All individuals struggle with periodic feelings of inferiority. These feelings emerge when one perceives the self as less than one's own ideals. These ideals might include feats of great achievement or simply the desire to not feel inferior in the presence of others. These ideals constitute the fictional goals of the individual. One may indeed be quite superior, but personal standards may be so high as to leave that individual feeling recurrently inadequate to his or her own standards, thus facing periods of felt inferiority. For others, feelings of inadequacy may predominate, and their perceptions of outside events are nearly constant reminders of their perceived inadequacy. Adler would describe the first as prone to inferiority feelings, which are inevitable in life; the second he would describe as facing an inferiority "complex," an old term used to describe the chronicity of those perceptions and associated feelings (Adler, 1959). Important to this discussion, individuals with chronically low self-esteem and general feelings of inadequacy struggle with feelings of self-contempt, contempt being the feeling that compels one to psychologically reject an object or person whom that individual associates with some form of derision (Rasmussen, 2010). When that source is something external to the individual, contempt is often expressed with signs of active indifference, through gossip, or perhaps through expression of the well-known symbol of contempt—the extension of the middle finger directed at the source of those feelings. When the source of that contempt is perceived to be the self, the individual is likely to be plagued by feelings of anguish, the emotion that reflects the strong need to enact some change in life in order to find both relief and validation—the foundational goals in the movement and striving of the individual.

Anguished self-contempt is the feeling that is likely to compel suicidal gestures, attempts, and completions. Indeed, depression, in its purest form, is likely to prevent suicide as a result of the retreat and inactivity of a depressed state. When the depression is inadequate and the individual struggles with anguish, suicide becomes a considerable risk. That suicide is associated with the manic phase of bipolar depression more than the depressed phase yields support for this description (Schneidman, 1998). Prior to suicide, an individual will deal with that self-contempt by seeking outcomes that provide some sense of validation and some resolution of the distress and unhappiness that has come to define life (criterion 6). The self-contemptuous, anguished feelings create a high level of urgency, and it is this urgency that compels what we might call "hopeful enthusiasm," but because of the dangerous nature of the actions (criterion 7), the term "mania" may be more appropriate. While these conditions may render one vulnerable to a variety of conditions, the critical factor, from the IP perspective, is what the person does in the face of these compelling feelings. Some may turn to a focus on somatic symptoms that serve to provide some safeguarding relief from the felt burden to achieve. For others, those feelings compel extreme, often impulsive behaviors, enacted to provide relief from that anguish and to produce feelings of worth. During that manic period, the individual is often hopeful and optimistic and engages in activities that he or she associates with some positive outcome, including shopping sprees, sexual seduction or coercion, impulsive travel, or engagement in a risk-taking adventure. In some cases, it may include quitting a current job and pursuing a complete career change. Indeed, mania itself is often a positive experience for the individual (e.g., Gruber, 2011), thus representing the superiority/validation striving of the human condition. The pain emerges when the bills come due, the pregnancy test is positive, the romance leads to stalking, the travel leads to debt that cannot be repaid, and when other, necessary activities are ignored. In some cases, self-contempt may lead one into a situation in which self-satisfaction can only emerge through the compliance of others to his or her ideals and ambitions. For instance, the individual who needs others to accept his or her standards without complaint may have to enact extreme behaviors in order to prompt that compliance. In these cases, the "mania" may be expressed through irritability, anger, criticism, and other manipulations intended to affect the choices and actions of others. To be sure, many cases of Bipolar Disorder are diagnosed because of the recurrent pattern of anger and rage; however, the addition of DMDD may be more appropriate. In each of the circumstances, we see individuals striving to overcome the challenges faced and seeking validating outcomes, and acting without social interest.

These descriptions do not exclude the role of biology. Biology must be involved and temperament undoubtedly sets an affective foundation and vulnerability for the Bipolar Disorder to emerge. The necessary question is whether the biology controls the convictions and reactions to circumstantial events, or whether biology merely allows what the mind creates? Perhaps biology starts the cycle by way of mood-state influences created by a variety of factors, then the mind finds self-serving rationalizations of the mood and facilitates what becomes a manic episode. If either condition were the case, it would suggest a psychological influence as a necessary mediating factor.

It is noteworthy that while Bipolar Disorder is an Axis I condition, it is often discussed as if it were an Axis II condition. Indeed, the condition is often conceptualized as a chronic condition with which the individual will always contend. Most Axis I conditions are thought of as disorders that might come and go with changing circumstance and thus are not necessarily chronic. Chronic conditions are more typically those that exist on Axis II; however, this has been abandoned in *DSM-5*. Nonetheless, there may be personality or life-style characteristics that render one more prone to feelings and actions that will be labeled as "manic" or "bipolar." What then might be chronic are the personality attributes, which may represent a borderline style or paranoid style (see Rasmussen, 2005; Millon, 1999), two Axis II styles of personality demonstrated to be associated with manic tendencies. Thus, Bipolar Disorder is not the chronic condition: What is chronic are the personality or life-style attributes that leave one vulnerable to the characteristic symptoms of Bipolar Disorder.

Treatment Considerations

Currently, Bipolar I Disorder is most commonly treated using a variety of mood-stabilizing medications, including lithium (Lithobid), valproic acid (Depakene), divalproex (Depakote), carbamazepine (Tegretal), and lamotigine (Lamictal). In some cases treatment includes antipsychotics such as risperidone (Risperdal), olanzapine (Zyprexa), and aripiprazole (Abilify). While the mood stabilzers or antipsychotics are typically sufficient, in some cases an antidepressant is included, but with caution, as antidepressants may lead to a manic episode in some patients (Baldessarini et al., 2013). These treatments presuppose the importance of mood as the critical factor energizing the manic and withdrawing actions. However, the emotions are not simply random occurrences affecting the unassuming, but processes that emerge from a variety of mediating sources, including temperamental predispositions, fatigue and energy level, metabolic processes and cognitive processes. While medication can help to regulate mood state, they will not necessarily change life-style habits, self-contempt or alter convictions that set the foundation for mania or depression.

From the IP perspective a comprehensive life-style analysis is often valuable to help the individual understand the unarticulated conviction, or convictions, precipitating the mania. Mistaken beliefs about one's self and one's place among others will have to be altered such that the individual can find some satisfaction in his or her current position, while making consistent and managed efforts toward growth and development. It is particularly useful to help the individual to identify an emerging manic episode, which likely occurs in the face of discouragement and self-contempt, in order to pre-empt the episode. Unfortunately, because the mania often includes indulgence in what appears to be desirable activities, this can be difficult. However, if the therapist is able to help the patient find validation from activities that preclude mania, this can be achieved more readily.

Case Example: Martha

The case of Martha (Peven, 1996) illustrates several dynamics of the bipolar disorders identified in this section. Martha was a 30-year-old married Caucasian female who presented for individual psychotherapy shortly after being hospitalized due to a manic episode. She had a four-year-old son. Precipitating events included relocating to Chicago when her husband accepted the position of vice-president of a medium-sized corporation. Here is the Adlerian case conceptualization.

Family constellation

Martha is a firstborn child with one younger sister. Martha strived to be the "goodest" girl in the world in which she was a people-pleaser and sought to be seen positively by others. Her family contains a biological predisposition to mood and bipolar disorders. Her mother struggled with Bipolar and was inconsistent with psychiatric and psychological treatment.

Early recollections

Her early recollections contained the following themes: "I want life to be beautiful, everybody to be happy and have a good time, and life to go smoothly. When life becomes unpleasant I suffer and I don't know what to do" (Peven, 1996, p. 105). One of her memories included a swing recollection. This interpretation depicts the extremes and up-and-down mood swings of those who struggle with Bipolar. Peven (1996) identified that swing recollections are often presented by bipolar clients, and the thematic content of the memories are strong metaphors for bipolar life-style convictions.

Life-style convictions

Martha views herself as happy and successful when her moods were high, but unhappy and unable to cope in highly stressful and demanding situations. She views the world as beautiful but demanding, with the expectation that she please and impress others with her goodness. Her life strategy, especially during stressful situations, is to try her hardest to please others, but when situations do not go as she wishes, her emotional arousal increases and triggers her cyclic moods.

BIPOLAR II DISORDER

Clinical Presentation

The primary difference between Bipolar I and Bipolar II is the extent of the mania. In Bipolar I, the mania is more extreme, suggesting that the beliefs are more irrational, the feelings more intense and the actions more perilous. Also, Bipolar II excludes psychotic features, which would suggest Bipolar I. Some evidence suggests that those with Bipolar I Disorder possess cognitive qualities that render them more prone to extreme beliefs, expectations and subsequently to more extreme reactions. Likewise, evidence suggests that those diagnosed with Bipolar I are characterized by tremendous creativity that renders them vulnerable to extreme positions (Jamison, 1993). The majority of mental health professionals recognize that those diagnosed with Bipolar I Disorder struggle with unique neurobiological attributes that render them vulnerable to mania. However, even with these unique attributes, those with a Bipolar I diagnosis are still individuals moving through time and circumstance, striving to overcome challenge and to find some joy and validation in life. It may be that their creativity and insightfulness provide more opportunity to find potential validations, but also more reason for self-contempt and the creation of more dramatic crises.

Bipolar II is characterized by hypomania, which includes less extreme periods of manic pursuit. Several factors could contribute to the extreme reactions of the Bipolar I patient, while those diagnosed with Bipolar II are less extreme during periods of mania. It may be that the Bipolar II patients have greater awareness of the potential consequences of their actions, and this inhibits the mania. Perhaps their ambitions are not as lofty or self-contempt as extreme. Perhaps their life-task commitments and social interest prompts reflection on the implications of their reactions, which serves to limit the mania. The emotions of anticipated shame and guilt associated with interpersonal failure and disappointment, and the fear of consequence could all serve to retard manic energy. Whether or not such limits would occur is a function of different life-style convictions. For some, those life-style qualities may not have developed and thus would not impede a manic episode. For one with convictions related to a need to be significant and to avoid failure at all cost, there is little to prevent a manic episode and perhaps to inhibit a retreat into depression. For those whose convictions include the fostering of relationships, meeting responsibilities, and developing closeness with others (i.e., social interest), both mania and depression would be less probable, although periods of enthusiasm and disappointment are inevitable for everyone. To be sure, there are qualities that will contribute to the emergence of the mania and qualities that will limit a mania. For most individuals, there are life-style attitudes that limit mania to periods of enthusiasm, interspersed with periods of disappointment.

DSM-5 Characterization

For the diagnosis of Bipolar II, the patient presents with at least one episode of major depression and at least one hypomanic episode. Importantly for the differential diagnosis, for Bipolar II there has never been a full manic episode and the individual does not present with psychotic features. Indeed, for the Bipolar II patient, the hypomania itself may not significantly contribute to problems in daily functioning. The more significant disruption emerges from the depressed symptoms.

Biopsychosocial–Adlerian Conceptualization

Because this disorder is a variant of Bipolar I Disorder, see the Adlerian conceptualization of the Bipolar I Disorder above. As with the other bipolar disorders, there is an obvious biological vulnerability for this disorder. However, there is also likely to be psychosocial vulnerability to this disorder, which can be inferred from an investigation of the individual's life-style convictions.

Treatment Considerations

Treatment for Bipolar II is very similar to that of Bipolar I, although the clinician will be more attentive to the depressed features than to the mania. Psychotherapy is also very similar to that of Bipolar I, but again will focus more attention perhaps on depression, and also on concerns directed toward those factors precipitating the hypomania.

Case Example: Chase

Chase is a 27-year-old male who has struggled to maintain relationships and employment. He was recognized years ago as being very bright and creative, but also as being rather undisciplined and inattentive. He was able to get through high school relying on his basic abilities, but struggled in college and eventually dropped out and pursued a variety of jobs and activities. He has relied on his family to support him financially and this has created recurrent conflicts. At 27, his family has finally decided to stop supporting him. He was brought to therapy after an episode at a party in which he threatened to jump off a balcony at a ski lodge.

Chase comes from a well-established family in the Northeast and the expectations are that he attend college and then go to either law school or medical school. Chase's three siblings, who are all older, are all professionals. Chase is thought to be the creative one in the family. Chase feels a great need to achieve, but feels burdened by the responsibility (Peven & Shulman, 1983). He goes through periods in which he strives to commit to school or to a job, but he finds it difficult to "buckle down" and get the work done. His quitting school or work consistently follows some emotional crisis. For Chase, the belief that he must achieve in order to have worth is felt as anguish, and his response to that anguish typically includes an extreme reaction that serves to remove attention away from the need to achieve.

CYCLOTHYMIA

Clinical Presentation

Cyclothymia may be a condition very similar to Bipolar I and II, but may characterize individuals who for a variety of reasons simply do not regulate their emotions well, but who do not go through periods of either mania or hypomania. While random activity of the limbic system could create chaotic emotional reactions, we would argue that changes in emotional reactivity occur in reaction to circumstantial events viewed as either desirable, and thus validating, or undesirable, and thus compelling. Importantly, emotional expression is the first means of interspecies communication for human beings. Verbal communication develops years after the young child has learned to interact with others, and verbal understanding of the self likewise develops years after the child has begun to form convictions. Parents of young children often plead with them to begin using words in hopes of limiting the child's use of emotional communications. In addition, many parents take active efforts to teach children how to manage emotional reactions, which includes teaching the child to tolerate periods of disappointment and unhappiness. Other parents may be more inclined to react simply to decease the child's distress, thus rescuing that child from challenge and teaching the child that when unhappy, advertise that distress and elicit rescue. When a child reaches an age in which extreme emotional reaction is inappropriate and undesirable to others, that child may be called moody, hyperactive, spoiled, or obnoxious by nonprofessionals. A professional may call the condition Cyclothymia, or if the behavior includes acts of aggression, Disruptive Mood Dysregulation Disorder. What may be lacking in these individuals, beyond simply emotional control, is the willingness to think beyond the self and consider their impact on others and to take the initiative to meet life-task obligations.

An important concern is whether or not we should call the inability to regulate emotions well a disorder. Since this inability creates problems for the individual, it constitutes a disorder. If we use the term "disorder" to indicate that we have a medical condition that is beyond the individual's control (like cancer), we may be thinking too narrowly. However, to say that it is not simply a medical condition is not to say that it is the person's fault or it is an intentional condition. In many cases, it may be that the person has not developed skills that have significant functional importance. Business skills have functional importance, but we don't call those people without developed business skills disordered. The reason that we don't call these unskilled folks disordered is because we don't expect everyone to have well-developed business skills. We do, however, expect people to control their emotions. Similarly, we expect school children to sit down, pay attention, and do what the teacher tells them. If they don't, we are inclined to call them disordered (i.e., ADHD). For bipolar patients (and unipolar patients), their difficulty in regulating emotions has a significant impact on their ability to function day to day, thus their problem clearly constitutes a disorder, using the DSM concept of disorder. Medications have proven to be helpful. That medicines help does not validate the idea of a purely medical disorder. Medicines will typically affect people whether they are disordered or not. The greatest challenge to bipolar patients is to learn to regulate their emotions better, which most can do. Unfortunately, the usefulness of the negative emotions is reinforced on a lean, partial schedule of reinforcement and thus hard to extinguish. In addition, the beliefs and attitudes (i.e., schema) related to the manic behaviors are maintained via cognitive consistency processes. So, people can learn to regulate and control their emotions better, but it is often not very easy.

DSM-5 Characterization

The critical factor in Cyclothymia is "chronic, fluctuating mood disturbance involving numerous periods of hypomanic symptoms and periods of depressive symptoms that are distinct from one another" (American Psychiatric Association, 2013, p. 140). The hypomania and depression is not sufficient to warrant either a Bipolar I or II diagnosis, yet sufficient to disrupt one's ability to function efficiently.

Biopsychosocial–Adlerian Conceptualization

From an IP perspective, Cyclothymia represents a person who does not regulate emotions well and who is handicapped in life because of that disregulation. What is important is *why* the individual does not regulate emotions well. In many ways mood fluctuation is a normal pattern of life, and what we see in Cyclothymia may not be dramatically different than normal fluctuation; what may be critical is how the individual interprets the mood fluctuations and how the individual reacts. For those who have come to believe that any unpleasant feeling is indicative of a problem and that "normal" is happy, normal fluctuations may be quite distressing. Alternatively, if one has learned to counter unpleasant feelings with positive activity, or has come to accept mood fluctuation and the necessity of "riding out" occasional emotional storms, the disruption is less likely to reach "disordered" severity. Most important of course in the case of disordered status is that the fluctuation is sufficient to disrupt the individual's ability to function efficiently in common areas of life.

Considering the adaptive nature of emotion (Rasmussen, 2010), people experience the emotions they need to energize the behaviors necessary to overcome challenges and meet individual goals. In the case of Cyclothymia, the individual's reaction to normal mood changes may become safeguards against the burdens of life that the individual finds aversive. By focusing attention on the emotions rather than the solution to the problem prompting the emotion, the individual is able to sidestep life-task responsibilities. Further, because emotions serve the purpose of interpersonal communication (Rasmussen, 2010), the individual may rely on emotional expression to prompt compliance in another. Indeed, the child learns to impact its environment through the expression of emotion. Many children come to rely less on emotion and use more verbal communication; others continue to rely upon emotions, and subsequently emotional reactions become part of the life style of the individual.

Treatment Considerations

Medicines may be used to help the individual manage emotions, although many providers may prefer referring the individual to a therapist to help the individual develop greater emotional regulation. IP is particularly well suited to help these individuals. The challenge is to help the individual understand how he or she has come to rely on emotions to manage many life challenges and overcome obstacles to desired outcomes. Consideration of life-style patterns through life-style analysis can reveal these patterns and the individual can then be assisted in life-style reorientation. The emotional reorientation strategy presented by Rasmussen (2006) can prove beneficial with this population.

Case Example: Leonard

Leonard is 19 years old and has been diagnosed with Cyclothymia. He is the middle child of three, with an older brother and younger sister. His older brother is a very well-disciplined individual currently working with their father in the family real-estate business. Their sister is finishing high school and is very popular among her peers. She is currently head varsity cheerleader at the high school they all attended. Leonard is a first-semester sophomore at college and is struggling to get through. He is observed to go through periods of high functioning, only to then go through periods of increasing frustration and irritability, periods of substance abuse, often followed by periods of social and academic withdrawal. Were Leonard younger he may be diagnosed with Disruptive Mood Dysregulation Disorder; however, he does not express extreme episodes of temper. In the face of frustrations and discouragement, Leonard is more likely to express heightened anxiety and agitation, then retreat into either drug or other substance use or into a state of depression characterized by social withdrawal and isolation.

Concluding Note

The human experience is a process of adjusting and readjusting to the ever-changing circumstances of life. In this adjustment, the individual seeks opportunities for validating outcomes that signify a superior position and the overcoming of inferiority. How an individual goes about deriving a plus state and overcoming minus states depends on how the inherent characteristics of the individual are shaped by experience and the creative potential of the individual. Regardless of the developing life style, each individual is striving to create for him or herself a validating and rewarding existence, while also contending with the challenges that emerge as consequence of one's pursuit of validating outcomes and the result of common life events. Success in life requires that one accept the responsibility of sustaining the self, getting along with others and managing one's need for sexual and psychological intimacy. All of which must be done with concern for the broader community, now and into the future. To the extent that one is unable or unwilling to meet the tasks of life and act with social interest, emotional distress is nearly inevitable.

In the case of depression, we observe individuals who have in many ways given up hope that they will be able to reliably overcome or derive the validation they seek. Often, the expectations are unrealistic and the result is discouragement, which is often manifested in various forms of depression. In the case of mania, we observe individuals struggling to derive consistent and reliable forms of validation, who are inclined to extreme and impulsive actions implemented to overcome distress and burden and/or to derive validation. Unfortunately, the mania often leads to outcomes that leave the individual hopeless, discouraged and depressed.

Individual Psychology offers treatment that helps the individual to reorient the self to the realities of the world and the necessities of living as a member of a civil community. Everyone has the potential for growth. Individual Psychology maintains a position of faith, hope, and encouragement, and through the encouraging assistance of the IP therapist, the individual is able to find better ways of overcoming the challenges that life presents, and via greater commitment to life-task fulfillment and social interest derive more reliable opportunities for validation.

References

Adler, A. (1938/1998). *Social Interest: Adler's Key to the Meaning of Life*. (Initially published as *Social Interest: A Challenge to Mankind*). Boston, MA: Oneworld.

Adler, A. (1959). In H.L. Ansbacher & R.R. Ansbacher (Eds.), *The Individual Psychology of Alfred Adler*. New York, NY: Basic Books.

American Psychiatric Association (2004). *The Diagnostic and Statistical Manual of Mental Disorders, Fourth Edition (Text Revision)*. Washington, DC: American Psychiatric Publishing.

American Psychiatric Association (2013). *The Diagnostic and Statistical Manual of Mental Disorders, Fifth Edition*. Arlington, VA: American Psychiatric Publishing.

Arney, W.R. & Bergen, B.J. (1984). *Medicine and the Management of Living: Taming the Last Great Beast*. Chicago, IL: University of Chicago Press.

Baldessarini, R.J., Faedda, G.L., Offidani, E., Vázquez, G.H., Marangoni, C., Serra, G., & Tondo, L. (2013). Antidepressant-associated mood-switching and transition from unipolar major depression to bipolar disorder: A review. *Journal of Affective Disorders*, 148(1), pp. 129–135.

Busner, L. & Turgum, S.D. (2007). The Clinical Global Impression scale. *Psychiatry*, 4(7), pp. 28–37.

Cloninger, C.R., Svrakic, D.M., & Przybecl, T.R. (1993). A psychobiological model of temperament and character. *Archives of General Psychiatry*, 50(12), pp. 975–990.

Dreikurs, R. & Soltz, V. (1964). *Children: The Challenge*. New York, NY: Hawthorne Books, Inc.

First, M.B. (2011). DSM-5 proposals for mood disorders: A cost-benefit analysis. *Current Opinion in Psychiatry*, 24, pp. 1–9.

Ghaemi, S.N., Vohringer, P.A., & Vergne, D.E. (2012). The varieties of depressive experience: Diagnosing mood disorders. *Psychiatric Clinics of North America*, 35, pp. 73–86.

Grisel, J., Rasmussen, P.R., & Sperry, L. (2006). Anxiety and depression: Physiological and pharmacological considerations. *Journal of Individual Psychology*, 62(4), pp. 397–416.

Grohol, J. (2013). DSM-5 Changes: Personality Disorders (Axis II). *Psych Central*. Retrieved on November 27, 2013, from http://pro.psychcentral.com/2013/dsm-5-changes-personality-disorders-axis-ii/005008.html.

Gruber, J. (2011). Can feeling too good be bad? Positive Emotion Persistence (PEP) in Bipolar Disorder. *Current Directions in Psychology Science*, 20(4), pp. 217–221.

Jamison, K.R. (1993). *Touched With Fire: Manic-Depressive Illness and the Artistic Temperament.* New York, NY: Free Press.

Kocsis, J.H. (2010). Melancholia as a distinct mood disorder? Recommendations for DSM-5. *American Journal of Psychiatry*, 167, p. 1534.

Kroewke, K., Spitzer, P.L., & Williams, J.B. (2001). Patient health questionnaire (PHQ-9). *Journal of General Internal Medicine*, 16(9), pp. 606–613.

Lamb K., Pies R., & Zisook, S. (2010). The Bereavement Exclusion for the diagnosis of major depression: To be or not to be? *Psychiatry (Edgmont)*, 7, pp. 19–25.

Maniacci, M.P. (2002). The *DSM* and Individual Psychology: A general comparison. *Journal of Individual Psychology*, 58, pp. 356–362.

Millon, T. (1990). *Toward a New Personality: An Evolutionary Model.* New York, NY: John Wiley & Sons.

Millon, T. (1999). *Personality-Guided Therapy.* New York, NY: John Wiley & Sons.

Mosak, H.H. & Maniacci, M.P. (2006). Of cookie jars and candy bars: Dysthymia in light of Individual Psychology. *Journal of Individual Psychology*, 62(4), pp. 357–365.

Nusslock, R. & Frank. E. (2011). Subthreshold bipolarity: Diagnostic issues and challenges. *Bipolar Disorders*, 13, pp. 587–603.

Parker, G., Fink, M., Shorter, E., Taylor, M.A., Akiskal, H., Berrios, G., Bolwig, T., Brown, W.A., Carroll, B., Healy, D., Klein, D.F., Koukopoulos, A., Michels, R., Paris, J., Rubin, R.T., Spitzer, R., & Swartz, C. (2010). Issues for DSM-5: Whither melancholia? The case for its classification as a distinct mood disorder. *American Journal of Psychiatry*, 167, pp. 745–747.

Peven, D. (1996). Anxiety disorders I. In L. Sperry & J. Carlson (Eds.), *Psychopathology and Psychotherapy: From DSM-IV Diagnosis to Treatment.* Washington, DC: Accelerated Development, pp. 77–114.

Peven, D. & Shulman, B. (1983). The psychodynamics of bipolar affective disorder: Some empirical findings and their implication for cognitive therapy. *Individual Psychology*, 39, pp. 2–26.

Rasmussen, P.R. (2005). *Personality-Guided Cognitive-Behavioral Therapy.* Washington DC: American Psychological Association.

Rasmussen, P.R. (2006). Pareto's Principle applied to life and therapy. *Journal of Individual Psychology*, 62(4), pp. 455–459.

Rasmussen, P.R. (2010). *The Quest to Feel Good.* New York, NY: Routledge.

Rasmussen, P.R. (2012). The infantile philosophy, private logic, and the task of maturity. In P. Prina, K. John, A. Millar, & C. Shelly (Eds.), *UK Adlerian Yearbook 2012* (pp. 151–167). London: Adlerian Society UK & Institute for Individual Psychology.

Rasmussen, P.R. & Dover, G.J. (2006). The purposefulness of anxiety and depression: Adlerian and evolutionary views. *Journal of Individual Psychology*, 62(4), pp. 366–396.

Schneidman, E.S. (1998). *The Suicidal Mind.* Oxford: Oxford University Press.

Shear, M.K. (2009). Grief and depression: Treatment decisions for bereaved children and adults. *American Journal of Psychiatry*, 166(7), pp. 746–748.

Slavik, S. & Croake, J. (2001). Feelings and spirituality: A holistic perspective. *Journal of Individual Psychology*, 57(4), pp. 354–362.

Thomas, A. & Chess, S. (1977). *Temperament and Development*. New York: Brunner/Mazel.

Wilson, T.D. (2002). *Strangers to Ourselves: Discovering the Adaptive Unconscious*. Cambridge, MA: Belknap Harvard.

Zisook, S., Corruble, E., Duan, N., Iglewicz, A., Karam, E.G., Lanuoette, N., Lebowitz, B., Pies, R., Reynolds, C., Seay, K., Shear, M.K., Simon, N., Young, I.T. (2012). The bereavement exclusion and DSM-5. *Depression and Anxiety*, 29, pp. 425–443.

6   Trauma- and Stressor-Related Disorders

Bret A. Moore and John F. Newbauer

Our understanding of trauma- and stress-related disorders is increasing at a rapid pace. Research funding focused on cause, course, prevalence, and intervention for related disorders is at an all-time high. Consequently, there has been a shift within the fields of psychiatry and psychology. For example, the complexity of trauma- and stress-based psychological disruption resulting from stressful events has become more apparent. Seldom do symptoms fit neatly within previously held nosological systems. In fact, the variability of symptom manifestation between individuals is so great that symptoms once believed to belong to non-trauma-based disorders are acknowledged as not only possible, but likely to occur from exposure to traumatic and stressful experiences. This is most evident when considering the prevalence of anger, irritability, aggression, and depressive symptoms in military personnel who have served in the recent wars in Iraq and Afghanistan. Generally not associated with traditional anxiety- or fear-based networks, these symptoms are both pervasive and prominent (American Psychiatric Association, 2013). Fortunately, the American Psychiatric Association has, at a minimum, acknowledged the complexity of trauma- and stress-based disorders and the tremendous overlap of symptoms between different classes of disorders. This understanding resulted in a new category—Trauma- and Stressor-Related Disorders— being added to the most recent edition of the organization's flagship publication, *Diagnostic and Statistical Manual of Mental Disorders, Fifth Edition (DSM-5)*.

The primary defining feature of the *DSM-5* chapter on trauma- and stress-related disorders—in contrast to the *Diagnostic and Statistical Manual of Mental Disorders (Fourth Edition—Text Revision) (DSM-IV-TR)*—is the listing of exposure to a traumatic or stressful event as part of the diagnostic criteria. A secondary feature, which has already been discussed above, is the heterogeneity of symptoms and their manifestation. This chapter begins by describing the addition of the category of Trauma- and Stressor-Related Disorders to include the shifting of disorders into this new category from the *DSM-IV-TR*, and assignment of a novel disorder to this new classification system, which is based on an existing disorder (i.e., Reactive Attachment Disorder). Subsequently, the chapter presents the Adlerian conceptualization of trauma- and stress-related disorders. Finally, the diagnostic criteria, clinical presentations, Adlerian conceptualizations, and treatment considerations for each of the following trauma- and stress-related disorders are described and illustrated: Reactive Attachment Disorder; Disinhibited Social Engagement Disorder; Post-Traumatic Stress Disorder; Acute Stress Disorder; and Adjustment Disorders. Although two other diagnoses are included in the Trauma- and

Stressor-Related Disorders grouping (Other Specified Trauma- and Stressor-Related Disorders and Unspecified Trauma- and Stressor-Related Disorders), they will not be discussed in detail as they are relatively non-specific and overlap with the five disorders listed above.

Trauma- and Stressor-Related Disorders in *DSM-5*

DSM-IV-TR versus DSM-5 Definitions

The changes that resulted in creation of the Trauma- and Stressor-Related Disorders category of the *DSM-5* are arguably some of the more significant ones. In the *DSM-IV-TR* there was no Trauma- and Stressor-Related Disorders category. The disorders that currently make up this new grouping were scattered throughout several diagnostic categories in the *DSM-IV-TR*. For example, Post-Traumatic Stress Disorder (PTSD) and Acute Stress Disorder (ASD) belonged to the Anxiety Disorders category in the *DSM-IV-TR*. The reasons behind removing PTSD and ASD from the Anxiety Disorders section were twofold: 1) The new Anxiety Disorders grouping reflects disorders in which excessive fear and anxiety result in behavioral disturbances (American Psychiatric Association, 2013, p. 189), and 2) PTSD and ASD have components of excessive fear and anxiety, but are more complex and overlap significantly with other disorders such as depression and impulse control (American Psychiatric Association, 2013, p. 265). Reactive Attachment Disorder (RAD) originally belonged to the category "Other Disorders of Infancy, Childhood, or Adolescence" in the *DSM-IV-TR*. Its new home in the Trauma- and Stressor-Related Disorders grouping is based on the idea that the specific stressor of social neglect and its relation to behavioral disturbances aligns with the intent of the new DSM-5 category. The related Disinhibited Social Engagement Disorder (DSED) is merely an acknowledgement that although RAD and DSED share a common etiology, the expression of symptoms is different. RAD is considered to be primarily an internalizing disorder, whereas DSED presents with considerable externalizing behavior not unlike disruptive and attention disorders (American Psychiatric Association, 2013, p. 265). The remaining collection of adjustment disorders has been shifted to the Trauma- and Stressor-Related Disorders category, due to their shared etiology of some form of psychosocial stressor. The subtypes (i.e., depression, anxiety, conduct, mixed) remain the same between the *DSM-IV-TR* and *DSM-5*.

Adlerian Conceptualization of Trauma- and Stressor-Related Disorders

Adler and Trauma, Stress, and Dysfunction

Adler was not unfamiliar with trauma. One morning, when he was four years old, he awoke in bed to find his brother dead, lying next to him (Bottome, 1957). He also reported an early memory of having pneumonia:

> The doctor, who had suddenly been called in, told my father that there was no point in going to the trouble of looking after me as there was no hope of my living. At once a frightful terror came over me and a few days later when I was well I decided

definitely to become a doctor so that I should have a better defense against the danger of death and weapons to combat it superior to my doctor's.

(Bottome, 1957, pp. 32–33.)

As a young physician, Adler served in the Austrian army during the First World War, and after the war treated working-class people who were often exposed to trauma and hazardous experiences. He wrote a paper in 1918 describing the war neurosis, which was a heated topic of debate in Germany and Austria following the war, as it had a tremendous impact on national and private health insurers. Adler referred several times to trauma and its role in the development of neurosis. He referred to this as "shock," which appears to include less threatening situations than one would experience in war or acts of terror:

> No experience is a cause of success or failure. We do not suffer from the shock of our experiences—the so-called trauma—but we make out of them just what suits our purpose. ... Meanings are not determined by situations, but we determine ourselves by the meanings we give to situations.
>
> (Ansbacher & Ansbacher, 1956, p. 208.)

The new section on Trauma- and Stressor-Related Disorders in the *DSM-5* shows recognition of the multi-faceted and creative ways people respond to traumatic events.

Adler's focus in his writings was obviously on the creative work of the individual in defining his or her unique life style. The earlier in life these shocks occurred, the more likely they would be to play an important role in the development of the life style. "It is not the child's experiences which dictate his actions; it is the conclusions which he draws from his experiences" (Ansbacher & Ansbacher, 1956, p. 209).

For Adler, people make sense out of all that is experienced and integrate it into their style of life, or life style. The individual's life style is a biopsychosocial map of the world that can be referred to as a reminder of who we are, what other people are like and what the world is like. We are most active in this endeavor as children, when we enter the world not having knowledge of the language, customs, or usual ways of doing things. Think of a tourist in a foreign land in which she or he does not know the language and is not familiar with the customs. Most people report paying close attention to how others behave, watching for facial cues, and listening for some familiar sounds in the language that is spoken in order to fit in to this new world experience. We may feel more attentive and more focused on our environment, trying to figure out what is appropriate and inappropriate.

On the other hand, at home, in our own culture, and among people who speak our language, we may be much more relaxed and less attentive to every movement and facial cues because we are more at ease. In many ways, this is the task of the infant and toddler as they grow and develop, learn the language, learn how to react to those around them, learn the meaning of various facial and behavioral cues, feel the fear and joy and excitement in their parents' bodies while being held and fed, and put all these experiences together in a way that makes sense to them.

Out of all these experiences the child formulates a concept of self, others and the world and what she or he must do in order to attain perfection, superiority, or power. Adler sees this striving for perfection as innate:

We all wish to overcome difficulties. We all strive to reach a goal by the attainment of which we shall feel strong, superior, and complete. … But whatever name we give it, we shall always find in human beings this great line of activity—this struggle to rise from an inferior to a superior position, from defeat to victory, from below to above. It begins in earliest childhood and continues to the end of our lives.

(Ansbacher & Ansbacher, p. 104).

Experiencing trauma or severe neglect during childhood, when the life style is being actively developed, may have a different impact on the person than experiencing trauma at a later age, when it is usually considered that one's life style has been well established.

Extension to DSM Trauma- and Stressor-Related Disorders

Adler's view of trauma and stressors is not a simple one. Adler believed that *Gemeinschaftsgefühl*, also translated as "community feeling" or "social interest," was necessary for a "useful" style of life. "Most accurate of these translations is community feeling, which encompasses the individual's awareness of belonging in the human community and the cosmos of which it is a part, and an understanding of his or her responsibility for the way the life of the community is being shaped by his or her actions" (Griffith & Powers, 2007, p. 11). Community feeling is an innate potential that humans have, but it must be developed in the same way that language and speech is trained. For Adler, community feeling was regarded as an index to successful adaption. The more developed the community feeling, the more diminished the individual's feelings of inferiority, alienation, and isolation (Griffith & Powers, 2007).

It follows that the more developed the sense of community feeling is in an individual, the better able they might be to handle traumatic situations. While a traumatic event may be one more life challenge that a person has to face, some traumatic events are long-lasting and so intense that they cause a dramatic shift in how the person views self, others, and the world, and as a result, there follows a reduction of community feeling and an increase of feelings of alienation, inferiority, and isolation. While there are typical responses to trauma, individuals vary in how they will use the trauma and the symptoms that may develop as a result of the trauma. Adler spoke of a psychology of use, not a psychology of possession. According to this view, it is not what happens to a person or what they have experienced that matters as much as the use to which the individual puts these things. For this reason it is difficult to speak about one way that trauma affects a person, and is more correct to speak about how the traumatic event and the resulting symptoms and behavior patterns will be used creatively by the person in pursuit of his or her life-style goals.

Ilan Strauch asks, "Put another way, is a traumatic reaction a lifestyle response to an extreme situation, or is it something that leads to a change in the person's phenomenological field and that effectively could change the lenses through which the individual perceives life?" (Strauch, 2001). Experiences of trauma that include actual or threatened death or serious injury to one's physical integrity, as well as situations of both acute and chronic neglect or threat to one's psychological integrity, result in major shifts in how the person views self, others, and the world and also their ability to reach their fictional goal of superiority and a satisfactory degree of community feeling. Feelings of positive regard for self, a sense of competence, and a sense of belonging to the human community are often severely impaired by exposure to traumatic experiences, especially when they are so overwhelming that they destroy one's sense of competence and feeling of belonging to the community of humankind, or shatter one's view of others or the world.

Having one's sense of self, others, or the world shattered, a variety of symptoms can be developed to safeguard one's now threatened self-esteem. Symptoms may develop ranging from anxiety and depression to anger and despair, to major shifts in one's life style, and even psychotic episodes. It seems very appropriate to organize these disorders into a category of their own in the *DSM-5* since they all represent the vast array of symptoms and disorders that may result from a disruption of the development of social interest, whether that be from lack of appropriate encouragement of social interest in the first formative years of life or from those who have been faced with experiences that have shattered their sense of personal identity, worth, and belonging (O'Connell & Hooker, 1996).

REACTIVE ATTACHMENT DISORDER

Clinical Presentation

The most prominent and obvious behavioral presentation of children with RAD is the avoidance of and withdrawal from caregivers, other adults, and peers. When distressed, RAD children tend to reject attempts at comforting and soothing. In fact, these children tend to be calmer when left alone and are often seen engaging in self-calming/soothing behavior. Young children with RAD smile infrequently, do not reciprocate when being hugged or picked up, and generally are not interested in playing typical childhood games such as hide-and-seek. Older children avoid social activities and become isolative, and when frustrated, may engage in aggressive behavior toward adults and peers.

The affective style of children with RAD tends to be of reduced positive affect. As noted above, they generally do not smile. Their affect can vacillate between sadness, anxiousness, irritability, and general distress. Therefore, as part of a comprehensive psychiatric evaluation, it is important to rule out mood, anxiety, and psychotic disorders.

Interpersonally, RAD children tend to have few friends. This is not only by choice, but a consequence of projecting a disinterested attitude toward social interaction and emotional reciprocation. This is true for peers and adults. In fact, with regard to the latter, child and caregiver can get caught in a negative loop of interpreting disinterest and avoidance in each other's behavior, leading to more disinterest and avoidance.

DSM-5 Characterization

Children with Reactive Attachment Disorder (RAD) exhibit an ongoing pattern of emotional distance and general inhibition with regard to interactions with adult caregivers. Specifically, the child is resistant to seeking out comfort and support from caregivers when distressed, as well to as responding adequately when comfort and support is provided. This inhibition and lack of emotional responsiveness extends to others within the child's environment, both within the extended caregiver structure (e.g., teachers, relatives) and peers. It is believed that children with RAD are able to form appropriate social attachments. However, due to significant social neglect and lack of opportunities for receiving developmentally appropriate comfort, affection, and stimulation from caregivers, this capacity is not fully realized. The diagnosis of RAD is not made unless the child is at least nine months of age and the symptoms have been present prior to five years of age (American Psychiatric Association, 2013, p. 266).

Biopsychosocial–Adlerian Conceptualization

Adler frequently emphasized the importance of the mutually beneficial relationship between mother and infant and later the child and the family. The encouragement of parents and teachers in the child's development of the life style was of primary importance in the development of social interest (Ansbacher & Ansbacher, 1956). In writing about "demoralized (neglected) children," Adler emphasized how children integrate experiences into their life styles in a unique way. Feeling put down and humiliated by parents who are often overwhelmed with the challenges of life, and further put down by their teachers and society at large, they develop a view of themselves, others, and the world in general based on their inadequate means and childish interpretations. These conclusions are often indecisive, pessimistic, and lacking in hope and self-confidence. Gaining a courageous attitude that is necessary to fulfill the life tasks (occupation, friendship, and love) afterwards requires much time and energy (Adler, 1925/1973). Without encouragement as a child, the individual develops few resources that are necessary for attachment to a caregiver, for dealing with stressors that are inevitable in life, and instead develops attitudes toward isolation and withdrawal rather than social interest.

Withdrawal and avoidance seem to be logical responses to an early childhood experience of being neglected and ignored. The *sine qua non* condition for Reactive Attachment Disorder is assumed to be the failure to form the normal attachment to the primary caregiver, which may be related to abuse, extreme neglect, abrupt separation from caregivers between the ages of six months and three years, or a repeated lack of responsiveness on the part of the caregiver(s) to the child's attempts to interact. Believing and feeling that one does not belong or is not good enough or accepted leads to a pattern of behavior based on these feelings and beliefs.

> Hostile or pampering family circumstances lead a child not to feel confident; not to himself, herself, or others; and to lack feelings of belonging. Once the child feels that she or he does not belong, behaviors are then directed toward self-protection rather than contribution to the community and the vicious cycle continues. … The more the person does not feel belonging, the more disturbing her or his behavior is likely to be, and in turn, this leads to even less reliable support from others.
>
> (Ferguson, 2010a, p. 4.)

There may also be some constitutional factors that contribute to this pattern of behavior, but so far nothing has been determined, except that attachment and bonding between the infant and the earliest caretakers was not established and further training of the child's social interest was not continued.

Treatment Considerations

Treatment of RAD consists primarily of psychosocial interventions. First and foremost, it is important that the child be in a secure, safe, and supportive environment. If the child is in a neglectful environment, referral to appropriate state, tribal, or federal agencies should be made. It is also critical that the professional work toward the goal of helping the child develop a secure attachment with a caregiver, whether it is with a biological or foster parent, relative, or other parental surrogate. This can be accomplished directly with the caregiver through parenting classes or individual psychotherapy.

The presence of empirically based studies on psychotherapy with RAD children is limited. However, there is some evidence supporting both play therapy and family therapy individually (O'Connor, Spagnola, & Byrne, 2012) as well as combining the two (Weir, 2011). Even more limited is research on the use of medications in the treatment of RAD. In fact, when medication is used it is typically for the purpose of treating co-occurring disorders (e.g., depression) or individual RAD symptoms (e.g., aggression).

Case Example: Thomas

Thomas was brought for evaluation when he was nine years old. He was adopted by an older couple, along with his 11-year-old brother. Both children showed signs of disturbance in attachment. Thomas was the son of Romanian parents and it appeared from the history that he and his brother had been removed from their parents' care because of repeated incarceration, drunkenness, and drug abuse by their parents. Thomas was three years old at the time of the placement in the orphanage and was adopted at age six.

At the time of his evaluation, he had lived with his new foster parents for approximately a year. His new parents brought him in because of his isolative behavior but also because of his aggressive and violent outbursts. They were very well-educated people and were aware that he may have problems with attachment, but did not expect those problems to be as intense as they were. They made a conscious decision to adopt both children in order to keep them together as they felt that things would only get worse for them if they were separated from each other. The brothers did seem to feel connected to each other. The older brother also had attachment issues, but appeared to meet criteria for Disinhibited Social Engagement Disorder (DSED) rather than RAD.

Due to his escalating violence in the home and neighborhood, the older brother was removed from the home shortly after Thomas came in for evaluation, and placed in a residential treatment center by the court. Emphasis in treatment for Thomas and his family was on parenting and encouraging the parents to remain engaged with the children and helping them develop a consistent and encouraging style of relating to them. This was a challenge as both parents had strong ideas about what should be done and were reared in autocratic families, but eventually through conjoint couple counseling and conjoint family therapy, they were able to work together in a healthier style.

Thomas seemed almost unable to control his emotional outbursts at times when he felt threatened. While there was a long history of learning that these kinds of outbursts would keep people away from him and allow him to be by himself, it was important to help him become more tolerant of other people in his environment, even when he was upset. Initial intervention with the family helped to teach them to allow Thomas to go to his room or to go outside in the yard when he was upset, rather than to continue to force him into a situation that was uncomfortable to him. This was a difficult task as they wanted to comfort him and control him, not realizing that their efforts to comfort him were perceived by him as threatening. The parents were then encouraged to seek him out after a short period of time and stay near him but at a comfortable distance, as part of the goal of his isolating behavior was to stay safe from others.

A feeling of mutual respect and trust as well as an understanding of Thomas' view of self, others, and the world was developed by asking Thomas to tell his story to the therapist, learning about where he was from, what he remembered of his time in the orphanage and what he remembered about his parents (which wasn't much). Through friendly and respectful discussion of his life and the ways in which he handled his frustrations growing up, we were able to develop a mutual understanding of how his new situation was viewed by him as temporary and not permanent, and his intention to take advantage of every possible thing or person that he met in order to get what he wanted. This was a very logical (private logic) point of view, although lacking greatly in social interest of any kind at this point. As Ferguson writes, "'Private logic' is the way we unconsciously or implicitly think about events that are counter to social interest" (Ferguson, 2010b).

Eventually, the therapist was able to teach some relaxation skills to Thomas and his parents and help Thomas learn to control his rage-like emotions through deep-muscle relaxation and deep-breathing techniques, but only after a beginning sense of trust was developed with the therapist. Moving from deep-muscle relaxation to deep breathing when upset helped him respond to challenging situations in a more appropriate way.

Once Thomas was able to tolerate frustration a bit more, some work on his private logic began. He grew up believing that no one cared about him, that no one would meet his needs. He had good reason to believe these things, based on his first few years of life. The therapist challenged these beliefs and pointed out that his new parents cared for him, met his needs and responded when he asked for something. The therapist encouraged the parents to do things with Thomas and his older sibling, once he had returned home, that were fun, and encouraged them also to do work around the house together, rather than assigning chores for the children to do on their own. In this way they were modeling the fact that they were a unit, a family, and that they all had responsibilities to each other.

Thomas also had the belief that if he acted out, people would leave him alone. The parents were challenged to give him some space but also to not let him stay alone, as the goal was to develop a sense of belonging. Through positive parenting, lots of encouragement by his parents and challenges to his private logic, Thomas was able to develop closer ties with his new family.

As Thomas slowly developed a sense of belonging in his new family, he also slowly began to consider others' needs. He began to offer to help around the home and even at school without any apparent design on his part to obtain anything for himself. He continues to be challenged by his sense of being alone in the world, but with the help of his parents is making strides in feeling a sense of belonging and in turn of contributing to others.

DISINHIBITED SOCIAL ENGAGEMENT DISORDER

Clinical Presentation

In essence, although there are several differences, DSED can be considered as the polar opposite of the inhibited nature of Reactive Attachment Disorder (RAD). In fact, DSED was considered a subtype of RAD in the *DSM-IV-TR*. The most prominent and obvious behavioral presentation of children with DSED is their indiscriminate interaction with strangers. For these children, there is little anxiety or distrust of unfamiliar people, which often manifests as culturally inappropriate physical contact and displays of affection. The young child's behavior may be dismissed as "attention seeking" by caregivers. The older child may be seen as disingenuous and "fake" with regard to displays of emotion. This is a result of the excessive and inappropriate nature of the interaction. DSED is often confused with Attention-Deficit/Hyperactivity Disorder since the disorder is primarily one that consists of externalizing behaviors. Behavior may be seen as impulsive and disruptive (American Psychiatric Association, 2013, p. 269).

The affective style of children with DSED tends to be of excessive affect. There is a general happiness around strangers, which may or may not be the same case for caregivers. Children with DSED may be seen by strangers as clingy. They may also be seen as emotionally sensitive and anxious if strangers are viewed as rejecting of their affection.

Interpersonally, DSED children tend to be viewed as having poor interpersonal boundaries. This often makes strangers uncomfortable and even suspicious of the child's behavior. The behavior is also distressing for the caregiver, as the child is generally unaware of the proximity of the caregiver, which raises concern about possible assault and/or abduction by a stranger.

DSM-5 Characterization

Children with Disinhibited Social Engagement Disorder (DSED) exhibit a pattern of behavior in which they seek out attention and contact with unfamiliar adults. In these children there is a noticeable and concerning familiarity with strangers, which is evidenced by inappropriate verbal and physical interactions. In some cases, the child with DSED will wander off with strangers, leading to extreme distress for the caregiver, but not the child. Similarly, the child may neglect to maintain awareness of his or her location to the caregiver in unfamiliar settings. The etiology of DSED is the same as RAD. It is believed that significant social neglect, repeated changes in the primary caregiver and limited opportunities to form developmentally appropriate connections with caregivers are at the root of the problem. DSED is not diagnosed if the child is less than nine months of age (American Psychiatric Association, 2013, p. 268).

Biopsychosocial–Adlerian Conceptualization

Unlike the child with RAD, there is some indication in research that the child with DSED may have some constitutional or biological basis for her or his behavior. In their 2010 paper for the American Psychiatric Association, Charles Zeanah and Mary Gleason (2010) indicated that indiscriminate social behavior similar to that found in children with DSED is also present in children diagnosed with Williams Syndrome and with Fetal Alcohol Syndrome, even in cases where there is no known history of pathogenic care. At this time, however, there is no known biological treatment of this particular aspect of the disorder.

While the child with Reactive Attachment Disorder developed isolative symptoms as a way of protecting herself or himself, the child with Disinhibited Social Engagement Disorder (DSED) developed an alternative approach. This may represent a different strategy, in which the person seeks engagement with others as a means of protection, or perhaps as a way of the child using his or her apparently friendly and placating demeanor to win approval of anyone who may appear to be a potential threat or protector (perhaps not able to differentiate one from the other). While desirous of protection from others, they have little concern about others' well-being. Adler speaks about movement as one aspect of the developing person's life style: "Wild, unbridled, stubborn, stealing, quarrelsome children obviously have a greater degree of activity than shy, reticent, frightened children, and those who are dependent on others" (Ansbacher & Ansbacher, 1956, p. 165). This sounds almost as if he is describing the child with DSED. Given the large number of orphans roaming the streets of Vienna after World War I, it is quite likely that there were many with DSED and RAD. Millon (1990) also discusses the importance of movement in the developing personality, and the different styles that are developed by those who are passive as compared to those who are more active.

A child may respond to the pathogenic early family environment, in which there is little encouragement and few displays of social interest, with a more active approach at finding security. Lacking trust and having learned that parents or early caretakers cannot be depended upon to take care of their needs or protect them, they seek out others who may protect them, with a friendly style and an engaging manner. However, when one spends much time observing them, one finds out that they have little or no remorse, guilt, or regret when they hurt or disappoint others, because of their lack of social interest, which was not nurtured during the early years of their lives. Lacking experience and training in empathy and belonging, they tend to treat others as things rather than as human beings deserving of respect.

Treatment Considerations

Similar to RAD, treatment of DSED consists primarily of psychosocial interventions. Establishing a sense of safety and security between the child and his or her primary caregiver is paramount. It is believed that once trust and consistency is formed, there will be less need on the child's part to seek out comfort from strangers. In addition to psychoeducation related to parenting and developmentally appropriate attachment, caregivers should be taught how to help their child set interpersonal boundaries. Supportive and solution-focused counseling can assist with the stress and negative emotions associated with caring for a child with DSED.

Not unlike RAD, the presence of empirically based studies on psychotherapy with DSED children is limited. In fact, there are no studies available on DSED as a new entity, as DSED has been considered as a subtype of RAD. The available evidence supports the use of play therapy and family therapy as primary psychotherapeutic interventions (O'Connor, Spagnola, & Byrne, 2012). There is no significant evidence available supporting pharmacotherapy as an effective treatment modality.

Case Example: Mike

Mike was 12 years old when he was arrested and brought to the juvenile center. His parents were very concerned about his aggressive behavior that was exhibited not only on the playground and in the neighborhood but also in the home and at school. He was labeled by the schools as a special-education child and had an Individualized Education Plan (IEP) for his aggressive behavior and also for his roaming the halls and apparent ADHD. Mike was adopted at six years of age. His pre-adoption history included placements in ten foster home, five of them during the first three years of his life. Most of the moves were because of aggressive behavior toward foster parents or toward foster siblings living in the home with him, although one of the earliest moves was because the foster family was deemed unfit for caring for the children placed with them after one of the teenagers in the house was involved in sexual abuse of some of the other foster children in the home. There was no evidence that Mike had been sexually abused.

Mike's parents were very desirous of being good parents but were going about it in different ways. Father was very authoritarian with lots of rules and limits, and Mother was more pampering and made excuses for Mike's behaviors. Two years after Mike was adopted, they had a daughter of their own. Mike was often cruel to his younger sister and it created a state of great tension in the house as the parents finally came to the realization that he did not seem to care about how much he hurt her, them, or anyone else. As a result, they were not at all hesitant to have Mike stay at the detention center for several weeks while his case was processed and a treatment plan worked out.

Mike's behavior in detention was appropriate but also showed little concern for the welfare of others. His behavior would vary from being very attentive to others and apparently seeking their friendship and attention, followed by periods of antagonizing those same persons, both residents and staff. Most of the staff felt he was manipulative, and shortly realized that he was often the person who started disturbances on the unit.

The parents were involved in a parenting group while Mike was in detention, and were confronted by the other group members about their conflicting roles. They learned how to work together as a team and how to use a positive approach to discipline with firm limits but lots of encouragement along the way. The group also challenged them about how they treated their daughter compared to how they treated Mike.

Counselors worked with Mike in terms of his private logic and feelings of isolation and betrayal by others. Mike was released after two months in detention and he and his family were referred to a home-based family therapist. Individual and family work was continued by the same therapist on an as-needed basis that often included several sessions each week. The home-based therapist was able to work with Mike and his family when they needed assistance, sometimes at their scheduled sessions but also at times that were not scheduled, such as late at night when problems erupted without warning. She was also able to meet with Mike's teacher and school IEP team and provide insights for working with Mike in school.

Eventually, with his therapist's encouragement, Mike became involved in group therapy. There he was often confronted about his manipulative behavior and acting out in school. The group helped challenge his belief that he had no one to count on, and much to the surprise of his parents, he began to form what seemed to be a mutual friendship with another boy in his class.

With the continued encouragement and friendly confrontations of his home-based family therapist, changes in his parents' behavior, and his work in group, Mike began to see that others did care for him. The group was very helpful for Mike to see that he did belong and had a lot in common with other people. His behavioral outbursts decreased and his relationship with his family improved, as did his relationship with peers and teachers.

POST-TRAUMATIC STRESS DISORDER

Clinical Presentation

Behaviorally, individuals suffering from PTSD are seen as avoidant, particularly with people who have some connection to the traumatic event. An example is a combat veteran who avoids local veterans' groups, as the telling of "war stories" causes significant distress for the individual. Individuals with PTSD are often hypervigilant (e.g., knowing where the nearest exit is located, acutely aware of strangers in the area). They are prone to angry outbursts, which can manifest either verbally, physically, or both. They may be easily startled when surprised, have difficulty initiating and maintaining sleep, and feel uncomfortable in social situations, which may lead to panic attacks and social isolation.

The affective style of many individuals with PTSD is one of dysphoric or depressed mood. There is a presence of excessive feelings of shame and guilt in some, as well as a noticeable and disturbing inability to be happy and enjoy life. Anger and aggression is a prominent feature of PTSD (Jakupcak et al., 2007). It is not unusual for an individual with PTSD to become enraged over seemingly benign events or with little provocation. A sense of emotional detachment and withdrawal from loved ones is also a defining feature of PTSD. An absence of loving feelings for a spouse, child, or other loved one is not uncommon. Understandably, this causes tremendous concern and disruption within intimate relationships, leading to increased guilt, shame, anger, and depression for the individual.

Interpersonally, as mentioned above, individuals suffering from PTSD are physically and emotionally detached from loved ones. Interpersonal conflict is common, and divorce and separation are often consequences of the relational discord. Related to the intentional avoidance of reminders of the traumatic event, the individual may have a reduced social network through avoiding people associated with event and/or not making new friends due to withdrawal from social activities.

DSM-5 Characterization

Resulting from political and social pressures after the Vietnam War (Keane, 2009), the formal diagnosis of Post-Traumatic Stress Disorder (PTSD) was included in the 1980 release of the *DSM-III* (American Psychiatric Association, 1980). Over the decades, there have been minimal but significant changes to the diagnostic criteria for the disorder. Arguably the latest change to the nomenclature for PTSD is the most extensive in its history. Ironically, these changes are significantly due in part to lessons gleaned from war (Moore, 2013).

PTSD has been moved from the Anxiety Disorders category of the *DSM-IV-TR* to the Trauma- and Stressor-Related Disorders category in the *DSM-5*. Major changes reflected in the *DSM-5* iteration are: 1) acknowledgement that trauma-related symptoms can develop vicariously (e.g., listening to repeated accounts of disturbing material); 2) responding to the traumatic event with a sense of "fear, helplessness, or horror"; 3) explicit mention of sexual violence as a potential precipitant; and 4) expansion and recategorization of the dysphoric/mood symptoms commonly associated with the disorder.

In general, the latest version of the diagnostic criteria for PTSD continues to focus on direct or indirect exposure to some aversive event that could result in death or serious injury. Symptoms can present in one of four categories: re-experiencing, avoidance, negative mood, and arousal. Re-experiencing symptoms include nightmares, intrusive thoughts, flashbacks, and general psychological and physiological distress when confronted with thoughts or experiences associated with the original traumatic event. Avoidance symptoms include attempts at avoiding external and internal reminders of the event. The negative-mood-symptom cluster includes inability to recall portions of the trauma, distorted cognitions, loss of interest in activities, emotional detachment, unremitting negative emotions, and the inability to experience happiness or joy. The arousal-symptom cluster includes irritable behavior and angry outbursts, recklessness, excessive vigilance, and problems with attention and concentration. The heightened arousal also includes an exaggerated startle response and sleep problems. There are criteria for children six years of age or younger suspected of having PTSD that are similar to the adult criteria, but some unique criteria are included (e.g., learning that a parent or caregiver was exposed to a traumatic event) (American Psychiatric Association, 2013, p. 272–273).

Biopsychosocial–Adlerian Conceptualization

Prolonged exposure to stressors, especially intense stressors such as one experiences in combat, sexual assault, or life threatening events has an effect on the brainstem/hypothalamus, the limbic system, and the neocortex. The most basic areas of life are controlled by these systems, including sleeping and activity, monitoring danger in the outside world, performance of routine tasks, feeding, reproductive cycles, and the most elemental forms of care of offspring (Van der Kolk, 1996, p. 215). The interconnections among these systems is extremely complicated and it's not possible to separate them or attribute various disruptions that occur to only one of the systems as they operate in cooperation with each other. A variety of approaches may be necessary to address the disruption that occurs in severe trauma, especially severe trauma that is experienced over an extended period of time. Medication may be needed to provide some regulation of systems that are essentially malfunctioning. Because of the changes in the adaptation system of the individual, medication is sometimes necessary (Freeman, Lundt, Swanton, & Moore, 2009).

> There are probably some events that are so horrific that they would likely be experienced as traumatic by the strongest and mentally healthiest of individuals. There is also likely an interaction between life-style and the severity of the event. PTSD might represent an emerging awareness that there is a problem (or threat) with no easy solution. PTSD, therefore, could be viewed as resulting from an individual (with varying psychological vulnerabilities) experiencing a traumatic event (of varying intensity) which has the end result of a fixation on the traumatic experience and discouragement (or further discouragement) in engaging productively with the tasks of life.
>
> (Hjertaas, 2013, p. 188.)

While the severe neglect and failure to nurture any sense of social interest was the focus on the first two forms of trauma-related disorders (RAD and DSED), the experience of extreme trauma is the focus of PTSD and Acute Stress Disorder (ASD). The extreme trauma could happen in childhood or it could happen after one is an adult. Trauma can be the result of very personal and up-close actions such as rape, incest, armed robbery, killing, or beatings. It can also be non-personal such as occurs in earthquakes, tornados, hurricanes, and bombings. No matter the proximity of the violence, the individual perceives the situation and attributes meaning to the event (apperception). In addition, they respond to it. In some way, the person tries to make sense of the situation in terms of their understanding of self, others, and life in general, and their particular fictional goals. Sometimes this is not possible, and the result is a shattered sense of self, others, life, and what one's fictional goals had been.

PTSD involves a disturbance in four different processes: re-experiencing, avoidance, negative mood, and arousal. Adlerians look at these in terms of the role they play or purpose they serve for the individual. Re-experiencing in the form of intrusive thoughts, flashbacks, nightmares, and other reminders of the horrific experience seem to serve the purpose of reminding the person that life is dangerous and that they are vulnerable and inadequate to meet the threat (O'Connell & Hooker, 1996). They may also be a way of reminding the person to stay alert, to stay on guard, and to be on constant look-out for potential harm.

Avoidance is an attempt to stay away from anything that reminds them of the shame, guilt, and sense of helplessness they experienced during the event or around the time of the event. Avoidance protects the individual from having to deal with feelings that are extremely uncomfortable. As the result of avoidance, however, the person does not readily engage in discussions about the event and this makes treatment more difficult, as it is necessary to discuss certain aspects of the event if one is to come to a different understanding of it.

Negative mood symptoms of inability to recall portions of the trauma, distorted cognitions, loss of interest in activities, emotional detachment, unremitting negative emotions, and the inability to experience happiness or joy reflect the extreme discouragement experienced by the individual. Private logic begins to take over, as evidenced by the distorted cognitions and the other symptoms in this cluster that are the result of that private logic and discouragement.

The arousal-symptom cluster of irritable behavior and angry outbursts, recklessness, excessive vigilance, and problems with attention and concentration reflect not only the biological component of extreme trauma but also the continuing interaction of private logic and discouragement, and the feeling of alienation and the increased self-boundedness of the individual as a result of the shattering of one's sense of belonging, which may be the result of exaggerated guilt feelings or shame. A continued state of arousal represents the individual's striving to be alert, to be on guard against further trauma.

The symptoms of PTSD are so intense that the individual feels unable to meet or unworthy of fulfilling the tasks of life: the tasks of work, social relationships, and love. Hence, in more severe cases all of these tasks are disrupted, while in less severe cases or cases in which there is some active recovery going on, only one or two of the tasks of life are disrupted. Of the tasks of life, the love task remains the most difficult and challenging and most likely to be disrupted.

The experience of severe trauma usually affects five areas or themes of private logic: safety, trust, power, self-esteem, and intimacy. These five areas are related to the individual's perception of self as well as others in each area. For example, safety is related to others by constantly questioning if others are safe to be around or if this is a safe place. Safety is related to the concept of self by frequently questioning if I am capable of determining if a situation is safe or if it is safe to be with a particular person or in a particular place. The private logic of the person has become so self-focused as a result of the alienation from others and the diminishing social interest, that every major aspect of life is questioned.

An enormous amount of encouragement is needed to restore the shattered sense of self and any possibility of restoring social interest and community feeling. The power of fear in the situation is not to be minimized, and the private logic that results continues to reinforce the person's sense of inadequacy, guilt, shame, and humiliation.

Treatment Considerations

Treatment of PTSD consists of psychotherapy, pharmacotherapy, or an integration of the two. Regarding psychotherapeutic approaches, there are several treatments, particularly within the military and veteran populations, considered to be "first line," which are all cognitively and behaviorally focused. These included Prolonged Exposure (PE), Cognitive Processing Therapy (CPT), Eye Movement Desensitization and Reprocessing (EMDR), and Stress Inoculation Training (SIT). There is significant clinical research supporting use of all four, with PE and CPT having the most robust literature available (Powers et al., 2010; Williams, Galovski, Kattar, & Resick, 2011; Chard, 2005). Other common treatments with less scientific evidence include Acceptance and Commitment Therapy and various psychodynamically oriented psychotherapies. The current push in the psychotherapeutic treatment of PTSD is the adherence to detailed and tested manualized treatment protocols (i.e., CPT and PE). One notable concern with trauma-focused treatments such as the ones mentioned above is that they are uncomfortable for the patient, which can lead to the patient dropping out of treatment.

Pharmacotherapy is a common and relatively effective aspect of PTSD treatment. There are a number of randomized controlled trials (RCTs) available indicating significant benefits beyond placebo (Stein, Ipser, & Seedat, 2006). Serotonin reuptake inhibitors such as fluoxetine and citalopram and serotonin-norepinephrine reuptake inhibitors such as venlafaxine and desvenlafaxine have become first-line treatments (Benedek, Friedman, Zatzick, & Ursano, 2009). Other medications, that include atypical antipsychotics (e.g., risperidone, quetiapine), adrenergic agents (prazosin, propranolol), and benzodiazepines (clonazepam, alprazolam), are also commonly used (even though the latter group is contraindicated with PTSD). One notable concern with pharmacological intervention is that medication side effects can be significant for the patient, which may lead to poor treatment compliance.

Adlerian psychotherapy is probably most closely related to Cognitive Processing Therapy in terms of its focus on challenging private logic and developing a positive view of self, others, and the world. Cognitive Processing Therapy as described on the Veterans Administration webpage sounds extremely similar to Adlerian psychotherapy:

> Cognitive Processing Therapy (CPT) helps you by giving you a new way to handle these distressing thoughts and to gain an understanding of these events. By using the skills learned in this therapy, you can learn why recovery from traumatic events has been hard for you. CPT helps you learn how going through a trauma changed the way you look at the world, yourself, and others. The way we think and look at things directly affects how we feel and act.
>
> (National Center for PTSD, Veterans Administration, 2009, updated July 26, 2013.)

Case Example: Jason

Jason was a 16-year-old white male admitted to a psychiatric hospital because of depression and aggressive behavior. He was living in a foster home at the time of his admission. He had been removed from his mother's home when he was eight years old because of her drug addiction and resulting lack of supervision and inability to provide a safe environment. His father had never been involved with him as long as he could remember. This was a third foster-home placement for him and it was a home with several other teenage boys. Jason had run away from the home about eight months before his admission to the hospital. He returned to his foster home after being picked up by the police in a large urban area about a month later. The foster family was willing to take him back and he was willing to return to the home. He denied that there was anything wrong at the foster home and indicated that his decision to run away was based on a desire to see the world and get off the farm (the foster home was in a rural area). Another male teenager from his school initially accompanied him, but the other teenager decided to return home after a couple of days on the run.

Since returning home, Jason's behavior was different than before he left. At first he was just quiet and stayed away from the other foster siblings. Over the course of several months he continued to be despondent and had become very irritable. He was quick to pick a fight with his peers. He had difficulty sleeping, as manifested by nightmares and difficulty going to sleep. He would become upset about little things that happened, and this was very different from his previous behavior. Jason did not want to talk with his foster parents or foster siblings about where he was or what he did when he ran away. All he would say was that he was in a big city and it was different than he expected. He spent a lot of time alone either in one of the rooms in the house or outside on the farm. He seemed to be lacking in energy and did not seem to enjoy doing things he used to do. In school, his teachers reported that he had difficulty concentrating and seemed to have a chip on his shoulder. He was in frequent fights and was suspended from school several times. The hospitalization occurred after he had struck his foster father during an argument about some chores.

On the unit, Jason was belligerent and spent a lot of time isolated from the other patients, and when he was around others he seemed to be looking for a fight. He was placed in the seclusion room almost every day because of aggressive acting-out behavior toward other patients or hospital staff. The psychologist was asked to see him by one of the mental health technicians who had been able to gain his trust. The mental health technician said that he thought part of his confusion may have to do with sexuality, and indicated that he learned this after Jason had become really angry at him during a temper outburst, and when confronted started sobbing and curled up in a ball. It was at that point that he said he was so messed up he couldn't even masturbate anymore. He was seen the first time in his hospital room, and the mental health technician introduced the psychologist to him and sat in on the session.

Jason was very nervous and apprehensive. He seemed reassured by the presence of the mental health technician, who encouraged him to talk freely. He was asked several questions about his present situation and how he came to be at the hospital. He said he didn't understand his present behavior and indicated that he didn't like the way he was acting. He talked about when his new behavior started and indicated that it was upon his return home from his runaway episode. Jason was asked what happened during the time he ran away, and he said it ended up much differently than he expected. He said that after his friend decided to return home he ended up living on the streets and sleeping in alleys. He did a few odd jobs here and there to earn some food and occasionally stole things that he needed. After a couple of weeks he said he ended up in a rough part of town. He didn't really know his way around town and had no idea where he was. Jason indicated that it was in this area that something bad happened and he didn't want to talk about it.

The psychologist switched topics for a while and asked more about his home situation and his earlier years growing up. Eventually, the psychologist focused on Jason's present situation and the fact that he was in a safe place, and no matter what it was he was going to say it wouldn't offend them or make them think less of him. Both the psychologist and the mental health technician emphasized this in a couple of ways. At this point, the psychologist decided that it was important to focus on some emotional containment exercises, and Jason was led through some progressive muscle-relaxation exercises. He seemed to calm down and was able to relax. He was asked to come up with an image of a place that was safe for him. He picked a place on the farm that was away from the other people. He was asked to focus on what it was like for him to be in that place: What did he see, what did he smell, what did he hear, and what did it feel like to sit on the ground there? The session was ended with Jason being asked to repeat this exercise on his own at least a couple more times later that day and before he went to sleep. He was told that they would return the next day.

On the second visit, Jason said that he had actually done the exercise one time and used the image of the safe place when he went to sleep that night. The psychologist encouraged Jason then to tell them what had happened, with the idea that they could stop any time and go back to his safe place. Jason then told the story of how he had been approached by a couple of older teens, who appeared to be 18 or 19 years old, and had been asked to perform oral sex on them. He said he refused, and when he did this, they called some of their friends and he was gang raped by approximately six older males who forced oral and anal sex on him. After it was over, a couple of them urinated on him and laughed at him as they left him lying in the alley.

Jason was asked to describe his feelings and his thoughts about what had happened and how this had affected him since then. He indicated that he blamed himself for putting himself in that situation; in his mind it was his fault. He blamed himself for running away in the first place, when his foster parents had been there for him in the past. He felt humiliated and shamed that he had been raped and violated in such a degrading manner, but knew that he deserved it because he was bad. He felt weak and emasculated because he believed he should have been able to fight them off, to stop them. He hated African-Americans now, because his perpetrators were all African-American. He was asked several times to stop and do some imaging work, relaxing as best he could. He was able to do this with some coaching.

One of the most difficult things for Jason was that they had laughed at him and made fun of him when it was over. Upon asking him to clarify this, he said that they laughed at him because he had had an orgasm during the rape and they said that meant that he enjoyed it. He admitted that he had had an orgasm during the rape and that he had felt pleasure at this point, but he denied that he enjoyed anal intercourse and started crying. He said he had begun to think that he must be gay and that he was less a man than he thought he should be. The psychologist discussed this with him and gave him some basic sex education information that he seemed to be missing about the function of the prostate gland and how it worked. He had no idea that the prostate gland, if massaged, could cause a man to have an orgasm and that it had nothing to do with whether he was gay or straight. Jason was then asked to use the relaxation exercises again and he was able to calm down. An appointment was set up for the next day to continue working on this with Jason.

The next morning Jason was seen, and indicated that he had actually slept through the night. Focus in this session was on some of the beliefs he had about himself, about others, and about the world. He was told that any kind of traumatic experience like this usually impacts the victim's sense of safety, trust, power, self-esteem, and capacity for intimacy. Those five themes were explained and discussed and he was able to identify aspects of all five areas that appeared to be changed as a consequence of his experience, including the capacity for intimacy, which was what led him to the statement earlier that he was so messed up he couldn't even masturbate. He said that he often had the urge and had been able to do so before the rape, but now when he became sexually aroused he would start thinking of the rape and it would end up with him being angry and not being able to focus on self-pleasuring. He seemed relieved to know that this was not an uncommon experience for others who had also been forced to engage in sexual activities.

This was an intensive treatment of Jason, and as one might expect, after he disclosed the rape to the psychologist and the mental health technician, he stopped having the aggressive episodes. He remained in the hospital for another two weeks, but was placed in seclusion only one time for some inappropriate verbal outbursts, as it was no longer an everyday occurrence. He did return to his foster home and school and was seen by an outpatient therapist to continue the work that was started in the hospital. His depression was lessened and his sleep improved. He had minor problems with behaviors but did not return to the hospital.

ACUTE STRESS DISORDER

Clinical Presentation

Behaviorally, individuals with ASD present similarly to those suffering from PTSD. They are confronted with intrusive and disturbing recollections related to the traumatic event, avoid reminders of the traumatic event, and experience myriad arousal (hypervigilance, insomnia) symptoms. One notable difference is the degree to which someone with ASD experiences dissociative symptoms. This is particularly the case immediately following exposure. As noted earlier, this may include a sense of depersonalization, derealization, or lack of awareness.

The affective style of many individuals with PTSD is either dysphoric or depressed and/or anxious mood. Although ASD has traditionally been considered an anxiety disorder, research and clinical experience has led to the acknowledgement that depressed or dysphoric mood is as common as anxious mood in many individuals. As noted earlier, this is reflected in the updated diagnostic criteria and classification in the latest version of the *DSM*.

Interpersonally, individuals with ASD may be seen as withdrawn, avoidant, and emotionally disconnected. This is true for both strangers and loved ones in their lives. Although the exact cause is unclear, it is likely that an increase in negative mood, reduced positive emotions, and increased agitation following the traumatic event are contributors. In other words, a reduced desire to connect with others and the inability of others to ease the person's distress following a traumatic event, likely lead to a bidirectional emotional disconnect.

DSM-5 Characterization

Added to the psychiatric nomenclature in 1994, Acute Stress Disorder (ASD) has been referred to as the precursor to PTSD. It shares virtually the same symptoms with PTSD, except for some minor but important differences. ASD differs from PTSD in two important ways. First, ASD is time limited. In order to meet diagnostic criteria and receive the diagnosis, symptoms must be present for at least three days and no longer than 30 days. Anything less than three days would be considered an acute stress reaction (or combat stress reaction in the military) and generally considered to be transient in nature. Trauma-based symptoms lasting longer than 30 days receive the diagnosis of PTSD. Second, ASD is characterized by the presence of significant dissociative-type symptoms. Although not universal, many individuals experience an altered sense of reality such as depersonalization (feeling disconnected from one's self) and derealization (being in a daze or feeling as if time has slowed or stopped), which can last from hours to a few days.

As already mentioned, the diagnostic criteria for ASD is similar to PTSD. After being exposed to actual or threatened death, serious injury, or sexual violence, intrusive (e.g., nightmares, flashbacks), avoidance (e.g., avoiding reminders of the traumatic event), arousal (e.g., sleep problems, hyperstartle), and mood (e.g., sadness, reduced positive emotions) symptoms emerge. The general course is that the symptoms either rapidly improve, leading to low-functional impairment, or continue, causing significant social and/or occupational impairment leading to the PTSD diagnosis (American Psychiatric Association, 2013, p. 280–281).

Biopsychosocial–Adlerian Conceptualization

As in PTSD, there may be a biological component with ASD since it also involves exposure to extremely threatening situations. The traumatic situation may be just as intense and prolonged as that in PTSD. ASD is very similar to PTSD in the Adlerian view as the differential diagnosis is purely based on time since the traumatic event (3 to 30 days).

Treatment Considerations

Treatment of ASD consists primarily of cognitive and behavioral strategies. One of the more common and effective strategies is exposure. Studies have shown that exposure therapy is effective at reducing subsequent PTSD symptoms in people with ASD or prior to onset of PTSD (Bryant et al., 2008; Cigrang, Peterson, & Schobitz, 2005). Other cognitive and behavioral strategies, such as cognitive restructuring, psychoeducation, and relapse prevention, have also shown to be beneficial. One approach that continues to be used, which is considered to be controversial, is the use of psychological debriefings. At best, the literature is mixed regarding the application of group-oriented discussion of potentially traumatic events. Some research has actually shown worse outcomes when psychological debriefings were compared to controls (see review by Nickerson and Bryant, 2013). Although pharmacological interventions are commonly used during the acute phase of trauma, little evidence supports the effectiveness of this approach. In fact, the use of some medications (benzodiazepines) has been shown to increase incidence of subsequent PTSD (Gelpin, Bonne, Peri, & Brandes, 1996).

Case Example: Officer Haley

Officer Haley was a police officer referred by his chief for treatment following an accident in which he observed a woman being burned alive in her car. His presenting symptoms were sleep problems, depressive affect, and re-experiencing the event through intrusive thoughts, images, sounds, and smells. He indicated that he had become more and more irritable, and as a result was spending more time alone and away from his wife and family for fear of having an angry outburst toward them. He was also isolating from his friends and fellow officers.

The incident happened one night when he was called to the scene of an accident. He and another officer came upon the scene and found a woman trapped in her car along with two children. One of the children was able to get out of the car by releasing her seat belt, and the other child was in a car seat in the rear. The woman's foot was trapped and she was not able to get it free to leave the car. The police officers summoned a wrecker that would be able to release her foot, but in the meantime the smell of gasoline became more and more intense. The car eventually caught fire and she was still trapped in the front seat. Officer Haley assured her that her children were safe and cut her seat belt to try and free her from the vehicle. The flames grew quickly and soon she was engulfed in flames and Officer Haley could only stand by and watch her die. He heard the sounds of her screams and saw her body writhe in pain.

The images of the woman dying became intrusive thoughts for Officer Haley over the next couple of weeks. He could also smell gasoline when there was none present, and the sounds of her screams were also part of his re-experiencing the event. He could not get to sleep without great difficulty and would awake with nightmares. He was prescribed some sleep medication and an antidepressant, which seemed to help but left him feeling lethargic the next day.

Treatment focused on providing information about trauma and critical incidents and the typical ways people react to these events, in an attempt to normalize somewhat his response. He was told that the nightmares and intrusive thoughts of the event would begin to lessen in frequency and intensity over time.

Officer Haley was introduced to relaxation using an autogenic relaxation approach. He seemed to be able to focus on some images that could help him reach a state of relaxation and was encouraged to practice this several times a day, at least once in the morning and once at night, and more often if possible. Once he was able to demonstrate some ability to contain his emotions in a helpful way, he was encouraged to share his experience of the event and his thoughts and feelings about the event as it happened and now that it was over. His thoughts during the event focused on what he was not able to do, rather than what he actually did (saved her two children from the fire). His thoughts after the event focused on retracing his steps and looking for mistakes that he had made. Despite the fact that he could identify none, he knew that he must not have done all he could or else she would be alive. His feelings were of inadequacy and guilt, and these were intense, as he had told her he would get her to safety and everything was going to be OK, but it turned out not to be for her. He blamed himself for lying to her and felt guilty and ashamed that he was unable to save her.

His intense feelings were based on his private logic that she would be alive if only he had done the right thing. He was led to explore this idea and to consider the possibility that perhaps he had done everything that was humanly possible and yet she still died. While not a pleasant thought, it was more acceptable, and eventually he began to see this as possibly true. He began to see his guilt as misguided and perhaps due to his private logic that he should be able to handle every situation that comes along.

He was encouraged to talk with the other officer who responded to the scene, and eventually was able to do so. They shared similar concerns but came to the conclusion that they did everything they could in the situation. Officer Haley continued to practice the relaxation techniques and added some soothing music of his own to it before going to bed at night. He reported this was as helpful to him as the medication and did not cause the lethargy for him the next day.

ADJUSTMENT DISORDERS

Clinical Presentation

Individuals with Adjustment Disorders present consistent with the prominent symptoms they are experiencing. In other words, those with more anxiety symptoms will present as anxious, and those with prominent depressive symptoms will appear as someone who is depressed. And others will present with mixed emotional features, leading to a more complex presentation, which often leads to greater challenges in making an accurate diagnosis. When children and adolescents are diagnosed with an adjustment disorder, it is usually with the specifier of conduct disturbance. This is due primarily to the fact that children and adolescents tend to engage in more externalizing behaviors (acting out) subsequent to a psychosocial stressor, whereas adults engage in more internalizing behaviors (mood disturbance).

DSM-5 Characterization

In essence, Adjustment Disorders are characterized by the development of emotional and behavioral symptoms shortly after experiencing some type of psychosocial stressor. This may include being laid off from work, break-up of a relationship, failing health of a loved one, and countless others. The key components with regard to diagnosing an adjustment disorder are: 1) The level of distress should be excessive or disproportional to what would be considered "typical" or "normal" for the stressor; 2) significant impairment in life functioning must occur; 3) symptoms are not due to normal bereavement; and 4) the symptoms do not persist beyond six months once the stressor is removed. Overall, the category of Adjustment Disorders has virtually been left unchanged from the *DSM-IV* to the *DSM-5*. For example, specifiers can be applied to the diagnosis (e.g., with depressed mood/anxiety, with disturbance of conduct, with mixed disturbance of emotions and conduct) and the disorder should not be better accounted for by Major Depression, an anxiety disorder, and so on (American Psychiatric Association, 2013, p. 286–287).

Biopsychosocial–Adlerian Conceptualization

The Adjustment Disorders represent to the Adlerian practitioner a milder form of trauma, or "shock," as Adler referred to it. It is highly unlikely that there is a causative biological component, but certainly the interplay of mind, body, and society need to be kept in mind. As in anxiety or depression, some symptoms may appear to be primarily biological (e.g., upset stomach, nausea, headaches) and yet remit as the social situation changes and as the person begins to give up some of their private logic.

While something that shocks us or upsets us can appear to be the cause of the problem, it is more likely that the cause of the problem is what we make of what has happened to us. This has already been stated earlier in this chapter, and so we won't repeat it here.

Treatment Considerations

Adjustment Disorders most often respond to psychosocial interventions. Cognitive, behavioral, psychodynamic, supportive, and interpersonal therapies are generally the treatment of choice. Depending on the symptom presentation, impact on functioning, and preference of the individual, pharmacotherapy can be employed. This can include antidepressant and/or anxiolytic medications, and hypnotic agents for sleep. However, by definition, adjustment disorders are transient in nature, and long-term use of medications would indicate a more severe condition. In many cases, internal resources and support from family and friends is sufficient to facilitate recovery. This is why it is important to avoid overpathologizing emotional and behavioral symptoms associated with a life stressor.

Case Example: Shelley

Shelley was 16 years old and brought to therapy by her mother, who was very concerned about her recent behavior. She had become more and more depressed and withdrawn from her family. She currently had no friends and did not seem interested in forming new friendships. Her schoolwork was suffering, and while she had once been an A and B student, she was now flunking three subjects and barely passing two others.

Shelley's symptoms started after moving from her previous home in a medium-sized city two states away to her new home. She was a sophomore in high school at the time of the move and did not want to leave her home. She had grown up in that city and had attended school with most of the same peers throughout the previous nine grades. She was looking forward to finishing high school and graduating with them. The move was precipitated by her father being transferred to another work location. Her younger siblings, who were ten and seven years old, seemed unaffected by the move and had made new friends and were doing well in school.

Shelley had found her place in her old school and in her old social network. She knew who she was and what was expected of her. In her new school, she was not known and was having a difficult time adjusting to the way things were done at her new school. While many youths may have initial adjustment problems, Shelley found herself not only not knowing anyone, but not caring to even meet any of the other students. Of course she went through the niceties of saying hello and so forth, but she really didn't care to get to know these people, as they were not the friends she had known all her life and wanted in her life.

The therapist worked with Shelley on her resentment toward her parents, which seemed to take the form of a passive-aggressive response, in which she would show them how terrible it was for them to move by refusing to accept the move itself. In her mind, her private logic was saying that it wasn't fair that they moved her to this new location, and since it wasn't fair, she wasn't going to make an effort to get along and certainly wasn't going to be happy in her new environment. In effect, she would rather suffer than adjust, and she did. Her private logic focused on all the things that had been unfair in her life, and the expectation became for her that nothing would ever be fair either.

Shelley finally was able to discuss her anger about the move. She said she did not feel she could really express herself to her parents about her anger and resentment, as she didn't want to hurt their feelings. She knew that her father had a good job with this company and enjoyed his work. She also sensed that her mother was not happy about the move either but was keeping it to herself and had not expressed it to anyone. A session was held with her and her parents with the intent to discuss her feelings with them. As a result, her parents became more aware that her depression seemed to stem from the recent move, and made arrangements to visit their old town during spring break and renew some of their acquaintances. This seemed to give Shelley some hope. She began to give up the idea that it was unfair to move and began to recognize that it was just something that happened, and that she may be able to maintain some relationships in her old town as well as develop some new friends. With support from her therapist and greater understanding from her parents, her depression began to diminish and her grades once more began to improve.

Concluding Note

Initially clinicians and students may be surprised that the category of Trauma- and Stressor-Related Disorders was added to the *DSM-5*. Moreover, the removal of Post-Traumatic Stress Disorder, Acute Stress Disorder, Disinhibited Social Engagement Disorder, Reactive Attachment Disorder, and the Adjustment Disorders from their respective previous nosological groupings may seem unwarranted. However, the shift in understanding that symptom manifestations are highly variable amongst individuals fits with moving these disorders into a broader category defined primarily by the stressful or traumatic origins of their symptoms. Indeed, consistent with Adler's teachings, this shift has moved even further away from viewing disorders through reductionist lenses, and now through the spectacles of individuality, meaning-making, and response to the environment.

References

Adler, A. (1973). *The Practice and Theory of Individual Psychology* (P. Radin, Trans.). Totowa, NJ: Littlefield, Adams & Co. (Original work published 1925.)

American Psychiatric Association (2013). *Diagnostic and Statistical Manual of Mental Disorders, Fifth Edition.* Arlington, VA: American Psychiatric Publishing.

American Psychiatric Association (2000). *Diagnostic and Statistical Manual of Mental Disorders, Fourth Edition (Text Revision).* Washington, DC: American Psychiatric Publishing.

American Psychiatric Association (1980). *Diagnostic and Statistical Manual of Mental Disorders, Third Edition.* Washington, DC: American Psychiatric Publishing.

Ansbacher, H.L. & Ansbacher, R.R. (Eds.) (1956). *The Individual Psychology of Alfred Adler.* New York, NY: Harper Torchbooks.

Benedek, D.M., Friedman, M.J., Zatzick, D., & Ursano, R.J. (2009). Practice guideline for the treatment of patients with acute stress disorder and posttraumatic stress disorder. *Psychiatry Online.* www.psychiatryonline.com/content.aspx?aid=156498 Accessed August 12, 2013.

Bottome, P. (1939). *Alfred Adler: A Biography.* New York, NY: G.P. Putnam & Sons.

Bryant, R.A., Mastrodomenico, J., Felmingham, K.L., Hopwood, S., Kenny, L., Kandris, E., & ... Creamer, M. (2008). Treatment of acute stress disorder: A randomized controlled trial. *Archives of General Psychiatry,* 65(6), pp. 659–667.

Chard, K.M. (2005). An evaluation of cognitive processing therapy for the treatment of posttraumatic stress disorder related to childhood sexual abuse. *Journal of Consulting and Clinical Psychology,* 73(5), pp. 965–971.

Cigrang, J.A., Peterson, A.L., & Schobitz, R.P. (2005). Three American troops in Iraq: Evaluation of a brief exposure therapy treatment for the secondary prevention of combat-related PTSD. *Pragmatic Case Studies in Psychotherapy,* 1(2), pp. 1–25.

Ferguson, E.D. (2010a). Adler's innovative contributions regarding the need to belong. *Journal of Individual Psychology,* 66(1), pp. 1–7.

Ferguson, E.D. (2010b). Mutual respect relates to need to belong and to contribute. Paper presented at NASAP Convention in Minneapolis, MN on June 11, 2010.

Freeman, S.M., Lundt, L., Swanton, E.J., & Moore, B.A. (2009). Myths and realities of pharmacotherapy in the military. In S.M. Freeman, B.A. Moore, & A. Freeman (Eds.), *Living and Surviving in Harm's Way.* New York, NY: Taylor & Francis, pp. 329–348.

Gelpin, E., Bonne, O., Peri, T., & Brandes, D. (1996). Treatment of recent trauma survivors with benzodiazepines: A prospective study. *Journal of Clinical Psychiatry,* 57, pp. 390–394.

Griffith, J. & Powers, R.L. (2007). *The Lexicon of Adlerian Psychology: 106 Terms Associated with the Individual Psychology of Alfred Adler* (2nd edn.). Port Townsend, WA: Adlerian Psychology Associates.

Hjertaas, T. (2013). Toward an Adlerian Perspective on Trauma. *Journal of Individual Psychology,* 69(3), pp. 186–200.

Jakupcak, M., Conybeare, D., Phelps, L., Hunt, S., Holmes, H.A., Felker, B., & ... Mcfall, M.E. (2007). Anger, hostility, and aggression among Iraq and Afghanistan war veterans reporting PTSD and subthreshold PTSD. *Journal of Traumatic Stress,* 20(6), pp. 945–954.

Keane, T. (2009). Improving models, methods, and measures: Contributions of CITRM to the field of psychological trauma. *Journal of Traumatic Stress,* 22(6), pp. 632–633.

McCann, I., Sakheim, D., & Abrahamson, D. (1988). Trauma and victimization: A model of psychological adaptation. *The Counseling Psychologist,* 16, pp. 531–594.

Millon, T. (1990). *Toward a New Personology: An Evolutionary Model.* Hoboken, NJ: John Wiley & Sons.

Moore, B.A. (2013). PTSD: Past, present, and future. *CNS Spectrums,* 18(2), pp. 71–72.

Nickerson, A. & Bryant, R.A. (2013). Acute stress disorder. In S.M. Stahl & B.A. Moore (Eds.), *Anxiety Disorders: A Guide for Integrating Psychopharmacology and Psychotherapy.* New York, NY: Routledge, pp. 155–175.

O'Connell, W.E. & Hooker, E. (1996). Anxiety Disorders II. In L. Sperry & J. Carlson (Eds.), *Psychopathology and Psychotherapy* (2nd edn.) (pp. 179–220). Philadelphia, PA: Accelerated Development.

O'Connor, T.G., Spagnola, M., & Byrne, J. (2012). Reactive attachment disorder and severe attachment disturbances. In P. Sturmey & M. Hersen (Eds.), *Handbook of Evidence-Based Practice in Clinical Psychology, Vol 1: Child and Adolescent Disorders* (pp. 433–453). Hoboken, NJ: John Wiley & Sons.

Powers, M.B., Halpern, J.M., Ferenschak, M.P., Gillihan, S.J., & Foa, E.B. (2010). A meta-analytic review of prolonged exposure for posttraumatic stress disorder. *Clinical Psychology Review,* 30(6), pp. 635–641.

Stein, D.J., Ipser, J.C., & Seedat, S. (2006). Pharmacotherapy for post-traumatic stress disorder (PTSD). *Cochran Database Systemic Reviews.* 1, CD002795.

Strauch, I. (2001). An Adlerian reconceptualization of traumatic reactions. *Journal of Individual Psychology,* 57(1), pp. 246–258.

U.S. Department of Veterans Affairs, National Center for PTSD (2013). Cognitive Processing Therapy. www.ptsd.va.gov/public/pages/cognitive_processing_therapy.asp Accessed August 12, 2013.

Van der Kolk, B.A., McFarlane, A.C., & Welseath, L. (1996). *Traumatic Stress: The Effects of Overwhelming Experience on Mind, Body, and Society.* New York, NY: Guilford Press.

Weir, K.N. (2011). Playing for keeps: Integrating family and play therapy to treat reactive attachment disorder. In A.A. Drewes, S.C. Bratton, & C.E. Schaefer (Eds.), *Integrative Play Therapy* (pp. 243–264). Hoboken, NJ: John Wiley & Sons.

Williams, A., Galovski, T., Kattar, K., & Resick, P. (2011). Cognitive processing therapy. In B.A. Moore and W.E. Penk, *Treating PTSD in Military Personnel: A Clinical Handbook* (pp. 59–73). New York, NY: Guilford Press.

Zeanah, C.H. & Gleason, M.M. (2010). *Reactive Attachment Disorder: A Review for DSM-V.* Department of Psychiatry and Behavioral Sciences, Tulane University School of Medicine, 2010. http://www.nrvcs.org/nrvattachmentresources/documents/APA%20DSM-5%20Reactive%20Attachment%20Disorder%20Review%5b1%5d.pdf. Accessed August 22, 2013.

7   Eating Disorders

Mary Frances Schneider

Feeding and eating disorders involve practices that limit or distort eating behavior in a way that threatens physical health and interferes with social and emotional performance. The eating disorders of most concern to mental health practitioners are Anorexia Nervosa, Bulimia Nervosa, and Binge-Eating Disorder, although they also need to be aware of Pica, Rumination Disorder, and Avoidance/Restrictive Food-Intake Disorders. The disorders covered in this chapter are: Anorexia Nervosa; Bulimia Nervosa; Avoidance/Restrictive Food-Intake Disorder; and Binge-Eating Disorder. Two others disorders, Pica and Rumination Disorder, will be briefly considered. The case studies selected for this chapter demonstrate typical clinical presentations of eating disorders, highlighting the value of team treatment and pinpointing the specific challenges associated with each disorder. The Adlerian case study analysis includes consideration of the family constellation, early recollections, and an Adlerian conceptualization of the case designed to help the practitioner anticipate the client's line of movement. Each case study demonstrates this issue of comorbidity and the necessity of treating both the eating disorder and the underlying comorbid condition in tandem or at least with conscious awareness of its presence.

Eating Disorders and *DSM-5*: Definitional Changes from *DSM-IV-TR* to *DSM-5*

The most sweeping change offered in *DSM-5*, the *Diagnostic and Statistical Manual of Mental Disorders*, is that Binge-Eating Disorder has been assigned its own category as an eating disorder. In *DSM-IV*, binge-eating was an over-used category under Eating Disorder Not Otherwise Specified (NOS).

Changes for Anorexia Nervosa involve the elimination of the word "refusal" in Criterion A; the elimination of amenorrhea in Criterion D (males do not experience menstrual cycles; birth-control pills may eliminate female cycles; post-menopausal females can be anorexic; and some female anorexics do experience menstrual cycles). Finally, regarding Bulimia Nervosa (BN), *DSM-5* has reduced frequency of binge-eating and purging (compensatory behaviors) from twice a week to once a week.

While the American Medical Association has designated obesity as a disease, obesity is not included in *DSM-5* as a major category in eating disorders. While obesity is definitely a medical disorder resulting in a cascade of medical problems and extreme challenges to treatment (King, 2013; Ogden et al., 2012; Swinburn et al., 2011; Weir, 2012), obesity can be associated with a wide range of mental health disorders.

Adlerian Conceptualization of Eating Disorders

Adlerian assessment tools, the life-style assessment and early recollection summary, essentially assemble the client's backstory, identify core family and cultural values, provide information regarding the client's beliefs about the self, others, ethics, and ideals, as well as highlight the client's line of movement (Manaster & Corsini, 2009).

The case studies selected for this chapter demonstrate that while the presenting problem is a challenge in eating or feeding, in each case, the eating disorder is actually more of a misguided coping strategy. This misguided strategy, or what Mosak (1979) would call "the sideshow," is developed and used by the client to divert cognitive focus from coping with real-life or more genuine life-task challenges such as learning emotional self-regulation, facing fears about growing up, accepting responsibility for personal independence, cultivating work skills, developing talents, evolving a sense of spirituality/life-meaning, and addressing relationship challenges. In addition, the eating disorder is often a safeguarding response to living in a particular family system and a greater subculture/culture that overvalues beliefs like perfection and thinness as a representations of health, success, and well-being.

Eating Disorders, Comorbidity, and Prevalence

Eating disorders are usually accompanied by underlying mental health challenges, with anxiety and mood disorders being most prevalent—40% to 70% of the cases. Obsessive-compulsive disorders are most prevalent in Anorexia Nervosa (Jordan et al., 2008). A large body of research exists that demonstrates the comorbidity of eating disorders and substance abuse (Courbasson, Nishikawa, & Dixon, 2012). Gadalla and Piran (2007), in their meta-analysis of the research on women and substance abuse, note the importance of recognizing and planning for the co-occurrence in the initial stages of treatment conceptualization.

Research on personality disorders demonstrates a wide range of findings on comorbidity (21% to 97%) with the Cluster C traits. Bipolar Disorder and Cluster B personality traits are most common in Bulimia Nervosa (Bulik, 2003).

Mehler and Anderson (2010) provide the overview. Eating disorders are more prevalent in Western cultures, and in higher socioeconomic classes in both Western cultures and developing countries; they are more prevalent in females, gay males, adolescents, and individuals in their early 20s; they appear to have 50% to 70% heritability (twin studies), and tend to effect groups with appearance demands, like dancers, models, actors, body builders, and wrestlers.

Female eating disorders begin in the early teen years and continue through young adulthood (Lewinsohn, Striegel-Moore, & Seeley, 2000). The increased incidence of eating disorders in males highlights the need for diagnostic awareness (Dalgliesh & Nutt, 2013).

Johnson, Cohen, Kasen, and Brook (2002) highlight the role of childhood adversities, difficult childhood temperament, and parental psychopathology in the development and persistence of an eating disorder. Low paternal affection, care, and empathy, as well as high paternal control, unfriendliness, overprotectiveness, and seductiveness were associated with the development of persistent eating disorders.

Popular books like *Never Goin' Back: Winning the Weight-Loss Battle for Good* (Roker & Morton, 2013) and *Obsessed: America's Food Addiction—And My Own* (Brzezinski & Smith, 2013) provide highly public examples of the rollercoaster struggle with eating disorders, and emphasize the parallel between eating disorders and addictions—an area of current research (Terence, 2010).

General Treatment Considerations

Treating eating disorders (ED) requires a team approach. Individuals interested in practicing psychology or counseling in the domain of eating disorders should plan practicum placements and internship experiences in hospitals, treatment centers, and practices with a reputation for successful treatment in ED. In addition to a team-based approach, most ED treatment programs offer flexibility between inpatient and outpatient treatment. The individual therapist trained in Adlerian psychotherapy will find the Adlerian tools extremely helpful when formalizing treatment paths within both Cognitive Behavioral Therapy (CBT) and Dialectical Behavioral Therapy (DBT) treatment for ED.

Team treatment typically involves the participation of a physician(s) (general practitioner, pediatrician, gynecologist), a psychiatrist who specializes in the treatment of eating disorders, a registered dietitian, a social worker, and therapists trained in family therapy, group, and individual therapy. Team members collaborate to keep the case on track with treatment, defined roles, delineated goals, consultation questions, and a treatment model.

Therapy models that have been effective in the treatment of BED have included Cognitive Behavior Therapy (CBT), Interpersonal Therapy (IPT), and Behavioral Weight Loss Therapy (BWL). Research demonstrates that clients with a higher baseline of pathology respond best to Dialectical Behavior Therapy (DBT). Dialectical Behavioral Therapy has demonstrated better long-term outcomes in the treatment of more resistant cases of binge-eating disorders and Bulimia Nervosa (Safer, Telch, & Chen, 2009).

Lazaro et al. (2011) studied the efficacy of group therapy for adolescents attending outpatient treatment for eating disorders. The results of their research support the usefulness of a group therapy in the development of self-esteem and social skills, as well as the value of family therapy in treatment.

ANOREXIA NERVOSA

Clinical Presentation

Anorexia Nervosa is diagnosed when the individual (adolescent or adult) displays a body weight significantly below what is normal or expected for the individual's current age and height. The individual is preoccupied with self-image and appears to be in denial regarding the severity of weight loss. The individual presents with perceptional distortions regarding his or her body ("fat thighs," "fat stomach"), when the individual actually lacks appropriate body mass. The extreme weight loss in Anorexia Nervosa is due to the individual's fear of gaining weight—a fear that translates into subtype patterns of restricting food intake and/or patterns of bingeing and purging. The body mass index

(BMI) is used to indicate the severity of the disorder, with ranges from mild to extreme. There are two subtype patterns of Anorexia Nervosa. These subtypes may be combined in any particular case. The subtypes involve patterns of food restriction and patterns of binge-eating followed by purging.

DSM-5 Characterization

Anorexia Nervosa (American Psychiatric Association, 2013) is diagnosed when an individual is significantly below normal levels in body weight, has an intense fear of gaining weight and exhibits practices of food restriction, and displays undue preoccupation with body weight or denial of current low body weight. Anorexia Nervosa can be either restricting type or binge-eating/purging type. Severity of mild, moderate, severe, and extreme is assessed by body weight.

Biopsychosocial–Adlerian Conceptualization

When conceptualizing any case from an Adlerian perspective, the biological, sociological, psychological, and teleological aspects of the case require a treatment focus. The biological challenges in Anorexia Nervosa are considerable. First, the disease takes a considerable toll on health, requiring both medical and dental examinations to determine the level of biological care required. In addition, research demonstrates that there are often significant neurological ramifications, especially to an extended practice of Anorexia Nervosa. Social aspects of this disease involve consideration of the family constellation and the role of anorexia in the family constellation. Within this social context the anorexic develops a psychological belief system and set of fictive goals, such as perfectionism or the desire to remain a child. These fictive goals draft the individual into sideshow dramas that focus, almost entirely, on excessive food restriction/body preoccupation while ignoring healthy life task development in areas of intimacy, work, friendships, spirituality, and the use of leisure time.

Treatment Considerations

Clinical considerations when a client presents with extremely low body mass index signals the need for medical, dental, and psychological examinations. Time spent in states of semi-starvation results in bone density concerns, loss of menses, and gastric disorders. Depression and social engagement issues as well as obsessive-compulsive behaviors around eating and exercise are also common. There are cautions that should be considered when treating Anorexia Nervosa. A meta-analysis of suicide rates in clients with Anorexia Nervosa demonstrated higher suicide rates among patients with Anorexia Nervosa when compared with the regular population (Pompili et al., 2004).

While the physical effects of Anorexia Nervosa (AN) are well documented, research has turned to the neurological and cognitive effects of the disorder. Meta-analysis documents brain changes and patterns similar to Alzheimer's disease from long-term client practices of Anorexia Nervosa (Titova, Hjorth, Schiöth, & Brooks, 2013).

AN is more common in females, with a 10:1 ratio; more common in higher-socio-economic countries (United States, Australia, Japan); lower in low- and middle-income countries. In the United States, the prevalence is lower among Latinos and African-Americans. The disorder often presents in adolescence or young adulthood. The disorder is found more often in vocational environments that value thinness. In terms of personality variables, anorexic clients often display patterns of obsessive-compulsive behavior. The disorder may be chronic, especially when hospitalization is required for the treatment of the medical side effects of the disease. Suicide and depression screening is warranted.

Case Study: Dana

Eve sits across from the family therapist, running her perfectly manicured finger around the top rim of a coffee cup. Her husband, Tom, sits to her right. Eve's daughter, Dana (age 24), sits to the left of her mother, with eyes downcast. In this family therapy session, Dana and her parents are revisiting the family history that provides the background narrative for Dana's eight-year battle with Anorexia Nervosa. It is an intergenerational story of eating disorders, offering a heritage common in families that struggle with adolescents and/or young adults captured by AN.

Dana's weight had dropped from 154 pounds (body mass index [BMI] of 26) to 90.2 pounds (BMI 14.7) with a height of 5'5". Dana had been hiding her changing body under layers of clothing. At the time of the admission, Dana was eating 600 calories a day, claiming to be vegan, and running 5 to 10 miles per day. Her periods had stopped for over one year. Her skin was dry and nails cracked. At the time of admission, 80% of her thoughts were about food, and the remaining about marijuana. Even after treatment for substance abuse, her addictive ideas about "food and weed never quiet down."

In the hospital, Dana began a treatment program called Dialectical Behavior Therapy (DBT) specifically designed for eating disorders. The plan was to begin treatment with hospitalization, and once initial weight goals were reached, move to outpatient treatment. The treatment program involved individual, group, and family sessions. Within two months Dana reached her target weight of 126 pounds.

In this session, the family celebrates Dana's graduation from inpatient treatment to outpatient treatment. This treatment plan follows Dana's fourth hospitalization. The first hospitalization was for substance abuse. The second through fourth hospitalizations involved Anorexia Nervosa. Hospitalized for two months, this was the first time Dana voiced personal responsibility: "This time I am learning tools that actually help me step up to my thoughts. I feel empowered."

Dana's team members include a psychiatrist, nurse practitioner, psychologist, dietitian, and a social worker. Individual and family therapy was the focus of the psychologist, while group therapy was conducted by the social worker. The entire practice was trained in DBT therapy. The lens of this case study summary is from the point of view of the team psychologist who, trained as an Adlerian and schooled in DBT, integrates the use of both models as she supports the individual and family therapy components of Dana's treatment.

Dana feels that family therapy, individual therapy, and group therapy—especially family therapy—has empowered not only herself but every member of her family. "We are all learning about my bipolar disorder and the issues that come with borderline behavior. Now we can stand up to these things." Dana feels that her mother can stop "fretting" and settle into supporting Dana's efforts to "talk back to the dark messages." Her family applauds the extent to which therapy has encouraged Dana to take personal responsibility, while supplying all family members with what her father called a "trunk full of tools and lots of support."

Dana's goals for therapy are to understand her mental health challenges and learn how to "talk back to the voices and feelings." She wants to "get steady on my feet" before returning to college in Florida.

Family constellation

The life-style inventory has brought understanding about the inter-generational patterns of eating disorders. As Dana walks through her own early years and family history, her reflections are laced with insight regarding the family guiding lines, the cultural politics of being a socially successful family, the stereotypic gender roles, as well as the lack of spiritual and psychological coping tools that were present in her early family life.

She sees her mother as a petite version of "the mother in _Leave it to Beaver_ or _Ordinary People_." "My mother is flawless. Perfect. I adored her. I thought this is the way to be a woman." The odd thing was that her mother, a Harvard graduate, "never did anything with her degree." While her father, also a Harvard graduate, was a successful businessman.

Dana's mother often-voiced goal was to "make her husband happy." She did this by excelling as a homemaker: cooking "Betty Crocker perfect" meals, keeping a spotless home, and using exercise classes and beauty consultations to keep herself "attractive." Dana's father provided the family with wealth beyond the socioeconomic level of most of her school friends. "We had the best house, the best cars, the best clothes, the best vacations. My parents had the 'best friends.'" This status often made Dana feel socially isolated.

While Dana's mother was the family chef, Dana never remembers her mother sitting down and eating a meal. "She sliced, diced, poured, served, and dished out food… she just never seemed to eat any of it." Dana was able to draw parallels between her own eating behavior, her mother's eating behavior, and her maternal grandmother's eating challenges. All three generations of women had eating disorders.

Diagnosed in childhood with learning disabilities, Dana thinks she has been an impulsive decision maker who escaped into alcohol and substance abuse. Dana acknowledges loving the effects of alcohol, marijuana, and "the drugs I have taken for pain."

Dana is the second of two children. Dana's brother, Mike (age 28), is a "chip off the block" of Eve and Tom. He is a young man who "never gave them a moment

of worry." A "perfect" student in grade school and high school, Mike attended private boarding school, graduated from Harvard, and is in a master's program at Northwestern. He was the "easy kid and the perfect adolescent." In this family he followed the guiding lines of being perfect.

Dana believed that she was a "handful" and often brought "chaos" to family life, while Mike was perfect. Dana feels that Mike is "my bright spot. I knew he loved me even if I wasn't perfect." Certainly Dana struggles with family values of perfection, high performance, high educational standards, and female guiding lines that formed early tutoring in the acquisition of eating disorders.

Early recollections

Dana's early recollections are laced with messages about eating disorders. Dana vividly remembers her mother pushing food around on her plate and finding distractions from eating, in the tasks of serving her little family—"running back into the kitchen to get things." Dana watched her mother in this memory, trying to see if her mother would eat even one bite of what was on her plate. She never saw her mother eat anything.

Dana had a memory of coming upon her mother in the kitchen and knowing that her mother was chewing a piece of meat. After chewing, her mother discreetly spit the chewed glob into a paper napkin. Dana is convinced that her "wafer thin" mother was restrictive in her own eating. When Dana retold this memory in family therapy, her mother did not deny it, but began to talk about *her* mother, who also had eating disorders. Dana recalled a memory in which she came to understand that she was petite and "could not eat whatever she wanted." She recalls standing in front of a mirror, with her mother pointing out Dana's "puff around the middle." Determined to remove the "puff," she began surveying her body on a daily basis.

Dana recalled bingeing as a very young child. She came upon a recently baked lemon meringue pie and guzzled down the pie, lying to her mother about having eaten it. Dana says that as she looks back on these memories she is aware of her eating behavior. Dana still wants "to remain thin" and worries what that means as she continues her recovery from Anorexia Nervosa.

Adlerian case conceptualization

Family therapy focusing on a discussion and inspection of the family constellation, family history, and family values provided tremendous insight to Dana and her parents. Including Mike in the sessions added additional interpersonal resources and support.

Eve, Tom, and Dana awakened to Eve's codependence with Dana as well as Tom's tendency to escape this atmosphere of worry and obsession by withdrawing from the family and overworking. Eve acknowledged her obsessive-compulsive traits and worrying. Eve suggested a return to Al-Anon. Dana feels her parents were more helpful when involved in Al-Anon.

Dana feels that she is "learning tools that help her manage her moods for the first time in her life." I have "things to do with my feelings rather than escape through the use of drugs or alcohol." The DBT skills (Linehan, 1993a; Linehan, 1993b) have been key tools.

Dana's bipolar and borderline challenges are best addressed through internalization of coping skills. In addition to the tools offered by DBT, the Adlerian therapist would study Adlerian treatment of these disorders in support of conceptualizing positive movement in Dana's recovery (Mosak, 1979; Schulman, 1982; Sperry, 1990; Sperry & Mosak, 1996).

Treatment considerations

While Dana and her family voice a new kind of optimism regarding Dana's current level of insight, responsibility, functioning, and recovery from Anorexia Nervosa, this disease is persistent and requires therapeutic vigilance. DBT treatment for eating disorders, combined with an Adlerian conceptualization, is currently successful and has resulted in Dana feeling more responsible and empowered. Supporting the parents in attending Al-Anon will encourage their compassionate detachment.

BULIMIA NERVOSA

Clinical Presentation

Bulimia Nervosa is a serious and potentially life-threatening eating disorder. Individuals with Bulimia will binge-eat food and then purge, trying to get rid of excess calories. Prevalence is approximately 10:1 female to male ratio and is found highest among young adults (American Psychiatric Association, 2013).

DSM-5 Characterization

Bulimia Nervosa (American Psychiatric Association, 2013) is a pattern of binge-eating followed by methods of purging or compensating to avoid weight gain, and it is not a pattern occurring as a practice within Anorexia Nervosa. The purging and/or compensation often involves vomiting, the use of laxatives, diets, and/or fasting. In this disorder the individual is preoccupied with thoughts about appearance, shape, and weight. The disorder can range from mild (one to three episodes of binge/purge per week) to extreme (14 or more episodes per week), based on the frequency and duration of the episodes of bingeing and purging.

Biopsychosocial–Adlerian Conceptualization

Clients presenting with Bulimia Nervosa (BN) will often display biological challenges. Medical and dental examinations are warranted, due to the health toll taken by practices of vomiting and use of laxatives. From a psychosocial perspective, clients with BN often begin this disorder in an effort to find social acceptance. Family constellation and early recollections often demonstrate patterns of attention-getting and dependency on others for approval. Issues of external beauty and preoccupation with the social value of "looking good" are common themes among clients with BN. In an effort to control weight in a society where food is prevalent and high-calorie fast food easily accessible, purging is often initially a short-term strategy for managing weight. As in all disorders, this sideshow strategy becomes the main show in the client's life—often to the neglect of other important life tasks.

Treatment Considerations

During binge-eating individuals report a lack of control—an inability to stop bingeing—often naming the binge experience as an addiction. Tremendous quantities of food may be consumed during binge-eating. The experience is often hidden, occurring during the night or when alone. Purging tends to involve voluntary vomiting following the binge-eating episode. Clients become skilled at practices of vomiting, diuretics use, and exercise.

Individuals with Bulimia Nervosa tend to be of normal weight, and "low calorie" or "careful restrictive" eaters between episodes of bingeing and purging. Challenges with menstrual cycles, laxative dependence, esophageal complications, dental disorders, and cardiac disorders are possible. BN is more common in females, beginning in adolescence and remaining a pattern through early adulthood. Depending on the number and duration of bingeing episodes per week, the disorder is given a severity rating of mild, moderate, severe, or extreme.

BN clients tend to present with symptoms of depression, anxiety, and/or social anxiety, with a focus on excessive ideation regarding weight concerns. The disorder is more prevalent in the West and is increasing with males. Suicide assessment is warranted with BN. Antidepressants and birth-control pills are contra-indicated during active phases of BN, due to drug-absorption issues. Comorbidity with other mental disorders, Bipolar Disorder, or mood disorders is often the case with Bulimia. Substance abuse with alcohol and/or stimulants is prevalent in about one-third of the individuals presenting with this disorder. Dentists and dental hygienists play an important role in identifying Bulimia, since they are often the first to see the damage caused by vomiting (Mehler & Anderson, 2010). BN is often found in social settings or professions that involve a body-performance aspect, for example, in sports, acting, modeling.

Case Example: Coty

Coty, aged 20, is a sophomore in college. Coty is a member of the dance team and was referred for treatment by her co-dancer, Amy, who is currently receiving treatment for an eating disorder. Coty came to therapy because Amy and their dance coach have been "evangelistic" about the problem of eating disorders in college athletes.

Coty resonated with Amy's "peer-generated diagnosis." Coty did not deny Amy's observation of her binge-eating and vomiting. Rather, Coty defended her practices as "normal" in the dance world, stating that she "had no other choices." After observing Amy's recovery success, elevation of mood, social achievements, body-building program, and dance vigor, Coty decided to give treatment "a chance." Coty said she decided to "ride Amy's coat tails."

Coty's engaged in approximately eight binge-eating and purging episodes per week—an increase from her high-school behavior of four episodes per week. The severity level of Coty's challenge with Bulimia resulted in the team treatment decision that Coty should enter the outpatient wing of the university hospital for ED treatment. While currently outpatient treatment appeared to be warranted, the inpatient option existed if Coty's symptoms became more involved. The team determined that Coty was experiencing a depression accompanied by thoughts of self-harm, and the profile of a Dependent Personality Disorder. Results of dental and medical examinations found that Coty displayed dental problems due to vomiting, serious anemia, but no gastric disorders. Due to drug-absorption issues, the gynecologist took Coty off of birth-control pills, and the psychiatrist refrained from prescribing antidepressants. Coty was shocked by these findings. Coty's goals for therapy involved stopping the BN disorder, having a recovery like Amy's recovery, and getting clarity on her own professional goals.

Family constellation

Coty is the youngest of three children. Her two older brothers, aged 25, are twins. Both graduated from college, with one persuing law school and the other getting a master's in Business. Both brothers had already joined their father in the successful family computer software business. Coty viewed her father as authoritarian with a "short fuse" and high expectations. "Ordering people around which worked better in the military than it did at home." The home atmosphere was tense and "everyone walked on egg shells when Dad was around." Coty viewed her mother as highly religious, kind, and a pleaser who always regretted not finishing college. Her mother was a homemaker, a great baker, always present at school activities, and Coty's greatest support. Her mother loved the arts and enrolled Coty at the age of two in dance class. Coty was "not a very good student, certainly not a star like my brothers."

Early recollections

Coty's two most favorite early recollections involved her "hide out—the family basement." This was where Coty danced "all the time." In one of her recollections, Coty's mother gave her a beautiful tutu and she felt like a princess. In her other most favorite early recollection, she got the "best birthday surprise ever": her mother hired a handyman to construct a stage in the basement. Coty created shows with her friends on that stage. One of Coty's early recollections involved her father. In this memory he was mad at the loud music and smashed her boom box. Coty realized that while she was following the pleasing style of her mother, she tended to be scared of men.

Adlerian case conceptualization

Coty displays the profile of the avoidant type of individual, with low activity and low social interest (Sperry & Mosak, 1996). Discouraged and outdistanced by her brothers, Coty sought contentment in dance. Coty followed her mother's guiding lines, avoiding conflict, pleasing others, and remaining aloof from her own aspirations. Even dance appears to be more a fantasy outlet than a career choice. Coty is fearful of men and has been avoiding dating. She has periodically wondered if she is gay, but is "not ready to explore that idea at this time." While Coty is currently considering majoring in the area of early childhood, she has no idea if she would like that career. Coty does not want to join her father's business and feels that she may be pressured into it if she leaves college.

Coty's parents attended the treatment-planning phase of the evaluation even though her father did not "see the value of therapy." Coty's mother was engaged and worried about Coty's physical and mental health. Coty liked the members of her treatment team, enjoyed the freedom of college life, and wanted to remain at the university.

Treatment considerations

Coty began therapy in the outpatient treatment program and was diagnosed with depression and suicidal thinking. Coty was nearly frozen by obsessive thinking, avoiding class, and not socializing with fellow students. Coty found relief in dance and dance rehearsal. Here Coty experienced moments of relief from obsessive thoughts. The dance team coach helped Coty by having her sing dance instructions out loud. This increased relief from the intrusive eating-disordered thoughts.

In group therapy, Coty began to develop social skills and assertiveness skills. Individual therapy was increased to two days a week. Coty reduced her university course load and began visiting early-childhood programs in an effort to investigate whether this academic major was viable. Coty has accompanied Amy and Amy's sorority sisters giving campus talks on eating disorders. This activity, paradoxically, provided relief from intrusive thoughts as Coty engaged in social interest around a challenge she faced in her own life. Coty is beginning to face the reality that she has a long journey to recover from Bulimia. She is currently engaged in therapy and able to measure her own progress in baby steps.

AVOIDANT/RESTRICTIVE FOOD-INTAKE DISORDER

Clinical Presentation

Avoidant/Restrictive Food-Intake Disorder is a new diagnosis in the *DSM-5*. This diagnosis includes symptoms that do not match the criteria for traditional eating disorder diagnoses, but includes clinically significant struggles with eating and food. The *DSM-5* has not reported any prevalence data on Avoidant/Restrictive Food-Intake Disorder; this disorder typically develops in infancy or childhood, but it can carry into adulthood.

DSM-5 Characterization

An avoidant and/or restrictive food-intake disorder (American Psychiatric Association, 2013) involves limiting the consumption of food to levels below those recommended as sufficient to meet daily nutritional needs. This limitation of food results in weight loss, lowered levels of energy, and health problems due to insufficient nutrition. This avoidant/restrictive pattern may become so extreme that inpatient treatment with enteral feeding or oral nutritional supplements are required. The pattern may impair psychological and social functioning. It is important to note that this disorder is not the result of cultural or religious practices that involve fasting; it is not the result of famine or food restrictions due to war or civil unrest. It may be attributed to other definable medical disorders or treatment, for example, loss of appetite due to chemotherapy treatment. It is only diagnosed when the restriction is beyond what would normally be associated with that medical condition. Food restriction may occur as a part of Anorexia Nervosa or Bulimia Nervosa—if so, these disorders are the primary diagnosis.

Biopsychosocial–Adlerian Case Conceptualization

The patterns of thoughts and behaviors that are designed to limit food intake get in the way of normal social functioning and form what Mosak (1979) has aptly termed "the sideshow." In every eating disorder, the relationship with food takes center stage in the client's life, limiting the energy and focus the client can devote to authentic life-task issues of work, intimacy, social relationships, spirituality, and leisure interests.

Treatment Considerations

As in all treatment of eating disorders, a team approach fosters a better outcome. It is important to make sure the client has a physical examination to rule out other possible health issues and to identify health problems that can be associated with food restriction (anemia, nutrition issues, or heart and thermal issues).

Clients with practices of restrictive eating may present for therapy with a focus on anxiety or depression. They may be experiencing challenges in life-task areas, such as work or intimacy, and not be totally aware that practicing an eating disorder is taking up significant amounts of time and energy. Including an intake question about eating practices and eating challenges opens space for this challenge to be addressed in therapy.

Case Example: Amy

Amy, aged 19, is Caucasian and a freshman in college. Experiencing intense social anxiety during the first month of freshman year, Amy sought therapy. Amy voiced depression and extreme challenges in adjusting to college life. Embarrassed at the idea of being a "college drop out," Amy decided to see a therapist.

Presenting as anxious, judgmental, and angry, Amy voiced anger at all aspects of college life. As an only child, Amy never shared a room with anyone, much less "this closet the university calls a room." College was a "major comedown with terrible food." Amy expressed concerns about not "fitting in" with girls in the dorm because many of them came to college with their high-school friends. Amy was anxious about shopping for a sorority bid as well as preparing and auditioning for the dance team. Preparation for the dance audition required hours of daily practice, and securing a place on the dance team was even more important than finding a sorority. "The competition is stiff—only the best of the best will make it."

"Obsessed" with dance practice, Amy fell behind on figuring out her sorority options. Amy viewed herself as athletic and a hard worker. In high school she was "smart and popular—very successful." Her tools for keeping this status were "dance, aerobics, and a strict diet."

When asked her goals for therapy, Amy did not want to quit school and go home. "I'm no quitter." She needed support to "get through the pressure of all this auditioning." She wanted to reduce the anxiety in her life and "get back to where I was in high school."

In the second session, the therapist began to hypothesize that Amy was suffering from an eating disorder. This awakening was the result of Amy's complaints about dorm life. The worst thing about the dorms was the trouble Amy was having with food. Fearing the "freshman 10 or 20" would be her fate, due to dorm food, Amy wanted to control her food intake. Amy felt that dorm food would ruin her body, torpedo her dance audition, and limit her sorority choices.

Exploration of food issues resulted in a lengthy conversation regarding Amy's restrictive food practices. Amy was savvy about Anorexia and Bulimia, having had two high-school friends who were "still practicing Bulimia" and one friend who had been hospitalized for Anorexia. She felt that while food is "an issue for most girls, and all girls on the dance team," she had found "healthy" ways to keep her good figure. Amy felt that "dance performers were like movie stars and models—thin is in." The only way she felt that she could accomplish this "underweight, but still healthy" life style was through a very strict diet.

Family constellation

Amy is the only child in an upper-middle-class family that values athletics. In her family, Amy was "everybody's favorite." Amy enjoyed the life-style inventory process. She liked talking about her parents, grandparents, and her family life. She expressed gratitude for her own "charmed life." Amy spoke about her father with admiration. A runner, her soccer and basketball coach, he was a devoted father. Weekends were family times filled with games, picnics, swimming, and parties.

Amy's mother was also athletic. A Physical Education major in college, she was an avid tennis player and an exercise instructor for the local park district. Amy's mother worked for a weight loss company for about eight years. Her mother said it was during those years that she learned how to create "good eating habits" and how to understand the pain of others who suffer from eating disorders. Amy felt that her mother also practiced a somewhat restricted diet plan—sets of favorite foods and careful weight monitoring.

High school affirmed Amy's athletic abilities, especially her dance talent. Her dance skills brought Amy an extremely important social status. "I was pretty, thin, and in charge of the dance team." Amy immediately made the connection with her parents' athletic pursuits and her own "dance fever." Amy already seemed to be living the family values of athletics, performance, and hard work.

Early recollections

Amy's early recollections were filled with stories about performances. She loved to perform her dance routines for parents and grandparents—"playing to a devoted audience." Amy was a ringleader in her neighborhood social groups—always "popular and filled with exciting ideas." She organized her friends into little performance groups. They would sing, dance, play instruments, enjoying "being our own neighborhood band." At the age of five she led a field trip of the kids in her neighborhood, walking six blocks to spend money at a candy store. Concerned about safety, the storeowner called Amy's parents. Her friends loved the adventure, but her parents grounded her. "Punishment? I had my own TV in my own room!"

Adlerian case conceptualization

Amy sought therapy, presenting with social anxiety and issues regarding the challenge of adjusting to college life. From an Adlerian perspective, Amy demonstrates the typology of the ruling type, with high activity levels and low social interest (Sperry, 1990; Sperry & Mosak, 1996). From her life-style information we see that Amy engages in an active life, providing a lot of leadership for herself as well as for others. She loves performance and expects to be appreciated for her performance efforts. Her engaging leadership style draws in a wide audience of family and peers. She is used to being valued in social circles for her achievements.

Amy is willing to work hard to achieve her goals. While her style may demonstrate aspects of obsessive-compulsive behavior, she is highly active in the pursuit of her own goals. She has high expectations in both work and social spheres. She is clearly motivated to do well in her college dance career and eager to find a place in sorority life. She likes to lead, is willing to work hard, and has vision for her immediate goals.

Treatment considerations

With Amy's permission, her therapist requested a consultation from the university hospital ED program. The team felt that Amy was already responding to treatment, and the hospital treatment center's screening supported the fact that Amy's eating patterns were restrictive, and that she was addicted to Diet Coke. The team recommended dental and medical screening. Amy had a complete physical and met with a gynecologist to answer concerns about Amy's irregular periods. Amy introduced the ED team to her dance coach. There was an immediate marriage between the coach's training philosophy and the hospital treatment center's position regarding the challenges of eating disorders on campus.

Medical examinations supported the presence of low weight, anemia, and an overly restrictive diet. The nutritionist consulted with Amy, the therapist, and Amy's coach, discussing a nutritional eating plan within dorm environments. The coach, backed by the university, was a part of a movement to help young athletes refrain from developing eating disorders and maintain healthy weight levels. The coach recommended that Amy gain five to eight pounds and develop muscle strength through good nutrition and strength training. The coach's strength-training philosophy targeted a gain in muscle strength while reducing fat-density measurements. Under this program, Amy gained muscle strength, increased stamina, lost inches of fat, and gained six pounds (of muscle).

Amy joined a sorority, qualified for the dance team, and began to feel like "a social success again." After five months of successful treatment, Amy saw an opportunity for service and leadership in this shared vision of helping young female and male athletes avoid and/or cope with eating disorders. Amy and a group of her sorority sisters began the "What's Eating You?" project, with the mission of educating students on the dangers of eating disorders as well as the paths of recovery. Amy enjoyed her hard work on the dance team, and found a place of respect among her peers for her dance skills and her personal candor. In sorority life, "I learned how to share and be a true sister. I came to see that what I thought was being a leader might have been being more of a dictator. Working on the 'What's Eating You?' project has given me great satisfaction. We are sure that we are making a difference."

BINGE-EATING DISORDER

Clinical Presentation

Binge-Eating Disorder is a chronic disorder that is characterized by an individual consuming a high amount of food and often engaging in a compensatory behaviors to avoid or cope with weight gain. This presentation is seen primarily among young adult females. Prevalence is approximately 10:1 female to male ratio and is found highest among young adults (American Psychiatric Association, 2013).

DSM-5 Characterization

Binge-Eating Disorder (American Psychiatric Association, 2013) occurs when an individual consumes excessive amounts of food in a relatively short amount of time (two hours or less) and engages in this bingeing behavior one or more times per week for at least a three-month period of time. A binge is an isolated period of eating in which the individual ingests enormous amounts of food, often at a rapid rate, eating to the point of physical discomfort. While it might be a common experience to witness one or two relatives engaging in binge-eating at events like Thanksgiving dinner, the binge-eating disorder involves engaging in this type of over-eating from one to over 14 times per week. Individuals experience the binge as an "out of personal control" experience unrelated to the feeling of hunger. Bingeing often occurs in isolation due to embarrassment regarding the amount of food ingested, and is usually accompanied by intense feelings of guilt. Binge-eating is diagnosed if the binge occurs without purging and is not an active component of eating disorders like Bulimia or Anorexia Nervosa. The degree of severity in binge-eating ranges from mild (one to three weekly episodes) to extreme (14 or more weekly episodes).

Biopsychosocial–Adlerian Conceptualization

The biological challenges of binge-eating are substantial. During the binge episode, the individual takes in enormous amounts of food (like an alcoholic binge), and may compensate through dieting. The client is often on the roller-coaster ride of living from one fad diet to another, with obese clients seeking bypass surgery. Ideation is captured by the need to lose weight, and maintain weight loss. The client may be extremely embarrassed by weight gain and self-isolate. Life-style themes of "not getting enough," "needing more," wanting to feel "filled up" are common. Binge episodes are experienced as a type of "out of body" or "trance-like" experience where the client experiences a loss of control. The bingeing life style lacks social interest, reducing both the time and the energy needed to focus on the development of other life-task areas. The therapist will want to identify and take into consideration other coexisting mental health challenges such as Bipolar Disorder and/or Cluster B and C disorders of personality.

Treatment Considerations

While not all binge-eating is associated with obesity, individuals who engage in binge-eating are often overweight or obese. Obesity is the result of eating more calories than the body needs, and not necessarily due to engaging in episodes of binge-eating. Obese individuals suffer significantly more medical challenges, such as hypertension, stroke, heart disease, sleep apnea, Type 2 Diabetes, colon cancer, and breast cancer (Center for Disease Control and Prevention, 2013).

Binge-Eating Disorder is more prevalent in females, but occurs more often in males than do other eating disorders (Spitzer et al., 1993). Binge-Eating Disorder is present across races and is more prevalent in industrialized countries where food supply is abundant. BED often occurs in individuals who seek treatment for weight loss (Brody, Walsh, & Devlin, 1994). Often the client lacks awareness of the psychological or psychiatric components of the disorder. Binge-eating is also seen in approximately 49% of those seeking bariatric surgery (Niego, Kofman, Weiss, & Geliebter, 2007). Researchers estimate that 71% of individuals attending Overeaters Anonymous were challenged with BED. Individuals engaging in binge-eating often seek diets to help control the binge-eating (Spitzer et al., 1993). This disorder usually begins in adolescence and does tend to run in families. Binge-eating has a more complicated course of treatment if bipolar and/or personality disorders are also diagnosed (Mehler & Andersen, 2010).

When seeking clinical treatment, individuals diagnosed with BED achieve only 55% of the weight loss achieved by fellow clients (Pagoto et al., 2007). Research also demonstrates that BED clients have poorer outcomes in bariatric treatment than clients who are not challenged with BED. They continue to suffer from BED even after surgical intervention, requiring more post-surgical support (Busetto et al., 2005).

BED clients report more distress and reduced quality of life when compared to obese individuals who do not have the disorder. They report more challenges in the domain of work (lower raises), public challenges (not fitting into public seats), challenges to sex life, and lower self-esteem (Rieger, Wilfley, Stein, Marino, & Crow, 2005). Inpatient and/or outpatient treatment for binge-eating is often appropriate when underlying personality challenges like bipolar behavior, Borderline Personality Disorder and/or other Cluster B challenges are present in the client. Inpatient or outpatient treatment programs based on Dialectical Behavior Therapy have been shown to be extremely effective with binge-eating challenges (Safer, Telch, & Chen, 2009).

Case Study Example: Dr. Lucy

Lucy, age 63, is a physiology professor with a German Jewish background. Lucy was referred for therapy by her daughter, who shared Lucy's concern about a recently developed binge-eating disorder and weight gain of 43 pounds. Since Lucy, a petite woman of 5"1', had maintained a weight of approximately 128 pounds since graduate school, she was extremely distressed at gaining 43 pounds in six months. Lucy felt "trapped in this ugly habit of bingeing." Lucy stated her goal was "to stop bingeing and return to her healthy and happy self."

Lucy eagerly offered the "backstory" on her life. She graduated from college with a B.S. in Biology and worked in a research laboratory before having her children. She married a physician, left her job, and began raising her family. When the last of her children graduated from college, Lucy and her husband planned "to take a year-long trip around the world." Her husband died before this planned retirement. Lucy "was a total mess" for several years. Initially surrounded by compassionate friends and family, soon people "went on with their lives, drifting away." Her social friendships diminished. "It's a couples' world." While she still phones and has lunch with old friends, "it is just not the same." Lucy shared that her problem with binge-eating began in early February and continued into the summer. Lucy told herself if she could not "get a hold" of her eating, she would see a therapist.

The integration of life-style questions within Lucy's articulate unfolding of the eating challenge was easily achieved. The current binge-eating problem began on evenings when Lucy attended bridge or Scrabble group. On her way home, Lucy would stop at a deli for a cup of tea and a dessert. She never invited anyone from either group to join her because she thought she "was actually making space for the eating problem." If she was alone it was possible "to have another piece of pie or another dish of ice cream," rather than having the single serving that would be her limit if she were with a friend. Friends would be "like a brake on the eating."

Lucy sensed she was "releasing the brake on her eating," or "going all out" with eating. After the deli visit, she would return home and eat enormous amounts of food. When asked about previous weight issues, Lucy told painful stories about bingeing in high school and college.

Family constellation

Lucy was the youngest child of four children, with three older brothers. Lucy delighted in the fact that she was the only girl and "the baby" of the family. Her two oldest brothers, "the twins," were eight years older. Her youngest brother, Simon, was only 13 months older. "We were Irish twins—Simon was my best friend." Lucy felt that she was the "darling of her father" and her mother's "little dolly." She believes that she was spoiled and "definitely could do no wrong" in the eyes of her parents. The family's social life was exclusively extended family— aunts, uncles, and cousins. Lucy depended on being with her brothers and their friends—she did not reach out to make her own friends. She felt that her own mother did not model relationships with other women at all. Her brother Simon had "lots of friends." She felt that "she never liked girls very much...I had my brothers, my brothers' friends and my family. My mother was maybe my best girl friend."

Early recollections

Lucy's early recollections held themes of being accidently injured and saved by one of her brothers. There were themes of having neighborhood children throw rocks at her, causing a large cut on her forehead and a trip to the emergency room for stitches. This event was followed by her mother's protective cautions about "wild" peers. In these memories, her brothers always took care of her. Even though she was small and not very coordinated, Simon included her in games of hockey, soccer, baseball, or skating. Her memories included joining in with her brothers' friends as they sang guitar music, went to movies, or played games. Lucy liked being the "tagalong little sister." She can still hear mother's voice saying, "Take care of your sister, Simon." Lucy also resonated with the idea that she liked "being saved, especially by men."

Adlerian case conceptualization

Lucy presented as depressed and isolated. In her discouragement, she has reverted to an old habit of bingeing that provides temporary soothing and serves as a "sideshow" in her life. Instead of moving out of isolation, she is following old guiding lines: avoiding taking action on her own life tasks. Old expectations that others should come to rescue her are not working. Lucy presents with obsessive-compulsive tendencies that speak to the desire for order and control in her life. This experience of being out of control shakes her at her roots. It will be important for the therapist to consult Adlerian conceptualizations in other chapters of this book and other resources that focus both on depression and on the obsessive-compulsive personality (Sperry, 1990; Sperry & Mosak, 1996).

Lucy has reverted to a pattern of bingeing that began during her last two years of high school and grew in difficulty during college. "My mother was a great baker. I just didn't seem to fill up." In college the extreme bingeing happened about "three times during the week and once on Sunday night." In that bingeing pattern, she would eat a normal dinner and then eat large amounts of desserts. Her brothers' eating "covered me." "I was maybe 40 pounds overweight. My mother didn't care about how I looked. Mum was overweight herself and didn't value exercise. She was happy that I liked her baking."

She knew weight was a problem because, unlike other girls, she was not attracting boys—other than her brothers' friends, but they were "just friends." Lucy felt that as graduate school approached she began to wake up. This was a "scary, but exciting time for me."

This waking up was Lucy's realization that she had her own dreams. "I woke up to the weight issue because I wanted to go to graduate school in France and date guys. I wanted to find someone and have a better social life. I liked one of my brother's friends, but he just joked with me, he didn't like me in a sexual way." It was this desire for a sexual partner and life beyond her family of origin that awakened Lucy. "I wanted to live on my own. I wanted to have romance in my life. I felt that my weight was the big barrier to having that life." She joined Weight Watchers and lost 40 pounds, achieving her goal weight. "I started to take charge and things started to flow in my life." She was leaving the baby role and developing independence.

Lucy took big steps: applying to graduate schools; seeking a professor mentor; finding an apartment in France; taking French emersion courses; and finding a roommate. Creating her own life induced a mixture of fear and excitement as she left the role of baby. She "was on fire" with the desire to make her own life. Once she began taking action, change rippled through all of the life-task areas. She returned from France, married one of Simon's friends, and settled into motherhood and family life. Life was great through all of this—no bingeing problem.

Her life-style summary and early recollection themes resonated deeply with her own perceptions of how she had functioned in life: The idea of being the baby in the family; the only and deeply treasured girl; being waited on "hand and foot and treated like a treasure—even though I could do it myself"; being rescued by wise and guiding men on many occasions, having "things come to me rather easily—these are big stories in my life." Studying was really the "only thing required of me and I was good at it." Lucy could see how the challenges in each of the life-task areas, especially the loss of her husband, and then two brothers, brought loneliness and depression into her life, as did the independence of her grown children. Lucy was not in the "wife role," the "mother role," "the sister role," or "in the grandparent role." She felt that her life lacked meaning. It was at this point that binge-eating began to grow as a desire in her.

Treatment considerations

Adlerian therapy begins as the client tells the stories that form the life-style inventory. The assessment invites the many stories that will form a picture of the family constellation, relationships with siblings, the guiding lines offered by parents, the social environment, and the early recollections that provide clues to clients' line of movement. Lucy easily saw the effects of her spoiled-baby status and life style of inaction. She could see that when she did take action, her life unfolded in meaningful ways.

Lucy could see that, "stopped" by the losses, depression grew and bingeing began.

She found herself speaking in her late mother's words—"What is there to live for?" Hearing the linkage between her own negative mantra and her mother's negative voice shocked Lucy.

Lucy shared that her mother had experienced several depressive episodes—each one resulting in a suicide attempt. Lucy scared herself with the idea that she might be turning into her mother. She did see that her mother's female guiding lines were much more in the area of service to her family, rather than discovery and service to herself. Lucy saw that her mother "never really got to have personal goals or ambitions." During the first weeks of therapy, Lucy began to "feel lighter." She had noticed that she had already stopped bingeing. She did not want to take antidepressants, preferring to "see what happens with therapy alone."

Over the course of four months of weekly therapy Lucy and her therapist went over the life-style assessment and identified the central themes in Lucy's life—the thoughts, feelings, and actions that fit with her stories of "independence", and the thoughts, feelings, and actions that fit with her times of "being the baby."

Lucy followed her science interests and began a course on genetics. The adults in this emeritus course formed a weekly lunch club. She noticed "one of the guys in the class has his eye on me." Lucy scanned her social environments for possible female friendships. She tried out each possible friendship by inviting the person to the movies. She began dating online, joined a church choir, and began taking guitar lessons. With her son's help, she bought a guitar.

"Not bingeing, but still thinking too much about it," Lucy rejoined Weight Watchers. As the "returning star," she found a new friend, and they began "cooking together." Bingeing began to fade as a behavior and then as an idea. She lost the extra weight at a rate of about two pounds per week, joined a gym, started walking, and joined a yoga class. With the inspiration of her new body and the help of her daughter, Lucy bought stylish clothes. She is currently dating "one special person."

When asked about the binge-eating challenge, Lucy stated that she's thinking about it a lot "in philosophical ways—having filled my life with joy, I don't seem to have the need to fill my body with ice cream and chips." Lucy currently states that she is doing well, but wants to come to therapy every four to six weeks "to stay awake in my life." She is still scared of the memories of her mother's depressive episodes and does not "want to become my mother."

At the time of this writing, the binge behavior has been in "remission" for ten months. Medication does not seem necessary at this point. Lucy plans to check in for "tune ups" once every six weeks, her physician is pleased with her progress, and the therapist is mindful that antidepressants could play a role in long-term recovery.

PICA AND RUMINATION DISORDER: BRIEF CONSIDERATIONS

PICA

Pica (American Psychiatric Association, 2013) is an eating disorder typically found in children with developmental or intellectual delays, usually only diagnosed in children over the age of two. Individuals displaying Pica have an appetite for non-nutritive substances, typically clay, dirt, sand, soap, wood, paint, coal, ice, or chalk. (Bryant-Waugh, Markham, Kreipe, & Walsh, 2010). To be classified as a disorder the eating of these substances must be developmentally inappropriate and not culturally prescribed. Pica can lead to physical and mental challenges. Intestinal obstructions, nutritional problems, and parasites may be evidenced in Pica cases. When Pica appears in individuals with Autism, Schizophrenia, or Kleine-Levin Syndrome, it is not an additional diagnosis unless the condition is severe.

Pica may be caused by mineral and iron deficiencies, with the individual ingesting a mineral in which they are deficient. Pica can be related to celiac disease or hookworm infections. Prevalence rates of between 21.8% and 25.8% of populations of institutionalized mentally retarded and cognitively disabled individuals have been reported (Casey, Cook-Cottone, & Beck-Joslyn, 2012), and Pica incidence rates of 74% of pregnant women have been reported in developing countries. Behavioral treatment has been effective with developmental cases, as well as with pregnant women (Blinder & Salama, 2008).

RUMINATION DISORDER

Rumination Disorder (American Psychiatric Association, 2013) is the repeated regurgitation of food that is re-chewed, re-swallowed, or spit out. This disorder is not a medical disorder; that is, it is not the result of a gastric or reflux disorder. It is not diagnosed if it occurs as a part of any other eating disorders discussed in this chapter. Rumination Disorder is most prevalent in neurodevelopmental and/or intellectual disorders and is only diagnosed if the frequency is so severe that it warrants focused clinical remediation. Weight loss and malnutrition may occur when infants have the disorder, especially if regurgitation occurs immediately after eating. Adolescents or adults with this disorder often try to hide the disorder and may experience social isolation due to the repulsive nature of the disorder (Chial et al., 2003). Like Pica, this disorder is found primarily in individuals with intellectual disabilities. It is important that medical examinations exhaust the possibility of gastrointestinal disorders. It is also important to consider that the Rumination Disorder may actually be a part of Anorexia Nervosa, Bulimia, or a symptom of a generalized anxiety disorder.

Treatment Considerations for Pica and Rumination Disorder

An examination by a medical practitioner is warranted as a starting point for treatment of Pica or Rumination Disorder. Ruling out and then supplying treatment for medical causes and complications is the first step in the treatment of both diseases. When Pica presents in infants and toddlers, it may be normal oral exploration unless the presentation is severe; however, the presentation of moderate to severe Rumination Disorder in infancy can pose a threat to development and even lead to lethal medical conditions. Making sure that a medical team is alert to the presence of these disorders is extremely important.

The second consideration in treatment for Pica or Rumination Disorder involves the use of psychological interventions. Both school psychologists and special educators provide the first line of diagnosis in children with developmental, neurodevelopmental, and/or intellectual disorders. Psychological interventions that have been effective in the treatment of cases of Pica and/or Rumination Disorder rely on the use of behavioral analysis and behavioral interventions. However, identification of the purpose of the behavior is often key to the development of a good treatment plan. These disorders may be the result of a desire for attention, or the avoidance of some task, or a desire for sensory feedback. Once a purpose is hypothesized, positive reinforcement, extinction, differential reinforcement, discrimination training, negative practice, overcorrection, or substitution of more positive oral stimulation may be employed (McAdam et al., 2004).

Concluding Note

This chapter reviewed the diagnostic features and current research on eating disorders, presenting an Adlerian conceptualization of each disorder as well as specific treatment considerations for each disorder. The case study examples offered in this chapter demonstrate Adlerian conceptualization of treatment within the frameworks of Cognitive Behavioral Therapy and/or Dialectical Behavioral Therapy, as well as offering examples of the co-occurrence of mental health challenges like Bipolar Disorder and personality disorders. The case studies demonstrate how elegantly Adlerian practices, like the life-style assessment and use of early recollections, fold into standard inpatient and outpatient CBT and DBT therapy for eating disorders.

References

American Psychiatric Association (2013). *Diagnostic and Statistical Manual of Mental Disorders, Fifth Edition*. Arlington, VA: American Psychiatric Publishing.

Blinder, B.J. & Salama, C. (2008). An update on pica: Prevalence, contributing causes, and treatment. *Psychiatric Times*, 25, p. 6.

Brody, M.L., Walsh, B.T., & Devlin, M.J. (1994). Binge eating disorder: Reality and validity of a new diagnostic category. *Journal of Consulting and Clinical Psychology*, 62(2), pp. 381–386.

Bryant-Waugh, R., Markham, L., Kreipe, R.E., & Walsh, B.T. (2010). Feeding and eating disorders in childhood. *International Journal of Eating Disorders*, 43(2), pp. 98–111. doi: 10.1002/eat.20795.

Brzezinski, M. & Smith, D. (2013). *Obsessed: America's Food Addiction—And My Own*. New York, NY: Weinstein Books.

Bulik, C.M., Tozzi, F., Anderson, C., Mazzeo, S.E., Aggen, S., & Sullivan, P.F. (2003). The relation between eating disorders and components of perfectionism. *American Journal of Psychiatry*, 160, pp. 366–368.

Busetto, L., Segato, G., De Luca, M., De Marchi, F., Foletto, M., & Vianello, M., (2005). Weight loss and postoperative complications in morbidly obese patients with binge eating disorder treated by laparoscopic adjustable gastric banding. *Obesity Surgery*, 15,(2), pp. 195–201.

Casey, C., Cook-Cottone, C., & Beck-Joslyn, M. (2012). An overview of problematic eating and food-related behavior among foster children: Definitions, etiology, and intervention. *Child & Adolescent Social Work Journal*, 29(4), pp. 307–322. doi: 10.1007/s10560-012-0262-4.

Center for Disease Control and Prevention. www.cdc.gov/eating disorders.

Chial, H.J., Camilleri, M., Williams, D.E., Litzinger, K., & Perrault, J. (2003). Rumination syndrome in children and adolescents: Diagnosis, treatment, and prognosis. *Pediatrics*, 111(1), pp. 158-162.

Cook, B., Hausenblas, H., Tuccitto, D., & Giacobbi, P.R. (2011). Eating disorders and exercise: A structural equation modelling analysis of a conceptual model. *European Eating Disorders Review*, 19, pp. 216–225.

Courbasson, C., Nishikawa, Y., & Dixon, L. (2012). Outcome of Dialectical Behaviour Therapy for concurrent eating and substance use disorders. *Journal of Clinical Psychology and Psychotherapy*, 19, pp. 434–449. doi: 10.1002/cpp.748.

Dalgliesh, J., Nutt, K. (2013). Treating men with eating disorders. *Nursing Standard*, 27(35), pp. 42–46.

De Zwaan, M., Mitchell, J.E., Howell, L.M., Monson, N., Swan-Kremeier, L., & Crosby, R.D., (2003). Characteristics of morbidly obese patients before gastric bypass surgery. *Comprehensive Psychiatry*, 44, pp. 428–434.

Fredericks, D.W., Carr, J.E., & Williams, W.L. (1998). Overview of the treatment of rumination disorder for adults in residential setting. *Journal of Behavior Therapy and Experimental Psychiatry*, 29, 1(6), pp. 31–40.

Gadalla, T. & Piran, N. (2007). Co-occurrence of eating disorders and alcohol use disorders in women: A meta-analysis. *Archives of Women's Mental Health*, 10(4), pp. 133–140.

Giorgio, A.T., Maxwell, H., Bone, M., Trinneer, A., Balfour, L., & Bissada, H. (2012). Purging disorder: Psychopathology and treatment outcomes. *International Journal of Eating Disorders*, 45, pp. 36–42.

Johnson, J.G., Cohen, P., Kasen, S., & Brook, J.S. (2002). Childhood adversities associated with risk for eating disorders or weight problems during adolescence or early adulthood. *American Journal of Psychiatry*, 159, pp. 394–400.

Jordan, J., Joyce, P.R., & Carter, F.A. (2008). Specific and nonspecific comorbidity in Anorexia Nervosa. *International Journal of Eating Disorders*, 41, pp. 47–56.

King, B.M. (2013). The modern obesity epidemic, ancestral hunter-gatherers, and the sensory/reward control of food intake. *American Psychologist*, 68(2), pp. 88–96.

Lazaro, L., Font, E., & Moreno, E. (2011). Effectiveness of self-esteem and social skills group therapy in adolescent eating disorder patients attending a day hospital treatment programme. *Journal of European Eating Disorders*, 19(5), pp. 398–406. doi:10.1002/erv/1054.

Lewinsohn, P.M., Striegel-Moore, R.H., & Seeley, J.R. (2000). Epidemiology and the natural course of eating disorders in young women from adolescence to young adulthood. *Journal of the American Academy of Child and Adolescent Psychiatry*, 39, pp. 1284–1292.

Linehan, M.M. (1993a). *Cognitive-Behavioral Treatment of Borderline Personality Disorder*. New York, NY: Guilford Press.

Linehan, M.M. (1993b). *Skills Training Manual for Treating Borderline Personality Disorder*. New York, NY: Guilford Press.

Linehan, M.M. & Chen, E.Y. (2005). Dialectical behavior therapy for eating disorders. In A.Freeman (Ed.), *Encyclopedia of Cognitive Behavior Therapy* (pp. 168–171). New York, NY: Springer.

McAdam, D.B., Sherman, J.A., Sheldon, J.B., & Napolitano, D.A. (2004). Behavioral interventions to reduce the pica of persons with developmental disabilities. *Behavior Modification*, 28(1), pp. 45–72. doi: 10.1177/0145445503259219.

Manaster, R.J. & Corsini, R.J. (2009). *Individual Psychology: Theory and Practice*. Chicago, IL: Adler School of Professional Psychology.

Masterson, J. (1976). *Psychotherapy of the Borderline Adult: A Developmental Approach*. New York, NY: Brunner/Mazel.

Mehler, P.S. & Andersen, A.E. (2010).*Eating Disorders: A Guide to Medical Care and Complications* (2nd edn.). Baltimore, MD: Johns Hopkins University Press.

Mosak, H. (1979). Mosak's typology: An update. *Journal of Individual Psychology*, 35(2), pp. 92–95.

Niego, S.H., Kofman, M.D., Weiss, J.J., & Geliebter, A., (2007). Binge eating in the bariatric surgery population: A review of the literature. *International Journal of Eating disorders*, 40, pp. 349–359.

Pagoto, S., Bodenlos, J.S., Kantor, L., Gitkind, M., Curtin, C., & Ma, Y. (2007). Association of major depression and binge eating disorder with weight loss in a clinical setting. *Obesity*, 15, pp. 2557–2559.

Pompili, M., Mancinefli, I., Girardi, P., Ruberto, A., & Tatarefli, R. (2004). Suicide in Anorexia Nervosa: A meta-analysis. *International Journal of Eating Disorders*, 36(1), pp. 99–103. doi: 10.1002/eat.20011.

Rieger, E., Wilfley, D.E., Stein, R.I., Marino, V., & Crow, S.J. (2005). A comparison of quality of life in obese individuals with and without binge eating disorder. *International Journal of Eating Disorders*, 37(3), pp. 234–240.

Roker, A. & Morton, L. (2013). *Never Goin' Back: Winning the Weight-Loss Battle for Good*. New York, NY: New American Library.

Safer, D.L., Telch, C.F., & Chen, E.Y. (2009). *Dialectical Behavior Therapy for Binge Eating and Bulimia*. New York, NY: Guilford Press.

Schulman, B. (1982). An Adlerian interpretation of the borderline personality. *Modern Psychoanalysis*, 7(2), pp. 137–153.

Sperry, L. (1990). Personality disorders: Biopsychosocial descriptions and dynamics. *Individual Psychology*, 48(2), pp. 193–202.

Sperry, L. & Mosak, H. (1996). Personality disorders. In L. Sperry & J. Carlson (Eds.), *Psychopathology and Psychotherapy: From DSM-IV Diagnosis toTreatment* (2nd edn.), pp. 279–335. Washington, DC: Accelerated Development/Taylor & Francis.

Spitzer, R.L., Yanovski, S., Wadden, T., Wing, R., Marcus, M.D., Stunkard, A., et al. (1993). Binge eating disorder: Its further validation in a multisite study. *International Journal of Eating Disorders*, 13(2), pp. 137–153.

Terence, W.G. (2010). Eating disorders, obesity and addiction. *European Eating Disorders Review*, 18(5), pp. 341–351.

Titova, O.E., Hjorth, O.C., Schiöth, H.B., & Brooks, S.J. (2013). Anorexia Nervosa is linked to reduced brain structure in reward and somatosensory regions: A meta-analysis of VBM studies. *BMC Psychiatry*, 13(1), pp. 1–11. doi: 10.1186/1471-244X-13-110.

Weir, K. (2012). Big kids. *Monitor on Psychology*, 43(11), pp. 58–63.

8 Schizophrenia Spectrum and Other Psychotic Disorders

Len Sperry and Jon Sperry

In 1994, John Nash, Ph.D., the American mathematician, was awarded the Nobel Prize in Economics for his contribution to game theory. Of surprise to many is that 35 years earlier, Nash was given the diagnosis of Schizophrenia. Starting with this first psychotic break at the age of 30, he was subsequently hospitalized several times. Attempts were made to treat him with medications, psychoanalytically oriented psychotherapy, and insulin shock therapy. In his estimation, none of these were successful. Yet, at the time of the award he was no longer psychotic. By John Nash's own account, after several years of essentially being homeless, he stopped listening to his auditory hallucinations and began refuting his delusions. That's right: He stopped listening to his hallucinations and began refuting his delusions. How could this be? Isn't psychosis a lifelong, decompensating disorder? Can individuals recover without conventional treatment? Can hallucinations and delusions be defeated, as Nash claims? From an Adlerian perspective, the answer to the last two questions is a qualified "yes." As the reader will soon learn, Nash's self-description of his delusions and hallucinations and how they develop and change is remarkably similar to the Adlerian conceptualization of psychosis.

So what exactly is Schizophrenia and the psychotic process? In brief, Schizophrenia is a syndrome consisting of a highly altered sense of inner and outer reality to which individuals respond in ways that impair their lives. This altered sense of reality, which is the core of this disorder, shows itself in disturbances of speech, perception, thinking, emotion, and physical activity. The most common form of psychosis is Schizophrenia. The term literally means "splitting of the mind," which in popular parlance connotes a "split personality" or multiple personality. Technically, however, Schizophrenia refers to the incongruity between different mental functions; that is, between thought content and feeling, or between feeling and overt activity. For example, an individual diagnosed with Schizophrenia may talk of being sad or terrified by a specific event, while laughing or showing no affect whatsoever. The case of John Nash and the other case examples in this chapter demonstrate these and other clinical features and dynamics.

This chapter consists of sections which describe the following psychotic disorders: Schizophrenia and Schizophreniform Disorder; Delusional Disorder; Schizoaffective Disorder; Brief Psychotic Disorder; and Substance- and Medication-Induced Psychotic Disorders. The plan for each section is to begin with a clinical description of the disorder and its DSM-5 characterization. Next, a biopsychosocial–Adlerian conceptualization of that disorder is provided. This is followed by a brief discussion of treatment considerations. Finally, a case example rounds out the discussion of the disorder.

However, before turning to specific psychotic disorders, the chapter begins with a general Adlerian conceptualization of psychosis and the psychotic process.

Adlerian Conceptualization of Psychosis

The theory of psychosis presented in this section reflects the Adlerian perspective particularly as it has been articulated by Bernard Shulman (1968, 1984), and supplemented with the research-based theory of Michael Gazzaniga (1988), the noted mind–body researcher.

Shulman's model (Sperry & Shulman, 1996) of the psychotic process can be summarized as follows:

Vulnerability + Life-Style Convictions + Decision + Self-Training and Discouragement ⟶ Psychotic Process and Symptoms

Briefly, vulnerability (i.e., positive family history for a major psychiatric disorder, some biological predisposition to psychosis, and/or faulty training) combined with psychotic-like life-style convictions, personal decision, self-training and discouragement can result in a psychotic process. One becomes schizophrenic over a period of time in response to cumulative life stressors and a feeling or failure. The "choice" is neither conscious nor planned ahead of time. It is a series of small steps—a self-training in which one step makes taking the next step easier, so that, in the end, one somehow arrives at one's own illness without recalling the past by which one came to it.

Like other Adlerians, Shulman espouses a cognitive theory of personality development and psychopathology. Cognitive theory offers a description, an explanation of the internal cognitive structures of the individual. This explanation includes the individual's consistent style of perceiving. For example, schizophrenics extract and process information differently from other persons. They are "over-inclusive"; that is, they include too many categories in their thoughts. They do not filter out extraneous information well. Furthermore, they do not abstract with precision, and thus make errors in logic. They do not pay proper attention to differences in the semantic context of language, and thus they do not understand precisely what others are saying to them. Therefore, they invest what they hear with meaning, prompted by the inner fantasies. In addition, cognitive theory describes the internal schemata apperception—the self-concepts of individuals, their world designs, and their plans for coping with the world. Kelly (1955) devised the term "personal constructs" for the idiosyncratic ways individuals construe events. The word "construe" is apt, since it implies that events are actually constructs devised by individuals themselves. It is a personal conclusion about life and themselves that produces a seemingly appropriate action. These personal constructs are contained in the memory organization of individuals, and influence how subsequent events are stored in their memory.

The personal constructs contain the world design and the plan of action in the schizophrenic, the extravagant ideals that Binswanger (1960) mentioned. Self-concept, world design, and plan of action are all part of what Adler called the life style (1926). Extravagant ideals grow from normal human motives that have gone awry. Finally, a cognitive theory describes the coping program devised by individuals. If we know the life style of individuals, we will know their cognitive blueprint for behavior. Then, we shall be able to see how those who become psychotic have followed a step-by-step progression in their journey toward psychosis. We shall understand how they integrate the events of their lives into this journey in accord with their unconscious blueprint. Thus, knowing their master plan for perceiving stimuli, we shall be able to understand their subjective experiences—the phenomenology of their life. From knowing their phenomenology, we also may reason backwards and plot out their cognitive blueprint.

Arieti (1974, 1980) and Binswanger (1960) have offered useful insights for understanding the psychotic process from a cognitive perspective. Arieti (1980) begins his inquiry by noting the importance of a child's subjective perceptions. Specifically, it is essential to understand the interpersonal world that the individual experienced early in life. This involves determining how the child experienced this world, how he internalized, and how such internalization affected the subsequent events of his life, which in turn acted as feedback mechanisms.

A more thorough cognitive-phenomenological theory of psychosis and Schizophrenia is offered by Binswanger (1960). Starting from the premise that individuals construct their own world design, he insists that schizophrenics construct a world design in which they set up a set of rigid alternatives, a hard and fast either/or. "These alternatives are totally inadequate to escape from an unescapable situation ... he shuts himself off from the world of others and himself, and most especially ... he shuts himself off from ... a loving relatedness with others" (Binswanger 1960, p. 160).

Binswanger was saying that those who will become psychotic have created an impossible situation for themselves. As part of their world design, they have constructed a distorted and misguided goal that is impossible to achieve. They do not give themselves permission to cease pursuit of this goal, and they believe they will be a total failure if they do not achieve it. This notion that schizophrenics have inordinate and inappropriate goals is similar to that of Adler (1926)—a concretized, rigid, and dogmatic aspiration to be in some way superhuman, and a greater interest in this personal goal than in fellowship or enjoyment of life. The few studies on level of aspiration that have been done on schizophrenics and those with other psychoses confirms that, unlike non-psychotic individuals, these individuals either maintain high levels of aspiration after repeated failure, or raise those levels (Lu, 1962).

A Neurobiological Explanation of Psychosis

Even in high-risk situations, most individuals do not experience the psychotic process. Specifically, why does one child in the family become psychotic while others do not? Vulnerability is an important consideration. The basic assumption here is that a person who has a vulnerability to a psychiatric illness has the propensity to develop or express symptoms of the disorder under certain stressful conditions. This is the basis of what is called the stress-diathesis model. Neuchterlein and Dawson (1984) and Liberman (1987) have described vulnerability-stress models of Schizophrenia in which the course and outcome of the disorder are in dynamic flux, influenced by biological, psychological, and social-environmental variables. This vulnerability is manifested by genetic predisposition, neurotransmitter abnormalities, and other unknown neurological factors, resulting in cognitive, autonomic, and attentional dysfunctions, as well as a host of premorbid psychosocial factors such as faulty early childhood training, high-flown goals, and life-style convictions, to name some.

Neuchterlein and Dawson (1984) emphasize the information-process deficits that come along with autonomic reactivity anomalies, and social competence and coping limitations, called enduring vulnerability characteristics. These characteristics interact with environmental stimuli (social stressors and non-supportive social networks) and transient intermediate states (processing capacity overload, autonomic hyperarousal, and deficient processing of social stimuli) to yield the psychotic symptoms of Schizophrenia.

Some schizophrenics seem to start life with what Alfred Adler called an organ inferiority, a central nervous system organization that is unstable or somehow defective. Gazzaniga (1988, 2006) and his colleagues (Gazzaniga, Ivry, & Mangun, 2008) developed and articulated a cognitive theory of psychopathology that addresses this issue of central nervous system dysfunction. It effectively integrates research findings from both the neurosciences and cognitive theory. Gazzaniga proposes that individuals generate a series of internally consisted schemas or beliefs about themselves and life, which allow daily living to be both predictable and meaningful. He labels these cognitive schemas the *brain's interpreter*, which is similar to what Adlerians call life-style convictions. Gazzaniga's "brain interpreter" is also reminiscent of Kurt Goldstein's (1939) compensatory tendency and Adler's theory of compensation. The interpreter does not always have correct data, but must interpret this information any way the brain can. Gazzaniga further postulated an urge to create order in the information being processed, which is an effort to compensate for central nervous system dysfunction, or "organ inferiority," as it was called by Adler. Gazzaniga (1988) believes that Schizophrenia is a disease in which the brain's interpreter, typically the verbal, left hemisphere, attempts to create order out of what is most likely endogenous, or inner-generated, brain chaos. By brain chaos, he referred to spurious neural actions precipitated by faulty biochemical brain states, such as sharp rises or decreases in neurotransmitters, which adversely affect the typically symbolic, image-generating right hemisphere. The interpreter makes decisions about what meaning to assign to chaotic events.

The psychotic process in general, and Schizophrenia in particular, reveals how powerful the interpreter may be and how much it wants to succeed in generating reasonable ideas about unreasonable experiences and thoughts that arise out of dysfunctional brain states. As the right hemisphere continues to generate odd, unexplainable images and impressions, the left hemisphere desperately attempts to "interpret" and integrate these aberrations, according to some consistent, logical, rule-governing system, which Adlerians would term the life style.

Endogenous brain changes, particularly changes in the levels of neurotransmitters such as dopamine, create new circumstances, to which the brain's interpreter must continually react. That reaction in turn produces perceptions that can become powerful guides for the mental outlook of the patient. An endogenous state that is quickly induced by a change of brain chemistry—such as with a mind-altering drug like LSD—can be fairly easily dismissed as an apparition after the brain's biochemistry returns to a more normal state. However, if the brain change lasts longer, then the interpretations generated by the altered state of mind become more embellished and the memories associated with them take on their own life, and can become powerful influences on the personal history of the individual. Gazzaniga noted that "crazy thoughts" are manageable for the normal person because they occur as part of some unusual context, and thus are easily rejected. On the other hand, continually crazy thoughts, evoked by chronic brain dysfunction, become harder to reject. This occurs because of the accumulative effect of one "crazy memory" welcoming other "crazy ideas."

Gazzaniga (1988) speculated that Schizophrenia is the fate of the human mind exposed to long-term distortions of reality. The brain's interpreter tries to bring order to the chaos brought about by biochemical or structural brain abnormalities. As a result of processing erroneous data about self, social relationships, and life circumstances over long periods of time, the brain's interpreter constructs strange and psychotic theories about reality, which become the bizarre images generated by the right hemisphere.

He was not saying that chronic brain dysfunction, such as Schizophrenia, is the result merely of the over production of the neurotransmitter dopamine. Rather, he believed that the dopamine abnormality impacts nerve circuits such that they misfire. In turn, the brain's interpreter creates a specific delusion or set of hallucinations that allow the patient to "make sense" of this phenomenon (Gazzaniga, 1988).

Gazzaniga (1988, 2006) offers a useful phenomenological description of the overwhelming feelings of vulnerability of individuals entering a psychotic state. The non-psychotic person's sense of worth is usually sustained by the positive feedback from social contacts, interactions, and personal relationships. While individuals may have doubts about the future in known and unknown situations, they can cope with such feelings, because life in the past with other people has worked out. But what happens if these individuals start to lose their perception of these automatic rewards? Assuming that accurate perceptions reflect brain circuitry that is functional, good feelings are automatically triggered when individuals have contact with a good friend. But what if seeing that friend did not trigger the response? Gazzaniga believed that this new, negative experience evolves into a state much like Schizophrenia. With their personal reference system at loose ends, because they had trouble producing those automatic rewards, they feel suddenly uncertain and vulnerable. In this disorienting state, they begin to see the world through a haze of paranoia. Such a change in neurotransmitter activity in the limbic system, also called the reward-generating system, alters brain circuits, so that pleasant associations and rewards are no longer produced. Thus, it is easy to imagine how bizarre thoughts fill this void. Without input of thoughts from the normal reward system, schizophrenics are in a chronic information vacuum. They search for information from their current environment, but because of their increasing social isolation, little is to be found. As consensual validation decreases, their interpreter creates an alternative reality, which accounts for hallucinations and delusions.

Intrusive thoughts may begin to flood this chronic informational vacuum. As schizophrenics cope with these unwanted intrusions into thought, thought itself becomes very disordered and interrupted. The first response can be wild embarrassment, and schizophrenics withdraw from social contact as much as possible. However, rather than helping, social isolation further compounds the problem. At first, the brain's interpreter had to deal with imagined sounds and voices, but it now has to comprehend them without the steadying influence provided by contact with friends and family. The same can be said about delusions. At times, all persons experience some paranoid thinking. Episodes of overwhelming vulnerability that arise in the absence of a threatening stimulus are usually due to some transitory biochemical balance in the neurocircuitry, which the brain's interpreter easily dismisses as unsubstantiated. But when the condition moves beyond the episodic to a chronic condition, the brain's interpreter can create prominent delusions in its attempt to "explain" its neurochemical dysfunction.

Hallucinations

Hallucinations, particularly auditory hallucinations, serve to support, and even reinforce, the psychotic process just described. In the past 60 years there have been many hypotheses put forward to explain how such hallucinations are produced and function. One of the longest enduring of these hypotheses, that has considerable support, is the subvocalization hypothesis (Green & Kinsbourne, 1990). Subvocalization, also called inner speech, is the subtle motor activity within the larynx and vocal cords that accompanies auditory hallucinations. It is postulated that psychotic individuals are actually producing the hallucination, i.e., talking to themselves, but do not recognize their voice. Presumably, this lack of recognition is due to a block in neural circuitry of the brain. This hypothesis is the basis for therapeutic interventions, primarily Cognitive Behavior Therapy, for reducing and even eliminating these hallucinations (Ritsher, Lucksted, Otilingam, & Grajales, 2004).

Other Predisposing Factors

Besides brain dysfunction, other vulnerabilities to Schizophrenia include a positive family history for a major psychiatric disorder, predisposing an individual biologically and psychosocially for an expression of psychotic process; and a difficult childhood, in which the individual has become systematically and persistently discouraged by the demands of life. The childhood of schizophrenics is characterized by unsatisfactory human relationships, not only with parents but also with siblings and peers. Such unsatisfactory childhood situations, containing deviant personal methods of relating, distorted and confusing methods of communication, marital problems, suppressive parental behavior, and other peculiar and unsatisfying interactions, have been described by many theorists and researchers. Adlerians believe that these unsatisfactory situations are not what result in psychosis, but rather the child's personal reaction to these childhood problems.

Shulman (1984) noted that the child must conspire with environment pressures to bring about situations that lead to Schizophrenia. He indicates four common syndromes that predispose or increase the individual's vulnerability to Schizophrenia. The four syndromes are the special child syndrome, the bossy child syndrome, the inadequate childhood syndrome, and the child who has to be something to satisfy others syndrome.

Schizophrenia seems to be a final common pathway to which different people can come. Perhaps these concepts do not yet explain who becomes schizophrenic. By looking at the internal schemata of the individual we inevitably find evidence of the kind of world design described by Binswanger (1960), and the kind of life style described by Kurt Adler (1958).

In addition, Shulman proposed that both a vulnerability to psychosis and an extreme stressor are necessary but insufficient conditions in the decision. Therefore, he proposed that the child with a predisposition toward psychosis can "choose" to be or not to be schizophrenic. The question is basically one of choosing a course of life that is likely to lead to Schizophrenia. In their study of families of schizophrenics, Hoover and Franz (1972) found that both normal and psychotic siblings selected their responses to parental demands and life situation stimuli, by either letting themselves become involved in intense embroilment with the parent or refusing to do so. In each case, some kind of decision or choice is made. Thus, in addition to hereditary and environmental determinants, a *creative self* is also at work. Shulman (1984) stated that this creative self becomes a crucial factor in the etiology of Schizophrenia, because it leads us to the notion that Schizophrenia is a personal choice; unconscious perhaps, but a choice nevertheless. Like Gazzaniga, Shulman is convinced that psychosis is more likely to be the result of a plan, rather than simply the result of a defect in brain functioning only.

Psychotic Process and Symptoms

The symptoms of psychosis themselves also can be understood as a form of surrealistic creation and its consequences. Psychotics can present with multiple symptoms, not all of them limited to psychotic processes. They can worry, be fearful, become despondent, self-conscious, suffer feelings of inadequacy, be cynical, be lonely, lose sleep and appetite, have obsessive thoughts, overindulge in alcohol, and be unable to concentrate, as can the so-called neurotic. On the other hand, some of their symptoms are specific manifestations of Schizophrenia, particularly those involving their refusal to use consensuality.

With this in mind, Shulman (1984) has classified the symptoms of psychosis as specific markers along the continuum, moving away from or toward consensuality. Symptoms are arranged in a developmental sequence rather than in the chronological order. As in any developmental sequence, stages may merge and overlap and are not always sharply distinguishable from one another. In addition, stages may be repeated, since psychosis sometimes proceeds through the same process over and over again. It is important to note that many with psychotic disorders will not pass through all these stages but will skip some of them in the course of their illness. Thus, one must not think that every patient follows this exact course of events. Note needs to be made that many psychotic disorders, such as acute organic brain syndromes and delusional disorders, will not fit into this scheme.

The sequence is described in terms of the symptoms evident to an observer and related to the psychotic individual's subjective experience at the time. Not all of the schizophrenic's symptoms are psychotic symptoms *per se*. Some can more rightly be called neurotic. The sequence of psychotic symptoms is as follows:

1. Symptoms with a purpose of permitting and facilitating the withdrawal from social integration. These include seclusiveness, secretiveness, apathy, shallow affect, lack of interest in normal events, deep concentration, practicing autistic thinking, and even suicide.
2. Symptoms with a purpose of defeating the appeal of social living and the insistence of social demands. These include inappropriate affect, loose associations, private language, Mutism, negativism, self-neglect, violence, disgusting behavior, and assaultiveness.

3.   Symptoms with a purpose of reinforcing their private logic in insuring the correctness of their position. These include hallucinations, delusions, provocation of others, impulsiveness, the need to prove self as no good, and playing the game of being "crazy."

4.   Symptoms with a purpose of admitting the re-establishment of conditional social relationships, which are sometimes so bizarre that we are constrained to consider them as indications of psychoses. These include some bizarre methods of behavior. However, obsessive-compulsive and hypochondriacal symptoms may be used for the same purpose. Perhaps these symptoms, bizarre as they may be, should be included among those we consider restitutive, because they are not intended to further separate the individual from society.

SCHIZOPHRENIA AND SCHIZOPHRENIFORM DISORDERS

Arriving at a diagnosis of Schizophrenia can be challenging. As currently understood, the symptom pattern of Schizophrenia consists of some combination of "positive" psychotic symptoms" (delusions, hallucinations, disorganized thinking, or bizarre behavior) and "negative symptoms" (flat affect, reduced motivation, and limited relationships). But these symptoms are not necessarily specific to Schizophrenia, since they can occur in other mental disorders. In other words, none of the symptoms that define Schizophrenia is pathognomonic (specific and always present). Some individuals will present with all or most of these diagnostic features, while most will present with only some of them. This means that while classic, textbook cases of Schizophrenia are unmistakable, diagnosing Schizophrenia is often difficult, given its variability in presentation and its overlap with other disorders. Two individuals who have been given the diagnosis of Schizophrenia may look very different from each other. Also, in some individuals, Schizophrenia may be difficult to distinguish from other disorders that can have psychotic features, such as Bipolar or Depressive Disorders, substance-related disorders, or medical conditions. In cases that are less clear, it is helpful to consider the longitudinal course of how symptoms have evolved. More specifically, look for the presence of psychosis, disorganized thinking and behavior, and negative symptoms, as well as the absence of other psychiatric and neurological conditions.

Clinical Presentation

As a diagnostic label, Schizophrenia includes a wide variety of clinical presentations. Symptoms can vary so greatly from one individual to another that to present a classic textbook picture of the disorder is difficult. For example, the diagnostic presentation could be that of a hypervigilant accountant who suspects that others are plotting against him, or the housewife who believes she is controlled by her dead mother's voice. Or, it could be that of a withdrawn and apathetic college student who broods incessantly about the reality of existence. Symptoms also can vary within the same individual over time, so that the individual may be floridly psychotic and totally unable to function one week, and then be capable of adequate reality testing and reasonable performance in the workplace the following week.

Generally speaking, this disorder first presents with the *prodromal phase*. Typically, it begins with a noticeable deterioration of functioning prior to the active phase and involves the presence of specific symptoms. The *active phase* is recognized by the presence of certain characteristic symptoms combined with gross impairment in the tasks of life: work, love, and friendship. These include primarily "positive" psychotic symptoms. The *residual phase* gradually follows from the active phase. It is manifested by the same symptoms already described for the prodromal phase, along with "negative" psychotic symptoms. An individual with a diagnosis of Schizophrenia who recovers fully is usually considered to be "in remission." If no recurrences intervene over a period of five years without medication, the diagnosis is then changed to that of "no mental disorder." Those in remission frequently experience an acute exacerbation of their symptoms, possibly requiring hospitalization. The clinical lore about this disorder includes the "rule of thirds." According to this rule, approximately one-third of all those who meet the criteria for a Schizophrenia diagnosis will recover fully after a single episode, and another one-third will experience periodic exacerbations of symptoms and periods of remission, while the remaining one-third will experience the ongoing chronic form of this disorder.

Schizophreniform Disorder and Schizophrenia are exactly the same in presentation and differ only in duration, with Schizophreniform Disorder presentation lasting less than one month. The main reason for differentiating the two disorders is that those who are able to recover more quickly have a better lifetime prognosis. There are indicators of good prognosis: the absence of prior episodes, an acute onset, the absence of bizarre behavior, the presence of specific stressors, as well as the presence of mood symptoms.

DSM-5 Characterization

Schizophrenia

Schizophrenia is a disorder characterized in *DSM-5* as having positive and negative symptoms and three phases: prodromal, active, and residual. Individuals who meet criteria for this diagnosis exhibit characteristic symptoms during the active phase. Positive symptoms include delusions, hallucinations, disorganized speech, and grossly disorganized behavior. Negative symptoms include flattened affect and avolition. Symptoms are experienced continuously over a period of at least six months. During this time, approximately one month involves active-phase symptoms, while prodromal and residual symptoms are experienced the rest of the time. Negative symptoms are more likely to be exhibited in the prodromal or residual phases of this disorder. Besides displaying such symptoms, the individual's functioning is also greatly affected. This is noted by markedly impaired functioning in interpersonal relations, work, and/or self-care. The diagnosis of Schizophrenia is not given if Schizoaffective Disorder, Depressive Disorder, or Bipolar Disorder with psychotic features are present. Nor can the diagnosis be made if there is evidence of the direct physiological effects of a medication, a drug of abuse, or a medical condition. When there is a history of a communication disorder beginning in childhood, or autistic spectrum disorder, the diagnosis of Schizophrenia can be added only if prominent delusions or hallucinations have been present for at least one month. Previously, the *DSM* had listed Schizophrenia subtypes: paranoid, disorganized, catatonic, undifferentiated, and residual type. But these subtypes have been removed from *DSM-5* because of limited diagnostic reliability and poor validity (American Psychiatric Association, 2013).

Schizophreniform Disorder

The symptoms of Schizophrenia and Schizophreniform Disorder in *DSM-5* are identical. The two disorders are distinguished only by the duration of symptoms and impairment. A diagnosis of Schizophreniform Disorder can be given if there has been an entire episode—prodromal, active, and residual phases—lasting one month but no more than six months (American Psychiatric Association, 2013).

Biopsychosocial–Adlerian Case Conceptualization

From an Adlerian perspective, schizophrenic individuals are understood to create their own meaning for their existence according to their underlying convictions. These same convictions are schizophrenogenic; that is, they predispose individuals to Schizophrenia. Shulman (1984) assumes that a teleological factor must be present, namely, a set of personal values that are largely self-determined and "call forth" the psychosis.

Such personal values are developed during childhood, in the context of the family. They include convictions about self and life drawn from childhood relationships, the raw material from which the individual must select data and fashion beliefs. These psychotogenic values or convictions grow out of faulty training in responding to life's demands and result in the syndromes of behavior described above. Individuals who will become schizophrenic are the recipient of faulty training, which leads to one or more of the following faulty beliefs.

1. The conviction that they have no place in the world because of their deficiencies and/or the hostilities of the environment.
2. The conviction that they must achieve some special state or position, which frees them from all defects in order to have a satisfactory life. This special state or position is always an exaggerated goal, e.g., to be perfect, to be godlike, to be impregnable, to hurt and humiliate, to be utterly masculine, to have "perfect" interpersonal relationships, and so on. Only this longed-for state can give them a place. Their goals are therefore relatively inflexible, have an all-or-none quality, and demand absolute fulfillment. They see few or no alternatives.
3. The conviction that any defeat or anticipated defeat, no matter how minor, in the pursuit of this goal is a major threat to their desperate attempt to overcome their defects and will "spoil" their life. From this grows the idea that schizophrenics are abnormally sensitive to slights or defeats, whereas normal individuals are able to withstand certain disappointments. Schizophrenics are thus seen as having "low frustration tolerance" and "weak egos." For Shulman, persons who are so "sensitive" to failure exaggerate the importance of succeeding in all endeavors. Life must not bring any defeat, because that would topple the whole structure. In this sense, schizophrenics have all their eggs in one basket. Thus they make unreasonable demands on life.

4. The conviction that common sense, social participation and acceptance of the rules of life according to which society operates interfere with their movement toward their chosen goal. Therefore, in order to better pursue the goals and/or avoid defeat in their pursuits, they make all other considerations of lesser value. Thus, good human relations, the customs of society, sex, health, and even life itself have less value than the continuation of their pursuits. In short, schizophrenics train themselves to be different, because being like others will not work for them.

The crisis occurs when they perceive that their life situation does not allow achievement of the goal in accord with "common sense" in a socially acceptable and useful way. Therefore, "common sense" and consensuality are discarded because they interfere with the pursuit of the goal. They decide to stop living in the consensual world. This is the *decision* that constitutes the "psychotic break." At this point they discard the obligation to function like other human beings.

Having discarded common sense, they are free to develop their own private logic, which permits them to create the fiction that they have reached or will reach their goal of superiority. For example, a Divinity student, convinced of his own sinfulness and failing in his schoolwork, spent three days and nights in prayer and fasting, eventually resulting in a state of confusion in which he felt himself drawn to Jesus. When found by the school authorities, he claimed that he *was* Jesus, and he was subsequently hospitalized. Schizophrenics-in-process systematically and autistically build a fantasy life to suit them. They become independent of the rules which others feel obliged to obey. They can even publicly defecate or masturbate without shame.

Because the world and other people, by their very existence, tend to intrude on their privacy, they must erect barriers to protect their private world. To this end, they isolate themselves and take steps to nullify the efforts of others who attempt to communicate with them. They remove themselves by stupor or drive others away by threats and bizarre behavior. They decide that what others do is wrong, harmful, silly, or crazy, and otherwise blunt, impede, or hide from the efforts of others to reach them. They make themselves immune to logic and sentiment: two consensual ways of communicating by which one person can possibly influence another. All this is made easier by having discarded "common sense." If one wants to stop being part of this world and live in the world of one's own making, the efficient procedure is not to accept "common sense."

Once the schizophrenogenic convictions have been reached and the crisis situation has occurred, the decision to discontinue social participation leads to forms of behavior that prevent continued social integration. Such behavior may be universal or limited to certain specific life areas, because sometimes schizophrenics can accomplish their goals by discarding only some aspects of consensuality. They need not discard all of them, nor all of them all of the time.

By continued isolation from social participation, what begins as a device for avoiding personal defeat or catastrophe becomes itself a catastrophe. Schizophrenics may start by playing a game of pretense, but often find themselves caught in their own devices. Scher (1962) said that schizophrenics begin to believe their own fanciful constructs; they discarded the social system and now have only their schizophrenic system as their standard mode of operation. Their only choice is to continue their attempts to strengthen their foundation, to work harder at reifying their private sense, till they succeed at reaching a state hospital or halfway house. There they are relatively free from the demands of life, or until their decompensation into Schizophrenia permits them to escape the defeats they fear, after which the "acute psychosis" may remit and they resume limited social participation. Otherwise, only strong intercurrent events affect their system. Psychotropic drugs, electroshock therapy, or a skillful therapist may sidetrack them from the pursuit of this fiction. However, if they are soldiers, and the military situation does not permit them to withdraw from social participation, they may be forced to make some kind of peace with the demands of life.

The "decision" to disregard consensuality is thus the *sine qua non* of the psychotic break. Boisen (1947) compared this to creative thinking, saying that observation of a person experiencing this psychotic process shows evidence of a "unsolved personal problem"; attempts at solution are made, which proceed by stages similar to the development of insight and creative thinking. Boisen considered the psychosis as a chosen "solution" to the problem.

Shulman (1984) also noted that schizophrenics must be convinced that common sense is an obstacle, rather than an aid to their purpose. Since common sense is not only sufficient but also necessary for the achievement of those personal goals that are chosen by the majority of persons, it becomes logical to assume that psychotics aspire to achievements that are impossible, or at least highly unlikely, when they remain within the bounds of consensuality. Research has shown that schizophrenics have a higher level of aspiration than non-schizophrenics, and they tend to raise these levels after repeated failures, rather than lowering them as normal persons do (Lu, 1962). Their goal may not only be very high and perfectionistic, it also may be extremely inappropriate, such as wanting to be the Messiah, God, super-sexed, nonhuman, wanting relationships only on their own terms, wanting to have no human relationships at all, or wanting to live in a completely different kind of world.

Schizophrenics also must decide that their private personal goals are imperatives that outweigh all other considerations and values. Nothing else has an appeal for them equal to this rigid goal. In their ambitions, all else is considered chaff for the wind. Only in dreams, in toxic states, in narcotic fantasies, in artificial psychoses, in experiments on sensory deprivation, or in times of severe exhaustion can those living by consensual rules arrange to discard common sense and operate according to a private sense which is completely personal and extra social. At other times, the *Weltanschauung* we accept constrains us to heed the commonly accepted forms of behavior and communication, even though we may resent their limitations.

Since "private sense" cannot stand too much daylight without crumbling, schizophrenics must protect it from close scrutiny. To this end, they severely limit interpersonal communications, either by not speaking at all or deliberately misleading those attempting to speak with them. They may be willing to transact business with others when such transactions do not threaten their private logic, either because the area of transaction is an innocuous or because a therapist or other person is willing to accept their rules of the game. This last situation is called "participating in the patient's psychosis."

Basically, schizophrenics remain well integrated in their *own way*. An outside observer may be impressed with the inappropriate quality of the psychotic solution and thinks he sees a person whose "defenses have disintegrated." Actually, psychotic individuals have discarded their previous consensual defenses, because they were related to consensual modes of functioning and are therefore no longer useful to them. This is why psychotic individuals do not use the usual "defense mechanisms," which require that they accept the rules of common sense. The decision to discard common sense still leaves psychotics with the continuing problem of reifying their private sense. In Gazzaniga's language, the brain's interpreter now has to make sense out of chaos. They must support, justify, and defend their point of view until it becomes an article of faith, as when paranoid individuals provoke others to abuse them, so they can feel justified in being "victims." At this point, some of their behavior will be exploratory in nature; that is, they will empirically determine which varieties of behavior best serve their purpose of keeping distance. This is why a far greater variety of behavior is seen in earlier stages of psychosis than in later stages. Eventually, effective ways of creating distant are evolved, tested, sharpened, and refined, and these behaviors become no longer exploratory and relatively open, but rigid, stereotyped, and concrete.

What others have called "poor ego functioning," "poor drive control," and "emergence of primary processes" are the schizophrenics' careful inattention to those stimuli and perceptions that they want to filter out, and the consequent availability of illogic, unreason, illusion, fantasy, and so on, both as modes of perception and as modes of communication. This allows them to be and act "crazy," since the consensual rejection of "crazy" behavior is absent. For example, psychotics' first fantasy is that the world is astride; then, they are justified in rejecting as unreal and false any evidence that the world exists. Now they are free from obligation to observe rules; they emancipate themselves from all powers other than their own and save their self-respect by blaming the outside world or refusing to acknowledge its existence.

The "decision" seems often to occur at times of physical exhaustion or illness. The crisis situation, with its attendant fear, indecision, restlessness, exhaustion, sleeplessness, and sleep deprivation, provides an easier transition into a psychotic state. When physical resistance is lowered, the integrating functions of the central nervous system is diminished as the brain's interpreter "tires," and nonconsensual experiences are more likely to occur. Perhaps if they set out to become reactively psychotic, an easy procedure perhaps is to work themselves into a state of frenzy, lack of clarity, exhaustion, and extreme subjectivity, just as warriors engage in a war dance to work themselves into frenzied readiness before a battle.

Treatment Considerations

Since the middle 1950s antipsychotic medications have been the treatment of choice for schizophrenics particularly in the active phase. The introduction of antipsychotic medications has had a powerful influence on the management of Schizophrenia. Some pharmacologists believe that the antipsychotic medication is the only proven mode of treatment and that psychotherapeutic interventions are of little use. On the other hand, advocates of psychotherapy for Schizophrenia argue that medication alone is not sufficient and that the effectiveness of medication depends on the psychosocial context in which it is given. They also contend that medication only reduces psychotic symptoms but does not affect the patient's social or personality functioning. For all practical purposes, talking about a single "correct" treatment is not useful since Schizophrenia is a syndrome consisting of a number of disorders. The range of treatments and combinations of treatments used reflects the variability inherent in this disorder. What is useful to some schizophrenic individuals may not be useful, or may even be harmful, to others. Most effective treatment regimens combine psychopharmacology and psychosocial therapies (Beitman and Klerman, 1986).

Shulman (1984) has described an Adlerian perspective on treatment. He noted that the decision to reverse the psychotic process requires that the individual be willing to consider alternatives to current behavior, to experiment with these alternatives, and to train oneself in new directions. The task is not a simple decision to "buck up and stop thinking that way," but a willingness to reorder one's perception in order to permit the growth of a new frame of reference in regard to life. Shulman noted that change must proceed through a kindling of hope, a reestablishment of consensual ways of behaving, and an experiencing of satisfaction in consensual living. The keynote of the therapist's behavior is, thus, encouragement. Patient, persistent encouragement is a necessity. "The approach is continued," stated Kurt Adler (1958), "until the patient becomes convinced that fruitful cooperation is possible, becomes more hopeful as to the achievement of some of his goals, learns to feel less of an isolate and more likely the human being."

For psychotic individuals, change involves a certain amount of learning.

> That they have mistaken high-flown goals; that they have misunderstood what it means to be human; that they can become successfully human with human practice; that life will be more satisfying when they join the human community; that they have been training themselves away from the common sense way of looking at life and practicing the use of an isolating private logic; and, that their psychotic symptoms are purposeful maneuvers more under their control than they have recognized.
>
> (Sperry & Shulman, 1996, p. 46)

Shulman (1984) noted that the great majority of schizophrenic individuals will not have any systematic individual psychotherapy, nor that the relationship between therapists and patients will be extended over a long enough term to be effective. However, even brief encounters can have far-reaching effects. While therapists may engage in long-term psychotherapy with relatively few schizophrenic individuals, they will briefly and perhaps casually come in contact with many more patients. Any of these encounters, while making ward rounds, while doing intakes in the clinic, while examining patients or emergency admissions, provide therapists opportunities to intervene therapeutically albeit briefly. Shulman noted that treatment such as group therapy, milieu therapy, family and recreational therapy, music therapy, psychodrama, social clubs, and even medication groups can be very useful treatment interventions. They are social processes and tools of communication with a purpose of encouraging and clarifying self-awareness and self-understanding, overcoming isolation, promoting the use of social skills, and correcting faulty perceptions.

Two cases examples of Schizophrenia are provided here. The first represents a relatively common presentation of chronic Schizophrenia that evolves over years, and does not resolve but worsens. The second example represents a case that evolves over years, but does resolve.

Case Example: Mr. P.

Mr. P. is a 41-year-old single white male who had been hospitalized for psychotic reactions five times in the previous 15 years. He presented as a Dependent Personality Disordered individual, who lived with an older married sister, and was supported by a Veterans Administration pension. Although unmarried, he had had girlfriends in the past and still maintained a sexual relationship with one of them. He had male friends and enjoyed drinking, playing cards, and going to ball games with them. His downfall always came at work. He was able to get a job whenever he felt well, and always showed himself to be a good worker. Soon he would be given more responsibilities. He feared and resisted, but he was not able to speak up affectively to his bosses. He would react by becoming slipshod in his work and taking days off. Shortly thereafter, he would begin to feel agitated, and worried about his job and his health. He would lose his appetite and become unable to sleep. For several sleepless nights, he would begin "having thoughts," which were obsessive ideas that he was getting sick or that he would lose his mind. Eventually he became exhausted and disoriented, would hear voices, imagine that he was dying, fear he was being poisoned, and so on. He would be brought to the hospital by his sister or sometimes would present himself for admission. His stays in the hospital tended to last from six months to two years. After a few months he would begin to calm down, recover his composure, and would slowly regain his confidence to leave the hospital and try working again. He had never been discharged from a job, but voluntarily left when he felt too sick to work. His greatest fear was that he would again have a psychotic episode.

During the psychotic episodes, this male fulfilled all the criteria for the diagnosis of Schizophrenia. During his periods of remission he was a dependent personality with reasonably superficial adjustment to others. He never felt able to undertake many responsibilities, such as marriage or advancement at work. He had dropped out of school in the 11th grade, because he felt it was too much for him. He was the baby of his family and had been overprotected by his mother until her death. His older sister now filled his mother's role. The pattern of his life is a common one, but why did he become psychotic in times of stress, rather than developing an anxiety disorder, which might have served his purpose just as well? For him, his psychotic episodes function as ordinary anxiety disorders, as a safeguarding device for avoiding a difficult situation, or for saving face in it. When faced with the responsibility that is perceived as overwhelming, this patient could defeat the demands of his life situation by "flipping his lid," by "throwing everything up for grabs." However, he has been able to maintain a "bridge" to the non-psychotic world in two ways: First, he always remains able to find a job; and second, he willingly returns to the dependent hospital situation, where he is relieved of responsibility and stress.

Case Example: John Nash, Ph.D.

John Nash was born in a small town in West Virginia in 1928. Nash is described as a solitary and introverted young boy who was more interested in books and experimenting than in friends (Naser, 1998). At the age of 15, Nash and two of his friends were experimenting with homemade explosives when one of the boys was killed by a pipe bomb they had made. The parents of the surviving boy sent him off to boarding school to shield him from Nash's influence. The result was that Nash lost his two friends and appears to have experienced survivor guilt, since this trauma was not worked through emotionally (Capps, 2005). Nash went on to complete a bachelor's and doctoral studies in six years. Thereafter, he took academic positions and worked to fulfill his goal of becoming the top mathematician in the world.

Family constellation

He was the firstborn child—his sister was two years younger—of parents with professional training and upwardly mobile aspirations. His biographer refers to the family as "social climbers," as they became Episcopalian and joined the town's new country club (Naser, 1998). His father was an engineer and his mother a school teacher, who in time relinquished her career to home-school her precocious son. Family values appeared to be achievement and social recognition.

Life style

Although there are some biographical and autobiographical accounts, no early recollections are provided. Nevertheless, there is information to make inferences about his beliefs about self and the world and speculate about his vulnerability to psychosis, the content of his hallucinations and delusions, and the precipitants for his psychotic break. His self-view, world-view, and life strategy are inferred as: "I am special and different but better than others. The world and other people may not want to, but they must recognize my specialness. Therefore, I will act differently, be ambitious, competitive, and achieve greatness, and do whatever is necessary to make others recognize my greatness." Nash achieved considerable success and stature in the beginning of his academic career as a mathematician. However, as he turned 30 years of age it became clear that he would not reach his high-flown goal of becoming the world's greatest mathematician.

Precipitating the psychotic process

The precipitant for his first psychotic break at age 30 seemed to have involved three converging themes. The first was his failure to win the coveted Fields Prize in Mathematics that year. He had expected to win it and was very bitter that it was awarded to someone else. The second was his feeling of being "trapped" in two relational situations without sufficient coping skills (Capps, 2005). The third was his wife Alicia's pregnancy, which would displace her affection and attention from him to an infant (Naser, 1998). Having a child appears to have been a major threat to his narcissistic self-view. A particularly telling photo of Nash, appearing in his biography, seems to support this hypothesis (Naser, 1998). It shows Nash at a New Year's Eve party, sitting in the same chair as his pregnant wife, clad only in a diaper and drinking from a baby's bottle. Presumably, he is "demanding" to remain as the center of attention. This was not to be, and over the next few days he started exhibiting increasingly bizarre behavior, which resulted in his first of several psychiatric hospitalizations.

Delusions

Over the ensuing years Nash exhibited both positive and negative symptoms of his psychotic process. These included both paranoid and grandiose delusions. In the 2002 PBS documentary, *A Brilliant Madness*, Nash provides a rather insightful description of his psychotic process: "Madness can be an escape. If things are not so good, you may be want to imagine something better. In madness, I thought I was the most important person of the world and people like the Pope would be just like enemies, who would try to put me down in some way." In describing his delusional thinking, he said: "A delusional state of mind is like living a dream. Well, I knew where I was, I was there on observation, but I was able to think that I was like a victim of a conspiracy. ... In madness, I saw myself as some sort of messenger, or having a special function. Like the Muslim concept with Muhammad, the messenger of Allah." From an Adlerian perspective Nash is describing the "arrangement" for his psychosis and the "safeguarding" function it played in his life. Essentially, his psychotic process allowed him to achieve his "high flown goal" (Adler, 1926) of being the world's greatest mathematician, not in this world, but in his imagined world. He also comments: "To some extent, sanity is a form of conformity." This comment addresses the distinction Adlerians make between "consensual reality" and "private logic." He continues: "People are always selling the idea that people who have mental illness are suffering. But it's really not so simple. I think mental illness or madness can be an escape." This second mention of psychosis as an escape reflects the Adlerian functions of arrangement and safeguarding.

Hallucinations

Not only did his delusions support his high-flown goal, but so also did his auditory hallucinations. They, too, serve a necessary function in maintaining the psychotic process. What is particularly instructive in the PBS documentary is that Nash appears to have considerable insight into his role in the production of the auditory hallucinations that he experienced. He said: "You're really talking to yourself, is what the voices are." Interestingly, this explanation is essentially the same as the subvocalization hypothesis of auditory hallucinations.

Reversing the psychotic process

Nash was able to outgrow the need for his psychotic process. He claims that none of the conventional treatments offered him, particularly medication and psychoanalytically oriented psychotherapy, were helpful. Instead, he insists the change occurred because he changed the way he thought about and responded to his hallucinations and delusions. "I don't really remember the chronology very well, exactly when I moved from one type of thinking to another. I began arguing with the concept of the voices. And ultimately I began rejecting them and deciding not to listen. ... I moved from one type of thinking to another. I began arguing with the concept of the voices. And, ultimately I began rejecting them and deciding not to listen."

In his autobiographical sketch that appeared after he was awarded the Nobel Prize in Economics, Nash comments further on the reversal of his delusional thinking. "Then gradually I began to intellectually reject some of the delusionally influenced lines of thinking which had been characteristic of my orientation. This began, most recognizably, with the rejection of politically oriented thinking as essentially a hopeless waste of intellectual effort. So at the present time I seem to be thinking rationally again in the style that is characteristic of scientists." (Les Prix Nobel, 1994).

DELUSIONAL DISORDERS

Clinical Presentation

Delusions are the signature feature of this disorder. This diagnosis requires the presence of persistent delusions, without the disorganized and negative symptoms that are characteristic of Schizophrenia. That means that hallucinations, odd speech, bizarre behavior, and blunting of emotions (affect) are not present. In fact, those with the diagnosis appear to be completely normal, charming, and intelligent, as long as their delusions are not triggered in conversation with them. But, as soon as they are, these individuals will begin expressing wildly strange beliefs. Their delusional beliefs are fixed, false, and resistant to compelling contrary evidence and rational disputation. Since their psychosis is tightly encapsulated, they are able to function reasonably well in other areas of their life. That means that professionals such as physicians, lawyers, and teachers who are floridly psychotic when discussing their delusions can still function in their jobs.

DSM-5 Characterization

Individuals who meet criteria for this diagnosis are characterized by the presence of one or more delusions. Such delusions are manifest for at least one month. In addition, there are no positive symptoms of Schizophrenia, particularly hallucinations. However, if hallucinations are present, they are not prominent and must be related to the theme of the delusions. Functioning at work or in relationships is not significantly impaired. Nor is the individual's behavior considered odd, bizarre, or eccentric. If a Major Depressive Episode or a Manic Episode has occurred concurrently, these episodes have been relatively brief. Furthermore, the disorder is not caused by the direct physiological effects of a medication or drug of abuse, nor by a medical condition. Unlike previous editions, *DSM-5* no longer requires that delusions be "non-bizarre" in nature. Several types of delusional disorders can be specified, each of which reflects a dominant delusional theme. These include the Erotomanic Type, with the theme that someone of a higher status is in love with the individual. In the Grandiose Type, the theme involves delusions of having some great power, talent, insight, or a special relationship to a deity or famous individual. In the Jealous Type, the theme involves the unfaithfulness of the individual's sexual partner. In the Persecutory Type, the theme involves being abused or treated malevolently. In the Somatic Type, the theme involves having a physical defect or medical condition.

Individuals who meet criteria for this diagnosis are characterized by prominent delusions and/or hallucinations that are not due to the physiological effects of a medication, drug of abuse, or toxic substance. This disorder is differentiated from other psychotic disorders by considering its onset and course. When the history, physical examination, or laboratory findings suggest that the cause of hallucinations or delusions were substance related, the diagnosis of Substance/Medication-Induced Psychotic Disorder is highly likely. These symptoms must develop during, or within one month of intoxication by or withdrawal from the substance, and the substance must be capable of producing these symptoms. It must be determined that the disorder is not better accounted for by a non-substance-induced psychotic disorder. Finally, this diagnosis cannot be given if symptoms occurred primarily during the course of a delirium.

There are two specifiers associated with this disorder. The designation "with onset during intoxication" is used when ingesting the intoxicating substance and the symptoms develop during the period of intoxication. Likewise, the designation "with onset during withdrawal" is used when withdrawal (symptoms) develop during withdrawal from the substance. Finally, severity can be rated with a quantitative assessment of the specific positive and negative psychotic symptoms present. Symptoms are rated on a 5-point scale ranging from 0 (no present) to 5 (present and severe) (American Psychiatric Association, 2013).

Biopsychosocial–Adlerian Case Conceptualization

Shulman (1984) differentiated the paranoid features of the schizophrenic from those seen in the Delusional Disorder and the Bipolar Disorder. In the Delusional and Bipolar Disorder, Shulman noted that individuals develop some private logic while retaining some consensuality. Patients can become very upset, but do not appear to have undergone an acute disoriented episode. They may have their own private explanation of "causes" and "evil forces at work," and have no intent to expose these explanations to rules of consensual logic. The Bipolar Disorder, on the other hand, so often can look as bizarre as the schizophrenic that the differentiations become difficult. The acute disoriented state in the manic phase of the bipolar is similar to that of a schizophrenic. Both states can show perceptual distortions and autistic thinking. *Manic states* may contain considerable paranoid features. However, manic individuals do not wish to keep a distance between themselves and others. Although they change the rules of the "reality game," they continue to want social relationships. Their behavior is that of those who constantly seek close relationships. Even in the distrust phase of the Bipolar Disorder, their behavior is designed to keep others involved with them. This is the essential difference between the Bipolar Disorder and the schizophrenic. Between attacks, individuals with the Bipolar Disorder usually accept the human role as the rest of us do, whereas schizophrenics do not.

Treatment Considerations

Generally speaking, treatment of delusional disorders is extraordinarily difficult. The longer the symptoms have been present, the more refractory they are to simple treatments such as psychoeducation, psychotherapy, or medication. However, some culturally induced syndromes may respond to relocation—i.e., returning to the patient's country of origin—even if they have taken months to come to clinical attention (Reid, 1989).

When individuals with this disorder agree to psychotherapy, it may be the treatment of choice, but it should be initiated in such a way that they see some benefit from it and some support from the therapist. Emphasis should be on developing a trusting relationship with a neutral and accepting therapist. Ritzler (1981) indicated that systematic desensitization has been effective in reducing delusional behavior. Antipsychotic medication has been noted to be effective in some cases. However, most patients are reluctant to take neuroleptics, either because of their suspiciousness of the treatment or because of their exquisite sensitivity to the side effects of medication. It has been shown that antipsychotic medication takes the "edge" off delusions, making psychosocial treatment much more possible. Recent use of antidepressants also has been noted to be effective (Reid, 1989).

Bullard's (1960) short paper on Adlerian psychotherapy with delusional individuals is a classic. Bullard described an approach to engaging the suspicious and distrustful patients. Shulman (1984) noted that, insofar as possible, he tries to save the pride of the paranoid.

> Our explanations and interpretations are egosyntonic: we treat him with courtesy and respect, while we do not let his delusions pay off; we try to discuss with him his feelings about life, and those areas where he feels threatened by defeat, and try to help him to feel that he is a worthwhile person. It will take longer to convince that he is not surrounded by a hostile world, and that he does not always need to win to be superior or to be right.
>
> (p. 156)

Case Example: Mr. D.

Mr. D. is a 45-year-old divorced New York City cab driver of Chinese descent. He was arrested for a disturbance that occurred when he was distributing flyers about various government conspiracies. He was taken to a psychiatric emergency room where he was evaluated. He was convinced that the government was oppressing poor homeless individuals and forcing budget cuts to anti-poverty programs. He believed it was his duty to distribute anti-government materials to force the government to back down. His resentment for the government dates to the time when his father's benefits were cancelled. Even though they were subsequently reinstated, Mr. D. and his family had to vacate their apartment and live in a homeless shelter. However, it was not until he was in his forties that he began to develop systematized persecutory delusions.

In tandem with this delusion, he also held the grandiose delusion of having the power to cause national calamities and deaths of prominent political figures by the sheer force of his prayers. He cited a politician's suicide that was caused by his prayers as support for this delusion. He did not manifest auditory hallucinations, a thought disorder, nor a medical condition to explain these delusions. Outside of these political beliefs he was otherwise normal. His friends and family did not consider his ideas to be abnormal, and he was able to support himself as a cab driver, living by himself. He refused to have any treatment, a decision that was strongly supported by his family.

SCHIZOAFFECTIVE DISORDER

Clinical Presentation

Schizoaffective Disorder is a diagnosis reserved for individuals who do not meet sufficient criteria for either Schizophrenia or a mood disorder but have features of both. For example, those with Major Depressive Disorder or Bipolar Disorder may have episodes of depression and/or mania, as well as delusions or hallucinations. Likewise, in Schizophrenia, individuals may present with delusions and/or hallucinations, and may present with prominent mood symptoms. This is the reason why Schizoaffective Disorder is referred to as a border diagnosis.

DSM-5 Characterization

Individuals who meet criteria for this diagnosis are characterized by an uninterrupted and continuous display of active or residual symptoms of psychosis. During this time, a Manic Episode or a Depressive Episode—with depressed mood—must be concurrent with positive symptoms of Schizophrenia. These must include delusions or hallucinations for at least two weeks. In addition, Manic or Depressive Episode symptoms must also be present during most of the active and residual phases of the disorder. Furthermore, this disorder cannot be caused by the direct physiological effects of a medication, drug of abuse, or medical condition. Two types are specified. In the Bipolar Type, the disorder involves Manic Episodes, Mixed Episodes, or a Manic or a Mixed Episode and Major Depressive Episodes. In the Depressive Type, the disorder involves only a Major Depressive Episode.

In contrast to previous editions, *DSM-5* now requires that a major mood episode be present for a most of the time the disorder is manifested. This change means that this disorder is a longitudinal, rather than a cross-sectional, diagnosis. In this respect, it is comparable to Schizophrenia, Bipolar Disorder, and Major Depressive Disorder, which are bridged by this condition (American Psychiatric Association, 2013).

Biopsychosocial–Adlerian Case Conceptualization

There is no specific Adlerian conceptualization of the Schizoaffective Disorder. However, since this is a variant of Schizophrenia, the basic conceptualization of Schizophrenia, including life-style convictions—as previously described—are applicable. If the individual's symptom presentation is largely mood based, consult the life-style convictions for depression and/or Bipolar Disorder described in other chapters of this book.

Treatment Considerations

The newer antipsychotic medications appear to be quite effective in Schizoaffective Disorder treatment. If the individual's psychotic symptoms are acute and accompanied by agitation, an older antipsychotic medication, Haldol, can be given as an injection to slow behavior. If depressive symptoms are prominent, an antidepressant is often added. Psychotherapy can be useful, particularly if it is focused on modifying the life-style convictions that provoke mood disturbance and thought disorder. Often, combined treatment with medication and psychotherapy is needed to effect change.

Case Example: Mrs. S.

Mrs. S. was a 36-year-old married woman with three children. She was reported to be a happy woman, but 11 months after her last child was born she began to complain of sleep difficulties. Her husband noticed that she was irritable, sometimes euphoric, and increasingly isolated and was unable to take care of the children. One night her husband received a phone call informing that his wife was in jail. She had secretly left the house, and gone to a bar, where she started a fight with a police officer who had observed her acting wildly and suspected her of drug abuse. She was taken to a psychiatric clinic where a drug screen was negative for alcohol and drugs of abuse. At that time she told the police and the psychiatrist that she was absolutely certain that somebody was using her social security card and was collecting her benefits. She had gone to the bar because a man's voice told her that the person who was using her social security number was in the bar. At the same time she also told them that she was one of the ten smartest people in the world. She was treated with antipsychotic medications, to which she quickly responded, and was discharged. One year later she was rehospitalized. Her husband confirmed that she was taking medicines as prescribed and was compliant. However, during the previous two weeks she had been complaining that someone had again stolen her social security card. The psychiatric evaluation found her to be depressed, thinking herself worthless, and she complained that the man's voice had returned. She was started on an antipsychotic and an antidepressant, and within two weeks she became asymptomatic. A diagnosis of Schizoaffective Disorder was given.

BRIEF PSYCHOTIC DISORDER

Clinical Presentation

This diagnosis is given to individuals who experience a stressor which precedes their psychotic disorders. They may experience hallucinations, delusions, dissociate (feel spacy), or become very agitated or impulsive. As the diagnostic label implies, this presentation is for a brief duration, after which individuals return to their previous level of functioning. Common triggering events (stressors) include ending a relationship, leaving home for college, travel to a foreign country, or a traumatic experience.

DSM-5 Characterization

Individuals who meet criteria for this diagnosis are characterized by the sudden onset of a positive psychotic symptom. "Sudden" means that within two weeks an individual shifts from a non-psychotic to a frankly psychotic state. Positive psychotic symptoms can include delusions, hallucinations, disorganized speech, and grossly disorganized or catatonic behavior. An episode of this psychotic disorder lasts at least one day but no more than a month. After this time there is a full return to the individual's previous level of functioning. The diagnosis is not given if Schizophrenia, Schizoaffective Disorder, Depressive Disorder, or a mood disorder with psychotic features are present. Also, this disorder cannot be caused by the direct physiological effects of a medication, drug of abuse, or medical condition. Three types of this disorder can be specified, as follows.

The designation Brief Psychotic Disorder with Marked Stressor(s)—also called Brief Reactive Psychosis—is given if symptoms occur just after and in response to situations that, separately or together, would be significantly stressful to others in similar circumstances in the individual's culture. The designation Brief Psychotic Disorder without Marked Stressor(s) is given if the psychotic symptoms do not occur immediately after or not in response to situations, or are not apparently in response to events that, singly or together, would be markedly stressful to almost anyone in similar circumstances in the person's culture. The designation Brief Psychotic Disorder with Postpartum Onset is given if the onset of the conditions occurs within four weeks following birth. Finally, severity can be rated with a quantitative assessment of specific psychotic symptoms present. Symptoms are rated on a 5-point scale ranging from 0 (no present) to 5 (present and severe) (American Psychiatric Association, 2013).

Biopsychosocial–Adlerian Case Conceptualization

Adlerians recognize that individuals who present with psychotic features do not completely fit the Adlerian conceptualization of Schizophrenia. This is particularly the case with Brief Psychotic Disorder. While they may experience some childhood difficulties, they were neither schizotypal nor paranoid personality types. They can relate interpersonally with families and peers, but from time to time become psychotic under stress. Once the acute psychotic state clears, their underlying personality disorder, usually histrionic, passive-aggressive, or borderline, becomes evident.

This disorder can be conceptualized as a partial retreat from reality in the face of a most unpleasant demand of a life task. It provides a temporary way out and starts to recede as soon as the life demand is no longer present. It can be compared to the behavior of a child losing a game: One child will lose graciously, another will hide its hurt, the third will depreciate the game, a fourth will accuse the others of cheating, a fifth will cheat to influence the outcome, the sixth will rationalize, and a seventh will grit its teeth and determine to win next time. The eighth child, however, will deny, distort, disturb, and even destroy the game, refusing to let it come to its natural end. This is the mode of reaction of a patient who fits the criteria for Brief Psychotic Disorder (Sperry & Shulman, 1996).

The main difference between these cases and Schizophrenia is that the psychosis in these cases is only temporary and not a way of existence. Typically, these individuals are not caught up in what Adler (1926) called the high-flown goal, and what Binswanger (1960) termed the extravagant idea. Of the four sets of convictions mentioned earlier in this chapter, seemingly they suffer only from the fourth. This distinction fits the criteria in *DSM-5* for Brief Psychotic Disorder as distinguished from Schizophrenia.

Treatment Considerations

Sometimes this psychotic presentation resolves spontaneously without treatment and individuals return to their previous level of functioning. More often, and to facilitate its resolution, a brief course of inpatient treatment is provided. Usually, this includes a course of antipsychotic medication to "break" the psychosis. However, intensive outpatient treatment may be just as effective. Psychotherapy can be useful in understanding the trigger or precipitant and the individual's biopsychosocial vulnerability for psychosis.

Case Example: Mrs. B.

Mrs. B. is a 39-year-old married female. Mrs. B. was responsible for most of the duties related to raising four children and maintaining the home. In the past, she had been treated for an episode of Postpartum Psychosis. However, until recently she functioned adequately and had not used nor needed any mental health services. Problems began the day that her husband informed her that he was having an affair and moved out of the house. Up to this time, she believed that her emotionally distant husband was not home because he was out of town on business trips. Actually, he was nearby having an affair with a woman whom Mrs. B. knew. Over the next four days, she became intensely agitated and depressed. While she seldom drank, she now drank heavily to diminish her agitation and insomnia. She ate and slept very little, and experienced extreme guilt about not taking better care of her children. She felt burdened over her "transgressions and sins." She described fearing that she would be doomed to "eternal damnation" and that she "had lost her soul" and would have to repent for the rest of her life. In the emergency room in which she was being evaluated she described a conspiracy by the Catholic Church to steal her soul. A diagnosis of Brief Psychotic Disorder was given.

SUBSTANCE/MEDICATION-INDUCED PSYCHOTIC DISORDERS

Clinical Presentation

This presentation of psychotic symptoms results from the use of medications or recreational drugs. Such symptoms occur as the result of intoxication with the substance, or less often, in withdrawal from it. Experienced clinicians consider this diagnosis when evaluating adolescents and young adults who abruptly present with psychotic symptoms, particularly when visual hallucinations are involved. Lab testing (drug screens) is invaluable in making this diagnosis.

DSM-5 Characterization

Individuals who meet criteria for this diagnosis are characterized by prominent delusions and/or hallucinations that are the physiological effects of a medication, drug of abuse, or toxic substance. This disorder is differentiated from other psychotic disorders by considering its onset and course. When the history, physical examination, or laboratory findings suggest that the cause of hallucinations or delusions were substance related, the diagnosis of Substance/Medication-Induced Psychotic Disorders is highly likely. These symptoms must develop during, or within one month of intoxication by or withdrawal from the substance, and the substance must be capable of producing these symptoms. It must be determined that the disorder is not better accounted for by a non-substance-induced psychotic disorder. Finally, this diagnosis cannot be given if symptoms occurred primarily during the course of a delirium.

There are two specifiers associated with this disorder. The designation "with onset during intoxication" is used when symptoms develop during the period of intoxication. Likewise, the designation "with onset during withdrawal" is used when withdrawal develops during the period of withdrawal. Finally, severity can be rated with a quantitative assessment of the specific positive and negative psychotic symptoms present. Symptoms are rated on a 5-point scale ranging from 0 (no present) to 5 (present and severe) (American Psychiatric Association, 2013).

Biopsychosocial–Adlerian Case Conceptualization

There is no specific Adlerian conceptualization of this disorder. Because there is an obvious biological vulnerability for this disorder, treatment is largely biological. The extent to which there is psychosocial vulnerability to this disorder can be inferred from an investigation of the individual's life-style convictions.

Treatment Considerations

Treatment of this disorder is directed at relieving the effects of the intoxicating medication or substance condition. This requires careful medical observation to control withdrawal symptoms, or for medical management of a continuing withdrawal process. If the symptoms were produced by the effects of a needed medication, reduction of the dose is made under close medical supervision. Typically, this takes place in an inpatient medical or psychiatric setting, since the first priority is the individual's safety and life-supportive measures. If the treatment is not successful, it may indicate that the diagnosis was incorrect and that the more likely diagnosis is Brief Psychotic Episode.

Case Example: Ms. M.

Ms. M. is a 19-year-old single female who was brought by Jason, her boyfriend, to the paramedics at a first-aid station at an outdoor arena. Since M. was unable to communicate, Jason expressed his concerns. He described the gradual deterioration he had noted in her over the past hour. At first, she displayed abrupt shifts in affect, with giddiness and laughter one moment and agitation and impulsiveness the next. Jason said that she was "talking crazy talk" and not making much sense. He also mentioned that M. had brief bursts of terror lasting a few seconds or minutes, during which he had to stop her from running away. He believed that she was responding to hallucinations. He also reported that M. had stopped speaking and appeared to have lost the ability to do so. She also had a hard time walking and tried to crawl away from him. By the time that the paramedics were able to examine her, M. was rigid, immobile, mute, and unable to communicate with others. When M. was coherent enough to talk to the consulting psychiatrist she described the experience of auditory hallucinations, image distortion, and amnesia. Later, Jason admitted that they had used Phencyclidine (PCP) earlier that day. All these symptoms were consistent with PCP use. Accordingly, the diagnosis of Substance/Medication-Induced Psychotic Disorders- Phencyclidine with Onset during Intoxication was made.

Concluding Note

Knowledge of the psychotic disorders is critical for clinical practice. At a minimum, clinicians need to know the clinical description and DSM criteria for these various disorders. They also need to understand something of the neuroscience and the psychodynamics of these disorders. This chapter has provided readers with essential information in all four of these areas. Presumably, it is the kind of information and understanding necessary for planning and implementing effective treatment. Particular emphasis has been on the Adlerian conceptualization of psychosis in general and for the five specific psychotic disorders in particular. As it happens, the Adlerian literature on the psychotic disorders, particularly Schizophrenia, is more rich and detailed than for any other mental disorder, and the breadth of this literature is shared in this chapter.

References

Adler, A. (1926). *Uber den Nervosen Charakter*. Wiesbaden: J.F. Bergman.
Adler, K. (1958). Life style in schizophrenia, *Journal of Individual Psychology*, 14, pp. 68–72.
American Experience (Producer) (2002). *A Brilliant Madness* (DVD). Boston, MA: WGBH Educational Foundation.

American Psychiatric Association (2000). *Diagnostic and Statistical Manual of Mental Disorders, Fouth Edition (Text Revision)*. Washington, DC: American Psychiatric Publishing.

American Psychiatric Association (2013). *Diagnostic and Statistical Manual of Mental Disorders, Fifth Edition*. Washington, DC: American Psychiatric Publishing.

Arieti, S. (1974). An overview of schizophrenia from a predominantly psychological approach. *American Journal of Psychiatry*, 131, pp. 241–249.

Arieti, S. (1980). Psychotherapy of schizophrenia: New or revised procedures. *American Journal of Psychotherapy*, 34, pp. 464–476.

Beitman, B. & Klerman, G. (Eds.) (1986). *Combining Psychotherapy and Drug Therapy in Clinical Practice*. New York, NY: S.P. Medical & Scientific Books.

Binswanger, L. (1960). Existential analysis, psychiatry, schizophrenia, *Journal of Existential Psychiatry*,1, pp. 157–165.

Boisen, A. (1947). Onset in acute schizophrenia, *Psychiatry*, 10, p. 159.

Bullard, D. (1960). Psychotherapy of paranoid patients, *Archives of General Psychiatry*, 2, pp. 137–141.

Capps, D. (2005). John Nash: Three phases in the career of a beautiful mind. *Journal of Religion and Health*, 44, pp. 363–376.

Gazzaniga, M. (1988). *Mind Matters: How Mind and Body Interact to Create our Conscious Lives*. Boston, MA: Houghton-Mifflin.

Gazzaniga, M. (2006). *The Ethical Brain: The Science of our Moral Dilemmas*. New York, NY: Harper Perennial.

Gazzaniga, M., Ivry, R., & Mangun, G. (2008) *Cognitive Neuroscience: The Biology of the Mind* (3rd edn.). New York, NY: Norton.

Goldstein, K. (1939). *The Organism: A Holistic Approach to Biology Derived from Pathological Data in Man*. New York, NY: American Book Co.

Green, M.F. & Kinsbourne, M. (1990). Subvocal activity and auditory hallucinations: Clues for behavioral treatments? *Schizophrenia Bulletin*, 16(4), pp. 617–625.

Hoover, G. & Franz, J. (1972). Siblings in the families of schizophrenia. *Archives of General Psychiatry*, 26, pp. 334–342.

Kelly, G. (1955). *The Psychology of Personal Constructs*. New York, NY: Norton.

Les Prix Nobel (1994). John Nash. Full text available on-line at http://www.nobel.se/economics/laureates/1994/nash-autobio.html.

Liberman, R. (1987). *Psychiatric Rehabilitation of Chronic Mental Patients*. Washington, DC: American Psychiatric Publishing.

Lu, Y. (1962). Contradictory parental expectations in schizophrenia. *Archives of General Psychiatry*, 6, pp. 219–234.

Nasar, S. (1998). *A Beautiful Mind*. New York, NY: Simon & Schuster.

Nash, J. (2001). *The Essential John Nash*. S. Nasar & H. Kuhn (Eds.). Princeton, NJ: Princeton University Press.

Neuchterlein, K. & Dawson, M. (1984). A heuristic vulnerability/stress model of schizophrenic episodes. *Schizophrenia Bulletin*, 10, pp. 300–312.

Reid, W. (1989). *The Treatment of Psychiatric Disorders: Revised for the DSM-III-R*. New York, NY: Brunner/Mazel.

Ritsher, J., Lucksted, A., Otilingam, P., & Grajales, M. (2004). Hearing voices: Explanations and implications. *Psychiatric Rehabilitation Journal*, 27, pp. 219–224.

Ritzler, B. (1981). Paranoia—prognosis and treatment: A review. *Schizophrenia Bulletin*, 7, pp. 710–728.

Scher, J. (1962). *Theories of the Mind*. New York, NY: Free Press of Glencoe.

Shulman, B. (1968). *Essays in Schizophrenia*. Baltimore, MD: Williams & Wilkins.

Shulman, B.(1984). *Essays in Schizophrenia* (2nd edn.). Chicago, IL: Alfred Adler Institute.

Sperry, L. & Shulman, B. (1996). Schizophrenia and delusional disorder. In L. Sperry & J. Carlson, (Eds.), *Psychopathlology and Psychotherapy: From DSM-IV Diagnosis to Treatment.*(2nd edn.) (pp. 23–50). Washington, DC: Accelerated Development/Taylor & Francis.

Torrey, E. (2014). *Surviving Schizophrenia* (6th edn.). New York, NY: Harper Perennial.

9   Dissociative Disorders

Jon Sperry and Len Sperry

On February 2013, a man was discovered unconscious in a motel in Palm Springs, California. He was transported to an emergency room where he regained consciousness. Subsequently, he was hospitalized after not recognizing his own face on his California driver's license. Nor did he recognize three other pieces of personal identification. The name on the license and other identification was that of Michael Thomas Boatwright. Instead, the man claimed to be Johan Ek. An interpreter was needed since he only spoke in Swedish. Four months later he remained hospitalized, still insisting he could not remember his past. During this time, it was learned that Boatwright was born in Florida and had a sister in the U.S. who said she had not been in contact with him for years. It was also learned that he did speak English, that he had served in the military, and did live for a while in Sweden. A psychiatric consultant speculated that Boatwright was likely experiencing Dissociative Amnesia, in which his "break from reality may be a form of 'self protection.'" Assuming that this man was not suffering from a stroke or other brain condition and was not fabricating the story to avoid some problem, the diagnosis of a Dissociative Disorder is most reasonable. Likewise, the psychological mechanism of dissociation as a form of self-protection is a common explanation among clinicians. Of course, Adlerians prefer the term "safeguarding" instead of self-protection to explain Dissociative Amnesia.

This chapter begins with some background information on dissociation, including its definition and history. Next, is a brief section describing the changes involving the dissociative disorders from *DSM-IV-TR* to *DSM-5*. This is followed by an Adlerian conceptualization of the dissociative disorders. Then, clinical descriptions of the *DSM-5* Dissociative Disorder are provided. Next, case conceptualizations of each disorder are identified and are followed by a brief discussion of treatment considerations. Lastly, a case example illustrates the disorder. More specifically, this chapter discusses and describes the following dissociative disorders: Dissociative Identity Disorder; Dissociative Amnesia; Depersonalization/Derealization Disorder; Other Specified Dissociative Disorder; and Unspecified Dissociative Disorder.

The Phenomenon of Dissociation and the History of Dissociative Disorders

Dissociation is a phenomenon that is commonly defined as a temporary alteration in the normally integrative functions of consciousness, identity, or memory. Dissociation involves a splitting off of thoughts, feelings, or behaviors that are ordinarily closely connected. Thus, thoughts can be dissociated from behaviors or from feelings. Dissociative phenomena are not necessarily associated with psychopathology. These phenomena may occur spontaneously, can be sought after, or be induced for therapeutic purposes. It is believed that the ability to have such experiences is related to the same phenomenon that underlies hypnotizability. Hypnosis requires concentrated focal alteration with a relative reduction in awareness of stimuli (Spiegel & Spiegel, 1978).

Beahr (1982) refers to the "dissociative continuum" ranging from milder, more common forms of dissociation to pathological dissociative states that are included in the *DSM-5* category of Dissociative Disorders. Commonplace dissociative events include daydreaming and absorption in reverie, such that one can drive past one's freeway exit or not hear one's name being called by a class instructor.

For a three-year-old child, having an imaginary playmate would be considered normal, as would a college student learning and practicing one of the many forms of meditation. Religious individuals may pursue spiritual practices such as meditation that a secular observer might interpret as autohypnotic. Our culture tacitly supports and reinforces some degree of dissociation. In the process of becoming socialized, an American child is taught to take on a variety of roles that exist simultaneously but are expressed sequentially, depending on the demands of the situation. Among adults, the "part self" nature of the psyche has been easily accepted by the lay public, and is a favorite theme in literature and the arts. We tacitly understand that we are not homogeneous, "singleminded" organisms, and that conflict, diversity, and disparity within the self-structure are central features of being human.

In early development, splitting represents a necessary and adaptive coping mechanism. According to object-relations theory, the infant protects itself by splitting its objects (others) into good and bad facets and keeping them separate. Infants use splitting to reduce distressing ambivalence, anxiety, and depression by separating mutually contradictory, alternating self- and object-representations and their resultant affects (Akhtar & Byrne, 1983). Splitting simplifies matters by changing the infant's complex relationship with mother into one that appears to be several simple relationships: a loving object and a gratified object, a hating object and a frustrated self, and so on. Splitting serves to disperse dangerous and aggressive impulses and feelings by keeping them separate from the gratified self. As object constancy is achieved, the child has less need for splitting. However, when object constancy is not achieved, severe pathology, including the Borderline and Narcissistic Personality Disorders, emerges, wherein pathologic splitting continues as a dominant coping mechanism.

Certain dissociative states are pathological forms in which complex behaviors take place outside the awareness of one's predominant consciousness. These include trances, blackouts, Dissociative Amnesia, fugue, Depersonalization/Derealization Disorder and Dissociative Identity Disorder. Although the etiology of dissociative states is considered to be functional or psychological in origin, they can have an organic etiology. Yaeger (1989) notes that blackouts and periods of amnesia can be caused by alcohol or other substance intoxication, as well as by head trauma. Furthermore, Yaeger notes that dissociative states, including Dissociative Identity Disorder, have been observed in individuals with temporal lobe epilepsy and with partial complex seizures.

History of Dissociative Disorders

Hysteria seems to have been highly prevalent among the leisure class of the late 19th century. Ellenberger (1970) believes this was due to cultural factors such as affectation and theatricality, as well as puritanical ethos. He insists that these factors fostered repression as a mechanism of defense or as a neurotic safeguard. The virtual disappearance of hysteria/dissociative disorders amid the change to a more compulsive and work-ethic-driven culture in the early and middle part of the 20th century may have accounted for the almost total disappearance of this disorder. However, through the 1960s, the "me" and "now" generation, and a shift to a more narcissistic ethos, an apparent reappearance of this class of disorders has been observed.

The phenomenon of dissociation has enthralled, as well as puzzled philosophers, clinicians, and the lay public since the beginning of recorded history. For instance, the early Greeks employed dissociation in their "sleep therapy." Medical interest in dissociative disorders was reported beginning in the late 19th century with systematic studies of hysteria and hypnosis. Pierre Janet is credited with introducing the term "dissociation." He hypothesized a model of idea complexes existing outside of consciousness as the cause of hysterical symptoms, as well as the basis for hypnotic and post-hypnotic phenomena. Janet used the term dissociation to describe a split in consciousness. He also believed that dissociation was the result of neuropsychological weakness (Sperry, 1990).

Freud and Breuer (1955) claimed that thoughts that were kept out of conscious awareness to ward off painful affects could and did cause hysterical symptoms. Freud used the term repression, rather than dissociation, as a label for this phenomenon of thoughts kept out of consciousness. Unlike Janet, Freud's understanding of dissociation referred to both the observation of the split in consciousness and the mechanism of defense; that is, repression. Furthermore, Freud preferred a psychological rather than an organic explanation for dissociation. Finally, his patients tended to be diagnosed as patients suffering from hysteria without a clear organic cause.

Prince (1906) also developed a theory of dissociation similar to Janet's, in which different conscious states could exist in a person without awareness, since his or her attention was not focused on them. He described co-consciousness as an explanation for phenomena seen in both hysterical symptoms and multiple personality. Like Janet, Prince primarily studied patients with amnesia, fugue, somnambulism (sleep walking), and multiple personality.

Freud and Prince had considerable impact on subsequent researchers and theorists on hysteria and multiple personality. So, it is not surprising that dissociative symptoms tend to be attributed to the existence of a split in consciousness, and not to organic etiologies. The fact that both postulated "dissociation" as the underlying mechanism led many investigators to "lump" the phenomena of amnesia, fugue, multiple personality, and hysteria together. This unwarranted assumption and consequent lumping of clinical presentations has led to diagnostic confusion.

One result of this was that *DSM-III*, *DSM-III-R*, *DSM-IV*, and *DSM-IV-TR* approached diagnosis on the basis of similarities of signs and symptoms or known organic etiologies, rather than on postulated psychological mechanisms. This change in focus has meant that some cases described in the literature as Psychogenic Fugue would actually meet criteria for Psychogenic Amnesia in *DSM-III* and *DSM-III-R*, or Dissociative Amnesia in *DSM-IV* and *DSM-IV-TR*. For example, while the main character in Hannah Green's book, *I Never Promised You a Rose Garden*, was diagnosed and was treated by her psychiatrist as a schizophrenic, today she would be classified as a Dissociative Identity Disorder.

For these, and perhaps other reasons, there is considerable skepticism in the mental health profession about dissociation and the dissociative disorders. From the 1970s through the 1990s, there was a resurgence of interest in the Multiple Personality Disorder, now known as the Dissociative Identity Disorder. Lawsuits involving clinicians "implanting" repressed memories in patients have significantly dampened such interest. Nevertheless, there remains a small group of clinicians who insist this disorder has been overlooked, leaving untold numbers of patients undiagnosed or not adequately treated if they received a different diagnosis. In contrast, most clinicians are of the mind that Dissociative Identity Disorder is very rare, if it exists at all.

Dissociative Disorders in *DSM-5*

Changes from DSM-IV-TR to DSM-5

Some changes occurred in the *DSM-5* Dissociative Disorders section. First, Derealization was added to the diagnosis formerly called Depersonalization Disorder, now called Depersonalization/Derealization Disorder. Second, Dissociative Fugue was added as a "specifier" to Dissociative Amnesia, as compared to being a separate diagnosis in the *DSM-IV-TR*. Lastly, symptoms resulting in disruption of identity may now be reported by the client or observed by others in the criteria for Dissociative Identity Disorder. This chapter will incorporate these changes in a discussion of each of the Dissociative Disorders and in the corresponding case vignettes.

Adlerian Conceptualization of Dissociative Disorders

This section describes the functional component of psychopathology and the usefulness of dissociation in the arrangement of a client's symptoms through an Adlerian conceptualization. An Adlerian conceptualization of the Michael Thomas Boatwright story at the beginning of this chapter, would consider his Dissociative Amnesia as a safeguarding mechanism to protect him from feelings of inferiority, physical or emotional threat, or his overall ability to tolerate a recent stressor. Parenthetically, other psychotherapeutic orientations consider safeguarding to be a form of self-protection or a defense mechanism.

Adler discussed several safeguarding mechanisms: symptoms, excuses, aggression, and distance seeking (Adler, 1956,1968). Dissociative Disorders are typically forms of safeguarding involving symptoms and distance-seeking. Distance-seeking is a form of safeguarding that allows individuals to reduce their feelings of inferiority or pain by distancing themselves from life tasks that could expose their feelings of inferiority (Carlson, Watts, & Maniacci, 2006). Symptoms serve the function of providing a rationalization for why an individual has not achieved a desired outcome or life task. This might include the private logic, "Yes, but I'm sick." This attitude serves the purpose of excusing individuals from taking risks of moving towards life tasks that might reveal their perceived inferior self-view. Individuals living with dissociative disorders may have achieved few life tasks as a result of significant instability due to their symptoms. The arrangement of symptoms allows individuals experiencing inferiority to avoid reality. This process is out of the awareness of the individual and is considered a nonconscious process (Sperry, 1996).

An Adlerian conceptualization would also examine precipitating events, perpetuating factors, pattern, and predisposing factors such as life-style convictions and family constellation (Sperry & Sperry, 2012). Exploration of precipitating events might consist of a traumatic event or acute stressor, which may have triggered the client's maladaptive pattern and life-style convictions. Perpetuating factors are any variable that maintains or exacerbates the presenting symptom or problem. The maladaptive pattern includes the client's interpersonal movement and the purpose of that movement. It is hypothesized that Michael Thomas Boatwright's movement was to "move away" from his experience of stress via Dissociative Amnesia, which served the purpose of safeguarding himself. Additionally, an Adlerian case conceptualization would examine his life-style convictions, his family constellation, themes from his early recollections, and his level of social interest (Sperry & Sperry, 2012). In short, safeguarding is a key element in an Adlerian case conceptualization of dissociative disorders.

Dissociative disorders are often linked to trauma, whether it be associated with war, terrorism, childhood medical procedures, or childhood abuse that could be sexual, emotional, or physical (American Psychiatric Association, 2013). Adler discussed "shock" rather than trauma, by which he believed that traumatized or discouraged individuals cling to the shock effect to safeguard themselves (Adler, 1956). The shock effect is utilized by never moving past that particular point in time, so that the individual can prevent the traumatic event from occurring again. This can be accomplished by focusing on the traumatic situation and remaining in a standstill position, by which the life tasks are avoided. Clearly, traumatized individuals are often discouraged, may lack social interest after the trauma, and often experience inferiority complexes that continue to interfere with their ability to achieve the tasks of life. As victims of trauma, individuals with pre-existing inflexible or rigid life-style convictions will often be less resilient and are more likely to utilize the standstill position.

Alfred Adler wrote relatively little about dissociation and nothing about the dissociative disorders. What accounts for this? Of course, we do not know, but we can speculate. First of all, it should be noted that prior to *DSM-III*, the dissociative disorders were usually known as Hysterical Neuroses—Dissociative Type, to distinguish them from the Conversion Type of the Hysterical Neuroses. In that regard Ellenberger (1970) notes that Freud tended to limit his practice to the treatment of higher-functioning, upper-middle-class patients who for the most part presented with Hysterical Neuroses of both types. Adler, on the other hand, reportedly treated a wider variety of patients, including many lower-functioning working-class individuals with obsessive-compulsive and character-logical features. Thus, it might be that Adler had little or no therapeutic contact with Dissociative Disordered patients.

Yet, Adler did allude to "dissociation" as synonymous with "the apparent double-life of the neurotic" (Adler, 1925, 1968 p. 21). He was fond of discussing daydreams, which are a form of dissociation (Adler 1956, 1964). His basic view of daydreams, and presumably of other dissociative phenomena, was consistent with his overall theory of psychopathology: "The findings of Individual Psychology point to the fact that all behavior of a human being fits into a unit and is an expression of the individual's style of life" (Adler, 1956 p. 358). In discussing the retrogressive movement of the neurosis, Adler mentions Psychogenic Amnesia as one such manifestation (Adler, 1925, 1968). Finally, Adler's aversion to hypnosis should be noted (Adler 1925, 1968 p. 161–2). Since hypnosis has and continues to be a basic diagnostic and treatment method of dissociative disorders, it would be even more unlikely that Adler or his protégés and later followers would focus much of their theoretical, clinical, and research efforts on the dissociative disorders. A review of the published Adlerian literature seems to support this observation (Sperry, 1996).

There are some indications that this trend might be changing. As more and more dissociative disordered individuals present for treatment, more and more clinicians, including Adlerians, are "gearing up" to meet this therapeutic challenge. A rediscovery of the pioneering efforts of Pierre Janet holds considerable promise for those clinicians who were unconvinced or uncomfortable with the prevailing theories based on Freud's formulation (Vander Kolk & Vander Hart, 1989). Not only does Janet's formulation of dissociation provide a broad integrative framework for understanding and unifying elements for other theories, but it is quite compatible with Adlerian thinking (Shulman, 1990).

Essentially, Janet prepared a broad theory of perceptive and cognitive processes and memory that is now being validated by research in the neurosciences. Janet hypothesized that consciousness consisted of a unified memory of all psychological facets related to a particular experience and that memory was an act of creation rather than a passive and static recording of events. He speculated that memories were synthesized into a perceptual system that provided a matrix for categorizing and integrating subsequent data into what we would today call cognitive schemas. Janet believed that dissociations were sentiments of incompleteness or idea complexes that were split off or existed outside of consciousness. He believed that therapy is a process of bringing these split-off ideas into consciousness and that his process would be curative. For Adler, therapy was likewise a process of bringing these mistaken and missing ideas into consciousness. Of course, the "missing" element is social interest (Shulman, 1990).

DISSOCIATIVE IDENTITY DISORDER

Clinical Presentation

Dissociative Identity Disorder is characterized by the presence of two or more distinct identities or "alter egos" within the same individual. Each alter is dominant at a particular time. It should not be surprising that because there can be a large number of alters in these individuals, it can be difficult to detect and diagnose, especially early in the course of the disorder. Putnam et al. (1986) note that the average duration of psychological treatment prior to the proper diagnosis of Dissociative Identity Disorder is over six years. Because of the waxing and waning character of this disorder and the innumerable permutations of symptoms, the patient may present differently on different occasions. Thus, it should not be surprising that these patients usually have a history of being given several diagnoses. Kluft (1985) notes that this variable clinical picture is characteristic of 80% of patients with this disorder.

Individuals with Dissociative Identity Disorder usually enter psychotherapy for any number of concerns from anxiety to sleep disorders. In the course of treatment these individuals may complain of new concerns, like the sudden onset of dizziness, difficulty finding their parked car, inordinate indecision about which clothes to wear, or denial of actions that were clearly observed by others. Upon further investigation, a different personality emerges or is discovered in the course of treatment. In some cases, alters continue to be produced. This may result from the indirect suggestion of the clinician, or through formal means like hypnotic induction or amytal interview.

Auditory hallucinations and some features of thought disorder are commonly noted in this disorder, as are sudden mood swings. In fact, depression is the most commonly identified symptom of Dissociative Identity Disorder. The more severely dysfunctional individuals living with dissociative disorders engage in para-suicidal behavior—including self-mutilation. Horevitz and Braun (1984) found that 70% of simple Dissociative Identity Disorder cases met the DSM-III criteria for Borderline Personality Disorder. Finally, amnesia is considered a pathognomonic sign of Dissociative Identity Disorder.

Etiologically, predisposing factors are a history of repeated childhood abuse and neglect, childhood medical procedures, war, childhood prostitution, sexual assaults, and terrorism, for which the child responded by dissociating. Approximately 90% of clients living with this disorder have experienced a repeated and severe history of physical and/or sexual abuse as children (American Psychiatric Association, 2013).

For these clients, dissociation becomes the predominant or only adaptive coping style. The onset is usually in early childhood, and the course tends to be more chronic than any of the other dissociative disorders. Most Dissociative Identity Disordered patients are diagnosed between the ages of late adolescence and early middle age. As they enter their late fifties, the majority begin to spend an increasing amount of time in one resilient personality with a wide range of functions. Some personalities may even integrate simultaneously. Prevalence for Dissociative Identity Disorder among adults in the U.S. was 1.6% for males and 1.4% for females (American Psychiatric Association, 2013).

DSM-5 Characterization

Individuals who meet criteria for this diagnosis are characterized by a disruption of identity, which involves the presence of two or more distinct identities or personality states in which the individual experiences altered affect, behavior, memory, consciousness, sensory motor functioning, or overall perception. Additionally, since the *DSM-IV-TR*, the *DSM-5* articulates that these symptoms may be reported by the individual, or observed by others. Memory impairment regarding important personal information, recall of daily events, and recall of traumatic events may occur in this disorder. Besides displaying such symptoms, the individual's functioning is also greatly affected in occupational, social, or other psychosocial domains. Furthermore, the disorder is not caused by the direct physiological effects of a medication, drug use, nor a medical condition. Lastly, the disturbance is also not a part of any cultural or religious practices (American Psychiatric Association, 2013).

The differential diagnosis of Dissociative Identity Disorder includes: substance-related disorders; personality disorders; Conversion Disorder (Functional Neurological Symptom Disorder); seizure disorders; and Factitious Disorder and malingering (American Psychiatric Association, 2013).

Biopsychosocial–Adlerian Conceptualization

From an Adlerian perspective, Dissociative Identity Disorder is a safeguarding mechanism utilized to help individuals deal with feelings of inferiority and to avoid further pain. As abused children, these individuals learned to survive by psychologically escaping their own body during trauma. The dissociation process becomes a coping mechanism that is utilized through adulthood. By activating different alters, an individual is able to disconnect from reality when feeling unsafe or threatened. By utilizing distance-seeking and standing-still strategies, the individual reinforces the conviction that if they never move past the initial trauma or shock, they can prevent the trauma from happening again. This process includes withdrawing from reality and disconnecting from the self, which are indicators of discouragement. Individuals with Dissociative Identity Disorder will typically display low levels of social interest during the alter-shifting process (Sperry, 1996).

Social isolation is frequent among individuals with Dissociative Identity Disorder, because the typical social response of others is to avoid such an unstable and unpredictable person. The interpersonal movement can be characterized as ambivalent, because some alters move away from others to safeguard the individual, while other alters may move towards others to please those others or to seek attention. An individual with Dissociative Identity Disorder develops as many alters as are necessary to cope. Kluft (1985) notes that these alter egos have names that reflect their functions. Most common are: the Protector, the Whore, the Little Girl (Child), and the Angry One. In their review of hundreds of confirmed diagnoses of this disorder Putnam et al. (1986) found an average number of ten alters, with a median of seven and a mode of under five. This maladaptive process serves the purpose of being able to meet one's needs by accessing various alters.

Treatment Considerations

Fortunately, recent developments in therapy tailored to Dissociative Identity Disorder suggest that individuals with this disorder may be quite responsive to therapy. The treatment of Dissociative Identity Disorder tends to be long, demanding, and painful. The initial goal is to establish a trusting relationship, and the intermediate goal is to optimize the patient's function and potential. The ultimate goal, of course, would be the achievement of total integration of the alters into one personality. However, a reasonable degree of conflict-free collaboration among the personalities may be the only realistic goal for some patients. Today, less emphasis is placed on examining past trauma, and more emphasis is placed on improving functioning and helping clients live more meaningful lives. Techniques that include confronting past abusers are discouraged as part of treatment planning, as a result of lawsuits filed by accused abusers and the lack of empirical data supporting the efficacy of that intervention (Kihlstrom, 2001).

Generally speaking, medications have been ineffective for this disorder, although some have been successful with treating accompanying symptoms such as depression, insomnia, and panic symptoms. Treatment success has been reported with hypnotherapy, psychoanalytical psychotherapy, group therapy with and without videotaping, and sodium amytal. Braun (1986) has described a series of 13 steps that are sequential, but overlap and continue throughout treatment, which have been found useful regardless of the treatment orientation.

Case Example: Ms. E.

Ms. E. is a 45-year-old Caucasian female who presented for treatment at the request of her youngest son (Jake), who told his mother (Ms. E.) that she would not be able to attend his wedding if she did not attend therapy regularly to treat her "condition." Ms. E. had been through many bouts of therapy to manage her Dissociative Identity Disorder symptoms. It is noteworthy to mention her long history of inconsistent diagnoses, and unsuccessful past treatment episodes. At the time of intake, Ms. E. reported that she was adhering to antidepressant medication, and felt "good" on most days. Jake came to the first session with Ms. E. and reported that she had been emotionally abusive to his family and fiancée over the past six months. Jake noted that Ms. E. rotated between three alters: Joan—the good little girl alter, Mike—the angry and abusive alter, and Julie—the responsible adult alter. Jake reported that his family had been through several family therapy treatment episodes in the past ten years. As a result, Jake was familiar with clinical terminology regarding his mother's condition, and he was also aware of signs that Ms. E. often displays when she is under significant stress. Ms. E. reported that she was raped by several of her cousins and uncles from ages four through nine, and was also forced to participate in Satanic rituals when one of her abusive uncles would babysit her.

DISSOCIATIVE AMNESIA

Clinical Presentation

Dissociative Amnesia, previously called Psychogenic Amnesia, is described as the sudden, but temporary loss of ability to recall important personal information. This loss of memory can involve information about a specific topic, or memories of the immediate or distant past. This memory loss is too extensive to be explained by ordinary forgetfulness, and it cannot be due to an organic etiology such as amnesia following a head injury, alcohol-induced blackouts, or amnesia associated with a seizure disorder or induced by electroconvulsive therapy (ECT). Predisposing factors for this condition are single or repeated traumatic experiences, sexual assault, exposure to combat, and extreme conflict or emotional stress (American Psychiatric Association, 2013). Unlike the common portrayal of amnesia in TV shows and movies, Dissociative Amnesia very rarely involves a total loss of recall.

A hallmark of Dissociative Amnesia is that both the onset and termination of amnesia are rapid, and complete recovery of amnesias secondary to organic etiologies tends to be gradual and rarely is complete. Appropriate assessment of amnesia requires a complete psychosocial evaluation, including psychosocial stressors, history of drug use, trauma, tasks of life, and life-style convictions. Referral for a medical evaluation must be considered to rule out physical trauma, neurological disease, and metabolic or drug-induced causes as primary or contributing factors. Prevalence rates from a small study that examined Dissociative Amnesia among adults in the U.S. were 1.0% for males and 2.6% for females (American Psychiatric Association, 2013).

DSM-5 Characterization

Individuals who meet criteria for this diagnosis are characterized by an inability to recall important information that is autobiographical in nature. This loss of memory can involve information about a specific topic or memories from the immediate or distant past, such as traumatic or stressful events. Localized or selective amnesia pertains to specific events or partial loss of memory, while generalized amnesia refers to a complete loss of memory pertaining to one's life history. This can include a loss of knowledge about one's identity or loss of previous knowledge about the world. Besides displaying such symptoms, the individual's functioning is also greatly affected in occupational, social, or other psychosocial domains. This memory loss is too extensive to be explained by ordinary forgetfulness, and it cannot be due to an organic etiology such as amnesia following a head injury, alcohol-induced blackouts, or amnesia associated with a seizure disorder (American Psychiatric Association, 2013).

The *DSM-5* relocated Dissociative Fugue Disorder from a stand-alone in the *DSM-IV-TR*, to a diagnosis as a specifier of the Dissociative Amnesia criteria. In the *DSM-5*, this is now categorized as Dissociative Amnesia with Dissociative Fugue. Individuals who experience Dissociative Amnesia with Dissociative Fugue often engage in travel from one's home or place of work, and it often includes an inability to remember one's past, confusion about personal identity, and even assuming a new identity in some cases.

The differential diagnosis of Dissociative Amnesia includes: Post-Traumatic Stress Disorder; neurocognitive disorders; substance-related disorders; Post-Traumatic Stress Disorder due to brain injury; seizure disorders; catatonic stupor; Factitious Disorder and malingering; and normal and age-related changes in memory (American Psychiatric Association, 2013).

Biopsychosocial–Adlerian Conceptualization

From an Adlerian perspective, Dissociative Amnesia can be conceptualized as a safeguarding mechanism. The utilization of distance-seeking and symptom arrangement can help individuals avoid intense feelings of inferiority or protect themselves after a traumatic event. The unique function of this disorder is that this type of memory loss can protect one from feelings of pain or inadequacy, by being unaware that it occurred. Presenting with an inability to remember stressful situations or traumatic events can serve the purpose of retreating from emotional pain or stress. While this striving is not always fully useful, it truly holds a functional purpose in protecting one's convictions by safeguarding one's self. This maladaptive pattern is characterized as moving away from others and the self to reduce inferiority feelings and emotional pain. Life-style convictions among this group might include themes of self-protection to belong, "Yes, but I'm sick," or to withdraw when an individual has not had his or her needs met. Unfortunately, these individuals are often unable to achieve the life tasks and live meaningful lives as a result of the safeguarding process (Sperry, 1996).

Treatment Considerations

The goal of treatment for both Dissociative Amnesia and Dissociative Amnesia with Dissociative Fugue, is to recover lost memories and identity and to integrate the traumatic antecedent event(s) into the patient's consciousness. Regardless of the clinician's theoretical orientation, the general treatment strategy is to elicit the history in a supportive manner and listen empathically. A supportive environment may be sufficient for spontaneous resolution to occur, and may be all that is needed in some cases. More active measures to recover missing memories are hypnosis, free association, suggestion, amytal interviews, and abreactive techniques. These methods are often utilized in conjunction with ongoing psychotherapy.

Case Example: Mr. X.

Mr. X. is a 35-year-old Asian-American male who presented for treatment through being referred for counseling by a local hospital, after being discharged after a two-month hospital stay due to injuries sustained in a severe car accident. The car accident story made local news, as two of Mr. X.'s friends died in the wreck. Mr. X. had no recollection of the accident, but could recall that he and his friends were driving to the grocery store just before the time of the accident. He also remembers entering the hospital just after the accident. Interestingly, the car crash investigators reviewed the surveillance footage of the car accident, which occurred at a major intersection: It revealed that Mr. X. was fully conscious after the wreck, and was even trying to pull his friends from the burning car. He reported having no recollection of the accident, and did not recall that he had attempted to pull his friends from the car. A thorough medical and neurological evaluation ruled out an organic etiology, while he denied any history of drug use, seizures, or head trauma.

DEPERSONALIZATION/DEREALIZATION DISORDER

Clinical Presentation

The Depersonalization/Derealization Disorder is unlike the other DSM-5 Dissociative Disorders in that consciousness is never actually segmented, nor is significant memory loss a factor; in fact, it bears little resemblance to any DSM-5 category. Probably because it includes the feature of dissociation and "fits" less well with other major DSM-5 categories, it was assigned to the Dissociative Disorders. In the *DSM-5*, Derealization was added to this diagnosis and is now called Depersonalization/Derealization Disorder.

Depersonalization is usually described as an alteration in the individual's perception of self. In this altered perception, individuals perceive and experience being estranged from their selves, feeling as though they were a separate observer of the self. Meditators and users of hallucinogens have reported "out of body" experiences, which is a form of depersonalization. Predisposing factors for this condition are emotional abuse and/or neglect, witnessing domestic violence, growing up with a mentally ill parent, a harm-avoidant temperament, both disconnection and over-connection schemata, poor adaptation skills, themes of defectiveness and incompetence, single or repeated traumatic experiences, and physical abuse (American Psychiatric Association, 2013).

It is estimated that 50% of all adults have had some experience of dissociation, suggesting that it is a very common phenomenon. In fact, some systems of meditation insist that the ability to regularly achieve a dissociative state in meditation is a marker of progress toward enlightenment. Prevalence rates from a study that examined depersonalization/derealization among individuals in the U.S. were approximately 2%, with a gender ratio of 1:1(American Psychiatric Association, 2013).

Since depersonalization is experienced by many individuals who are not bothered by it, the criteria for a diagnosable disorder then depends on its frequency or the extent of distress brought about by the experience. To meet full criteria for the diagnosis, it must impact the individual's psychosocial functioning. A corollary phenomenon, called derealization, refers to alterations in one's perception of one's environment or object; it is as if it were alien or unreal. Derealization frequently accompanies depersonalization. Depersonalization is a symptom that is present in a number of psychiatric syndromes, particularly Panic Disorder, partial complex seizures and Schizophrenia.

The etiology of depersonalization is uncertain. A number of investigators, following Janet, have postulated a biological basis. Others have suggested that depersonalization/derealization follows the attempt to repudiate a self-image associated with unacceptable drives or alterations of ego boundaries, while others point to interpersonal influences. In addition to purely biological and psychological explanations, Putnam, Guroff, Silberman, et al. (1986) believe that data on severe social stressors and life-threatening circumstances demonstrates that dissociation has a social basis. Perhaps a biopsychosocial explanation better explains and predicts this disorder.

The course of the disorder is generally chronic and marked by remissions and exacerbations. The degree of impairment is minimal but can be exacerbated by anxiety or the fear of becoming insane. In that sense, it is similar to the conditioned anxiety response that many argue is the cause of the flashbacks occurring with certain drug experiences.

DSM-5 Characterization

Individuals who meet criteria for this diagnosis are characterized by the presence of depersonalization, derealization, or both. Individuals who experience depersonalization may experience detachment, unreality, or a sense of being observer of their body, thoughts, feelings, or actions. This can also include feeling emotionally and/or physically numb, feeling absent from oneself, or experiencing a distorted sense of time. Individuals who experience derealization often report feeling detached from reality, experiencing unreality, or feeling that they are in a dream or lifeless. Derealization frequently accompanies depersonalization. Besides displaying such symptoms, the individual's functioning is also greatly affected in occupational, social, or other psychosocial domains. Furthermore, this disorder cannot be caused by the direct physiological effects of a medication, drug use, or medical condition (American Psychiatric Association, 2013).

The differential diagnosis of Depersonalization/ Derealization Disorder includes: Illness Anxiety Disorder; Major Depressive Disorder; Obsessive-Compulsive Disorder; other dissociative disorders; anxiety disorders; psychotic disorders; substance/ medication-induced disorders; and mental disorders due to another medical condition (American Psychiatric Association, 2013).

Biopsychosocial–Adlerian Conceptualization

From an Adlerian perspective, depersonalization and derealization can be conceptualized as a safeguarding mechanism. The utilization of distance-seeking and symptom arrangement can help individuals avoid intense feelings of inferiority or protect themselves after a traumatic event. Feeling detached from one's body, or that life is "unreal," can serve the purpose of retreating from pain or potential inferiority-provoking situations (Sperry, 1996).

Through depersonalization and/or derealization, withdrawing from reality and disconnecting from the self is often associated with a decrease in social interest. By making the choice to discontinue social participation and focusing on one's symptoms, this leads to continued social isolation. Beyond social interest, life-style convictions are particularly significant in the conceptualization of this presentation. Life-style convictions that are inflexible and rigid can predispose individuals to having difficulty "bouncing back" after a traumatic event, or coping with stressful situations. This interpersonal and intrapersonal movement can be characterized as "moving away from." "Moving away from" can serve the purpose of protecting one's self from hurt, pain, discomfort, distancing one's self from others, and to increase feelings of safety. Some examples of faulty life-style convictions of individuals who experience depersonalization and/or derealization are:

1. "I am too inadequate to manage the stressors of life; therefore, I will withdraw when feeling unsafe or threatened."
2. "Life is too risky to take chances, I can find my place in the world by avoiding pain."
3. "Through withdrawal from reality I can prevent threatening situations from happening again."
4. "Being in my body is too threatening during times of conflict; it is easier to disconnect from myself and attend to my confusion and feelings of unreality" (Sperry, 1996).

Treatment Considerations

The literature on Adlerian treatment of Depersonalization/Derealization Disorder is scant and inconclusive. Since the Depersonalization/Derealization Disorder is as much an identity development disorder as it is a dissociative phenomenon, the goal of

~~treatment is a fuller integration of the personality, and correlatively, a more accurate~~ perception of self and external reality. Treatment approaches that hold promise include hypnosis—especially for those with high hypnotizability—imagery techniques, and cognitive-behavioral approaches.

Generally speaking, medications have been ineffective for the disorder, although they have been of some use with targets such as symptomatic depression, insomnia, and panic symptoms. Treatment success has been reported with hypnotherapy, psychoanalytical psychotherapy, group therapy with and without videotaping; and sodium amytal. Braun (1986) has described a series of 13 steps that are sequential, but overlap and continue throughout treatment, which have been found useful regardless of the treatment orientation.

Case Example: Mrs. V.

Mrs. V is a 26-year-old Latina female who presented for treatment, and identified that she was seeking treatment due to "feeling disconnected from my body" on her intake form at the student health services clinic. She described the ongoing episodes as feeling like she could look down at her body from the sky, and feeling that she was "going crazy." She explained that it was as though she was watching herself in a movie, because she felt physically and emotionally numb during the episodes. These episodes had persisted for over a year, and made socializing and meeting friends very difficult for her. In addition, she has reported feeling highly concerned about "failing after college", which she started over two years ago. After further intake, she identified that the episodes typically occurred within several days of major exams, or when group projects were required in her courses. She admitted that she was on academic probation due to missing two different final exams as a result of feeling too detached to study, and avoiding the entire exam week last semester. A thorough medical and neurological evaluation ruled out an organic etiology, while she denied any history of drug use, or head trauma.

OTHER SPECIFIED DISSOCIATIVE DISORDER

Clinical Presentation

This category is intended for those disordered presentations in which dissociation is the predominant feature, but which do not meet full criteria for any of the other dissociative disorders in this section, but meet criteria for one of the four specified categories: chronic and recurrent syndromes of mixed dissociative symptoms; identity disturbance due to prolonged and intense coercive persuasion; acute dissociative reactions to stressful events; and dissociative trance. Some examples include dissociated states following brainwashing in prison camps, duress associated with hostage situations, or indoctrination in cults. Dissociative trance disorders such as *ataque* or spirit/demon possession is another example.

DSM-5 Characterization

Individuals who meet criteria for this diagnosis are characterized by symptoms and characteristics of a dissociative disorder that cause psychosocial impairment, but do not meet the full criteria for any of the Dissociative Disorder diagnostic disorder categories. Examples of the categories that can be specified using "other specified" include: chronic and recurrent syndromes of mixed dissociative symptoms; identity disturbance due to prolonged and intense coercive persuasion; acute dissociative reactions to stressful events; and dissociative trance.

First, chronic and recurrent syndromes of mixed dissociative symptoms include identity disturbance or alterations in identity, but no dissociative amnesia. Second, identity disturbance due to prolonged and intense coercive persuasion involves individuals who are exposed to intense coercive persuasion, such as brainwashing or extended torture, which may include changes in consciousness, or questioning one's identity. Third, acute dissociative reactions to stressful events is a category in which acute, but transient, conditions that last less than one month, or even as little as a few hours, occur. This category includes a shift in consciousness such as depersonalization, derealization, or other perceptual disturbances. Lastly, dissociative trance is an acute loss of awareness of one's surroundings. This presentation might include stereotyped behaviors, transient paralysis, or even loss of consciousness.

Besides displaying such symptoms, the individual's functioning is also greatly affected in occupational, social, or other psychosocial domains. Furthermore, the disorder is not caused by the direct physiological effects of a medication or drug of abuse, nor a medical condition.

Biopsychosocial–Adlerian Conceptualization

Similar to the conceptualizations identified in the other dissociative disorders in this chapter, the safeguarding mechanism coping response can also be used when conceptualizing the Other Specified Dissociative Disorders. An Adlerian conceptualization of this diagnosis would also examine the life-style convictions, the level of discouragement and social interest, and an individual's achievement of their life tasks (Sperry, 1996).

Case Example: Mr. B.

Mr. B. is a 51-year-old African-American man who presented for counseling due to "feeling that I am not alive" and experiencing that "time feels like it is moving so slow that I can't focus on any of my studies." His presenting concern was most recently triggered by news of being offered an internship in another state. His acute confusion and derealization were also accompanied by his report of perceptual distortions in which he identified that "it seems like my feet get really big or really small and I just can't think straight". He reported that he has experienced two of these episodes in the past year, which typically last about one to three days. His first episode resulted in him being admitted to a psychiatric facility for five days. Documentation from the first hospital visit indicated a diagnosis of Other Specified Dissociative Disorder—Acute Dissociative Reactions to Stressful Events. The evaluation concluded that although Mr. B. presents with some dissociative symptoms, the diagnosis of Other Specified Dissociative Disorder—Acute Dissociative Reactions to Stressful Events was accurate, given his presenting symptoms and his report of an acute stressor. A thorough medical and neurological evaluation ruled out an organic etiology, while he denied any history of drug use, or head trauma.

UNSPECIFIED DISSOCIATIVE DISORDER

Clinical Presentation

This catch-all category is intended for those disordered presentations in which dissociation is the predominant feature but does not meet criteria for one of the four aforementioned dissociative disorders. Some examples include dissociated states following brainwashing in prison camps, duress associated with hostage situations, or indoctrination in cults. Dissociative Trance Disorders such as *ataque* or spirit/demon possession is another example.

DSM-5 Characterization

Individuals who meet criteria for this diagnosis are characterized by symptoms and behaviors of a Dissociative Disorder that cause psychosocial impairment but do not meet the full criteria for any of the Dissociative Disorder diagnostic categories. A clinician may assign this diagnosis when an individual presents traits suggestive of a Dissociative Disorder, but they may not have sufficient information to make a specific diagnosis. This provisional diagnosis may be assigned in an emergency-room type setting, when dissociative-type symptoms are reported but information is unclear and further assessment will be indicated.

Concluding Note

Relatively minor changes have occurred in the Dissociative Disorders section of the *DSM-5*. The Adlerian conceptualization of safeguarding can help clinicians bridge the gap between assessment and treatment planning when dealing with the dissociative disorders. Integrating the Adlerian perspective with *DSM-5's* perspective of dissociative disorders might well increase clinical outcomes.

References

Adler, A. (1956). In H.L. Ansbacher & R.R. Ansbacher (Eds.), *The Individual Psychology of Alfred Adler*. New York, NY: Basic Books.

Adler, A. (1968). *The Practice and Theory of Individual Psychology*. (Trans. P. Radin) Totawa, NJ: Littlefield, Adams, & Co. (Original work published 1925).

Adler, A. (1964). In H.L. Ansbacher & R.R. Ansbacher (Eds.), *Superiority and Social Interest: A Collection of Later Writings*. Evanston, IL: Northwestern University Press.

Akhtar, S. & Byrne, J. (1983). The concept of splitting and its clinical relevance. *American Journal of Psychiatry*, 140, pp. 3–10.

American Psychiatric Association (1986). *Diagnostic and Statistical Manual of Mental Disorders, Third Edition (Revised)*. Washington DC: American Psychiatric Publishing.

American Psychiatric Association. (2013). *Diagnostic and Statistical Manual of Mental Health Disorders, Fifth Edition*. Arlington, VA: American Psychiatric Publishing.

Beahr, J. (1982). *Unity and Multiplicity: Consciousness of Self in Hypnosis, Psychiatric Disorder and Mental Health*. New York, NY: Brunner/Mazel.

Braun, B. (1986). Issues in the psychotherapy of multiple personality disorder. In B. Braun (Ed.), *Treatment of Multiple Personality Disorder*. Washington, DC: American Psychiatric Publishing, pp. 3–28.

Carlson, J., Watts, R.E., & Maniacci, M. (2006). *Adlerian Therapy: Theory and Practice*. Washington, DC: American Psychological Association.

Ellenberger, H. (1970). *The Discovery of the Unconscious*. New York, NY: Basic Books.

Freud, S. & Breuer, J. (1955). Studies on hysteria. In J. Strachey (Ed.), *The Pre-standard Edition of the Complete Psychological Works of Sigmund Freud* (Vol 2), London: Hogarth Press, pp. 3–305.

Horevitz, R. & Braun, B. (1984). Are multiple personalities borderline? *Psychiatric Clinics of North America*, 7, pp. 69–88.

Kihlstrom, J. (2001). Dissociative disorders. In P.B. Sutker & H.E. Adams (Eds.), *Comprehensive Handbook of Psychopathology* (3rd edn.). (pp. 259–276). New York, NY: Plenum.

Kluft, R. (1985). The natural history of Multiple Personality Disorder: A study of thirty-three cases. In R. Kluft (Ed.), *Childhood Antecedents of Multiple Personality*. Washington, DC: American Psychiatric Publishing, pp. 167–196.

Prince, M. (1906). *The Dissociation of Personality*. New York, NY: Green.

Putnam, F. (1985). Dissociation as a response to extreme trauma. In Kluft, R. (Ed.), *Childhood Antecedents of Multiple Personality*. Washington, DC: American Psychiatric Publishing, pp. 285–293.

Putnam, F. (1989) *Diagnosis and Treatment of Multiple Personality Disorder*. New York, NY: Guilford.

Putnam, F., Guroff, J., Silberman, E., et al. (1986). The clinical phenomenology of multiple personality disorder: Review of 100 recent cases. *Journal of Clinical Psychiatry*, 47, pp. 285–293.

Shulman, B.(1984). *Essays in Schizophrenia* (2nd edn.). Chicago, IL: Alfred Adler Institute.

Spiegel, H. & Spiegel, D. (1978). *Trance and Treatment*. New York, NY: Basic Books.

Sperry, L. (1990). Dissociation, multiple personality and the phenomenon of evil, *Journal of Pastoral Counseling*, 25, pp. 90–100.

Sperry, L. (1996). The dissociative disorders. In L. Sperry & J. Carlson (Eds.), *Psychopathology and Psychotherapy: From DSM-IV Diagnosis to Treatment* (2nd edn.) (pp. 245–261). Washington, DC: Accelerated Development/Taylor & Francis.

Sperry, L. & Sperry, J. (2012). *Case Conceptualization: Mastering this Competency with Ease and Confidence*. New York, NY: Routledge.

Van der Kolk, B. & Van der Hart, O. (1989). Pierre Janet and the breakdown of adaptation in psychological trauma, *American Journal of Psychiatry*, 146, pp. 1530—1540.

Wilbur, C. & Kluft, R. (1989). Multiple personality disorders. In *Treatment of Psychiatric Disorders: A Task Force Report of the American Psychiatric Association* (Vol. 3). Washington, DC: American Psychiatric Publishing, pp. 29–60.

Yager, J. (1989). Manifestations of psychiatric disorders. In H. Kaplan & B. Sadockleds (Eds.), *Comprehensive Textbook of Psychiatry* (5th edn.). Baltimore, MD: Williams & Wilkins, pp. 553–582.

10 Somatic Symptoms and Related Disorders

Laurie Sackett-Maniacci and Michael P. Maniacci

"Pain is pain" and "suffering is suffering." When people experience a loss or other significant life stressor, they suffer. When people experience frequent headaches, stomach aches, or chronic fatigue, they suffer. In their suffering they oftentimes seek help for their distressed symptoms, and via medication, counseling, or psychotherapy, these people recover and move on from their painful situations and symptoms. Sometimes, however, relief is not always so clear cut. This is often seen when individuals develop somatic symptoms and are unable to get immediate relief. More often than not individuals seek help via their primary care physician or other medical personnel. They start to react to their symptoms in such a way that little time or space is left for other areas of life. Others, including family, friends, and professionals who are trying to help them, become frustrated and may slowly withdraw their support. These individuals continue to suffer and may begin to feel alienated, at worst, or misunderstood, at best. The individuals in this scenario may in fact be suffering from one of a number of somatic symptom or related disorders as categorized by the *DSM-5* (American Psychiatric Association, 2013).

The *DSM-5* has sought to increase the clarity in understanding and differentiating between somatic disorders as compared to the *DSM-IV-TR* (American Psychiatric Association, 2000). This chapter will begin by presenting the changes made in the *DSM-5* and the general criteria for somatic disorders. Following will be a presentation of an Adlerian conceptualization of somatic disorders. Lastly the diagnostic criteria and clinical presentation, dynamics, and treatment considerations for each of the following disorders will be presented: Somatic Symptoms Disorder; Illness Anxiety Disorder; Conversion Disorder; Psychological Factors Affecting Other Medical Disorder; and Factitious Disorder.

Somatic Symptom and Related Disorders in the *DSM-5*

Changes in definition from DSM-IV-TR to DSM-5

Considerable changes in the definition of disorders involving somatic symptoms have been made and indeed are reflected in the manner in which these disorders are now labeled in the *DSM-5*. What used to be considered Somatoform Disorders are now referred to as a new category of disorders called Somatic Symptom Disorders (American Psychiatric Association, 2013, p. 309). This change came about due to lack of clarity in the previous system regarding what is needed to diagnose these disorders, as well as a considerable amount of overlap of symptoms that occurred from one Somatoform Disorder to the next (American Psychiatric Association, 2013, p. 309). A crucial difference in the definition of these disorders is in conceptualization of the symptoms. In the *DSM-IV-TR* the emphasis was on diagnosing when there were somatic symptoms in the absence of a medical explanation. The problem with this approach was that oftentimes the discomfort experienced by patients was dismissed and they were given the impression that their symptoms were not real. This approach also created a challenge in that it did not allow for the possibility that a medical condition could also include a comorbid mental disorder.

DSM-5 Characterization for Somatic Symptom Disorders

With the rejection of diagnosing Somatic Disorders based on the *absence* of a medical condition (i.e., diagnosing based on what is *not* there), the *DSM-5* requires diagnosing based on *positive* symptoms (i.e., symptoms that are present). More specifically, all of the disorders categorized in the Somatic Disorders section require the presence of somatic symptoms that are associated with significant distress and impairment. The distress is created by the patient's focus on the somatic symptoms themselves and includes abnormal thoughts, feelings, and behaviors experienced or exhibited by the patient. Emphasis is placed on how the patient presents and interprets his or her symptoms. Moreover, the patient's suffering is considered authentic, regardless of whether or not symptoms can be explained medically.

Adlerian Conceptualization of Somatic Symptom Disorders

Adler (1956) was an early voice in understanding and discussing the problem of psychosomatic disorders, and offered a comprehensive framework for understanding the mind–body relationship in general and the somatic symptom disorders in particular. Early on, Adler (1956, p. 223) saw the connection between physical symptoms and psychological symptoms, indicating that "mental tension affects both the central nervous system and the autonomic nervous system which can then alter blood circulation, the muscle tonus and almost all of the organs." Blushing or body trembles are simple examples of this connection. Understanding the somatic symptom disorders from an Adlerian framework calls for the understanding and incorporation of many of the key assumptions and concepts inherent in the theory. Adlerian theory is holistic, preferring to look at the person and not just the "parts" (e.g., the psychological or biological). Moreover, the teleological, phenomenological aspects of the clients' experience are also considered, as we truly understand somatic sympton disorders from all angles.

Adler (1917) described organ inferiority as an inherited defect in an organ or organ system, which resulted in inhibited growth. Examples of this inferiority could be seen in the respiratory tract, genito-urinary apparatus, circulatory organs, or nervous system (Adler, 1956). How does an organ inferiority become problematic? One way described by Adler is in regard to the interplay of the organ inferiority and the demands placed on that organ via stress. This notion parallels the thinking in the current biopsychosocial and stress-diathesis models. This stress could originate either from outside the individual (i.e., demands that the environment places on the person) or within the individual (i.e., the demands the individual places on him or herself). Regardless of the source of stress, the demands experienced by the individual negatively affect the person in general and the inferior organ in particular. When a person experiences enough stress, symptoms will often emerge. For example, when an individual has an inherited predisposition to migraine and the person comes under a good amount of stress, migraine attacks may occur.

Another way in which an organ inferiority manifests itself is in the body's attempt to gain equilibrium. This is done through what Adler (1917) referred to as compensation. When the body experiences an inferiority, it must do something about it in order to keep its balance. In a sense, the body continues to strive for wholeness, functionality, and continued survival. If a problem exists in any part of the body, the body will respond to overcome that problem created by the "weakest link."

Somatic symptoms can also be understood from a phenomenological perspective, and Adler (1956) emphasized this method. The phenomenological approach calls for the recognition of the people's frames of reference and perspectives. With this approach also lies the notion that people are meaning-makers. Beginning early in life, people create a template for understanding their world. Moreover, this template helps to direct their attention to what is important. They create and give meaning to their experiences, and bodily symptoms are no exception. When people present with physical symptoms, there is often a meaning attached, be it known or unknown to the person, and the physical symptoms themselves often "voice" this meaning, so to speak. This has been referred to as organ dialect (Wolfe, 1934) or as organ jargon (Griffith, 1984). A gateway to understanding and treating people's symptoms is to investigate the meaning of the symptoms and what they may be expressing for the individual. For example, when a person complains of chronic lower back pain, it could be that the person is really expressing, "I have been stabbed in the back." Another example might be the frequent headache, which could express, "I have been thinking too much and I am tired of it," or "I am so angry I have had it up to here."

We are also interested in the "meaning behind the meaning" of symptoms. This is often related to the person's inferiority feelings. Shulman (1973, pp. 106–109) presents an array of meanings related to "dangers" that people perceive. These dangers are threats to what the people believe about themselves or the world, and in general are experienced as threats to their self-esteem. These dangers include threats such as "the danger of being defective," "the danger of being exposed," "the danger of disapproval from others," or "the danger of having to submit to order." Again these meanings are often not readily acknowledged by the person, but nonetheless may hold significant meaning in relation to the symptoms from which the people suffer.

While exploring the meaning of the bodily symptoms can aid in providing both an understanding of the patient and providing direction of treatment, this is often only part of the picture. A teleological approach, that is, understanding the purpose that any given symptom may serve, also enhances understanding of the person and treatment direction. This approach stands in contrast to the current trend to consider symptoms as only reactive. Vomiting serves the purpose to rid our body of something noxious, and other bodily symptoms can serve to do something for the person. An allergic reaction can alert the person that something has gone wrong, and the body seeks to protect itself. Symptoms can serve to "gain," "protect," and have survival value on a biological level, and the same can also be said for symptoms of a psychological nature. Physical symptoms can serve to protect a person's self-esteem, maintain control over self or others, allow a retreat from a situation that threatens what the person believes about him or herself, and so on.

The next several pages will present the various somatic symptom disorders and will include a detailed description of each, their clinical presentation, treatment considerations and case examples. Also, an Adlerian conceptualization of each will be presented. It is important to note that most, if not all, of the following disorders share similar dynamics. In general, people with somatic disorders typically have an external locus of control. There is a reduced sense of their own personal power in dealing with the challenges of life. Given this, there is a tendency to look outside of themselves for help. The problem is that while they want someone to help them, they believe that there is no one who is capable of helping. This pessimistic attitude toward others plays out in their quest for someone to help (i.e., a physician or other healthcare provider), coupled with a tendency to idealize, depreciate, or accuse of others of not being able to help. They never quite seem to get help for their symptoms, and so the search continues.

Other dynamics can be understood from a developmental perspective. Early on, these people confused bodily sensations with emotions. These individuals grew up in a family that taught them that their feelings were not important. Sensations in general, and ill health in particular, then became overemphasized and often become a device for communication (Sullivan, 1956). People with somatic disorders often come from homes that are chaotic, abusive, dysfunctional, and hostile. As children, these people learned that others could not be trusted. These families frequently emphasized that "you are what you do and you better have a good reason for not doing something." Physical symptoms became a prime tool used for justification in those situations where these people felt they did not "do" enough.

SOMATIC SYMPTOM DISORDER

Clinical Presentation

People with this disorder typically suffer a good deal from their symptoms and often are troubled by one or more symptoms. Regardless of whether or not these symptoms can be explained by physical causes, these people are hurting. In addition to their suffering, the lives of these people are greatly disrupted by a preoccupation with symptoms, frequent efforts to attain medical help for their symptoms, and also a general moving away from many aspects of their lives. They limit participation in social and work activities. Their suffering and pursuit of relief often becomes the focal point of their lives. Their striving to "feel better" becomes a primary goal. In their social interactions, symptoms often become the primary focus, and become the way they connect with others.

DSM-5 Characterization

Somatic Symptom Disorder is less restrictive than the previous Somatization Disorder and is characterized by the presence of one or more somatic symptoms which contribute to a good deal of disruption in the person's life. The disruption experienced by the person is related to how the person responds to these symptoms. The response becomes problematic in that the person has excessive worry and anxiety regarding the seriousness of the symptoms, regardless of the fact that medical evidence does not warrant it. These people may spend a good deal of time utilizing medical services but typically do not find relief for their symptoms. Risk factors for this disorder include a temperament that is more negative and a tendency to be hypervigilant to bodily symptoms.

Biopsychosocial–Adlerian Conceptualization

People with Somatic Symptom Disorder have a strong frame of reference that is focused on the body. These are people who are very aware of physical sensations They tend to focus on how they are feeling. Oftentimes this is related to underlying temperamental style that can be characterized as highly reactive to internal stimuli. This sensitivity is lifelong.

The heightened sensitivity is not problematic in and of itself. It is when this temperament is combined with the belief system and coping style of the individual that Somatic Symptom Disorder can emerge. These individuals feel a heightened sense of inferiority with regards to surviving a world where bad things happen. Life is experienced as a very threatening place. The worldview of these individuals is often one of, "Life gives me pain and I am to suffer." Oftentimes these individuals grew up in an environment where they experienced a good deal of threatening situations, such as abuse. It was not uncommon for these people to feel victimized by others (and most often they were), and at the mercy of them. Their past experience is often a feeling of suffering at the hands of life and of others. That there is heightened sensitivity to bodily sensations often leads to a sense of threats coming from "within" as well as from the outside world. This contributes to a sort of "double whammy," in that it is not bad enough that these people feel negative physical sensations, but these people also want to fight that experience, only contributing to more focus on what hurts.

The self-concepts of these people is often one where they view that not only is life a threatening place, but that security lies outside of themselves, and they can not do a whole lot to protect themselves or get what they want. This external locus of control contributes not only to confirm and perpetuate their suffering, but also contributes to a heavy reliance upon help-seeking from medical professionals.

Treatment Considerations

Many individuals with Somatic Symptom Disorder will not initiate seeking help from a mental health professional, given that they believe their symptoms are of a physical nature. Often these individuals only come to such services via a referral from their physician. Many times, especially when the referral to the mental health professional is handled less than delicately, these people display a good deal of resistance. One way to remedy this is for the clinician to establish a strong collaborative relationship with the healthcare professional, both ahead of time and ongoing over the course of treatment with the patient. It is best to take a team approach and to let the patient know that the clinician will be working as part of a team in helping to reduce the his or her suffering. The current milieu is one of integrating primary care and mental health services. As this integration continues to emerge, it is hoped that referrals of patients to mental health professionals will continue to be met with less and less resistance.

Treatment with these people should emphasize increasing their functioning in general and decreasing the emphasis on symptoms and preoccupation in particular. Given the tendency to focus on the somatic, intervention strategies should target the patients' physical functioning via teaching relaxation and other stress-reduction skills. Training these patients in deep breathing, progressive muscle relaxation, and yoga techniques can both help these people feel better physically, and increase their sense of self-efficacy. Meditation and mindfulness strategies can also serve to increase skills that assist with minimizing the preoccupation on physical symptoms. These strategies can also help the patients accept the symptoms rather than "fight" them, which typically only serves to increase discomfort.

Other important interventions surround helping to increase the self-efficacy of these patients, so as to decrease the subjective experience of suffering and believing that security and help lies only outside of themselves. Strategies that can be useful here include helping the patients verbally express feelings and learn assertive communication, teaching them ways of limiting worry, and increasing their overall activity.

Effective treatment should also include assessment of the purpose and meaning that the symptoms might hold. The use of "The Question" is beneficial here. Adler (1956) proposed the use the use of "The Question" as a method for differentiating between somatogenic and psychogenic disorders. Asking the patient "What would you do if you were completely well?" (Adler, 1956, p. 331) can help in both assessment and treatment planning. How patients respond to this question can provide insight into the extent of which symptoms are more organic or functional in their etiology. Responses such as "I would feel better" suggest an organic etiology. However, responses such as "If I didn't have these headaches then I would be able to go out and look for a job" point to a functional etiology. Here we have some understanding of what might be stressful for patients and what patients may be avoiding due to inferiority feelings. This then points to important issues to explore during treatment. To the extent that responses to "The Question" represent somatogenic etiology, treatment interventions should include those activities that help them feel better, such as relaxation exercises. To the extent that those responses represent functional etiology, treatment interventions should include helping patients to change what it is that is stressful for them. This includes helping them to modify their belief system, try new behaviors, or alter their situation in some way. More often then not, treatment interventions for both somatogenic and psychogenic etiology are necessary.

Another similar strategy to help glean potential meaning of symptoms is to ask patients, "If your symptoms had a voice what would they be saying?" The response to this question may provide understanding of what patients are not directly expressing. For example, responses such as "My headache is telling me that I have had it up to here with anger" suggest that patients are angry but not articulating their anger verbally. Given such a response, treatment would include an exploration of what patients are angry about and also what it is that keeps them from expressing their anger in more direct ways. Together these two strategies for understanding potential meaning and purpose of symptoms help to bring the phenomenological and idiographic nature of patients' health challenges into focus.

Case Example: Nina

Nina is a 40-year-old female who was referred for psychological services by her primary care physician. She is married and has three school-age children who are very busy with outside activities. Her husband is a high-powered executive who travels frequently, and when he is home he is psychologically absent, as he often brings his work home. Nina reports a recent worsening of long-term health issues that she has struggled with over the years. She suffers frequent migraine headaches, Irritable Bowel Syndrome, back pain, and fibromyalgia-like symptoms. She also believes that she is starting to experience menopausal symptoms that are interrupting her sleep. She is quite busy running the home, caring for her children, and frequenting physicians' offices in search of relief for her symptoms, which has been minimal at best. Nina reports growing up in an abusive family where her father was an alcoholic who could not keep a job, and her mother, a nurse, was frequently absent, trying to support the family. She decided early on that she would not make waves, and keep to herself so as to not bring about more physical or emotional abuse. In her family, feelings were discouraged and were considered signs of weakness. As an adult, Nina remains pessimistic that things will turn out her way and steers away from self-assertion in order to keep the peace.

ILLNESS ANXIETY DISORDER

Clinical Presentation

People with Illness Anxiety Disorder tend to misinterpret otherwise insignificant physical symptoms as signs of a more serious or fatal problem. For example, a headache is feared to be a sign that the person has a brain tumor, or mild congestion in his or her lungs is a sign of lung cancer. Given their concerns these people will frequent medical assessment, often seeking numerous opinions when no medical findings are present, and these individuals often conclude that the physician is incompetent or has overlooked a serious problem. Needless to say, physicians and other health professionals who try to convince these patients that all is well can become highly frustrated and end up discounting or dismissing them. This sets the stage for a problematic cycle of hostility and anxiety.

DSM-5 Characterization

Illness Anxiety Disorder is characterized by a preoccupation with health in general and a fear of serious illness in particular. This preoccupation occurs despite the fact that there are no somatic symptoms present. Moreover, medical assessment declares no physical evidence of illness outside of perhaps the normal symptoms or sensations that anyone would experience. People with Illness Anxiety Disorder have a good deal of anxiety related to their health and well-being and believe that they suffer from a serious disease. Not only do people with this disorder believe that they are suffering ill health, but "being ill" becomes a significant part of their self-identities. The strong anxiety contributes to considerable avoidance of daily activities.

Biopsychosocial–Adlerian Conceptualization

People with Illness Anxiety Disorder believe that "life is dangerous" and that a focus on their health is paramount. What makes life so dangerous is not necessarily the things that could go wrong in the world; rather, these people are impressed with what could go wrong within themselves. These individuals go through life with a hypervigilance regarding their physical health, and the smallest pain, sensation, and so on is cause for alarm. Growing up, these people tended to be influenced by two experiences. First, these individuals grew up learning that others cannot be trusted. Oftentimes as children these individuals experienced neglect and a misreading of their needs, especially where physical sensations were concerned. Experiences such as hunger, or other physical discomfort, may not have been attended to, and as such these children began to associate physical pain with not getting needs met (Erikson, 1950). A second influence for these individuals was in the training in the advantages of being sick. While in childhood, these individuals may have experienced neglect, and therefore they may have been able to acquire attention when they were more obviously ill. In some situations, this may have been the only avenue for getting caretakers involved with them. They may have also witnessed the attention that others in the family received when they were sick, thus impressing them with the value of sickness in receiving caring and nurturing. Moreover, they may have experienced overprotection from caregivers who overemphasized every bump, bruise, or fever. This set the stage for children to be overly impressed by what could go wrong with their bodies.

The dynamics listed above often perpetuate the continued focus on the body and vigilance to what can wrong for individuals with Illness Anxiety Disorder. Much time is spent in frequent worrying or obsessing about their health. Socially, these people keep others very busy with them and seek to get their concern and nurturance. Physicians, especially, are frequently sought out, although the persons' concerns are rarely of significance or as life threatening as these people believe them to be. These individuals often defeat the physician by claiming that something has been missed and that the physician is incompetent. They then move on to the next physician. In this way, they not only remain worried and focused on their health, but also demonstrate to the world their heroic existence for carrying on as sick as they are. For some people with Illness Anxiety Disorder, there is an element of excitement-seeking.

Treatment Considerations

Evidenced-based interventions mentioned in the literature point to the effective use of cognitive behavioral interventions in the treatment of Illness Anxiety Disorder. Like the Somatic Symptom Disorder, people with Illness Anxiety Disorder often come to mental health professionals via a referral from a physician. Given this, it is imperative that the concerns regarding physical health that these patients bring be taken seriously and delicately. Educating the patient on the harmlessness of the vast physical sensations that anyone experiences is important. In this way the patients become desensitized to many physical sensations and learn to take a nonchalant attitude regarding them. For example, clinicians need to help them understand that a pain in the head is just a temporary, uncomfortable nuisance, and not a sign of a potential brain tumor. This desensitization to the normal physical sensations that everyone experiences can be aided by educating patients on the physiological changes that occur during the stress response. Mindfulness and acceptance-based strategies can also be of aid here. Teaching patients to accept their symptoms in a nonjudgmental way helps to minimize their impact. It also can help patients to not "fight" their symptoms, which often only makes them feel worse. Moreover, teaching patients relaxation training and stress management can not only help to reframe physical sensations, but help give them a sense of self-efficacy in helping themselves feel better.

To the extent that the Illness Anxiety Disorder is perpetuated by social motivations for obtaining care and connection, interventions surrounding this social piece are crucial. Helping patients to find ways of connecting with others, other than through emphasizing their health issues, can be beneficial. Assertiveness training can be helpful here as well. The immense focus that these people have on their physical health can also be ameliorated by helping to turn their attention to others and ways in which they might be helpful to them. It is not uncommon for these individuals to be quite angry or maintain hostile feelings. Identifying and modifying the beliefs that underlie these feelings should be addressed.

Case Example: Jack

Jack is a 59-year-old male who was referred for psychological services by his cardiologist. Jack reports that he has been having heart palpitations for many years and is afraid he is going to have a "heart attack and die." His cardiologist has put him through numerous tests, including stress tests, echocardiogram, Holter monitor, and MRI, and all have been inconclusive. His cardiologist has even referred him for second and third opinions, and all have come up the same results. His cardiologist has also noted Jack's tendency to be concerned about other bodily symptoms for which he has not been able to get adequately diagnosed. She referred him for counseling after it was clear that he was becoming very stressed and agitated by a lack of definitive diagnosis. The cardiologist indicated that this stress could have a negative impact on his health and referred him for a psychological evaluation.

Jack is quite preoccupied with his health and spends a good deal of time talking with his friends and family about his concerns, and they are getting frustrated, too. He has backed off of some of his work and exercise, as he is afraid to tax himself too much, given his heart palpitations. He is irritated with the many physicians who have not helped him and reports that he feels "they are incompetent."

CONVERSION DISORDER

Clinical Presentation

Conversion Disorder is more often diagnosed in women than men. The reason for this could be that in general, women are often more sensitive to changes in their bodies. Situations such as the changes brought on by menstruation may offer the opportunity to be more in tune and aware of bodily changes. Another reason that Conversion Disorder is more often diagnosed in women is that it is often more socially acceptable for women to report physical symptoms than it is for men. People with Conversion Disorder complain of one or more bothersome symptoms that affect how they move or sense the world. While these individuals can go into great detail regarding their symptoms, they often express only limited concern regarding them. Historically this has been referred to as La Belle Indifference, and while it is sometimes seen in these individuals, it is important to note that this tendency is not specific to Conversion Disorder (American Psychiatrist Association, 2013). It is not uncommon for the onset of symptoms to occur in concert with a significant change, loss, trauma, or other stressor. Oftentimes these individuals are not psychologically minded, and their histories often included experiences of abuse, especially sexual abuse. The tendency toward dissociation and depersonalization is commonly seen with these individuals. In other words, these people often deal with stressors by removing themselves psychologically from stressful situations as a way of safeguarding themselves. In this way, they do not pay attention to certain events in the first place and therefore they do not remember them.

DSM-5 Characterization

People diagnosed with Conversion Disorder experience symptoms of voluntary motor function or of sensory function (e.g., symptoms such as weakness or paralysis of a limb, or reduced ability to see or hear). What makes these symptoms problematic is that clinical findings cannot explain why these symptoms are occurring or if there is a neurological disorder present—the symptoms cannot be accounted for by such illness. However, these symptoms contribute to significant impairment in these people's work, social, and family life. The onset of symptoms oftentimes coincides with a psychological or physical stressor or other trauma. One change from the *DSM-IV* to the *DSM-5* is that the identification of a specific stressor may not be apparent and is not needed to make the diagnosis of Conversion Disorder.

Biopsychosocial –Adlerian Conceptualization

From an Adlerian perspective, conversion disorders include two common styles, referred to as the feeling-avoider and the getter (Mosak, 1968). Feeling-avoiders are people who tend to minimize their feelings. Those who embrace more of a getting style focus on what they can get from life and others, be it admiration, attention, or material things. How these styles might develop and their relationship to Conversion Disorder will be presented as follows.

How might some people become feeling-avoiders? By understanding feeling-avoiders, we can understand the process of dissociation (Sullivan, 1956). As mentioned earlier, these people often confuse physical sensations as emotions. Developmentally, this tendency can come about given a number of situations. While Adler (Mosak & Maniacci, 1999) did not propose a developmental theory *per se,* attachment theory (Allen, 2013) and Erickson's (1950) stages of development can augment our understanding of how someone might be inclined to discount feelings. From an attachment theory perspective, those who have early experiences characterized by limited empathic experiences go on to discount feelings in themselves and others. Growing up, these people were not empathized with. They may value logic over feelings and cut themselves off not only from their feelings but their bodies as well. As these people get older, they may appear as if all is well on the outside, but physiological measures will tell a different story. For example, it is not uncommon for these people to have elevated heart rates even though they look calm on the outside. From Erikson's (1950) point of view, conversion disorders often come about as a result of problems at the initiative stage of development. Here children's wishes, thoughts, and feelings were often discouraged or punished. Subsequently, these children stop paying attention to their feelings and wishes and pull back from initiating actions. This contributes to a lack of psychological mindedness, which is commonly seen in conversion disorders.

Both of those theories describe situations that Adler thought would be problematic for the development of most children and could contribute to the tendency to avoid feelings. These situations include *discouragement* and lack of a sense of *belongingness.* Part and parcel of encouraging children is validating who these children are and empathizing with their feelings. Also, a lack of sense of belonging can come about from early experiences of emotional neglect. Moreover, a lack of sense of belonging in and of itself can have a deleterious effect on one's health, as research has shown that threats to belonging can contribute to both emotional and physical numbing (Gere & MacDonald, 2010).

The "getter" provides understanding of another common dynamic seen in conversion disorders; it can also provide further explanation for why some people might avoid feelings as well. People who develop Conversion Disorder place a high value on looking good, especially in the eyes of others. This makes sense when viewed in conjunction with their wish of getting from others. This striving has special significance in the psychodynamics of the disorder and includes a couple of important points. The striving to look good does not always lend itself well to dealing with the negative feelings that are common to the human experience, and the reason for this is twofold. First, to acknowledge and voice a negative feeling requires that people take a stand. But someone could disagree with the stance and therefore show disapproval. This would be upsetting to the individuals, because then they would not be able to "get" something from that person. It is not uncommon for people with this disorder to have a history of abuse in their early development. They may fear that to acknowledge and voice negative feelings would result in being like the abuser. Then what to do about feelings, especially negative ones? For these people it is better to bite their tongues or not acknowledge the feeling at all. But the tension still exists, and it is this tension that is often manifested in the physical symptoms.

The second way in which the getter can become problematic is when the person is confronted with a stressor that he or she is feels unprepared for. In this situation, an increased focus on physical symptoms can allow for a retreat from the challenges, but doing so in a way that he or she still can "look good." While it would probably be difficult to find people who have not found a retreat from stress in physical symptoms, this is often a frequent movement with people with Conversion Disorder, although he or she is typically unaware that that dynamic is taking place.

Treatment Considerations

Research proposing evidenced-based intervention for Conversion Disorder is limited at best (Seligman & Reichenberg, 2012). However, there are a number of considerations and general treatment approaches that can be helpful. Given the tendency for limited psychological mindedness, combined with the fact that patients are typically referred to clinicians via their physicians or other healthcare providers, it is important to refrain from any suggestion that their symptoms are not "real." It should be emphasized that symptoms are real, despite lack of clinical findings. Educating patients that physical symptoms can be brought on by stress, and is rather common, may be emphasized with discretion. In general, supportive therapy is of benefit to these individuals. It is not uncommon for conversion disorders to be precipitated by a stressor or trauma. Allowing the patients to talk about the stressor in the context of a safe, warm, therapeutic environment can go a long way. Teaching the patients relaxation skills and other stress-management techniques can help them to feel better. If the patients are amenable, a life-style assessment (Mosak & Maniacci, 1999) can be conducted, and the purpose of this is twofold. First, in the process of telling their story, these patients can have the opportunity to be clearly understood and feel empathized with. Second, identification of the patients' life style can provide understanding as to what will stress them out.

Case Example: Penny

Penny is a 48-year-old woman who was attending a psychiatric partial hospitalization program. One day she called in sick, claiming that she could not walk. Her "elderly" parents were concerned and she was brought to the hospital emergency room for a full neurological workup. According to Penny, her legs were "paralyzed and totally useless." This had happened in the morning, when just the night before she had been fully mobile. There were no neurological findings to support her loss of functioning. Psychiatric consult was ordered and her therapist from the hospital's partial program was brought in as well. Penny had been living with her parents for the past three years and was unemployed. The staff at the partial program were working in family therapy with Penny and her parents to move her into a supervised living arrangement nearby. The night before the "paralysis," a family therapy session had been held to firm up the date when Penny would be transitioned to the apartment. Her parents were enthusiastic and relieved. Penny reported feeling enthusiastic and happy about the move until the next morning. When she was asked "The Question" she responded, "Well, this means we are going to have to put off the move." The meaning of the symptom: "I can't stand up for myself and I am unable to stand on my own two feet." The purpose became clear: The staff were moving too quickly in arranging the independent living.

PSYCHOLOGICAL FACTORS AFFECTING OTHER MEDICAL CONDITION

Clinical Presentation

The clinical presentation of this disorder can be as varied as there are individuals and medical disorders. That being said, there are a number of medical disorders where psychological factors are deemed potential contributing or exacerbating factors. Diseases such as heart disease, diabetes, or cancer are commonly impacted by psychological factors. So, too, are immune and endocrine disorders. Illnesses such as migraine, Irritable Bowel Syndrome, fibromyalgia, and pain disorders are also impacted. There are many general ways in which psychological factors can contribute to or worsen a medical disorder. One example of the relationship would be how psychological distress causes hyperactivity in the hypothalamus–pituitary–adrenal system, exacerbating thyroid issues. Another example is how chronic activation of the stress response negatively impacts the immune system via altering bacteria in the gut, which exacerbates immune problems such as asthma or allergies. Mood disturbance can play a role in medical disorders. For example, depression has been implicated as both a risk factor in heart disease and a factor that negatively impacts recovery (Langosch, Budde, & Linden, 2007). Maladaptive coping strategies can impact a medical condition, such as the case where a person with chronic hostility develops heart disease or a person who tends to overutilize an avoidance strategy denies worsening chest pain. An additional common clinical presentation is the use of poor health behaviors, such as overeating or non-adherence to treatment, as seen in the diabetic who does not monitor his or her blood sugar and eats too many sugary, high-processed foods.

DSM-5 Characterization

The biggest change in this disorder from the *DSM-IV-TR* is that it has become a part of the Somatic Symptoms Disorder; it is no longer considered under Other Conditions That May Be a Focus of Clinical Attention, and is not officially listed among the mental disorders (American Psychiatric Association, 2013). This speaks to the prevalence of these disorders so often being seen in medical settings. The emphasis on the relationship between psychological factors and physical illness is gaining widespread recognition. As this chapter is being written, much action is underway that integrates psychological services into primary care, and is an important initiative of healthcare reform. Psychological Factors Affecting Other Medical Condition includes those diagnoses where an actual medical condition exists. However, there are psychological factors that are judged to play a role not only in the development of the medical illness, but also either in exacerbating the illness or impeding the recovery of the illness. Psychological factors can include mental disorders such as depression or anxiety, stressful life events, or maladaptive coping and health behaviors.

Biopsychosocial–Adlerian Conceptualization

Adlerian theory provides a sound basis for understanding these disorders. Diagnosing these disorders inherently calls for an incorporation of biopsychosocial factors. Adler's

(1917) notion of organ inferiority and compensation can also shed light on conceptualizing these disorders. As both the ideas of holism and organ inferiority were discussed earlier in this chapter, not much more will be said here. The *life style* is a useful construct and will be elaborated on here (Adler, 1956; Mosak & Maniacci, 1999).

Understanding people's life styles illuminates what they might strive for or move toward in life. It is important to not only understand what they strive for, but how they strive for it. While each life style is unique and it would be impossible to discuss its relationship to medical illness in a detailed way, constructs like *personal priorities* can be utilized to put us in the ball park of understanding the role of life style and medical illness. Four personal priorities (Pew, 1976) have been highlighted, and include the strivings toward *comfort, pleasing, control,* and *superiority.* An individual will most likely experience stress of sorts when his or her main priority is not realized. For example, in striving for *comfort* a person will feel stressed out when there are too many demands, there is chaos at home or work, or there is unresolved conflict. The *pleasing* styles will feel stressed out when they feel criticized or rejected, are faced with conflict in a relationship, or have little structure in their environment. The *control* styles will probably be stressed out when there is disorder in their environment or when someone is challenging them. The *superiority* styles may commonly feel stressed out when they feel overextended, do not receive enough acknowledgement, lack a sense of accomplishment, or feel that their authority is being challenged. When any of these particular styles experience chronic stress in these areas, chances are they will start to develop physical symptoms. Interestingly, Bitter (1987) has posited that each of the styles tend to lean toward particular symptoms or health issues. For instance the *comfort* style often develops headaches, dizziness, or other nervous system problems; the *pleasing* style often develops stomach or digestive problems, or chronic tension in the shoulders; the *control* style often develops neck and back problems or complaints that defy diagnosis; the *superiority* style often develops back pain, muscle-tissue problems, and high blood pressure.

Other common life-style themes have been identified in relationship to physical illness. For example, Sackett-Maniacci (1999) found a tendency for chronic migraine headache sufferers to commonly embrace a *going along* style (a style similar to *pleasing*), characterized as a tendency to be flexible yet sometimes passive or unassertive. Moreover, these headache sufferers also tended toward a low sense of *entitlement.* Together, these traits can create stress for migraine sufferers in terms of having a reduced sense of self-efficacy and ability to get what they want in life. This can culminate in chronic stress and subsequent increase in migraine.

To summarize, understanding a person's life style can help to not only understand what stressors may have contributed to the development of medical illness, but may also provide some insight into how the person may negotiate recovery. Maladaptive personality strivings may negatively impact full recovery.

Treatment Considerations

The treatment of these disorders should include an integrative, mind–body approach. Like with the other disorders in this section, a team approach where clinicians collaborate with physicians or other healthcare providers involved is recommended to help enhance

patient compliance and ensure continuity of care. While there are a number of general treatment interventions that are recommended for these disorders, there are also more specific interventions, given the nature of the psychological factors involved. For example, if there is an anxiety, mood, or substance abuse disorder that is affecting the medical treatment, then interventions specific to those disorders are recommended. Given their specificity, these will not be mentioned here, and readers are directed to those chapters in this text.

Another consideration in providing specific treatment recommendations surrounds the fact that while the emphasis is on Psychological Factors Affecting Other Medical Condition, there appear to be a good deal of treatment recommendations specific to some medical conditions that need to be taken into account. For example, much research has been done that validates interventions specific to recurrent headaches, such as thermal biofeedback or cognitive behavioral treatment of chronic pain (Mercer & Duckworth, 2006). Interventions such as stress management, yoga, and group support for heart disease is another example (Langosch, Budde, & Linden, 2007). Providing the wide range of evidence-based interventions for these disorders is beyond the scope of this chapter. Instead, the following general interventions will be provided.

With these disorders, psychoeducation can go a long way in helping the patients cope with their medical disorder. Given that so many medical disorders are brought on or exacerbated by stress, and that the experience of having a medical disorder is stressful in and of itself, helping the patients learn better stress management is key. General stress-management strategies, such as relaxation exercises and mindfulness meditation, can be taught as methods for helping the patient decrease the impact of stress. Additionally, identifying the idiographic aspects of what makes something stressful for the patient to begin with can be undertaken. Here we are talking about understanding life-style themes or personal priorities. What is stressful for one person may not be stressful for the next, so we want to understand the subjective experience of the patient so as to best create individualized treatment goals. After all, to paraphrase Shakespeare, "Nothing is good or bad, but thinking makes it so." We want to understand how and what patients perceive and think.

Educating and counseling the patients on other behavioral changes to increase coping is crucial. Helping them to learn more effective communication strategies, such as assertiveness training, can help patients become better advocates for themselves both in their relationships and in navigating their healthcare. Encouraging exercise, in conjunction with their physicians' recommendations, can help decrease pain and increase patients' sense of self-efficacy. Since lack of sleep can perpetuate many health or psychological disorders, instructing them on adequate sleep hygiene is crucial. We have come a long way in understanding the impact that diet has on our health and the issues that come with frequent consumption of highly processed, chemically laden foods on our physical health and mood. Therefore educating patients on nutrition and having them work with a nutritionist is important. Finally, helping patients increase their support network and sense of connection to others are other important factors that have been implicated as buffers against stress and health problems. Linking patients to ancillary services, such as support groups, or alternative approaches such as acupuncture or yoga therapy, can also aid in helping them more effectively deal with their medical disorder and gain relief of symptoms.

Case Example: Gloria

Gloria is a 60-year-old divorced female who was referred for psychological evaluation and stress management by her physician. Gloria lives alone and has two adult children who live out of state. She recently was laid off of a supervisor job that she had held for the past 25 years and is devastated. She is a recovering alcoholic and former smoker. She has been in treatment for Chronic Obstructive Pulmonary Disease (COPD) and Diabetes for the past three years. She is overwhelmed by the loss of her job and is feeling isolated. She remains sober but has recently started sneaking a few cigarettes to help her cope with the stress. Additionally, she has been eating more sugary and processed foods, which are making her Diabetes worse. Gloria told her physician that she is "just so overwhelmed" and is "unsure what to do" to deal with the loss of her job. She believes that it will be difficult for a 60-year-old to find work given the current economic milieu. While she is not suicidal, it is clear that she is significantly stressed and her methods for coping are maladaptive.

FACTITIOUS DISORDER

Clinical Presentation

People with Factitious Disorder seek or continue medical consultation for symptoms that are consciously created and can appear anywhere on a continuum, from an unrealistic exaggeration of symptoms occurring with an existing medical disorder on one end, to actually creating symptoms on the other end. Persons with this disorder may report symptoms such as dizziness, stomach pains, blackouts, seizures, and so on, that do not really happen. They may also go as far as contaminating samples or injecting themselves with substances in order to create symptoms or influence medical assessment procedures to reflect pathology. Examples of this are taking a thyroid-stimulating drug to create hyperthyroidism, injecting themselves with insulin to produce hypoglycemia, or manipulating catheters with fecal material to produce sepsis. People with Factitious Disorder may undergo many unnecessary surgeries or other procedures. While many people would not welcome most surgeries or procedures, these individuals seem to be quite open and accepting of them.

People with Factitious Disorder may not only produce or falsify symptoms in themselves, but may produce or falsify symptoms in others. This is often seen with their children, elderly adults whom they have frequent contact with, or even with pets. The movie *The Sixth Sense* presents an excellent portrayal of a mother who not only produces symptoms in her daughter by poisoning her, but also ultimately kills her daughter. In this way this is a disorder that can include the abuse of others and involve criminal behavior.

It is not uncommon for people with Factitious Disorder to have a childhood history of frequent illness or surgeries, or psychological symptoms. Abuse and neglect is often seen in the history of these individuals. There may have also been a pattern of lying as children. In adulthood, there is a high frequency of this disorder occurring with those in the healthcare industry. It is also not uncommon for this disorder to co-occur with depression, anxiety, or personality disorders.

DSM-5 Characterization

People with Factitious Disorder report physical or psychological symptoms with or without a precipitating event or illness; however, these symptoms are deliberately and knowingly falsified. These individuals are deceiving others that an illness or symptoms exist, when in fact there are none. These individuals are not delusional and the hallmark of this disorder is one of conscious deception. Moreover, this deception is not aimed at gaining obvious external rewards, such as seen in malingering. These patients are striving to have others see them as "sick." People with this disorder may also seek to falsify the illness or injury of another, such as a child, pet, or other adult.

Biopsychosocial–Adlerian Conceptualization

An Adlerian approach to understanding the Factitious Disorder emphasizes identifying the underlying motivations that perpetuate the conscious creation of symptoms and the subsequent deceiving of others. These motivations are to be considered consistent with the life style of these individuals, and the purpose of their behavior is viewed in accordance with their life style. Common life-style themes that can be seen with Factitious Disorder include those themes that emphasize getting, excitement-seeking, and going against. For example, consciously created symptoms can serve to "get" something from others, and in this case, it is most likely created to get the attention and care of others. Being viewed as sick in our society warrants a certain social protocol where others cater to and give to those whom are sick. This might possibly be a prime goal of those with Factitious Disorder. In those situations where these individuals are actually fabricating or inducing symptoms in someone else, this disorder can serve the same purpose, although it now becomes one of getting attention, concern and care for having a sick child, relative, or pet. Most people are inclined to empathize with and offer to help those who are nursing a sick family member, and may offer to help by providing meals, rides to the doctor, or just a sympathetic ear. These may be the very things that people with Factitious Disorder crave.

There is also an element of "excitement" in being diagnosed and treated for physical symptoms. Indeed the energy needed to generate and tend to a medical illness, and the opportunity for conversation and focus from a social perspective, can be experienced as exciting and can also serve as a goal of these people. The development of symptoms can add structure and color to an otherwise mundane existence.

Inherent in Factitious Disorder is the element of dishonesty and of "pulling something over on others," albeit only in lying about symptoms. This striving may represent a more encompassing attitude and goal of "going against." This may play out as these people lie outright to their physicians and may secretly have a sense of rebelling against them or having superiority over them. Moreover, this may also play out as an overall "going against" the requirements of living in our society, which calls for contribution and involvement with our fellow human beings. Certainly friends and family who become unknowing participants in the illness drama based on lies can very likely be the social situation that these people "go against."

An additional dynamic to consider from an Adlerian perspective is in understanding their self-concepts. Many of these individuals have concluded that they are sick, weak, or in need of care, and this becomes what they know about themselves. Creating or fabricating of symptoms may simply serve to confirm what they believe to be true about themselves. Perhaps this conclusion came out of frequent early experiences of being sick, or of getting attention only when they were sick, but in any event this is what they believe. As they enter into adulthood and are faced with the challenges that adulthood brings, they may not know how else to be if not "sick," and may not know how to connect with others outside of the sick role.

Treatment Considerations

The treatment of Factitious Disorder becomes challenging in that the inherent dishonesty seen in this disorder makes it difficult for these individuals to come for treatment, given the high probability that they will deny they have a problem. That being said, these individuals can certainly benefit from treatment once they decide to pursue help. The first aspect of treatment includes ensuring the safety of these people and of those other individuals who may be considered a victim of their fabrications and symptom creation. Certainly if these people are hurting others, steps need to be taken to provide for victims' safety. Legal intervention is almost always required, and reporting to the relevant authorities is ethically and legally demanded.

Other treatment considerations include cognitive-behavioral and supportive approaches. Helping these individuals decrease their use of medical resources by helping them create a different structure is crucial not only for the individuals, but for society as a whole. Including the family to help decrease the enabling that happens can go a long way. More specific interventions recommended are those that can identify and modify maladaptive beliefs surrounding their self-concepts. In addition, helping these individuals to explore more socially useful ways of connecting and contributing is crucial.

Concluding Note

The Somatic Symptoms and Related Disorders represent one of the true interfaces between the biological and the psychosocial. Individuals with these disorders are using the body to speak instead of their mouths. Clinicians need to be sensitive, compassionate, and capable of interpreting these symbolic representations of psychological conflicts.

References

Adler, A. (1917). *Study of Organ Inferiority and Its Psychical Compensation: A Contribution to Clinical Medicine* (S.E. Jelliffe, Trans.). New York, NY: Nervous and Mental Diseases Company. (Original work published 1907.)
Adler, A. (1956). In H.L. Ansbacher & R.R. Ansbacher (Eds.), *The Individual Psychology of Alfred Adler*. New York, NY: Basic Books.

Allen, J.G. (2013). *Restoring Metallization in Attachment Relationships: Treating Trauma with Plain Old Therapy*. Washington, DC: American Psychiatric Publishing.

American Psychiatric Association (2000). *Diagnostic and Statistical Manual of Mental Disorders, Fourth Edition (Text Revision)*. Washington, DC: American Psychiatric Publishing.

American Psychiatric Association. (2013). *Diagnostic and Statistical Manual of Mental Health Disorders, Fifth Edition*. Arlington, VA: American Psychiatric Publishing.

Bitter, J.R. (1987). Communication and meaning: Satir in Adlerian context. In R. Sherman & D. Dinkmeyer (Eds.), *Systems of Family Therapy: An Adlerian Integration* (pp. 109–142). New York, NY: Brunner/Mazel.

Erikson, E.H. (1950). *Childhood and Society* (2nd edn., revised & enlarged). New York, NY: Norton.

Gere, J. & MacDonald, G. (2010). An update of the empirical case for the need to belong. *The Journal of Individual Psychology*, 66, pp. 93–115.

Griffith, J. (1984). Adler's organ jargon. *Individual Psychology: The Journal of Adlerian Theory, Research & Practice*, 40, pp. 437–444.

Langosch, W., Budde, H-G., Linden, W. (2007). Psychological interventions for coronary heart disease: Stress management, relaxation, and Ornish groups. In J. Jordan, B. Barde, & A.M. Zeiher (Eds.), *Contributions Toward Evidence-Based Psychocardiology: A Systematic Review of the Literature* (pp. 231–254). Washington, DC: American Psychological Association.

Mercer, V.E. & Duckworth, M.P. (2006). Recurrent headache disorders. In J.E. Fisher & W.T. O'Donohue (Eds.), *Practitioner's Guide to Evidence-Based Psychotherapy* (pp. 567–582). New York, NY: Springer.

Mosak, H.H. (1968). The interrelatedness of the neuroses through central themes. *Journal of Individual Psychology*, 25, pp. 56–63.

Mosak, H., Maniacci, M. (1999). *A Primer of Adlerian Psychology: The Analytic-Behavioral-Cognitive Psychology of Alfred Adler*. Philadelphia, PA: Brunner/Mazel.

Pew, W.L. (1976). The number one priority. *Monograph of the International Association of Individual Psychology*.

Sackett-Maniacci, L.A. (1999). *Lifestyle Factors of Chronic Migraine Headache Sufferers*. Unpublished doctoral dissertation, Adler School of Professional Psychology, Chicago, IL.

Seligman, L. & Reichenberg, L.W. (2012). *Selecting Effective Treatments: A Comprehensive, Systematic Guide to Treating Mental Disorders* (4th edn.). Hoboken, NJ: John Wiley & Sons.

Shulman, B.H. (1973). Psychological disturbances which interfere with the patient's cooperation. In B.H. Shulman (Ed.), *Contributions to Individual Psychology* (pp. 105–121). (Original work published 1964.)

Sullivan, H.S. (1956). *Clinical Studies in Psychiatry*. New York, NY: Norton.

Taylor, S., & Asmundson, G.J.G. (2006). Hypochondriasis. In J.E. Fisher & W.T. O'Donohue (Eds.), *Practitioner's Guide to Evidence-Based Psychotherapy* (pp. 313–323). New York, NY: Springer.

Wolfe, W.B. (1934). *Nervous Breakdown: Its Cause and Cure*. London: George Routledge & Sons.

11 Sleep-Wake Disorders

Jennifer N. Williamson and Daniel G. Williamson

This chapter identifies six of the ten disorders described in the *DSM-5* and includes Insomnia, Hypersomnolence, Narcolepsy, Obstructive Sleep Apnea, Central Sleep Apnea, and Nightmare Disorders. Descriptions provided in this chapter identify clients' dissatisfaction with the quality, quantity, patterns, and timing associated with sleep, as well as varying expressions of distress and impairment that accompany these disorders.

DSM-IV-TR versus *DSM-5* Descriptions

The transition between descriptions and definitions associated with sleep-wake disorders between the *DSM-IV-TR* and the *DSM-5* demonstrates a simpler approach, as disorders have been grouped or split, depending on presentation, reflecting the presence of characteristics derived from research in physical origins and treatment considerations. The authors of the *DSM-5* suggest that the purpose of this presentation is to help facilitate accuracy in diagnosing conditions, while clarifying when referral to a sleep specialist may be required (American Psychiatric Association, 2013).

DSM-5 Criteria for Sleep-Wake Disorders

Sleep-wake disorders, described in the *DSM-5*, encompass an integrated approach, as considerations for comorbid conditions are included. The authors of the *DSM-5* suggest that the inclusion of comorbid conditions is essential to the diagnosis, rather than the exception. Included among these comorbid conditions are breathing-related sleep disturbances, heart and lung diseases, neurological and degenerative disorders, and diseases of the skeletal system. The authors also indicate that while many of these coexisting conditions may interfere with sleep, they may also be exacerbated during sleep. Classification of the sleep-wake disorders in the *DSM-5* includes language and descriptions associated with the International Classification of Sleep Disorders (ICSD-2) as well as the International Classification of Diseases (ICD) (American Psychiatric Association, 2013).

Adlerian Conceptualization of Sleep-Wake Disorders

Adlerian Psychology is a holistic theory embracing a biopsychosocial approach (Garrison & Libby, 2010; Sperry, 2008). Sperry (1988) described this biopsychosocial approach to treatment as "an integrative and systems perspective for understanding a person and the relationship of the system outside and inside of the person that influences health as well as illness" (p. 226). This model asserts that a client can only be understood fully when a therapist examines all areas of functioning in three distinctive and interrelated stages— evaluation, formulation and creation, and implementation of a treatment plan (Sperry, 1988)—and in all areas of functioning: biological, psychological, and social (Sperry, 2008).

Adler perceived sleep disorders to be connected to an individual's waking life. Adler professed, "Any theory which treats sleep and waking, dream thought and day thoughts as contradictions is bound to be unscientific" (Ansbacher & Ansbacher, 1956, p. 229).

> In sleep … we are still in contact with reality. The fact that … we can make the adjustments which prevent us from falling out of bed shows that connections with reality are still present. A mother can sleep through the loudest noises in the street and yet awaken at the slightest movement of her child.
>
> (Adler, 1956, as cited in Ansbacher, 1982, p. 230)

An individual's personality or style of life is present both in sleeping and waking states. An Adlerian approach to sleep disorders must address the individual's private logic, or the meaning an individual assigns to the sleep disorder. Adler (1992, p.15) extrapolated that

> Human beings live in the realm of *meanings*. We do not experience things in the abstract; we always experience them in human terms. Even at its source our experience is qualified by our human perspective. … Anyone who tried to consider circumstances, to the exclusion of meanings, would be very unfortunate: he would isolate himself from others and his actions would be useless to himself or anyone else; in a word, they would be meaningless. But no human being can escape meanings. We experience reality only through the meaning we ascribe to it: not as a thing in itself, but as something interpreted.

As the therapist explores and assists individuals in constructing meaning, the Adlerian therapist should embrace an encouragement-focused approach. Treatment of sleep disorders must be encouragement focused, as many individuals may become discouraged because of their sleep disruption and the social turmoil that often accompanies sleep distress.

> Encouragement focuses on helping counselees become aware of their worth. By encouraging them, you help your counselees recognize their own strengths and assets, so they become aware of the power they have to make decisions and choices … Encouragement focuses on beliefs and self-perceptions. It searches intensely for assets and processes feedback so the client will become aware of her [or his] strengths. In a mistake-centered culture like ours, this approach violates norms by ignoring deficits and stressing assets. The counselor is concerned with changing the client's negative self-concept and anticipations.
>
> (Dinkmeyer, Dinkmeyer, & Sperry, 1987, p. 124.)

An encouragement-focused approach to treatment is critical, as many sleep disturbances produce symptoms that impact social, educational, and vocational functioning. Clients often become discouraged because of ridicule, task-oriented failure, social isolation, or interpersonal conflict connected to sleep concerns. Counseling may help clients better identify styles and strategies for coping with both the sleep disturbance itself, as well as the biological, psychological, and social consequences associated with these conditions. Shulman (1973) discussed Adler's idea about how an individual's intrapersonal opinion impacts his willingness to strive. He stated, "The individual's own opinion of himself determined how hard he would strive and his opinion of where his best chance for growth and development lay would influence the direction of his endeavors" (p. 93). He concluded that it is the "conviction of inferiority" that is important in this situation (Shulman, 1973, p. 93). An individual's attitude concerning his/her disordered sleep will likely be critical in the treatment process.

Adler's approach to sleeplessness was very practical. He asked individuals who struggled with sleep, "What could you do if you could sleep?" (Adler, 1944, p. 60). In answering this question, individuals would clarify worries and fears. The therapist can also ask, "What are you thinking about if you do not sleep during the night?" (Adler, 1944, p. 62). Adler recommended that individuals use the time in which he or she cannot sleep for treatment (Adler, 1944). Watts (2003, 2013) expanded this approach further with the development of the *Reflecting "As If"* technique. Adlerians have utilized *acting as if* when encouraging clients to act as if "they were already the person they would like to be" (Watts, 2003, p. 73). Watts developed the "reflecting as if" technique as a preliminary and safer way to approach new or uncertain situations. "Reflecting as if" persuades clients to take a reflective step forward in the safety of their own minds to try out a new manner of being. In utilizing this technique, therapists can tap into the creativity and imagination of the client as a resource for problem solving and co-constructing a plan.

In the treatment of disordered sleep, Adlerians recognize the socially embedded nature of human existence. The implications for sleep disorders do not end with the individual, but rather impact those with whom they are most closely and socially connected. Dinkmeyer (1997) suggested:

> All behavior has social meaning. Each of us is socially embedded in an interactive social system. We are a continuous influence upon each other. Any movement by the individual or the family creates movement in all other components of the system.
>
> (p. 456)

Garrison and Eckstein (2009) echoed this belief as it relates to sleep behaviors. They asserted that "because humans spend one third of their lives sleeping, the impact of sleep disruption, both personally and on relationships, is significant" (p. 58).

With growth in medical science and the development of advanced technology, the health-related community possesses a better understanding of the physiological effects related to sleep maladies. Because the multitude of sleep disorders is more complicated and, oftentimes, has a greater physiological impact than mere sleeplessness, therapists are frequently a part of a larger treatment team of health professionals. The *DSM-5* recommends that sleep disorders are treated by a multidisciplinary team because of the many dimensions present with these conditions (American Psychiatric Association, 2013). This fits very well with the Adlerian conceptualization, as Adler maintained a teleological and phenomenological approach to understanding human nature

(Ansbacher & Ansbacher, 1956). He recognized individuals could *use* their disorder to strive toward a goal like revenge or ambition (Adler, 1944). Private logic and life style might severely impact one's approach to, or avoidance of, medical and psychological treatment (Ansbacher & Ansbacher, 1956). Therefore, a holistic or wellness approach is well aligned with Adlerian Psychology (Myers, Sweeney, & Witmer, 2000).

INSOMNIA DISORDER

Clinical Presentation

Individuals encountering this sleep-related disorder experience complications with falling asleep and remaining asleep, and often awaken early in the morning and cannot easily return to sleep. Individuals feeling anxious about this concern may experience distress due to the inability to fall asleep, resulting in dissatisfaction and frustration, which further impairs their ability to sleep. Individuals who recurrently experience this sleep disorder may develop increased fatigue, lower energy, and significant changes in mood, which can result in the adoption of erratic and maladaptive sleep patterns. These inconsistencies in sleep may further develop into difficulties with social, work, academic, and behavioral areas of functioning (American Psychiatric Association, 2013).

DSM-5 Characterization

Insomnia Disorder is characterized by difficulties falling asleep and/or remaining asleep. Different presentations of Insomnia include Sleep-Onset Insomnia, whereby individuals experience difficulty falling asleep, Sleep-Maintenance Insomnia, whereby recurrent or lingering periods of awakening occur throughout the sleep cycle, and Late Insomnia, whereby individuals have difficulty returning to sleep after awakening early in the morning (American Psychiatric Association, 2013).

Biopsychosocial–Adlerian Conceptualization

The following biopsychosocial formulation may be helpful in understanding factors that contribute to Insomnia. Biologically, there might be a genetic and familial link to Insomnia, and it is more common among first-generation family members. Insomnia is more prevalent among females, and the first onset is most commonly associated with the birth of a child or with the onset of menopause. Associated features with Insomnia include increased fatigue, lower energy, and significant changes in mood that may lead to difficulties with social, work, academic, and behavioral areas of functioning (American Psychiatric Association, 2013).

Rasmussen and Moore (2012) stated that "Adler was clearly ahead of his time and we might argue, certainly in the case of Insomnia, we are still waiting for others to catch up" (p. 243). Consistent with the *DSM-5*, Adler recognized that Insomnia can be present due to psychological or organic conditions. If an organic reason can be excluded, it is important to identify how the Insomnia fits with an individual's style of life. Adler saw sleep as an activity, and there are often reasons why individuals struggle with sleep. Furthermore, Adler determined sleeplessness to be a symptom of ambition. Often, it can be used as a tool of competition. Typically, individuals who do not sleep have a certain purpose in not sleeping (Adler, 1944; Ansbacher & Ansbacher, 1956). To Adler, individuals who struggle with Insomnia may be attempting to manage life's quandaries and challenges. Insomnia can serve as a protective function from the risks of success or failure, as they relate to the most basic strivings away from inferiority (Rasmussen & Moore, 2012).

Treatment Considerations

Adlerians and the authors of the *DSM-5* both recognize that the effective diagnosis and treatment of Insomnia require a multidisciplinary approach to treatment (Garrison & Libby, 2010; American Psychiatric Association, 2013). The sleep-wake disorders identified in the *DSM-5* address criteria for both diagnostic and referral purposes (American Psychiatric Association, 2013). Treatment should begin with a medical exam and a sleep study, conducted by an appropriately trained professional (Garrison & Libby, 2010). Additionally, clients should be assessed for comorbid conditions and co-occurring psychological disorders (American Psychiatric Association, 2013). Garrison and Libby (2010) asserted that Insomnia is often intertwined with pain and psychological distress. The *DSM-5* identifies the bidirectional nature of sleep disturbances with other physiological and psychological disorders and allows for independent diagnosis and treatment (American Psychiatric Association, 2013). Haack, Sanchez, and Mullington (2007) recognized the exacerbating effects of lack of sleep on conditions such as depression, immune-related diseases, and pain. The National Institute of Health (2005, 2011) and the National Sleep Foundation (2011b) concurred that sleep disturbances often occur with other disorders.

Adler asserted that the sleeplessness might serve a variety of purposes, including "hitting at" [sic] another person, bolstering ambition, and supporting melancholia (Adler, 1944, p. 61). Understanding the individual's private logic concerning his/her sleeplessness is a key aspect of therapy. Adler suggested that "you will find that every person who does not sleep has a certain purpose in which he is supported by not sleeping" (Adler, 1944, p. 61). Within the context of Insomnia, he recommended asking the client "The Question," "What could you do if you could sleep?" (Adler, 1944, p. 60).
In answering this question, the client will indicate what is worrying him or her or what he or she fears. The therapist can also ask "What are you thinking about if you do not sleep during the night?" In answering this question, the sleepless person may identify how to use the time in which he or she cannot sleep to further his/her treatment (Adler, 1944).
Rasmussen and Moore (2012) asserted that:

> the good news for the insomniac is that prognosis for treating an insomniac improves when, as Adler suggested, the individual accepts responsibility for his or her role in perpetuating the disorder. Specifically, what is it about the individual's lifestyle and current life circumstance that is creating the opportunity for insomnia?
> (p. 248)

Success in treatment is dependent upon the client's willingness to accept responsibility for his/her role in life-style adjustment. Additionally, people are socially embedded creatures in need of social connection, and must be willing to reach out to those who can provide emotional and practical support. Failure to reach out may perpetuate or exacerbate the disorder.

In identifying with the client's concerns, the therapist might work with the client to evaluate his/her sleep environment and identify subjective sleeping habits. It may be productive to consider other contributing factors that inhibit sleep, including the timing and use of technology, as well as caffeine intake, that affect the ability to fall and remain asleep. The National Sleep Foundation (2011a) recommended behavior modifications, including maintaining a consistent sleep schedule, exposing oneself to bright light in the morning and avoiding it at night, exercise, establishing a bedtime routine, creating a comfortable sleep environment, keeping stress out of the bedroom, avoiding caffeine, nicotine, alcohol, and stimulating medication, and keeping a worry-book next to the bed.

Case Example: Ms. I.

Ms. I. is a 37-year-old career woman who "has it all." She was referred by her primary care physician, following her yearly routine physical examination due to complaints of Insomnia. She has struggled with mild sleeplessness throughout her life, but it seems to have worsened after launching her career, marriage, and family. She had considerable difficulty sleeping during graduate school, and she attributed her inability to sleep to her need for more time to accomplish school tasks and study. She indicates that she lies in bed at night thinking about the tasks she has to perform during the next day. She typically works on her laptop prior to trying to fall asleep, and her phone stays on during the night, charging on the table next to her bed. She has tried medication and counting to help her to sleep, but she has not been satisfied with the results. She occasionally uses alcohol to promote sleepiness, but indicates that she might just be one of those people who do not sleep much. Ms. I. reports feeling sleepy during the day, and she compensates for her sleepiness with caffeinated beverages approximately four to six times per day.

Family constellation

Ms. I. is the oldest of three children. She reports that she was considered "the responsible one" out of the three children. As a child and adolescent she had many friends, and made good grades in school. Typically, she found ways to belong through achievement. She mentions that her parents and husband were, and continue to be, supportive and proud of her. Three family values worth addressing in her family of origin are "good people take care of their business," "your value depends on what you achieve," and "you need to be there for the people you love."

Early recollections

Ms. I.'s earliest recollection involves feeling successful and in charge of her younger brother and sister. When she was five years old, she recalls her mother cutting her hand while playing with the children in the front yard. Her father rushed home to take her mother to the hospital. He asked her to watch the other children until Grandma could arrive. Her father told her he was so proud that she was able to take care of the other children, and did not cry. Another recollection included her parents being angry with her younger brother, because he forgot his permission slip and coat at school. She felt very bad that she did not remind him.

Adlerian case conceptualization

Ms. I.'s inability to sleep seems to be exacerbated by her strong sense of obligation and achievement. She reported having a history of struggling with sleep, but it seems to have worsened upon the growth of her career and family. Ms. I.'s presenting problems are understandable when viewed from the perspective of her style of life. She connects with significant others by being responsible to them and through success. She tends to connect through achievement and responsibility.

Treatment plan and implementation

After Ms. I. received a medical exam, and a physical cause for her Insomnia was not detected, she was evaluated for other psychological disorders, but no diagnosis was rendered other than for Insomnia. Treatment would involve an examination of the client's style of life. Her perfectionism and need to be responsible seem to play some part in this condition. The therapist would employ an encouragement-focused approach, as Ms. I. examined her life and ultimately attempted to find the courage to be imperfect while not accepting others' burdens to accomplish and succeed. The therapist might also consider helping the client to examine environmental factors that might exacerbate her sleeplessness. *Reflecting as if* she had completed all of her tasks and could now sleep, might prove to be an effective technique and provide her with a new goal toward which she can strive (Watts, 2003, 2013).

HYPERSOMNOLENCE DISORDER

Clinical Presentation

Individuals encountering this sleep-related disorder report disproportionate sleepiness, despite having slept an appropriate amount of time the preceding night. Individuals may experience periodic drifting into sleep during the day and may report that prolonged periods of sleep fail to be revitalizing (restorative). Problems may arise as individuals have difficulty awakening from sleep, and may encounter abrupt and unintended sleep during quiet, low-stimulus activities. This increased need for sleep may adversely affect a person's concentration and memory during daily work, social, and school-related activities. Concomitantly, the individual may report arriving late for work or other social engagements, struggling to fulfill typical obligations, and having difficulty driving (American Psychiatric Association, 2013).

DSM-5 Characterization

This sleep-related disorder is characterized by extreme sleepiness, regardless of having adequate sleep (at least seven hours). Individuals reported experiencing repeatedly falling asleep during the day, sleeping excessively without feeling refreshed, and having difficulty fully awakening after being suddenly aroused from sleep. Individuals enduring this disorder may also have difficulty with concentration, connecting with others, and work-related activities (American Psychiatric Association, 2013).

Biopsychosocial–Adlerian Conceptualization

Clients encountering Hypersomnolence may report feeling excessively sleepy, increasingly physically fatigued, and lethargic, with attenuated concentration and memory recall during daytime hours. Clients may also report having difficulty awakening in the morning. These characteristics may adversely affect the individual's concentration and memory during daily work, social, and school-related activities. As a result of this excessive need for sleep, clients may also report unexpected episodes of sleep that intrude during waking hours. These unintentional and intrusive moments of sleep may be dangerous for individuals if they occur when the client is operating machinery, heavy equipment, or a motor vehicle (American Psychiatric Association, 2013).

Little has been written in the Adlerian literature concerning Hypersomnia; however, Adler (1944) recognized the existence of organic reasons for sleep issues. It is clear that Hypersomnolence can lead to physical problems as well as problems in work and relationships. Excessive daytime sleepiness is associated with poor school performance, behavior issues, and emotional difficulties. In a study of college students, it was also found that increased daytime sleepiness was associated with more general irregular life-style patterns (De Volder, Rouckhout, & Cluydts, 2000). As little is understood concerning this condition, a holistic wellness approach might offer a good launching point for treatment. Britzman and Henkin (1992) described wellness as

> a proactive, multidimensional philosophy. It necessitates self-responsibility and self-care to make useful, daily, health-related choices concerning physical activity, nutritional awareness, stress management, spirituality, and environmental sensibility, including cultivating social interest. The pursuit of wellness entails courage and discipline to discover opportunities for growth and change throughout the lifespan with a resulting commitment to self-betterment.
>
> (p. 194.)

From an Adlerian vantage point, it might be important to examine the whole individual, identifying contributions from environmental and situational issues that create or exacerbate this disordered sleep pattern.

Treatment Considerations

The National Sleep Foundation described Hypersomnia as "a serious and debilitating disorder with no known cause" (2011c, para. 1). Treatment of Hypersomnolence should begin with a comprehensive evaluation by a sleep specialist. This might include a polysomnography and a multiple sleep latency test. While most of the direct treatment for Hypersomnolence will be administered by a general-practice physician or sleep specialist, psychological treatment might address the social and psychological effects of this condition.

Hypersomnolence Disorder can impact individuals in many ways, as excessive sleepiness can be embarrassing, or even dangerous when individuals operate heavy machinery or a motor vehicle (American Psychiatric Association, 2013). Client safety is a primary concern, especially when the individual is engaged in a vocation where sleepiness might put the individual or others in danger. Hypersomnia might also cause a pattern of disconnection and disengagement. Helping clients to reconnect with those in their families and communities would be an important consideration.

Case Example: Mr. H.

Mr. H. is a 52-year-old independent cross-country truck driver. He has recently been diagnosed with Hypersomnolence Disorder after a routine company physical. He also has high blood pressure and symptoms associated with acid reflux. He has been divorced for the last ten years, and he is the father of a 12-year-old son. He does not see his son often, as the son lives with his mother, and she has sole custody. Mr. H. has struggled with daytime sleepiness for years, but assumed it was due to an irregular schedule and "road hypnosis."

NARCOLEPSY/HYPOCRETIN DEFICIENCY

Clinical Presentation

Individuals encountering this sleep-related disorder yield to uncontrollable moments of sleep during non-sleep-related, daytime activities. Sleep paralysis or sudden muscle weakness often accompanies the sudden and unexpected onset of an incident, leading to loss of movement, slurred speech, and drooping eyelids. Conversely to Hypersomnolence Disorder, individuals enduring Narcolepsy reported that the sleep, while brief, was restorative. The sudden paralysis associated with Narcolepsy can lead to physical harm, as the person may uncontrollably fall or drop, resulting in injury. Persons enduring this type of sudden paralysis may find themselves restricted from legally being able to independently drive a car or operate machinery. Narcolepsy may also occur concurrently with other concerns, including changes in mood and increased anxiety. The medical community has found a strong relationship between this condition and hypocretin deficiencies in the brain. Concomitantly, these individuals may also experience unintended eating as well as sudden paralysis or loss of muscle tone when experiencing strong emotions (i.e., laughter, sadness, and intense anger) (American Psychiatric Association, 2013).

DSM-5 Characterization

Persons enduring Narcolepsy will often experience sudden, uncontrollable moments of sleep, accompanied by loss of purposeful muscle movement. The client will often report that the sleep, while brief, was restorative. Associated with this disorder, clients may experience other concerns including sleep-related hallucinations, nightmares, vivid dreams, sleepwalking, teeth-grinding, excessive movement, nightmares, and/or bed-wetting. Occasionally, clients may also encounter unintentional eating while asleep (American Psychiatric Association, 2013).

Biopsychosocial–Adlerian Conceptualization

Clients encountering Narcolepsy may experience sudden paralysis or intense muscle weakness associated with the sleep episode or when expressing an intense emotion, leading to loss of purposeful movement and possibly collapse. Research and clinical history has revealed that sleepwalking, teeth-grinding, and bed-wetting are comorbid conditions with Narcolepsy. Left untreated, individuals may be at risk for injury to themselves or others as well as the loss of driver's license and ability to work (American Psychiatric Association, 2013).

Although Narcolepsy is often treated as primarily a physical condition, an Adlerian approach would involve a more holistic examination of the individual client's circumstances. Narcolepsy occurs in many cultures and ethnic groups; however, untreated individuals may face injury and/or social isolation (American Psychiatric Association, 2013). Clients often grapple with discouragement and disconnection in conjunction with their Narcolepsy, creating the need for psychological forms of treatment and not merely a pharmacological intervention. Britzman and Henkin (1992) recommended the use of Adlerian encouragement as part of an Adlerian holistic-wellness approach, especially as it relates to coping with physical ailments. "The Adlerian philosophy of altering perception and supporting efforts to expand behavior repertoires can awaken inner resources, lead to feelings of significance and well-being, and facilitate one's wellness process" (Britzman & Henkin, 1992, p. 201). Carns and Carns (2006a, 2006b) concurred and asserted that encouragement is perceived as helpful in promoting behavior change.

Treatment Considerations

As with many sleep disorders, Narcolepsy is most effectively treated through a holistic biopsychosocial approach. A formal sleep study should be conducted by a sleep specialist, including a screening for hypocretin deficiency and a nocturnal sleep polysomnography. Britzman and Henkin (1992) proposed a proactive wellness approach in the treatment of physical problems. They asserted an Adlerian approach to enhance encouragement strategies and to treat individuals as a holistic system, as "the physical, psychological, intellectual, social, emotional, and environmental processes are intimately connected" (p. 194).

Treatment of Narcolepsy is typically focused on the symptoms of the disorder (American Psychiatric Association, 2013). Longstreth, Koepsell, Ton, Hendrickson, and Belle (2006) found "the search for etiologic risk factors has yet to yield important results" (p. 13); however, with advances in technology and research, the *DSM-5* has divided Narcolepsy into multiple subcategories (American Psychiatric Association, 2013). Individuals with Narcolepsy often struggle in work or school with perceptions of being lazy or unmotivated. Many face social or sexual side effects to medication, become anxious or irritable, and often avoid treatment altogether for fear of losing their freedom to drive a vehicle (Douglas, 1998). There is currently no cure for Narcolepsy, but symptoms can be managed to a near normal range of functioning. Avoiding alcohol and heavy meals, while maintaining a regular sleep schedule with regular naps, has proven to be beneficial to many enduring Narcolepsy (National Sleep Foundation, 2011d). The National Sleep Foundation (2011d) recommends counseling, as individuals might feel uncomfortable, depressed, or alienated, as symptoms are not widely understood. Stress in marital, family, and social relationships is also a common occurrence (American Psychiatric Association, 2013; Douglas, 1998).

Case Example: Mr. N.

Mr. N. has been referred to therapy by his parents and his sleep specialist. He is an 18-year-old high-school student with average grades, and he feels very discouraged, as he will no longer be allowed to drive a car or play football. His cataplexy seems to be triggered when he is teased or, for his own protection, when he is restricted from going somewhere. His sleep specialist has prescribed several medications for the condition. His parents hope that counseling will help him overcome feelings of discouragement while developing more effective strategies for emotional regulation. They hope this will, in turn, increase his ability to control the cataplexy.

Family constellation

Mr. N. is an only child and reports that he has always been able to negotiate and solve problems. He identifies seldom being unable to work out a logical issue. As a child and adolescent, he had a few close friends, and made good grades in school. Typically, he found ways to belong through control. He mentioned that his parents were currently overprotective and overly strict. Three family values worth commenting on in his family of origin were "Be first or go home," "No excuses," and "If you can't hang with the big dogs, stay on the porch."

Early recollections

Mr. N.'s earliest recollection involves feeling free and strong. He would play in the yard from an early age. Sometimes, he would play with cousins, but was always able to win at games. When he did not win, he would renegotiate the rules or find an exception. The adults would usually laugh at this behavior, and his cousins would give in.

Adlerian case conceptualization

Mr. N.'s struggle with his current condition seems to be exacerbated by his style of life. He has traditionally resolved dilemmas through strength, talent, and negotiation, and he seems to feel as though his typical means for coping with problems have been taken away. His two current venues for achievement, freedom, and connection were his car and playing football. He is not allowed to engage in either function, and he does not feel as though he has had a choice in the decision. Additionally, for the first time, his coping mechanism of negotiation with adults has proven to be unsuccessful. He is feeling very discouraged, disconnected, and powerless.

Treatment plan and implementation

Mr. N.'s treatment would likely involve two aspects. First, Narcolepsy would involve a holistic, team-based approach to treatment. The therapist would collaborate with medical professionals to ensure all aspects of a biological treatment would be conducted. Additionally, the therapist would focus on the psychological and social implications of Narcolepsy by recognizing the discouraging aspects of this condition and assisting the client in reconnecting with individuals in his or her perceived social world. The encouragement-focused goal of treatment is to help Mr. N. identify tools within himself that can be used to effectively cope with his condition. Mr. N. has previously found belonging through competition. Finding other ways to belong or achieve might fit with the client's style of life.

SLEEP APNEA AND OBSTRUCTIVE SLEEP APNEA HYPOPNEA SYNDROME

Clinical Presentation

Individuals experiencing this breathing-related sleep disorder will encounter abnormally shallow breathing or complete breathing cessation during normal periods of sleep, accompanied by snoring, gasping for air, snorting, and pauses in breathing. While the client may not be able to provide an accurate accounting of his/her sleep, collateral sources (i.e., spouses or partners) may be helpful in establishing a history of sleep patterns. Clients enduring this sleep disorder will often report daytime sleepiness, fatigue, and non-restorative sleep (American Psychiatric Association, 2013).

DSM-5 Characterization

The Obstructive Sleep Apnea Hypopnea Syndrome involves excessive disruptions in normal breathing patterns associated with excessive snoring, snorting, gasping, and prolonged pauses. Individuals and collateral sources encountering this syndrome report dissatisfaction with quantity and quality of sleep due to the abnormal breathing that interferes with sleep (American Psychiatric Association, 2013).

CENTRAL SLEEP APNEA

Clinical Presentation

Central Sleep Apnea is characterized by abnormally shallow breathing and complete cessation of breathing during scheduled sleep. During an hour of sleep, individuals will repeatedly engage in unusually shallow breathing or simply stop breathing for short periods of time. Following the cessation, the individual will often recover with a rapid deep breath. The inconsistency associated with the periodic breathing and the cessation is followed by sudden recovery resulting in alternating hyper- and hypoventilation (American Psychiatric Association, 2013).

Central Sleep Apnea is experienced by individuals with heart failure, stroke, or renal failure, who often encounter an atypical breathing pattern called Cheyne-Stokes breathing. This pattern may consist of several deep breaths followed by a series of very shallow breaths, or periods of several short, shallow breaths followed by a large, deep, recovery breath. Occasionally, the deep recovery breath can interrupt the client's sleep, resulting in an abrupt awakening. In both cases, this persistent variation in breathing patterns often results in and is directly associated with the Central Sleep Apnea. Individuals encountering this type of irregular breathing report experiencing inconsistent sleep patterns, awakening with shortness of breath, and excessive sleepiness during daytime hours (American Psychiatric Association, 2013).

DSM-5 Characterization

Individuals encountering this sleep disorder experience frequent periods of abnormally shallow breathing or cessation of breathing during sleep. The breathing cessation associated with Central Sleep Apnea typically lasts longer than ten seconds and is followed by a sudden and rapid inhalation. Patterns of cessation and shallow breathing associated with Cheyne-Stokes breathing concerns may also occur with this disorder. A characteristic that differentiates Central Sleep Apnea from other breathing-related sleep disorders is the absence of obstructive sleep phenomena (snoring, snorting, gasping, etc.). The Cheyne-Stokes breathing syndrome is also characterized by significant changes in heart rate, blood pressure, shortness of breath, and feelings of shakiness. Diagnosis of this type of disorder can be best achieved through a sleep-study. The cause of this sleep disorder is of unknown origins (American Psychiatric Association, 2013).

Biopsychosocial–Adlerian Conceptualization

Both Obstructive Sleep Apnea and Central Sleep Apnea involve breathing-related concerns, which have implications associated with dysfunctional sleep and other health concerns. Obstructive Sleep Apnea identifies obstructions in an individual's sleep patterns caused by excessive snoring, snorting, gasping, and pauses in breathing during sleep. Physical experiences and sensations associated with Obstructive Sleep Apnea include heartburn, increased need to urinate during the night, headaches in the morning, dry mouth, high blood pressure, attenuated libido, and erectile dysfunction. Central Sleep Apnea identifies cessation in breathing or irregular breathing patterns during sleep, resulting in occasional sudden awakening upon the breathing recovery period. Both conditions may result in non-restorative sleep leading to excessive sleepiness, fatigue, and/or Insomnia (American Psychiatric Association, 2013).

Obstructive Sleep Apnea affects 1% to 2% of children, 2% to 15% of adults in middle age, and over 20% of older adults. The prevalence rates for Central Sleep Apnea are unknown, although it is thought to be rare (American Psychiatric Association, 2013). This is not an area often addressed by Adlerian Psychology; however, it is garnering more attention, as technology is allowing for a greater understanding and diagnosis of the condition.

Sleep Apnea can impact cognitive, behavioral, and physiological functions (American Psychiatric Association, 2013; Garrison & Eckstein, 2009; Hansen & Vandenberg, 1997). The National Sleep Foundation (2011e) reported that 18 million American adults experience Sleep Apnea, and it can be a life-threatening condition. Recognizing the signs and symptoms is necessary for accurate diagnosis and treatment. Hansen and Vandenberg (1997) indicated that "The effects of pediatric apnea appear similar to characteristics of other childhood disorders, most notably attention deficit disorder" (p. 304).

Sleep Apnea could be considered a chronic illness and treated as such by Adlerian Psychology. Sperry (2006, pp. xi–xii) identified that

> chronic illness is the subjective experience of chronic disease, and such diseases tend to have multiple causes and treatments. This means that the experience of chronic illness is quite variable, depending on several biopsychosocial factors, including biomedical, personality, coping, and cultural factors.

An individual's approach to his or her health impacts multiple facets of treatment and wellness. In addition to the physical impairments of Sleep Apnea, it poses a great barrier to one's ability to connect to others (Garrison & Eckstein, 2009).

As Sleep Apnea is primarily a physiological condition, it is important to recognize that clients will present for counseling not merely for the condition, but also for the psychological and social impairment which accompany this disorder. Garrison and Eckstein (2009) addressed the impact that sleep issues have upon a couple's ability to connect. They asserted that "sleeping with someone may be more intimate than having sex with him or her" (p. 58). Sleep Apnea may impair mood memory, relational abilities, intimacy functioning, and daytime functioning. Keeping this in mind, it is imperative to examine how it is impairing one's ability to perform in all life-task areas (Garrison & Libby, 2010; Myers, Sweeney, & Witmer, 2000).

Treatment Considerations

Dreikurs (1967) described the process of therapy in four stages: relationship, psychological investment, interpretation, and reorientation. In the treatment of Sleep Apnea, it might be tempting for the client or therapist to jump directly to reorientation; however, the Adlerian clinician must remember to first develop the appropriate therapeutic alliance. Additionally, Sleep Apnea poses further challenges of gaining accurate and reliable information concerning specifics of the disorder. Collateral sources may be valuable, although good information might be a challenge. Schreck and Richdale

(2011) indicated that health professionals have limited knowledge about childhood sleep, and their study concluded that parents' knowledge of their children's sleep was generally poor, with the quality of information declining as the children aged. This highlights the need for therapists to work with parents to help them observe their children's sleep in a more consistent manner.

Sleep Apnea treatment should begin with a professional sleep evaluation, including polysomnography. It is recommended that clients avoid sleeping pills, alcohol, and nicotine (American Psychiatric Association, 2013). Losing weight and elevating the head when sleeping may also help with symptoms (Garrison & Eckstein, 2009). While these approaches may provide initial help, analysis of an individual's life style may reveal patterns that impact his or her styles of coping. Individuals who approach life by avoiding problems might refuse or avoid treatment of Sleep Apnea.

Case Example: Child Q.

Child Q. is a 12-year-old boy whose sleep specialist and parents referred him to counseling. Initially, he was referred to a sleep specialist by his pediatrician because of extreme sleepiness coupled with symptoms that looked similar to ADHD. Additionally, he has appeared to have trouble in school. He has difficulty sustaining attention, taking tests, and analyzing new information. He had been evaluated at school for ADHD; however, he did not meet the diagnostic criteria. His parents answered "I don't know" to many of the sleep screening questions asked by the pediatrician, so the pediatrician made a referral in an effort to be thorough. The sleep specialist diagnosed him with Obstructive Sleep Apnea after a thorough sleep evaluation.

Case Example: Mr. O.

Mr. O. is a 62-year-old factory worker who was referred to counseling on the insistence of his wife. His Sleep Apnea symptoms have been present for a number of years, but they have become increasingly more severe in the last nine months. Additionally, he has become more forgetful, sleepy, and grumpy, thus impairing his ability to manage the line at work, and he has received complaints from coworkers on his shift. His wife complains of his excessive snoring, as he awakens her frequently. She is also concerned that this will exacerbate other health issues. This has impacted their level of marital satisfaction, as he has low energy, low sex drive, and his wife regularly asks him to sleep on the couch. Mr. O. is moderately overweight, smokes one pack of cigarettes each day, and drinks a moderate amount of beer. He has not been evaluated by a sleep specialist, and he is reluctant to have a sleep evaluation.

Family constellation

Mr. O. is a middle child with two siblings. He has a brother who is older and a sister who is younger. Mr. O. reports that he was a quiet child, and he spent most of his childhood trying to be invisible. As a child, he blended with peers and tried not to stand out. Typically he tried very hard to be part of a team. His parents were busy with jobs, family, and life. Three family values worth noting are "Try not to be a burden," "Don't make a fuss," and "Cowboy up."

Early recollections

Mr. O.'s earliest recollection involves traveling with the family to visit relatives. He was in the back seat between his brother and sister, who were fighting while he was trying to be very still and quiet to avoid trouble. Another recollection involved fishing with his father and cutting his finger with the hook. His father laughed and told him that was just a part of life.

Adlerian case conceptualization

Mr. O. has spent his life attempting to "blend." He addresses problems by ignoring them while trying to not stand out. He currently does not want to make a change in his behavior; however, he is attempting to avoid conflict and make his wife happy. Mr. O. reports feeling discouraged by his circumstances as well as the disruption to his interpersonal relationships. Addressing this discouragement and helping him to find the courage to seek treatment will be an important first step for Mr. O. It would also be important to assess if this condition and treatment have an impact upon other parts of his life or emotional wellbeing (i.e., increased anxiety, depression, weight gain, etc.). The biopsychosocial model suggests that "a person can only be adequately understood if all levels of an individual's functioning are considered" (Sperry, 2008, p. 370).

Treatment plan and implementation

Building rapport with Mr. O. is going to be of paramount importance, as he is already "grumpy," short on patience, and does not seem committed to seeking treatment. The therapeutic process itself will likely seem uncomfortable, as he will be the center of attention. Previously, Mr. O.'s life style has allowed him to remain invisible. If Mr. O. chooses to seek treatment with his wife, he might attempt to allow her to be in the lead. Encouragement will be important, as this disorder is often discouraging, and he might feel as though he has limited choice or power. It would be important that Mr. O. is referred for a sleep study conducted by a sleep specialist.

NIGHTMARE DISORDER

Clinical Presentation

The Nightmare Disorder involves disturbing and distressing imagery often associated with efforts to evade danger, resulting in increased anxiety, fear, and other discomforting emotions. Clients encountering the Nightmare Disorder often report recurrent, past, unpleasant events and display unfavorable changes in personality. Changes in typical sleeping schedules and sleep deprivation may contribute to increased risk for experiencing this sleep disorder. While disturbing dreams may result in individual distress, there is less evidence of social or occupational impairment. However, if the persistence of dreams results in sleep aversion, individuals may encounter excessive sleepiness during waking hours, accompanied by difficulty with concentration, increased anxiousness, sadness, and irritability (American Psychiatric Association, 2013).

DSM-5 Characterization

Individuals encountering this sleep disorder report experiencing repetitive, discomfiting, and frightening dreams for which they retain full memory of the dream. Content of the disturbing dreams often involves efforts to evade or cope with perceived danger. Individuals who experience a traumatic event may have distressing dreams that possess elements of the event. Clients report feeling increased fear and anxiousness associated with the dream, even after fully awakening from the dream. Awakening from the distressing dream, individuals report rapidly regaining orientation and alertness (American Psychiatric Association, 2013).

Biopsychosocial–Adlerian Conceptualization

The following biopsychosocial formulation may be helpful in understanding Nightmare Disorder. Nightmares typically occur during rapid eye movement (REM) sleep, often occurring during the second half of a major sleep period. Associated with nightmares, individuals may report physical characteristics such as sweating, rapid heartbeat, and rapid breathing. Collateral sources may also report excessive movement and vocalizations during the sleep episode. Jet-lag or sleep disruptions might also impact the occurrence or timing of nightmares. Nightmares are often reported to co-occur with varying medical conditions, mental disorders, and substance withdrawal (American Psychiatric Association, 2013).

Psychologically, Adler recognized the value of dreams as a key to understanding the self (Ansbacher & Ansbacher, 1956). The therapist seeks to understand the dreamer and his or her world and to help dreamers to better understand themselves. Corsini and Wedding (1995) recognized that "One cannot understand a dream without knowing the dreamer" (p. 71). Bird (2005) described dream work as cooperative, allowing the client and therapist to work within an egalitarian alliance to examine the meaning and affective influence the dream has on the client's life. Bird (2005) and Yalom (2001) both suggested that they use dreams in pragmatic ways that facilitate movement in therapy.

Peven (2012), as well as Peven and Shulman (2002), identified that people dream to feel and that the Adlerian purpose for dreams is to create an emotion. As the emotions are created, they energize behavior and produce movement. Individuals utilize the emotions in pursuing aspirations. Adler (2010) asserted "the purpose of dreams, therefore, is to support the style of life against the demands of common sense" (p. 100). He further stated, "The style of life is the master of dreams" (p. 101). Dreams attempt to bridge the presenting problem with the current life style without having to adjust the current style of life. The dream supports the life style by creating the emotion needed to continue, without modifying the way of life. Adler explained that "The dream strives to pave the way toward solving a problem by a metaphorical expression of what it is … Naturally the dreamer does not recognize his own metaphor for what it is" (Adler, 1929, as cited in Ansbacher, 1982).

Brink and Matlock (1982) found that there was a relationship between birth order and nightmares. In their study, they discovered that older siblings were less likely to have nightmares, while youngest siblings were the most likely to report nightmares in adulthood. Therapeutically, the Adlerian approaches dream work with complete respect for the unique individual, their subjective apperception, and the emotional reactions that accompany the dreams (Bird, 2005).

In addition to the history of Adlerian dream work, it would be important to note that the *DSM-5* recognizes the possible connection between Nightmare Disorder and dangerous or traumatic events. Adler recognized that the significance of dreams depended upon the meaning to which an individual assigns the dream. Adler possessed a similar stance on trauma. In Ansbacher and Ansbacher (1956, p. 208) he asserted:

> No experience is a cause of success or failure. We do not suffer from the shock of our experiences—the so-called trauma—but we make out of them just what suits our purposes. We are self-determined by the meaning we give to our experiences, and there is probably always something of a mistake involved when we take particular experiences as the basis for our future life. Meanings are not determined by situations, but we determine ourselves by the meanings we give to our situations.

Therefore, if one recognizes the most important aspect of dreams and trauma to be the meanings individuals make of them, the construction or reconstruction of meaning becomes a primary aspect of treatment.

Treatment Considerations

A Nightmare Disorder can be concomitant with other disorders, when separate clinical attention is needed. It is important to note the onset of the Nightmare Disorder. An independent diagnosis might be considered when nightmares occur with PTSD or Acute-Stress Disorder, if the Nightmare Disorder preceded the other mental disorder, or if the nightmares continue after the other symptoms have been resolved. Nightmare Disorder should be differentiated from Sleep Terror Disorder. While both disorders include being aroused from sleep and an autonomic activation occurs, individuals who suffer with nightmares can clearly and vividly recall the dream. Nightmares typically occur later in the night than sleep terrors, and individuals typically wake up completely once the nightmare has occurred. Cultural significance may impact the meaning and the emotional consequences of nightmares. Women tend to report suffering from nightmares more frequently than men, and the themes of nightmares typically vary by gender (American Psychiatric Association, 2013).

Counselors can invite their clients to make notes of dreams that they experience and bring them to session. The therapist can help the client to examine the disturbing dream in a safe location, in an effort to gain insight and better understand how the dream related to the client's life. The therapist can also help the client to examine the meaning the client is assigning to the nightmare. Dreamers may be able to bring a dream to conclusion by constructing an ending, as often an individual's creativity and style of life are the same in sleeping as in waking states. After the client has described the dream, the therapist might ask, "And what happened next?" This allows the client to examine the dream as well as its relationship to his/her waking life (Bird, 2005, p. 213). Adler believed dreams to be related to one's style of life, suggesting that the person's imagination cannot create anything but that which his style of life commands. The dreamer's made-up dreams are just as good as those genuinely remembered, for imagination and fancy will also be an expression of his style of life (Adler as cited in Ansbacher & Ansbacher, 1956).

Case Example: Mr. N.M.

Mr. N.M. is a 43-year-old male who presented for therapy because his partner insisted he seek treatment. Mr. N.M. experiences terrible dreams four to five times each week. The typical theme of his distressing dreams involves falling. Many times he tries to stop himself or another person from falling, but is not successful. He is often awakened by the dreams, and he can usually recall the dreams in great detail. When asked if he has ever witnessed or experienced a traumatic fall, his response is "I can't remember." Mr. N.M. has suffered with nightmares since his early childhood. It is helpful when his partner is kind and soothing; however, she is often visibly shaken when awakened by his reaction to the nightmares. His partner reports that after nights when he has nightmares, he seems tired and grumpy during the next day. He has no known history of substance abuse, and he is not taking a large amount of medication. He does not have children. When asked about his early recollections, he indicated that he does not remember much before middle school. Mr. N.M. did not meet the diagnostic criteria for PTSD.

Concluding Note

Throughout this chapter, arrangement of the disorders between the *DSM-IV-TR* and the *DSM-5* reveals a simpler approach, as disorders have been grouped or split, depending on presentation, reflecting the presence of characteristics derived from research in physical origins and treatment considerations. Readers are encouraged to utilize a referral to a sleep specialist for the most effective treatment of these conditions. Lastly, the Adlerian conceptualization and treatment strategies of sleep-wake disorders might well increase clinical outcomes.

References

Adler, A. (1944). Sleeplessness. *Individual Psychology Bulletin*, 3, pp. 60–64.

Adler, A. (1964). *Problems of Neurosis*. New York, NY: Harper Torchbooks. (Original work published 1929.)

Adler, A. (1992). *What Life Could Mean to You* (C. Brett, Trans.). Oxford: Oneworld Publications. (Original work published 1931.)

Adler, A. (2010). *What Life Should Mean to You*. Mansfield Centre, CT: Martino Publishing. (Original work published 1932.)

American Psychiatric Association (2013). *Diagnostic and Statistical Manual of Mental Disorders, Fifth Edition*. Arlington, VA: American Psychiatric Publishing.

Ansbacher, H.L. (1982). Alfred Adler's views on the unconscious. *The Journal of Individual Psychology*, 38(1), pp. 32–41. Retrieved from http://0-search.ebscohost.com.library.acaweb. org/login.aspx?direct=true&AuthType=ip,url,uid,cookie&db=aph&AN=9096216&site=eho st-live.

Ansbacher, H.L. & Ansbacher, R.R. (Eds.) (1956). *The Individual Psychology of Alfred Adler*. New York, NY: Basic Books.

Bird, B.E.I. (2005). Understanding dreams and dreamers: An Adlerian perspective. *Journal of Individual Psychology*, 61(3), pp. 200–216. Retrieved from http://0-search.ebscohost.com. library.acaweb.org/login.aspx?direct=true&AuthType=ip,url,uid,cookie&db=aph&AN=1954 2385&site=ehost-live.

Brink, T.L. & Matlock, F. (1982). Nightmares and birth order: An empirical study. *Journal of Individual Psychology*, 38(1), pp. 47–49.

Britzman, M.J. & Henkin, A.L. (1992). Wellness and personality priorities: The utilization of Adlerian encouragement strategies. *Individual Psychology*, 48(2), pp. 194–202. Retrieved from http://0-search.ebscohost.com.library.acaweb.org/login.aspx?direct=true&AuthType=ip,url,u id,cookie&db=aph&AN=9103672&site=ehost-live.

Carns, M.R. & Carns, A.W. (2006a). An overview of the current status of Adlerian encouragement. In S. Slavik & J. Carlson (Eds.), *Readings in the Theory of Individual Psychology* (pp. 267–276). New York, NY: Routledge.

Carns, M.R., & Carns, A.W. (2006b). A review of the professional literature concerning the consistency of the definition and application of Adlerian encouragement. In S. Slavik & J. Carlson (Eds.), *Readings in the Theory of Individual Psychology* (pp. 277–293). New York, NY: Routledge.

Corsini, R.J. & Wedding, D. (Eds.) (1995). *Current Psychotherapies*. Itasca, IL: F.E. Peacock Publishers.

DeVolder, I., Rouckhout, D., & Cluydts, R. (2000). Explaining hypersomnolence in young adults. *Journal of Sleep Research*, 9(1) p. 53.

Dinkmeyer, D. (1997). Adlerian family therapy: An integrative therapy. In J. Carlson & S. Slavik (Eds.), *Techniques in Adlerian Psychology* (pp. 456–465). New York, NY: Routledge.

Dinkmeyer, D.C., Dinkmeyer, D.C., Jr., & Sperry, L. (1987). *Adlerian Counseling and Psychotherapy* (2nd edn.). Columbus, OH: Merrill.

Douglas, N.J. (1998). The psychosocial aspects of narcolepsy. *Neurology*, 50(1) pp. 27–30.

Dreikurs, R. (1967). *Psychodynamics, Psychotherapy, and Counseling: Collected Papers of Rudolf Dreikurs*. Chicago, IL: Alfred Adler Institute.

Garrison, M. & Eckstein, D. (2009). A sleep satisfaction interview for couples: Recommendations for improving your nights together. *The Family Journal*, 17(1), pp. 58–63.

Garrison, R. & Libby, L. (2010). Insomnia treatment: Interdisciplinary collaboration and conceptual integration. *Individual Psychology*, 66(3), pp. 237–252. Retrieved from http://0-search.ebscohost.com.library.acaweb.org/login.aspx?direct=true&AuthType=ip,url,uid,cooki e&db=aph&AN=58112951&site=ehost-live.

Haack, M., Sanchez, E., & Mullington, J. (2007). Elevated inflammatory markers in response to prolonged sleep restriction are associated with increased pain experience in healthy volunteers. *Sleep*, 30, pp. 1145–1152.

Hansen, D.E. & Vandenberg, B. (1997). Neuropsychological features and differential diagnosis of sleep apnea syndrome in children. *Journal of Clinical Child Psychology*, 26(3), pp. 304–310.

Longstreth, W.T., Koepsell, T.D., Ton, T.G., Hendrickson, A.F, & Belle, G. (2006). The epidemiology of narcolepsy. *Sleep*, 30(1) pp. 13–26. Retrieved from http://www.journalsleep. org/Articles/300102.pdf.

Myers, J.E., Sweeney, T.J., & Witmer, J.M. (2000). The wheel of wellness counseling for wellness: A holistic model for treatment planning. *Journal of Counseling and Development*, (78)3, pp. 251–266. Retrieved from http://0-search.ebscohost.com.library.acaweb.org/login.aspx?direct= true&AuthType=ip,url,uid,cookie&db=aph&AN=3310761&site=ehost-live.

National Sleep Foundation (2011a). Annual sleep in America poll exploring connections with communications and sleep. Retrieved from http://www.sleepfoundation.org/article/press-release/annual-sleep-america-poll-exploring-connections-communications-technology-use-.

National Sleep Foundation (2011b). Can't sleep? What to know about insomnia. Retrieved from http://www.sleepfoundation.org/article/sleep-related-problems/insomnia-and-sleep.

National Sleep Foundation (2011c). Extreme sleepiness. Retrieved from http://www. sleepfoundation.org/article/sleep-related-problems/idiopathic-hypersomnia-and-sleep.

National Sleep Foundation (2011d). Narcolepsy and sleep. Retrieved from http://www. sleepfoundation.org/article/sleep-related-problems/narcolepsy-and-sleep.

National Sleep Foundation (2011e). Sleep apnea and sleep. Retrieved from http://www. sleepfoundation.org/article/sleep-related-problems/obstructive-sleep-apnea-and-sleep.

National Institutes of Health (2005). NIH state-of-the-science conference statement on manifestations and management of chronic insomnia in adults. Retrieved from http:// consensus.nih.gov/2005/insomniastatement.pdf.

National Institutes of Health (2011). Your guide to healthy sleep. Retrieved from http://www. nhlbi.nih.gov/health/public/sleep/healthy_sleep.pdf

Peven, D.E. (2012). Dreams and dream-interpretation. In J. Carlson & M. Maniacci (Eds.), *Alfred Adler Revisited* (pp. 155–169). New York, NY: Routledge.

Peven, D. & Shulman, B. (2002). *"Who is Sylvia?" and Other Stories: Case Studies in Psychotherapy.* New York, NY: Taylor & Francis.

Rasmussen, P.R. & Moore, K.P. (2012). Nervous Insomnia. In J. Carlson & M. Maniacci (Eds.), *Alfred Adler Revisited* (pp. 243–249). New York, NY: Routledge.

Schreck, K.A. & Richdale, A.L. (2011). Knowledge of childhood sleep: A possible variable in under or misdiagnosis of childhood sleep problems. *Journal of Sleep Research*, 20(4), pp. 589–597. doi: 10.1111/j.1365-2869.2011.00922.x

Shulman, B.H. (1973). *Contributions to Individual Psychology.* Chicago, IL: Bernard H. Shulman, M.D.

Sperry, L. (1988). Biopsychosocial therapy: An integrative approach for tailoring treatment. *The Journal of Individual Psychology*,44(2), pp. 225–235. Retrieved from http://0-search.ebscohost. com.library.acaweb.org/login.aspx?direct=true&AuthType=ip,url,uid,cookie&db=aph&AN= 9095527&site=ehost-live.

Sperry, L. (2006). *Psychological Treatment of Chronic Illness: The Biopsychosocial Therapy Approach.* Washington, DC: American Psychological Association.

Sperry, L. (2008). The biopsychosocial model and chronic illness: Psychotherapeutic implications. *The Journal of Individual Psychology*, 64(3), pp. 369–376. Retrieved from http://0-search. ebscohost.com.library.acaweb.org/login.aspx?direct=true&AuthType=ip,url,uid,cookie&db= aph&AN=41672145&site=ehost-live.

Watts, R.E., (2013). Reflecting "As If." *Counseling Today*, 55(10), pp. 48–53. Retrieved from http://www.counseling.org/docs/counseling-today-archives/april-2013.pdf?sfvrsn=4

Watts, R.E., (2003). Reflecting "As If": An integrative process in couples counseling. *The Family Journal: Counseling and Therapy for Couples and Families*, 11(1), pp. 73–75.

Yalom, I. (2001). *The Gift of Therapy*. London: Piatkus.

12 Sexual Disorders

Sharyl M. Trail

Disordered sexual behavior has been of interest to philosophers, theologians, psychiatrists, psychologists, and other healthcare providers throughout the ages. Sexual deviance has been conceptualized by many in society as illness, immoral behavior, and "unnatural." Non-normative sexual behavior/gender expression has also at times been criminalized/pathologized and then decriminalized/depathologized, depending on the politics and ethos of the current society. The amount of curiosity and historical constraints societies and religions have placed on private sexual acts begs the question, "Why are we as a species concerned about people's private sexual activity?" (Cohen-Baker, 2006; Hegarty, 2012; Jordan, 1997; Weiss, 2011).

As Adlerians, the above question can be answered in many ways. Individual Psychology is concerned with the underlying *meaning* of a specific sexual behavior not only for the individual client, but also the meaning this behavior has for others and the larger community. Private sexual acts and gender identity/gender expression have far-reaching implications in the public sphere. The private and public life intersect, informing us as a community about beliefs on issues such as consent, violence, manipulation, power, exploitation, equality, and freedom (Anbacher & Ansbacher, 1956; Dreikurs, 2000). Throughout this chapter, we will be exploring Adlerian concepts such as social interest, social equality, inferiority/superiority, organ jargon, masculine protest, and life-style construction (including gender guiding lines) as it relates to the DSM-5 diagnosis of sexual psychopathology.

In the *DSM-5*, sexual disorders have been broken into three categories, including Sexual Dysfunctions, Gender Dysphoria, and Paraphilic Disorders. These categories each have their own chapter in Section II of the *DSM-5* (American Psychiatric Association, 2013). It should be noted that in the *DSM-IV-TR* all three of the above categories were placed under one heading, "Sexual and Gender Identity Disorders" (American Psychiatric Association, 2000).

Sexual Dysfunctions, Gender Dysphoria, and Paraphilic Disorders in *DSM-5*

Changes from DSM-IV-TR *to* DSM-5

Due to the *DSM-5* breaking up Sexual and Gender Identity Disorders into three separate chapters, we can no longer lump sexual dysfunctions, gender identity, and paraphilic behaviors into one category. Therefore, the remainder of this chapter will be broken into three distinct categories as defined by the *DSM-5*.

The Sexual Dysfunctions category had multiple changes from the *DSM-IV-TR* to the *DSM-5*. The *DSM-5* defines sexual dysfunctions as a "heterogeneous group of disorders that are typically characterized by the clinically significant disturbance in a person's ability to respond sexually or to experience sexual pleasure" (American Psychiatric Association, 2013, p. 423). Highlighted changes include: (a) deletion of the distinction between the desire and arousal stages of sexual activity; (b) the addition of gender-specific sexual dysfunctions; (c) all sexual dysfunctions (except substance/medication-induced sexual dysfunction) now require a minimum time duration. All changes were created to improve the precision of diagnosis and to reflect the most current research findings. One new diagnosis was added to the Sexual Dysfunctions category. Genito-Pelvic Pain/Penetration Disorder is a new diagnosis, which is a merging of the *DSM-IV* categories of Vaginismus and Dyspareunia. Finally, the subtype *due to psychological factors versus due to combined factors* was deleted. Instead medical and non-medical correlates—including partner factors, relationship factors, individual vulnerability factors, cultural or religious factors—and medical factors can be mentioned in the diagnosis (American Psychiatric Association, 2013, *Highlights of Changes from DSM-IV-TR to DSM-5*).

The most significant change in all three categories of sexual disorders is the change of diagnosis of Gender Identity Disorder in the *DSM-IV-TR* to Gender Dysphoria in the current *DSM-5*. According to the American Psychiatric Association fact sheet:

> DSM-5 aims to avoid stigma and ensure clinical care for individuals who see and feel themselves to be a different gender than their assigned gender. Persons experiencing gender dysphoria need a diagnostic term that protects their access to care and won't be used against them in social, occupational, or legal areas.
>
> (American Psychiatric Association, 2013)

Gender Dysphoria is also given its own chapter and separated from the other sexual disorders. The *DSM-5* defines many terms such as *sex, gender, gender assignment, gender-atypical, gender non-conforming, transgender*, and *gender reassignment* at the beginning of the Gender Dysphoria chapter. For the purposes of this chapter we will focus on the new *DSM-5* definition of Gender Dysphoria. "*Gender Dysphoria* refers to the distress that may accompany the incongruence between one's experienced or expressed gender and one's assigned gender" (American Psychiatric Association, 2013, p. 451). Rationale behind the change from Gender Identity Disorder to Gender Dysphoria is so clinicians and researchers focus on the dysphoria as the clinical problem, rather than the identity itself (American Psychiatric Association, 2013). In addition to the name change, Gender Dysphoria in the *DSM-5* can now be diagnosed in children and adults, with specific criteria for both age groups.

The final major change to the sexual disorders focuses on the Paraphilic Disorders. These disorders were labeled Paraphilias in the *DSM-IV-TR*. The Paraphilic Disorders cover a variety of atypical sexual interests and behaviors. The eight types of Paraphilic Disorders have not changed since the *DSM-III*. The significant change is the diagnostic criteria for these disorders. Through research and collective clinical expert knowledge, the DSM-5 Sexual and Gender Identity Disorders work group decided atypical sexual behavior is not in and of itself a mental disorder. In fact, they state most people with atypical sexual interests do not have a mental disorder. In the *DSM-5* an individual must meet one of two criteria to be diagnosed with a paraphilia. The first criterion states the person must feel distress about their atypical sexual interest, and not just distress stemming from society's disapproval of their sexual behavior. The second criterion states that the atypical sexual interest/behavior causes psychological distress or injury to another person or is not consensual/legal. Only one of the eight paraphilic conditions, Transvestic Disorder, has a specific change to the criteria. In the *DSM-IV-TR* the individual could only meet criteria for this disorder if the individual identified as a heterosexual male. Now, women and gay men can qualify for the diagnosis, but only if the interest causes them significant distress (American Psychiatric Association, 2013).

Sexual Dysfunctions in DSM-5

In the *DSM-5* there are ten diagnoses within Sexual Dysfunctions. These are: Delayed Ejaculation; Erectile Disorder; Female Orgasmic Disorder; Female Sexual Interest/Arousal Disorder; Genito-Pelvic Pain/Penetration Disorder; Male Hypoactive Sexual Desire Disorder; Premature (Early) Ejaculation; Substance/Medication-Induced Sexual Dysfunction; Other Specified Sexual Dysfunction; and Unspecified Sexual Dysfunction.

These diagnoses are grouped together and are characterized by a disturbance in the client's ability to respond sexually or experience sexual pleasure. Within each of these dysfunctions, specific symptoms are identified. Symptoms should be identified as originating during first sexual experience or as beginning after a period of normal sexual function. Additionally, it should be identified if they have symptoms, no matter what the sexual experience or partner, or if the symptoms only arise during a specific sexual act or with a specific partner. Other biopsychosocial factors should be considered when making a specific sexual dysfunction diagnosis. Examples include: partner issues; relationship issues; body image; history of sexual abuse; co-occurring psychiatric/substance-abuse disorders; external stressors; cultural or religious factors; and possible medical issues. Finally, a client only meets the diagnosis for a sexual dysfunction if it is causing significant distress.

As a part of the rule-out process, it is important to consider other medical or psychological disorders, along with extreme external stressors, that may better explain the client's symptoms. For example, a client would not meet criteria for Female Sexual Interest/Arousal Disorder if she is experiencing partner violence. Many other psychological disorders, such as mood and anxiety disorders, can present with sexual dysfunction symptoms. If the specific sexual dysfunction is a symptom of another mental disorder, then the sexual dysfunction diagnosis should not be used, with the sexual symptom(s) better explained by the mental disorder. If the sexual dysfunction is caused by substance abuse or medication, this should be indicated in the diagnosis. Lastly, if the sexual dysfunction is medical in origin, a psychiatric diagnosis is not indicated.

Gender Dysphoria in DSM-5

Gender Dysphoria in both children and adults is described as a significant inconsistency between the client's experienced gender and their assigned gender. This inconsistency causes psychological distress and negatively impacts functioning in school, work, or other social settings. With both children and adults, the clinician should indicate if the client also has a disorder of sex development. In addition, it should be noted if the client has begun or completed any medical treatments or is living full-time as his or her experienced gender.

In children, symptoms of Gender Dysphoria are focused on concrete behaviors that represent distress or dysphoria concerning their assigned gender. Symptoms include the client demanding they are the other gender than their assigned gender, wanting to play with stereotypical toys of the other gender, wearing stereotypical clothing of the other gender, disdain for their sexual anatomy and wanting sex characteristics to match their experienced gender. Behavior issues such as tantrums, refusal, and extreme crying may be experienced when adults ask the child to dress or act in a way incongruent with their experienced gender. For example, a child assigned female but who experiences herself as male is asked to wear a dress for school picture day.

In adults and adolescents, symptoms of Gender Dysphoria are focused on chronic and severe anatomic-sex-characteristic dysphoria. Symptoms include attempting to eliminate or prevent sex characteristics of their assigned gender, a longing to have the sex characteristics of their experienced gender, a desire to be treated as the other gender by society, and a strong belief that they experience the world as the other gender might.

Paraphilic disorders in DSM-5

In the *DSM-5* there are ten diagnoses within Paraphilic Disorders. These are: Voyeuristic Disorder; Exhibitionistic Disorder; Frotteuristic Disorder; Sexual Masochism Disorder; Sexual Sadism Disorder; Pedophilic Disorder; Fetishistic Disorder; Transvestic Disorder; Other Specified Paraphilic Disorder; and Unspecified Paraphilic Disorder.

The above disorders have a common denominator of all being atypical sexual thoughts and/or behaviors. Some, but not all diagnoses, include behaviors that can potentially injure other people and are also identified as criminal behavior. Other diagnoses in this category are only considered a disorder if they cause significant distress in the client, and do not meet criteria if the behavior is between consenting adults. The *DSM-5* splits the diagnoses into two categories, the first being disorders that are atypical sexual activities, and the second being atypical sexual preferences. The first category is then subdivided into "courtship disorders" (relational) and "algolagnic disorders" (pain and suffering).

Symptoms for all Paraphilic Disorders include chronic and extreme sexual arousal based on the specific disorder, and acting on the sexual desire with a non-consenting person and/or experiencing psychological distress or impairment in social functioning. In addition, each diagnosis should identify if the behavior occurs in an institutional setting, such as jail or prison or residential treatment facility, and if the client has been able to abstain from the behavior in an uncontrolled environment.

Adlerian Conceptualization of Sexual Disorders

Alfred Adler did identify many of the sexual disorders that are currently in the *DSM-5*, with some labeling differences. Adler discusses Vaginismus, frigidity in women, premature ejaculation, and lack of sex interest/satisfaction. In the *DSM-5* each sexual dysfunction explanation contains information on the risk and prognostic factors. These factors are broken into three categories including "temperamental," "environmental," and "genetic and physiological" (American Psychiatric Association, 2013, p. 431). Alfred Adler's theory on the cause and maintenance of sexual dysfunctions is also multi-factoral and focuses on the individual's ability to make creative meaning out of their lived experience. Temperamental factors for Adlerians include life-style development, mistaken goals and beliefs, degree of movement, sense of belonging, feelings of inferiority or superiority, safeguarding behavior, and the development of other mental disorders (Ansbacher & Ansbacher, 1956; Adler, 1979). It should be noted that throughout Adler's writings, the greatest emphasis is placed on the above temperamental factors when explaining the possible cause of sexual dysfunctions. For example, Adler remarks:

> The impotence, or whatever sexual disability is produced, is dictated by a neurotic goal of superiority and a mistaken style of life. Investigation always reveals a fixed intention to receive without giving, and a lack of social interest, courage, and optimistic activity.
>
> (Ansbacher & Ansbacher, 1956, p. 313)

However, Adler does identify environmental (social) and physiological factors that also contribute to sexual dysfunctions. Adlerians are interested in the social aspect of sexual experience and how issues such as the masculine protest, gender equality, cooperation, religious beliefs, and mastery of the *love task* can impact sexual dysfunctions for the positive or negative. It should be noted that the majority of sexual dysfunctions in the *DSM-5* also address history of trauma, including sexual abuse, and/or current trauma as environmental factors that impact risk and prognosis. Adler did not explicitly identify abuse and trauma as contributing factors to sexual dysfunctions, but emphasized the importance of equality and safety for the development of healthy sexual relationships. Adler (1979) states, "Sexuality, love and marriage are tasks of two equal persons, tasks of forming a unit, and can be rightly solved only if persons are trained for sufficient social interest" (p. 220).

Rudolf Dreikurs continued and built on Adler's theory of social interest, with an additional focus on social equality. In his book, *Social Equality: The Challenge of Today,* Dreikurs writes men historically have had dominance politically, economically, socially, and sexually (2000). As this reality has evolved at different rates in different cultures, men and women have had to re-evaluate their role in their sexual relationships. This can at times result in sexual dysfunctions. One example of the intertwining of sex and power in society is the concept of masculine protest. Adler states:

> Many men, and especially many women, through mistakes in their development, have trained themselves to dislike and reject their sexual role... This is what I have called the masculine protest which is very much provoked by the over evaluation on men in our present culture. Both men and women will overstress the importance of being manly, and will try to avoid being put to the test. We can suspect this attitude in all cases of frigidity and impotence in men.
>
> (Ansbacher & Anscacher, 1956, p. 433)

Lastly, we will identify genetic and physiological factors through the lens of Adlerian theory. The *DSM-5* lists many medications and medical conditions which can contribute to sexual dysfunction. Adler was also interested in the physical body and the interaction between body and mind. Therefore, Adlerians are not only interested in a client's medical conditions, but also how the client interprets and makes sense of his or her medical condition. Adler described this process as Organ Jargon/Organ Dialect. Adlerian theory explains that the body speaks a language and that "emotions and their physical expressions tell us how the mind is acting and reacting in a situation which it interprets as favorable or unfavorable" (Ansbacher & Ansbacher, 1956, p. 223).

GENITO-PELVIC PAIN/PENETRATION DISORDER

Clinical Presentation

Pain related to penetration/intercourse is quite common, with around 15% of North American women reporting symptoms. Once the client has experienced pain rather than pleasure when attempting intercourse or penetration, she can become avoidant of sexual activity as a way to manage anxiety. What seems to develop is a connection between pain, fear, and muscular tension during penetration/intercourse. Women may also develop other sexual dysfunctions such as reduced sexual arousal/interest as a way to avoid pain (American Psychiatric Association, 2013). As with many phobias, clients develop an appropriate aversion to physical pain, which can then develop into an anxiety/aversion behavioral pattern.

DSM-5 Characterization

Genito-Pelvic Pain/Penetration Disorder is one of ten disorders in the Sexual Dysfunctions chapter, and is diagnosed only in women. Women with this condition have some, but not all of the following symptoms: difficulty with penetration during intercourse; pain during vaginal intercourse or penetration attempts; fear and anxiety connected to the anticipation of intercourse/penetration; and tightening of the pelvic-floor muscles while attempting intercourse. These symptoms do not meet criteria for the diagnosis if they are better explained by a non-sexual mental disorder or as a consequence of extreme social stressors. Women can experience the above symptoms life long, or they can be acquired over time.

Biopsychosocial –Adlerian Conceptualization

It is unclear whether biological, psychological, or social factors are the initial contributor to physical pain during penetration, but once pain is experienced, all three factors may continue to reinforce pain avoidance. Possible contributing factors to this disorder include partner factors, relationship factors, individual factors such as poor body image and possible sexual/emotional abuse history, cultural/religious factors, and medical factors. These factors help the clinician understand the possible cause for the disorder as well as the maintenance of symptoms (American Psychiatric Association, 2013).

It is important when evaluating the purpose of the symptoms, along with the life-style beliefs/convictions, to determine the etiology of the Genito-Pelvic Pain/Penetration Disorder. If the etiology of the disorder is biological and due to a physical condition of the sex organs, then the clinician would work with the client to seek treatment from a medical professional who treats this disorder. If the origin of the disorder is more psychological in nature, the clinician would begin to explore the purpose of the symptom and the life-style convictions that perpetuate the symptoms. For example, how might pelvic pain reinforce avoidance of sexual activity and intimacy? What core convictions does the client have about sexual intimacy and gender guiding lines that may reinforce pain avoidance? What is the client's sense of self-worth and are there any inferiority feelings connected to her understanding of herself as a sexual being? Finally, social or external factors should also be taken into account. How might external stressors such as a history of sexual abuse or domestic violence impact the client's expression of this disorder? Does the client struggle with a sense of connection, and how do safety concerns get expressed through the symptoms of this disorder? Ultimately, there are many psychological and social factors that contribute to the development and perpetuation of Genito-Pelvic Pain/Penetration Disorder. The role of the Adlerian clinician, through life-style analysis, is to help the client make meaning out of her symptoms, resulting in the treatment of the underlying anxiety or inferiority feelings.

Treatment Considerations

Prior to any psychological treatment for this disorder, the client should be examined by a medical professional to rule out any organic or medical problems contributing to sexual pain. Once these conditions have been treated and the client is still experiencing pain, fear, and tension, there are multiple interventions to explore. Due to the emotional and physiological components that reinforce the pain–fear–tension cycle, this disorder is best treated with a team approach, involving medical, physical therapy, and mental health professionals. Rosenbaum (2011) recommends clients see a physiotherapist who works specifically to relax pelvic-floor muscles by teaching exercises that can be completed at home, as well as providing manual therapy that a psychotherapist could not ethically provide. In conjunction with physiotherapy, the client would benefit from traditional psychotherapy using desensitization and exposure techniques, CBT, and/or trauma informed interventions.

Case Example: Ms. B.

Ms. B. is a 23-year-old Latina female who recently graduated from college and is a first-year math teacher. She has been dating her current boyfriend for about one year and has starting having intercourse in the past six months. She feels guilty about being sexually active since her culture, family, and Catholic religion all disapprove of premarital sex. Ms. B. lives with her roommate, who is also a teacher at the school she works at. She was referred by her primary care provider after reporting extreme pain during intercourse. Ms. B. was treated for a yeast infection, which has been cured, and has no other medical problems contributing to her sexual pain at this time.

Family constellation

She is the youngest of four siblings, with three older brothers, two, four, and eight years older than her. Ms. B. was treated like "one of the boys" growing up, and as

---

the youngest and only girl always tried to keep up with her brothers. Ms. B. reports she has a strong and loving family, including a large extended family that lives in the same community. Ms. B. attended parochial schools as well as a Catholic college. Catholicism was integrated into her family, social, and cultural experiences. Ms. B. considers her Catholic faith to be a large part of her identity, and it gives her strength and comfort. As a child, she was sexually abused by a priest, but has never shared this information with her family or boyfriend for fear they will blame her or that she will bring shame on the Church.

Early recollections

Her earliest recollection involves playing with her siblings and cousins in the playground next to the church. She is the youngest, but is able to keep up with the other kids as they play tag in the churchyard. She feels free and is thinking this is one of the best days of the summer. Another recollection around age nine involved being with her priest at the school and being told that she must never tell anyone what she and the priest were doing alone. The priest explained that she would be punished by her parents, and that she was to obey. Ms. B. stated she felt terrified and confused.

Adlerian case conceptualization

Ms. B.'s increased pelvic pain when having intercourse seems to be related to her history of sexual abuse and her anxiety about breaking a religious and family moral value by have premarital sex. Ms. B. has many secrets related to sexuality and sexual activity. Feelings of shame seem to result in anxiety about current sexual experiences. This anxiety then results in muscular tension, which then reinforces experiences of pain. Ms. B.'s presenting problems are understandable when viewed from the perspective of her life style. Early in her childhood she experienced adults as safe and supportive, but after experiencing sexual abuse, authority and its connection to morality became confused and unclear. Ms. B. developed a strong sense of self and competence as the youngest child. She was competitive with herself and never let being the "little one" get in the way of her achievements. She also developed a strong sense of community and faith, since her religion, ethnicity, and family values were strongly integrated. Ms. B. is trying to develop her own core beliefs and values informed by her childhood, but not identical to her childhood. Ms. B. and her boyfriend are both still practicing Catholics, but do not believe in all the moral constrictions and are planning to move in together. This has caused some level of cognitive dissonance. Ms. B. sees herself as independent, hard working, and committed to community. Until becoming sexually active she has experienced few anxiety or depression symptoms.

The primary goal is to address the anxiety and fear related to sexual intercourse and penetration. Adlerians have many interventions to work on anxiety, such as "Naming the Demon" and "Interpretation," as described by Mosak and Maniacci in *Tactics in Counseling and Psychotherapy* (1998). Psychotherapy could also help the client work through previous traumatic experiences using exposure therapy and interpersonal interventions. Lastly, the client would likely benefit from exploring life-style convictions and identifying core beliefs that may exacerbate anxiety symptoms.

GENDER DYSPHORIA

In Adler's original writings he did not refer to either Gender Identity Disorder or Gender Dysphoria, but did discuss homosexuality and hermaphroditism. Adler defined hermaphroditism as "the union of the two sexes in the same individual" (Ansbacher & Ansbacher, 1956, p. 46). Adler confounded the concept of sexual orientation (the gender an individual is sexually attracted to) with the concept of gender identity (the gender an individual experiences even when incongruent with his or her assigned sex at birth). Adler understood gender nonconformity as a form of neurosis, and was displayed in homosexuals. Adler stated, "Thus we find feminine habitus in male neurotics and masculine habitus in female neurotics, as a rule together with inferiority of other organs" (Ansbacher & Ansbacher, 1956, p. 46). Adler questioned whether there was a genetic relationship with the psychological when individuals expressed hermaphroditism, but stated it could not be proven at the present time. While Adler seemed to make sense of Gender Dysphoria as a psychological neurosis in homosexuals, the current *DSM-5* makes it explicitly clear that gender expression and gender nonconformity are not in and of themselves a psychological disorder. Rather, it is the dysphoria related to incongruence between the individual's biological sex and assigned gender that is cause for the disorder.

There has been only one contemporary article written on transgendered individuals published in the *Journal of Individual Psychology*. In Shelly's 2009 article, the author does not focus on critiquing Adler's understanding of hermaphroditism, but rather focuses on the social exclusion, lack of belonging, and inferior position transgendered individuals face in today's current society. Shelly (2009) makes the point that being rejected by individuals' family/community/society can in fact "deprive them of the opportunity to express their own socially interested links" (p. 389). This inability to belong and express social interest is then connected to mental health problems such as depression and anxiety. It should be noted though that in the *DSM-5*, Gender Dysphoria cannot be diagnosed if the dysphoria is only coming from societal rejection, therefore decreasing the possibility of societal inequality and discrimination being pathologized in the individual.

The etiology of Gender Dysphoria is still unclear, with the majority of research addressing treatment and advocacy needs of the client, rather than causal factors. Kirk and Belovics (2008) state, "The causes of gender dysphoria and gender identity disorder remain a mystery" (p. 30). Similar to the chapter on Sexual Dysfunctions, the *DSM-5* lays out temperamental, environmental, and genetic and physiological risk and prognostic factors for Gender Dysphoria *without* a disorder of sex development. These risk factors are not considered causal factors, but rather correlated factors that may or may not be present in the client who meets criteria for Gender Dysphoria. According to the *DSM-5*, temperamental factors include exhibiting a high degree of atypical gender behavior from an early age, making Gender Dysphoria in adolescence and adulthood more likely. From an environmental perspective, there is some evidence that males with Gender Dysphoria more commonly have older brothers than do males without the condition. Lastly, the *DSM-5* states that there is insufficient current evidence for genetic or physiological factors unless the Gender Dysphoria is associated with a disorder of sex development (2013).

GENDER DYSPHORIA: CHILDREN

Clinical Presentation

Children with Gender Dysphoria, often from a young age, assert they are the opposite/ experienced gender than their biological/assigned gender. They often state that they plan to grow up and be their experienced gender. These children also may present as oppositional and refuse when parents encourage them/force them to wear clothing typical of their assigned gender or to play with stereotypical toys for their assigned gender. Distress in children can express itself as irritability, depression, anxiety, and oppositional behavior.

It is important to note that children who do not gender conform and like to play with more stereotypical toys associated with the opposite gender do not automatically qualify for this disorder (Dragowski, Scharron, & Sandigorsky, 2011). In contrast, children with Gender Dysphoria often explain they feel trapped in the wrong body or were born with the wrong genitalia. Research has not shown a correlation between non-normative gender identification and mental illness, yet children display symptoms of depression and suicidality as they experience the pain of transitioning through puberty (Gibson & Catlin, 2011).

Lastly, children with Gender Dysphoria and non-normative gender expression are at greater risk for experiencing peer bullying and violence. One study (Goldblum et al., 2012) showed children who experienced school-based violence (SBV) and gender-based victimization (GBV) were four times more likely to attempt suicide compared to those who had not experienced this type of discrimination. Hostile and unwelcoming school environments for these children is well documented, and as a result can lead to negative self-concept, self-destructive behaviors, and low self-esteem. Children are not only exposed to unwelcoming schools, but often experience discrimination and social rejection by family, church, and even their medical provider. Therefore, children can experience distress related to their assigned gender as well as from bullying/exclusion.

DSM-5 Characterization

As noted earlier in this chapter, due to page constraints we will look at one case study from each *DSM-5* chapter. The following case study focuses on a child with Gender Dysphoria, yet Gender Dysphoria can be diagnosed in adolescents and adults with a different set of criteria. Children with Gender Dysphoria present with a significant incongruence between their assigned gender and their experienced/expressed gender. This incongruence leads to symptoms such as a strong desire to wear stereotypical clothing and play stereotypical children's games connected to their expressed gender. A strong preference is demonstrated for playing with children of the other gender, and taking on cross-gender roles in make-believe/fantasy play. Lastly, children with Gender Dysphoria have a strong dislike for their sexual anatomy, and a longing to have the primary and secondary sex traits that match their experienced gender. A child must exhibit almost all of these symptoms as well as experience significant distress or social impairment for at least six months to meet the criteria.

Biopsychosocial –Adlerian Conceptualization

The following biopsychosocial formulation may be helpful in understanding how Gender Dysphoria is likely to have developed. Thus far, the main research focuses on biological factors over psychological and social factors when addressing the etiology of Gender Dysphoria (American Psychiatric Association, 2013). It is actually unclear the true etiology for Gender Dysphoria at this time. Psychological and social factors will be addressed when explaining how the child handles the rejection that often goes hand in hand with non-normative gender behavior.

Biologically, children with Gender Dysphoria, but without a disorder of sex development, have some weak genetic contribution. Children with a disorder of sex development have multiple biological factors contributing to symptoms of Gender Dysphoria and should have their condition addressed with the appropriate medical specialist. Medical interventions include hormone blockers, hormone replacement, surgical, and nursing care (Gibson & Catlin, 2011).

As mentioned earlier in this chapter, Adler did not specifically address Gender Dysphoria in his original writings. Although Adlerian theory gives us very little for understanding the etiology of Gender Dysphoria, the theory can help the reader identify ways in which social exclusion and inferiority messages impact a child with non-conforming gender expression (Shelly, 2009).

Psychologically, children with Gender Dysphoria view themselves as the opposite of their assigned gender. This is different from children who are flexible in their gender interests and at times present as androgynous. Instead, these children are rigid in their stereotypical behavior linked to their expressed gender (Perrin, 2003). So how does a child know what it means to be male or female? Powers and Griffith (1993) lay out an excellent conceptualization of Adler's theory of gender guiding lines (GGL). They explain that children look to their same-sex parent as a guide of what it means to be their assigned gender. As children get older they can then question if they want to move away from their parental role model or if they want to embrace the values their parent instilled about their gender. There have been no studies or publications looking at how children with Gender Dysphoria understand and experience GGL in their family. It would be interesting to see if these children follow the GGL of the opposite-sex (the child's expressed/experienced gender) parent, and in a similar fashion understand what it means to be male or female based on parental models.

Socially, parenting and environmental factors can contribute to either the child's sense of self and belonging, or their sense of rejection and non-acceptance. Children who have non-normative gender expression will likely be exposed to higher levels of bullying, teasing, and transphobia (fear or hatred of transgender people, expressed as violence, harassment, and discrimination), sending overt as well as subtle messages about the child's inferior status in society as a sexual minority. Children and their families can experience this type of bullying or discrimination at home, school, doctor's office, or any other community or social setting (Gerouki, 2010). This form of bullying/ victimization has been correlated to young adult psychosocial maladjustment, including depression and decreased life satisfaction (Toomey, Ryan, Diaz, Card, & Russell, 2010). According to Adlerians, messages of inferiority sent to a child by segments of society as well as the family unit can have a negative impact on life-style development and their understanding of self, others, and the world. This experience of inferiority status in the form of discrimination should be differentiated from Adler's concept of the inferiority complex, in which a client believes he or she is not strong enough to solve his or her life problems (Ansbacher & Ansbacher, 1956). Children may develop a need to safeguard against negative messages and therefore have greater focus on personal and emotional safety. When a child's energy and creativity is focused on safeguarding, it makes it difficult to fully contribute his or her skills and gifts for the good of society.

Treatment Considerations

Because children with Gender Dysphoria can also be diagnosed with a disorder of sex development, the child should also be medically evaluated to address biological factors impacting the child's Gender Dysphoria. With or without a disorder of sex, a child can meet criteria for Gender Dysphoria, which should be addressed. According to the DSM-5, atypical gender expression/identity in and of itself is not a disorder, but rather the symptoms of dysphoria attached to the client's assigned gender. Therefore, any treatment that tries to "repair" or "convert" the client's gender expression is considered unethical, and in some states (New Jersey and California) even considered illegal.

Therefore, treatment implications shift to addressing the needs of families, schools, and other community entities to better ensure these children do not experience violence, bullying, discrimination, or victimization in relation to their atypical gender expression. Adlerian/Dreikursian parent and teacher education, focusing on interventions such as encouragement, positive identity development, and social contribution, could be of great help to the child. Mental health providers can be of great to help to families and schools, providing professional support, knowledge, and resources, and advocacy for children with Gender Dysphoria (Vanderburgh, 2009). Adlerian play therapy could be used to address associated symptoms such as anxiety, depression, and low self-esteem in the child (Kottman, 1999). This specific form of therapy focuses on how the child can build connections and feel like he or she counts in his or her society, despite experiences of bullying/discrimination.

Case Example: Sarah (Born male with the given name Lucas)

Sarah is a 13-year-old self-identified female, although she was assigned the gender of male at birth. She was referred to the clinical psychologist after a teacher noticed some self-injurious behavior. Sarah also told her teacher there were a few students at the school who had been calling her names and bullying her on Facebook. Sarah's parents noticed their child (born male) by about age three was insistent she was a girl. Sarah played with stereotypical female toys, and most of her peers in the daycare were girls rather than boys. Sarah does not have a disorder of sex, and therefore no biological/medical treatment is needed at this time. Sarah and her parents have been working closely with their pediatrician, who has recently set them up with a support group for families with transgendered children. Sarah is also seeing her school counselor since the self-injury incident, to address depression and anxiety symptoms.

Family constellation

Sarah lives with her married heterosexual parents and is the oldest of three. She has two younger brothers. Sarah's father works for the federal government and they live in a suburb outside of Washington, DC. Sarah's parents are very concerned about their child's gender expression, but have allowed her to wear female clothing to school and go by a female name. There has been some conflict between her parents, with her father being extremely concerned their child will be bullied or even physically hurt by adults or children.

Early recollections

Sarah reported a memory as early as age four when she bit a child in preschool when the child insisted Sarah was a boy. Sarah stated she felt angry, sad, and confused as to why her peer kept insisting she was a boy. A second memory was around age eight when she and her father went to the grocery store. She stated she remembers the adult in the check-out line talking in a quiet voice, saying Sarah's father was "disgusting for letting his son wear a dress." Sarah reported her father became angry and made a comment to the person in line, telling them to "mind their own business." Sarah said at that time she felt bad that what she was wearing made it hard on her father, and that she was embarrassed about her identity.

Adlerian case conceptualization

Based on Sarah's clinical symptoms and early recollections, it is clear she is having difficulty with identity development, feelings of self-worth, and self-esteem. Although her nuclear family is supportive of her gender identity, Sarah has received multiple overt and covert messages from society that she is not fully accepted by others. This can lead to safeguarding behavior, unexpressed creativity, and inferiority feelings.

Adlerian treatment for children usually entails working with the child and their family. Since Sarah's main challenge is feelings of worthlessness and exclusion, treatment should utilize techniques that promote *The Crucial Cs*: to connect, to feel capable, to feel as if I count, and to have courage (Bettner & Lew, 1989). One specific technique that reinforces *The Crucial Cs* is a group activity utilizing the participants' early recollections (Shifron & Bettner, 2003). A child/ adolescent is asked to volunteer, and shares three memories with the group. The other members of the group write the memory down and identify strengths and abilities. These strengths and abilities are then shared with the volunteer, who is then asked to share his or her reaction. At the end of the session, the child goes home with a written list of his or her strengths and abilities. For Sarah this could be a very powerful intervention, especially if the group therapy session also includes other children with Gender Dysphoria.

PARAPHILIC DISORDERS

In Ansbacher and Ansbacher, 1956, the editors lay out a chapter on crime and related disorders. Sexual perversions, including sadism, masochism, fetishism, exhibitionism, and masturbation are covered as part of this chapter. All of these disorders, minus masturbation, are included in the *DSM-5*. Additional perversions and sexual deficiencies discussed by Adler include homosexuality, sodomy, necrophilia, promiscuity, and "exclusive frequenters of prostitutes" (Ansbacher & Ansbacher, 1979, pp. 222–223). Many of these disorders, including masturbation, homosexuality, sodomy, promiscuity, and exclusive frequenters of prostitutes, are no longer considered mental disorders and are not included in the *DSM-5*.

Similar to Sexual Dysfunctions and Gender Dysphoria, the *DSM-5* offers some risk and prognostic factors related to Paraphilic Disorders. Of the eight specific disorders in this category, some but not all provide temperamental, environmental, and genetic factors. Themes for temperamental factors include antisocial behaviors and traits, along with alcohol abuse. The main environmental factor for the majority of these disorders is a history of sexual abuse/child abuse. It should be noted that Sexual Masochism Disorder, Sexual Sadism Disorder, Fetishistic Disorder, and Transvestic Disorder do not provide any possible risk or prognostic factors.

According to Adler, Paraphilic Disorders originate from mistaken life-style beliefs, inferiority feelings, lack of social interest, egocentrism, and organic differences in sexual stimulation (Ansbacher & Ansbacher, 1979). No specific mention was made in Adler's original writings about childhood sexual abuse as a risk factor for developing Paraphilic Disorders, yet it can be surmised that childhood abuse of any kind has an impact on life-style development, including extreme private logic and complex safeguarding techniques.

PEDOPHILIC DISORDER

Clinical Presentation

Males have a much higher prevalence of Pedophilic Disorder than do females, with approximately 3% to 5% of the male population meeting criteria for the disorder. The prevalence in females is uncertain, but significantly lower than males (American Psychiatric Association, 2013). Clients with Pedophilic Disorder likely became aware of their sexual interest in children around the time of puberty, but may not be diagnosed until later in the client's adult life. Many males with this disorder report they were sexually abused as a child. Clients with Pedophilic Disorder also often present with

put out everything

Thurs:

BM

8:30 - 2.5 onzes

BM

9:15 - 10:05 - sleep - easy
        rock - !!

2 diapers

4 onzes 11am

diaper

sleep stroller 12:30 - 1:20

1145 - 2 onzes

diaper

2 pm - 3 onzes

2:50   sleep

Antisocial Personality Disorder (American Psychiatric Association, 2013), and as a result may not admit to their sexual behavior harming children.

In much of the literature, a distinction is made between offenders who view child pornography and those who complete sexual-contact offenses. Thus far, there has been no empirical research proving a causal relationship between offenders who view child pornography and sexual-contact offenses against children. One study did find a vulnerable subgroup of men who are at greater risk for committing a contact offense. The men who used child pornography as well as committed sexual-contact crimes, had much higher antisociality. These men also had less education and lower career attainment, compared to men who only used child pornography. The majority of men who are arrested for possession of child pornography never complete a contact sexual act against a child. These men still meet criteria for Pedophilic Disorder, since their sexual fantasies, facilitated by online child pornography, are focused on children (Lee, Li, Lamade, Schuler, & Prentky (2012).

DSM-5 Characterization

Of the ten specific disorders covered in the Paraphilic Disorders chapter, we will explore a case study of a client diagnosed with Pedophilic Disorder. Pedophilic Disorder is described as intense, reoccurring sexual fantasies, urges, or behaviors toward a prepubescent child or children. The individual must experience significant distress or interpersonal problems as a result of these fantasies, urges, or sexual behaviors. When making a diagnosis, it should be clarified whether the client is sexually interested in children only, or whether he or she is also sexually aroused by adults, as well as whether the client is attracted to males, females, or both. Diagnosis should also distinguish if the arousal is specific to incest.

Clients can only be diagnosed with this disorder if their self-report, legal history, or objective assessment shows they have acted on their sexual impulses with children. If the client does not express guilt or shame, and it can be proven they have never acted on their fantasies, then the client has pedophilic sexual orientation, but not Pedophilic Disorder. In contrast, if a client does not admit to pedophilic urges or sexual behaviors, but it is proven the client has engaged in these behaviors, they meet criteria for the diagnosis.

Biopsychosocial –Adlerian Conceptualization

The following biopsychosocial formulation may be helpful in understanding how Pedophilic Disorder is likely to have developed.

The *DSM-5* states, "There is some evidence that neurodevelopmental perturbation in utero increases the probability of development of pedophilic orientation" (p. 699). There are few to no published articles researching the biologic basis for Pedophilic Disorder, with the majority of research focusing on the psychological and sociological factors contributing to the disorder.

As discussed earlier, clients with Pedophilic Disorder are at higher risk of also having Antisocial Personality Disorder and a history of sexual abuse themselves. As Adlerians, we explore how the life-style convictions were developed, including information about family make-up, abuse/neglect history, and the development of beliefs and values around sexual activity. It could be hypothesized that clients who have Pedophilic Disorder and Antisocial Personality traits were exposed to an environment and family system that did not express socially interested core beliefs regarding how we treat our fellow man with respect and cooperation. This can then turn into mistaken beliefs for the child in understanding how to develop connection and how to find purpose in his or her family and in society. When a child is in an unsafe or hostile environment, he or she will likely develop safeguarding behaviors, including hurting others before they are hurt themselves.

There is some controversy about males with Pedophilia and their history of childhood sexual abuse, yet abuse is often reported by these clients (American Psychiatric Association, 2013). In one longitudinal study (Salter, McMillan, Richards, Talbot, Hodges, Bentovim, et al., 2003), the authors make the point that most male victims of child sexual abuse do not become pedophiles, yet the authors were able to identify a vulnerable subgroup based on psychological and social risk factors. Children who were victims/abusers experienced maternal neglect, lack of supervision, sexual abuse by a female person, physical abuse, parental emotional rejection, and had witnessed greater levels of family violence. These offenders had also been more likely to be cruel to animals, as well as to commit other crimes against people and property.

Treatment Considerations

Due to the degree this disorder destroys children, families, and societies (as well as the client with the disorder), the main focus should be on prevention of this disorder, rather than treatment of the disorder. Both Adler and Dreikurs were influential proponents of both parent and teacher education. Out of this passion to prevent mental illness, through building strong connections and character in children and families, these practitioners have influenced many contemporary parent/teacher education curriculums in the United States. One way to possibly prevent or reduce the incidence of Pedophilic Disorder is for Adlerian parent-educators to work with high-risk abusive/neglectful parents, whose children are at greater risk for developing Pedophilic Disorder. Adlerian parent-educators could also work with child protective service workers and juvenile probation and detention centers, providing information on how children develop prosocial behavior.

In terms of treatment, one study found that as a pedophile's social interest increased, the number of committed sexual offenses decreased. The authors (Miranda & Fiorello, 2002) conclude, as a result of their findings, that increasing social interest should be included as one of many different interventions. The main intervention often thought of with this disorder is containment or incarceration, yet this intervention will only be effective if the client is also provided mental health treatment. Level-of-care assessment should be based on the severity of symptoms and the client's level of rigid private logic or lack of conscience. Treating sex offenders is a highly specialized field, with most clinicians needing additional training and supervision while working with this population.

Case Example: Mr. P.

Mr. P. is a 43-year-old male who presented for therapy after transitioning from a federal prison to a halfway house for registered sex offenders. Mr. P. was caught in an online child pornography ring at the age of 30. After evaluation and criminal investigation it was also discovered Mr. P. had been sexually abusing the ten-year-old boy in the apartment next door.

Family constellation

Mr. P. grew up in a suburban community right outside of a large metropolitan area. He is the middle child of four children, with two older sisters and one younger brother. Mr. P.'s mother was rarely home while he was growing up, due to an untreated drug and alcohol problem. When his mother was home, she often had many strange men and women at the house, who Mr. P. and his siblings did not feel comfortable around.

Early recollections

Mr. P. reported he and his siblings would go weeks without seeing their mother and would have to scavenge for food until their mother came home with more supplies. Mr. P. had both academic and behavior problems at school. Teachers found him to be aggressive and oppositional. He spent a large part of instructional time in suspension, and was identified as a bully to other children. In the fifth grade, his teacher reported concerns of abuse and neglect to Child Protective Service (CPS), who investigated and later removed the client and all his siblings from the home. CPS discovered upon physical exam that Mr. P. had a sexually transmitted infection, likely due to sexual abuse from his mother's previous boyfriend. It was also discovered Mr. P. had been sexually abusing his younger brother for about six months. Mr. P. did not graduate high school, and ultimately was placed in a boys' home after multiple failed foster-care placements. Mr. P. reported an inability to identify any specific memories as a child, but has feelings of anger, sadness, and fear when examining his childhood abuse and neglect.

Adlerian case conceptualization

Due to Mr. P.'s extensive abuse and neglect history, including sexual abuse, Mr. P. developed severe mistaken life-style beliefs about himself, others, and the world. As a result of trying to survive during childhood, Mr. P. developed elaborate and rigid private logic about intimacy and boundaries. He experiences little to no guilt over his pedophilic behavior, and does not believe he is hurting children when he engages in sexual acts with minors.

Mr. P. has extremely underdeveloped social interest. Due to his almost complete denial of his problem, Mr. P. needs to be in specialized sex-offender treatment in a controlled environment. Mr. P. will likely need lifelong monitoring and treatment to address the safety needs of society and the client. Treatment should also focus on basic life skills, citizenship skills, and increasing social interest through restitution and community service.

Concluding Note

In the *DSM-5* there have been some substantial changes to the sexual disorders, including how they are organized, as well as criteria for specific disorders. The main change was separating the Sexual Dysfunctions, Gender Dysphoria, and Paraphilic Disorders into three separate chapters. Within each of these chapters, changes were made to some specific diagnoses and criteria attached. Of greatest interest to the psychological as well and the LGBT community was the change from Gender Identity Disorder in the *DSM-IV-TR* to Gender Dysphoria in the *DSM-5*. This change took the shift of pathology away from the identity of the client, and placed it on the dsyphoria non-gender conformity can cause. Clinicians should also take note that throughout all the sexual disorders, variance of sexual behaviors is not in and of itself psychopathology, but rather the behavior must be proved to be hurting the client, hurting a non-consenting adult, or a child. Utilizing Adlerian theory while treating these disorders can address not only treatment of the patient, but also prevention of certain disorders through advocacy, promoting equality, and providing good parent and teacher education.

References

American Psychiatric Association (2000). *Diagnostic and Statistical Manual of Mental Disorders, Fouth Edition (Text Revision).* Washington, DC: American Psychiatric Publishing.

American Psychiatric Association (2013). *Diagnostic and Statistical Manual of Mental Disorders, Fifth Edition.* Arlington, VA: American Psychiatric Publishing.

American Psychiatric Association (2013). *Gender Dysphoria.* Retrieved from http://www.dsm5.org/Documents/Gender%20Dysphoria%20Fact%20Sheet.pdf.

American Psychiatric Association (2013). *Highlights of Changes from DSM-IV-TR to DSM-5.* Retrieved on September 15, 2013, from http://www.dsm5.org/Documents/changes%20 from%20dsm-iv-tr%20to%20dsm-5.pdf.

Ansbacher, H.L. & Ansbacher, R.R. (Eds.). (1956). *The Individual Psychology of Alfred Adler.* New York, NY: Harper & Row.

Ansbacher, H.L. & Ansbacher, R.R. (Eds.) (1979). *Superiority and Social Interest.* New York, NY: W.W. Norton & Co.

Bettner, B.L. & Lew, A. (1989). *Raising Kids Who Can.* Newton Centre, MA: Connexions Press.

Cohen-Baker, N. (2006). Sex from Plato to Paglia: A philosophical encyclopedia. *Library Journal,* 131(6), p. 120.

Dragowski, E.A., Scharron-del Rio, M.R., & Sandigorsky, A.L. (2011). Childhood gender identity … disorder? Developmental, cultural, and diagnostic concerns. *Journal of Counseling & Development,* 89(3), pp. 360–366.

Dreikurs, R. (2000). *Social Equality: The Challenge of Today.* Chicago, IL: Adler School of Professional Psychology.

Gerouki, M. (2010). The boy who was drawing princesses: Primary teachers' accounts of children's non-conforming behaviours. *Sex Education,* 10(4), pp. 335–348.

Gibson, B. & Catlin, A.J. (2011). Care of the child with the desire to change gender—Part I. *Urologic Nursing,* 31(4), pp. 222–229.

Goldblum, P., Testa, R.J., Pflum, S., Hendricks, M.L., Bradford, J., & Bongar, B. (2012). The relationship between gender-based victimization and suicide attempts in transgender people. *Professional Psychology: Research and Practice,* 43(5), pp. 468–475.

Hegarty, P. (2012). Beyond Kinsey: The committee for research on problems of sex and American psychology. *History of Psychology,* 1(3), pp. 197–200.

Jordan, Mark D. (1997). *The Invention of Sodomy in Christian Theology*. Chicago, IL: University of Chicago.

Kirk, J. & Belovics, R. (2008). Understanding and counseling transgender clients. *Journal of Employment Counseling*, 4(1), p. 29.

Kottman, T. (1999). Integrating the crucial C's into Adlerian play therapy. *Journal of Individual Psychology*, 55(3), pp. 288–297.

Lee, A., Li, N., Lamade, R. Schuler, A., & Prentky, R. (2012). Predicting hands-on child sexual offenses among possessors of Internet child pornography. *Psychology, Public Policy, And Law* [serial online],18(4), pp. 644–672.

Miranda, A.O. & Fiorello, K.J. (2002). The connection between social interest and the characteristics of sexual abuse perpetuated by male pedophiles. *Journal of Individual Psychology*, 58(1), pp. 2–75.

Mosak, H.H. & Maniacci, M.P. (1998). *Tactics in Counseling and Psychotherapy*. Belmont, CA: Thomas Learning.

Perrin, E.C. (2003). Helping parents and children understand "Gender Identity Disorder." *Brown University Child & Adolescent Behavior Letter*, 19(1), p. 1.

Powers, R.L. & Griffith, J. (1993). Gender guiding lines theory and couples therapy. *Individual Psychology: The Journal of Adlerian Theory, Research, and Practice*, 49(3/4), p. 361.

Rosenbaum, T. (2011). Addressing anxiety in vivo in physiotherapy treatment of women with severe vaginismus: A clinical approach. *Journal of Sex & Marital Therapy*, 37(2), pp. 89–93.

Salter, D., McMillan, D., Richards, M., Talbot, T., Hodges, J., Bentovim, A., & ... Skuse, D. (2003). Development of sexually abusive behaviour in sexually victimised males: A longitudinal study. *Lancet*, 361(9356), p. 471.

Shelley, C.A. (2009). Trans people and social justice. *Journal of Individual Psychology*, 65(4), pp. 386–396.

Shifron, R. & Bettner, B. (2003). Using early memories to emphasize the strengths of teenagers. *The Journal of Individual Psychology*, 59(3), pp. 334–344.

Sperry, L. & Sperry, J. (2012). *Case Conceptualization*. New York, NY: Routledge.

Toomey, R., Ryan, C., Diaz, R., Card, N., & Russell, S. (2010). Gender-nonconforming lesbian, gay, bisexual, and transgendered youth: School victimization and young adult psychosocial adjustment. *Developmental Psychology*, 46(6), pp. 1580–1589.

Vanderburgh, R. (2009). Appropriate therapeutic care for families with pre-pubescent transgender/gender-dissonant children. *Child & Adolescent Social Work Journal*, 26(2), pp. 35–154.

Weiss, M. (2011). Beyond Kinsey: Judith Butler's impact on the feminist and queer studies. *Association for Feminist Anthropology Blog*, doi:10.1037/e583522012-010.

13 Neurodevelopmental and Conduct Disorders

Larry Maucieri

In this chapter, we will explore the diagnostic changes, theoretical conceptualizations, and treatment options for some of the neurodevelopmental and conduct disorders, as they have been modified and presented in the *DSM-5* (American Psychiatric Association, 2013). This will be accomplished with a review and exploration of the current related literature written from a modern Adlerian perspective. Because of space constraints, and gaps in the extant literature, not every condition or disorder within these *DSM-5* groupings is included here. However, a number of major disorders from these sections of the *DSM-5* have been included.

Before proceeding directly into the disorders, however, it may be helpful to review some of the general principles and tenets of Adlerian theory and methods. I will then discuss the context within which DSM-5 diagnostic conceptual changes have occurred. It might be particularly useful to provide readers with some brief information regarding the transition from the *DSM-IV-TR* to the *DSM-5* (American Psychiatric Association, 2000, 2013). This chapter includes the following disorders with DSM and Adlerian conceptualizations: Autistic Spectrum Disorder; Specific Learning Disorder; Attention Deficit Hyperactivity Disorder; Tourette's Syndrome; Conduct Disorder; and Oppositional Defiant Disorder. Intellectual Disability is also briefly covered.

Adlerian Conceptualization

Adlerian theory and concepts were under-appreciated in their own time, yet still remain remarkably germane today (Peluso, 2008). In this section, some key concepts of Adlerian theory and the context within which they developed will be discussed, particularly in relation to the DSM-5 disorders considered in this chapter.

Organ Inferiority

Some scholars have noted the relationship between Adler's own life experiences and some of his theoretical tenets. Monte (1995), for instance, argues that Alfred Adler's childhood was punctuated with illness, death, and danger, that Adler was struck by a car as a child, and that his brother died when Adler was only three years old. From these early developmental traumas Adler may have been influenced and subsequently developed some of his primary psychological concepts, such as *organ inferiority* (Monte, 1995).

Organ inferiority, which initially suggested a physical deficiency in a bodily organ, might be conceptually broadened to more globally reflect one's feelings of inferiority in relation to others and the world. Among those with neurodevelopmental disorders, this Adlerian idea appears quite relevant, as issues of shame, inferiority, and despair frequently occur in individuals struggling with learning disorders, Autism, tic disorders, and Attention Deficit Hyperactivity Disorder (ADHD). The feeling of inferiority is likely due not only to the actual symptoms of the disorders, but also to the negative effects that they have on the individual's self-esteem, mood, and social life (Maucieri, 2013). In the case of a tic disorder, for instance, a sense of self-degradation and shame might develop not only from embarrassing vocal and motor tics themselves, but also from the social and emotional alienation that occurs as a result of these behaviors. Particularly in children and adolescents, the nagging sense of being intractably different is likely to lead to a strong sense of inferiority, stemming in this example from one's neurodevelopmental or other behavioral challenges.

According to Adler, the sense of inferiority is ultimately intolerable. To compensate for this deeply rooted, innate sense of worthlessness, we may strive for superiority and perfection. How this might occur in an individual with a neurodevelopmental or conduct disorder is of primary clinical interest, but may be idiosyncratic to the individual. Since Adlerian theory is teleological, or forward-focused, in nature, however, it tends to place considerable importance on goal strivings and direction toward one's ultimate life aims (Monte, 1995). Beyond the specific struggles and unique challenges of each individual, a teleological framework may ultimately provide an effective context within which one's sense of inferiority, and compensatory behaviors for his/her inferiority, may be examined, challenged, and successfully modified.

Social Context and Social Interest

It might have already been evident in the brief discussion about organ inferiority above, but Adler's theories of personality and psychological functioning are not those of Freud's. The two colleagues remained in regular contact for about nine years in Vienna, early in Adler's career. Adler was invited to join Freud's psychoanalytic discussion group in 1902. Monte (1995) argues that Adler never fully accepted Freud's psychoanalytic approach, however, and that by 1911 they were at an impasse.

Adler's separation from Freud and from the psychoanalytic group in 1911 was contentious. Their ideas involving personality and psychology clearly differed, and there was not much room for differences of opinion on key Freudian concepts in the group. Adler therefore resigned and left. Unlike the early Freudian theorists, Adler conceptualized the human experience within a specifically *social context* (Mosak, 1995). This was in stark contrast to the Freudian emphasis on sexuality and, later, aggression, which incidentally Adler identified well before it was adopted into Freud's model in the 1920s (Monte, 1995).

Adler rejected fundamental orthodox Freudian concepts on a number of levels. These included the functions of the ego in relation to the id, and the sexual nature of the Oedipal rivalry (Monte, 1995). For Adler, humans are generally innately good and social in nature. They strive for personal competence, trying to defeat their challenges, rather than merely suffering through the misery of daily existence (Monte, 1995). For Adler, a signature of sound psychological adjustment is having a strong sense of social interest and charitable concern for one's fellows (Monte, 1995). A similar incorporation and valuation of social interest is not easily found, if even present at all, in classic Freudian theory. Conversely, Freud's later scholarship appears to reflect an increasingly negative and portentous view of humanity.

Adler stood alone among his Viennese contemporaries in terms of the relevance of social context and social interest in psychological functioning. These valued concepts remain vital in Adlerian theory. An essential and enduring concept of Adlerian theory is encapsulated in the German term of *Gemeinschaftsgefühl*. This aggregated noun represents a concept not easily translated into an equivalent English definition. It means something comparable to the concept of social interest, or perhaps more specifically, "the feeling of being connected to all of humanity—past, present, and future—and to an interest in the welfare and interests of others" (Sonstegard, 1998, p. 243). Underlying this concept is a sense of belonging, social connection, and deep concern for others (Sonstegard, 1998).

Given the difficulty with social and interpersonal relationships that individuals with conduct disorders and neurodevelopmental disorders experience as part of their symptoms, Adler's concepts of social interest and social context are quite relevant. Interventions based in part on the Adlerian notions of social interest and fellowship may be beneficial, and one such program is described in the section on Autistic Spectrum Disorder below.

In sum, Adler's emphasis is distinctly holistic, relational, and sociocultural in nature. It is uniquely different from its contemporary model of classic Freudian theory in a number of ways. Adler's model is more social and optimistic in character. Mosak (1995) notes that the Adlerian approach is interpersonal, and that for Adlerians, "all behavior occurs in a social context" (p. 52). At heart, it is a theory that is realistic, pragmatic, and hopeful. Like behavioral and cognitive-behavioral models it is also active: From an Adlerian perspective, learning and change come from taking actions (Sonstegard, 1998).

The Problem of "Choice"

Another Adlerian concept that diverges from Freudian theory involves a de-emphasis, and in some instances an outright rejection, of determinism. Adlerian theory is more likely to posit that conscious or unconscious personal choices may play key roles in one's behaviors and their consequences. The Adlerian approach allows for a more functional interpretation of behaviors and symptoms than do most other theoretical models. This position has nonetheless caused problems, with some writers criticizing Adlerian theory for "blaming the victim" for his/her struggles, and others balking at the idea that choice might somehow be involved in the development of certain disorders (e.g., Autism, Schizophrenia) that clearly have very solidly documented biological bases, from the scholarly and empirical literatures.

In the present era, the concept of choice must be adjusted to allow for the known genetic and biological underpinnings of certain disorders that were simply not recognized at the time of Adler. An insistence that personal choice plays a key role in the onset of Autism or Schizophrenia, for instance, is simply untenable with our present knowledge base. Put another way, there is a mountain of evidence supporting the role of genetics and other biological processes in the development of Schizophrenia and Autism, and not a lot of evidence supporting the role of conscious or unconscious choice in the development of these disorders.

Given what is now known about the biological antecedents of certain mental health issues, a more reasonable calibration of the role of choice in something like Autism or even ADHD might be that these disorders emerge as a result of complex interactions between a biological predisposition and certain environmental stressors (the diathesis stress model), but that the expression of individual symptoms, or perhaps one's personal reactions and coping methods to the conditions, are in part guided by conscious and unconscious choice.

Similarly, Mosak (1995) discusses using "The Question" as a helpful tool in possibly discerning between symptoms and problems of a primarily psychological nature versus those of a primarily physical (what he terms "organic") nature. Its use in counseling and therapeutic approaches has already been well documented. As a sole diagnostic tool, however, it could not be currently recommended in this capacity, since its validity and reliability for such queries are unknown, and there are a broad range of highly precise neuroimaging techniques (e.g., MRI, PET scans) and psychometrically sound inventories and psychological tests available, which would much more accurately answer such a question. Using a method such as "The Question" within a set of other instruments and assessment tools might be helpful and provide *additional* insight into the current struggles of the individual, but not as a sole litmus for the physical or psychological bases of symptoms. Beyond that point, there is a greater appreciation now of the interactive and symbiotic nature of psychological and physical processes in mental health, that was absent before, so a discrete categorization of physical versus psychological problems has become murkier in recent decades.

The issue of the diagnostic use of "The Question" is brought up here as a parallel to the concept of choice as discussed. In both instances these are valuable concepts from Adlerian theory when trying to understand and help the individual. However, the original interpretation of choice as a causal component of a presenting disorder, like the application of "The Question" by itself for diagnostic clarification, is not presently supported by our extant clinical and research knowledge, and so these concepts must be reconfigured a bit within the full clinical literature relating to the questions being asked.

Life Approaches

Adlerian theory indicates that we all consciously and unconsciously develop *life styles* that guide us on the path of our hopeful life pursuits, goals, and achievements (Monte, 1995). Mosak (1995) clarifies that a life style "is neither right nor wrong, normal nor abnormal, but merely the 'spectacles' through which people view themselves in relationship to the way in which they perceive the world" (p. 52). Cognitive-behavioral theorists might equate this to an overarching schema involving one's self and the world.

A life style, however, also has a functional component; it might also be understood as one's "answer" to the unique challenges and feelings of inferiority that occur over the course of life. Adlerian clinicians obtain life-style information from such techniques as the published life-style inventory and the collection and interpretation of early memory recollections. Other tools used to understand a client's concerns and difficulties involve analysis of dreams and the investigation of birth order in one's family of origin.

In Adler's conceptualization, we are all faced with three main life tasks or goals, which involve work, love, and social and relational pursuits. Some of Adler's followers later added life tasks involving spirituality and our relationships with ourselves (Mosak, 1995). Social connection again plays a core role in Adlerian theory, not only with others, but even with ourselves. Adler was among the first to recognize these important components of a balanced life. Berger and Felsenthal-Berger (2009) succinctly define Adler's theory as the first to recognize "the human being as primarily a social creature, with the need to relate to others" (p. 351).

DSM-5 Changes

Transition to DSM-5

After a prelude of controversy and fierce debate, the *DSM-5* was released in late May 2013 (American Psychiatric Association, 2013; Wakefield, 2013). The new edition of the *DSM* was met with a range of concerns. Some mental health professionals expressed trepidation that involved incomplete field trials, while others wondered if normal human behaviors were sometimes being pathologized (Wakefield, 2013). Allen Francis, for instance, remarked that "[the] DSM-5 will turn temper tantrums into a mental disorder... Normal grief will become Major Depressive Disorder" (Francis, 2012, as cited in Wakefield, 2013, p. 140). The degree to which these concerns may actually manifest is of course not yet clear.

Spectrum-Based Models

One major change in the *DSM-5* involved a reorganization of many clinical conditions into more deliberately spectrum-based or dimensional representations. Specificity, it seems, was de-emphasized in favor of larger groupings of common or similar clinical conditions. This approach represented a movement away from the categorical classification model that had dominated the *DSM-IV* and *DSM-IV-TR* (American Psychiatric Association, 2000; 2013).

A salient illustration of this change was the fusion of several related pervasive developmental disorders (e.g., Autism, Asperger's Disorder) into a single DSM-5 entity called Autistic Spectrum Disorder (American Psychiatric Association, 2013). These disorders, which were previously conceptualized as separate but related, are now nested within a common spectrum. Thus, instead of the subtype specificity evident in the *DSM-IV* and *DSM-IV-TR*, the authors of the *DSM-5* embraced a more encompassing configuration, including a range of possible and perhaps at times even rather divergent clinical presentations within a common spectrum (American Psychiatric Association, 1994, 2000, 2013). This change is particularly relevant for a number of the neurodevelopmental disorders, which will be discussed and considered below.

The reasons for this shift in diagnostic conceptualization are not without precedent. Coghill and Sonuga-Barke (2012), for instance, indicated that categorical diagnostic conceptualizations were problematic, in that they reflected not only clinical and scientific reasoning, but also include political, economic, and psychological influences that were beyond the scope of clinical diagnosis. For therapists and counselors who rely on the

DSM diagnostic system, the inclusion of these superfluous elements and influences was also awkward.

Criticism of the General DSM Model

Given the range of opinions and criticisms leading up to its release, the *DSM-5* was unlikely to satisfy critics of it or of the previous editions of the manual. Vanheule (2012), for example, criticized the DSM model of case conceptualization and diagnosis in general. He noted that classification was not necessarily synonymous with diagnosis, and he explored the sometimes unclear, or even disputed, scientific bases for disorders being included in the *DSM*. While Vanheule (2012) mentioned some interesting challenges to the DSM approach of diagnosis, a few important points seemed to be missing in this discussion. First, although this author concluded that the DSM model might not be beneficial for psychotherapy practice, no workable alternative system of diagnosis was mentioned in any detail. Second, the writer did not clarify that one of the reasons that the *DSM-IV, DSM-IV-TR*, and *DSM-5* more explicitly referenced the neuropsychiatric bases of some disorders was because of the vast emerging literature that directly or indirectly supported these findings. An enormous amount of empirical support for biological bases (but not solitary causation) has accumulated for Schizophrenia, Bipolar Disorder, substance use, ADHD, and Autism. This should be considered when discussing possible reasons why neurobiological aspects of mental illness have been increasingly represented in recent editions of the *DSM*. From an opposite perspective, other writers have even criticized the *DSM-5* for *not including enough* on clinical genetic research in the understanding and treatment of neurodevelopmental disorders (Addington & Rapoport, 2012).

With that being said, a continued criticism of the *DSM-5* and previous editions of the manual has involved the "overmedicalization" of human behavior and mental illness. This issue likely creates difficulties for those who closely apply DSM criteria when new editions are released. Vanheule (2012) remarked in this regard that the DSM model tended to employ a "neo-positivist" model (p. 130). In a neo-positivist model, symptoms and behaviors are understood as palpable "evidence" of a true disorder, in much the same way that there are physical symptoms for viral meningitis or asthma.

While this approach probably evolved in large part from the medical matrix (psychiatry) within which the *DSM* had developed (Vanheule, 2012), it is difficult to defend the sometimes large changes in diagnostic criteria or other diagnostic requirements made during manual revisions, when they are done without much external evidence supporting them. Also, the issue of removed and added diagnoses tends to strain the applicability of this model to mental health. When the *DSM-5* was released in May 2013, for instance did a diagnosis that had previously been included in the *DSM-IV-TR*, but not in the *DSM-5*, really just cease to exist? Did new disorders included in the *DSM-5*, but not the *DSM-IV-TR*, suddenly exist where they had not been before? Were they there all along and now just discovered? It is these sorts of questions that make the medical model of mental health, as codified in the *DSM*, a vexing and challenging approach to diagnosis.

However, the *DSM-5* may prove to be more malleable in time. Unlike its predecessors, the *DSM-5* uses Arabic numbers rather than Roman numerals (5 rather than V) because, according to Wakefield (2013), it was planned to be a flexible, "living document" (p.

140), that allowed for targeted updates, as the pertinent scholarship and clinical literature advanced.

In the past, Adlerian theorists have tended to de-emphasize diagnosis and psychopathology as inconsistent with their core values and beliefs (Peluso, 2008). However, diagnostic systems such as the DSM-5 are a modern reality in American behavioral healthcare. One way then to potentially bridge these two divergent viewpoints is to recontextualize the DSM-5 system *from an illness model*, which suggests that someone's struggles are pathological and medical in nature, *to a strengths-based approach*, which is more congruent with the counseling perspective and consistent with Adlerian principles (Peluso, 2008).

Neurodevelopmental Disorders

By grouping together the conditions that have a largely developmental component, the authors of the *DSM-5* shifted focus from the onset period of these disorders (childhood and adolescence) to their neurodevelopmental nature. This change has redirected our attention to their etiology and developmental processes (APA, 2013; Wakefield, 2013). The neurodevelopmental disorders of DSM-5 include, among others, Intellectual Disability (formerly Mental Retardation), the Autistic Spectrum Disorders, Specific Learning Disorders, and Tourette's Syndrome. We will briefly look at each of these major disorders in succession.

Intellectual Disability

Consistent with the scholarship in this area, the diagnostic category of Mental Retardation has been redefined as "Intellectual Disability" (ID) in the *DSM-5* (American Psychiatric Association, 2013). Like Mental Retardation, ID is diagnosed based on: (a) the presence of subpar scores on standardized individual measures of intelligence; (b) impairments in adaptive skills; and (c) evidence of early (roughly speaking, under the age of 18 years) neurodevelopmental processes as part of the cause (American Psychiatric Association, 2000, 2013). Hare (2012) suggested that for a majority of individuals, ID may have biological origins. The estimated prevalence of ID is about 3% in North America, with a majority of individuals falling into the mild or moderate severity ranges (Matson et al., 2012).

In the previous diagnosis of Mental Retardation, severity level was strongly determined by individual standardized intelligence test global scores (American Psychiatric Association, 2000). The DSM-5 definition of ID has instead placed greater emphasis on independent skills and adaptive impairments, and less weight on composite intelligence scores, to establish a diagnosis and severity level for ID (American Psychiatric Association, 2013; Wakefield, 2013). Perhaps to operationalize this process more uniformly, the *DSM-5* has provided a detailed chart (American Psychiatric Association, 2013, pp. 34–36) to help clinicians define ID severity level (i.e., mild, moderate, severe, or profound). The established severity level is based largely on adaptive, communication, cognitive, and independent living skills and behaviors. This approach appears more consistent with work done by the American Association of Mental Retardation (AAMR) decades ago, documenting the importance of adaptive skills when assessing neurodevelopmental disorders (Wilmshurst, 2011).

Additionally, *DSM-5* appears more flexible in allowing clinicians to weigh evidence and use their own judgments when considering a number of intelligence test scores, other cognitive skills, and a range of adaptive functioning skills in determining the severity level of an individual's ID (American Psychiatric Association, 2013). Prior editions of the manual, such as the *DSM-IV-TR*, more specifically incorporated global intelligence scores as core in the diagnosis of Mental Retardation (American Psychiatric Association, 2000).

Like Autistic Spectrum Disorder (discussed below), a number of behavioral modification techniques have been frequently employed to help individuals with ID. These methods, including positive behavioral support methods such as applied behavior analysis (ABA) (Matson et al., 2012), are briefly described below.

AUTISTIC SPECTRUM DISORDER

Clinical Presentation

The amalgamation of several pervasive developmental disorders into a single broad classification, now called Autistic Spectrum Disorder (ASD), was among the most significant and controversial changes from the *DSM-IV-TR* to the *DSM-5*. This modification removed the separate diagnoses of Autism, Asperger's Disorder, Rett's Syndrome, Childhood Disintegrative Disorder, and the residual group of Pervasive Developmental Disorder—Not Otherwise Specified (PDD—NOS). In *DSM-5* they have all been merged into ASD (American Psychiatric Association, 2013).

While these conditions have been all grouped together into the new diagnosis of ASD, the ASD criteria most closely reflect the symptoms of Autism and perhaps to a lesser degree Asperger's Disorder. Autism is typically defined by impairments in social and interpersonal interactions, repetitive and restricted interests and behaviors, and lags in language development (Lord & Jones, 2012; Moseley et al., 2011).

A concern of many critics, though, was the uncertain reason for obviating the diagnosis of Asperger's Disorder and combining it with Autism. In *DSM-IV* and *DSM-IV-TR*, Asperger's Disorder was similar to Autism, but it lacked the history of language delays (American Psychiatric Association, 1994; 2000). While many clinicians regarded Asperger's Disorder and Autism as related and even overlapping, the distinction in language development and skills had long been accepted as a differential factor between the two disorders.

A second feature of *DSM-5* regarding ASD involves a greater number of specifiers and severity level indicators, perhaps to provide more information within the broadly defined spectrum diagnoses. ASD for instance may include a range of specifiers (e.g., "with catatonia"). There is also a chart to assist clinicians in determining a severity level for ASD (American Psychiatric Association, 2013, pp. 51–52).

While the prevalence of Autism has been estimated at slightly less than 1% of the general population, or about 1 in 110 individuals (Axelrod, McElrath, & Wine, 2012), the rates of Autism diagnosis have increased for uncertain reasons. Like ID, comorbid conditions are common in ASD. A recent investigation by Australian researchers suggested that nearly half of their sample of adolescents and young adults with Autism met criteria for comorbid psychiatric conditions, such as anxiety, mood, and disruptive behavior disorders (Moseley et al., 2011). Other investigators have mentioned a link between Autism and neurologic disorders (Ryland et al., 2012).

DSM-5 Characterization

Similar to the *DSM-IV* and *DSM-IV-TR*, *DSM-5* defines ASD by a pattern of behaviors exhibiting social communication and social interactions, and narrowly defined and repetitive interests and behaviors (American Psychiatric Association, 2013). These must be from neurodevelopmental causes, and may not be attributable to other syndromes, such as Intellectual Disability. As noted above, the spectrum criteria include problems with or without language impairments to subsume to formerly defined Asperger's Disorder (American Psychiatric Association, 2013).

Cognitive deficits often occur with Autism, but are not necessarily diagnostic of the disorder. The cognitive symptoms among those with ASD vary widely, as individuals may range from profoundly intellectually disabled to intellectually gifted. Individuals in the latter subgroup had previously been referred to as having "high-functioning Autism." ID is not a diagnostic feature of ASD. Rather, core symptom areas in ASD involve social and interpersonal interactions, language and communication skills, and repetitive and stereotyped behaviors (Axelrod et al., 2012). Autism has also been linked with behavioral difficulties and increased family stress (Lord & Jones, 2012), both of which may be ameliorated with a number of interventions mentioned below.

Biopsychosocial–Adlerian Conceptualization

Huber and Zivalich (2004) linked the work of Lovaas (described below) with Adlerian principles and techniques in treating autistic children. In doing so, the authors cited the work of Tolman, who used behavioral concepts while conceptualizing behavior in a more social context. In this and related work, Huber and Zivalich (2004) noted a more teleological perspective. The writers argued that the behaviorists' methods to augment self-efficacy were congruent with the Adlerian aims of reducing feelings of inferiority. Hartshorne and Herr (1983) similarly concluded that behavioral interventions for Autism and related disorders are consistent with Adlerian models. A difference might arise in the interpretation of behavior according to these authors, such that Adlerians may be more likely to understand behaviors as goal directed rather than reinforced.

Huber and Zivalich (2004) developed the Meredith Autism Program (MAP), which is based on the behavioral principles developed by Lovaas. MAP uses a strong behavioral approach, while still incorporating Adlerian theory and principles into the treatment model. Like many forms of Applied Behavioral Analysis (ABA), long weeks of intensive behavioral training are required in MAP. This is consistent with certain aspirations of Adlerian training, in which "behavioral improvement is seen as part of an educational process involving all those involved" (p. 351). It is also congruent with Adler's approach to education, in which students are helped to cope in their own worlds: The children in MAP are behaviorally reinforced to learn basic social concepts (e.g., colors, shapes), develop basic communication skills, and follow directions (Huber & Zivalich, 2004). In the MAP approach, imperfection is tolerated, punishment is not used, and programs are individualized to the specific needs of the child (Huber & Zivalich, 2004). In these and other ways, operant conditioning based on the seminal work of Lovaas is fused with core Adlerian values.

Treatment Considerations

The work of Lovaas and others helps us to appreciate how much is available when working therapeutically with individuals who sometimes have profound deficits due to neurodevelopmental conditions, such as ASD. Before Lovaas' groundbreaking work, children with Autism and intellectual disabilities were considered largely unreachable, and their parents were often blamed for them developing ASD (Hartshorne & Herr, 1983). Whether behavioral or other methods tend to be employed, the overarching sense of community and social interest, which reflect Adlerian principles, remains of primary importance when we work with clients who have neurodevelopmental challenges.

Current interventions for both ID and ASD draw on behavioral models. For Adlerian therapists and counselors, the challenge is in fusing their guiding theory with these behavioral intervention methods. Generally speaking, more abstract methods, as might be used in directive forms of Adlerian therapy or cognitive-behavioral therapy (CBT), may be less applicable for individuals with moderate, severe, or profound levels of ID. Sturmey (2012) clarified that while Applied Behavioral Analysis (ABA) and behavioral modification methods are well established and supported for individuals with ID, interventions that assume a greater degree of cognitive abstraction, like CBT, are less supported from the scholarly scientific literature.

For individuals with ASD, treatment methods involve behavioral training, as well as adaptive-skills training, teaching replacement behaviors, and even relaxation techniques (Wilmshurst, 2011). By far, the most effective treatment for ID and ASD has involved systematic behavioral training. Klintwall et al. (2012) identified ABA-based intervention programs as "first line treatments" (p. 139) for young autistic children. Accordingly, these methods will be described here in a bit more detail for the interested reader.

Applied Behavioral Analysis (ABA) and Related Models

As with other behavioral methods, the emphasis in ABA is on external factors and influences to control, alter, or otherwise modify an individual's behaviors, rather than an exploration of intrapersonal psychological processes (Sturmey, 2012). Although quite repetitive and time consuming, ABA has been largely credited with helping individuals with neurodevelopmental disabilities to learn and to acquire an array of personal skills and adaptive behaviors (Axelrod et al., 2012; Sturmey, 2012).

Common behavioral difficulties that arise in individuals with ASD or ID include tantrums, aggression, self-harm, and repetitive, stereotyped movements. These behaviors are often amenable to change or extinction using behavioral methods, such as ABA or similar interventions (Matson et al., 2012; Sturmey, 2012).

Early on, Lovaas sometimes used aversive training to decrease self-harm or other undesirable behaviors in children. While possibly effective, this approach is not consistent

with Adlerian principles and values. It was also controversial at the time, and Lovaas was criticized for some of these methods (Smith & Eikeseth, 2011). In later years, though, other ABA methods were developed that employed more positive approaches to behavioral change while remaining quite effective (Smith & Eikeseth, 2011). A newer model related to ABA, called Positive Behavior Support (PBS), for example, minimizes punishment and aversive methods to influence behavior, and emphasizes systems-level (class, family) changes that may positively influence targeted behaviors (Wilmshurst, 2011)

Another ABA-related empirically validated approach is called Pivotal Response Therapy (PRT) (Koegel, 2000). To address the problem of scarce resources, PRT aims for more efficient time usage than is usually observed in standard ABA, and for more direct parent involvement (Koegel, 2000).

Finally, a highly intensive, early-intervention application of ABA, called Early Intensive Behavior Intervention (EIBI), appears particularly beneficial in the remediation of language skills and intellectual functions for long durations of time in children (Axelrod et al., 2012).

In addition to behavioral training, other common interventions for ASD and ID involve social skills therapy, occupational therapy, language/speech therapy, psychoeducation, and family therapy.

Case Example: S.

S. is an eight-year-old girl with a history of academic excellence. She consistently scores well above her age and grade levels on school tests and assignments, and is intellectually very curious. Like her father, however, S. has very limited social skills and minimal awareness of the feelings of others. She does not recognize emotions in herself or others, has difficulty empathizing, and strongly prefers to play alone, and enjoys systematic and repetitive tasks involving stacking her blocks. When talking to others, S. gives the appearance of "looking through" them in a largely emotionless way, and her use of language is sophisticated for her age, but also overly complex, formal, and "professorial," making her unpopular with her classmates.

SPECIFIC LEARNING DISORDER

Clinical Presentation

Specific learning disorders (SLD) (often referred to as "learning disabilities" in more common parlance) have also been redefined into a spectrum-based configuration, but less drastically so than with ASD. The subtypes of SLD are still available for clarification in the *DSM-5*, which makes this change less sweeping for SLD. These subtypes involve reading, math, and written expression.

An SLD may involve academic topics such as reading, math, and writing (American Psychiatric Association, 2013). In the transition from *DSM-IV-TR* to *DSM-5*, the diagnosis of an SLD was updated to remove the embedded "discrepancy model" of diagnosis. In that model, test scores on measures of academic achievement in a given area (e.g., math) needed to be significantly lower than expectation, based on the individual's intelligence test scores (American Psychiatric Association 2000, 2013; Kaufmann & von Aster, 2012). This was considered to be outdated and challenged by federal legislation, such as the Individuals with Disabilities Education Act (IDEA), by the time that the *DSM-5* was released in 2013.

The *DSM-5* conceptualization of Specific Learning Disorder (SLD) attempts to reflect current models of etiology and intervention. It has loosened the emphasis on psychometric measures of achievement and intellect, provided other possible methods to establishing and documenting learning problems, and allowed greater latitude about when academic performance difficulties might emerge (American Psychiatric Association, 2013; Kaufmann & von Aster, 2012).

Reading

Perhaps the most common and widely known subtype of an SLD is Dyslexia, which of course involves reading. Dyslexia has been described as a decoding deficit, such that speech–sound relationships are misunderstood (Snowling & Hulme, 2012). Dyslexia, however, is not the only type of reading problem. A second major form of SLD in reading involves poor reading comprehension (Snowling & Hulme, 2012). Some have argued that the *DSM-5* provides minimal coverage for this form of an SLD (Snowling & Hulme, 2012). Their concern was that the *DSM-5* conceptualization of reading-related learning problems is too simplistic, does not reflect the heterogeneous etiologies or symptoms of these disorders, and does not adequately present the comorbid or atypical presentations of these conditions (Snowling 2012; Snowling & Hulme, 2012).

Math

A second major area of SLD involves numeracy and mathematics. Similar to Snowling and Hulme's (2012) concerns involving reading elements of SLD in the *DSM-5*, the same criticisms of lack of specificity may be made for math skills. Like Dyslexia for instance, Dyscalculia represents one well-documented (but not the only) area of math learning problems in the literature. Kaufmann and von Aster (2012) described Dyscalculia as "difficulty acquiring basic arithmetic skills that is not explained by low intelligence or inadequate schooling" (p. 767). And like Dyslexia, Dyscalculia is but one form on the larger spectrum of SLD, with the additional specifier of "With Impairment in Mathematics" (American Psychiatric Association, 2013).

DSM-5 Characterization

As mentioned above, DSM-5 criteria for SLD involves a pattern of learning difficulties and academic performance persisting greater than six months in a specific area of academic skill, such as reading, math, or written expression (American Psychiatric Association, 2013). Criteria involve the specific skills that are deficient, such as aspects of spelling, reading, and math. Other possible causes of these impairments, such as Intellectual Disability and neurologic problems, are specifically ruled out, and the onset of at least some of these academic-related problems must occur in the school years.

Biopsychosocial–Adlerian Conceptualization

The Adlerian concept of organ inferiority once again appears relevant for this set of difficulties. The literature suggests that Adler was more responsive to the concepts of innate struggles and difficulties of a biopsychosocial origin than some of his contemporaries.

Part of Adler's detachment from Freud involved his refusal to concede that anatomy was destiny (Rasmussen & Watkins, 2012). This is a germane perspective when considering the implementation of interventions and remediation tools for individuals with SLD and other neurodevelopmental disorders. Adler's questioning of genetic determinism does not inherently refute the challenges and the sometimes innate aspects of SLD and other neurodevelopmental conditions mentioned here, so much as help us to appreciate the environmental and contextual components within which the individual exists when trying to master these challenges (Rasmussen & Watkins, 2012).

Treatment Considerations

Modern interventions for SLD tend to be highly school based or involve outside tutoring and support for academic skills. For Dyslexia, for instance, there may be education-based skill development focused on enriching a child's phonological skills and phonological awareness (Snowling & Hulme, 2012).

That said, there is a place for Adlerian treatment methods in the remediation of SLD. The incorporation of Adlerian values, such as encouragement and innate human value, when guiding students in the development and strengthening of their problematic academic skills, is particularly suitable. Moreover, drawing on the Adlerian intervention methods of natural consequences leading to less desired outcomes, acting "as if" while skills are being mastered, and appreciating the social context within which these challenges occur, are all helpful approaches to include with the more skill-based school interventions for SLD.

Interventions for SLD typically occur in the context of special education support, educational interventions, and skill-building approaches (Kaufmann & von Aster, 2012; Snowling & Hulme, 2012). From an Adlerian perspective, however, the spirit of these methods, involving skill and conceptualization development in areas of weakness, encouragement, and in augmenting a sense of community, are vital. To assist the individual in a more holistic manner, Individual Psychology foci involving social interest, belongingness, and encouragement within the school and home settings would be optimal for individuals being treated for SLD (Brigman et al., 2011).

Case Example: M.

M. is a 15-year-old boy who is the middle of three children in his family. M. is a gifted athlete, socially skilled, and amiable with his teachers and fellow students. His visual-spatial skills are well developed and he seems to have little difficulty with math. M.'s reading skills have long been below his grade level. As a small child he had significant problems with phonics, or matching words and their respective sounds. He read slowly, lost track of passages easily, could not automatically read certain information, such as letters and numbers, as quickly as his peers. M. sometimes guessed words by the beginning sounds, rather than painfully trying to sound out words to recognize them. He attempted to get by using his logic, making guesses while answering homework questions, or having his mother or girlfriend read and summarize passages for him. As he transitioned to high school, however, these strategies no longer worked for M., and his grades and school performance for reading-intensive classes plummeted.

ATTENTION DEFICIT HYPERACTIVITY DISORDER (ADHD)

Clinical Presentation

ADHD is among the most commonly diagnosed behavioral conditions in American children. Although frequency figures vary somewhat, about 3% to 7% of American school children have been diagnosed with some form of ADHD (Wehmeier et al., 2011). It remains a controversial diagnosis in the academic and treatment settings.

Core symptoms of ADHD involve distractibility, inattention, restlessness, hyperactivity, and disorganization. Symptoms must be present in childhood for the diagnosis of ADHD to be given, and there has been growing evidence in recent decades that remnants of the disorder may persist into adulthood (Maucieri, 2013). Recognizing ADHD can be confusing to clinicians, however. For one thing, it remains difficult to differentiate from other behavioral disorders, and there is a fair amount of comorbidity among these disorders. It appears uncertain whether this is due to symptom overlap or a co-occurrence of different conditions within the same individuals. Webster-Stratton et al. (2011) noted that young children with ADHD were at greater risk for subsequent development of Oppositional Defiant Disorder (ODD) and Conduct Disorder (CD). Other writers have reported that there is a high degree of comorbidity among ADHD, ODD, and CD (Poulton, 2011; Wehmeier et al., 2011). These findings have ramifications for the potential treatment interventions that may be helpful for individuals with ADHD, ODD, and/or CD.

DSM-5 Characterization

Unlike ASD or SLD, ADHD has remained largely categorical in its diagnostic criteria, with less inclusion of a spectrum-oriented model for it in *DSM-5*. The primary symptom clusters of Attention Deficit Hyperactivity Disorder (ADHD) involve inattention and hyperactivity-impulsivity (American Psychiatric Association 2000, 2013). These have remained relatively unchanged over successive versions of the *DSM*. What has changed is some of the wording of the individual symptoms, as well as some related diagnostic criteria, such as the required age of onset. The main modifications of ADHD in *DSM-5* include: an increase in the maximum age of symptom onset from 7 to 12 years; symptom wording with less explicit emphasis on childhood behaviors and experiences; and a decrease in the number of symptoms (for adults).

Three types of ADHD are diagnosable: those with primarily inattentive symptoms; those with primarily hyperactive and impulsive symptoms; and those with a significant number of inattentive, hyperactive, and impulsive symptoms (referred to now as "ADHD, Combined Presentation" in *DSM-5*, as per American Psychiatric Association, 2013). Interestingly, the *DSM-5* now provides for a specifier of "in partial remission" for ADHD, which was not previously available.

Officially, the diagnosis of "Attention Deficit Disorder" (ADD) was discontinued with the *DSM-IV* in 1994, in favor of the subtype ADHD—Predominately Inattentive Type (American Psychiatric Association, 1994). Unofficially, however, the term "ADD" is still pervasively used and referred to in the popular press (Maucieri, 2013).

One criticism of the *DSM-IV* and *DSM-IV-TR* criteria for ADHD was that they were too heavily geared toward the experiences and behaviors of children (American Psychiatric Association, 1994, 2000). This was because ADHD was originally conceptualized as a disorder of childhood; only recently has it been considered to possibly persist into adulthood (Maucieri, 2013). The *DSM-5* has adjusted for the increased acceptance of adult lifespan ADHD symptoms, with symptom criteria for ADHD that are more encompassing of the full lifespan (American Psychiatric Association, 2013; Maucieri, 2013).

Biopsychosocial–Adlerian Conceptualization

In an Adlerian conceptualization, certain characteristics and behaviors may correspond with the birth order of a child within a family (Berger & Felsenthal-Berger, 2009; Monte, 1995). Drawing on this theory, Berger and Felsenthal-Berger (2009) investigated if birth order might influence which children in a family might be more likely to develop ADHD. While they did not find a statistically significant difference among specific birth positions and probability of developing ADHD, the authors did reasonably investigate the complex environmental and genetic bases that are thought to interact and lead to the emergence of ADHD early on in the lifespan. Focusing on this biopsychosocial conceptualization of ADHD, a range of Adlerian techniques and ideas may be applied with children who have conduct issues and neurodevelopmental concerns, including ADHD. Some of these are mentioned in the section on ADHD treatment considerations.

Treatment Considerations

The current standard of care for ADHD often involves stimulant medication and ancillary behavioral, cognitive-behavioral, family, and/or psychoeducational therapeutic interventions (Maucieri, 2013; Wehmeier et al., 2011). All of these counseling interventions may draw upon core Adlerian values of encouragement, empowerment, and the family as a community.

Webster-Stratton et al. (2011) supported the potential efficacy of psychosocial interventions that include parent training in young children with ADHD.

Another recent phenomenon in the remediation of ADHD symptoms has been the use of computerized training programs—such as CogMed, Jungle Memory, or Cognifit—to train working memory skills, which may be impaired in individuals with ADHD. Individual studies of these programs were initially optimistic, although a meta-analysis of 23 studies completed by Melby-Lervåg and Hulme (2013) suggested that the positive effects were time limited and did not tend to generalize to other tasks.

Unlike ASD and SLD, medication has been used quite extensively in the treatment of ADHD. It has been accepted as a core component of the treatment of ADHD, and has typically involved psychostimulants (Maucieri, 2013). Medication, in particular, has been effective in treating the distraction and reduced focus in ADHD, rather than the social or organizational challenges of the disorder (Maucieri, 2013).

For other elements and problems related to ADHD, interventions and support come from behavioral and CBT therapy, psychoeducation, parent training, coaching, couples therapy, and involvement in peer-support groups, such as CHADD and ADDA (Maucieri, 2013). Because of the often long history of personal struggles and sense of failures associated with ADHD, Adlerian values involving encouragement and value within a community are particularly important within the therapeutic process.

One recent article documented clinical success by using a combination of adventure-based and Adlerian play therapy models for children with ADHD (e.g., Portrie-Bethke et al., 2009). In this program the authors adopt a strengths-based approach rooted in the counseling wellness model, which tends to de-emphasize pathology and places greater weight on encouragement, prevention, experiential learning, and active teaching (Portrie-Bethke et al., 2009). These concepts are congruent with Adlerian values and ideas, including use of an action orientation, de-emphasis on psychopathology, creation of an encouraging, supportive environment, and a pragmatically rooted treatment program.

Case Example: L.

L. is a 35-year-old female working in a high-stress law firm. She has a long history of distractibility, poor focus, disorganization, anger problems, and severe procrastination. As early as first grade, L.'s teachers noted her behavioral problems, restlessness, and hyperactivity. In her teens and early 20s L. used marijuana to help her focus and relax, but this led to other concerns for her, and so she stopped using the drug at 25. She is often able to "pull through" on her tasks and assignments with an eleventh-hour injection of hyperfocus and increased arousal and energy when her deadlines are fast approaching. In addition to her innate cognitive skill, these methods were largely how she completed law school. In her current position, however, the structure of the job, the highly regulated oversight of all employees, and the persistent demands of her work have all combined to undermine her usual coping and work skills. At the point that L. initiated counseling and a medication evaluation for her ADHD, she was on probation at her employer and had begun to falsify some of her timesheet documents to try to cover up for her persistent struggles.

TOURETTE'S SYNDROME

Clinical Presentation

Tourette's syndrome (TS) is relatively well known to the general public due to its portrayal in films and television. These portrayals are not always totally accurate, however. Not all individuals with TS for instance experience *copralalia* (involuntary utterance of obscene and/or offensive language), and individual symptoms of TS can be transient and changing, even while the syndrome itself persists. The diagnostic criteria for TS in *DSM-5* have changed little from prior editions of the manual. The combination of motor and vocal tics—though not necessarily simultaneously—are the hallmark symptoms of TS (American Psychiatric Association, 2000, 2013; Leclerc et al., 2011). The condition overwhelmingly impacts males over females. TS is also frequently comorbid with other neuropsychiatric conditions, such as OCD, ADHD, SLD, and anxiety (Leclerc et al., 2011).

Unlike some of the other neurodevelopmental disorders mentioned in this chapter, the onset of TS may not be evident very early on in the lifespan. This is in part because early tics, such as repetitive eye blinking, may not be highly noticeable, or may be covered up for some time. The *DSM-5* indicates that tic onset usually begins between ages four and six years old, but the peak severity of TS symptoms may not manifest until ages 10 to 12 (American Psychiatric Press, 2013). Tics may change over time and increase or decrease in severity due to factors such as fatigue, anxiety, or excitement (American Psychiatric Press, 2013).

DSM-5 Characterization

Tourette's syndrome (TS) is virtually unchanged in the *DSM-5* relative to early editions of the manual (American Psychiatric Press 2000; 2013). The key elements of TS involve: an onset before age 18 years; the presence of both motor and vocal tics at some time (not necessarily simultaneously) in the course of the condition; persistence of tic symptoms for more than a year since the initial onset; the tics must not be due to another cause or condition. Individuals who have only ever had motor tics or vocal tics, but not both in the course of the condition, would likely meet criteria for Persistent Motor or Vocal Tic Disorder, rather than TS.

Biopsychosocial–Adlerian Conceptualization

Remediation of TS, like other neurodevelopmental disorders, must consider Adler's three life tasks of love, work, and friendship (Wolf et al., 2012). With TS, though, symptom presentation and severity may be particularly problematic for these tasks, due in part to the reactions and misperceptions of others about the behaviors of the individual with TS. More than the other disorders, the symptoms of TS are often first interpreted as willful misbehavior or intentional efforts to disrupt order. Even in childhood it is common for those with TS to be mislabeled as defiant, rebellious, and impulsive within the school setting.

While awareness of TS has increased in the past few decades, it is still not well recognized or understood in some school and treatment settings. From an Adlerian view, more needs to be done to help individuals with TS and the often comorbid conditions of OCD, ADHD, or depression. While the usual interventions employed for TS (see below) may decrease the problematic tic symptoms of TS, considerable damage in self-esteem and social efficacy remains from the after effects of the disorder itself and the reactions of others to the individual with TS. A successful counseling approach for individuals impacted by TS would include not only a reduction in tics, but assistance to help the individual feel more encouraged, proficient, and connected with his/her greater sense of community (Brigman et al., 2011). Conditions like TS are often such isolative experiences for the individual impacted directly by them, and a reduction in tics alone does not address these struggles.

Treatment Considerations

Tourette's Syndrome (TS) is often treated with a combination of medication and cognitive-behavioral therapy (CBT). The most prescribed medications for TS include clonidine, haloperidol, and risperdone (Leclerc et al., 2011). Areas of focus in CBT interventions for Tourette's Syndrome involve psychoeducation, exposure and response prevention, and habit reversal for the tics themselves (Leclerc et al., 2011). As noted in the passage above, while the core treatment for TS involves the reduction or extinction of tics, the enhancement of social skills, strengthened self-esteem, psychoeducation, and community-based support are essential in the complete remediation approach for TS.

Case Example: J.

J. is a ten-year-old boy who struggles with his grades in fourth grade. About two years ago he developed motor tics, which began as repetitive eye blinking. Since that time the location and severity of his tics have changed. More recently J. has exhibited vocal tics, such as barking, grunting, and coughing loudly, which initially caused him to be labeled as a behavioral problem in his school. With intervention and special education advocacy, the school personnel have come to appreciate that these are symptoms of J.'s TS, rather than willful attempts to misbehave. J.'s tics worsen with stress and fatigue. He has benefitted from medication, psychoeducation, and behavioral therapy to manage his TS, although the symptoms have not completely remitted.

Conduct Disorders in the *DSM-5*

The conduct disorders tend to involve difficulties with behavioral control, aggression, and violations of social norms. Two major disorders within this group are Conduct Disorder (CD) and Oppositional Defiant Disorder (ODD). In *DSM-IV* and *DSM-IV-TR* these disorders were grouped with the conditions that tend to manifest in childhood or adolescence (American Psychiatric Association 1994, 2000). In the *DSM-5*, these disorders are more clearly linked with the diagnosis of Antisocial Personality Disorder.

CONDUCT DISORDER

Clinical Presentation

The diagnosis of Conduct Disorder (CD) represents the more severe spectrum of behavioral problems occurring within childhood or adolescence. Barry et al. (2013) described Conduct Disorder as a condition in which the individual repeatedly violates social norms and the rights of others. *DSM-5* indicates that the prevalence of Conduct Disorder is fairly consistent across several countries, and that CD is diagnosed more in males than in females (American Psychiatric Association, 2013). The *DSM-5* briefly mentions that CD might be overdiagnosed in certain settings, such as high-crime areas, but the manual does not directly address past concerns about racial bias and rater bias in the diagnosis of CD, ODD, and Antisocial Personality Disorder (American Psychiatric Association, 2013). Common comorbid conditions with CD include both ADHD and ODD (American Psychiatric Association, 2013),

DSM-5 Characterization

Symptomatic behaviors in Conduct Disorder by *DSM-5* criteria may include bullying, fighting with others, theft, property damage, and/or physical harm to animals (American Psychiatric Association, 2013; Barry et al., 2013). Broad symptom groupings in the *DSM-5* conceptualization of CD may also involve aggression to people and animals, theft, deceit, and significant violation of rules (American Psychiatric Association, 2000, 2013).

The diagnosis of CD has been used as a precursor to the diagnosis of Antisocial Personality Disorder in adulthood, although not all individuals who meet criteria for CD would necessarily later meet criteria for Antisocial Personality Disorder. Still, many of the criteria for both of the disorders do actually overlap (American Psychiatric Association, 2013). This is, in part, due to the fact that the diagnosis of Antisocial Personality Disorder has long required the individual meets the criteria for CD as a minor, first (American Psychiatric Association, 2000, 2013).

While *DSM-IV-TR* provided subtypes of Conduct Disorder based on age of onset (American Psychiatric Association, 2000), the *DSM-5* provides not only these subtypes, but also specifiers involving behavioral constellations (e.g., involving lack of remorse, lack of empathy, shallow or limited affect), as well as symptom severity levels (American Psychiatric Association, 2013). These additional codes may be important for case conceptualization and treatment planning, as the literature on Conduct Disorder suggests that earlier onset is correlated with a poor adult outcome (Barry et al., 2013).

Biopsychosocial–Adlerian Conceptualization

From an Adlerian perspective the limited opportunities, lack of encouragement, and distressed social environments in the development of individuals who develop Conduct Disorder play important roles in the eventual manifestation of their behavioral problems and symptoms. While genetic or biological factors may predispose an individual toward some of these problems, the lack of an enriching, supportive, and encouraging environment is ultimately what unlocks this potential and induces the development of a conduct or related disorder. The key intervention from an Adlerian view in the management of conduct or related disorders is therefore preventative and wellness based.

At a social level, can environmental components be altered through parent training, school-based interventions, and the augmentation of social interest, such that conduct and other related disorders do not develop? This is a question likely to be posed by an Adlerian theorist. For once these conditions take hold in an impacted individual, they are fiercely resistant to change and have profoundly negative effects on the social interest of the individual him/herself, and those around the individual. Proactive and preventative methods to reduce the development of Conduct Disorder and Oppositional Defiant Disorder are therefore vital.

Treatment Considerations

Early intervention for CD is crucial, since delays lead to poorer prognosis. Earlier onset is also less positive for a hopeful prognosis: Webster-Stratton et al. (2011) noted that early-onset Conduct Disorder was among the most refractory of all psychiatric disorders. The impetus for early intervention for CD is consistent with the Adlerian conceptualization described above, and the need to focus more distinctly on preventive measures that enhance social interest and encouragement, such that the environmental factors that often lead to the development of Conduct Disorder are minimized,

Compared with the neurodevelopmental disorders, and more similar to Antisocial Personality Disorder, the treatment of CD may be more challenging for clinicians. Complicating issues may involve commitment to treatment; highly refractory symptoms and behaviors; strong environmental reinforcement of behaviors; and perhaps biologically based temperament. Nonetheless, several treatment approaches have been explored for CD, and interventions with younger children may be more effective. CBT methods may be used with social modeling, but issues of motivation and generalization to everyday life remain problematic. One method, using a program called the Incredible Years, described below to help treat ODD (Webster-Stratton et al., 2011), might also apply to treating CD.

Case Example: R.

R. was born into an upper-class suburban family, but his home life was marred with parental substance abuse, inconsistent and extreme disciplinary methods, and neglect. The family was unpredictable and emotionally unsafe for the children. Although a bright youngster, by age 10 R. had begun to skip school; by age 12 he stayed out until with friends until the following morning on weekends, stole petty items frequently from stores, smoked cigarettes, and burned down his neighbor's shed for fun. At age 14 he stole a golf cart from a local golf course and faced legal charges for it. R. was quite charming and cunning, and was able to have the charges dropped with probation. Within months of the charges being dropped, though, R. was accused of trying to engage in sexual contact with a non-consenting classmate, whom he thought had a crush on him. R. began to use alcohol and marijuana frequently, fought occasionally with classmates, and failed most of his classes in school.

OPPOSITIONAL DEFIANT DISORDER

Clinical Presentation

Oppositional Defiant Disorder (ODD) reflects a less severe form of behavioral problems and defiance than may be found with either CD or Antisocial Personality Disorder. Some individuals, however, may progress from ODD to CD, and then finally to Antisocial Personality Disorder in adulthood. Whereas violation of social norms, interpersonal aggression, rule and law violations, and destructive behaviors tend to dominate the *DSM-5* diagnostic criteria for CD and Antisocial Personality Disorder, the issues that occur with ODD are milder (American Psychiatric Association, 2013). ODD-related behaviors involve irritability, difficulty managing anger, defiance, purposefully annoying others, and deflecting blame on others.

DSM-5 Characterization

The *DSM-5* criteria for ODD involve hostile and negative behaviors, irritability, deliberately irritating others, and lack of personal responsibility for one's own behaviors (American Psychiatric Association, 2013). Changes in criteria for ODD from the *DSM-IV-TR* to *DSM-5* were relatively small, but a few were made. In both the *DSM-IV-TR* and the *DSM-5* a specific time duration is specified for the individual A criteria. The *DSM-5* does, however, provide guidelines of symptom frequency to distinguish ODD behaviors from more normal presentations (American Psychiatric Association, 2013). These frequency guidelines subjectively appear roughly similar to those that have been used in previous editions of the *DSM* for symptom frequency in Major Depressive Disorder (American Psychiatric Association, 2000).

Biopsychosocial–Adlerian Conceptualization

Similar to the Adlerian conceptualization involving CD, for ODD there is a sense of diminished social interest, a developmental matrix of discouragement and minimal support, and a lack of behavioral consequences, which all interact with a biological predisposition, and thus lead to the development of ODD symptoms. The symptoms and social effects are less severe and problematic for ODD than they are for CD, however, and so the hope for changing behaviors and nullifying symptoms of ODD with psychoeducation, parent training, environmental modifications, and encouragement are more germane for this disorder than for CD. Even so, the remediation of ODD, particularly later in life or in situations with highly entrenched negative environments, remains challenging.

Treatment Considerations

There are a number of comprehensive treatment programs available for ODD, which are empirically promising. One such treatment program developed for ODD is called the Incredible Years Parent Training program. It has also been applied to working with young children who have ADHD (Webster-Stratton et al., 2011).

The Incredible Years Parent Training program as administered by Webster-Stratton et al. (2011) was comprehensive, and it involved two-hour weekly group sessions over a course of 20 weeks. Among other things, the groups focused on support and helped the children to develop skills in a range of areas, including problem solving, regulating emotions, and establishing and maintaining regular home and school patterns. Problem solving between parents and teachers was also incorporated into the program. Coaching methods were employed, and other skills, such as identifying and expressing feelings, anger management methods, and developing teamwork, were introduced in a related program.

Case Example: T.

T. is the second oldest child in his family of origin, and the oldest male of the children. Early on, T. showed signs of behavioral impulsivity and spitefulness in kindergarten, by easily losing his temper with peers, challenging his teacher and other authority figures, and enjoying getting on the nerves of others. When another child angered him, T. caused damage to the other child's bike. As he grew up T. bullied his younger siblings, displayed hostility toward his peers and instructors, and frequently ignored rules at home and at school. He had difficulty taking responsibility for his actions and typically attempted to coerce others into redirecting the blame for his misdeeds toward his siblings or classmates. In adolescence, T.'s behavioral issues have spiked. More than anything T. has enjoyed causing strife, shifting conversations to upset others or to intentionally create conflict, and persistently "needling" others with accusations and negative comments, thrilled when they finally express frustration and exasperation with his comments and behaviors.

Concluding Note

A number of changes and adjustments have been made in the transition from the *DSM-IV-TR* to the *DSM-5*. The *DSM-5* was initially met with some skepticism and controversy, but the long-range assessment of the document is yet to be determined. Major changes in the areas of neurodevelopmental disorders and conduct disorders have involved the development of a spectrum-based approach for the autistic-related disorders and the specific learning disorders. Other diagnostic and related changes and adjustment for conditions such as ADHD, Intellectual Disability, Tourette's Syndrome, Conduct Disorder, and Oppositional Defiant Disorder have been less drastic, but have still modified the conceptualization of these disorders for clinicians and researchers, to some extent.

Intervention methods for most of these disorders have been directive in nature, typically relying on various forms of behavioral, or sometimes cognitive-behavioral, treatment approaches. This does not necessarily preclude Adlerian theory from playing an important role in working with individuals impacted by neurodevelopmental or conduct disorders. The use of encouragement, fostering a sense of community, and helping clients to appreciate the natural consequences of problematic behaviors will all greatly enrich this therapeutic work, regardless of the other methods and interventions upon which we draw. Adler and Dreikurs both emphasized that we know and appreciate what is needed in a given situation (Rasmussen & Watkins, 2012), and this is particularly salient when we help individuals with sometimes complex challenges, due to neurodevelopmental or conduct disorders.

References

Addington, A.M. & Rapoport, J.L. (2012). Annual research review: Impact of advances in genetics in understanding developmental psychopathology. *Journal of Child Psychology and Psychiatry*, 53, pp. 510–518.

American Psychiatric Association (1994). *Diagnostic and Statistical Manual of Mental Disorders, Fourth Edition*. Washington, DC: American Psychiatric Publishing.

American Psychiatric Association (2000). *Diagnostic and Statistical Manual of Mental Disorders, Fourth Edition (Text Revision)*. Washington, DC: American Psychiatric Publishing.

American Psychiatric Association (2013). *Diagnostic and Statistical Manual of Mental Disorders, Fifth Edition*. Arlington, VA: American Psychiatric Publishing.

Axelrod, S., McElrath, K.K., & Wine, B. (2012). Applied behavior analysis: Autism and beyond. *Behavioral Interventions*, 27, pp. 1–15.

Barry, C.T., Golmaryami, F.N., Rivera-Hudson, N., & Frick, P.J. (2013). Evidence-based assessment of conduct disorder: Current considerations and preparation for DSM-5. *Professional Psychology: Research and Practice*, 44, pp. 56–63.

Berger, I. & Felsenthal-Berger, N. (2009). Attention-deficit hyperactivity disorder (ADHD) and birth order. *Journal of Child Neurology*, 24, pp. 692–696.

Brigman, G., Villares, E., & Webb, L. (2011). The efficacy of individual psychology approaches for improving student achievement and behavior. *Journal of Individual Psychology*, 67, pp. 408–419.

Cebula, K.R. (2011). Applied behavior analysis programs for autism: Sibling psychosocial adjustment during and following intervention use. *Journal of Autism and Developmental Disorders*, 42, pp. 847–862.

Coghill, D. & Seth, S. (2011). Do the diagnostic criteria for ADHD need to change? Comments on the preliminary proposals of the DSM-5 ADHD and disruptive behavior disorders committee. *European Child and Adolescent Psychiatry*, 20, pp. 75–81.

Coghill, D. & Sonuga-Barke, E.J.S. (2012). Annual research review: Categories versus dimensions in the classification and conceptualisation of child and adolescent mental disorders—implications of recent empirical study. *Journal of Child Psychology and Psychiatry*, 55, pp. 469–489.

Day, S.X. (2007). *Groups in Practice*. Boston, MA: Lahaska Press.

Hare, D.J. (2012). Letters: Defining learning disability. *The Psychologist*, 25, p. 562.

Hartshorne, T.S. & Herr, M.D. (1983). An Adlerian approach to autism. *Individual Psychology: The Journal of Adlerian Theory and Research, and Practice*, 39, pp. 394–401.

Huber, R.J. & Zivalich, D.M. (2004). Loovas's behavioral treatment of autism viewed from an Adlerian perspective. *Journal of Individual Psychology*, 60, pp. 348–354.

Jones, K.D. (2012). Dimensional and cross-cutting assessment in the DSM-5. *Journal of Counseling and Development*, 90, pp. 481–487.

Kaufmann, L. & von Aster, M. (2012). The diagnosis and management of dyscalculia. *Deutsches Aerzteblatt International*, 109, pp. 767–778.

Kehle, T.J., Bray, M.A., Byer-Alcorace, G.F., Theodore, L.A., & Kovac, L.M. (2012). Augmented self-modeling as an intervention for selective autism. *Psychology in the Schools*, 49, pp. 93–103.

Kennan, K. (2012). Mind the gap: Assessing impairment among children affected by proposed revisions to the diagnostic criteria for oppositional defiant disorder. *Journal of Abnormal Psychology*, 121, pp. 352–359.

Klintwall, L., Gillberg, C., Bölte, S., & Fernell, E. (2012). The efficacy of intensive behavioral intervention for children with autism: A matter of allegiance? *Journal of Autism and Developmental Disorders*, 42, pp. 139–140.

Koegel, L.K. (2000). Interventions to facilitate communication in autism. *Journal of Autism and Developmental Disorders*, 30, pp. 383–391.

Leclerc, J., O'Connor, K.P., Forget, J., & Lavoie, M.E. (2011). Behavioral program for managing explosive outbursts in children with Tourette syndrome. *Journal of Developmental and Physical Disabilities*, 23, pp. 33–47.

Lord, C. & Jones, R.M. (2012). Annual research review: Re-thinking the classification of autistic spectrum disorders. *Journal of Child Psychology and Psychiatry*, 53, pp. 490–509.

Matson, J.L., Neal, D., & Kozlowski, A.M. (2012). Treatment for the challenging behaviours of adults with intellectual disabilities. *Canadian Journal of Psychiatry*, 57, pp. 587–592.

Maucieri, L. (2013). ADD, ADHD, and adults: Sorting it all out. In L. Maucieri & J. Carlson (Eds.), *The Distracted Couple: The Impact of ADHD on Adult Relationships*. London: Crown House.

Melby-Lervåg, M. & Hulme, C. (2013). Is working memory training effective? A meta-analytic review. *Developmental Psychology*, 49, pp. 270–291.

Mosak, H.H. (1995). Adlerian psychotherapy. In R.J. Corsini & D. Wedding (Eds.), *Current Psychotherapies* (5th edn.). Itasca, IL: F.E. Peacock.

Monte, C.F. (1995). *Beneath the Mask: An Introduction to Theories of Personality* (5th edn.). Fort Worth, TX: Harcourt Brace.

Moseley, D.S., Tonge, B.J., Brereton, A.V., & Einfeld, S.L. (2011). Psychiatric comorbidity in adolescents and young adults with autism. *Journal of Mental Health Research in Intellectual Disabilities*, 4, pp. 229–243.

Peluso, P.R. (2008) Book review of *Adlerian Therapy: Theory and Practice*. *Journal of Counseling and Development*, 86, pp. 505–506.

Portrie-Bethke, T.L., Hill, N.R., & Bethke, J.G. (2009). Strength-based mental health counseling for children with ADHD: An integrative model of adventure-based counseling and Adlerian play therapy. *Journal of Mental Health Counseling*, 31, pp. 323–338.

Poulton, A.S. (2011). Time to redefine the diagnosis of oppositional defiant disorder. *Journal of Paediatrics and Child Health*, 47, pp. 332-334.

Rasmussen, P.R. & Watkins, K.L. (2012). Advice from the masters II: A conversation with Robert L. Powers and Jane Griffith. *Journal of Individual Psychology*, 68, pp. 112–135.

Ryland, H.K., Hysing, M., Posserud, M.B., Gilberg, C., & Lundervold, A.J. (2012). Autism spectrum symptoms in children with neurological disorders. *Child and Adolescent Psychiatry and Mental Health*, 6, p. 34.

Smith, T. & Eikeseth, S. (2011). O. Ivar Lovaas: Pioneer of applied behavior analysis and intervention for children with autism. *Journal of Autism and Developmental Disorders*, 41, pp. 375–378.

Snowling, M.J. (2012). (Editorial) Seeking a new characterisation of learning disorders. *Journal of Child Psychology and Psychiatry*, 53, pp. 1–2.

Snowling, M.J. & Hulme, C. (2012). Annual research review: The nature and classification of reading disorders—a commentary on proposals for DSM-5. *Journal of Child Psychology and Psychiatry*, 53, pp. 593–607.

Sonstegard, M.A. (1998). The theory and practice of Adlerian group counseling and psychotherapy. *Journal of Individual Psychology*, 54, pp. 217–250.

Sturmey, P. (2012). Treatment of psychopathology in people with intellectual and other disabilities. *Canadian Journal of Psychiatry*, 57, pp. 593–600.

Sweeney, T.J., Myers, J.E., & Stephan, J.B. (2006). Integrating developmental counseling and therapy assessment with Adlerian early recollections. *Journal of Individual Psychology*, 62, pp. 251–269.

Vanheule, S. (2012). Diagnosis in the field of psychotherapy: A plea for an alternative to the DSM-5.x. *Psychology and Psychotherapy: Theory, Research and Practice*, 85, pp. 128–142.

Wakefield, J.C. (2013). DSM-5: An overview of changes and controversies. *Clinical Social Work Journal*, 41, pp. 139–154.

Webster-Stratton, C.H., Reid, M.J., & Beauchaine, T. (2011). Combining parent and child training for young children with ADHD. *Journal of Child and Adolescent Psychology*, 40, pp. 191–203.

Wehmeier, P.M., Schacht, A., Dittman, R.W., Helsberg, K., Schneider-Fresenius, C., Lehmann, M., ... & Ravens-Sieberer, U. (2011). Effect of atomoxetine on quality of life and family burden: Results from a randomized, placebo-controlled, double-blind study in children and adolescents with ADHD and comorbid oppositional defiant or conduct disorder. *Quality of Life Research*, 20, pp. 691–702.

Wilmshurst, L. (2011). *Childhood and Adolescent Psychopathology: A Casebook* (2nd edn.). Los Angeles, CA: Sage.

Wolf, C.P., Thompson, I.A., & Smith-Adcock, S. (2012). Wellness in counselor preparation: Promoting individual well-being. *Journal of Individual Psychology*, 68, pp. 164–181.

14 Substance Use and Addictive Disorders

Mark T. Blagen

Substance use and abuse, including alcohol and illicit drug use, costs in the United States are estimated to be nearly $400 billion annually (National Institute on Alcohol Abuse and Alcoholism, 2008). Although the economic costs are extremely high, the human tragedy of these costs goes well beyond what can be calculated in terms of lost potential, shattered families, individual and family stress, and loss and grief. This chapter will provide ways of understanding and treating addiction with the hope that a better understanding will assist in alleviating some of the national tragedy addiction has become.

Over the years, as with other mental disorders, the *Diagnostic and Statistical Manual of Mental Disorders (DSM)* has evolved its definition of what addiction is. The latest iteration, the *DSM-5*, is certainly not without critics, but nonetheless has evolved our understanding of what addiction is in a very profound way.

Perhaps the most significant change relates to how the abuse and dependence categories of the *DSM-IV* have now been combined into a single continuum labeled Use Disorders, for ten classes (alcohol, opiates, stimulants, cannabis, etc.) of drugs, with specific modifiers of mild, moderate, and severe, depending on the degree of use.

Another major change the *DSM-5* has made is the inclusion of Gambling Disorder. This is a radical departure from the *DSM-IV*, which considered pathological gambling an impulse-control disorder not elsewhere classified. So deciding that Gambling Disorder is a substance-related and addictive disorder rather than an impulse-control disorder is an important change. However, why has activity such as compulsive spending, exercise, work, and Internet use not found its way into the Substance-Related and Addictive Disorders section of the *DSM-5*, even though ample neurological imaging empirical data (Amen, Willeumier, & Johnson, 2012; Blum et al., 2012; Karim & Chaudri, 2012; Yin, 2008) suggests that these activities are indeed similar to addictive disorders? The short answer is that the authors feel that there is not enough peer-reviewed data to support such a move (American Psychiatric Association, 2013). Clinically, what has been seen is an uncanny resemblance between compulsive use and addiction to such drugs as cocaine and alcohol. The same can be said for numerous other activities and behaviors. The movement of Gambling Disorder to this section, and including Internet addiction in the appendix (conditions for further study), seems to indicate that as the empirical and peer-reviewed studies continue to support these conditions as addictions, the *DSM* will include these also.

So, if criticism from both ends of the spectrum means those who developed the *DSM-5* did a good job, a good job they have done. From one end of the spectrum there are those who decry that "normal" behavior is being pathologized, and from the other end of the spectrum there are those who state that behaviors that become extreme, take away from normal life processes, and are not modified by negative life circumstances (in other words meet Substance Disorder milestones) should be included in the *DSM*.

Disorders to be covered in this chapter are: Alcohol Use Disorder; Cannabis Use Disorder; Opioid Use Disorder; Stimulant Use Disorder; Sedative, Hypnotic, or Anxiolytic Use Disorder; and Gambling Disorder.

Biopsychosocial Conceptualization of Addiction

With many diseases it is the confluence of multiple risk factors that causes the disease, with no definitive smoking gun. So too it is with addiction; however, with addiction we have had a model that has gained a great deal of acceptance in recent times. This model is commonly referred to as the biopsychosocial theory of causality.

What follows is a closer look at each specific component—biology, psychology, and sociology—which conspires to cause addiction. And even though we will initially look at each factor separately, keep in mind that these discrete factors work together to cause addiction.

Biological (Neurological) Factors

As early as the 1960s the American Medical Association declared alcoholism a disease (American Medical Association, 1966), but unfortunately in the 1980s the Supreme Court, in a disputed decision, determined alcoholism to be "willful misconduct" (Miller & Hester, 1995). But by 1997, primarily due to technological advances, the evidence for determining addiction to be a "brain disease" was clear and mounting. Leshner (1997), in an article entitled "Addiction Is a Brain Disease, and it Matters," clearly stated the evidence and argument for this premise. And since 1997 the neurological understanding of addiction has greatly increased, and is compelling and impressive. The American Society of Addiction Medicine (ASAM) determination in March of 2011 (ASAM, 2011a) and subsequent press release in September of 2011 (ASAM, 2100b) were a natural consequence of this evolution of the evidence. The following will briefly explain the meaning of some of this research.

How does this neurological imperative occur? In general there seem to be three basis for this. The first basis has to do with "dysregulations (abnormalities in neurotransmitter functioning) of mesolimbic neurotransmitter systems in the brain" (Erickson & White, 2009, p. 339). A second basis is related to prolonged exposure of the brain due to drug use. This causes brain changes leading to deficits in cognition and memory (Gatley et al., 2005). A third cause relates to psychosocial stressors such as trauma (Erickson, 2007). In the first case there is ample evidence that this dysregulation can, and often does, pre-exist substance use. In other words, a genetic component for addiction does exist (Erickson, 2007). And, according to Erickson (2007), prolonged use can cause both dysregulation and cognitive deficits. In many individuals it is a combination of factors that creates this neurologically based out-of-control use.

Even in a brief conservation with someone who has experienced this out-of-control usage there is a sense of driving a car that has suddenly lost its steering. No matter how hard the driver attempts to steer the car, the car is hopelessly out of control. That seems to be the experience of addiction—no matter how hard the addict tries to control their usage, the addiction will not be controlled. Neurologically, the necessary components are not working properly to allow for appropriate decision-making and control.

Psychological Factors

Psychological factors generally fall into three categories. The first factor relates to issues such as self-esteem and self-worth (Regier et al., 1990). The second factor relates to the self-medication of pre-existing psychological conditions, such as depression or anxiety, that initially seem to respond to alcohol or other drug usage (Regier et al., 1990). And the third factor relates to the correlation of Antisocial Personality Disorder and addictive behavior (Moos, 2007). In general, psychological factors explain why a person may initially use alcohol or other drugs, and why they may continue this usage. Psychological factors often lead to addiction. Psychological addiction can occur to any psychoactive substance (Fisher & Harrison, 2009).

Low self-esteem and self-worth will often create in individuals a negative feeling state that will often lead to using alcohol or other drugs as a way of feeling better and escaping (Burrow-Sanchez, 2006). With this comes learning (that this actually works, even if for a very short period), and with the learning more use. Early intervention is often effective, in many counseling strategies helping to help an individual to experience him or herself in a more real and positive way (Burrow-Sanchez, 2006). However, without this intervention an individual may become psychologically addicted, or either rapidly or over time alter neurological functioning that then leads to physiological addiction. It is important to recognize that developmentally, achievement motivation or recognizing what a person is good at or has a passion for occurs in adolescence and young adulthood. Achievement motivation is a strong protective factor or moderator for alcohol or drug abuse. Unfortunately, early use of alcohol or other drugs can derail this normal development. Also, it is important to understand that the adolescent brain is still developing, so early exposure to alcohol and drugs is related to greater likelihood of addiction later in life (American Society of Addiction Medicine, 2011b).

The self-medication of pre-existing psychological conditions as an explanation for alcohol or drug use makes intuitive sense and often does exist, but, in general, this self-medication only works for a period of time, and in fact can make the pre-existing condition worse. Clinically this is seen as a strategy that once worked but that no longer does; however, the continued alcohol or drug use does at least provide minimal relief, so it continues. The strong correlation between childhood trauma and Post-Traumatic Stress Disorder with alcohol or other drug use suggests that this kind of self-medication is common and at least somewhat helpful for the individual (Brady, Back, & Coffey, 2004). There are also correlations between various forms of psychosis and problematic alcohol or other drug use, and between Bipolar Disorder and alcohol or other drug use (Regier et al., 1990). Motivation of alcohol and other drug use (AOD) use with these disorders varies from relief to enhancement of certain symptoms.

Individuals who have been diagnosed with Conduct Disorder or Antisocial Personality Disorder are at increased risk for drug abuse or addiction. The increased risk is estimated to be approximately 30% of those with this diagnosis, and this is a 300% increase over the general population (Krueger et al., 2002). The explanation for this increase is not complete, but most likely relates to executive functioning within the brain and poor impulse control.

Sociological or Environmental Factors

As with psychological factors, environmental factors explain the initiation of AOD use, the continuation of the use that can result in addiction. These factors include easy availability, cultural or sub-cultural normalization, peer influence, parental influence, low socio-economic class and associated environmental stressors, and existing in a condition of little or no hope (Connors & Tarbox, 1985; McCarty, 1985).

Although easy availability may need no further explanation in how this is a factor for AOD use and abuse, several points should be made. The first is that alcohol marketers know that availability is the key to selling their product. As a result, the alcohol industry is very aggressive in rescinding any policies that restrict availability. The premise of this factor is that if a drug is available, it will be used by a larger percentage of the population, abused by a larger percentage, and some will become addicted.

Anytime a drug is "normalized" within a segment of a population, that drug will be used by a percentage of that population. We see this with underage drinking by college students, smokeable heroin use by young servicemen in Southeast Asia during the Vietnam conflict, and cocaine use in the '80s by young professionals. In each of these populations, use and addiction are at higher rates than in the general population.

Peer and parental influence are consistently seen in the prevention literature as primary motivations for teens to use nicotine and other drugs (Burrow-Sanchez, 2006). Even when other prosocial factors exist, these two influences remain key factors for the commencement of AOD use.

Environmental stressors, such as securing the basic life necessities of shelter, food, and safety, have been correlated with higher use of AOD and with a present versus future-time orientation. A mediating factor or explanation as to why so many who struggle with day-to-day living do not succumb to AOD use includes the condition of hope.

When hope exists, the realization that a behavior or activity is counterindicated becomes a part of the reality, and a choice can be made to discontinue that activity or behavior. The converse is also true. If a person exists with little or no hope, AOD use is viewed very differently.

From the above, it is clear as to why the biopsychosocial theory of addiction causality is so attractive. In reality, from a clinical perspective, a vast majority of addicted individuals experience a combination of these factors—the more factors, the more likely a person will become addicted. But the over-riding factor seems to be neurological dysregulation. This is the risk factor that is more than likely to cause addiction. And as mentioned above, this dysregulation can pre-exist prior to exposure to psychoactive substances (a genetic predisposition), as a result of prolonged use of psychoactive substances, or as a result of trauma.

Adlerian Conceptualization of Substance-Use and Non-Substance-Related Disorders

Adlerian psychology is well suited to both describe addiction etiology and to provide a helpful framework for clinicians to treat addicted individuals. This is in part because Adlerian Psychology is phenomenological, teleological, and holistic. These three characteristics of Adlerian Psychology have yielded important interventions for understanding and treating addictions.

Arguably one of the most important concepts of Adlerian Psychology is that all behaviors (and symptoms) are purposeful. So what is the purpose of addictive behavior? Again Adler helped us to understand that behavior that appeared to the outside world to be harmful, hurtful, or not helpful was in fact providing a purpose for the addicted individual. Addicted individuals, in general, are discouraged, and to a greater or lesser degree have given up on pursuing the original three life tasks Adler described (love, work, and relationships), and the two additional life tasks neo-Adlerians have described (relationship with self and relationship with the cosmos). A justification is needed to "explain" both lack of progress and symptoms: "I am poor at relationships because of my depression, and I am depressed because I am poor at relationships"—a somewhat perfect fit for a discouraged individual. "You would drink too if you had my job," when in fact the job is so unagreeable because of the drinking. So, our addicted individual is a discouraged, fearful cynic who has found a perfect fit for his or her symptoms (drug use).

I was amazed when I began my career as a drug and alcohol counselor at how similar each individual seemed to be, and yet after a couple of weeks of treatment a more complete representation of personality began to emerge. I learned two important lessons from this observation, the first lesson being that addiction greatly constricts an addict's repertoire of thoughts, behaviors, and feelings. As a result, addicts in the throes of their addiction often seem similar. The second lesson was that as their personalities began to emerge, it was clear that each addict was indeed a unique individual. Adler was one of the first to articulate this phenomenological concept. Each addict is indeed unique, views their world from their perspective, and counselors must respond with this understanding. An example of the importance of this follows. Early in my counseling career I was biased toward thinking that those in my field who were recovering themselves were best suited for this work. But soon I discovered that this bias was not accurate, in that those counselors who seemed to get the best responses from clients were both recovering themselves and those with no history of addiction. And counselors who seemed ill suited for this work were likewise represented by both recovering and non-recovering counselors. In part, what I concluded from this is that those counselors who understood the uniqueness of their clients, and understood the unique worldview of each client, were better at developing rapport and an effective counseling relationship.

Holism is another important concept of Adlerian Psychology. Holism is about *not* attempting to dissect or organize an individual into distinct parts or aspects, but understanding the totality of the person as one interacting system. What this means for understanding addiction is understanding etiology as being multi-causal, and understanding the addict in all of his or her unique aspects and treating all of these aspects. The ramifications of this are many, and will be discussed more fully in other sections of this chapter.

In the course of the addictive process virtually all addicts must work hard to protect their addiction from others and as much as possible from themselves. This requires an enormous amount of effort. In this process an addict becomes more and more self-centered, and in this process he or she violates social norms. Adler (1979) stated that the measure of an individual's mental health is in direct relationship with an individual's social interest. The German term for social interest is *Gemeinschaftsgefühl*, and although this word is normally translated as "social interest," the term "community feeling" is perhaps closer to the actual meaning. Important concepts of social interest are concern for others, self, and community, in a healthy balance (Adler, 1979). Adler (1956) stated that in part, social interest moves a person to the socially useful side of life. Addiction is the opposite. Addiction becomes the protection of self at the expense of others and community, and any individual productivity is not socially motivated but self-motivated.

Clinical Presentation of Substance-Related Addictive Disorders

Clinically, three important concepts of addiction are presented. First is the concept of degree of addiction. Over the years many terms have been used to describe this concept. In textbooks the continuum of use is described as beginning with use, progressing to misuse, then to abuse, and to addiction. And for many years clinicians drew a very specific line between an abuser and an addict, and thus treatment was more education for the abuser and more intense psychotherapy for the individual addicted. A more contemporary way of viewing addiction is to assess the number and severity of addiction-related symptoms (American Psychiatric Association, 2013). These symptoms include: using more than intended; attempts to cut back or cease use; medical, social, and personal problems related to use; the continuation of use in spite of medical, social, and personal problems related to use; craving when not using; requiring more of the substance to achieve desired effects; anxiety, depression, headaches, or other psychological or physical symptoms when not using the substance, etc. The more of these symptoms or the longer these symptoms have existed, the more severe the addiction is considered. As an example, if a person presents with say only three symptoms and all of the symptoms are recent, the treatment may be less intense than if a person presents with all of the symptoms and the symptoms have existed for some time.

Second, a person who presents with several symptoms, and his or her drug of choice is marijuana, will have drug-specific issues that could be different than a person whose drug of choice is alcohol or cocaine, or someone who whose drug choice is various prescription drugs used in combination. The remainder of this chapter will consider separately five classes of drugs (cannabis, opioids, sedatives, stimulants, alcohol), and gambling in terms of clinical presentation, an Adlerian case conceptualization, treatment considerations, and a case example.

Third, it is very common for an addicted individual to use various drugs simultaneously. Clinically, what we see is that most individuals addicted to drugs have a drug of choice, meaning that a specific drug is the one they gravitate toward, prefer, and which seems to cause them the most problems. In general, individuals addicted to drugs clearly know what their drug of choice is. This is not to suggest that their use of other drugs is not a problem, but the problem with their use of other drugs may be different than their use of their drug of choice.

Several treatment concepts will be introduced here and expanded on as treatment considerations for each class of drugs are discussed. Most addicted individuals seldom understand how drugs have impacted their lives, and most addicted to drugs have a skewed view of their present functioning (their reality).

In the last three decades two related and helpful strategies have been introduced that greatly assist those who work with addicted individuals. These strategies are "Stages of Change" (DiClemente, 2003), and Motivational Interviewing (Miller & Rollnick, 2013).

Assessing what stage of change an individual is in is very helpful. The following are the stages of change with a brief descriptor:

- Precontemplation—client does not think he or she has a problem and is not thinking about change.
- Contemplation—the client is beginning to think there is a problem and he or she is thinking about change.
- Preparation (sometimes called determination stage)—the client decides to do something to change.
- Action—the client is actively doing something to change.
- Maintenance—working on and maintaining change strategies.

The goal of the therapist is to develop treatment strategies, based on the stage the client is in, that assist the client to move forward one stage at a time.

Motivational Interviewing, also developed in the '80s, is an excellent strategy for working with an addicted client. Motivational Interviewing is partially based on a client-centered therapy premise, but with an obvious twist. The following is a clinical definition: "A person-centered counseling style for addressing the common problem of ambivalence about change" (Miller & Rollnick, 2013, p. 410). As the definition indicates, resolving ambivalence in favor of change (verses the status quo) is at the core of working with an addicted person. The therapist will probe and direct the client to discover, explore, and resolve ambivalence. In several of the case examples that follow, ambivalence will be explored.

ALCOHOL USE DISORDER

Clinical Presentation

Short-term effects of alcohol, based on blood-alcohol concentration from lower to higher, includes lowered inhibitions, relaxation, some loss of muscular coordination, decreased alertness, reduced social inhibitions, impaired ability to drive, clumsiness, exaggerated emotions, slurred speech, inability to walk without help, life-threatening unconsciousness, coma, death from lung and heart failure. Even with moderate use, such as a blood-alcohol content (BAC) of .05, scientific studies have shown that at this level most drivers have slower reaction time and are a danger to themselves and others driving a vehicle.

Long-term effects include various digestive and liver diseases, such as alcoholic hepatitis, cirrhosis, gastritis, and pancreatitis, hypoglycemia, and other malnutrition related problems. Long-term effects of alcohol also cause cardiovascular disease and nervous-system problems including Dementia, Wernicke's encephalopathy and Korsakoff's psychosis. Some of these long-term effects can occur in as little as, or less than, ten years of alcohol use.

DSM-5 Characterization

The use of alcohol in a manner that causes great difficulty in normal life roles, where use is not modified even as significant problems persist. Unpredictability in how often and how much the drug is used is a common symptom. Craving, needing more for the desired effect, and ill physical effects when not consumed can occur.

Biopsychosocial– Adlerian Case Conceptualization

In addition to a strong neurological imperative, other important contributing factors include the cultural acceptability and availability, and association of use with fun. Early use of this drug is associated with impulsivity and lifelong problematic use.

Substance- and non-substance-use disorders from an Adlerian perspective serve a specific purpose. In general, these disorders serve the purpose of evading life tasks. To paraphrase Adler (1954), these individuals are inadequately prepared for meeting the demands of living. Discouragement and fear of failure are at the core of a life style that is full of sadness and isolation. Alcohol is commonly used as way of coping when other ways have failed or not longer work. In the following case study, alcohol became the primary way of surviving a life that was seen as a failure and loveless. Melanie was inadequately prepared for life.

Treatment Considerations

An important first consideration is an assessment of the severity of addiction, the role alcohol plays in a person's life, and the degree of motivation to change. Also, an important clinical consideration relates to the involvement with other drugs.

Detoxification from alcohol is difficult and must be monitored by trained professionals. With a higher level of severity, clouded thinking could linger for several weeks or longer after alcohol has been discontinued.

The American Society of Addiction Medicine has developed a patient-placement criteria guide that places an individual into one of five levels of care assessed over six dimensions (ASAM, 2001). The ASAM criteria are required in over 30 states and are considered the gold standard for determining the proper level of care.

Case Example: Melanie

Melanie is a 38-year-old single mother of two children, a boy aged 12 and a girl aged 10. Melanie's father was an autocratic alcoholic who died of an alcohol-related accident when Melanie was in college. Melanie was the oldest of three siblings and swore she would never drink. She did not drink until her marriage of eight years ended when her children were aged five and seven. Even though the marriage ended due to an unfaithful husband, Melanie blames herself for the marriage breakup. In the five years she has been drinking she has received two driving-under-the-influence citations, and lost her job as a registered nurse due to her drinking.

Family constellation

Melanie was the oldest of three siblings, and true to form she was the responsible one. She did a bulk of the housework, caring for her younger siblings and helping her mother pick up the pieces of her father's drinking. She even began working at an early age to help her mother pay bills. Melanie was an outstanding student and graduated from high school with a perfect A average, and graduated from college in four years while helping her younger siblings survive family life after her father had died. Melanie does not have any fond memories of growing up, and worked hard at achieving as a way of dealing with her home life.

Early recollections

Melanie reported two distinct early recollections from her pre-school childhood, and one from the first day of kindergarten. The first recollection took place when she was about three years old, and it was of her father standing in the driveway laughing hysterically at the badly damaged car he just drove home. Her mother was crying uncontrollably, asking the father what he was laughing at. The second early memory is of her father waking the family up in the middle of the night, after her mother had changed the locks of the door to prevent her father from returning too late from drinking. Several people in the neighborhood were also awakened and were watching through their windows. Her third recollection was of her first day of kindergarten, being both excited but also wanting to be home to take care of her mother.

Adlerian case conceptualization

Although Melanie excelled in school, she received virtually no training in how to live life in other than a fearful way. Because of her home life she had many casual friends, but none she would get close to, so as to avoid having to confide in them about her home life. In terms of intimacy, Melanie had no idea what true intimacy was, in that she did not feel love from either of her parents and believed that interpersonal relationships would always let you down. Her marriage was problematic from the beginning, since she was hypervigilant, always expecting her husband to disappoint and betray her. She experienced a great sense of joy when her first child was born, but also was overcome by the fear that she had to care for him herself. Melanie was an outstanding employee until her drinking began. In a short amount of time Melanie went from being a hard-working, dependable person, to being fired because of excessive absenteeism and poor performance.

Treatment plan and implementation

Although Melanie's addiction was considered moderate, she did not need detoxification. Melanie knew very early on she needed help and was a willing participant, knowing she would lose her children if she did not change. Melanie had a great deal of anger, mostly toward her deceased father, but also toward her mother. Slowly Melanie began to understand that her parents had done the best they could with what they had, and that her response to anger, fear, and anxiety by using alcohol only made things worse. For the first time Melanie began to focus on who she was as a person and who she wanted to be. Working intently with her group members and her counselor, she began to understand what friendship could be and what true intimacy was. By the time Melanie finished treatment she learned that she was not responsible for the actions of others and that she could be a part of a group without having to be responsible.

For Melanie, as for most who leave treatment for an addiction problem, affiliation with a group such as Alcoholics Anonymous is a good way to continue to learn, to give, and to be a part of something that contributes to society. Melanie also learned that much of what she had been exposed to in her childhood could be left there, and that how she lived her life now did not have to be dictated by what happened to her then.

CANNABIS USE DISORDER

Clinical Presentation

With all drug use there is a cultural component, but with cannabis, for a variety of reasons, this cultural component is much more pronounced. With cannabis, there is a cultural component that "accepts" this drug in a way that creates confusion for many users. As an example, in the legalization debate, marijuana is often compared to alcohol, with compelling evidence that marijuana is safer than alcohol. Alcohol is legal, therefore many young users conclude marijuana is safe, or at least safer than alcohol. But missed in all this is that for many, due mostly to neurological dysregulation, addiction is the result of use of this "safer" drug. Due to the potency of marijuana, many more accidents occur than most believe; and perhaps most problematic is the negative impact marijuana use has on the developing adolescent brain and personality (Inaba & Cohen, 2007).

Unless a national conversation occurs concerning the place of drugs in our society, the place the alteration of consciousness has in our society, and the responsibility each of us has toward the other, the legalization of marijuana will lead to more use and addiction, and, most troubling, more use at a younger age. Brain science should be an integral part of this conversation.

When discussing cannabis, the societal context must be considered. This context makes the treatment of this drug more difficult. As an example, many individuals who willingly accept alcohol or heroin as a problem refuse to see their marijuana use in that same way, even when objective data clearly shows their marijuana use as a problem. And there are too many parents who excuse their child's use of marijuana because marijuana is a "safe" drug, and at least it is not crack cocaine.

Problematic use of marijuana includes short-term physical and mental effects. Physical effects include such things as relaxation or mild sedation, impaired ability to follow a moving object, an increase in hunger, and enhancement of sensory appeal, such a food tasting and smelling better and music sounding better. Mental effects include confusion, drowsiness, difficulty concentrating, exaggerated mood and personality, short-term memory difficulties, time distortion, and based on potency, distortions of sound and color and possible hallucinations. The above effects tend to be individualized, meaning that some who use marijuana will be energized, whereas most will be more relaxed and sedated. Some report using marijuana only in a specific context, to be more sociable or to hear music more deeply or differently.

Long-term effects include respiratory problems, immune system impact, and acute mental effects. Although there is not a direct relationship between long-term marijuana use and cancer, such as there is with nicotine use, other respiratory problems include acute and chronic bronchitis and lung-tissue damage. The literature remains mixed on the influence of marijuana use and mental disorders. The general consensus at this point is that some individuals do experience a great deal of anxiety and paranoia while using marijuana, which persists after usage. There are also reports of marijuana use precipitating psychosis (Os et al., 2002; Grinspoon, Bakalar, & Russo, 2005) in individuals who have a pre-existing tendency toward this condition. Although the percentages are low, clinically this is observed, and complicates treatment.

DSM-5 Characterization

The use of cannabis in a manner that causes great difficulty in normal life roles is not modified, even as significant problems persist. Unpredictability in how often and how much the drug is used is a common symptom. Craving, needing more for the desired effect, and ill psychological effects such as depression when not consumed, are common.

Biopsychosocial–Adlerian Case Conceptualization

In addition to a strong neurological imperative, other important contributing factors include the poor development of coping skills to deal with frustration, early lack of interest in social conventions such as community and family, and poor success in school. Often this drug is thought to be a safe drug. This belief increases the likelihood of use and lack or recognition of problems associated with its use. Early use of this drug is associated with the of lifelong problematic use.

Substance- and non-substance-use disorders from an Adlerian perspective serve a specific purpose. In general, these disorders serve the purpose of evading life tasks. To paraphrase Adler (1954), these individuals are inadequately prepared for meeting the demands of living. Discouragement and fear of failure are at the core of a life style that is full of sadness and isolation. Cannabis use provides an escape from a reality that is full of discouragement. As the following case illustrates, John had much reason to be discouraged, and escape provided a perfect way of blunting out his discouragement.

Treatment Considerations

Using the "Stages of Change" and Motivational Interviewing approach discussed above, most clients will begin to see how marijuana use has negatively impacted their life and how constricted their response to life has become. Most clients have some initial difficulty abstaining, in that their life has been so centered around the use of marijuana, but once they have developed strategies for not using, most do well, with very little craving. However, complacency is a problem that most marijuana users underestimate. A typical example is "forgetting" both how bad and good marijuana use was for them, and as a result, relapse episodes are common and often problematic. With all drug treatment, relapse prevention is an important aspect, but with those involved with marijuana, relapse prevention is even more important, due to the sneaky and seducing nature of marijuana memory.

Another important clinical consideration is making sure that the individual who has been addicted to say alcohol and marijuana does not downplay their marijuana use. Proper acceptance of their marijuana use is the key.

Case Example: John

John is a 15-year-old mixed-race ninth grader who reports multiple times a day use of marijuana. John is a foster child whose mother is deceased and was addicted to crack cocaine, and who will never know his father. John has a learning disability that makes school very difficult for him.

Family constellation

John is an only child to a single foster-mother professional. Since age three John has been with his foster mother. John reports always feeling different and less than, due to his mixed race and difficulty in school. John also reported feeling "disconnected," since he will never know his father and his mother is deceased.

Early recollections

John's earliest recollections involve feeling distant and apart. One early recollection involves crying and no one responding, and another involves being left alone for long periods of time.

Adlerian case conceptualization

Although John grew up in a stable environment since age three, his life prior to that was conflicted and chaotic. Due to a learning disability John has had great difficulty meeting normal educational milestones. John has always felt he did not belong, felt isolated, and felt he was different. As a result, John had little success in the three life tasks of relationship (I am too different to be liked), school (school is too difficult for someone like me), and love (the one person who was suppose to love me abandoned me). John developed intense inferiority, and essentially developed a style of life in which he would never be good enough. John would put in just enough effort to get by, and bring as little attention to himself as possible by accepting below-par performance, not attempting to make friends, and rejecting the love his foster mother attempted to give him.

Treatment plan and implementation

John needed encouragement and to discover the power he possessed to engage the world. From the beginning it was clear that John had a great amount of ambivalence about his marijuana use (he was a self-referral). He quickly discovered that this ambivalence was based on a desire to not disappoint his foster mother. He also soon discovered that not only did his foster mother love him, but he loved her as well. Within a short period of time John began to discover ways to be successful by using the resources that were available to him. As he became less discouraged, he began to be more involved in his church community and to take interest in his foster mother's activist politics. As John began to make strides toward fulfilling life tasks, his desire to use marijuana was extinguished.

OPIOID USE DISORDER

Clinical Presentation

Opioid addiction generally comes through prescription drug use and/or the use of heroin. Prescription drugs that individuals become addicted to include such substances as Oxycodone, Oxycontin, Percoset, Percodan, and Vicodin, to name but a few. These drugs are prescribed by physicians to relieve moderate to severe pain. These drugs are extremely effective, and a vast majority of those who use them do not become addicted.

It is estimated that the addiction rate for all opiates including heroin is approximately 1% of the adult population of the United States (American Psychiatric Association, 2013) (Inaba & Cohen, 2007). For other developed countries the addiction rate is 50% to 75% less. In recent years there has been a significant increase in the addiction rate for opiates, due in large part to how widely they are prescribed. It is estimated that the ratio of heroin users to illicit prescription drug users is one heroin user for every six addicted illicit prescription drug users (SAMHSA, 2006).

There are similarities and differences between illicit prescription drug use and heroin use. Heroin is a highly addictive drug and it is estimated that 23% of those who use heroin, even one time, will become addicted to it (American Psychiatric Association, 2013). For prescription drug use the percentage most likely is less than 1%. Also, the effects are different. With heroin there is an initial rush that has been described as so intense that those who experience this spend a lifetime attempting to feel that rush again. This powerful, initial rush is followed by a euphoric dreamlike state of drowsiness, an increase in self-esteem and decreased concern with problems and stressors in one's life (National Institute for Drug Abuse, 2010). Except for the powerful initial rush, prescription drug use provides many of the same feelings and experiences. As a result, these drugs have a high potential for addiction.

Chronic use of prescription drugs often leads to loss of energy, tolerance, physical addiction, and lack of ambition and drive.

DSM-5 Characterization

The use of opioids in a manner that causes great difficulty in normal life roles, where use is not modified even as significant problems persist. Unpredictability in how often and how much the drug is used is a common symptom. With this class of drug, the need to use more for the desired effect develops very rapidly, and significant physical ill effects when use is discontinued are extremely common and expected. Although not life threatening, physical ill effects are intense and a motivation for continued use.

Biopsychosocial–Adlerian Case Conceptualization

In addition to a strong neurological imperative, other important contributing factors include impulsivity and novelty-seeking. Abuse of this class of drugs often begins with exposure to a legitimate prescribed need. The user finds a desirable psychological feeling that leads to procuring more of the drug for this need. Adolescent abuse of this class of drug often begins by experimenting with an unused portion of a prescription found in the home.

Substance- and non-substance-use disorders from an Adlerian perspective serve a specific purpose. In general, these disorders serve the purpose of evading life tasks. To paraphrase Adler (1954), these individuals are inadequately prepared for meeting the demands of living. Discouragement and fear of failure are at the core of a life style that is full of sadness and isolation. Opiates are typically referred to as painkillers, and this is indeed an apt description. In addition to making physical pain manageable, opiates also numb psychological pain.

Treatment Considerations

Most who are addicted to this class of drug have no difficulty recognizing the devastation this drug causes. The cycle of procuring, using, suffering the consequences of using, and withdrawing from this drug are all too familiar. Once in treatment they are usually very motivated to get clean and stay clean.

Withdrawal symptoms from opiates are extremely unpleasant and have been described as a bad, bad, bad case of the flu. Depression is common for several days or weeks after the acute withdrawal.

The use of Motivational Interviewing is very helpful in the identification of the reasons an individual wants to stop using. In the beginning of treatment these reasons often are as simple as not wanting to experience the negative effects of the drug. However, as treatment progresses, clients usually begin to identify important life goals they would like to achieve. Once these broader goals are articulated, the client is encouraged to develop short- and middle-term goals for accomplishment.

An important treatment consideration for this drug is that environmental cues can cause intense craving. As a result, it is often very helpful for a client to develop realistic and meaningful strategies for countering these cravings.

Case Example: Mark

Mark was 33 years old when he was hospitalized for intestinal blockage. The resulting surgeries nearly cost him his life, and Mark spent 50 days in the hospital, during which there was not a day he did not experience severe pain and was given powerful opiate drugs to counter the pain. Upon leaving the hospital the pain had dissipated and he was given a large quantity of opiates to take as needed. Mark realized that he was now mostly taking these opiates to feel better psychologically, or for the effect.

Family constellation

Mark was adopted when he was very young and had a brother in his adopted family who was nine years older than him. He essentially was an only child.

Early recollections

Mark had two distinct early recollections that both related to wanting to belong and be a part of a community.

Adlerian case conceptualization

Mark was independent from an early age, was very shy, began to experience difficulty in school at an early age, and was fearful of his parents. During middle school Mark began to read a great deal and became very interested in politics and current affairs. Mark learned to work very hard and stayed away from trouble, but constantly fought with his parents over such things as politics and religion. After barely graduating from high school (mostly because of lack of effort) he joined the U.S. Navy. And although he had some initial success, he found it very difficult being close to others. Once he was exposed to opiates he discovered that he felt exactly the way he wanted to feel. He felt connected and that he belonged and that anything was possible. After one year of hiding his addiction, he asked for help and was referred for treatment.

From an Adlerian viewpoint, Mark had never moved toward accomplishing the life tasks of love, relationships, and work, but instead took on a victim stance, had a very low opinion of himself, and found ways of avoiding being with others although he longed to feel connected to others. What treatment provided him was a goal and a way to feel the way he wanted to feel.

Treatment plan and implementation

Treatment was life changing for Mark. He immediately began to discover aspects of himself that that he did not know. As an example, he learned that he was very intelligent, but because of a mild learning disability he did poorly in school. He also learned how to find ways of overcoming his learning disabilities. Mark also became very close to his group members and began to learn how to initiate and maintain friendships. And perhaps most importantly he learned that all he wanted from life could be obtained in cooperation with others and by contributing to society.

STIMULANT USE DISORDER

Clinical Presentation

In general the stimulants that are abused fall into the categories of amphetamine-type stimulants and cocaine. Each will be briefly discussed separately.

It is estimated that approximately 0.2% of the adult population is addicted to amphetamine-type stimulants and 0.3% is addicted to cocaine (American Psychiatric Accociation, 2013).

Amphetamines produce feelings of euphoria, provide relief from fatigue, increase mental alertness, and enhance mood. Negative short-term side effects include anxiety, confusion, paranoia, and aggression. Chronic-use side effects include psychotic behavior, hallucinations, respiratory problems, cardiovascular problems, and extreme weight loss. Other associated dangers include risk of infectious disease due to shared needle use, depression, intense cravings, and development of extremely poor oral hygiene.

Cocaine produces feelings of profound well-being, enhanced alertness, intense energy/strength, decrease in anxiety, increase in self-confidence, heightened sexual drive, and an increase in sense of mastery and power. Dangers include severe cardiovascular problems, irritability, nervousness, and agitation. Long-term impact includes reduction in number of dopamine receptors, which decreases the ability to experience pleasure, nasal-cavity irritation, problems swallowing, and lung damage.

DSM-5 Characterization

The use of stimulants in a manner that causes great difficulty in normal life roles, and where use is not modified even as significant problems persist. Unpredictability in how often and how much the drug is used is a common symptom. With this class of drug the need to use more for the desired effect develops very rapidly. Also with this class of drug, when not using, or attempting to be abstinent, substantial cravings occur. These cravings, in addition to being intense, also last for a very long time. Withdrawal is unpleasant, and with intense cravings makes relapse likely for many.

Biopsychosocial–Adlerian Case Conceptualization

In addition to a strong neurological imperative, other important contributing factors include impulsivity and similar personality traits. Use of this class of drug is also common for those suffering from bipolar and schizophrenic disorders. Other risk factors include prenatal cocaine exposure and postnatal cocaine use by parents. Community and family violence during childhood are also predictors for problematic use of this class of drug.

Substance- and non-substance-use disorders from an Adlerian perspective serve a specific purpose. In general, these disorders serve the purpose of evading life tasks. To paraphrase Adler (1954), these individuals are inadequately prepared for meeting the demands of living. Discouragement and fear of failure are at the core of a life style that is full of sadness and isolation. Cocaine is often used as a shortcut for empowerment. And as is the case for other substance use, cocaine provides relief from discouragement.

Treatment Considerations

Often individuals addicted to stimulant drugs will also use depressant drugs to counteract the effects of stimulants, to reduce anxiety, and to sleep. Individuals will sometimes become addicted to those drugs as well.

The inability to experience pleasure long after cessation of the use of cocaine is an issue that will often lead to resuming the use of cocaine or resorting to other drugs to experience pleasure. Treatment for stimulant addiction is often longer in duration, due to the depression these drugs cause. And unlike marijuana and opiate drugs, the craving for stimulant drugs is much more pronounced and protracted.

Case Example: Bill

Bill was a 42-year-old successful investigative journalist who seemingly disappeared for four days before being found in an alley outside of a "crack" house in Denver, Colorado. Bill had used cocaine off and on since his early 20s, but more recently intensified his use to several times a day. Once he was introduced to crack cocaine, nothing else mattered. In the four days of his final use, Bill had withdrawn over $4,000 from his bank accounts.

Family constellation

Bill was the youngest of five brothers. His parents worked hard to ensure that all five boys got the best education possible. Both parents had only high school educations and wanted more for their children. All five children were also hard workers and successful professionals.

Early recollections

Bill's earliest recollections are of his family, mostly his brothers, participating in outdoor activities and enjoying life. One early recollection is of the time Bill was all alone in the house and how scared he felt.

Adlerian case conceptualization

From an early age Bill remembers feeling supported by his siblings and, to a lesser degree, his parents. Bill never had to work very hard for anything, in that most everything came naturally. He attributes this in part to his brothers' willingness to teach and help him. He took advantage of this, as he did very well in school, and specifically athletically. His dream of being a professional athlete ended when he was in college. He remembers this being the single most devastating thing to ever happen to him. It was about this time that Bill began to use cocaine. Through the years Bill used cocaine as his primary support system to deal with frustration, loss, and difficulty in general. After a difficult divorce his cocaine use was out of control until a friendly colleague (older brother figure) helped him stop. This was three years before his current binge.

Treatment plan and implementation

Although not in the classic sense, Bill was a pampered child. Bill was always supported and never had to face or accept any real adversity or failure until college. His life style had been set at an early age, that all he had to do was give life his best effort and he would come out on top. Bill never came to appreciate others, except in how they could benefit him. Once Bill began to face difficulty, he looked to others to assist him. Cocaine became to him another older brother.

While in treatment Bill began to learn that it was OK to be imperfect and that adversity and failure was as much a part of life as success was, and that both were imposters. Bill began to learn that others were not just there to provide for his needs, but were there to form community. Bill learned that his great abilities could be used in the service of others and in community.

SEDATIVE, HYPNOTIC, OR ANXIOLYTIC USE DISORDER

Clinical Presentation

This class of drugs relates to barbiturates and benzodiazepines. These are both prescribed drugs used to control anxiety and aid in sleep. Due to a very low therapeutic index (TI), a ratio of the effective dose to the lethal dose, barbiturates are not considered safe and must be used with caution. Benzodiazepines were introduced in the 1960s, have a much higher TI, and are used for most of the same conditions barbiturates are prescribed for. Since benzodiazepines are safer, this drug is much more common and has a tendency of being abused.

These drugs lead to mild sedation, muscle relaxation, and lowered anxiety, and even when not abused, physiological addiction for this class of drug is common when used over several months. Problematic use of these drugs occurs when they are combined with other drugs, such as methadone, to increase the effect, or used to counter the effect of stimulant-type drugs. Individuals have also been known to use these drugs during working hours, when drinking alcohol would be too easily detected. Like alcohol, the effect of these drugs includes slurring of speech, difficulty with coordination, and poor judgment.

DSM-5 Characterization

The use of sedatives, hypnotics, or anxiolytics in a manner that causes great difficulty in normal life roles, and where use is not modified even as significant problems persist. Unpredictability in how often and how much the drug is used is a common symptom. With this class of drug, the need to use more for the desired effect develops extremely rapidly, and significant physical ill effects when use is discontinued are expected. Abrupt discontinuation of this class of drug can be life threatening, including suicidal thoughts.

Biopsychosocial–Adlerian Case Conceptualization

In addition to a strong neurological imperative, other important contributing factors include impulsivity and novelty-seeking. As with prescription opiate use, abuse of this class of drugs often begins with exposure to a legitimate prescribed need. The user finds a desirable psychological feeling that leads to procuring more of the drug for this need. Adolescent abuse of this class of drug often begins by experimenting with the unused portion of a prescription found in the home.

Substance- and non-substance-use disorders from an Adlerian perspective serve a specific purpose. In general, these disorders serve the purpose of evading life tasks. To paraphrase Adler (1954), these individuals are inadequately prepared for meeting the demands of living. Discouragement and fear of failure are at the core of a life style that is full of sadness and isolation. Use of this type of drug is effective in relieving anxiety, and often is effective when used in the short term, but is obviously a problem when used for every disappointment or frustration.

Treatment Considerations

Although a person addicted strictly to benzodiazepines is rare, it does occur. What is much more likely is an addiction to benzodiazepines and other central nervous system depressants, such as alcohol, or opiates. When these drugs are used in combination with others, detoxification is complicated.

Case Example: Jennifer

Jennifer is a 32-year-old, divorced mother of a ten-year-old son. She shares joint custody of her son with his father. Jennifer was recently arrested for driving under the influence. In order to maintain joint custody, Jennifer agreed to be evaluated for a drug or alcohol problem.

Family constellation

Jennifer was an only child, born when her father was 45 and her mother was 41. Jennifer was considered a miracle, in that her parents had attempted to have children since they were married in their late 20s. Both of Jennifer's parents had experienced problems with alcohol, and had warned her that she too might experience problems with alcohol. Jennifer never drank alcohol in fear that she too might develop a problem. After her son was born, Jennifer began to develop anxiety-related problems including mild panic attacks. Her doctor prescribed a benzodiazepine that gave her the relief that she needed. But Jennifer also began to take more of this medication than prescribed when she was feeling upset with her husband or experienced difficulty at work. Within a short period of time Jennifer was going to multiple doctors, and even finding the medication she needed from street suppliers.

Early recollections

Jennifer reports that her earliest recollection was related to her desire to play with other children her age. She also remembers asking for a baby brother or sister and her parents telling her how special she was.

Adlerian case conceptualization

Because Jennifer was a miracle child in the eyes of her parents, she never wanted for anything and seldom had to work hard to achieve. Jennifer did average in school and in college. Jennifer did not have a job until after college, and she remembers the work being so demanding that she wanted to call her dad so he could help her. Although she adjusted to the work environment, she longed to not have to work. After the birth of her son she just stayed home to take care of him, until her husband was injured and as a result lost his well-paying job. Jennifer remembers her life falling apart when she had to go back to work and take care of her son, who was not yet in school. Jennifer felt overwhelmed and the benzodiazepines provided relief.

Treatment plan and implementation

Jennifer at first resisted treatment, believing that she was special and not like common drug addicts and alcoholics. Gradually Jennifer began to understand that she was indeed as much a drug addict as her group members. And Jennifer also began to understand that the pampered childhood she experienced inhibited her from taking responsibility for herself. In a short period of time Jennifer began to appreciate who she was as an individual and that she possessed both weaknesses and strengths. And through the group process Jennifer began to develop empathy that had been badly missing in her earlier life. As a result, she began to connect with others.

GAMBLING DISORDER

Clinical Presentation

Most estimates indicate there are over 2.5 million pathological gamblers in the United States (Blume & Travares, 2005). This makes up about 0.9% of the adult population. Due to greatly increased accessibility, the number of pathological gamblers has increased and is expected to continue to increase. The similarity of gambling to substance addictions is emphasized by the high rates of other addictions among pathological gamblers. These rates are estimated to be about 50% (NORC, 1999). And another troubling statistic is that gambling often becomes a problem when a person abstains from their substance addiction (Petry, Stinson, & Grant, 2005). In the past the ratio of male to female pathological gamblers was approximately 2–3 to 1. This ratio is rapidly evening out, and more pathological gamblers are now those seeking to escape from depression, trauma, or relationship problems.

DSM-5 Characterization

Problematic gambling that causes great difficulty in normal life roles, and gambling behavior that is not modified even as significant problems persist. Increase in gambling behavior. Has great difficulty in not gambling or cutting back. Preoccupied with gambling, and great desire to gamble when not doing so. Use of gambling when feeling stressed or distressed.

Biopsychosocial–Adlerian Case Conceptualization

In addition to a strong neurological imperative, other important contributing factors include impulsivity, competitiveness, and becoming easily bored. Gambling often begins in adolescence and is frequently influenced by family patterns of gambling. Gambling is associated with Antisocial Personality Disorder, Bipolar and Depressive Disorder, and other substance abuse disorders, particularly Alcohol Use Disorder.

Substance- and non-substance-use disorders from an Adlerian perspective serve a specific purpose. In general, these disorders serve the purpose of evading life tasks. To paraphrase Adler (1954), these individuals are inadequately prepared for meeting the demands of living. Discouragement and fear of failure are at the core of a life style that is full of sadness and isolation. Gambling is a form of distraction from an unfulfilled or discouraged life, which provides a way of being that in and of itself substitutes for life tasks.

Treatment Considerations

Formal treatment for gambling problems is relatively new, with 17 states funding some kind of gambling treatment program. Usually, when pathological gamblers come into treatment they have hit a bottom that many could never understand. Often they are depressed, over $1,000,000 in debt, and have no meaningful kind of support. And as mentioned above, a co-occurring disorder is likely.

Case Example: Eddie

Eddie was a 14-year veteran of a major city police department. Due to his gambling he lost his family, and was arrested as he made a feeble attempt to rob a bank to cover gambling debts. Although he may still face a long prison sentence, he was diverted into a gambling-addiction treatment program.

Family constellation

Eddie grew up the third of four children. His father was a factory worker and his mother was a school teacher. Eddie was the only child who did not go to college. He described himself as an outsider and a rebel. Eddie married outside his faith and did not have very much connection with his parents until his divorce.

Early recollections

Eddie remembers how proud his father was when they bought their first new car when Eddie was five years old. Another early recollection is of Eddie breaking his arm when he fell out of a tree, and his mother scolding him all the way to the hospital.

Adlerian case conceptualization

Eddie felt he was rejected by both his father and mother at an early age, and as a result he sought a life outside the family. Eddie was always popular with schoolmates, due to his hyperactivity and class clowning. Eddie never sought conventional ways of being accepted, and even though he was a police officer, he never felt he was ever fully accepted by his peers.

Treatment plan and implementation

Eddie did not initially respond well to treatment. Eddie felt enormous shame for his lack of responsibility and did not want to get close to anyone. Over time Eddie began to share, and soon he felt something he had seldom felt before, and that was acceptance. By the time Eddie finished treatment he was confident that he could start over again, no matter what might happen with his legal problems, reunite with his family, and be of service in some capacity to his community.

Concluding Note

Although the changes in the *DSM-5* as to how substance- and non-substance-use disorders are diagnosed are significant, most will become very comfortable with these changes rapidly if they think about problematic use on one continuum, as opposed to the two distinct continuums in previous editions. Although many are disappointed that more non-substance-use disorders were not included in this most recent update, there is obvious movement in that direction. And, of course, clinician discernment is required to differentiate normal behavior from diagnosis of a use disorder.

References

Adler, A . (1956). In H.L. Ansbacher & R.R. Ansbacher (Eds.), *The Individual Psychology of Alfred Adler* (p. 167). New York, NY: Harper & Row.

Adler, A. (1979). In H.L. Ansbacher & R.R. Ansbacher (Eds.), *Superiority and Social Interest: A Collection of Later Writings* (3rd rev. edn.). New York, NY: Norton.

Amen, D.G., Willeumier, K., & Johnson, R. (2012). The clinical utility of Brain SPECT imaging in process addictions. *Journal of Psychoactive Drugs*, 44, pp. 18–26.

American Medical Association (1966). Drug dependencies as diseases. *Policy Finder*. H-95.983. Chicago, IL: American Medical Association.

American Psychiatric Association (2013). *Diagnostic and Statistical Manual of Mental Disorders, Fifth Edition*. Arlington, VA: American Psychiatric Publishing.

American Society of Addiction Medicine (2011a). Public policy statement: Definition of addiction. Chevy Chase, MD: American Society of Addiction Medicine.

American Society of Addiction Medicine (2011b). Press Release: ASAM releases new definition of addiction. Chevy Chase, MD: American Society of Addiction Medicine.

American Society of Addiction Medicine (2001). Patient Placement Criteria. Available at www.asam.org/PatientPlacementCriteria.html.

Blum, K., Werner, T., Carnes, S., Carnes, P., Bowirrat, A., Giordano, J., Oscar-Berman, M., & Gold, M. (2012). Sex, drugs, and rock 'n' roll: Hypothesizing common mesolimbic activation as a function of reward gene polymorphisms. *Journal of Psychoactive Drugs*, 44 , pp. 38–55.

Blume, S.B. & Tavares, H. (2005). Pathological gambling. In J.H. Lowinson, P. Ruiz, R.B. Milman, & J.G. Langrod (Eds.), *Substance Abuse: A Comprehensive Textbook* (4th edn.), (pp. 488–498). Baltimore, MD: Williams & Wilkins.

Brady, K.T., Back, S.E., & Coffey, S.F. (2004). Substance abuse and posttraumatic stress disorder. *Current Directions in Psychological Science*, 13, pp. 206–209.

Burrow-Sanchez, J.J. (2006). Understanding adolescent substance abuse: Prevalence, risk factors, and clinical implications. *The Journal of Counseling and Development*, 84, pp. 283–290.

Connors, G.J. & Tarbox, A.R. (1985). Macroenvironmental factors as determinants of substance use and abuse. In M. Galizio & S.A. Maisto (Eds.), *Determinants of Substance Abuse: Biological, Psychological, and Environmental Factors* (pp. 439–446). New York, NY: Plenum Press.

DiClemente, C.C. (2003). *Addiction and Change: How Addictions Develop and Addicted People Recover*. New York, NY: Guilford.

D'Onofrio, G & Degutis, L.C. (2004). Screening and brief intervention in the emergency department. *Alcohol Research and Health*, 28, pp. 63–72.

Erickson, C.K. (2007). *The Science of Addiction*. New York, NY: W.W. Norton.

Erickson, C.K. & White, W.L. (2009). The neurobiology of addiction recovery. *Alcoholism Treatment Quarterly*, 27, pp. 338–345.

Fisher, G.L. & Harrison, T.C. (2009). *Substance Abuse: Information for School Counselors, Social Workers, Therapists, and Counselors* (4th edn.). Boston, MA: Pearson.

Gatley, S.J., Volkow, N.D., Wang, G.J., Fowler, J.S., Logan, J., Ding, Y.S., & Gerasimov, M. (2005). PET imaging in clinical drug abuse research. *Current Pharmaceutical Design*, 11, pp. 3203–3219.

Grinspoon, L., Bakalar, J. B., & Russo, E. (2005). Marijuana: Clinical aspects. In J.H. Lowinson, P. Ruiz, R.B. Milman, & J.G. Langrod (Eds.), *Substance Abuse: A Comprehensive Textbook* (4th edn.) (pp. 263–76). Baltimore, MD: Williams & Wilkins.

Hoffman, J. & Froemke, S. (2007). *Addiction: Why Can't They Just Stop? New Knowledge. New Treatment. New Hope.* New York, NY: Rodale Press.

Inaba, D.S. & Cohen, W.E. (2007). *Uppers, Downers, All Arounders.* Medford, OR: CNS Publications.

Karim, R. & Chaudhri, P. (2012). Behavioral addictions: An overview. *Journal of Psychoactive Drugs*, 44, pp. 5–17.

Krueger, R.F., Hicks, B.M., Patrick, C.J., Carlson, S.R., Iacono, W.G., & McGue, M. (2002). Etiologic connections among substance dependence, antisocial behavior, and personality: Modeling the externalizing spectrum. *Journal of Abnormal Psychology*, 111, pp. 411–424.

Leshner, A.L. (1997). Addiction is a brain disease and it matters. *Science*, 278, pp. 45–47.

Miller, W.R. & Hester, R.K. (1995). Treatment for alcohol problems: Toward an informed eclecticism. In R.K. Hester & W.R. Miller (Eds.), *Handbook of Alcoholism Treatment Approaches: Effective Alternatives* (2nd edn.) (pp. 83–137). Boston, MA: Allyn & Bacon.

Miller, W.R. & Rollnick, S. (2013). *Motivational Interviewing: Helping People Change* (3rd edn.). New York, NY: Guilford.

Moos, R. (2008). Conservation with Rudolph Moos. *Addiction*, 103, pp. 13–23.

National Institute on Alcohol Abuse and Alcoholism (2004). National epidemiologic survey on alcohol and related conditions. Bethesda, MD: U.S. Department of Health and Human Services.

National Institute on Drug Abuse (2008). Drug abuse costs the United States economy hundreds of billions of dollars in increased healthcare costs and lost productivity. Retrieved August 14, 2013, from http://www.drugabuse.gov/publications/addiction-science-molecules-to-managed-care/introduction/drug-abuse-costs-united-states-economy-hundreds-billions-dollars-in-increased-health.

National Institute on Drug Abuse (2010). NIDA drug facts: Heroin. Retrieved August 14, 2013, from from www.nida.nih.gov/infofacts/heroin.html.

National Opinion and Research Center (1999). Gambling impact and behavior study. Report to the National Gambling Impact Study Commission. Retrieved August 13, 2013, from http://govinfo.library.unit.edu/ngisc/index.htm.

Os, J., Bak, M.,Hanseen, R.V., Bijl, R.V., Graff, R, & Verdous, H. (2002). Cannabis use and psychosis: A longitudinal population-based study. *American Journal of Epidemiology*, 156, pp. 39–27.

Petry, N.M., Stinson, F.S., & Grant, B.F. (2005). Cormorbidity of DSM-IV pathological gambling and other psychiatric disorders: Results from the National Epidemiologic Survey on Alcohol and Related Conditions. *Journal of Clinical Psychiatry*, 66(5), pp. 564–74.

Regier, D.A., Farmer, M.E., Rae, D.S., Locke, B.Z., Keith, S.J., Judd, L.L., & Goodwin, L. (1990). Comorbidity of mental disorders with alcohol and other drug abuse: Results from the Epidemiologic Catchment Area (ECA) study. *Journal of the American Medical Association*, 264, pp. 2511–2518.

Substance Abuse and Mental Health Services Administration (2006). Summary of findings from the 2005 National Household Survey on Drug Abuse. Rockville, MD: SAMHSA, Office of Applied Studies.

Yin, H.H. (2008). From actions to habits: Neuroadaptions leading to dependence. *Alcohol Research & Health*, 31(4), pp. 340–344.

15 Neurocognitive Disorders

Michael P. Maniacci and Len Sperry.

The recent *Frontline* documentary, *League of Denial*, and the book on which it was based (Fainaru-Wada & Fainaru, 2013), have begun a national conversation about sports-related, traumatic brain injuries. The concern is broader than concussions sustained by NFL players; the concern extends to kids who play football and "head" soccer balls in school and community sports leagues. The concern is about the long-term impact of repeated blows to the head and eventual neurocognitive disorders (NCD). This chapter is about NCDs, including those due to traumatic brain injury. While NCDs are ostensibly brain disorders, questions arise. Do they have a psychological or personality component? Specifically, what are the DSM-5 and Adlerian formulations or case conceptualizations of these disorders?

This chapter addresses these questions. It examines what is known about NCDs, their DSM characterization, and how they are viewed from an Adlerian perspective. It describes Adler's (1956) early work on organ inferiority and compensation, as well as his theory of life-style types and family constellation dynamics. The chapter consists of sections which describe the following neurocognitive disorders: Delirium; Neurocognitive Disorder due to Alzheimer's Disease; Neurocognitive Disorder Due to Traumatic Brain Injury; Neurocognitive Disorder Due to Parkinson's Disease; and Unspecified Neurocognitive Disorder. In addition, some other NCDs are briefly discussed. They include frontotemporal lobar degeneration, Lewy body disease, vascular disease, substance/medication use, HIV infection, Prion disease, Huntington's disease, and other disorders.

The plan for each section is to begin with a clinical description of each disorder and its DSM-5 characterization. Next, a biopsychosocial–Adlerian conceptualization of that disorder is provided. This is followed by a brief discussion of treatment considerations. Finally, a case example rounds out the discussion of the disorder. However, before turning to these specific disorders, the chapter begins with a cautionary statement and a general Adlerian conceptualization of the neurocognitive disorders.

A Cautionary Statement

By definition, all NCDs are brain disorders, i.e., medical conditions. Generally speaking, medical management, supervision, and consultation are required when non-medically trained professionals deal with such disorders. Psychotherapy cannot cure these conditions. But, as Laurence Miller (1993) has documented in his treatment manual,

Psychotherapy of the Brain-Injured Patient: Reclaiming the Shattered Self, counseling and psychotherapy of the patient and family can be crucial with treatment compliance, management, rehabilitation, self-esteem, and even prognosis. Patients who accept their condition, work collaboratively with physicians and nurses, and stick to treatment and rehabilitation plans have a significantly better prognosis, and counseling and psychotherapy, including family therapy, can increase compliance and adaptation.

Psychotherapists and other non-medical clinicians working with individuals experiencing NCDs would do well to become familiar with the neurological and neuropsychological literature. Two excellent resources for interested clinicians would be *The Mental Status Examination in Neurology* (4th edn.), by Strub and Black (2000), and *Neuropsychological Assessment* (5th edn.), by Lezak, Howieson, Bigler, and Tranel (2012). These texts provide extensive research and how-to guides for conducting diagnostic evaluations. From an Adlerian perspective, an invaluable resource is *Lifestyle Counseling for Adjustment to Disability,* edited by Rule (1984). In this textbook, Rule and his colleagues present many Adlerian-based tactics and guidelines for working with medically impaired individuals and their families.

Adlerian Conceptualization of the Neurocognitive Disorders

From an Adlerian perspective, there are five central factors useful in understanding the NCDs. The five are *nature of the inferiority, childhood training, family training, clinging to the shock effects,* and *private logic* (Maniacci, 1996). Each will be detailed.

The *nature of the inferiority* is important. As Dreikurs (1948/1967b) detailed, it is helpful to distinguish inferiority from inferiority feeling and inferiority complex. An inferiority is objective; that is, it can be measured according to some situationally determined standard. Inferiority feelings are subjective and have nothing to do with actual inferiorities. Inferiority complexes are open declarations of bankruptcy; that is, they are behavioral manifestations of subjective feelings of inferiority (Mosak & Maniacci, 1999). For example, Mary may have cerebral palsy, an actual inferiority. She may feel inferior because of it and declare bankruptcy, refuse to participate, and demand others take care of her. Carole, with the same actual inferiority, may not feel inferior. She may overcompensate and become exceptionally helpful and productive. The nature of the inferiority imposes certain limits upon what is possible, but not the attitude adopted.

Adler (1917, 1956) wrote about organ inferiority. Technically, an organ inferiority is inherited. When it is, the law of compensation takes place (Dreikurs, 1967b). Compensation takes place in three domains:

(a) Somatic level
(b) Sympathetic level
(c) Psychic level

When an organ is inferior in structure or function, compensatory efforts take place in each of the three areas. On the somatic level, the unaffected areas will assume a greater role, such as when one kidney enlarges to compensate for the troubled one. On the sympathetic level, the person may assume a gait and posture that unconsciously leans toward the unaffected kidney in order to protect the weaker side. On the psychic level, the person may overdevelop personality traits that make him or her feel stronger, more competent. In his 1907 monograph, Adler detailed what he believed to be the psychic compensations for numerous organ inferiorities (Adler, 1917).

When it comes to *childhood training*, Adler (2012) classified three situations he considered to be extremely problematic and potentially decisive in leading to mental disorders. The first, as discussed previously, is organ inferiority.

The second situation he called pampering. Pampering can be operationally defined as doing anything for children they can do for themselves (Dreikurs & Soltz, 1964). Pampered children do not grow up learning to count on themselves, and because so much has been regularly done for them, they typically begin to doubt their own instrumental skills. As they expect so much to be done, and often it is, when life and other people finally start to say "No!" to them, they feel victimized, deprived, and often grow up feeling neglected.

The third situation Adler called neglect. Neglect occurs when caregivers do not do for children what they are not capable of doing for themselves. Neglect can take many forms, such as outright deprivation, but Adler also included in this category children who grow up hated, unloved, and abused.

With *family training*, emphasis is placed upon the system itself (Barlow, 1984; Rule, 1984; Traver, 1984). According to Barlow (1984, p. 63), the "systemic life styles" of certain families can affect onset, adjustment, exacerbation, and maintenance of many physical conditions and disabilities.

Adler (1956, p. 295) spoke of certain patients who tended to *"cling to the shock effects"* of some situations. Bad things happen to everyone. Some people are shocked by these events, and understandably so. However, many move on, while some do not. Why? According to Adler, it is because some people cling to the effects of the shock for a payoff, classically a social payoff that provides them with a sense of compensation.

Finally, *private logic* is a factor in all of these disorders. Common sense is that which is shared by the community. It is a sign of empathy, identification with others, and community feeling. Private logic is not (Mosak & Maniacci, 1999). As Dreikurs (1967a, p. 135) stated, in cognitive disorders, "as perception of our common world vanishes or disintegrates, the inner world of the patient becomes dominant." The more people lose touch with reality, the more apparent their private logics will become; that is, their idiosyncratic, unique view of themselves, the world, and others will become exposed. If their private logic is problematic, their behavior will be as well, and therefore so will the management of their conditions.

It is in private logic that self-ideal statements can be found. As Adler (1956; Mosak & Maniacci, 1999) detailed, people strive for significance. Self-ideal statements can be summarized as, "In order to belong, I should…" What follows such a statement would entail what Adler originally referred to as the fictional final goal. Some common self-ideal statements would be:

I should be the best (type: superiority seeker)
I should be right (type: needs to be right)
I should be liked (type: pleaser)
I should be in control (type: controller)
I should be taken care of (type: baby)

Certain convictions, or beliefs, will coincide with these statements, and these cluster into recognizable patterns, or types (Mosak, 1971). Adlerians have identified numerous types, such as controllers, pleasers, babies, excitement seekers, and victims. In the pages that follow, for various NCDs, along with the relevant markers within the cognitive domains, examples will be provided of the various Adlerian types who either are prone to develop such NCDs, or use them in a socially unhelpful manner. In addition, how family members with different life-style types handle these challenging diagnoses in loved ones will be discussed.

Not all private logic is "exposed" for psychological reasons, however. In the NCDs, the private logic can be revealed because of neurobiological reasons. How can one tell the difference?

Cummings (1988) has detailed a useful set of guidelines for differential diagnosis. He listed seven characteristics that are indicative of clear-cut organic impairment once clinicians believe the client's private logic is manifesting:

1. Late onset—typically after age 45
2. Atypical features—that is, features that do not typically occur in Schizophrenia or mania
3. A coexistent deficit syndrome—such as Delirium or Aphasia
4. A normal premorbid personality
5. An absent history of psychiatric disability
6. An absent history of family psychiatric disability
7. A coexisting neurological disorder.

In addition, two other signs of which clinicians should be aware are visual hallucinations and making the unfamiliar familiar (Maniacci, 1996). In the first case, visual hallucinations are typically (but not exclusively) indicative of toxic processes in the blood work of patients. In the second, patients who claim to know strangers, or treat people they have never met before as if they knew them (e.g., confusing a nurse with a relative), are confabulating, a sign of impaired perceptual or memory systems. Besides the markers listed in the *DSM-5*, clinicians looking for possible indications of NCDs should be aware of these factors.

To sum up, patients with NCDs are people with histories, personalities, and psychologies. Except for late in the course of many of these disorders, they have styles of life that can influence how the disorders are managed. The family members, as well, have styles of life that can play a crucial role in the treatment, rehabilitation, and management of their loved ones with NCDs.

The relationship of NCDs to life style is fourfold, and can be summarized as:

1. The NCD can be a direct outgrowth or consequence of the life style
2. The NCD can develop completely independently of the life style and not be used in any way
3. The NCD can be independent of the life style, but then can be used either positively or negatively
4. The NCD can develop independently of the life style, and then change the life style for better or worse.

Neurocognitive Disorders in the *DSM-5*

How does the *DSM-5* (American Psychiatric Association, 2013) view the neurocognitive disorders? To begin with, the *DSM* says that the "NCDs are unique among DSM-5 categories in that these are syndromes for which the underlying pathology, and frequently the etiology as well, can potentially be determined" (American Psychiatric Association, 2013, p. 591). It states that all these disorders adversely affect cognition in a unique way. "The NCDs are those in which impaired cognition has not been present since birth or very early in life, and thus represents a decline from a previously attained level of functioning" (American Psychiatric Association, 2013, p. 591).

In prior editions of the *DSM*, terms such as "Organic Mental Disorders," and "Delirium, Dementia, and other Cognitive Disorders" were used (Maniacci, 1993, 1996). While the label "Delirium" has been kept, the new manual is dropping the formal use of the term "Dementia." Among the reasons for this change is that Dementia is commonly associated with the cognitive disorders in the elderly, "the term *neurocognitive disorder* is widely used and often preferred for conditions affecting younger individuals, such as impairment secondary to traumatic brain injury or HIV infection" (American Psychiatric Association, 2013, p. 561). While the term Dementia is still referred to throughout the section, and acknowledgment is made that professionals in various settings will continue to use it, the preferred term in *DSM-5* is "neurocognitive disorder."

Major and Mild Neurocognitive Disorder

Major Neurocognitive Disorder and Mild Neurocognitive Disorder are new diagnostic categories in the *DSM-5*, where "Major" and "Mild" exist on a spectrum of cognitive and functional impairment. The threshold between Mild NCD and Major NCD may seem somewhat arbitrary. However, the *DSM* insists that each represents different levels of impairment, and that the "mild" designation is a necessary diagnosis. They point to the need to recognize individuals who need care for cognitive issues that go beyond normal aging. The impact of these problems is noticeable, and identifying the mild level as early as possible can increase the likelihood that interventions will be more effective. "Major" and "mild" neurocognitive disorders are subtyped according to the known or presumed causes that underlie cognitive decline, as well as to the degree of impaired functioning.

Major Neurocognitive Disorder

With major NCDs, there are significant declines in "cognitive function" and "cognitive performance." This subtype or category includes a set of existing mental disorder diagnoses from the *DSM-IV*, including Dementia and Amnestic Disorder. In addition, these deficits "interfere with independence in everyday activities (i.e., at a minimum, requiring assistance with complex instrumental activities of daily living such as paying bills or managing medication)" (American Psychiatric Association, 2013, p. 602).

Mild Neurocognitive Disorder

Mild Neurocognitive Disorder represents a functional loss between normal aging and that of a major neurocognitive disorder. Mild NCD describes a level of cognitive decline that requires the individual to engage in compensatory strategies and accommodations to maintain independence and perform activities of daily living. With mild NCDs, cognitive decline is present but to a lesser degree. "Evidence of modest decline" in functioning and performance is noted, but such declines "do not interfere with capacity for independence" (American Psychiatric Association, 2013, p. 605). To meet the criteria for Mild NCD requires changes that impact cognitive functioning. These symptoms are usually observed by the individual, a close relative, clinician, or assessed by objective testing.

Cognitive Domains

A welcome addition to the manual is the inclusion of specific neuropsychological guidelines for diagnosing each of the disorders. These "cognitive domains" (American Psychiatric Association, 2013, pp. 592–595) are explained in detail, with specific examples provided. The six key domains are the following:

1. Complex attention (sustained attention, divided attention, selective attention, processing speed)
2. Executive functioning (planning, decision making, working memory, responding to feedback/error correction, overriding habits, inhibition, mental flexibility)
3. Learning and memory (immediate, recent, long term)
4. Language (expressive, receptive)
5. Perceptual-motor (visual, visuo-constructive, perceptual-motor, praxis, gnosis)
6. Social cognition (recognition of emotions, theory of mind).

Perhaps the importance of a biopsychosocial perspective is nowhere more evident than with these disorders. Adlerian theory has long been a holistic theory (Adler, 1956; Maniacci, Sackett-Maniacci, & Mosak, 2014; Mosak & Maniacci, 1999). Adlerians treat the whole person and the system in which the person lives. With these disorders, that is crucial.

DELIRIUM

Clinical Presentation

Delirium is basically a disorder of attention. It develops quickly and tends to fluctuate throughout the day. Most times, because of the disturbance in attention, some other domain is adversely affected (e.g., language, perception, etc.). It is often indicative of a medical emergency that requires immediate diagnosis and treatment. Rarely does it last more than one week, and typically, the younger the patient, the more hyperactive the presentation, with the elderly usually manifesting the hypoactive subtype. A sundown syndrome is quite common, with this disorder getting worse in the evening (as the sun sets and external stimulation decreases, and the patients' internal resources diminish due to fatigue). The majority of patients with Delirium recover with or without treatment, but early intervention helps shorten the length considerably. Anyone can develop Delirium. A high fever that goes untreated may quite easily produce it. Many drugs can trigger it as well.

On the mental status examination (MSE), the typical markers will be trouble repeating digits presented in sequence. New information will not be recalled (e.g., repeat back these four unrelated words). Mental calculations will be very difficult (e.g., divide 54 by 9). Patients will be slow and inaccurate in their tasks (e.g., putting together puzzles or block designs).

DSM-5 Characterization

Delirium is a disorder characterized in *DSM-5* as a disturbance in attention and awareness. This is shown by the reduced capacity to focus and shift attention and to be oriented to the environment. Delirium develops within hours to a few days and represents a sudden change not solely attributable to another neurocognitive disorder. Furthermore, it tends to fluctuate in severity over the course of a day. Other changes include memory deficit, disorientation, language disturbance, or a perceptual disturbance not due to a pre-existing neurocognitive disorder. Nor do they occur in the context of a coma. Finally, there is evidence of a physiological cause such as a medical condition, drug intoxication or withdrawal, or toxin exposure (American Psychiatric Association, 2013).

Biopsychosocial–Adlerian Case Conceptualization

Can life-style factors be involved in Delirium? From an Adlerian perspective, excitement seekers, superiority seekers, and controllers are rather prone to it. How so? An elaboration is needed. Excitement seekers are sensation seekers who court novelty and stimulation. Not all of them seek out drugs or abuse substances, but many do. This leads them to a higher risk. Superiority seekers and controllers are more prone to Delirium as well, for one common reason: Neither will seek out medical attention nor admit illness quickly. Both are likely to ignore signs that something with medication is not right or a low-grade fever is getting worse. Why? Because both are driven. They will keep focused on external goals until they are exhausted, even sick, but they must complete their tasks. They are too hesitant to admit "weakness." They fail to realize they are not "weak," they are "ill." Such a distinction typically falls on deaf ears. They believe in the supremacy of the will, and that they are going to "push through," even if it kills them. Without care, it might. Family dynamics are not usually that important in the development and management of Delirium for one basic reason: it is of such short duration.

Treatment Considerations

The vast majority of Delirium patients are cured within hours with simple treatment and rest. The substance and medication-induced varieties require rapid medical intervention, usually a brief inpatient stay for detoxification, and psychoeducation about their response to specific medications or substances.

Case Example: Bill

Bill arrived at the emergency room in restraint. He was thrashing about, swearing, and looking disheveled. Toxicology revealed he was filled with amphetamines. He was treated and psychiatric and psychological consultation was requested. He was 27 years old and still living at home with his widowed mother and younger sister. He had a sporadic work history and barely finished high school. Substance abuse counseling was recommended, as was family therapy. He refused both, claiming he was just having too much fun and things got out of hand. His mother reported that he regularly abused drugs. She felt he was best left to her care, that she would be able to handle him, and there was no need to worry. They left against medical advice 24 hours after detoxification.

Bill was an excitement seeker. He loved driving fast, taking risks, and having fun. Boredom was equivalent to dying, he believed; life without thrills was not worth living. The diagnosis of Delirium was clearly biological. His drug taking was tied to his life style: He sought out stimulants as his drug of choice; therefore he fell into category 1 of the aforementioned factors: His NCD was an outgrowth of his life style.

MAJOR OR MILD NEUROCOGNITIVE DISORDER DUE TO ALZHEIMER'S DISEASE

Clinical Presentation

In Alzheimer's disease, genetic testing and evidence of a genetic marker are crucial, but in addition, the MSE will reveal evidence of a decline in memory and learning. The decline, in either the major or mild variant, will be progressive without extended plateaus. It is terminal. The memory decline will show up as disturbance in the sensorium. A clear sensorium will have a person "oriented times four," meaning the patient will be able to identify correctly person, place, time, and situation. As the disease progresses, the decline will typically follow this progression: First, patients will have trouble articulating why they are where they are ("situation"); then they will have difficulty identifying where they are ("place"); as the disease progresses, they will have trouble identifying how long they have been with the examiner, and even what day or year it is ("time"); finally, in advanced cases, they will lose a sense of who they are ("person"). New learning, such as the ability to listen to a story and repeat it, will decline.

DSM-5 Characterization

Neurocognitive Disorder Due to Alzheimer's Disease is a disorder characterized in *DSM-5* by an insidious beginning and a slow, steady progression of impairment of memory, learning, language, perception, or another cognitive domain. For the diagnosis of Major NCD, there must be evidence of Alzheimer's disease from family history or genetic testing. In addition there must be obvious evidence of decline in learning and memory, and this decline must be progressive. Furthermore, the absence of other neurodegenerative or other neurological conditions is required. In contrast, for the diagnosis of Minor NCD, no evidence of Alzheimer's disease from family history or genetic testing is required. However, there must be obvious evidence of decline in learning and memory, steady progressive cognitive decline, and the absence of other neurodegenerative or other neurological conditions (American Psychiatric Association, 2013).

Biopsychosocial–Adlerian Case Conceptualization

There is no specific Adlerian conceptualization of this disorder. Because there is an obvious biological vulnerability for this disorder, treatment is largely biological. The extent to which there is psychosocial vulnerability to this disorder can be inferred from an investigation of the individual's life-style convictions.

Treatment Considerations

Generally, treatment that will be useful for those experiencing this disorder is best tailored to specific considerations unique to the individual patient. Typically, these include the type of symptoms, level of severity and impairment, personality and system dynamics, and quality-of-life considerations. It may include medication, psychiatric consultation, and family therapy with a focus on assisting family members to understand, accept, and adjust to the patient's progressively deteriorating condition.

Neurological determinism is the belief that improvement is not possible in progressively deteriorating neurological conditions. This form of hard determinism is alien to Adlerian Psychology. Instead, Adlerians believe that individuals can find meaning and increase their courage to persist in the face of disabling conditions.

Two promising Adlerian therapeutic interventions have been found to be useful in increasing meaning, courage, and quality of life in individuals with Alzheimer's disease, particularly in the early stages of the disorder. One of these is the use of a form of Adlerian play therapy using the sand tray. Parsons (2013) found that individuals in the early stages of Alzheimer's responded positively to this action-focused intervention, which increased both cognitive and emotional responsiveness and appeared to slow disease progression during the courses of this intervention. Pinke (2009) describes Adlerian Dementia resistance in working with individuals experiencing Dementia. She describes several strategies for encouraging resilience in individuals with Dementia. She also describes strategies for encouraging resilience in their caregivers.

Case Example: Hester

Hester is an 81-year-old female who was brought to a memory disorders clinic by her daughter. Although she did not believe that anything was wrong, her daughter reported that her mother's thinking and memory had deteriorated slowly over five years. Her phone had been disconnected because she forgot to pay the bills. She continued to buy the same canned food items whenever she went to the store. The refrigerator was full of spoiled food. When Hester was evaluated there were pauses in her speech, and her daughter often filled in missing words for her. On the Mini Mental Status Exam Hester was not oriented to the day, date, month, or year. Neither could she recall any of the three items she was instructed to remember. Furthermore, she was unable to name even common items. A CT scan of her head showed atrophy of hippocampi, lateral temporal lobes, and parietal lobes. There was clear evidence of a decline in prior cognitive abilities that interfered with function, noted in her phone being disconnected, buying the same food repetitively, and having spoiled food in the refrigerator. Cognitive impairments in both memory and language were present. That her memory deteriorated slowly over five years suggests a gradual onset. In addition, the CT scan of her head ruled out a vascular dementia. Therefore, she met DSM-5 criteria for Major Neurocognitive Disorder Due to Alzheimer's Disease.

MAJOR OR MILD NEUROCOGNITIVE DISORDER DUE TO TRAUMATIC BRAIN INJURY

Clinical Presentation

Another class of neurocognitive disorders is those that involve traumatic brain injury (TBI). As the name suggests, this disorder requires clear evidence of traumatic brain injury. Usually, this involves a head injury that has led to a change in cognitive functioning. The most common variation would be Post-Concussion Syndrome. The key diagnostic signs are loss of consciousness, amnesia after the evident (i.e., the patient cannot remember the injury), confusion and disorientation, and neurological signs on various structural tests (e.g., brain scans showing lesions, insults or injuries).

DSM-5 Characterization

Neurocognitive Disorder Due to Traumatic Brain Injury is a disorder characterized in *DSM-5* by evidence of a traumatic brain injury. This injury must involve disorientation and confusion, neurological signs, post-traumatic amnesia, or the loss of consciousness. This diagnosis also requires that these symptoms and signs appear immediately after the brain injury occurs, or right after recovery of consciousness. Criteria must also be met for either Major or Mild Neurocognitive Disorder. This NCD can be coded with or without behavioral disturbance. There is a three-point scale for assessing the severity of the TBI, which is reproduced in the *DSM-5* (American Psychiatric Association, 2013, p. 626).

Biopsychosocial–Adlerian Case Conceptualization

From an Adlerian perspective, this disorder is potentially tied to category 1. While many TBIs are purely accidental, some are a byproduct of life-style choices. Superiority seekers and drivers (Mosak, 1971) are prone to push too hard, do too much, and push the envelope. Football players, racecar drivers, and extreme-sports enthusiasts (e.g., skateboarding) can and often do experience TBIs.

Treatment Considerations

Generally, treatment that will be useful for those experiencing this disorder is best tailored to specific considerations unique to the individual patient. Typically, these include the type of symptoms, level of severity and impairment, personality and system dynamics, and quality-of-life considerations. It may include medication, psychiatric consultation, and family therapy with a focus on assisting family members to understand, accept, and adjust to the patient's progressively deteriorating condition.

Case Example: Doris

Doris was brought into family therapy at age 16, the youngest of five siblings. She was irritable, nasty, and argumentative. She was also an elite soccer player, being scouted by nationally ranked, big-time schools since the age of 12. She played on national championship teams, played soccer year round, and rarely could be found without a soccer ball nearby. She had trouble tracking in session. She could not repeat what was said without help, which she received on a regular basis from her mother. Her grades were declining, she was not sleeping well, and would often cry with little provocation. Besides family therapy, an MSE was administered. She had difficulty with attention, concentration, and immediate memory. She was oriented times four, but impatient. She had trouble with higher-cognitive functions, particularly with decoding others' motivations on storytelling tests. A referral was made to a neurologist, who found evidence for multiple TBIs, most likely due to several concussions. Doris admitted to getting her "bell rung" quite often from heading the soccer ball, and on at least three occasions, smacking heads with other players while attempting to head the ball.

Her earliest recollection (Mosak & Di Pietro, 2006; Mosak & Maniacci, 1999) was the following: "Age three: I was trying to keep up with my siblings. They were running and I couldn't keep up. I started to lose my balance and fell right on my face. Blood squirted out of my nose and I screamed. I got up and kept running—I wasn't going to lose to them. Mom saw me, ran over, and picked me up. She hugged me and put her sleeve on my nose, all the while yelling at my siblings to include me or else! The most vivid part of the ER was: Me trying to keep up and Mom hugging me. Feeling: Loved, but frustrated. Why was I so small?"

As Mosak (1971) has written, Doris was a combination of two types: driver and baby. Her father was a semi-professional athlete most of his life, and a youngest born who vowed to outdo his siblings, and did. He never made it to the "big leagues" and felt unfulfilled. Mother was an oldest born who nurtured and cared for her ailing mother and three challenging siblings while growing up. Doris took advantage of both parental styles. Father kept pushing her to excel, overidentified with her, and called her "daddy's superstar." Mother was always available to "clean her up" when she got bumps and bruises. Doris was going to succeed even if it killed her.

The neurologist recommended several months off of soccer. The family would not hear of it, despite the diagnosis of Mild Neurocognitive Disorder Due to Traumatic Brain Injury, post-concussion type. Family therapy was challenging. They wanted her calmer, nicer, but not less competitive. How much of her symptom presentation was due to her competitive, driven style versus the sequelae of the repeated TBIs is unclear. Both were considered important and interactive with each other.

MAJOR OR MILD NEUROCOGNITIVE DISORDER DUE TO PARKINSON'S DISEASE

Clinical Presentation

Notable in Neurocognitive Disorder Due to Parkinson's Disease is a decline in cognitive functioning, with insidious onset and gradual progression, but the MSE markers will include apathy, anxious and depressed mood, hallucinations, personality changes, and excessive daytime sleepiness. As the Parkinson's disease progresses, patients will shake, tremble, and have severe movement disturbances.

DSM-5 Characterization

Neurocognitive Disorder Due to Parkinson's Disease is a disorder characterized in *DSM-5* by the presence of Parkinson's disease. Also required is an insidious beginning and a slow, steady progression of impairment. The disorder cannot be caused by another medical condition, nor can there be evidence of mixed etiology, and Parkinson's disease must precede the onset of the NCD. Criteria must also be met for either Major or Mild Neurocognitive Disorder. This NCD can be coded with or without behavioral disturbance (American Psychiatric Association, 2013).

Biopsychosocial–Adlerian Case Conceptualization

There is no specific Adlerian conceptualization of this disorder. Because there is an obvious biological vulnerability for this disorder, treatment is largely biological. The extent to which there is psychosocial vulnerability to this disorder can be inferred from an investigation of the individual's life-style convictions.

Treatment Considerations

Generally, treatment that will be useful for those experiencing this disorder is best tailored to specific considerations unique to the individual patient. Typically, these include the type of symptoms, level of severity and impairment, personality and system dynamics, and quality-of-life considerations. It may include medication, psychiatric consultation, and family therapy with a focus on assisting family members to understand, accept, and adjust to the patient's progressively deteriorating condition.

Case Example: Pedro

Pedro presented to therapy reluctantly. He was 67 years old and exhibiting bizarre behavior, such as hallucinations, frequently falling asleep during the daytime, delusions that someone was stealing his money, and extreme tension and fear. Four years earlier he had been diagnosed with Parkinson's disease, and it was progressing. He had inconsistently taken his medications and had not regularly followed up with physicians. His wife, daughters, and niece requested a family "intervention" to "get through to him." His tremors were so pronounced that he had difficulty maintaining balance and he needed assistance to drink from a glass.

Careful screening was conducted with the MSE. He failed many items quickly. He could not maintain attention. He was hostile to any feedback that attempted to correct his mistakes. Once it became obvious he could not solve a particular problem, he dug his heels in, and kept trying the same strategy. On the FAS portion of the assessment, a task that required him to list as many words as he could in 60 seconds that began with the letters "F," then "A," and finally "S," he could barely produce five or six each during the allotted times (despite being a native English speaker). It was even worse with the animal-naming portion of the same test. He was oriented times two (person and place, but he had real trouble with time and situation). His complex drawing tasks were scored at the age of five to seven years, a sharp deterioration for him. Pedro was severely impaired and getting worse. He could not empathize with his wife and children, often claiming that they were out to get him and pushing him needlessly. On a few occasions, he had wandered out of the house alone and gotten lost.

According to all in the room, Pedro was an intelligent, sweet man, until the last couple of years. His wife thought he was becoming "schizophrenic," and his children and niece thought he was abusing drugs or alcohol. Unfortunately, none of those was true. After considerable pressure and two extended family therapy sessions, Pedro agreed to see his neurologist, who confirmed the diagnosis of Major Neurocognitive Disorder Due to Parkinson's Disease. The family was seen regularly to discuss home healthcare options, the use of home nurses and aids, and to plan for the eventual use of a nursing home or supportive living arrangement.

The case of Pedro is a clear example of a category 4. Pedro's life style was being changed by his disease. He was no longer the man he was. The family had a hard time accepting this and delayed what they knew had to be done. They kept hoping family therapy would "get through to him." It could not. Environmental manipulation was the issue: Pedro's environment had to be changed to protect him and prolong his life. He was no longer capable of changing himself.

UNSPECIFIED NEUROCOGNITIVE DISORDER

Clinical Presentation

Unspecified Neurocognitive Disorder represents a diagnosis of exclusion. "It is a useful placeholder in the not uncommon situation of uncertainty whether cognitive deficits are due to Delirium, Dementia, or a combination of both" (Frances, 2013, p. 129).

DSM-5 Characterization

Unspecified Neurocognitive Disorder is characterized in *DSM-5* as disorders in which symptoms of a specific NCD are present but do not meet the full criteria for any other NCD. However, such disorders must cause significant distress or impairment in social, occupational, or relational functioning. In addition, this diagnostic category is used in situations in which the exact cause cannot be determined with sufficient certainty (American Psychiatric Association, 2013).

Biopsychosocial–Adlerian Case Conceptualization

For the majority of these NCDs, they would fall into the categories of 2, 3, and 4. These develop independently of the life style, but can be used by it or significantly change it. In some cases, they have no effect upon the life style until the disease progresses, and the cognitive deterioration (basically) destroys all personality functioning. The disease overwhelms the personality.

Treatment Considerations

No general treatment recommendations are possible for disorders in this category. Instead, treatment is best tailored to the unique presentation, which typically will be focused on symptoms, degree of impairment, and quality-of-life considerations.

Case Example: George

George was 13 years old when he was referred by his cardiologist. He was clinically depressed, fighting with his family, doing poorly in school, and frequently had thoughts of suicide. He did not edit himself when he spoke, often using crude language and insults. He grabbed people inappropriately when aroused either sexually or in anger. He had received a heart transplant some four years prior, and was not functioning as well as medical tests indicated he should. He was the eldest of three. He had waited more than two years for the transplant, been given "last rites" by the family's Catholic priest on two occasions because his medical condition had worsened so much, and had missed almost three years of school, having to be home schooled or tutored in the hospital because of his grave condition. A full neuropsychological workup was performed.

George had a superior IQ (120), but an extremely patchy presentation. Some areas were well above the mean, while others were well below. Processing speed was extremely poor (5th percentile), short-term memory was poor (26th percentile), and calculating abilities were impaired (23rd percentile). Despite these scores, other scores were "off the chart," such as comprehension, visual memory, and reasoning skills (90th percentile or above). He admitted that at school, once he "got it," he "got it." "Getting it," however, was a "nightmare." He could not follow in class, especially if there were distractions. Reading was slow. He knew he was smart, but he had trouble showing it. The findings were discussed with his cardiology transplant team, a pediatric neurologist, and the family therapist (a psychologist). The diagnosis was Mild Vascular Neurocognitive Disorder with behavioral disturbance related to cardiac transplant.

His earliest recollection was this: "Age four: I was weak and knew it. I could never keep up with other kids and nobody knew why. One day, I was at the playground and I couldn't chase the ball my father threw. Another kid got it and brought it to my dad. Most vivid part: I failed again. Feeling: I'm a loser."

George felt like a failure. According to Mosak (1971), he would be a combination of the victim and inadequate types. His heart condition was undiagnosed until he was almost six, and only after a severe infection put him in the hospital and almost by accident was it discovered his already poorly functioning heart was weakened by the runaway fever and infection. It did not help that his two-year-younger brother was large for his age, precocious, and aggressive, taking every advantage he could to prove he was "better than" his big brother. This was a category 3 situation. The medical condition developed independently of the life style, but then reinforced what was already there. Now, on top of the weak constitution and small size, with a larger younger brother, George had a bad heart, which really drove him down. He was not able to control his outbursts and attention problems, but individual and family therapy was instituted to try and both develop some focusing skills and teach the family to not be provoked by his style or overly fearful of his cardiac condition (Jordan, Barde, & Zeiher, 2007). In addition, they had to learn how to not provoke him. This proved to be an on-going struggle. After five years of cognitive rehabilitation, individual and family therapy, many positive changes have occurred, but the underlying dynamics of the family, in particular, are unchanged. Father is a combination of "needs to be liked" and "needs to be right" (Mosak, 1971). Through religion and "niceness" he hopes to save his son. Mother is a panicked controller who on several occasions almost lost her firstborn son, and this only exacerbated her pre-existing tendency to control. Now she is what she laughingly refers to as a "super controller." She reports, somewhat accurately, that if she were not, George might be dead. She is partially correct.

OTHER NEUROCOGNITIVE DISORDERS

Frontotemporal Neurocognitive Disorder

This disorder involves a disturbance of the lobes of the brain associated with the ability to plan, inhibit impulses, and use reason, located at the front and sides of the head. It has an insidious onset and gradual progression. There is behavioral disinhibition (e.g., taking off clothes at inappropriate times and places), compulsive/ritualistic behaviors, along with hyperorality and significant changes to diet. The main declines are in social cognition, executive functions, and sometimes language skills. Interestingly enough, and diagnostically significant, there is little disturbance in learning, memory, and perceptual-motor functioning. On the MSE, patients can repeat numbers, do calculations, and reproduce complex drawings and puzzles. They cannot identify the feelings of others, have difficulty decoding social situations (e.g., Why do you think this person would do this?), and seem to not care about much. They will not stop themselves from doing what they feel (e.g., eating too much, touching others inappropriately, or checking and rechecking things).

Major or Mild Neurocognitive Disorder with Lewy Bodies

Lewy bodies are lesions of the brain, mostly cortical in nature but sometimes in the basal ganglia. This disorder has an insidious onset and gradual progression. These patients will have fluctuating cognitive skills that can be quite confusing to examiners. The most noticeable disturbances will be in attention and alertness, but two key factors are present: visual hallucinations and a rapid onset of Parkinson's disease-like symptoms. They will have trouble moving, fall frequently, they will have urinary incontinence, orthostatic hypotension (i.e., low blood pressure upon standing up), and frequently depression, delusions, and misidentifications of people.

Major or Mild Neurocognitive Disorder Due to Vascular Disease

This disorder is diagnosed when the cognitive decline is linked to a vascular incident (i.e., something related to blood flow to the brain). The decline is most noticeable in complex attention and frontal-executive functioning. On the MSE, patients will have trouble with processing speed, keeping multiple stimuli in focus, and general attention. They may not be able to inhibit their responses to strong emotions, and often will yield to whatever strong impulse they have.

Substance/Medication-Induced Major or Mild Neurocognitive Disorder

This disorder produces the impairment immediately after ingesting the substance, or after prolonged exposure. What the MSE shows is dependent upon the type and quantity of substance ingested, and any pre-existing conditions that might be exacerbated by the substance.

Major or Mild Neurocognitive Disorder Due to HIV Infection

The presentation of this disorder is very much dependent upon the progression of the Human Immunodeficiency Virus. Like the substance-induced variation, it will have a fluctuating presentation on the MSE.

Major or Mild Neurocognitive Disorder Due to Prion Disease

In this disorder the onset is insidious, and rapid progression is common. The disturbance will be in the motor areas, with ataxia being prominent. The two most common causes of this are Creutzfeldt-Jakob disease, and bovine spongiform encephalopathy ("mad cow disease"). The decline noted in the MSE common to all NCDs is present, but the motor piece is there as well. They will have difficulty with coordination (therefore, reproducing drawings may be difficult); their gait, when walking, will be disturbed (e.g., they will lean, or tilt, to one side, or slap their feet on the ground while walking).

Major or Mild Neurocognitive Disorder Due to Huntington's Disease

This disorder is similar to some aspects of NCD Due to Parkinson's Disease. However, there are also notable differences. Irritability, obsessive-compulsiveness, and psychosis are more common presentations, which are added to the clear, documented changes in cognitive functioning and performance.

OTHER DISORDERS

There are some non-NCD disorders that can mimic NCDs. These include Bipolar Disorder, Mood Disorder, Anxiety Disorder, Obsessive-Compulsive Disorder, Psychosis, and Personality Change Due to Another Medical Condition. These six diagnoses were previously considered part of the "Organic Mental Disorders" section of the *DSM* (Maniacci, 1993, 1996). They have been moved to the respective categories alongside their more psychologically based diagnoses. Nonetheless, clinicians should still be aware of their appearances. Patients with these disorders present as if they were depressed, anxious, even psychotic, yet the underlying mechanisms are biologically based, not psychologically determined. The guidelines by Cummings (1988) are helpful, and Taylor (1989) has detailed two additional categories of which clinicians should be aware: alerting and presumptive clues.

"Alerting clues" are those presentations that should raise suspicion of a possible biological cause. The five alerting clues are:

1. No history of similar symptoms
2. No readily identifiable cause
3. Age 55 or older
4. Chronic physical disease
5. Drug use.

"Presumptive clues" indicate a "strong possibility" of biological causes (Taylor, 1989, p. 586). The seven presumptive clues are:

1. Symptoms of brain syndrome (i.e., cognitive disorders)
2. Head injury
3. Change in headache pattern
4. Visual disturbances
5. Speech deficits
6. Abnormal body movements
7. Changes in consciousness.

Adlerians have two other criteria they use. Adler (1956), Adler (1989), Brown (1995), and Mosak and Maniacci (1998) have discussed how to use them. One tactic is called "The Question." Adlerians ask patients, "What would be different in your life if you did not have these symptoms?" Their responses fall into one of three categories (Brown, 1995).

Response one: "I would be able to work, love, socialize, etc." When the response to "The Question" is that the patients would be able to engage in a social activity of some sort, the chances are that the anxiety, depression, obsession, psychosis (or whatever specific symptom) would be functional; or in other words, primarily psychological.

Response two: "I wouldn't be in so much pain or discomfort, etc." If, even upon pressing, there is no social purpose given, chances are the symptoms are primarily somatic. The person with this type of response is most likely medically, not psychologically, ill.

Response three: "I wouldn't hurt so much, and then I would be able to socialize/work/love, etc." This is a combination response. It has the social purpose listed in response one, but also the medically based emphasis of response two. In such a case, the chances are that their symptoms are primarily medical, but being used psychologically as well.

The other tactic is to use "diagnosis by purpose." Most diagnoses are based upon "inclusion." A checklist is presented, and depending upon how many items the patients endorse, clinicians can say, "Yes, you meet the criteria for ____." If the items on the checklist are not endorsed to a sufficient degree, clinicians then use "exclusion." When all is ruled out, it must be "this." Until very recently, Alzheimer's disease was diagnosed this way. When all other dementias were ruled out, the leftover category was Alzheimer's.

Adlerians have a third way to diagnose: by purpose. "Diagnosis by purpose" means that the symptom must serve psychological purpose. As K. Adler (1989, p. 63) wrote:

(a) The symptom must be usable and necessary in the pursuit of the patient's goal....
(b) The use of this particular symptom must be traceable throughout his history from childhood on. (c) The symptom, which is thus part of his lifestyle, must be found to pervade all his attitudes, all his movements, his dreams, his memory, and all his feeling life and relations. ... If these criteria are not fulfilled, the chances are that his condition has some organic basis.

People have life styles. As Mosak (1971) has identified, clinicians can assess the type by looking at the private logic, particularly the self-ideal statements. Some of the types he identifies are victims, martyrs, controllers, babies, drivers, superiority seekers, pleasers, getters, and so forth. If the symptom presentation does not match the life-style type, chances are the symptoms are either a response to extreme stress, or biologically based.

For example, if a woman presents with a "pleasing/needs to be right" blend of types, chances are she would never be violent, aggressive, and cruel. If she is, clinicians should first check to see if she is under extreme stress, such as severe abuse or some major crisis. If no such cause can be found, then, as K. Adler (1989) noted, the chances are that there is some organic basis prompting her outbursts.

Case Example: Gerry

Gerry was just past his 30th birthday when he presented for counseling complaining of anxiety, sweating, dry mouth, and difficulty sleeping. He was becoming confused because his general practitioner had prescribed an anxiolytic, which was ineffective. Thirty-five sessions of psychoanalytically oriented individual psychotherapy was not helpful, either. His wife insisted he try one more time. He was asked "The Question": "What would be different in your life is you weren't so anxious?" His answer was quick and sure: "I'd be able to sleep. My hands wouldn't shake and I wouldn't sweat through my shirts!" Despite pressing, there was no social purpose stated. When asked, he affirmed two other symptoms he had, but to which he had not really paid too much attention: hair thinning and body temperature regulation problems (e.g., often too hot or too cold). He was sent to an endocrinologist, who ran three blood tests (TSH, T3, and T4), and the results indicated an extremely overactive thyroid. The diagnosis: Anxiety Disorder Due to Hyperthyroidism.

Gerry had no history of control issues. People do not develop anxiety disorders without a history of control in their life styles (Mosak, 1973). His early recollections, dreams, and family constellation interview all reflected the life style of a feeling-avoider (Mosak, 1971). He did not value feelings, but he was not into control, either. He could be rather messy, even disorganized, and considered himself an "absent-minded professor." He taught philosophy at a university, specialized in teaching logic and rhetoric, and was very dry in his humor. Anxiety is an intense type of fear, and Gerry never really paid much attention to feelings. Things simply did not add up. His symptoms had to originate from outside his life style.

Concluding Note

The NCDs are challenging. All clinicians, particularly those who are not physicians, should be aware of when more may be going on than psychodynamics and life-style issues. If a biopsychosocial perspective is to be maintained, clinicians should pay attention to more than the "psychosocial" end of the spectrum, and give more attention to the "biological" end of the "biopsychosocial" continuum.

Whether it is Delirium, or Major Neurocognitive Disorder, or one of the masquerading disorders such as Obsessive-Compulsive Disorder Due to Another Medical Condition, a holistic, teleological, phenomenological, and social perspective greatly increases the chances of helping patients. Adlerian theory is well suited to working with these patients. A thorough grounding in neuropsychology and a good working relationship with physicians and other healthcare professionals is required as well.

References

Adler, A. (1917). *Study of Organ Inferiority and Its Psychical Compensation: A Contribution to Clinical Medicine* (S.E. Jelliffe, Trans.). New York, NY: Nervous and Mental Diseases Company. (Original work published 1907.)

Adler, A. (1956). In H.L. Ansbacher & R.R. Ansbacher (Eds.), *The Individual Psychology of Alfred Adler: A Systematic Presentation of his Writings.* New York, NY: Basic Books.

Adler, A. (2012). The structure of neurosis. In J. Carlson & M.P. Maniacci (Eds.), *Alfred Adler Revisited* (pp. 218–228). New York, NY: Routledge. (Original work published 1935.)

Adler, K. (1989). Techniques that shorten psychotherapy: Illustrated with five cases. *Individual Psychology: The Journal of Adlerian Theory, Research & Practice*, 45, pp. 62–74. (Original work published 1972.)

American Psychiatric Association (2013). *Diagnostic and Statistical Manual of Mental Disorders, Fifth Edition.* Arlington, VA: American Psychiatric Publishing.

Barlow, M.S. (1984). Lifestyle and the family of the disabled. In W.R. Rule (Ed.), *Lifestyle Counseling for Adjustment to Disability* (pp. 61–80). Rockville, MD: Aspen Publications.

Brown, P.R. (1995). The reliability and validity of "The Question" in the differential diagnosis of somatic and psychogenic disorders. Unpublished doctoral dissertation, Adler School of Professional Psychology, Chicago, IL.

Cummings, J.L. (1988). Organic psychosis. *Psychosomatics*, 29, pp. 16–26.

Dreikurs, R. (1967a). Psychological differentiation of psychopathological disorders. In R. Dreikurs, *Psychodynamics, Psychotherapy and Counseling* (pp. 5–24). Chicago, IL: Alfred Adler Institute. (Original work published 1945.)

Dreikurs, R. (1967b). The socio-psychological dynamics of physical disability. In R. Dreikurs, *Psychodynamics, Psychotherapy, and Counseling* (pp. 167–188). Chicago, IL: Alfred Adler Institute. (Original work published 1948.)

Dreikurs, R. & Soltz, V. (1964). *Children: The Challenge.* New York, NY: Dell, Sloan, & Pearce.

Fainaru-Wada, M. & Fainaru, S. (2013). *League of Denial: The NFL, Concussions, and the Battle for Truth.* New York, NY: Crown Archetype.

Frances, A. (2013). *Essentials of Psychiatric Diagnosis: Responding to the Challenges of DSM-5.* New York, NY: Guilford.

Jordan, J., Barde, B., & Zeiher, A.M. (Eds.) (2007). *Contributions toward Evidence-Based Psychocardiology: A Systemic Review of the Literature.* Washington, DC: American Psychological Association.

Lezak, M.D., Howieson, D.B., Bigler, E.D., & Tranel, D. (2012). *Neuropsychological Assessment* (5th edn.). New York, NY: Oxford University Press.

Maniacci, M.P. (1993). Organic mental disorders. In L. Sperry & J. Carlson (Eds.), *Psychopathology and Psychotherapy: From Diagnosis to Treatment* (pp. 57–79). Muncie, IN: Accelerated Development.

Maniacci, M.P. (1996). Mental disorders due to a general medical condition and other cognitive disorders. In L. Sperry & J. Carlson (Eds.), *Psychopathology and Psychotherapy: From DSM-IV Diagnosis to Treatment* (2nd edn.) (pp. 51–75). Washington, DC: Accelerated Development.

Maniacci, M.P., Sackett-Maniacci, L., & Mosak, H.H. (2014). Adlerian psychotherapy. In D. Wedding & R.J. Corisini (Eds.), *Current Psychotherapies* (10th edn.) (pp. 55–94). United States: Cengage Learning.

Miller, L. (1993). *Psychotherapy of the Brain-Injured Patient: Reclaiming the Shattered Self.* New York, NY: Norton Books.

Mosak, H.H. (1971). Lifestyle. In A.G. Nikelly (Ed.), *Techniques for Behavior Change: Applications of Adlerian Theory* (pp. 77–81). Springfield, IL: Charles C. Thomas.

Mosak, H.H. (1973). The controller: A social interpretation of the anal character. In H.H. Mosak (Ed.), *Alfred Adler: His Influence upon Psychology Today* (pp. 43–52). Park Ridge, NJ: Noyes Press.

Mosak. H.H. & Di Pietro, R. (2006). *Early Recollections: Interpretative Method and Application.* New York, NY: Routledge.

Mosak, H.H. & Maniacci, M.P. (1998). *Tactics in Counseling and Psychotherapy.* Itasca, IL: F.E. Peacock.

Mosak, H.H. & Maniacci, M. (1999). *A Primer of Adlerian Psychology: The Analytic- Behavioral-Cognitive Psychology of Alfred Adler.* Philadelphia, PA: Brunner/Mazel.

Parson, M. (2013). Using the symbolic expression of sand tray to kinesthetically connect to the inner cognitions of individuals diagnosed with a neurocognitive disorder. (Unpublished doctoral dissertation.) Florida Atlantic University, Boca Raton, FL.

Pinke, J. (2009). *An Adlerian Framework for Encouraging Dementia Resilience* (Master's thesis). Retrieved from http://www.alfredadler.edu/sites/default/files/Pinke%20MP%202010.pdf.

Rule, W.R. (Ed.) (1984). *Lifestyle Counseling for Adjustment to Disability.* Rockville, MD: Aspen Publications.

Strub, R.L. & Black, F.W. (2000). *The Mental Status Examination in Neurology* (4th edn.). Philadelphia, PA: F.A. Davis.

Taylor, R.L. (1989). Screening for medical referral. In R.J. Corsini & D. Wedding (Eds.), *Current Psychotherapies* (4th edn.) (pp. 585–588). Itasca, IL: F.E. Peacock.

Traver, M.D. (1984). Using selected lifestyle information in understanding multigenerational patterns. In W.R. Rule (Ed.), *Lifestyle Counseling for Adjustment to Disability* (pp. 81–103). Rockville, MD: Aspen Publications.

Index

abuse 7, 12, 15, 45–47, 73, 78, 83, 87, 90, 119,
    148, 152, 155–156, 159, 185, 189, 195,
    197–199, 201, 209, 211–212, 216, 219, 227,
    229, 232–233, 237–238, 261, 267–273,
    278–281, 283, 304, 311, 313–314, 316,
    323–324, 326, 328–334, 337, 341–342, 353
acting "as if" 18, 20, 22, 245–246, 297
Acute Stress Disorder 123–124, 127, 136, 142,
    147–148, 260
Adjustment Disorders 123–124, 145–147
Adler, Alfred 1, 10, 12–14, 19, 24–25, 28, 59,
    93, 120, 147–148, 180, 203, 209, 221,
    240–241, 262–263, 268–269, 282, 285, 333,
    354–355
Adlerian assessment 18, 21, 24, 82, 128–129, 133
affect 33, 42, 45, 54, 56, 59, 113, 118, 127, 131,
    143, 177, 180, 183–185, 188–189, 194, 202,
    211, 225, 303
affective style 30, 37–38, 43, 48, 52, 54, 57, 127,
    131, 134, 142
Agoraphobia 49–51, 64–65, 68, 77–79, 91, 118
alcoholism 11, 27, 79, 311–312, 333–334
Alcohol Use Disorder 312, 317–318, 331
alter ego 210, 212
Alzheimer's disease 154, 335, 342–344, 352
amenorrhea 151
American Medical Association 151, 312,
    333–334
amnesia 202, 205–215, 220, 344; localized 214;
    psychogenic 208, 210, 213; selective 214
Amnestic Disorder 339
amphetamines 326, 342
anger management 39, 306
Anorexia Nervosa 7, 151–157, 162, 166,
    172–175
Antisocial Personality Disorder 27–28, 45–46,
    53, 56, 58, 61, 278–279, 302–305, 313, 331

Anxiety Disorders 37, 49, 63–64, 68, 71, 78,
    91–94, 100, 121, 124, 135, 148, 191, 217,
    267, 253
approach-specific elements 15–17, 24
arousal 31, 115, 135–137, 142, 266–268, 279,
    300
Asperger's Disorder 289, 292–293
assertiveness training 31–32, 231, 237
attachment 45, 65, 68–70, 128–129, 133, 233
Attention Deficit Disorder (ADD) 256, 299
Attention Deficit Hyperactivity Disorder
    (ADHD) 131, 285–286, 298–299, 307
auditory hallucinations 177, 182, 193, 197,
    202–203, 211
Autism 171, 286–290, 292–294, 307–308
Autistic Spectrum Disorder (ASD) 285, 292
autonomic-nervous-system reactivity 35, 43
Avoidance/Restrictive Food-Intake Disorders
    151
Avoidant Personality Disorder 28, 30–31,
    43–44, 49, 55

basic Adlerian constructs 18
behavioral disturbances 124
Behavioral Weight Loss Therapy (BWL) 153
biochemical therapies 4
biological considerations 8
Biopsychosocial–Adlerian Case
    Conceptualization 10, 29, 162, 186, 195,
    198, 199, 201, 318, 321, 324, 327, 329, 331,
    341, 343, 344, 346, 348
biopsychosocial perspective 3, 340, 353
Bipolar I Disorder 95, 110, 113, 115–116
Bipolar II Disorder 53, 95, 115–116
blackouts 206, 213–214, 238
Body Dysmorphic Disorder 64–65, 85–87, 92
body mass index (BMI) 153–155

Borderline Personality Disorder (BPD) 6, 12, 28–29, 33, 36, 42, 167, 174, 211; dependent type 35; histrionic type 35–36; passive-aggressive type 35–37
bossy child syndrome 18
bovine spongiform encephalopathy (mad cow disease) 351
brain's interpreter 180–182, 189
Brief Psychotic Disorder 177, 199–200
breathing-related sleep disturbances 243
Bulimia Nervosa 151–153, 158–159, 162

Cannabis Use Disorder 320
case conceptualization 4; Adlerian approach to 20; biopsychosocial – Adlerian 29; distinctive Adlerian elements 20
case of Geri: case conceptualization elements 22
catastrophic thinking 31
celiac disease 171
Childhood Disintegrative Disorder 292
circadian rhythms 34
clinical formulations 4
Clinical Global Impression Scale 100
Clinician-Rated Dimensions of Psychosis Symptom Severity chart 7
Cluster B traits 152
Cluster C traits 152
cocaine 326
cognitive assessment 63
cognitive constriction 41
cognitive decline 340
cognitive disorders 339
cognitive domains 340
cognitive focus 8
cognitive function 339
cognitive performance 339
Cognitive Processing Therapy (CPT) 138
cognitive restructuring 39
cognitive style 30
common elements 15
Common Elements of an Integrative Case Conceptualization 16
common sense 2
community feeling 66
comorbidity 151
compulsions 64
compulsive behavior 64
Conduct Disorder (CD) 285, 302, 303
conduct disturbance 145

conjoint family therapy 129
consciousness 205
controllers 338, 341, 353
Conversion Disorders 49–50, 232
conversion symptoms 45
copralalia 301
courage 79
cravings 326
creative self 183
Creutzfeldt-Jakob Disease 351
crisis-oriented psychotherapy 39
cultural considerations 7
cultural formulation 4
cultural identity 4
culture 152
Cyclothymic Disorder 95, 117

defense mechanism 31
delayed ejaculation 267
Delirium 335
Delusional Disorder 58, 194
delusions 176; Erotomanic 195; Grandiose 195; Jealous 195; Persecutory 195; Somatic 195
Dementia 339
Dependent Personality Disorder 28
depersonalization 33
Depersonalization Disorder 55
depressed/depression 3
depressive symptoms 32
derealization 34
desensitization 31
detachment/detached 217
Diagnostic and Statistical Manual, Fifth Edition (DSM-5) 1
diagnostic formulations 4
Dialectical Behavioral Therapy (DBT) 153
Diffuse identity 36
dimensional diagnosis 7
discouragement 2
Disinhibited Social Engagement Disorder 123
disinterest 127
Disruptive Mood Dysregulation Disorder 95
dissociation 33
dissociative continuum 206
Dissociative Disorders 205; types of: Amnesia 205; Identity Disorder 205; Not Otherwise Specified (NOS) 205; Other Specified 205; Unspecified 205
dissociative symptoms 142

distorted cognitions 135
dream work 259–260
dreams; frightening 259; disturbing 259
Dreikurs, Rudolf, 27
DSM-IV-TR 5
Dyscalculia 296
Dyslexia 296
Dyspareunia 266
Dysphoria 36
dysphoric mood 35
Dysthymia 107
dysthymic or neurotic depression 4

early recollections 19
Eating Disorder Not Otherwise Specified
    (NOS) 151
eating disorders 151
electroconvulsive therapy (ECT) 213
emotional detachment 135
empathic mirroring 39
encouragement 2
entitlement 236
environmental considerations 7
environmental factors 36
episodic depression 103
Erectile Disorder 267
euthymic mood 35
exaggerated startle response 135
excitement seekers 9, 111, 338, 341
Excoriation 64, 85
Exhibitionistic Disorder 268
extravagant ideals 178
Eye Movement Desensitization and
    Reprocessing (EMDR) 138

Factitious Disorders 50, 238
factitious symptoms 45
family constellation 19
family interventions 70
faulty conceptions 2
fear 63
Feeding Disorders 151
feeling-avoiders 67
Female Orgasmic Disorder 267
Female Sexual Interest/Arousal Disorder 267
Fetal Alcohol Syndrome 132
Fetishistic Disorder 268
fibromyalgia 235
flashbacks 135
Freud, Sigmund 41

frontotemporal lobar degeneration 335
Frotteuristic Disorder 268
fugue 206; Dissociative 207; Psychogenic 207

gambling 331
Gambling Disorder 311
gemeinschaftsgefühl/community feeling 126
Gender Dysphoria 265
gender equality 269
gender guiding lines (GGL) 275
gender identity 34
Gender Identity Disorder 266
Generalized Anxiety Disorder (GAD) 58, 80
Genito-Pelvic Pain/Penetration Disorder 266
"getter", the 232
Global Assessment of Functioning Scale
    (GAF) 5
Goldstein, Kurt 180
grandiosity 37
grief 99

helplessness 135
heroin 232
Histrionic-Antisocial Personality Disorder 53
Histrionic-Borderline Disorder 53
Histrionic Personality Disorder 51
HIV infection 335
Hoarding Disorder 64, 89
homosexuality 276
Huntington's disease 335
Hypersomnolence 243, 249
hypervigilant 134
hypnosis 206
Hypochondriasis 49
hypomanic symptoms 109
hypothalamus 136
hypothalamus–pituitary–adrenal system 235
hysteria 207
Hysterical Neuroses, types of: Conversion 209;
    Dissociative 209
Hysteroid Dysphoria 53

ICD-10 6
identity 205
Illness Anxiety Disorder 223
impulsive vacillation 36
inadequacy 31, 86, 112, 214
Inadequate Child Syndrome 182
Individual Psychology 1
individualized education plan 133

Individuals with Disabilities Education Act (IDEA) 296
inferiority complex 112
inferiority-superiority striving 27
insight-oriented therapy 41
insomnia 243; Late 247; Sleep-Maintenance 247; Sleep-Onset 247
integrative case conceptualization model 15
Intellectual Disability (ID) 285
intellectualization 55
International Classification of Diseases 243
International Classification of Sleep Disorders 243
interpersonal style 30
Interpersonal Therapy (IPT) 153
interpretation 33
intimacy 66
Irritable Bowel Syndrome 229, 235

Journal of Individual Psychology 95

Klein-Levin Syndrome 171

La Belle Indifference 232
level of acculturation 5
Lewy Body Disease 335
life style 2
life-style convictions 20
lifestyle assessment 68
life tasks 2, 18, 66, 91, 162, 289
locus of control, external 226

major depression 53
Major Depressive Disorder (MDD) 4, 101
Major Depressive Episode (MDE) 3
maladaptive pattern of functioning 16
maladaptive sleep patterns 247
Male Hypoactive Sexual Desire Disorder 267
manic/mania 58
masculine protest 265
medical considerations 8
Melancholia 100
memory 205
Mental Retardation 5
micropsychotic episodes 34
mindfulness strategies 228
motivational interviewing 317
movement; types of 8, 29, 209, 212
Mrs. A, case of 1

Multi-Axial (5-axes) System 5
Multiple Personality Disorder 208

naming the demon 92
Narcissistic Personality Disorder 28, 37
Narcolepsy 234, 251
Nash, John, case of 76
National Institute of Health, The 247
National Sleep Foundation 247
negative mood 135
negative-mood-symptom clusters 135
neglect 87
Neurocognitive Disorders (NCD) 335; due to Alzheimer's Disease 335; due to Parkinson's Disease 335; due to Traumatic Brain Injury 335; Major, 339; Mild 339
Neurodevelopmental and Conduct Disorders 285
neurotic disposition 2
Nightmare Disorders 234
nightmares 135
nosology 4

obesity 151
object constancy 206
object-relations theory 206
obsessions 64
Obsessive-Compulsive Disorder 64, 82
Obsessive-Compulsive Personality Disorder 28
Obstructive Sleep Apnea Hypopnea Syndrome 2
Opioid Use Disorder 323
Oppositional Defiant Disorder (ODD) 285
organ dialect/organ jargon 3
organ inferiority(ies) 3
Organic Mental Disorders 339
other conditions that may be a focus of clinical attention 235
other psychotic disorders 176
Overeaters Anonymous 167
overprotection 69

pampered/pampering 3, 69
Pancner, R. 4
panic attack(s) 64
Panic Disorders 49, 75
para-suicidal behavior 211
paranoid/paranoia 35
Paranoid Personality Disorder 28

Paraphilias 266
Paraphilic Disorder 265, 278
parenting style 36
passive-infantile pattern 35
patient health questionnaire 100
pattern/s 16
pattern change 16
pattern recognition 16
Pedophilic Disorder 268, 278
perfectionism 40
Persistent Depressive Disorder (PDD)
    (Dysthymia) 4, 107
personal constructs 178
personal priorities 236
personal superiority (*see* Superiority)
Personality Disorder (PD) 5
personality dysfunction 1
Pervasive Developmental Disorder—Not
    Otherwise Specified (PDD—NOS) 292
phase; active 185; prodromal 185; residual 185
phobia; simple 49; social 49
Pica 151
Pierre, Janet 207
play therapy 129; Adlerian 276, 300, 343
positive social regard 90
Post Traumatic Stress Disorder 123, 134
power 38, 137, 244, 265
predisposition 16
Premature (Early) Ejaculation 267
Prince, Morton 207
principal diagnosis 6
Prion Disease 335, 351
private logic 2
private sense (*see* private logic)
progressive muscle relaxation 228
projective identification 34
prolonged exposure (PE) 138
psychodynamic focus 8
psychoeducation 143
psychological convictions 2
psychological factors affecting other medical
    disorder 223
psychology of possession 9
psychology of use 9
psychomotor agitation 101
psychomotor retardation 101
psychopaths 45
psychosis 27; transient 33
psychosocial considerations 7
psychosomatic theories 3

psychotic break 176
psychotic disorders; Medication-Induced 176;
    Substance-Induced 176
psychotropic drugs 68
purging 151
purpose/purposefulness 106, 184, 246, 260,
    315, 352

rapid eye movement (REM) sleep 259
"Rat Man" (Freud) 41
Reactive Attachment Disorder 123, 127
recurrent depression 103
reflecting "As If" 246
reflection 39
regression 36
relapse prevention 143
Rett's Syndrome 292
rule of thirds (recovery from Schizophrenia) 185
Rumination Disorder 151, 171

safeguarding mechanism 66
safeguarding methods 9
schemata apperception 178
Schizoaffective Disorder 176, 197
Schizoid Personality Disorder 28, 54
Schizophrenia(s) 42; Catatonia 55;
    Disorganized 55; Spectrum 176
Schizophreniform Disorder 55
schizophrenogenic 186
Schizotypal Personality Disorder 28, 42
Sedative, Hypnotic, or Anxiolytic Use
    Disorder 328
Selective Mutism 64, 70
self-calming/self-soothing 127
self-image 34
self-training 178
separation anxiety 34
Separation Anxiety Disorder 64, 68
sex 265
Sexual and Gender Identity Disorders 265
sexual behavior 265
sexual deviance 265
sexual dysfunctions 265
Sexual Masochism Disorder 268
sexual psychopathology 265
Sexual Sadism Disorder 268
shyness training 31
sick/sickness 230
single-axis diagnosis 5
sleep 243

Sleep Apnea 166; Central 234; Obstructive 234
sleep disturbances 243, 244, 247
sleep paralysis 251
Sleep-Wake Disorders 243
sleepiness; disproportionate 249
sleeplessness 246
Social Anxiety Disorder 53, 73
social interest 1
social isolation 32
social task 66
sociopaths 45
Somatic Symptoms and Related Disorders 223
Somatic Symptoms Disorder 223, 226
Somatization Disorders 50
Somatoform Disorders 223
special child syndrome 182
Specific Learning Disorder (SLD) 285; math 295; reading 295; written expression 295
Specific Phobia 64
specifiers 7
spectrum disorder 3
spirituality 152
splitting 34
stages of change 317
Stimulant Use Disorder 326
stress-diathesis model 179
Stress Inoculation Training (SIT) 138
Stressor-Related Disorders 123
striving for perfection 125, 286
styles; comfort 236; control 236; getting along 236; pleasing 236; superiority 236
substance abuse 152
Substance Disorders 7, 311
substance intoxication 201
Substance/Medication-Induced Sexual Dysfunction 267
substance/medication use 335
Substance Use and Addictive Disorders 311
subtypes 7
subvocalization hypothesis 182
superiority 1

superiority seekers 341, 344, 353
symptoms; positive and negative 185
systemic focus 8

tailored treatment 9
temperament 30; anhedonic 41; difficult child 47; fearful infantile 43; ill-tempered infantile 47
"The Question" (Adler and Dreikurs) 74
"The Sideshow" (Mosak) 152
Tic Disorder 83
Tourette's Syndrome (TD) 285
trance 206; dissociative 218
Transvestic Disorder 267
trauma 123
Trauma-and-Stress-related Disorders 124
treatment formulations 4
Trichotillomania 64, 85

Unipolar Disorders 55
Unity of Personality/Holism 67
Unspecified Eating Disorder 27
Unspecified Neurocognitive Disorder 335
Use Disorders 311

V-code 5
Vaginismus 266
vascular disease 335
Voyeuristic Disorder 268
vulnerability 178

withdrawal symptoms 195, 201, 327
work/occupational task 66
World Health Organization Disability Assessment Schedule 2.0 (WHODAS 2.0) 6

"Yes-but" 2

Z-code 6
Z-factor 67